OSx86: Creating a Hackintosh

OSx86: Creating a Hackintosh

Peter Baldwin

WILEY

Wiley Publishing, Inc.

OSx86: Creating a Hackintosh

Published by
Wiley Publishing, Inc.
10475 Crosspoint Boulevard
Indianapolis, IN 46256
www.wiley.com

For general information on our other products and services or to obtain technical support, please contact our Customer Care Department within the U.S. at (877) 762-2974, outside the U.S. at (317) 572-3993 or fax (317) 572-4002.

Library of Congress Control Number: 2009942441

Trademarks: Wiley and the Wiley logo are trademarks or registered trademarks of John Wiley & Sons, Inc. and/or its affiliates, in the United States and other countries, and may not be used without written permission. All other trademarks are the property of their respective owners. Wiley Publishing, Inc., is not associated with any product or vendor mentioned in this book.

Wiley also publishes its books in a variety of electronic formats. Some content that appears in print may not be available in electronic books.

*To Darrell for putting up with an obsessive author
over the last eight months!*

About the Author

Peter Baldwin began programming when computers used punch cards to enter programs and data. Since then, he's written programs in just about every language from Applesoft BASIC on the Apple to Ada, through Pascal, C, C++, HTML, Javascript, and others. He has written many user manuals and spent several years teaching computing and developing training courses in various computer topics.

He first became interested in running Leopard on his own Intel-based computer in late 2008 after reading a story on a Web site. Since then, he's installed Leopard to a few different computers, with varying degrees of success. At present, he uses Leopard on both a desktop computer he assembled himself and on a netbook.

Credits

Acquisitions Editor
Aaron Black

Executive Editor
Jody Lefevere

Project Editor
Martin V. Minner

Technical Editor
Jaison Lewis

Copy Editor
Gwenette Gaddis

Editorial Director
Robyn Siesky

Editorial Manager
Cricket Krengel

Business Manager
Amy Knies

Senior Marketing Manager
Sandy Smith

Vice President and Executive Group Publisher
Richard Swadley

Vice President and Executive Publisher
Barry Pruett

Project Coordinator
Lynsey Stanford

Graphics and Production Specialists
Joyce Haughey
Jennifer Mayberry
Ronald G. Terry

Quality Control Technician
Melanie Hoffman

Proofreading
Christine Sabooni

Indexing
BIM Indexing & Proofreading Services

Contents

Acknowledgments

I do not know what I may appear to the world, but to myself I seem to have been only like a boy playing on the seashore, and diverting myself in now and then finding a smoother pebble or a prettier shell than ordinary, whilst the great ocean of truth lay all undiscovered before me.

~Sir Isaac Newton

So many people deserve credit for making this book possible. Without them putting hours and hours of their time into smoothing the path for others, this book would be impossible. It's not something any one person could do.

I owe a huge debt to many, many people, none of whom I've ever met face-to-face. As do most people, I know them only through their online names.

In no particular order, here are my thanks to these people: ~pcwiz, dfe, munky, ramjet, macgirl, superhai, everyone at ToH, Brazilmac, zephyroth, f41qu3, auzigog, mechdrew, bmcclure937, bmaltais, meklort, blackosx, d00m42, UnaClocker, Type11, buddymalec, and many others. If I've left your name out, please accept my apologies.

Without you talented and dedicated people, this book could never have happened.

I am extremely grateful to everyone at Wiley, particularly Marty Minner, my project editor, for guiding me and holding my hand via e-mail through the whole project; to Gwenette Gaddis, copy editor, for ensuring that each sentence made sense, and to Jaison Lewis, technical editor, for many helpful comments, suggestions, and corrections. Many thanks also to Aaron Black, acquisitions editor at Wiley, for starting the whole project and getting me involved.

Introduction

In June 2005, Apple unwittingly threw down the gauntlet to experimenters by announcing that from early in 2006, Apple would replace its line of PowerPC computers with computers based around Intel chips. Because these chips are the same as those used in the majority of computers that have run Windows, Linux, and other operating systems for several years, it seemed that at last it might be possible to get Apple's OS X operating system running on non-Apple computers.

Indeed it was. In February 2006, a couple of weeks after Apple released the first Intel Macintoshes running OS X Tiger (10.4.4), a programmer managed to get Tiger running on non-Apple hardware. Since then, Tiger went through revisions until Leopard (10.5) was released in late 2007 and Snow Leopard (10.6) in late August 2009.

About This Book

Through this book, you will journey through installing OS X Leopard on your own non-Apple computer, to explore the differences between Leopard and Windows, to getting the most out of the Apple software applications, and finally to extending the power of OS X by creating new applications.

My aim is to take you from wanting to know about how to install Leopard on your home computer, through setting the computer up to your own personal preferences, using the standard Macintosh software, and finally extending the power of your system by creating new programs to perform tasks that the base system cannot do, using the Apple Developer tools.

The book is organized into four parts:

- Installing Leopard
- Customizing Leopard
- Using the Leopard applications
- Extending the power of Leopard

Part I helps you install Leopard without having to make the commitment to purchase new Apple hardware. It takes you through several different options for installation. You learn how to install it on a separate USB hard disk, how to install it on a data disk inside your computer, and how to install it on a new partition on your Windows Vista, Windows 7, or Windows XP system disk.

Part II takes you on an exploration of the differences between Leopard and Windows and then helps you to set up the computer according to personal preference, ranging from network preferences and sound effects, to your desktop and screen saver, to printers and faxes.

In Part III, you explore the standard software applications supplied with Leopard, ranging from mail to Web browsing. You then can integrate Leopard into the rest of your computer system by learning to read and write to your Windows disk.

If you really miss your Windows operating system, you can install two different products that allow you to run your existing Windows or to install a different Windows system and run them without ever leaving Leopard. Or if you prefer, you can even run Leopard while never leaving your Windows system, though you miss out on most of the good parts of Leopard.

In Part IV, I introduce you to the power of scripting and programming. I show you how to create and add new widgets to your Dashboard and how to create new applications using the Apple Developer tools.

Who Should Read This Book?

Part I is for people who want the enjoyment of getting a computer to do something it was not designed to do: run Apple's Leopard system on a computer not made by Apple. It appeals strongly to those who enjoy these challenges. It gives step-by-step instructions for several different types of installations to several different types of computer.

Part II is for people who have switched from Windows to a Macintosh or who have installed Leopard to a non-Apple computer. This part takes you through the differences between Windows and Leopard and guides you through setting up Leopard to your liking. It is not necessary to have installed Leopard on your own computer.

Part III is for people who want a concise guide to using the standard Leopard software, whether they have created their own installation or are using a Macintosh. It makes an excellent guide to using Leopard applications and to creating a bridge between Windows and Leopard using virtualization software. It also appeals to existing Macintosh users who want to find out more about their computers.

Part IV is for people who want to extend the power of Leopard. It takes you through the programming required to create new and useful applications. For the most part, you do not need a background in programming, simply a desire to create something new. This part appeals to Macintosh users who want an easy-to-understand guide to creating new applications, regardless of whether they are using a Hackintosh or a genuine Apple Macintosh.

About the Future

In late August 2009, Apple released the newest version of the OS X family: Snow Leopard (OS X 10.6). With this release, Apple finally said goodbye to the PowerPC: Snow Leopard runs only on Intel Macintoshes. It also runs in 64-bit mode, though some applications may not be 64-bit capable.

Because of deadlines in writing this book, I could try out Snow Leopard on the Dell Mini 9 and on my desktop computer. This was possible only because of extremely active communities dedicated to running OS X on the Dell computer and on the Gigabyte motherboard. Very active communities exist for other computers, such as for Acer, MSI Wind, among others.

Given the early state of development of Snow Leopard on non-Apple hardware, I'd recommend that you install Leopard first, because the methods have been around much longer and far more help is available.

Installing OS X 10.5

This is where your journey begins. You have access to several different installation options for Leopard on a non-Apple computer, each of them with its own good points.

Unlike Windows operating systems, Leopard doesn't mind if it is installed to an external disk, so you can install and run Leopard without affecting your existing installation. Of course, you need to select which disk to boot from, but having done that, Leopard runs while still giving you access to your existing data.

You may want to install Leopard to your existing Windows boot disk. You can do this also, but then you must select the operating system from a menu when you start your computer from your Windows disk.

Each of these possibilities is explored in depth, with hands-on instructions and many illustrations guiding you through every step of the process.

Getting Started

Y ou can take the Apple Leopard Install DVD, insert it in your DVD drive, and start trying to install Leopard on your computer. Unless you are using a genuine Macintosh, you are unlikely to succeed, and you won't get the best experience of Leopard possible.

Many people have combined their expertise and experiences so those who follow can take a shorter path, bypassing many of the pitfalls. Why not capitalize on this experience?

In this chapter, you learn how to find out exactly what hardware your computer contains so you can be sure whether Leopard will run on your computer. You complete a table showing your hardware so you can find and use the additional resources you need. This becomes important in later chapters.

Determining Your Computer Hardware

Before you start trying to install Leopard, you should find out what hardware is inside your computer. The Windows Device Manager built into Vista and XP tells you most of the information you need to know; however, the *System Information for Windows* (SIW) software makes this very easy.

Although SIW shows details of all the software on your computer, you are interested only in the hardware details.

SIW was written by Gabriel Topala and is freeware for individual use. At the bottom of the download page is a link saying "If you like SIW, you can buy me a coffee." Click the link to send him a donation via PayPal.

To download and install this software, follow these steps:

1. **Point your Internet browser to** www.gtopala.com/.

2. **Click Download SIW.**

3. **When the file has downloaded, install the software.**

If you use Internet Explorer, click Run; if you use Firefox, click Save.

SIW adds itself to your programs list, available through the Start menu.

Figure 1.1 shows the start screen for System Information for Windows. The left pane is a collapsible list showing Software, Hardware, and Network components. To collapse a part of the list, click the – (minus) sign beside the major heading. To expand it again, click the + (plus) sign.

Figure 1.1

System Information for Windows—start screen

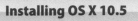

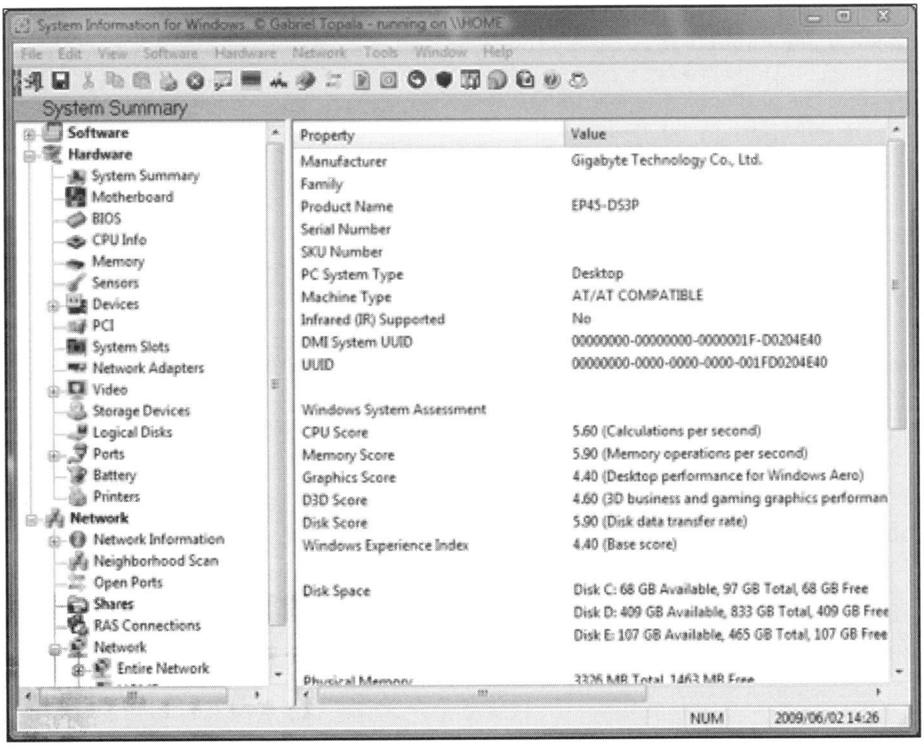

In the remaining parts of this chapter, you use SIW to find the information to complete the following table of hardware in your computer.

When you have completed Table 1.1, you will have enough information about your computer to know whether you are likely to be able to install and run Leopard.

Table 1.1 Your Computer Components

Item	Description
Motherboard	
Processor	
Display adapter	
Network (wired)	
Network (wireless)	
Sound	
Printer	
Other peripherals	
Webcam	
Scanner	
Others	

Finding Specifications for Your Motherboard

The most important part of your computer specification is the motherboard. This is sometimes called the mainboard, and it's where the processor chip plugs in. It also holds the BIOS (Basic Input Output System) chip, which is the very lowest level of interaction between your software and hardware.

Most motherboards also contain the sound and networking chips; some also contain the graphics chips.

You need to know details of the motherboard and the BIOS. To find the motherboard details, follow these steps:

1. **Click the – (minus) sign beside Software.**

   This collapses the Software part of the list and brings you to the Hardware details.

2. **Click Motherboard.**

3. **Read your motherboard details from the right pane, and write them in the table.**

4. **Read your BIOS details on the next line, and write them in the table.**

When I clicked Motherboard on the computer I used to write this, I found the following:

Manufacturer	Gigabyte Technology Co., Ltd.
Model	EP45-DS3P

When I clicked the BIOS line, I found the following information:

BIOS vendor	Award Software International, Inc.
BIOS version	F8
BIOS date	09/30/2008

Now you can fill in the first line of your table. Here is my table as an example:

Motherboard	Board: Gigabyte EP45-DS3P BIOS: Award F8 09/30/2008

Finding Your Processor Specifications

In this section, you use SIW to find your processor specifications.

1. **Using SIW, highlight the next line to find your processor specifications.**

On my computer, SIW showed me the following information:

CPU full name	Intel(R) Core(TM)2 Duo CPU E8400 @ 3.00 GHz

For my computer, this would be the next entry in the table:

Processor	Intel Core Duo E8400

You can now fill in that line in your table.

Working with older processors

For compatibility with older software, modern processors still have to work with instructions from earlier processors. In order to speed up processors, Intel developed the technique of using one instruction to operate on more than one set of data. This allows the code required to be much smaller so that, rather than having one set of instructions for each bit of data, one instruction works with all of them at once, effectively carrying out operations in parallel—hence the speed gain.

This technique is called Single Instruction, Multiple Data (SIMD). It is especially useful in putting graphics on the screen because several pixels can be processed at once.

SIMD comes in several versions, the most recent being SSE2 and SSE3. SSE stands for Streaming SIMD Extension. You don't need to understand exactly what that means, but you do need to know whether your processor can do it.

SSE2 was introduced in 2001, and SSE3 was introduced in 2004. Leopard cannot run on processors that don't support at least SSE2 instructions, and preferably SSE3.

While you are still on CPU Info, look down the right pane until you come to the line called Instructions. SIW shows you the instructions that your processor can process. This is the result for my computer:

Instructions	MMX, SSE, SSE2, SSE3, SSSE3, SSE4.1, ET64, XD, VMX, SMX, EST

Using an early Pentium chip

Pentium chips made since the Pentium 4 released in 2001 have supported SSE2, but SSE3 was not supported until 2004. If your chip was made before 2001, you can be almost certain that it is not capable of running Leopard.

Chips made after 2006 can almost certainly be made to run Leopard, though the task may not be simple. The most compatible chips are those of the Intel Core 2 family (either Core 2 Duo or Core 2 Quad) because Apple uses these chips in its own branded computers.

Finding Specifications of Your Video Setup

After the processor and the motherboard, the most important component for Leopard is your graphics chip. Unless it is reasonably fast and uses hardware acceleration, you can't get the full graphics effects of Leopard. Your graphics chip should also use its own memory, rather than using the main computer memory. However, almost any video setup allows you to use Leopard.

Since the Intel Macs were released, Apple has used a small range of video processing chips. The most common is the Intel GMA950 series, which has appeared in many of Apple's laptops and Mac Minis. Other chips that have been used are either nVidia or ATI.

Manufacturers supply two types of video: integrated into the motherboard or a separate graphics card. Where the chip is integrated into the motherboard, it usually uses shared memory. This means part of the main system memory is used for video.

The advantage, for the manufacturer, is that it saves on a separate video card, especially in a laptop where space is at a premium; the disadvantage is that you are stuck with that chip's performance.

Using a separate video card

1. **In System Information for Windows, click Video in the left pane.**

This shows the name of your display adaptor.

For my computer, SIW shows:

Display adapter	NVIDIA GeForce 7600 GS

What this doesn't show is whether your video is generated from a separate card or if it's on the motherboard. If your computer is a desktop, it likely uses a separate graphics card. If your computer uses a separate video card, the card has its own memory onboard. In Windows XP, this is the amount of graphics memory available, but in Windows Vista, the system can steal some of the main memory as well as its own to increase the memory available to the video card.

A graphics card with its own memory is the ideal situation because it can then function as a separate entity, without you worrying about whether the processor is trying to access the motherboard memory at the same time. This means it is highly likely (but not certain) that you can use the full power of the Leopard graphics: Quartz Extreme and Core Image.

Using integrated video

If your computer is a laptop, it almost certainly uses integrated video. If Apple has used that chip then you will get good graphics performance. For older chips it's a bit of a lottery: if it is popular enough then someone will develop drivers for it.

Unfortunately, I can't talk in certainties about graphics performance; all I can say is that most likely you can see graphics regardless of what your graphics processor and memory are. But the quality and speed depend completely on the exact specifications of your display adapter.

For my computer, the next line of the table is:

Display adapter	NVIDIA GeForce 7600GS

Finding Your Audio Hardware Specifications

Apart from wireless networking, sound is the most difficult area to get working. Sometimes manufacturers even give incorrect specifications for their sound chips, which makes configuring sound even harder than it should be!

SIW gives information about your sound hardware, although it doesn't have a separate heading. Follow these steps to find the info:

1. **In the left pane of SIW, click the + (plus) sign beside Devices.**

2. **Click the + (plus) sign beside Sound, video, and game controllers.**

3. **Look for the word Audio, and click it.**

Figure 1.2 shows the information that SIW gave me for my computer.

Figure 1.2

System Information for Windows—audio

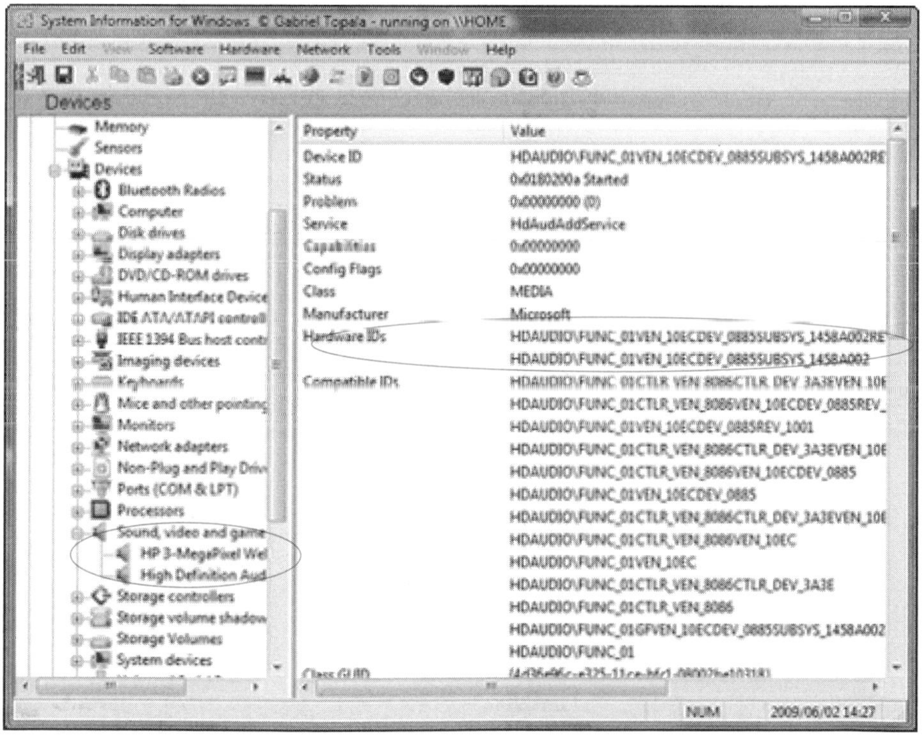

Because my computer has a Bluetooth dongle for synchronizing with my mobile phone, it shows three entries for Bluetooth audio, but we can ignore that.

My main audio is the Realtek High Definition Audio. This is a generic term, much like saying that your car has disk brakes: That's nice to know, but it's not much help if you want to replace the pads. Realtek uses many different sound chips, as do other audio output manufacturers.

When your motherboard was installed, the correct drivers for Windows were installed. These are supplied on a CD that comes with your computer. But, sadly, that CD is useless for Leopard. You need to dig much deeper to find drivers.

Look in the right pane to the Device ID. In this case, the Device ID line is:

Device ID	HDAUDIO\FUNC_01VEN_10ECDEV_0885SUBSYS_1458A002REV_1001

You need to divide this information into parts before you can find out exactly what your audio system is.

Following "HDAUDIO\FUNC_01" are the letters VEN followed by four characters. This is the vendor (manufacturer) ID. In this case, the characters are 10EC, which is a hexadecimal number.

1. **Write this number in the second column of the following table in the Vendor ID row.**

You can ignore the HDAUDIO\FUNC_01 part.

Vendor ID	
Device ID	

Immediately following the vendor ID is the device (DEV) identifier. This is another four-digit hexadecimal number—in this case, 0885.

2. **Write this number in the following table in the Device ID row.**

As an example, here is the table completed with my details:

Vendor ID	10EC
Device ID	0885

Finding the manufacturer

To find the name of the vendor and the device, search in the PCI database at `www.pci database.com`.

Searching for vendor 10EC shows that the vendor is Realtek, which we knew from the SIW display.

Finding the device name

Searching on 0885 shows that the device is a "7.1+2 Channel High-Performance HDA Codec with Content Protection," which doesn't get you much further!

Follow these steps using the table in the online database:

1. **Click the Realtek Semiconductor link.**

    This lists all the devices made by that manufacturer.

2. **Look down the Device ID column to 0x0885, which shows that the device is an ALC885.**

This becomes important later when trying to find drivers.

Interestingly, in its promotional literature, Gigabyte (the motherboard manufacturer) identifies it as an ALC889A, which is not correct. It's hard enough installing Leopard without manufacturers giving you incorrect information!

This line in the table becomes:

Sound	Realtek ALC885

Fill in the appropriate line in your own table.

Finding Your Networking Hardware Specifications

Now you need to find the specifications of your networking hardware. Your computer may have both wireless and wired networking abilities, as mine does. If you are going to use only one or the other, you can skip one part.

Using System Information for Windows again, follow these steps:

1. **Click the – (minus) sign to close the Sound, video, and game controllers line.**
2. **Click the – (minus) sign to close the Devices line.**
3. **Click Network Adapters.**

This shows all the network adapters that have been used on your computer. Figure 1.3 shows a display of networking hardware for my computer.

Figure 1.3

System information—network adapters

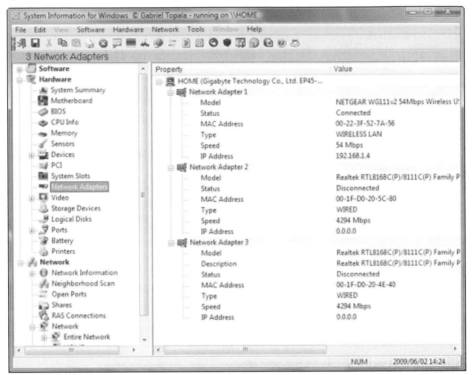

My computer has three network adapters: one wireless and two wired. Adapter 1 is my wireless adapter, and 2 and 3 are the adapters built in to the motherboard.

The primary network connector in use is the ASUS USB wireless adapter.

Wired networking

My motherboard has two wired network adapters, both Realtek RTL8168C. This is a common network adapter chip and is highly likely to work with Leopard.

Adding another line to the hardware list for my computer, we now have:

Network (wired)	Realtek RTL8168C

Add the appropriate information for your own computer to your table.

Wireless networking

Getting wireless networking to work is one of the most difficult parts of building a Hackintosh. Apple uses basically the same wireless adapter, with its chip made by Broadcom, in all its computers. If you can use that, you should have no problems. But, and it's a big but, finding what chip your wireless adapter uses is not easy, nor is finding wireless network adapters using the same Broadcom chip, or even finding wireless adapters that work at all, mainly because of a lack of drivers.

After all, if almost every Mac comes with built-in wireless networking, what incentive do manufacturers have to develop drivers to make them work with a Mac?

SIW and the Windows Device Manager list my wireless adapter simply as ASUS USB Wireless Network Adapter. You need to find out what model it is.

This should be relatively easy: Look on the box it came in or on the device itself. The box for this adapter is labeled WL-167G. You would expect to be able to go to the manufacturer's Web site and download the appropriate drivers.

A Google search on WL-167G shows that it's made by Asus. Digging deeper shows a single driver for Mac Leopard, dated 15 September 2006, and it supports only OS X 10.3 and 10.4 (Panther and Tiger) but not Leopard.

Using the Properties panel in the same way as you did for the sound, the hardware vendor ID is 0b05 and the device ID is 1723.

Again, you need to dig a bit deeper! Several Hackintosh Web sites often (but not always) have answers to questions about drivers. All sites have a search facility, but some work better than others.

One way to improve your success is to use a targeted Google search. To do this, add the name of the site at the end of what you're searching for. This restricts the search to that site only.

Let's search for information about the device on `insanelymac.com`. To do this, type **WL-167g site:insanelymac.com** into Google.

You end up with lots of queries about the device from users, and maybe you will be able to get drivers that way. The end of this chapter features a list of useful Hackintosh sites.

The next line in my table reads:

Network adapter (wireless)	ASUS WL-167G USB

Fill in the table with your own details.

Finding Your Other Hardware

All the other hardware, if it is relatively recent, should have drivers available at the manufacturer's Web site because the hardware can be connected to a genuine Apple Macintosh. Nevertheless, enter the identifiers into the table.

For my computer, the table now looks like Table 1.2.

Table 1.2 Hardware for my Computer

Item	Description
Motherboard	Board: Gigabyte EP45-DS3P BIOS: Award F3 05/29/2008
Processor	Intel Core Duo E8400
Display adapter	NVIDIA GeForce 7600GS
Network (wired)	Realtek RTL8168C
Network (wireless)	ASUS WL-167G USB
Sound	Realtek ALC885
Printer	Fuji-Xerox FX203A
Other peripherals	
Webcam	HP 3-MegaPixel Webcam GX607AA
Scanner	Epson Perfection 1670
Bluetooth	Broadcom Bluetooth 2.0+EDR USB dongle

Determining Your Hardware Compatibility

Now that you have listed all the devices, it's time to find out how compatible they are with Leopard. Remember that this is not an exact science; it relies on other people contributing to help the whole community because no support is available from Apple.

Although your exact hardware may be shown as compatible, almost invariably you'll encounter small glitches. Of course, your hardware may not even be shown in the lists.

Hardware compatibility lists (HCL) are found on the OSX86 Project Web site at `http://wiki.osx86project.org/wiki/index.php/Main_Page`.

Several compatibility lists exist, but the most complete at the time of this writing is the list for Leopard 10.5.2.

If you are using a name-brand desktop or laptop, you can go straight to the appropriate table by selecting either Portable Computers or Desktop Computers. These are listed alphabetically by manufacturer. Figure 1.4 shows part of the list for desktop computers.

Figure 1.4

Hardware compatibility list for systems

Contents [hide]

1 Acer
- 1.1 Aspire L100
- 1.2 Aspire T180
- 1.3 Aspire E380
- 1.4 Aspire L3600 7200
- 1.5 AcerPower 2000

2 Compaq
- 2.1 Presario SR1222NX
- 2.2 Presario SR5518F
- 2.3 Evo D 51 SFF
- 2.4 Evo 510 (P4 2.4ghz with 512Mo SDRAM / Nvidia FX5200@128Mo (Integrated Graphics Card disable)
- 2.5 Evo 510 SFF (P4 2.4ghz with 2 Gig mem / Nvidia Geforce FX6200@256M (Integrated Graphics Card disable)

3 Dell
- 3.1 Dimension 2400
- 3.2 Dimension 4550
  - 3.2.1 iATKOS v2.0i without options (Version 1)
  - 3.2.2 iATKOS v2.0i without options (Version 2)
- 3.3 Dimension 5150
- 3.4 Dimension 8400
- 3.5 Dimension 9100
- 3.6 Dimension 9150

If your exact computer is listed, you are halfway there! Click the link, and read what people have said about installing and running Leopard on your computer.

Under the heading Graphics, "no QE/CI" means that hardware acceleration (Quartz Extreme, Core Image) does not work, which affects the way images are displayed in Time Machine, wDashboard, and other Mac applications, for example.

If your particular computer is not listed in the HCL for 10.5.2, check the other lists, up to 10.5.6 at the time of this writing. If you still can't find it, you need to look up each individual component.

Finding my motherboard

Unfortunately, I found no exact matches for my motherboard. These are close:

Compatibility List for Leopard Version	*Motherboard*
10.5.1	GA-EP35-DS3P, GA-EP45-DS4P
10.5.2	GA-EP45-DS3, GA-EP45-DS3L, GA-EP45-DQ6
10.5.4	GA-EP45-DS4

After reading the user comments about each of these, I can reasonably conclude that the EP45-DS3P will work, but I'll need patching to get the audio working. In fact, this is what I found.

Finding my processor

Intel CoreDuo E8400: working with vanilla kernel. (Vanilla kernel refers to the unmodified Leopard core operating system.)

Finding my graphics card

NVIDIA GeForce 7600GS: all resolutions work; QE/CI supported.

Finding my wired network

Realtek RTL8168C: The chip is built into the motherboard, so the motherboard entry covers it. No mention of networking problems. This is what I found.

Finding my sound device

Realtek ALC885, although Gigabyte's documentation says it is an ALC889A.

I posted a query on an OSX86 forum, and another user e-mailed me drivers that work perfectly.

Finally you have enough information about your computer to be able to make a good attempt at installing a retail copy of Leopard.

Summary

By now, you have completed a table showing the complete specifications for all the hardware in the box your computer sits in—from the motherboard and processor chip to sound, networking, and video.

From the various hardware compatibility lists, you have a good idea of how likely it is that Leopard will run on your computer.

In addition, you have summaries of your peripheral equipment—the stuff that sits outside your main computer box. You need this summary in the next few chapters.

2

Installing Leopard to a Separate Hard Disk

nstalling OS X Leopard to an external hard disk that is separate from your main hard disks is a painstaking process, and you may have to install it a couple of times before you have it working properly. Installing it on a separate hard disk means you don't have to worry about erasing your existing hard drive. After you feel comfortable about installing Leopard and getting it working to your satisfaction, you can install it to your boot disk.

You need a retail copy of OS X Leopard, which you can buy from an Apple store or dealer, or even from eBay or such. If you buy it from anywhere except an authorized Apple dealer or retailer, be sure it is shrink-wrapped in the original packaging; otherwise, it may have been installed on another computer. You cannot use the disk that came with a friend's computer because it just won't work.

In Chapter 1, you carried out the preliminary work to find out exactly what hardware your computer contains, so you have an excellent chance of succeeding with the installation.

CAUTION

If you feel comfortable about opening up your computer and you won't risk voiding any warranty on your computer, I recommend disconnecting your fixed hard disk(s). This ensures that you don't inadvertently overwrite your existing operating system.

Booting from a Boot CD

In this section, you learn how to boot your computer from a separate boot CD. This is necessary because Leopard cannot boot from the CD/DVD drive on any computer except for a genuine Apple. You learn how to check your computer BIOS, to be sure it can start from an external hard disk, find a suitable boot disk, and burn it to a CD.

All Windows operating systems are made to install only to a fixed hard disk inside your computer. You cannot install and run a Windows system from an external hard disk.

Leopard, on the other hand, installs and runs perfectly well from an external hard disk, such as a USB hard drive. You can install Leopard to an external disk and keep it completely separate from your Windows system. A perfectly adequate 2.5-inch USB hard disk in an enclosure costs around $90–100.

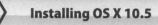

CAUTION

If you want to install to a hard disk that already has a Windows operating system on it, you should jump to either Chapter 4 (for Vista and Windows 7) or Chapter 4 (for XP).

Checking your BIOS

BIOS stands for Basic Input Output System. It is the part of your computer that gets control when you first turn it on. First it checks your computer memory and then checks the other attached hardware.

After it has finished its checks, it hands control over to the boot device; normally, that's your hard disk, but it can also be a CD/DVD drive, an external hard disk, or even a USB pen drive.

CROSS-REF

Appendix B includes an explanation of the boot process on a Windows computer compared with booting a Macintosh computer.

Before you start, you need to check that your computer can boot from an external hard disk, so you need to examine your computer's BIOS.

To do this, you press a key when the computer first starts up. Generally, the key is either F2 or Delete, although other keys may be used. Follow these steps to look at the BIOS:

1. **Switch off your computer.**
2. **Connect your external hard drive.**
3. **Wait a few seconds, and then restart the computer.**
4. **On the screen, look for text that says something like Press Delete to Enter Setup.**
5. **Press that key, and wait a few seconds.**

TIP

You may need to try these steps a few times because sometimes the information about the key to press doesn't stay on the screen for very long. By the time you've read it, it's too late to press the key!

After you have entered the BIOS, you see a screen that looks something like that shown in Figure 2.1.

At this point, your mouse doesn't work, so you need to use the keyboard. Use the right arrow key to move across to the Boot tab, and you arrive at the screen shown in Figure 2.2.

Figure 2.1

Typical BIOS setup screen

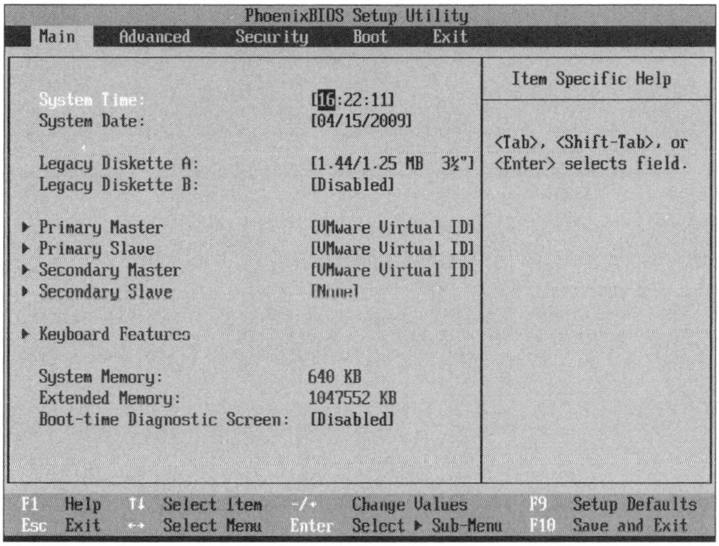

Figure 2.2

BIOS boot options

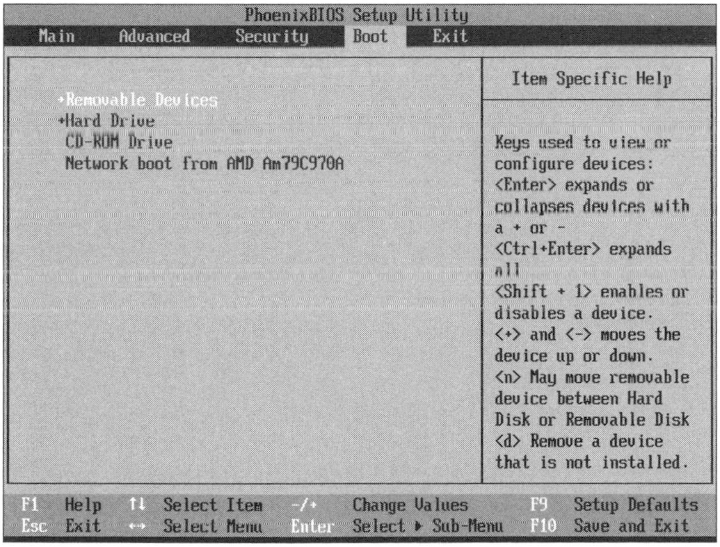

Your USB disk should appear in the section for hard disks, although it may appear in the removable devices section.

Finding a boot disk

Because it is not a Macintosh, your computer cannot boot from your Leopard retail DVD. To install Leopard, you need to have your computer boot the way a real Macintosh does.

TIP
Many people have created boot disks for this purpose. In essence, they contain software that bridges the gap between your hardware and what Leopard expects to find in a genuine Apple.

Probably the most common is a boot disk created by a team called Kabyl-Bumby. Search for it on Google. It is most likely hosted on a file-sharing site such as mediafire.com or rapidshare.com.

NOTE
These boot disks are always supplied as an image file (.iso), which you need to burn to a CD. An image file is an exact image of what is on a CD. Because it is a bootable image, when you burn it to CD, the CD is bootable.

Creating your boot disk

You can't simply copy the .iso to a CD because it just ends up as a file sitting on a CD, and you won't be able to boot your computer. Since the .iso file is an exact image of the CD, you need to copy that image exactly to the CD.

CAUTION
Whatever CD/DVD-burning software you are using, be sure you use the option to burn an image. A very good, free program to burn CDs and DVDs is ImgBurn, available from www.imgburn.com/.

If you are using ImgBurn, follow these steps to burn your .iso file to your CD:

1. **Start ImgBurn running.**

2. **Insert a blank CD in your drive.**

3. **Click the "Write image file to disk" option.**

4. **Click the file finder icon (with the magnifying glass) and navigate to where your .iso file is located.**

5. **Check the Verify box to verify that the CD contains exactly the same data as the image file.**

6. **Click the large button to start the burn process.**

7. **Label your disk Boot Kabyl Bumby.**

Checking that you have everything

Complete the checklist in Table 2.1 to be sure you have everything you need to install Leopard. Place a check mark in each box after you've verified that item.

Table 2.1 Checklist

Item	Check
Computer can boot from USB disk	
Have Leopard Retail Disk	
Have boot disk	

Specifying the Hard Disk Identifier

This section explains how to boot the Leopard Retail DVD using your boot CD as an intermediary.

Booting from the Leopard Retail DVD is a two-step process unless you are using a Macintosh. First, start the computer using the boot disk, and start the Leopard disk.

When your computer first starts, you see a screen that looks something like that shown in Figure 2.3.

Figure 2.3

Boot menu

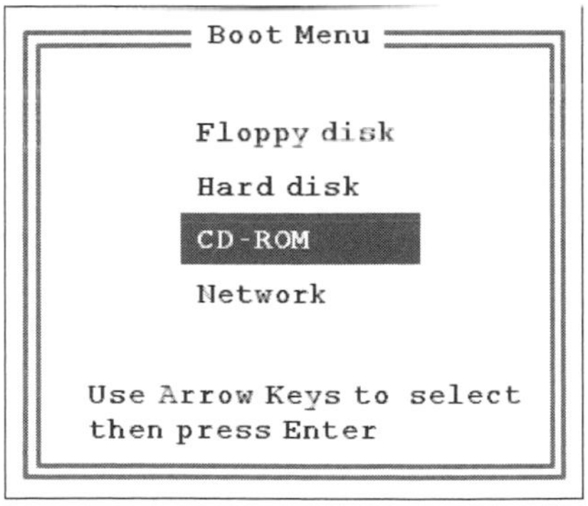

1. **Insert your boot disk in the CD/DVD drive.**

2. **Restart your computer.**

3. **Press the key required to change your boot device.**

   Usually F12 works, but not always.

4. **Select CD/DVD, and press Enter.**

5. **Wait for the boot disk to start up and finish at a prompt.**

   You then see the screen shown in Figure 2.4, which is where you start the next stage of the boot process.

Figure 2.4

Darwin boot screen

```
Darwin/x86 boot v5.0.132_dfe_r146_Chameleon_pre
1023MB memory
VESA v2.0 128MB (V M ware, Inc. VBE support 2.0)

Press Enter to start up Darwin/x86 with no options, or you can:
   Type -v and press Enter to start up with diagnostic messages
   Type ? and press Enter to learn about advanced startup options

boot: _
```

At this point, the boot disk is waiting for you to boot Darwin, the Unix operating system on which Leopard is based. Of course, Darwin itself is not on that disk; it is on your Leopard Retail DVD, so you need to tell it which disk that is and then swap disks.

6. **Press Esc.**

Now the boot prompt changes to look like the screen shown in Figure 2.5.

Figure 2.5

Darwin boot selector

```
Darwin/x86 boot v5.0.132_dfe_r146_Chameleon_pre
1023MB memory
VESA v2.0 128MB (V M ware, Inc. VBE support 2.0)

Typeical boot devices are 80 (First HD), 81 (Second HD)
Enter two-digit hexadecimal boot device [9F]: _
```

In this case, the boot disk has identified the boot device as 9f, the decimal number 159 in hexadecimal.

NOTE

If you want to convert hexadecimal to decimal and vice versa, use the calculator at `http://easy calculation.com/hex-converter.php`.

1. **Remove the boot disk from the CD drive.**

2. **Insert the Leopard Retail DVD in the CD drive.**

3. **Wait a few seconds for the drive activity to stop, and press Enter.**

You see a second Darwin prompt, with the correct disk specified in the brackets.

Specifying Boot Options

This section explains how to specify boot options for the Leopard Retail DVD and the effect of each.

At the boot prompt, you can type options that control the boot process. Table 2.2 lists the options you can type at the Darwin boot prompt.

Table 2.2 Darwin Boot Options

Option	Meaning
-v	Verbose: all output is sent to the screen
-f	Rebuild the kext cache
-x	Safe mode: similar to Windows safe mode
-s	Single user mode

CROSS-REF

Appendix B contains explanations of various terms such as kext, kext cache, and so on.

At this point, don't worry about specifying any options other than -v because the kext cache can't be rebuilt; it's stored on the DVD, which can't be overwritten. Safe mode and single-user mode do not affect whether the disk boots.

1. **Type -v, and press Enter.**

A few lines of text appear on the screen, and then it clears and switches to graphics mode. The text continues down the screen.

At this point, the text looks like gibberish, but you should see one important line as highlighted in Figure 2.6.

Figure 2.6

Verbose boot screen

```
mig_table_max_displ = 79
Local APIC version not 0x14 as expected
Skipping duplicate extension "com.apple.iokit.IOAHCISerialATAPI" with older/same verison (1.0.0 -> 1.01).
Replacing extension "com.apple.iokit.IOAHCIBlockStorage" with newer versio (1.0.3 -> 1.1.0).
ACPI CA 20051117 [debug level-0 layer=0]
dsmos: Initializing...
dsmos: Hook and decryption contexts set†
dsmos: Starting
AppleACPICPU: ProcessorApicId=0 LocalApicId=0 Enabled
Loading security extension com.apple.security.TMSafetyNet
calling mpo_policy_init for TMSafetyNet
Security policy loaded: Sagety net for Time Machine (TMSafetyNet)
Loading security extension com.apple.security.seatbelt
calling mpo_policy_init for mb
Seatbelt MACF policy initialized
Security policy loaded: Seatbelt Policy (mb)
Loading security extension com.apple.nke.applicationfirewall
Copyright (c) 1982, 1986, 1989, 1991, 1993
        The Regents of the University of California. All rights reserved.

MAC Framework successfully initialized
using 5242 buffer headers and 4096 cluster IO buffer headers
IOAPIC: Version 0x11 Vectors 0:23
Extension "com.apple.driver.ACPI_SMC_PlatformPlugin" has immediate dependencies on both com.apple.kernel and com.apple.kpi compo
nents; use only one style.
mbinit: done
Security auditing service present
BSM auditing present
From path: "uuid",
Waiting for boot volume with UUID 2F9E0D53-A722-3F30-B8C6-AFBDE806C18
Waiting on <dict ID="0"><key>IOProviderClass</key><string ID="1">IOResources</string><key>IOResourceMatch</key><string ID="2">bo
ot-uuid-media</string></dict>
Apple16X50ACPI1: Identified Serial Port on ACPI Device=COMA
Apple16X50ACPI2: Identified Serial Port on ACPI Device=COMB
Apple16X50UARTSync1: Detected 16550AF/C/CF FIFO=16 MaxBaud=115200
Apple16X50UARTSync2: Detected 16550AF/C/CF FIFO=16 MaxBaud=115200
ACPI: Button driver prevents system sleep
Got boot device = IOService:/AppleACPIPlatformExpert/PCI0@0/AppleACPIPCI/IDE@7,1/AppleIntelPIIXATARoot/CHN1@1/AppleIntelPIIXPATA
/ATADeviceNub@0/IOATAPIProtocolTransport/IOSCSIPeripheralDeviceNub/IOSCSIPeripheralDeviceType05/IODVDServices/IODVDB
BSD root: disk1s3, major 14, minor 3
Jettisoning kernel linker.
```

You should look for a line starting `BSD root: disk1s3`. The numbers you see may be different, but when you see it, you know that Leopard is at least going to boot on your computer.

NOTE

BSD root is the disk from which Darwin boots the main operating system. If Darwin can't identify it, then it can't boot.

After you see that line, you should see more messages scroll up the screen. The boot process takes quite a few minutes when you boot from the DVD. Be patient!

Finally, the screen goes blue and then black with the spinning beach ball in the top-left corner, and you see the Leopard Aurora desktop. Hooray!

Figure 2.7 shows the Leopard Aurora desktop.

If you get stuck at a blank desktop, a blue desktop, or the spinning beach ball, turn to the troubleshooting section in Chapter 6.

Figure 2.7

Leopard Aurora desktop

Preparing Your Hard Disk

This section explains how to prepare your external USB drive so Leopard can be installed to it. You partition and format the disk, ready for use.

Right now, you have a bare-bones version of Leopard running from the DVD. The first thing you need to do is to prepare your hard disk for the full installation of Leopard.

You need to select a language to use for the installation at the language selection screen, as shown in Figure 2.8a.

After you have selected your language, you proceed through a few more screens, which ask you to agree to the license conditions and then you arrive at a screen asking which disk you want to install Leopard to. You may or may not see any other disks at this point, although you may see your Windows disk(s) with a red exclamation mark on each one, if you haven't disconnected them.

This destination selection screen is shown in Figure 2.8b.

Figure 2.8

Language selection (a); the Select a Destination screen (b)

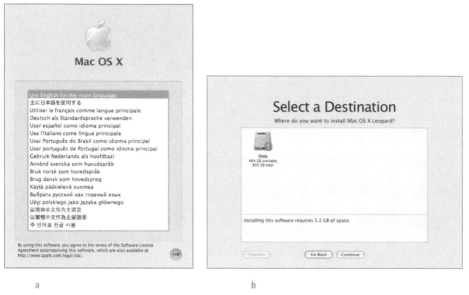

a   b

At this point, you should see a blank area for the destination. You need to prepare your disk so Leopard can use it. On Windows computers, this is called *formatting;* on Macintosh computers, it's called *erasing.* Leopard has its own disk format known as *Mac OS Extended (Journaled).*

N O T E

Leopard can read and write to Windows FAT disks, but it requires additional software (free) to be able to read and write to NTFS disks. This is covered in Chapter 14.

To format your disk, you use the Leopard Disk Utility. Figure 2.9 shows how to start the disk utility from the menu bar.

1. **Click Utility on the Leopard menu bar.**

2. **Select Disk Utility.**

This launches the Leopard application Disk Utility. You use this to format the disk that's ready to load Leopard.

Figure 2.9

Start disk utility

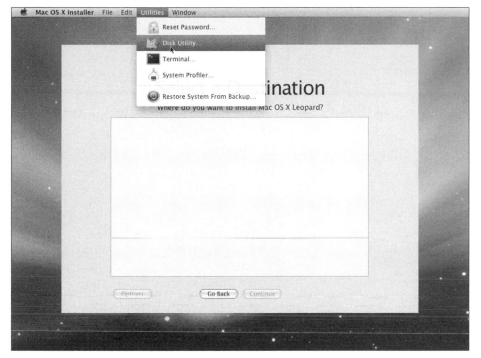

Although the Select a Destination screen you saw a moment ago may not show any disks, Disk Utility shows every disk attached to your computer. Figure 2.10 shows the initial screen with two hard disks.

In the left pane of the display, Disk Utility shows the disk drives attached to your system. In this case, I used VMware virtualization software to be able to capture screens. In your case, Disk Utility will show different disks. If you have disconnected your fixed hard disks, you should see only your external USB drive.

CAUTION

One of the disks shown may be your Windows system disk. Be very careful not to accidentally format it! Your Windows disk should be the first one shown, but double-check and triple-check by looking at the bottom right of Disk Utility to check the size.

First, you need to create a partition on the disk, as shown in Figure 2.11.

Figure 2.10

Disk Utility select disk

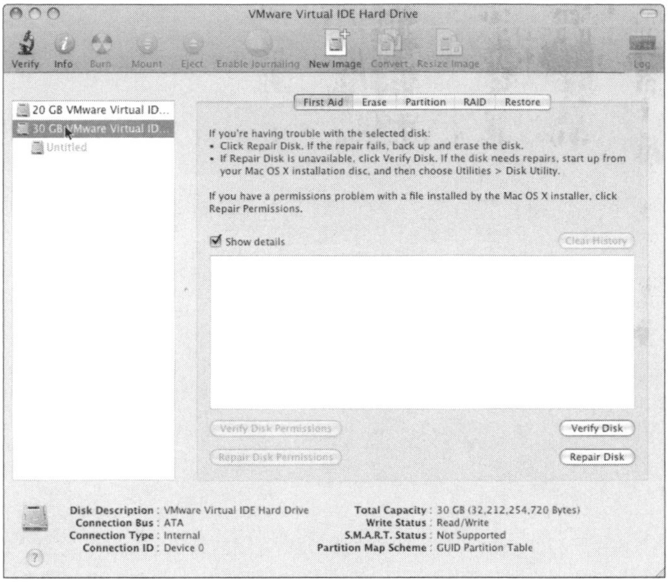

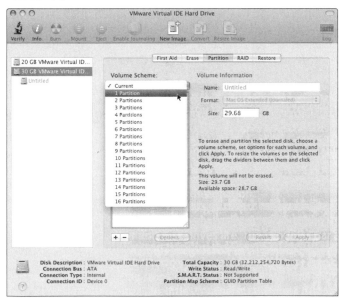

Figure 2.11

Partition disk

1. **Select your USB disk by clicking it in the left pane.**

2. **Click the Partition button at the top of Disk Utility.**

3. **Click the drop-down box under Volume Scheme, and select 1 Partition.**

4. **Type a name for the disk in the Name box on the right side.**

   Why not use **Hackintosh**?

5. **Select Mac OS Extended (Journaled) in the Format box.**

6. **Click the Options button, and select GUID Partition Table from the new panel.**

NOTE

The retail version of Leopard will not install a disk formatted with an MBR.

Figure 2.12a shows the drop-down sheet, with GUID Partition Table selected.

Figure 2.12

Disk partition scheme (a); the Select a Destination screen (b)

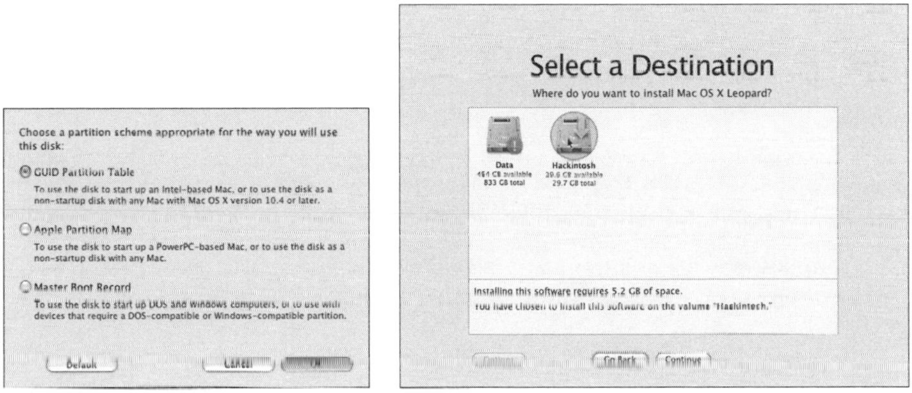

a   b

7. **Click Apply.**

   You have to wait while Disk Utility formats your disk, but it should be very quick.

CROSS-REF

Appendix B contains explanations of various disk formatting options.

8. After your disk has been formatted, click Disk Utility on the menu bar, and select Close.

The Select Destination panel reappears, showing your newly formatted disk.

9. Click that disk (Hackintosh, if you named it that).

A green arrow appears on the disk icon, as shown in Figure 2.12b.

The arrow indicates that Leopard can be installed to that disk.

10. Click Continue.

11. On the next screen, click Customize.

Specifying Installation Options

This section explains the Leopard installation options and how to select or deselect them. The Leopard retail version has these options:

- Printer drivers
- Additional fonts
- Language translations
- X11, a Unix windowing system

Unless your specific printer is in the list, you need not install any printers because you can add these later.

If you plan to always use English as your language, you can leave out the language translations.

You should include the additional fonts, unless you are very short on hard disk space.

Unless you are going to be running or developing applications that use X11, you can ignore that. Figure 2.13 shows the customize options screen.

Follow these steps to select customize options:

Each small triangle beside a heading expands or contracts the list. If the individual box is blue, it means that option is selected. If the heading box is blue, it means that all options under that heading are selected.

1. Place a check mark in each option that you want to select.

2. Click Done to proceed to the actual installation.

Finally, you are ready to install Leopard. Figure 2.14a shows the Install Summary screen.

3. **Click Install.**

   Leopard first wants to check your DVD. Because you've gotten this far with it and it's the first time you've used it, checking the DVD is probably pointless, so you can click the Skip button.

   Figure 2.14b shows this stage of the installation.

Figure 2.13

Customize options

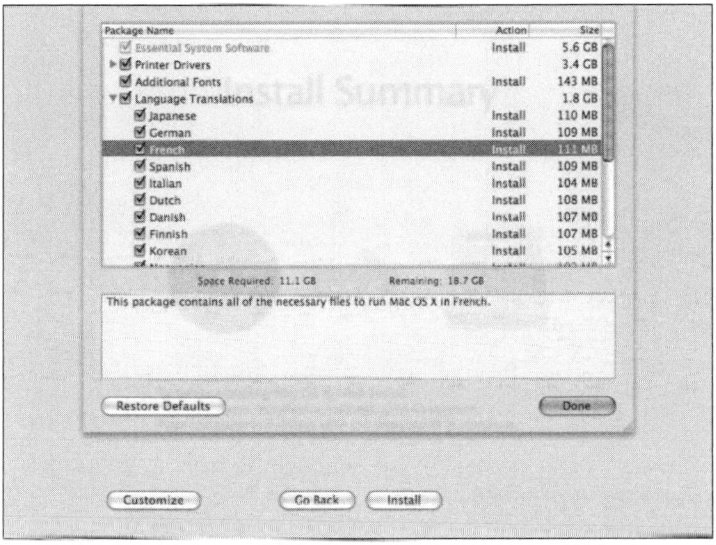

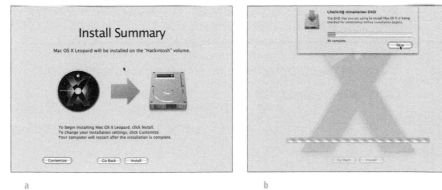

Figure 2.14

The Install Summary screen (a); checking the installation (b)

a   b

Leopard is now being installed. Normally, it takes between 20 and 60 minutes, depending on how fast your computer and disk drives are. The progress bar at the bottom of the screen gradually moves as the installation progresses, as shown in Figure 2.15a.

Occasionally, this display stops moving, but it shows how much more time the installation will take. Wait until all CD and hard disk activity has stopped for two or three minutes, and then restart your computer.

Eventually, you see the screen saying Leopard has been installed, as shown in Figure 2.15b.

Figure 2.15

Installing Leopard (a); installation succeeded (b)

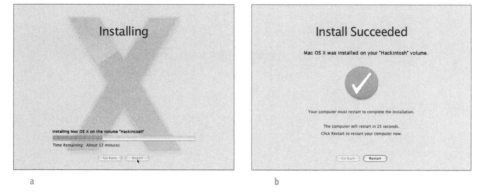

a   b

Watching the Welcome Video

After you have finished installing Leopard, you should watch the Leopard welcome video. This section explains how to do that and what you'll learn about Leopard from this video.

Booting your computer to run Leopard

Before you can watch the Leopard welcome video, you need to restart your computer and boot from the boot CD. Follow these steps:

1. **Open the CD/DVD drive, and remove the Leopard Retail DVD.**

2. **Insert the boot CD.**

3. **Press the reset switch on your computer (or power off and power back on).**

4. **Use whatever keystrokes your BIOS uses to boot from the CD drive.**

5. **At the Darwin boot screen, press the Esc key.**

This results in the boot selector screen as before, as shown in Figure 2.16.

Figure 2.16

Darwin boot selector

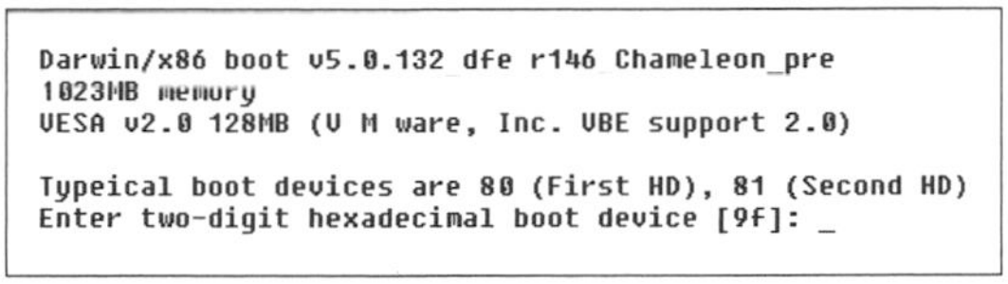

```
Darwin/x86 boot v5.0.132 dfe r146 Chameleon_pre
1023MB memory
VESA v2.0 128MB (V M ware, Inc. VBE support 2.0)

Typeical boot devices are 80 (First HD), 81 (Second HD)
Enter two-digit hexadecimal boot device [9F]: _
```

This time, however, you want to start from your hard disk, not the install disk.

If your USB drive is your only disk (in other words, you disconnected your fixed hard disks), then it is disk 80 (hexadecimal for 128). If you have a single hard disk, besides your external USB disk, then it is disk 80 and your USB disk is disk 81. If you have two internal hard disks, your USB disk is disk 82 and so on.

6. **Type the number of your hard disk, and press Enter.**

Figure 2.17 shows the boot screen for the case where the Hackintosh is the second hard disk.

Figure 2.17

Darwin boot disk

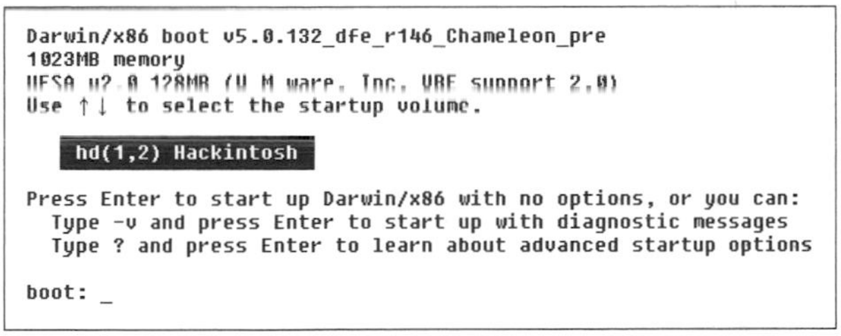

```
Darwin/x86 boot v5.0.132_dfe_r146_Chameleon_pre
1023MB memory
VESA v2.0 128MB (V M ware, Inc. VBE support 2.0)
Use ↑↓ to select the startup volume.

    hd(1,2) Hackintosh

Press Enter to start up Darwin/x86 with no options, or you can:
   Type -v and press Enter to start up with diagnostic messages
   Type ? and press Enter to learn about advanced startup options

boot: _
```

CAUTION

If, instead of your disk name (Hackintosh), you see something like "Foreign Operating System," you have selected the wrong disk. Press Esc again, and type a different number.

When you first boot your Leopard installation, you should force a rebuild of the kext cache.

CROSS-REF

Kexts and kext cache are explained in Appendix B.

7. Press F8 within a few seconds so that you can enter boot options.

8. Type `-v -f`, and press Enter

Again you see the commands roll up the screen. This time, you see many more commands because Leopard is reading each kext and placing it in the cache. Eventually, the screen clears and the lines roll down the screen.

At this point, you need to be sure that you see the `BSD root:` line again. The numbers are different, but it must be there.

CAUTION

If you don't see the BSD root: line, go to the troubleshooting section in Chapter 6.

Watching the welcome video

Eventually, the screen turns blue and then black or gray with the spinning beach ball. If you have the correct video kexts installed, you then see the Leopard welcome video. If you were using a real Macintosh, you would also hear sound from the video, although the music is rather banal.

Figure 2.18a shows the start of the welcome video. Figure 2.18b shows a screen from the middle of the video. Figure 2.18c shows the start of the final sequence.

Don't worry: The video is only a few seconds long.

CAUTION

If your screen stays stuck at the spinning beach ball or you don't see the welcome video, you don't have the correct video kexts. Refer to the troubleshooting section in Chapter 6.

Figure 2.18

Welcome video 1 (a); Welcome video 2 (b); Welcome video 3 (c)

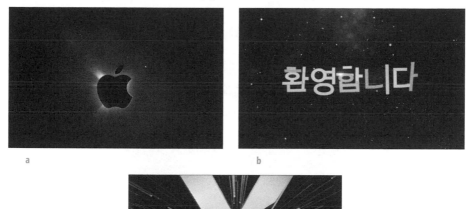

a

b

c

Entering Details About Yourself

This section walks you through the process of setting up your Leopard installation. This includes gathering information about your computer and you, and then setting up your login and home folder.

Figure 2.19 shows the Welcome to Leopard screen.

Selecting your keyboard

If Leopard doesn't recognize your keyboard, it asks you to press a couple of keys so it can be identified. After it has done that, it asks which country you are in so that it can use the correct keyboard layout.

TIP

The language you set here determines the dictionary that Leopard uses. Yes, it has a built-in dictionary.

Figure 2.20 shows the keyboard selection screen, with Australian highlighted.

Figure 2.19

Welcome to Leopard

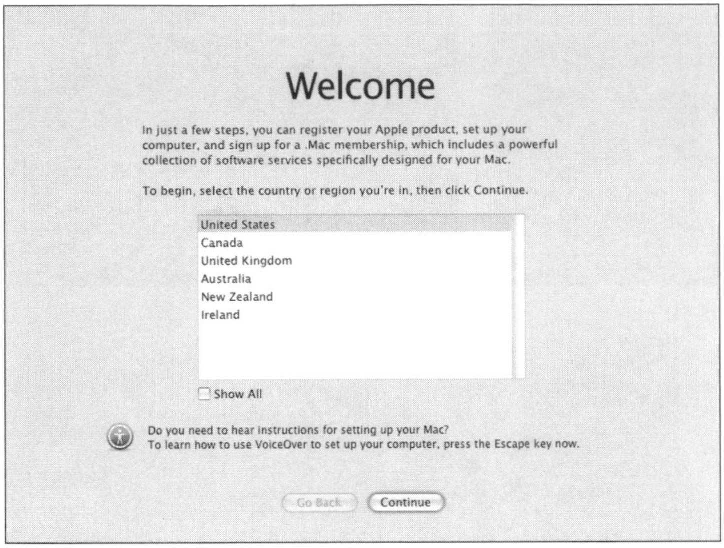

Figure 2.20

The Select Your Keyboard screen

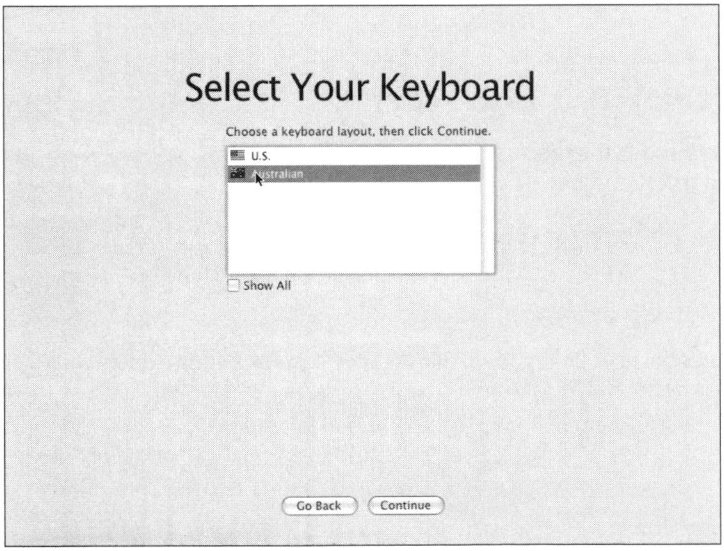

Transferring data from another Mac

If you already have a Mac computer, you can transfer data from it to your new installation. If you want to transfer data, you can do so by connecting to the Mac in a few different ways. Unless you really do want to transfer information, select Do not transfer my information now.

C R O S S - R E F

Leopard can read and write to your Windows disks if they are formatted as FAT disks. For NTFS disks, free software is available to enable it to read and write to them too. This is explained in Chapter 14.

Figure 2.21 shows the screen that asks if you want to transfer information from another Mac.

Figure 2.21

Already own a Mac?

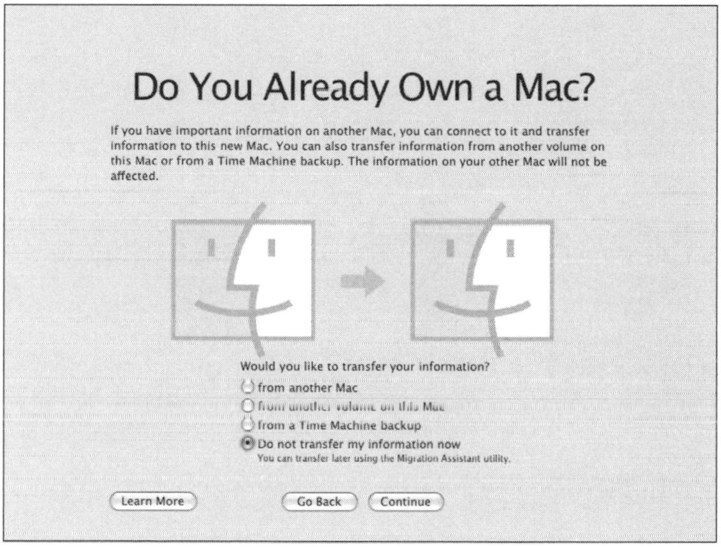

Entering your networking details

Next, Leopard wants to know how you connect to the Internet.

T I P

If you are using wired networking, Leopard may have already detected that and tries to connect you to the Internet.

If you are using wireless networking, however, Leopard probably won't automatically detect your network hardware, although some models of Dell computers use exactly the same chipset as Apple, so they connect wirelessly as though you had a real Apple Airport.

Unless Leopard automatically detects your network, select My computer does not connect to the Internet. You can set up your networking later.

Figure 2.22 shows the Internet connection screen.

Figure 2.22

How do you connect?

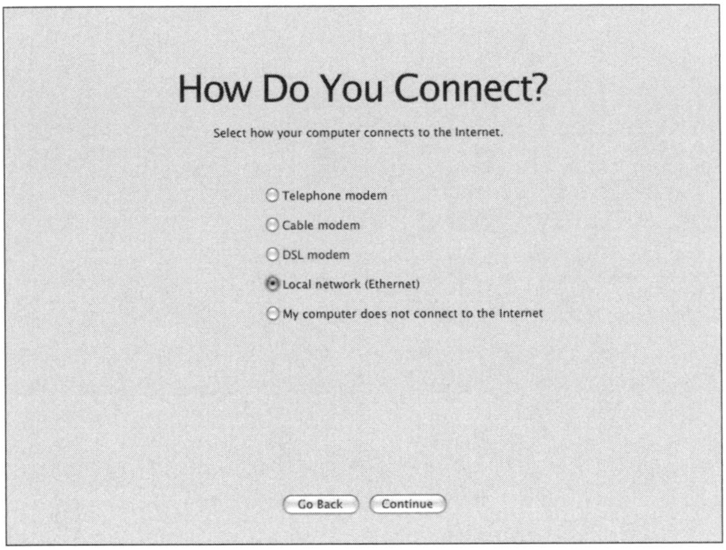

Entering your personal details

Now Leopard wants to know your most intimate personal details. This is used for a couple of purposes: It is used as the first index card in your Leopard address book, and it is the information sent to Apple to register your Leopard. Figure 2.23a shows the screen used to gather your personal information.

In this case, I gave my real name: Peter Baldwin. That is the name for my account on the computer. The other information is fake!

Apple is really nosy and wants to know where you are using the computer and what you are using it for. This is so that they can send you targeted information if you check the box allowing them to do just that. Figure 2.23b shows the drop-down box to select the other information.

Figure 2.23

Registration information (a); a few more questions (b)

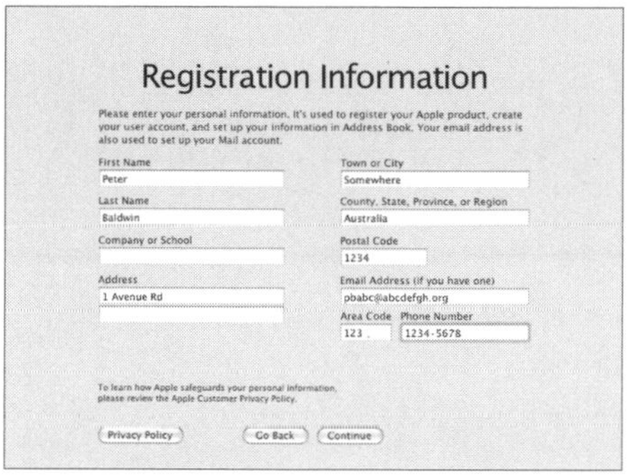

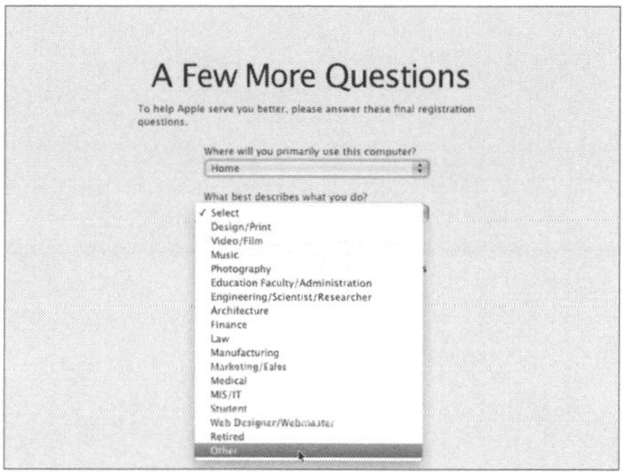

Leopard won't let you continue to the next screen until you select something for each box. You can either tell the truth or invent something; the choice is yours!

Leopard is about to set up a user account for you. The name you type here is the name Leopard uses for the account and the name of your home folder where your documents are stored. You need to choose carefully because changing these details later is very difficult. Figure 2.24a shows the screen gathering your user information and password.

Leopard automatically creates your home folder name from the name you type. In this case, it has called my home folder peterbaldwin. Leopard drops the capital letters and joins the two names together to form the name.

As always, Leopard blanks the password details. Leopard won't let you continue to the next screen until you have entered a password hint, nor will it let you just enter the password itself as the hint.

Leopard now requests that you send off your registration information.

TIP

If you select Register Now and you are connected to the Internet, your registration is sent. The choice is yours.

Figure 2.24b shows the registration screen.

If you don't wish to send the registration details (or if you can't because you don't have a network at this point), Leopard saves the information and places it in your home folder.

Figure 2.24

Create your account (a); register with Apple (b)

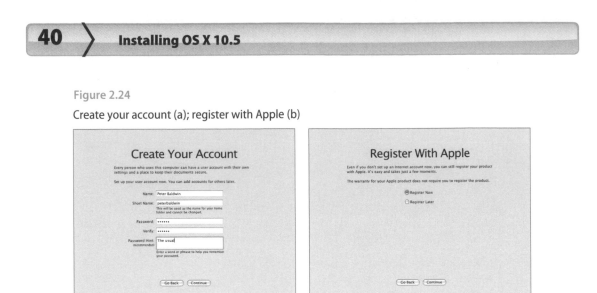

a   b

Setting time and date

You're in the home stretch now. Leopard wants to know where you are located so it can keep the time display in sync with local time. The time zone setting shows a map of the world for you to click where you are located, as shown in Figure 2.25.

Figure 2.25

Select a time zone

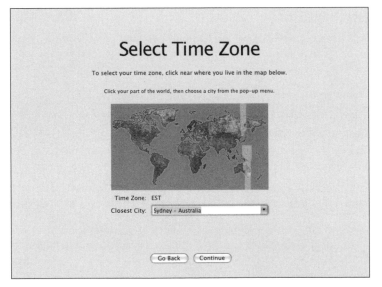

Leopard then allows you to set your local time and date. If you've been using Windows up to now, you will find the time that Leopard reads from your computer's hardware real-time clock is different from the time you saw in Windows.

C R O S S - R E F

Leopard uses a different timekeeping method from Windows, which can cause some issues with Windows time. See Appendix B for an explanation.

Seeing your Leopard screen for the first time

After one last entreaty to register your Leopard, you finally see your first Leopard screen. Figure 2.26 shows the first Leopard screen you see.

Figure 2.26

Your first look at Leopard

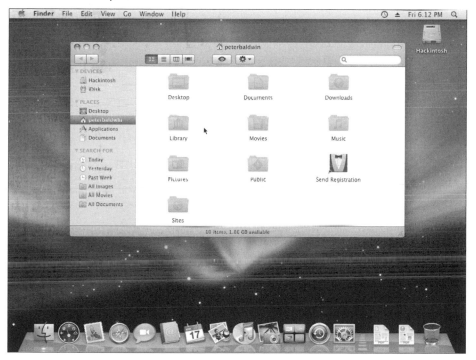

Congratulations! You achieved what used to be impossible: running an Apple operating system on non-Apple hardware.

Troubleshooting

If your installation doesn't start or you can't get the Leopard Retail DVD to boot, see Chapter 6 for some suggestions on things to try.

Summary

In this chapter, you learned how to install OS X Leopard to an external hard disk. Along the way, you learned about the insides of your computer and how it works.

If you are happy with the way Leopard runs from your external hard disk, you can go straight to the latter part of Chapter 6 and then on to Part II of this book.

If you want to dual-boot Leopard with Windows XP, go to Chapter 5. If you want to dual boot with either Windows Vista or Windows 7, go to Chapter 4.

3

Avoiding the Need for the Boot CD

Now that you have installed Leopard on your external drive, you need to start it by using the boot disk. This is not only an inconvenience, but it also prevents you from enjoying the full experience of Leopard.

When the separate boot disk was created, it used syslinux. Syslinux is a boot loader originally developed to load Linux systems, but it was modified to create rescue boot disks and other special purpose disks, such as OS X boot disks.

In this chapter, you learn how to download some software, install it on your Leopard disk, and use it to modify your Leopard installation so it can boot without using the boot disk. You also update Leopard to the latest version.

Finding and Downloading the Relevant Software

In this section, you locate the software to allow you to update your Leopard installation and transfer it to your Leopard disk.

Don't worry if your Leopard is not connected to the Internet because you can download the software to a Windows disk and then transfer it to Leopard using a USB key.

Downloading the file to update Leopard

Before you modify your Leopard installation, you need to first update to the latest version, because some modifications made during the update may remove some of your customizations—for example, sound drivers.

At the time of this writing, Leopard is up to its ninth version. Each version is identified by a number after a second decimal point. The first version of Leopard was OS X 10.5.0; the first update was 10.5.1. The latest at the time of writing is 10.5.8.

You can download the latest version from Apple's Web site. Two versions are available: the regular update and the combo update.

You should use the combo update because the regular update is for use only when you have the version immediately prior to the latest.

To go from version 10.5.5 to 10.5.6, you can use the regular update; to go from a version earlier than 10.5.5, you must use the combo update. This section uses 10.5.6 as the example, but it works exactly the same regardless of the update you use. Follow these steps:

CAUTION

Each combo update is around 650MB, so it may take some time to download. As always, be sure you don't go over any download cap from your ISP.

1. **Navigate to** www.apple.com/downloads/macosx/apple/macosx_updates/.

2. **Scroll down until you find the 10.5.6 combo update.**

3. **Click Download.**

4. **Save the file to your Windows hard disk or to a USB key.**

TIP

A USB key is always formatted with the FAT file system, which Leopard can read, so you don't need a special Mac formatted key.

Downloading the file to modify your boot system

This file converts your Leopard disk so it can boot directly from your hard disk, rather than requiring the boot CD each time.

You can do this in several ways, but the easiest by far is to use a Mac application called Universal Installer, or UInstaller, created by a Hackintosh expert known as pcwiz. Here's how you do it:

1. **Navigate to pcwiz's Web site at** http://pcwizcomputer.com.

2. **Click Downloads.**

3. **Click [Mac OSx86] Universal OSx86 Installer.**

4. **Scroll down to the line: Download Universal OSx86 Installer here, and click the link labeled *here*.**

5. **Save the file to your Windows hard disk or a USB key.**

Using the Installer to Complete Your OS X Installation

In this section, you learn to update your Leopard installation to the latest version and then install a boot loader so you are freed from using the boot disk every time you want to boot.

CAUTION

Ensure that your boot disk is still in your CD/DVD drive.

1. **Use the boot disk to boot your computer to Leopard.**

Remember to type the number of the disk holding the installation, as you did in Chapter 2.

Installing the combo update

First, you need to copy the update file to your Leopard disk. Leopard can read and write to FAT disks (such as a USB key) and can read but not write to NTFS disks. So if your file is on one of your Windows disks, you can copy it.

Most Mac install files are supplied as .dmg files. A .dmg file is a disk image and mounts on your Leopard in the same way that a DVD or USB key does. For all intents and purposes, Leopard sees it as another disk drive and displays an icon on your desktop. Follow these steps:

1. **Double-click the icon for the disk that contains your Windows data or your USB key.**

2. **In the Finder window that opens, navigate to where you have stored the file** MacOSXUpdCombo10.5.6.dmg**.**

Figure 3.1a shows the combo update for 10.5.6 in the Finder window on my computer.

3. **Drag the file icon from the Windows disk to your desktop.**

Because it is coming from a disk external to your Leopard disk, it is copied to your desktop.

4. **Double-click the desktop icon to open the disk image.**

Figure 3.1b shows the installer package for the update after double-clicking the installer.

In OS X, a package is a bundle of files that are installed using the Mac OS X Installer. This is very similar to a Microsoft Installer file (.msi) in Windows.

Figure 3.1

Combo update in Finder (a); combo update package (b)

a   b

5. **Double-click the .pkg icon.**

This launches the Leopard installer, in the same way that double-clicking an .msi file in Windows opens the Windows installer.

Figure 3.2a shows the introductory screen for the updater.

6. **Click Continue.**

Figure 3.2b shows the ReadMe screen giving locations where you can find out more information about the update.

Figure 3.2

Combo update introduction screen (a); combo update readme screen (b)

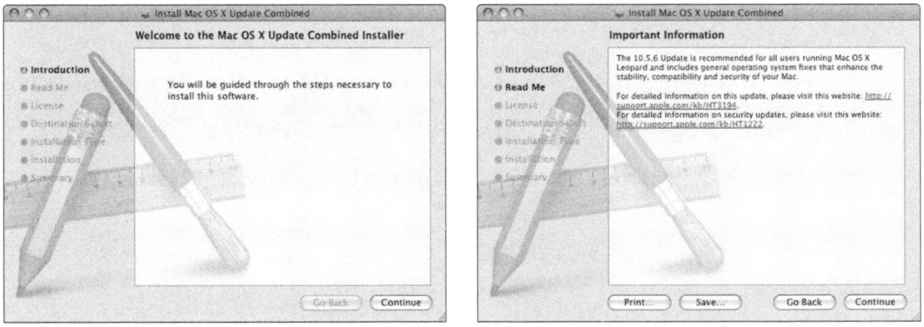

a   b

7. **Click Continue.**

Leopard asks you to read and agree to the license agreement. Figure 3.3a shows the small window (known as a sheet) that slides out of the main window.

8. **Click Agree.**

Leopard asks you where you want to install the update. Naturally, you want to install it to your Leopard disk. If you were updating a different computer on a network, you could click Change Install Location.

Figure 3.3b shows the dialog box to change location or continue to install on the default disk.

Figure 3.3

License agreement (a); combo update standard install (b)

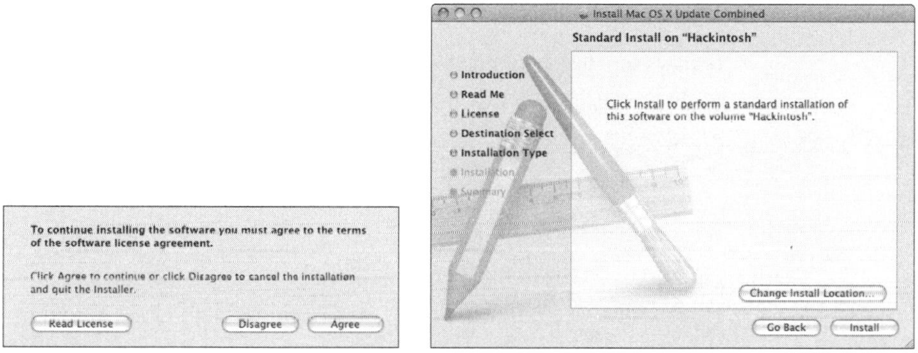

a   b

9. **Click Install.**

Leopard wants to be sure that you have enough privilege to carry out the installation, so it asks for your password. Unless a user has administrator privileges, the update cannot be installed. You'll encounter this frequently while using the Leopard computer, so you should get used to this small pop-up.

Figure 3.4a shows the password request box.

Leopard gives you one last chance to back out of the installation, as shown in Figure 3.4b.

The installer updates your installation. Normally, this takes 5 to 10 minutes.

Figure 3.5a shows the installation screen at the start of the update.

Figure 3.5b shows the screen partway through the update.

Figure 3.4

Combo update password request (a); combo update continue installation screen (b)

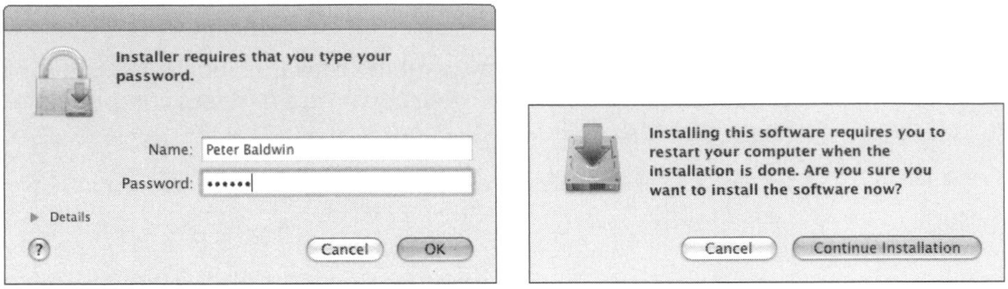

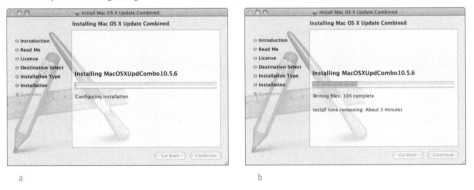

a

b

Figure 3.5

Combo update configuring installation screen (a); combo update installing (b)

a

b

Wait until the installation is complete.

Figure 3.6 shows the screen you hope to see at the end of the installation.

Many (but not all) software installations in Leopard require you to restart your computer. In the case of the update, many system files have been changed. Because most of them are required from the very start of booting, the old ones have to be unloaded and replaced by the new ones by rebooting.

10. **Click Restart.**

Your computer now shuts down and restarts.

Figure 3.6

Combo update installation complete screen

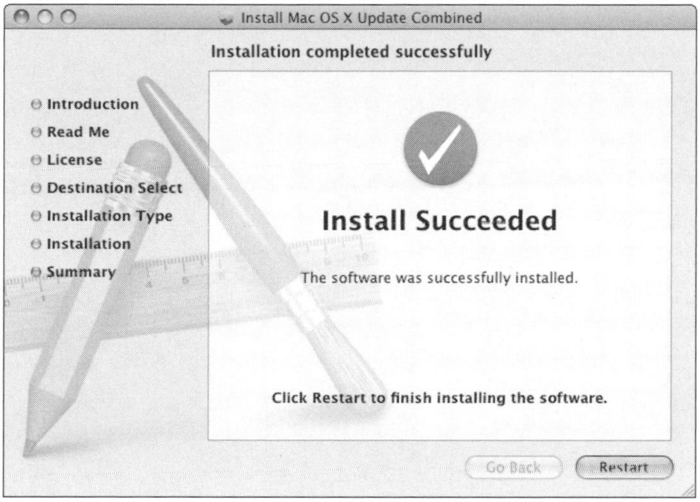

CAUTION

Be sure that your boot disk is still in your CD/DVD drive and that you select to boot from the CD/DVD as you did earlier. Enter -v and -f as boot options to be sure your kext cache is rebuilt and all the new kexts are being used.

After Leopard has restarted, you should first check that you have updated successfully.

1. Click the Apple icon on the menu bar to open the Apple menu.

2. Click About this Mac.

You see a small display that tells you a little about your "Mac." Check that the software version is the same as the version you updated to.

Figure 3.7 shows the small window giving you information about your Mac.

TIP

If you click the version number shown (10.5.6), it shows you the exact internal Apple description of the version you are using.

Figure 3.7

About this Mac

Installing the boot loader

Now it's time to install the boot loader so you no longer need the boot CD. You'll also install a couple of small niceties for your installation. First, you need to copy the loader from either your Windows disk or your USB key drive. Follow these steps:

1. **Using Finder, locate the UInstaller (.zip) file you downloaded earlier.**

2. **Drag the zip file to your desktop.**

3. **Double-click the zip icon.**

Leopard automatically unpacks the zip file and places a new folder on your desktop.

4. **Double-click the folder icon to open it.**

Figure 3.8 shows what is contained in the folder when the zip file is unzipped.

 CAUTION

You should only run UInstaller from within that folder because it contains support files required by the installer.

5. **Double-click UInstaller.**

This opens the UInstaller main screen. Figure 3.9 shows the main screen for UInstaller.

Figure 3.8

Inside UInstaller folder

Figure 3.9

UInstaller

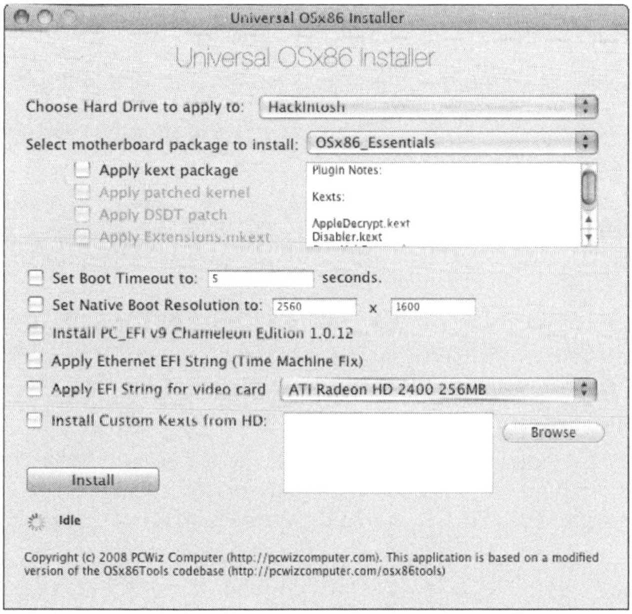

Installer may or may not show your Leopard disk first up. They are usually listed in alphabetical order, so if you have a disk whose name starts with a letter before the name of your Leopard disk, that one is listed before it.

6. **Click the drop-down box on the top line and select your install disk.**

Pcwiz and other authors have developed additional packages specifically for particular motherboards. At this point, if you are connected to the Internet, you can look for a package for your motherboard. If not, you can always run UInstaller again later.

NOTE
If you are not connected to the Internet, skip ahead to Step 12.

7. **Click UInstaller on the menu bar.**

8. **Click Download more plugins….**

9. **If you see your motherboard listed, click the line with its name and then click Download selected.**

10. **Close UInstaller, and restart it by double-clicking it.**

11. **From the drop-down menu for Select motherboard package to install, select the appropriate package.**

12. **Place a check in the box for Apply kext package.**

If you downloaded a motherboard package, you also see an Extensions.kext file with it.

13. **Click Apply extensions.mkext if you have downloaded a motherboard package.**

Setting boot timeout

When you boot your computer, the Darwin boot loader waits a certain time to give you the chance to press a key and enter startup options. You can change the length of this timeout using UInstaller.

1. **Enter the number of seconds you want Darwin to wait so you can press a key.**

Setting native boot resolution

If you allow Leopard to boot with the graphic boot screen, it uses an image 1024 pixels wide by 768 pixels tall. If your screen uses another resolution (such as 1920x1080), you can change the resolution of the image on the boot screen so the Apple logo is not distorted.

CAUTION
Be forewarned that this option often does not work! Leopard reads this line in the boot file, but it hasn't yet loaded the drivers for your graphics. Still, it's worth trying.

1. **Enter the x and y resolutions you want your boot resolution to be.**

My monitor is 1920 pixels wide by 1080 pixels high, so I would enter 1920 and 1080 in the two boxes.

Installing PC_EFI Chameleon

This next part is really the heart of what you are doing here: installing PC_EFI v9 Chameleon.

CROSS-REF

You can read more about EFI in Appendix B, but in essence it is the Macintosh equivalent of the BIOS in your non-Apple computer, but much smarter.

EFI stands for Extensible Firmware Interface; it's a method of adding much more "intelligence" to the BIOS. It stores information mostly about your hardware and has small programs that check the state of your hardware, in the same way that your BIOS checks your keyboard and memory.

Because your computer doesn't have a real EFI, you need to fake it. PC_EFI is a method of putting the type of information into the computer's memory that Leopard expects to see when it boots. When you selected Apply motherboard kexts in Step 12 and Apply Extensions.mkext in Step 13 (in the instructions earlier), you were telling the boot loader to add them to the EFI.

1. **Check Install PC_EFI v9 Chameleon Edition 1.0.12.**

Applying the Time Machine fix

On some systems, Time Machine doesn't work correctly because of a problem with detecting the Ethernet address of the system on which it's running. Using UInstaller, you can correct that. Even if you don't need the fix for Time Machine, you can install it anyway.

1. **Check Apply Ethernet EFI String (Time Machine Fix).**

Applying the EFI string for your video card

On a real Macintosh, the EFI contains lots of information about your video system. Using UInstaller, you can add that information to your fake EFI by selecting your video card from the drop-down box. UInstaller comes with more than 70 video cards supported, although only 8 of them are not nVidia cards.

My video card is an nVidia 7600GS, with 256MB of memory, as explained in Chapter 1.

1. **Select your video card from the drop-down box, and check Apply EFI String for video card.**

Installing customs kexts

Finally, UInstaller allows you to install some custom kexts from your hard disk. Because you don't have any kexts you want to install, you can leave that box unchecked.

Figure 3.10 shows the screen when I have selected everything for my system.

Figure 3.10

UInstaller configured

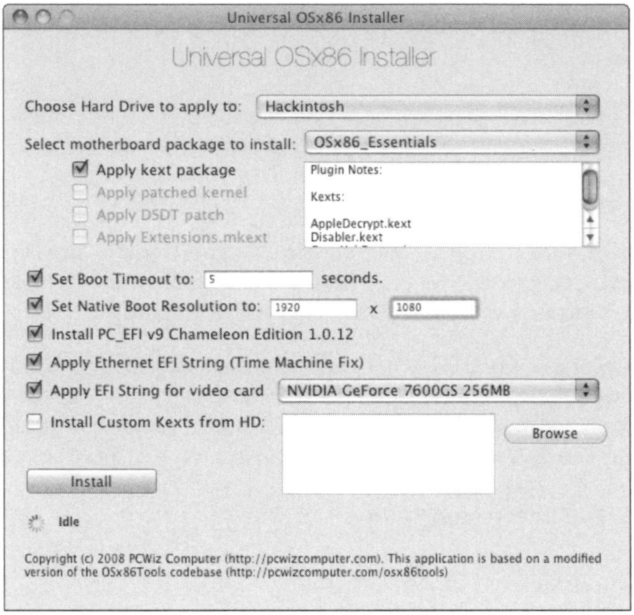

After just a couple of minutes, UInstaller has done its work and you get to the completed screen.

1. **Select Shutdown from the Apple menu.**

Selecting the Boot Disk from the Menu

This section walks you through restarting Leopard without using the boot disk. If all has gone according to plan, you can select the correct disk and have it boot directly to Leopard. Because you are not using your primary disk to boot, you need to select the external disk in your BIOS.

After UInstaller has finished, shut down Leopard and restart your computer. Follow these steps:

1. **Select Restart from the Apple menu.**

   When your computer restarts, you need to tell it to boot from your Hackintosh disk.

2. **Press the key you found in Chapter 2 that controls which device your computer boots from (usually F12).**

   Figure 3.11 shows the boot screen in the BIOS for VMware, showing the hard disks available.

Figure 3.11

Select external hard disk

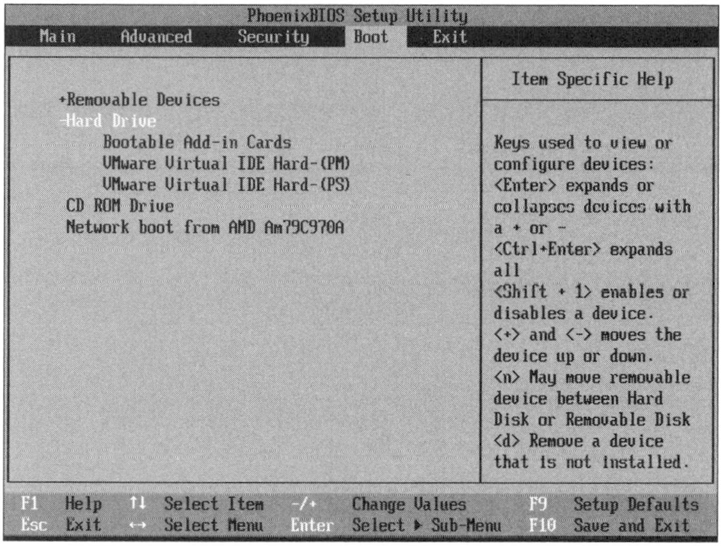

```
                    PhoenixBIOS Setup Utility
    Main     Advanced     Security     Boot     Exit

                                              Item Specific Help

      +Removable Devices
      -Hard Drive
          Bootable Add-in Cards              Keys used to view or
          VMware Virtual IDE Hard-(PM)       configure devices:
          VMware Virtual IDE Hard-(PS)       <Enter> expands or
      CD ROM Drive                           collapses devices with
      Network boot from AMD Am79C970A        a + or -
                                             <Ctrl+Enter> expands
                                             all
                                             <Shift + 1> enables or
                                             disables a device.
                                             <+> and <-> moves the
                                             device up or down.
                                             <n> May move removable
                                             device between Hard
                                             Disk or Removable Disk
                                             <d> Remove a device
                                             that is not installed.

    F1   Help   ↑↓  Select Item    -/+   Change Values    F9   Setup Defaults
    Esc  Exit   ↔   Select Menu   Enter  Select ▶ Sub-Menu  F10  Save and Exit
```

Remember that I used VMware so I could capture screen shots; other than taking photographs of the screen, this is the only way. Your disks will have different identifications, with your external hard disk most likely the last on the list.

3. **Select the external disk, and press Enter.**

This time, because the Darwin boot loader is loading from a hard disk, it is much faster than when loading from the CD.

You should finish at the same Darwin prompt as you had when starting from the CD.

Figure 3.12 shows the Darwin startup options screen.

Figure 3.12

Darwin startup options screen

```
Darwin/x86 boot v5.0.132 - Chameleon v1.0.11
Build date: 2008-05-09 20:12:22
1023MB memory
VESA v2.0 128MB (V M ware, Inc. VBE support 2.0)
Press any key to enter startup options. (5) _
```

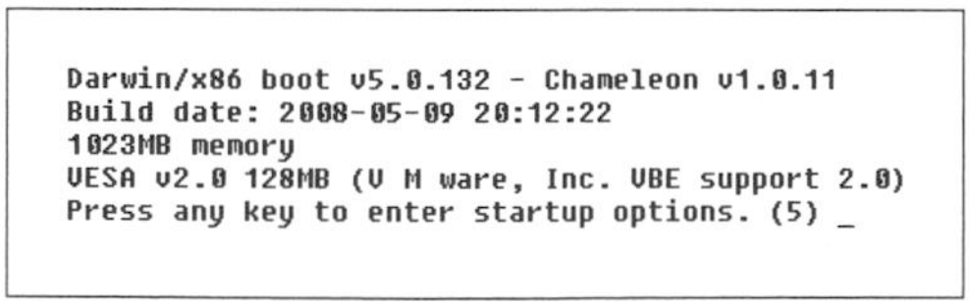

Again, you should start Leopard with the verbose option and to rebuild the kext cache.

Can you remember how to do this?

4. Press a key during the five-second pause.

This takes you to the Darwin boot options screen, as shown in Figure 3.13.

Figure 3.13

Darwin boot options screen

```
Darwin/x86 boot v5.0.132_dfe_r146_Chameleon_pre
1023MB memory
VESA v2.0 128MB (V M ware, Inc. UBE support 2.0)

Press Enter to start up Darwin/x86 with no options, or you can:
   Type -v and press Enter to start up with diagnostic messages
   Type ? and press Enter to learn about advanced startup options

boot: _
```

5. At the Darwin prompt, enter -v -f

Option $-v$ specifies verbose mode so you can see what is happening on the screen; $-f$ forces Darwin to rebuild the kexts cache (see Appendix B).

Again, you should look for the `BSD root:` line in the verbose boot screen.

Finally, you arrive at the Leopard screen. This time, you don't get any dialog boxes because you have already set up Leopard.

Now you need to start configuring Leopard to your own personal preferences. Chapter 9 walks you through that procedure.

Installing a Different Bootloader

While PC_EFI allows you to boot from your external hard disk, it is still necessary to select the Leopard hard disk in the BIOS as the disk to boot from. By using an alternative bootloader, you can use either your existing Windows system disk or your Leopard disk when you boot.

CAUTION

Be warned that this modifies the boot sector of your Windows disk. To return to your normal Vista or Windows 7 boot-loader, you need to boot from your Windows install disk to repair your Windows installation.

At the time of writing, the Chameleon 2 installer is at the Release Candidate 2 (RC2) version. Although the files for RC3 are available, installing them is not as straightforward as using the installer. If, by the time you read this, there is an installer available for RC3, use it in place of RC2.

Follow these steps to install the Chameleon bootloader:

1. **Navigate to** `http://chameleon.osx86.hu/` **and scroll down the page to the heading "Chameleon 2.0-RC2 is available …"**

2. **Click the link and then scroll down to the heading "Download information."**

3. **Click the link "Installer package" and then click the link "here."**

4. **Download the file and save it your Leopard drive.**

NOTE

If you can't access the Internet from your Leopard computer you can download the installer to your Windows computer and use a USB drive to install to your Leopard disk.

5. **Double-click the "Chameleon-2.0-r431.pkg" file.**

Figure 3.14 shows the installer's greeting screen.

Figure 3.14

Chameleon installer screen

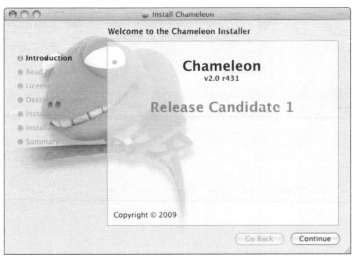

6. **Click Continue until you get to the software license agreement screen.**

7. **Click Agree.**

8. **At the next screen, click Install and enter your password to confirm the install.**

9. **Wait while Chameleon is installed and then restart your computer.**

Now you see a graphical boot screen that shows your Leopard install disk and your Windows disks, with a Windows symbol and a label NTFS. This is shown in Figure 3.15.

Figure 3.15

Chameleon bootloader screen

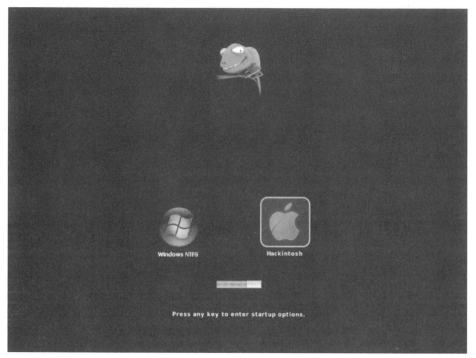

Summary

In this chapter, you learned to update your Leopard installation to the latest version, and you made it possible to start your computer without requiring a boot disk.

If you are happy with starting either Windows or Leopard by selecting the boot disk from your BIOS, you can go straight to Part II, "Setting Up and Customizing OS X."

If you prefer to have both operating systems on the same disk, you should go to either Chapter 4 if you are using Windows Vista or Windows 7 or go to Chapter 5 if you are using Windows XP.

4

Installing to a Hard Disk with Windows Vista Already Installed

In the preceding chapters, you've installed OS X to a separate hard disk. The advantage of this method is that it isolates your Leopard disk from the rest of your system. The downside is that it requires you to use your BIOS to choose which disk to boot from.

In this chapter, you learn how to install Leopard to a hard disk that already contains a Windows Vista or Windows 7 installation.

First you back up your Vista installation in case of errors. Then you create a new partition on your Vista or Windows 7 disk to allow OS X to be installed. Then you modify your Leopard installation disk so that it will install to a Windows disk.

After installing Leopard, you check that both operating systems start correctly and install a boot loader so you can choose which operating system to run at boot time.

Performing a Complete Image Backup of Your Vista Hard Disk

In this section, you completely back up your Vista or Windows 7 installation so that if anything goes wrong, you can restore to exactly where your system was before you started. This is essential disaster insurance!

Most people back up their files using a file backup method. In a file backup, your data is written to the backup medium file by file. When you want to recover a file, you simply select it from the list on the backup medium and copy it to where you want it.

An image backup is different from a file backup. An image backup knows nothing about files: It simply copies every single bit of data from the disk to the backup medium. In effect, the backup is like a photographic snapshot of everything on your hard disk. An image backup backs up your files, your programs, your preferences, and even your hard disk's boot sector.

You can use a series of DVDs to do an image backup, but more likely you use an external hard disk.

CAUTION

If you restore from an image backup, you restore the entire disk, not file by file. This is important because if your user files have changed since you last did a complete image backup, they will be overwritten by the old files when you restore.

Finding and downloading the software

If you have the Ultimate, Business, or Enterprise version of Vista or Windows 7, you already have image backup software on your computer. This is known as the Backup and Restore Center.

Otherwise, you need to download and purchase some image backup software. Table 4.1 shows a selection of the best known ones.

Table 4.1 Image Backup Software

Application	URL
Macrium Reflect (Free)	www.macrium.com/reflectfree.asp
DriveImage XML (Free)	www.runtime.org/driveimage-xml.htm
Drive Backup Free	www.paragon-software.com/home/db-express/features.html
Acronis True Image	www.acronis.com/
Norton Ghost	www.symantec.com/norton/ghost
Paragon Hard Disk Manager	www.paragon-software.com/home/hdm-personal/
O&O Disk Image 3	www.oo-software.com/home/en/products/oodiskimage/index.html
Terabyte Image for Windows	www.terabyteunlimited.com/image-for-windows.htm

Although the first three in the list are free, I have no experience with them, but you should certainly try one of them out. Just be sure you have a restore disk to boot your computer.

My favorite is O&O Disk Image 3, but any of those will work fine. I also use the Vista Backup and Restore Center: call me paranoid! I also use separate file backup software that I run every day. Because I don't store my data on the C: drive I only do an image backup once a week or so. File backups run every day.

Choose one of these, download it, and install it.

CAUTION

Be sure that you download the image backup software's restore disk and burn it to a CD. Without it you can't restore your image to your computer.

My preference would be to test the backup software first, just to be certain that it's going to rescue me if I make a mistake. And yes, I did manage to completely wipe my hard disk while writing this book. But I had two image backups to choose from.

Creating a disk image

Regardless of which software you use for your image backup, you need to be sure that everything is backed up. Every backup solution has an option to verify the backup. Be sure that it is turned on. This means that once you have written every byte to the backup media it reads what it has written and compares it with what is on the original disk.

Using Vista Ultimate, Business or Enterprise editions

Follow these steps to back up your data before installing the Mac software:

1. **Click the Vista Start orb.**

2. **Type Backup in the search box.**

3. **Click Backup and Restore Center when it appears in the programs section at the top of the window.**

   Figure 4.1 shows the greeting screen of the Backup and Restore Center.

4. **Click Back up computer.**

Figure 4.1

Backup and Restore Center

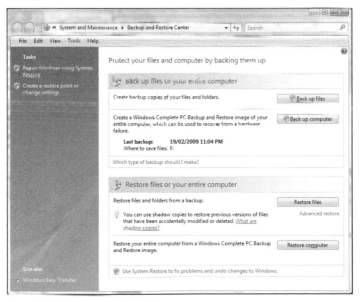

5. **Click Continue on the User Account Control window.**

   Backup and Restore then searches for a suitable hard disk attached to your computer. If you have already done an image backup and it is online, the computer finds it and defaults to that disk. Otherwise, it shows all your disks in the drop-down box.

6. **Select the disk to use in the drop-down box.**

7. **Click Next.**

8. **Select the disks you want to back up by putting a check in each box.**

   Normally, this is simply your C: drive, which is already checked.

9. **Click Next.**

10. **Click Start Backup, and wait while the backup is done.**

Using other downloaded software

You need to read the documentation that comes with the product you bought. Be sure to save your backup to a disk other than your system disk!

Restoring your system from the disk image

If the worst happens and you erase your system disk or make it unusable in some other way, you need your recovery CD or DVD.

Using the Vista install DVD

If you used Vista Backup and Restore, you simply boot from your Vista install DVD. Figure 4.2 shows the initial display when you boot from the Vista install DVD.

Figure 4.2

Vista install DVD

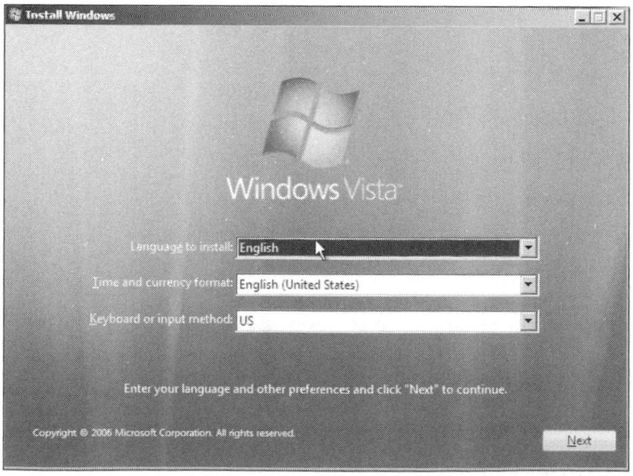

1. **Click Next.**

Figure 4.3 shows the startup options screen.

Figure 4.3

Vista startup options

2. **Click Repair your computer.**

The Vista installer looks for an existing copy of Vista. In Figure 4.4, you can see that it can't find an existing copy of Vista.

Figure 4.4

System recovery options

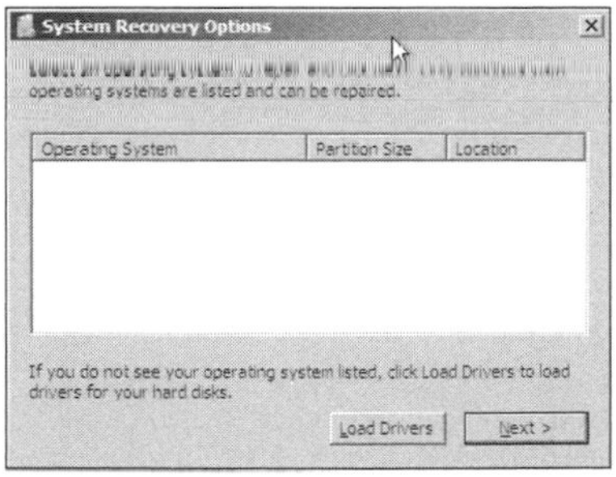

3. **Click Next.**

In Figure 4.5, you see that Vista provides you with a few recovery options.

Figure 4.5

Vista recovery options

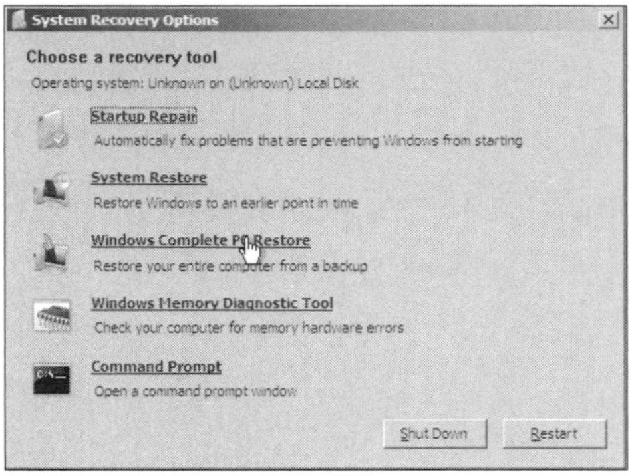

4. **Click Windows Complete PC Restore.**

In Figure 4.6, you can see Vista searching for a hard disk containing the image backup.

Figure 4.6

Restore your computer

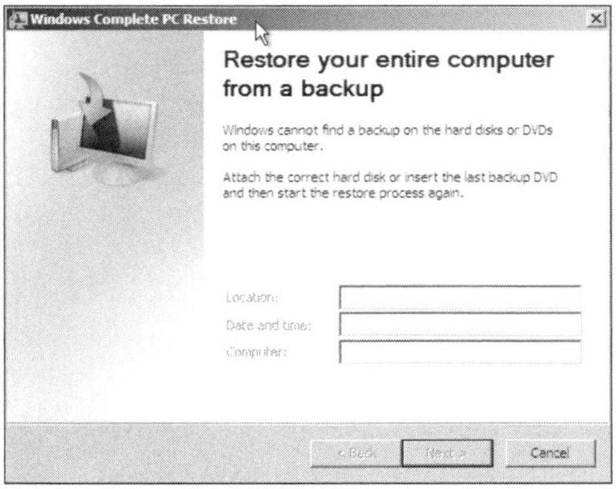

In this case, because it was recorded using VMware, no disk contains the Vista backup, but if you had a disk with the backup, it would be shown in the box.

5. **Select the backup you want to restore, and wait while Vista completes the restore.**

Using the recovery disk for the software you downloaded

Although the details and screens will be different depending on the software you are using, the basic principles are exactly the same:

- Boot from the recovery disk
- Select the backup you want to restore
- Select where you want to restore to
- Wait while it restores

Downloading Required Software to Start Vista and OS X

This section walks you through the process of downloading two more items of essential software you need before you can install OS X to your Vista disk:

- Software to partition your system disk
- Software to modify the Vista boot loader

In addition, you need to use your Vista or Windows 7 installation DVD to repair the boot sector.

If your computer came with Vista preinstalled, you likely do not have a complete installation DVD, but rather a repair disk. If this is the case, be sure to follow the steps in the section "Downloading software to repair your Vista boot disk," later in this chapter.

Downloading software to partition your Vista system disk

Vista has a built-in utility called diskpart that partitions disks. You access it through the command prompt. Diskpart can be used to expand a partition, provided you have enough free space on the disk. It also can be used to shrink a partition, but only under certain circumstances.

During normal operation of your computer, files are not written in a neat fashion to the same area of the disk but are scattered around the disk. This is done for performance reasons, but it results in lots of blank areas on the disk. For example, you might expect that a 120GB disk with 60GB of free space would have a so-called high water mark at 60GB, leaving the second half of the disk empty. But because of the way the files are written, the high water mark might be at 110GB, leaving only 10GB of space at the end of the disk. In this case, diskpart would be able to shrink the partition only to 110GB.

What is required is software that can move the files into the same area of the disk and thus make space for a larger partition.

Several programs are capable of doing this. Table 4.2 shows a selection of these.

Table 4.2 Partition Management Software

Application	URL
Acronis Partition Manager	www.acronis.com/
Partition Magic	www.symantec.com/norton/partitionmagic
Paragon Partition Manager	www.paragon-software.com/home/pm-personal/

These are all commercial software programs, but an excellent partition manager is free. It is GPartEd (pronounced "gee part ed"). It is available for download from http://gparted. sourceforge.net/.

GPartEd is supplied as a disk image (.iso file). You need to burn it to a CD and use it to boot your computer. Several programs can do this (Nero Burning ROM, AShampoo Burning Studio, Roxio Creator, among others), but my particular favorite is ImgBurn, available from www.imgburn.com/.

If you already have commercial software, use that; otherwise, give ImgBurn a try. Follow these steps:

1. **Download GPartEd, and save to your disk.**

2. **Use image-burning software to burn GPartEd to a CD.**

Be sure to burn it as an image; don't simply copy the iso file to the CD.

Downloading software to modify the Vista boot loader

Unfortunately, Vista and Windows 7 don't always play nicely with other operating systems: Windows tends to see itself as the only operating system on your computer. In order to be able to use your computer to boot either system easily, you need to modify the Vista boot loader. This is the small program that takes control after the ROM BIOS has finished its work. Its function is to load the first part of the operating system.

 CROSS-REF
Appendix B contains more discussion of the boot process for a computer.

Vista (and Windows 7) is different from earlier versions of Windows in that rather than store the details about the boot process in a single file, it uses a Boot Configuration Database. Vista provides a utility called BCDEdit that allows you to modify the database.

Unfortunately, like diskpart, it is command line driven, and unless you type the commands exactly, it either does not work or sets parameters that are inappropriate and may render your computer unable to boot.

Fortunately, a programmer named Mahmoud H. Al-Qudsi has written a utility called EasyBCD, and it is exactly that: It makes editing the BCD easy!

Download the latest version from `http://neosmart.net/` and install it. Please also consider making a donation to keep the site operating.

Downloading software to repair your Vista boot sector

If you are using an HP or Dell computer, skip straight to the third paragraph, because you definitely cannot repair your boot sector with the disks the manufacturers supply to you!

Before you download this software, insert your Vista install (or repair) disk and boot from it. If you see screens like those shown in Figures 4.2, 4.3, and 4.4, then you can use it to repair your boot sector. If your disk looks different or gives you different options, then you should download a disk specially created for exactly what you need to do.

On the same Web site where you downloaded EasyBCD (`http://neosmart.net/blog/2008/windows-vista-recovery-disc-download/`), you find a copy of the Vista recovery disk. Follow these steps:

1. **Go to** `http://neosmart.net/blog/2008/windows-vista-recovery-disc-download/`**, and download the .torrent file.**

2. **Use your bit torrent software to download the actual recovery disk.**

3. **Burn it to a CD (it's small enough to fit on a CD).**

At last you have enough software to be able to actually start installing.

Partitioning the Vista System Disk

Now that you have downloaded all the software you might need and made an image backup of your hard drive, it's time to tackle the hard stuff: partitioning your disk and installing Leopard. This section explains how you partition your hard disk.

As standard, the retail Leopard installation disk will not install to a disk partitioned as MBR (Master Boot Record). Instead it requires a disk partitioned as GPT (GUID Partition Table).

To install to an MBR disk you need to modify the installer. To do this, create an extra partition as a temporary measure, copy the Leopard installer to that partition, and modify it. You then use that partition to carry out the installation.

CROSS-REF

Appendix B contains explanations of different disk partition types. In the screen shots, I use GPartEd and partition a VMware drive. Details of your disk are, of course, different; likewise, if you are using different partitioning software, your screens look different.

Shrinking your existing partition

First, you need to shrink your existing partition to leave space for the new partition. Follow these steps:

1. **Insert your GPartEd disk, and boot from it.**

Figure 4.7 shows the startup screen from GPartEd.

Figure 4.7

GPartEd startup screen

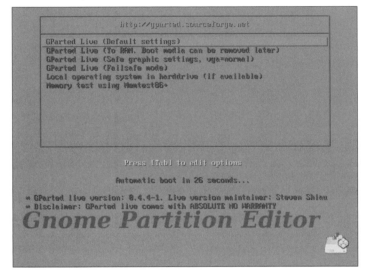

2. **Select GPartEd live CD.**

3. **Select the keyboard mapping you want.**

If you want the U.S. keyboard mapping, press Enter.

4. **Select the language you want to use.**

Simply press Enter if you want to use U.S. English.

A drop-down box on the right side of the screen allows you to select the disk you want to work with. If you only have a single disk drive, it has only one entry: /dev/hda. If you have more than one disk, the others are identified as /dev/hdb, and so on.

If your hard disk has two partitions, the first partition is identified as hda1, the second as hda2.

Your boot disk is always listed as `/dev/hda1`. You can cross-check that it's the correct disk because it should have the disk label (Windows 7, in this case) in the label column.

5. **Click in the part of the screen labeled /dev/hda1.**

   It becomes surrounded by a dotted green box, indicating it is the active partition.

6. **Click Resize/Move.**

7. **In the pop-up window, move the right edge of the green box to the left until the box labeled Free Space Following reads around 25GB or so.**

   If you have plenty of room on your disk, you can try larger partitions for Leopard, but 10GB is the minimum you should use.

   Figure 4.8 shows the display after the partition has had the new size selected.

Figure 4.8

Select size for new partition

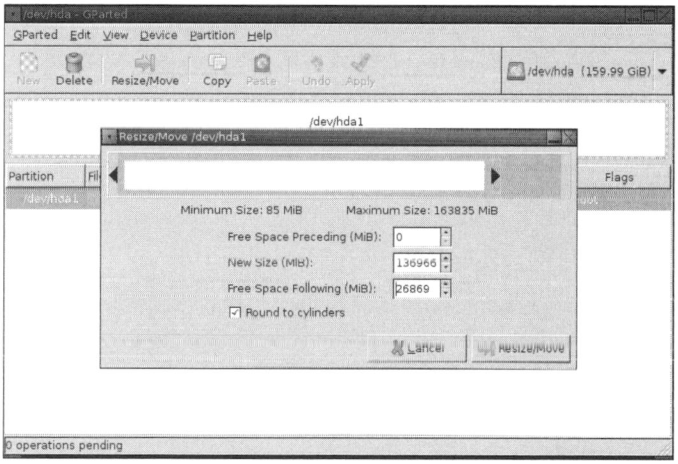

8. **Click Resize/Move.**

   To give you a second chance to be sure of what you are doing, GPartEd doesn't change the partition size immediately; it gives you time to double-check.

 CAUTION

Be sure to check and double-check exactly what you are asking GPartEd to do: A mistake here could lose data!

9. **Click Apply in the toolbar.**

   A dialog box, as shown in Figure 4.9, pops up, asking you to confirm that you really want to resize the partition.

Figure 4.9

Confirmation dialog box for resizing partition

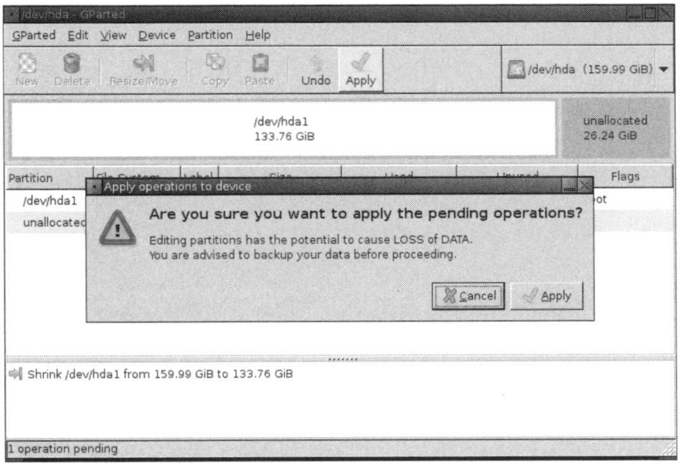

10. **Click Apply in the dialog box.**

Resizing of the partition may take some time because GPartEd has to move all the data from the part of the disk that no longer belongs to the partition.

Creating the new partitions

Creating the new partitions is a much quicker process than shrinking the existing partition. Here's how it goes:

1. **Click in the gray area to the right of the shrunk partition.**

2. **In the toolbar, click New.**

   Enter 5GB as the partition size.

3. **Ensure that the Primary Partition is selected for Create As.**

4. **Select hfs+ or FAT32 as the File System.**

   You can use either hfs+ or FAT32 because you will format the disk for Leopard during installation.

5. **Enter a label for the disk.**

I suggest you call it TempPart so that you can follow the instructions given later.

Figure 4.10 shows the result of these actions.

Figure 4.10

Creating a new partition for the temporary disk

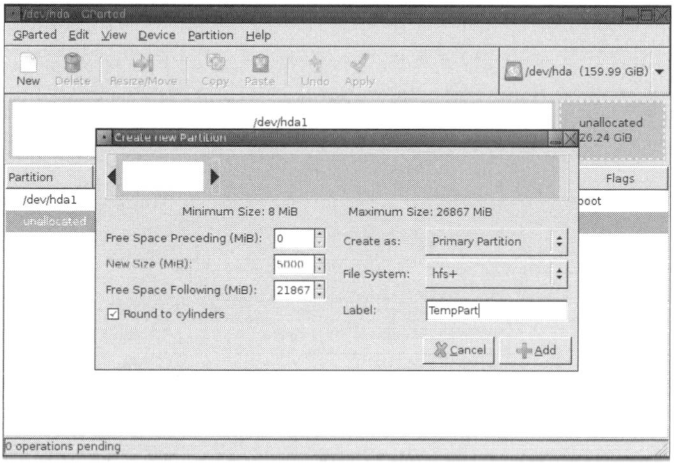

6. **Click Add.**

7. **On the toolbar, click Apply.**

8. **In the dialog box click Apply.**

Now you need to create the partition to which you will install Leopard.

9. **Click in the remaining gray area to the right of the TempPart partition.**

10. **In the toolbar, click New.**

Use the whole of the remaining disk space for your Leopard installation.

11. **Ensure that the Primary Partition is selected for Create As.**

12. **Select hfs+ or FAT32 as the File System.**

You can use either hfs+ or FAT32 because you will format the disk for Leopard during installation.

13. **Enter a label for the disk.**

Use whatever name you choose. I used Hackintosh as the name.

Creating the new partitions is quick because no data needs to be moved. The final outcome is shown in Figure 4.11.

Figure 4.11

New partitions created

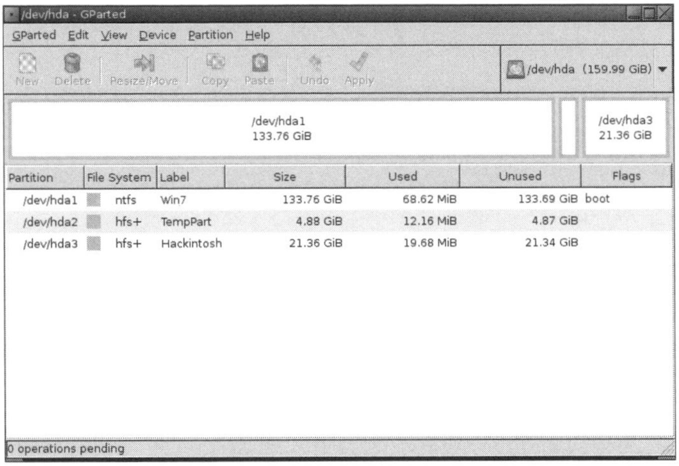

14. **Finally, be sure that your Vista or Windows 7 partition is still marked as the boot partition.**

If it is not, use GPartEd to flag it as the boot partition.

Now you have a disk with your Windows Vista or Windows 7 in the first partition, a temporary partition for installation and space to install Leopard in the third partition.

Booting the Leopard Installer

In this section, you boot the Leopard retail DVD, ready to modify its installation parameters so that you can install it on your Windows disk.

Finding a boot disk

Because it is not a Macintosh, your computer cannot boot from your Leopard retail DVD. To install Leopard, you need to have your computer boot the way a real Macintosh does.

TIP
Many people have created boot disks for this purpose. In essence, they contain software that bridges the gap between your hardware and what Leopard expects to find in a genuine Apple.

You can find a collection of boot disks for specific motherboards at www.insanelymac. com/forum/lofiversion/index.php/t125438.html. Many thanks to MACinized for collecting them together in one place. If your exact motherboard is not listed, try one from the same manufacturer.

Failing that, try one that sounds close. Remember, this is not an exact science!

N O T E

These boot disks are always supplied as an image file (.iso), which you need to burn to a CD. An image file is an exact image of what is on a CD. Because it is a bootable image, when you burn it to CD, the CD is bootable.

Creating your boot disk

You can't simply copy the .iso to a CD because it just ends up as a file sitting on a CD, and you won't be able to boot your computer. Since the .iso file is an exact image of the CD, you need to copy that image exactly to the CD.

C A U T I O N

Whatever CD/DVD-burning software you are using, be sure you use the option to burn an image. A very good, free program to burn CDs and DVDs is ImgBurn, available from www.imgburn.com/.

If you are using ImgBurn, follow these steps to burn your .iso file to your CD:

1. **Start ImgBurn running.**

2. **Insert a blank CD in your drive.**

3. **Click the Write image file to disk option.**

4. **Click the file finder icon (with the magnifying glass) and navigate to where your .iso file is located.**

5. **Check the Verify box to verify that the CD contains exactly the same data as the image file.**

6. **Click the large button to start the burn process.**

7. **Label your disk Leopard Boot.**

Specifying the hard disk identifier

This section explains how to boot the Leopard retail DVD using your boot CD as an intermediary.

Booting from the Leopard retail DVD is a two-step process, unless you are using a Macintosh. First, start the computer using the boot disk, and start the Leopard disk.

When your computer first starts, you see a screen that looks something like that shown in Figure 4.12. Then follow these steps:

Figure 4.12

Boot menu

Boot Menu
Floppy disk
Hard disk
CD-ROM
Network
Use Arrow Keys to select
then press Enter

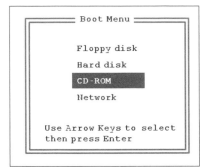

1. **Insert your boot disk in the CD/DVD drive.**
2. **Restart your computer.**
3. **Press the key required to change your boot device.**

   Usually F12 works, but not always.
4. **Select CD/DVD, and press Enter.**
5. **Wait for the boot disk to start up and finish at a prompt.**

   You then see the screen shown in Figure 4.13, which is where you start the next stage of the boot process.

Figure 4.13

Darwin boot screen

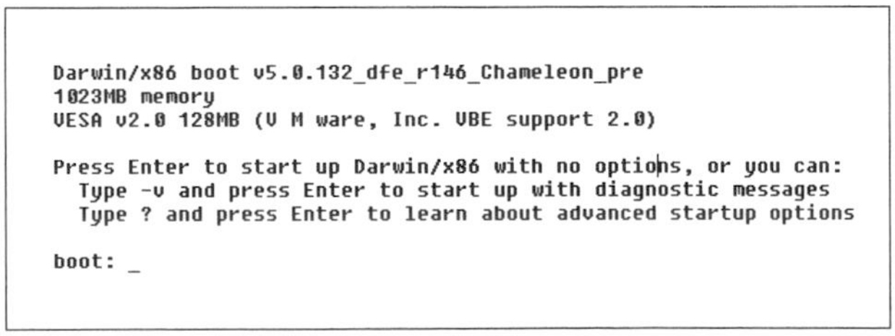

Darwin/x86 boot v5.0.132_dfe_r146_Chameleon_pre
1023MB memory
VESA v2.0 128MB (V M ware, Inc. VBE support 2.0)
Press Enter to start up Darwin/x86 with no options, or you can:
Type -v and press Enter to start up with diagnostic messages
Type ? and press Enter to learn about advanced startup options
boot: _

At this point, the boot disk is waiting for you to boot Darwin, the Unix operating system on which Leopard is based. Of course, Darwin itself is not on that disk; it is on your Leopard retail DVD, so you need to tell it which disk that is and then swap disks.

6. Press Esc.

Now the boot prompt changes to look like the screen shown in Figure 4.14.

Figure 4.14

Darwin boot selector

```
Darwin/x86 boot v5.0.132_dfe_r146_Chameleon_pre
1023MB memory
VESA v2.0 128MB (V M ware, Inc. VBE support 2.0)

Typeical boot devices are 80 (First HD), 81 (Second HD)
Enter two-digit hexadecimal boot device [9f]: _
```

In this case, the boot disk has identified the boot device as 9f, the decimal number 159 in hexadecimal.

NOTE

If you want to convert hexadecimal to decimal and vice versa, use the calculator at http://easy calculation.com/hex-converter.php.

Continue with these steps:

1. Remove the boot disk from the CD drive.

2. Insert the Leopard retail DVD in the CD drive.

3. Wait a few seconds for the drive activity to stop, and press Enter.

You see a second Darwin prompt, with the correct disk specified in the brackets.

Specifying boot options

This section explains how to specify boot options for the Leopard retail DVD and the effect of each.

At the boot prompt, you can type options that control the boot process. Table 4.3 lists the options you can type at the Darwin boot prompt.

Table 4.3 Darwin Boot Options

Option	Meaning
-v	Verbose: all output is sent to the screen
-f	Rebuild the kext cache
-x	Safe mode: similar to Windows safe mode
-s	Single-user mode

C R O S S - R E F

Appendix B contains explanations of various terms such as kext, kext cache, and so on.

At this point, don't worry about specifying any options other than -v because the kext cache can't be rebuilt; it's stored on the DVD, which can't be overwritten. Safe mode and single-user mode do not affect whether the disk boots.

Type -v, and press Enter.

A few lines of text appear on the screen, and then it clears and switches to graphics mode. The text continues down the screen.

At this point, the text looks like gibberish, but you should see one important line as highlighted in Figure 4.15.

Figure 4.15

Verbose boot screen

You should look for a line starting `BSD root: disk1s3`. The numbers you see may be different, but when you see it, you know that Leopard is at least going to boot on your computer.

N O T E
BSD root is the disk from which Darwin boots the main operating system. If Darwin can't identify it, then it can't boot.

After you see that line, you should see more messages scroll up the screen. The boot process takes quite a few minutes when you boot from the DVD. Be patient!

Finally, the screen goes blue and then black with the spinning beach ball in the top-left corner, and you see the Leopard Aurora desktop. Hooray!

Figure 4.16 shows the Leopard Aurora desktop.

Figure 4.16

Leopard Aurora desktop

Select the language you want to use to install Leopard and then pause at the next screen.

If you get stuck at a blank desktop, a blue desktop, or the spinning beach ball, turn to the troubleshooting section in Chapter 6.

Formatting your disks

Your computer is now running a bare-bones version of Leopard, running from the install DVD. Note that it has the Apple menu bar at the top of the screen. You now need to format the disk to which you want to install Leopard, as well as the temporary partition. To do that, you use Disk Utility, as shown in Figure 4.17.

Figure 4.17

Start Disk Utility

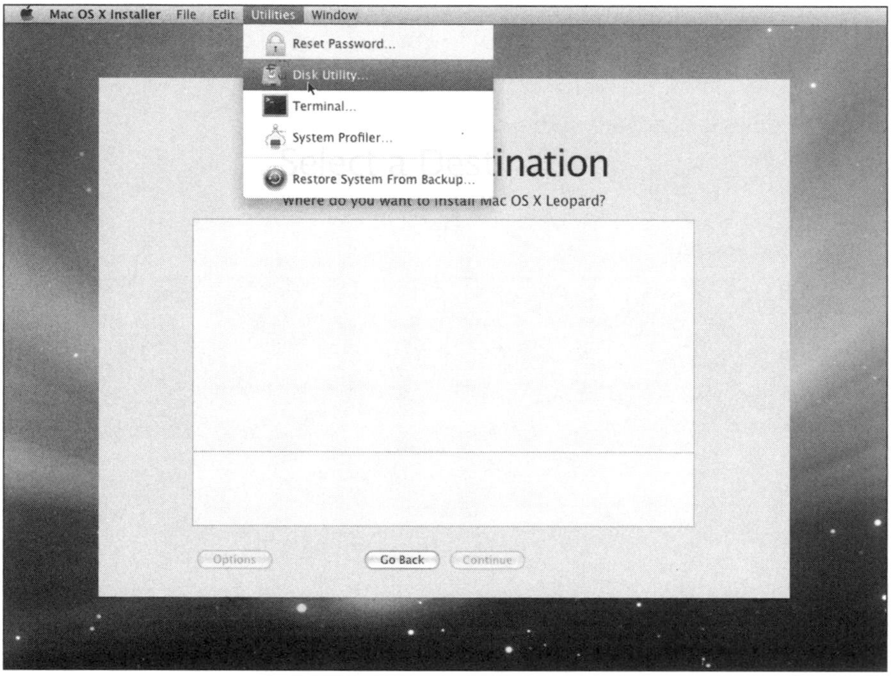

1. **Click Utilities on the Apple menu bar.**

2. **Click Disk Utility.**

After some whirring from the DVD, Disk Utility starts up, showing you the disks connected to your computer. In this example, the only disk shown is a VMware virtual disk, because I captured the screens using VMware. Your disk should show three partitions, though the numbers on them may be different.

Select each partition in turn to be certain which is the new Hackintosh partition, which is the temporary partition and which is your existing Vista partition. Follow these steps to format your disks:

CAUTION

Be very sure to select the correct partition: If you select the wrong one, you will erase your Vista or Windows 7 partition.

1. **Select Erase at the top of the Disk Utility window.**

2. **Select the small TempPart partition.**

3. **Select** Mac OS Extended (Journaled) **as the Volume Format.**

4. **Type the name for the partition.**

   Figure 4.18 shows the small temporary partition ready to be erased and formatted.

Figure 4.18

Ready to format TempPart using Disk Utility

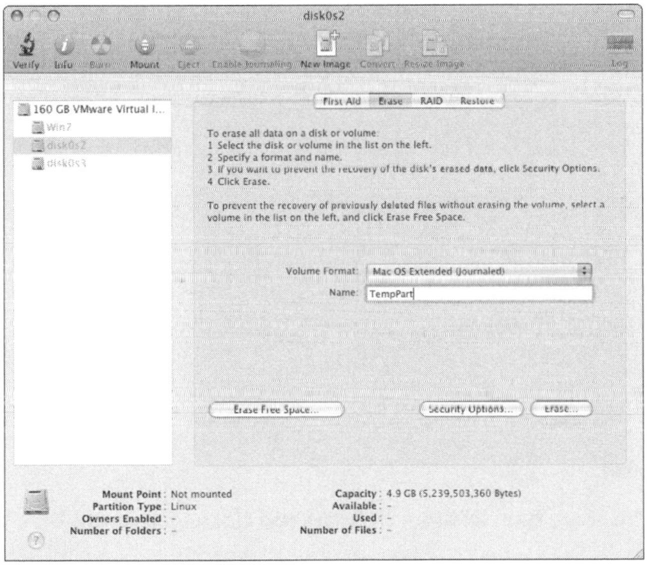

5. **Click Erase.**

   Disk Utility then formats your disk ready for installation.

6. **Select the main Hackintosh partition.**

7. **Select** Mac OS Extended (Journaled) **as the Volume Format.**

8. **Type the name for the partition.**

   Why not call it Hackintosh?

   At this point, Disk Utility should look something like that shown in Figure 4.19.

Figure 4.19

Disk Utility ready to format Hackintosh partition

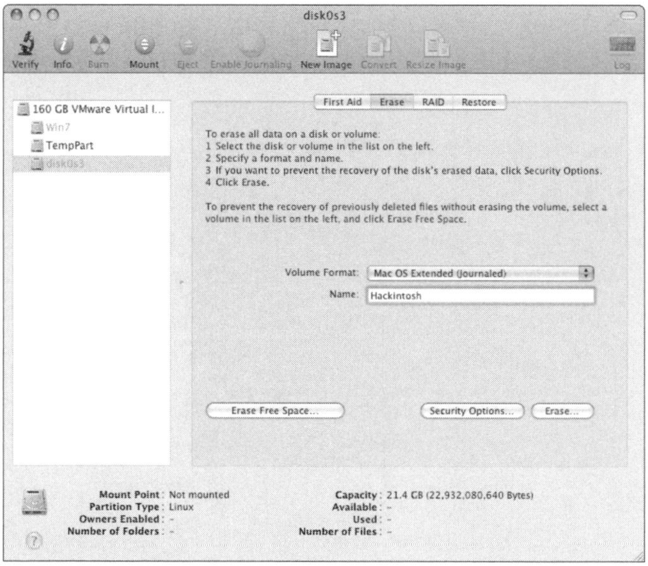

9. **Click Erase.**

10. **When the erase has finished, click the red close icon in the Disk Utility window.**

    You now return to the disk install select screen, as shown in Figure 4.20.

    This time, your newly formatted partitions show up.

Figure 4.20

Select install disk

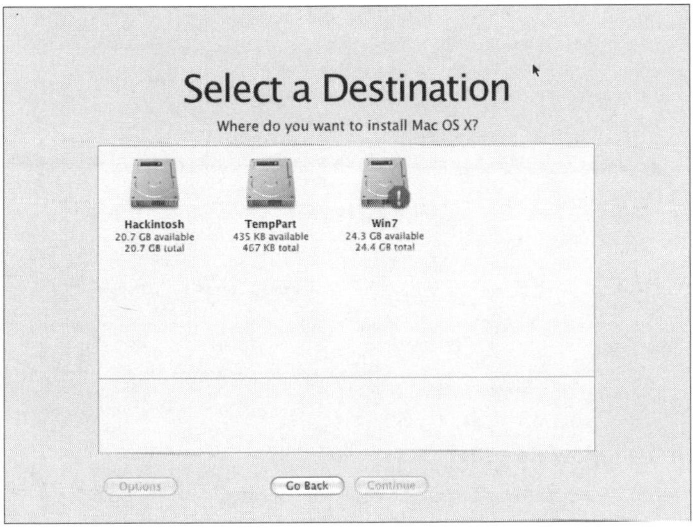

Select a Destination
Where do you want to install Mac OS X?

Hackintosh
20.7 GB available
20.7 GB total

TempPart
435 KB available
467 KB total

Win7
24.3 GB available
24.4 GB total

Options   Go Back   Continue

Modifying Your Leopard Installer

In order to install to an MBR disk, you need to remove the code in the installer that checks that the disk is formatted as GPT. As you would expect, while it sounds simple, you need to carry out a number of Unix commands, and you need to get each one exactly right or it will not work.

For this method I am greatly indebted to Fredde87, llauqsd, and STLVNUB. The original article is on the Insanely Mac Web site at www.insanelymac.com/forum/lofiversion/index.php/t181287.html.

CAUTION

Before you press Enter after entering each line of code, be sure to check your typing. If the command cannot be carried out, you receive an error message. If the command works, all that happens is that you get the prompt again. It works on the principle that no news is good news: If it didn't fail, then it must have worked!

Follow these steps to modify your installer:

1. **From the Apple menu bar, select Utilities then Terminal.**

This opens a terminal window as shown in Figure 4.21.

Figure 4.21

Terminal window in installer

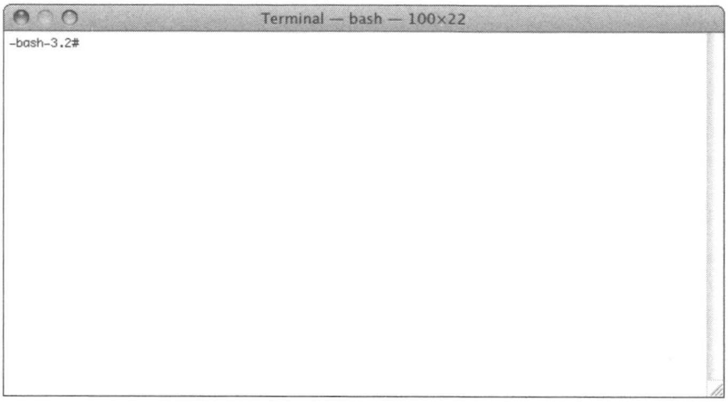

2. **Type the following code:**

```
cp -R /System/Installation/Packages/* /Volumes/TempPart
```

 CAUTION

Be careful of spacing. There should be a space after cp, after –R, and after *. Also be careful with capitalization because –r is not the same as –R. Be patient; copying the files takes a while.

This command copies everything in the System/Installation/Packages folder to your temporary partition.

3. **Type**

```
cd /Volumes/TempPart
```

This changes your working directory to the TempPart disk.

4. **Type**

```
mkdir temp
```

This creates a new folder called temp on your TempPart disk.

5. **Type**

```
mv OSInstall.mpkg temp/
```

This copies the installer to your new temp folder.

6. **Type**

```
cd temp
```

This changes your working directory to the temp folder.

7. **Type**

```
xar -x -f OSInstall.mpkg
```

xar is an archiving program. In this case you are using it to extract the files from the installer so that they can be modified.

8. **Type**

```
cat Distribution | sed "s/eraseOptionAvailable='true'//g"¬
    > Distribution2
```

NOTE

The ¬ character is a line continuation character. You don't type it in; it is just there to show you that everything in that command should be on one line. Also, be careful of the single (') and double (") quotes.

This is a classic Unix command and explains why so many people love using Unix. First, cat reads everything in the file Distribution and writes it out to a new file Distribution2. If the command was simply cat Distribution > Distribution2 the two files would be identical.

But sed is a stream editor: it takes everything that is input to it, changes it, and writes it back out. The s/.../.../g means substitute everything between the first /.../ with whatever is in between the second /.../. The /g means globally.

So this compact command reads through everything in the file Distribution, replaces every occurrence of eraseOptionAvailable='true' with a blank then writes it out to a new file Distribution2.

9. **Type**

```
mv Distribution2 Distribution
```

This command copies the new Distribution2 to overwrite the Distribution file.

10. **Type**

```
rm -Rf OSInstall.mpkg
```

This removes everything in the OSInstall.mpkg file.

11. **Type**

```
xar -c -f OSInstall.mpkg *
```

This repacks everything into the OSInstall.mpkg file.

12. **Type**

```
mv OSInstall.mpkg ../
```

This moves OSInstall.mpkg back into the top directory on the temporary disk.

13. **Type**

```
cd ..
```

This moves your working directory back up to the top directory.

14. **Type**

```
rm –Rf temp
```

This removes everything in the temp directory.

At this point your Terminal screen should look like the screen shown in Figure 4.22.

Figure 4.22

Terminal screen

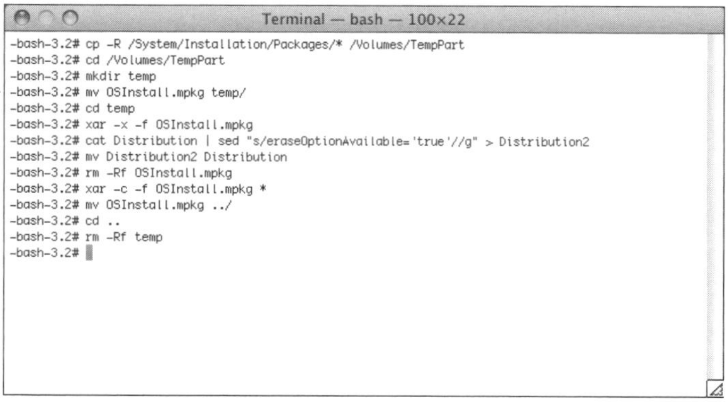

Don't close Terminal as you require it again in the next part.

All the commands up to this point have been to create a modified Leopard installer. The remaining part of the exercise is to have the installer use your modified installer, rather than the one that is on the DVD.

If you have access to a Macintosh, you can create a new installation DVD with the modification, but this way is much easier if you don't have easy access to a Mac. If you want to create a modified DVD using a Mac, follow llauqsd's tutorial at www.insanelymac.com/forum/lofiversion/index.php/t116505.html.

Forcing the installer to use your modifications

Having created the new installer, you now need to be able to use it.

Follow these steps to set up your installer:

1. **Still using Terminal, type**

```
mount
```

This command shows all the disks that are mounted on your Leopard computer as shown in Figure 4.23.

Figure 4.23

Result of mount command

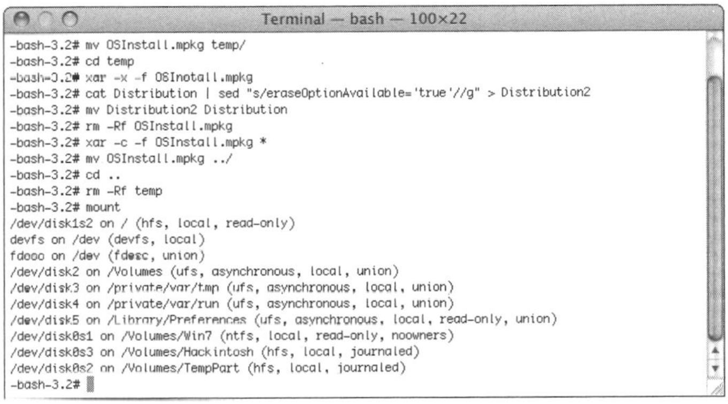

```
                     Terminal — bash — 100×22
-bash-3.2# mv OSInstall.mpkg temp/
-bash-3.2# cd temp
-bash-3.2# xar -x -f OSInstall.mpkg
-bash-3.2# cat Distribution | sed "s/eraseOptionAvailable='true'//g" > Distribution2
-bash-3.2# mv Distribution2 Distribution
-bash-3.2# rm -Rf OSInstall.mpkg
-bash-3.2# xar -c -f OSInstall.mpkg *
-bash-3.2# mv OSInstall.mpkg ../
-bash-3.2# cd ..
-bash-3.2# rm -Rf temp
-bash-3.2# mount
/dev/disk1s2 on / (hfs, local, read-only)
devfs on /dev (devfs, local)
fdesc on /dev (fdesc, union)
/dev/disk2 on /Volumes (ufs, asynchronous, local, union)
/dev/disk3 on /private/var/tmp (ufs, asynchronous, local, union)
/dev/disk4 on /private/var/run (ufs, asynchronous, local, union)
/dev/disk5 on /Library/Preferences (ufs, asynchronous, local, read-only, union)
/dev/disk0s1 on /Volumes/Win7 (ntfs, local, read-only, noowners)
/dev/disk0s3 on /Volumes/Hackintosh (hfs, local, journaled)
/dev/disk0s2 on /Volumes/TempPart (hfs, local, journaled)
-bash-3.2# 
```

As you can see at the bottom of the window, the list of disks on my computer Is:

- dev/disk0s1: /Volumes/Win7
- dev/disk0s2: /Volumes/TempPart
- dev/disk0s3: /Volumes/Hackintosh

2. **In the list of disks shown by the mount command, look for one that is shown as** `/Volumes/TempPart`

In my case it is `/dev/disk0s2`

3. **Move up one level in the folder hierarchy by typing**

```
cd /
```

In other words, move to the root of the disk.

4. **Now unmount the disk by typing**

```
umount /Volumes/TempPart
```

CAUTION

Although the command is used to unmount the disk, it is written as umount: without the first "n". Also, be careful of spacing in the command.

5. **Type**

```
mount -t hfs /dev/disk0s2 /System/Installation/Packages
```

TIP

Remember to change the disk0s2 to whatever your TempPart disk is shown as.

This command remounts the disk, calling it `/System/Installation/Packages` so that when the installer looks for the packages, it finds the one on your disk, rather than the one on the install DVD.

6. **Close Terminal.**

This returns you to the part of the installation where you choose the disk to install to.

7. **Click the Back arrow to return to the Choose your Language screen.**

8. **Click the arrow to go through the copyright and licensing screens and then choose your Hackintosh disk for the installation.**

Note that your TempPart disk shows as a folder because you mounted the disk as /System/Installation/Packages which is a folder. This is shown in Figure 4.24.

Figure 4.24

Installation options showing disks and folder

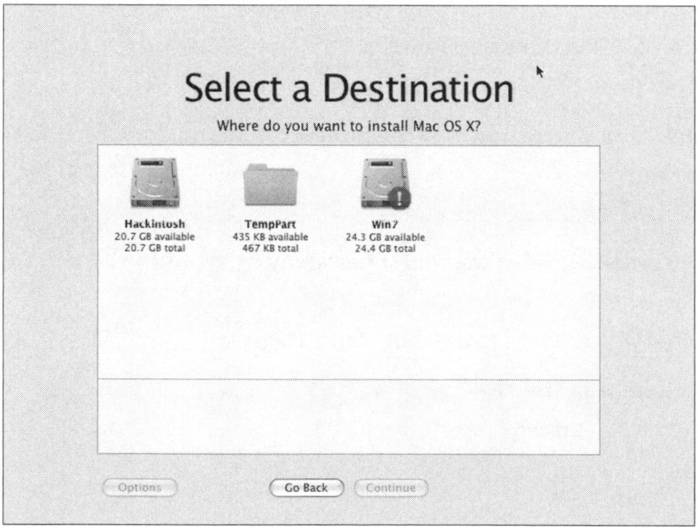

Select a Destination

Where do you want to install Mac OS X?

Hackintosh	TempPart	Win7
20.7 GB available	435 KB available	24.3 GB available
20.7 GB total	467 KB total	24.4 GB total

Options   Go Back   Continue

CAUTION

Be very careful that you choose your Hackintosh disk, not your Vista or Windows 7 disk!

Specifying installation options

This section explains the Leopard installation options and how to select or deselect them. The Leopard retail version doesn't have many installation options. You have these options:

- Printer drivers
- Additional fonts
- Language translations
- X11, a Unix windowing system

Unless your specific printer is in the list, you need not install any printers because you can add these later.

If you plan to always use English as your language, you can leave out the language translations.

You should include the additional fonts unless you are very short on hard disk space.

Figure 4.25 shows the customize options screen.

Figure 4.25

Customize options

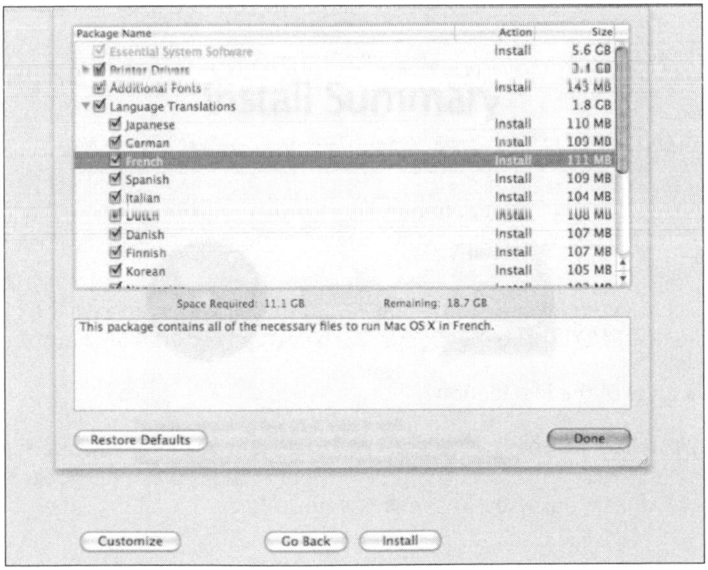

Follow these steps to select customize options:

> Each small triangle beside a heading expands or contracts the list. If the individual box is blue, it means that option is selected. If the heading box is blue, it means that all options under that heading are selected.

1. **Place a check in each option that you want to select.**

2. **Click Done to proceed to the actual installation.**

> Finally, you are ready to install Leopard. Figure 4.26 shows the Install Summary screen.

Figure 4.26

The Install Summary screen

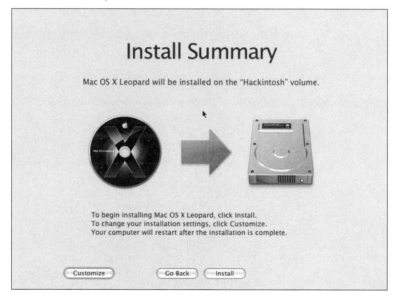

3. **Click Install.**

Leopard first wants to check your DVD. Because you've got this far with it and it's the first time you've used it, checking the DVD is probably pointless, so you can click the Skip button.

Figure 4.27 shows this stage of the installation.

Leopard is now being installed. Normally, it takes between 20 and 60 minutes, depending on how fast your computer and disk drives are. The progress bar at the bottom of the screen gradually moves as the installation progresses, as shown in Figure 4.28.

Figure 4.27

Checking the installation

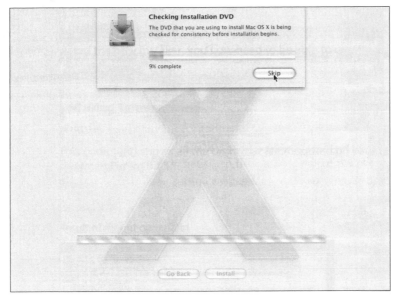

Figure 4.28

Installing Leopard

Occasionally, this display stops moving, but it shows how much more time the installation will take, as shown in Figure 4.28. If this happens, wait until all CD and hard disk activity has stopped for two or three minutes, and then restart your computer.

Otherwise, you eventually see the screen saying Leopard has been installed, as shown in Figure 4.29.

Figure 4.29

Installation succeeded

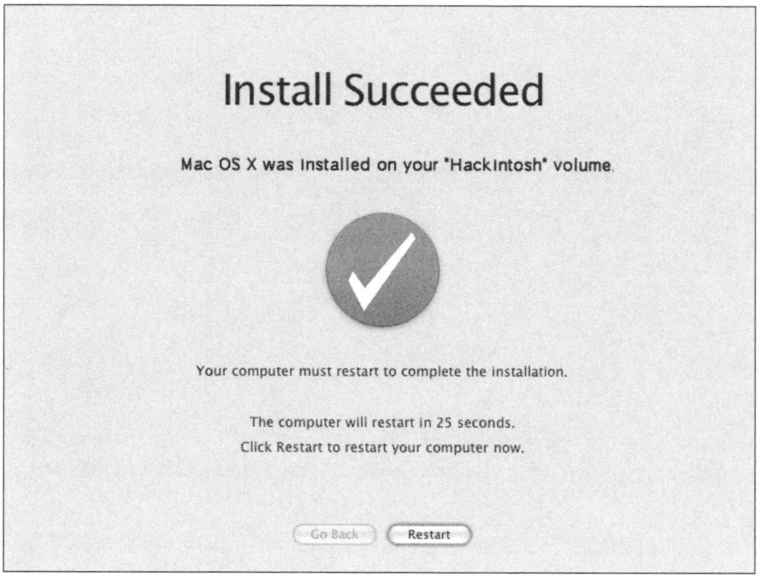

Restarting your computer

Now is the moment of truth! Will your computer restart?

Press the Reset button on your computer. If all has gone according to plan, you should see the Darwin boot prompt, but this time with three choices, as shown in Figure 4.30.

Let's not try the OS X partition for a moment; let's try to start Vista or Windows 7.

1. **Select Windows NTFS at the Darwin boot loader screen.**

What you probably see is the screen shown in Figure 4.31.

Don't despair! You are prepared for this.

Figure 4.30

Restart computer

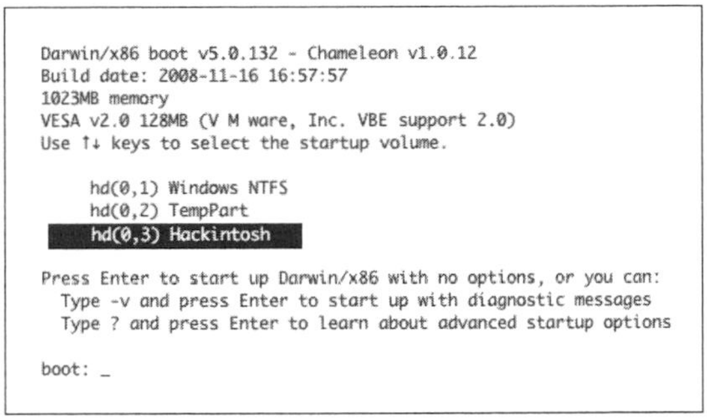

```
Darwin/x86 boot v5.0.132 - Chameleon v1.0.12
Build date: 2008-11-16 16:57:57
1023MB memory
VESA v2.0 128MB (V M ware, Inc. VBE support 2.0)
Use ↑↓ keys to select the startup volume.

      hd(0,1) Windows NTFS
      hd(0,2) TempPart
      hd(0,3) Hackintosh

Press Enter to start up Darwin/x86 with no options, or you can:
   Type -v and press Enter to start up with diagnostic messages
   Type ? and press Enter to learn about advanced startup options

boot: _
```

Figure 4.31

Trying to restart Vista

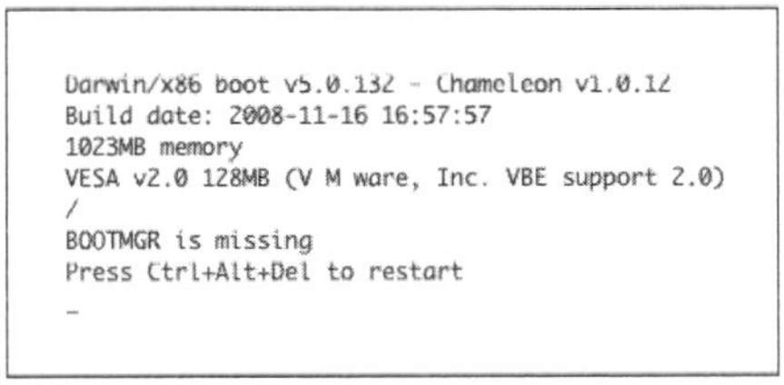

```
Darwin/x86 boot v5.0.132 - Chameleon v1.0.12
Build date: 2008-11-16 16:57:57
1023MB memory
VESA v2.0 128MB (V M ware, Inc. VBE support 2.0)
/
BOOTMGR is missing
Press Ctrl+Alt+Del to restart
 _
```

It is because GPartEd has made changes to the boot sector of your hard disk and has wiped out the boot loader. In the next section, you see how to restore your Vista installation to be able to boot again.

Using the Downloaded Software to Restore the Vista Partition

In this section, you use the Vista Recovery Disk to repair your boot sector and hence restore the partition.

1. **Boot from the Vista Recovery Disk.**

2. **At the Install Windows screen, click Next.**

3. **Click Repair your computer.**

Wait while System Recovery Options determines your operating system. After that step is complete, the recovery disk displays System Recovery Options, as shown in Figure 4.32.

Figure 4.32

System Recovery Options

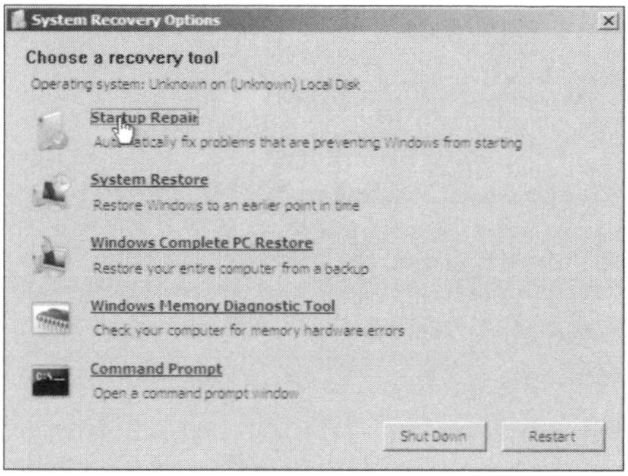

4. **Click Startup Repair.**

5. **Click Next.**

Wait while Vista attempts to repair your boot sector. When the repair is complete, reboot your computer.

Ensuring That Vista Starts

Now comes the moment of truth! You should be able to boot normally into Vista and have your computer working as it was before you began this.

If that does not happen, try the following things.

First, repeat the steps above, because occasionally more than one problem is preventing Vista from starting, and another pass fixes that.

In my experience, the problem has always been repaired on the first pass.

If all else fails, read the instructions on the EasyBCD Web site at `http://neosmart.net/wiki/display/EBCD/Recovering+the+Vista+Bootloader+from+the+DVD`.

TIP

Don't forget to donate to help keep the Web site going: It provides a great set of tools for people like you.

Second, if all else has failed, you have a recovery image of your disk so you can restore and start again. In my experience, however, that has never been necessary. The issues have always been resolved at least one step short of that!

Starting OS X

In this section, you start Leopard for the first time. For the first boot, I always recommend doing a verbose boot, so you can see what is happening, and rebuilding the kext caches, just in case the installer has not updated them. Follow these steps:

1. **Reboot your computer and press F8 when you see the Darwin boot prompt.**

2. **This time select hd(0,3) or whatever your Hackintosh shows as.**

3. **Type -v -f, and press Enter.**

In a minute or two, you should see the Leopard welcome video. Otherwise, you go straight to the Leopard desktop: With most distributions, this is the Aurora image.

If you fail to get through to the Leopard desktop, go to Chapter 6 for some troubleshooting advice.

Using a Different Boot Loader

During the time I've been writing this book, the Hackintosh scene has developed rapidly. One big development is the Chameleon boot loader. This is a graphical boot loader that automatically detects the disk drives connected to the computer and the operating systems installed on them and then allows you to select which to boot from.

CAUTION

If you install the Chameleon boot loader you may not be able to return to the Vista or Windows 7 boot loader you set up using EasyBCD unless you restore from your image backup and repair the Vista boot loader.

At the time of writing, the Chameleon 2 installer is at the Release Candidate 2 (RC2) version. Although the files for RC3 are available, installing them is not as straightforward as using the installer.

Follow these steps to install the Chameleon boot loader:

1. **Navigate to** `http://chameleon.osx86.hu/` **and scroll down the page to the heading "Chameleon 2.0-RC2 is available …".**

2. **Click the link and then scroll down to the heading "Download information."**

3. **Click the link Installer package and then click the link "here."**

4. **Download the file and save it to your Leopard drive.**

NOTE

If you can't access the Internet from your Leopard computer, you can download the installer to your Windows computer and use a USB drive to install to your Leopard disk.

5. **Double-click the Chameleon-2.0-r431.pkg file.**

    Figure 4.33 shows the installer's greeting screen.

    Figure 4.33

    Chameleon Installer screen

    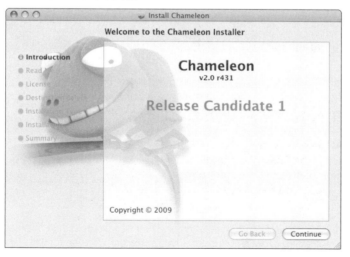

6. **Click Continue until you get to the software license agreement screen.**

7. **Click Agree. At the next screen, click Install and then enter your password to confirm the install.**

8. **Wait while Chameleon is installed and then restart your computer.**

   Now you see a graphical boot screen that shows your Leopard install disk and your Windows disks with a Windows symbol and a label NTFS. This is shown in Figure 4.34.

   Figure 4.34

   Chameleon boot loader screen

   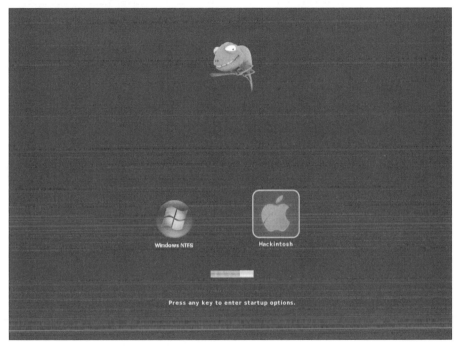

9. **From the boot screen, select the disk from which you want to boot.**

Expanding Your Windows Partition

After you have installed Leopard, you no longer need the partition (TempPart) that you used to modify Leopard. You can use GPartEd to first delete the partition and then expand the Windows partition to use the extra space.

CAUTION
Don't try to expand your Leopard partition because GPartEd cannot create an OS X partition that is recognized by Leopard, and you will have to repeat the install.

Summary

In this chapter, you backed up your Vista or Windows 7 installation and moved the files already on the disk into a smaller area so that you could create a new partition. Then you booted your Leopard installation disk and formatted the new partition to receive Leopard.

After booting from the Leopard installation disk you chose, you modified the Leopard installation and then installed it to your hard disk after choosing appropriate customizations. After checking that Leopard and Vista or Windows 7 booted, you modified the boot loader to give you a choice of starting either Vista or Leopard.

5

Installing to a Hard Disk with Windows XP Already Installed

Chapters 2 and 3 walked you through installing OS X to a separate hard disk. The advantage of this method is that it isolates your Leopard disk from the rest of your system. The drawback, though, is that to use Leopard you have to remember to select your Leopard hard disk through the BIOS each time you start your computer.

In this chapter, you learn how to install Leopard to a hard disk that already contains a Windows XP installation.

First, you back up your XP installation in case of errors. Then you create a new partition on your XP disk to allow OS X to be installed. Next, you install a modified version of Leopard that installs to a Windows disk.

After installing Leopard, you check that both operating systems start correctly, and you install a boot loader so you can choose which operating system to run at boot time.

Performing a Complete Image Backup of Your XP Hard Disk

In this section, you completely back up your Windows XP installation so you can restore your system to where it was before you started, in case anything goes wrong. This is essential disaster insurance!

Most people back up their files using a file backup method. In a file backup, your data is written to the backup medium file by file. When you want to recover a file, you simply select it from the list on the backup medium and copy it to where you want it.

An image backup is different from a file backup. An image backup knows nothing about files: It simply copies every single bit of data from the disk to the backup medium. In effect, the backup is like a

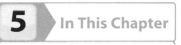

photographic snapshot of everything on your hard disk. An image backup backs up your files, your programs, your preferences, and even your hard disk's boot sector.

You can use a series of DVDs to do an image backup, but more likely you use an external hard disk.

CAUTION

If you restore from an image backup, you restore the entire disk, not file by file. This is important because if your user files have changed since you last did a complete image backup, they are overwritten by the old files when you restore.

Finding and downloading the software

First, you need to download and purchase image backup software. Table 5.1 shows a selection of the best-known ones.

Table 5.1 Image Backup Software

Application	URL
Acronis True Image	`www.acronis.com/`
Norton Ghost	`www.symantec.com/norton/ghost`
Paragon Hard Disk Manager	`www.paragon-software.com/home/hdm-personal/`
O&O Disk Image 3	`www.oo-software.com/home/en/products/oodiskimage/index.html`
Terabyte Image for Windows	`www.terabyteunlimited.com/image-for-windows.htm`

I use O&O Disk Image 3, but all of these work fine. In this chapter, the screen shots are taken using O&O Disk Image 3.

Choose one of these programs, download it, and install it.

CAUTION

Be sure that you download the image backup software's restore disk and burn it to a CD before you start. Without it, you can't restore your image to your computer.

My preference is always to test the backup software first, just to be certain that it's going to rescue me if I make a mistake. And yes, I did manage to completely wipe my hard disk while writing this book. But I had two image backups to choose from.

Creating a disk image

You need to read the documentation that comes with the product you buy. Be sure to save your backup to a disk other than your system disk!

In my case, I used O&O Disk Image, as shown in Figure 5.1.

Figure 5.1

O&O start screen

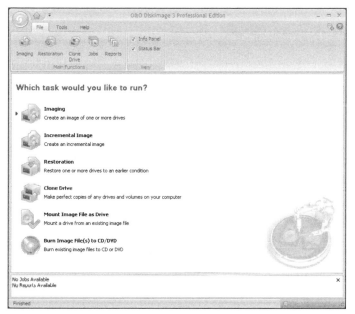

After you click Create and select the disk you want to image, O&O Disk Image asks where you want to save the image, as shown in Figure 5.2.

Figure 5.2

Disk image creation screen

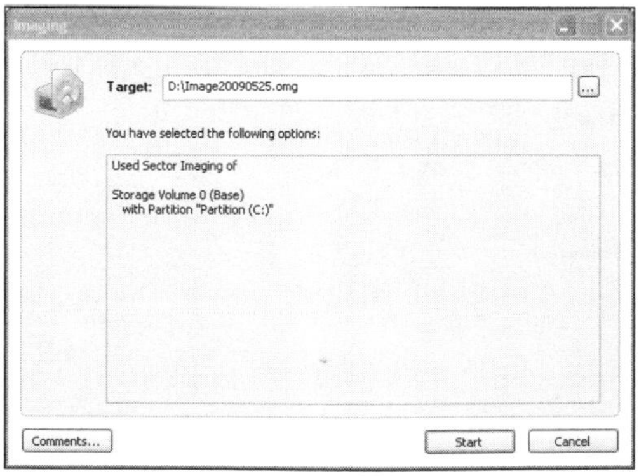

In this case, I'm saving the image on a removable USB hard disk, which is Drive D:. Figure 5.3 shows the screen when O&O is partway through the imaging process.

Figure 5.3

Part of the imaging process

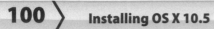

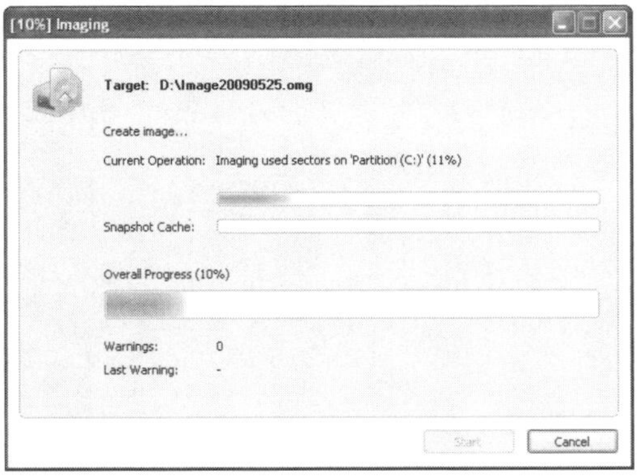

Restoring your system from the disk image

Should the worst happen and you erase your system disk or make it unusable in some way, you need your recovery CD or DVD. In this example, I use the recovery disk for O&O Disk Image. The software you chose to download will have a similar process.

Figure 5.4 shows the initial display when you boot from the O&O Disk Image CD.

In this case, I click Start to get O&O to the restore image screen, as shown in Figure 5.5.

For your imaging software, the details and screens will be different, but the basic principles are exactly the same:

1. **Boot from the recovery disk.**

2. **Select the backup you want to restore.**

3. **Select where you want to restore to.**

4. **Wait while it restores.**

O&O then restores the image to the original disk.

Figure 5.4

O&O Disk Image greeting screen

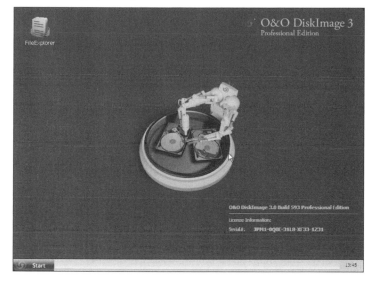

Figure 5.5

Image to restore

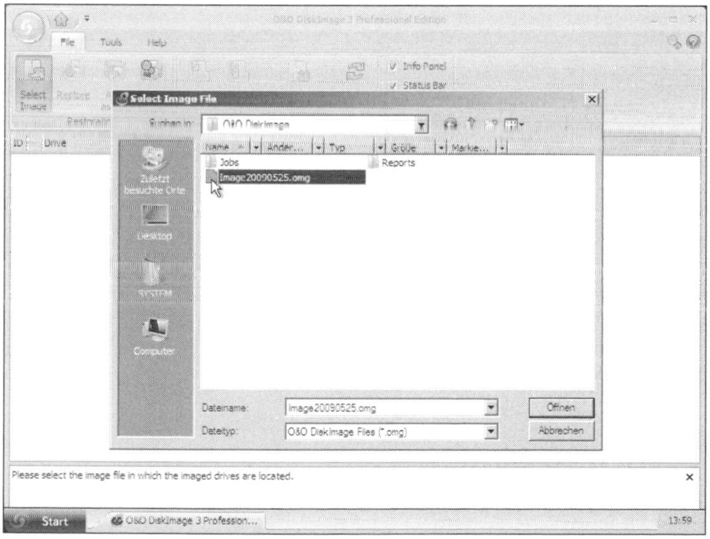

Downloading Required Software to Start XP and OS X

In this section, you download three more items of essential software you need before you can install OS X to your XP disk:

- Software to partition your system disk
- Software to modify the Windows XP boot loader

Downloading software to partition your XP system disk

Windows XP has a built-in utility to partition disks called *diskpart* that is accessed through the command prompt. Diskpart can be used to expand a partition, provided you have free space on the disk. It also can be used to shrink a partition, but only under certain circumstances.

During normal operation of your computer, files are not written in a neat fashion to the same area of the disk, but are scattered around the disk. This is done for performance reasons, but it results in lots of blank areas on the disk. Consider a 120GB disk that has 60GB of free space. You might expect that the so-called high water mark of the disk would be at 60GB, leaving the second half of the disk empty. But because of the way the files are written, the high water mark might be at 110GB, leaving only 10GB of space at the end of the disk. In this case, diskpart could shrink the partition only to 110GB.

What you need is software that can move the files into the same area of the disk and thus make space for a larger partition.

Several programs are capable of doing this. Table 5.2 shows a selection of these.

Table 5.2 Partition Management Software

Application	URL
Acronis Partition Manager	www.acronis.com/
Partition Magic	www.symantec.com/norton/partitionmagic
Paragon Partition Manager	www.paragon-software.com/home/pm-personal/

These are all commercial software, but an excellent partition manager is free. GPartEd (pronounced "gee part ed") is available for download from http://gparted.sourceforge.net/.

GPartEd is supplied as a disk image (.iso file). You need to burn it to a CD and use it to boot your computer. Several programs are capable of doing this (Nero Burning ROM, AShampoo Burning Studio, Roxio Creator, and others), but my favorite is ImgBurn, available from www.imgburn.com/.

If you already have commercial software, use that; otherwise, give ImgBurn a try. Follow these steps:

1. **Download GPartEd, and save it to your disk.**

2. **Use image-burning software to burn GPartEd to a CD.**

Be sure to burn it as an image; don't simply copy the iso file to the CD.

Downloading software to modify the XP boot loader

Windows XP uses a different boot loading method from Vista and Windows 7. The boot process is controlled by a file called boot.ini. It is a simple text file.

On my computer, it contains the following:

```
[boot loader]
timeout=30
default-multi(0)disk(0)rdisk(0)partition(1)\WINDOWS
[operating systems]
multi(0)disk(0)rdisk(0)partition(1)\WINDOWS="Microsoft Windows XP
    Professional" /noexecute=optin /fastdetect
```

Note that you must enter the last two lines as a single line: the line is only broken because the page in this book is not wide enough.

To be able to dual boot, you need to download a file called chain0 (that's a zero, not the letter O). You can find several different sources for this by searching Google. It is simply a file that tells the boot loader where to find your Leopard partition.

You can find a download location for it at http://rs279.rapidshare.com/ files/110576025/Chain0_.rar or at TinyURL http://preview.tinyurl.com/ qr68u3.

After you've installed Leopard, we'll look at how to use chain0 to allow dual booting.

CROSS-REF
Appendix B contains more discussion of the boot process for a computer.

Partitioning the XP System Disk

You have downloaded all the software you might need, and you have done an image backup of your hard drive, so now it's time to tackle the hard stuff: partitioning your disk and installing Leopard. In this section, you partition your hard disk.

As standard, the retail Leopard installation does not install to a disk partitioned as MBR (Master Boot Record). Instead it requires a disk partitioned as GPT (GUID Partition Table).

To install to an MBR disk you need to modify the installer. To do this, create an extra partition as a temporary measure, copy the Leopard installer to that partition, and modify it. You then use that partition to carry out the installation.

CROSS-REF

Appendix B contains explanations of different disk partition types. In the screen shots, I use GPartEd and partition a VMware drive. Details of your disk are, of course, different. Likewise, if you are using different partitioning software, your screens look different.

Shrinking your existing partition

First, you need to shrink your existing partition to leave space for the new partition. Here's how:

1. **Insert your GPartEd disk, and boot from it.**

   Figure 5.6 shows the startup screen from GPartEd.

   Figure 5.6

   GPartEd startup screen

   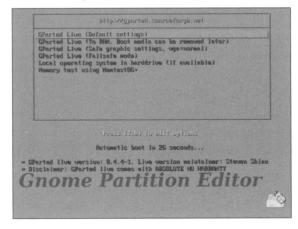

2. **Select GPartEd live CD.**

3. **Select the keyboard mapping you want.**

   If you want the U.S. keyboard mapping, simply press Enter.

4. **Select the language you want to use.**

Press Enter for U.S. English.

After much threshing of the CD, you eventually arrive at the main screen for GPartEd, as shown in Figure 5.7.

Figure 5.7

GPartEd main screen

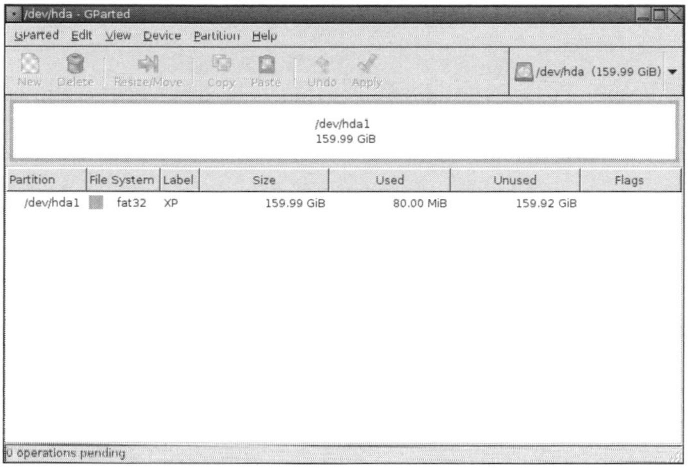

The right side of the screen contains a drop-down box that allows you to select the disk you want to work with. If you have a single disk drive, it has only one entry: /dev/hda. If you have more than one disk, the others will be identified as /dev/hdb and so on.

If your hard disk has two partitions, the first partition is identified as hda1, the second as hda2.

Your boot disk is always listed as /dev/hda1. You can cross-check that it's the correct disk because it should have the disk label (XP, in this case) in the label column.

5. **Click in the part of the screen labeled /dev/hda1.**

It becomes surrounded by a dotted green box, indicating it is the active partition.

6. **Click Resize/Move.**

7. **In the pop-up window, move the right edge of the green box to the left until the box labeled Free Space Following reads around 25GB or so.**

If you have plenty of room on your disk, you can try larger partitions for Leopard, but 10GB is around the minimum you should use.

Figure 5.8 shows the display after the partition has had the new size selected.

Figure 5.8

Select size for new partition

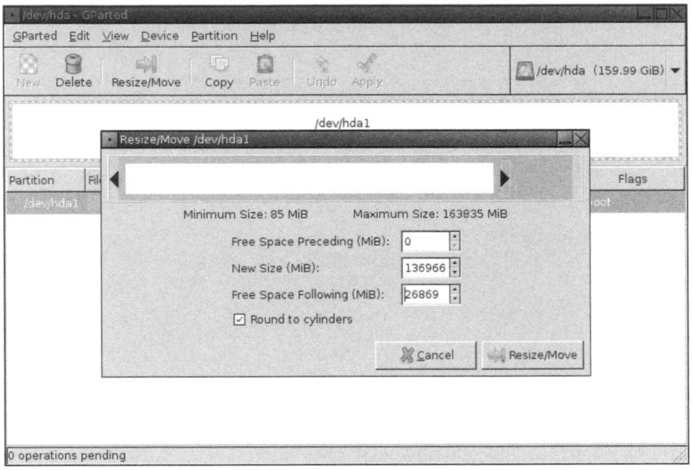

8. **Click Resize/Move.**

   To give you a second chance to be sure of what you are doing, GPartEd doesn't change the partition size immediately but gives you time to double-check.

CAUTION

Be sure to check and double-check exactly what you are asking GPartEd to do: A mistake here could lose data!

9. **Click Apply in the toolbar.**

   A dialog box, as shown in Figure 5.9, pops up asking you to confirm that you really do want to resize the partition.

10. **Click Apply in the dialog box.**

Resizing of the partition may take some time because GPartEd has to move all the data from the part of the disk that no longer belongs to the partition.

Figure 5.9

Confirmation dialog box for resizing partition

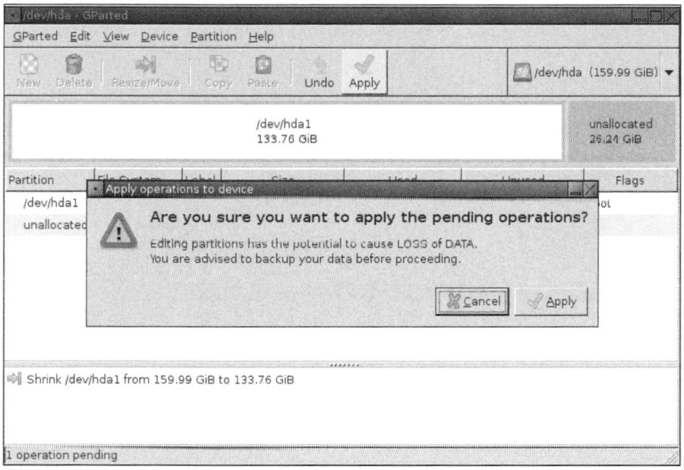

Creating the new partitions

Creating the new partitions is a much quicker process than shrinking the existing partition. Follow these steps:

1. Click in the gray area to the right of the shrunken partition.

2. In the toolbar, click New.

Enter 5GB as the partition size.

3. Ensure that the Primary Partition is selected for Create As.

4. Select hfs+ or FAT32 as the File System.

You can use either hfs+ or FAT32 because you will format the disk for Leopard during installation.

5. Enter a label for the disk.

I suggest you call it TempPart so that you can follow the instructions given later.

Figure 5.10 shows the result of these actions.

6. Click Add.

7. On the toolbar, click Apply.

8. **In the dialog box, click Apply.**

Now you need to create the partition to which you will install Leopard.

Figure 5.10

Creating a new partition for the temporary disk

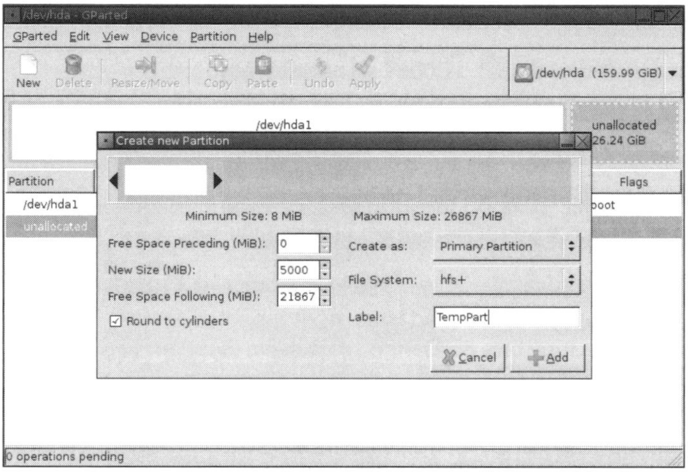

9. **Click in the remaining gray area to the right of the TempPart partition.**

10. **In the toolbar, click New.**

Use the whole of the remaining disk space for your Leopard installation.

11. **Ensure that the Primary Partition is selected for Create As.**

12. **Select hfs+ or FAT32 as the File System.**

You can use either hfs+ or FAT32 because you will format the disk for Leopard during installation.

13. **Enter a label for the disk.**

Use whatever name you choose. I used Hackintosh as the name.

Creating the new partitions is quick because no data needs to be moved. The final outcome is shown in Figure 5.11.

14. **Finally, be sure that your XP partition is still marked as the boot partition.**

If it is not, use GPartEd to flag it as the boot partition.

Now you have a disk with your Windows XP in the first partition and space to install Leopard in the second partition.

Figure 5.11

New partitions created

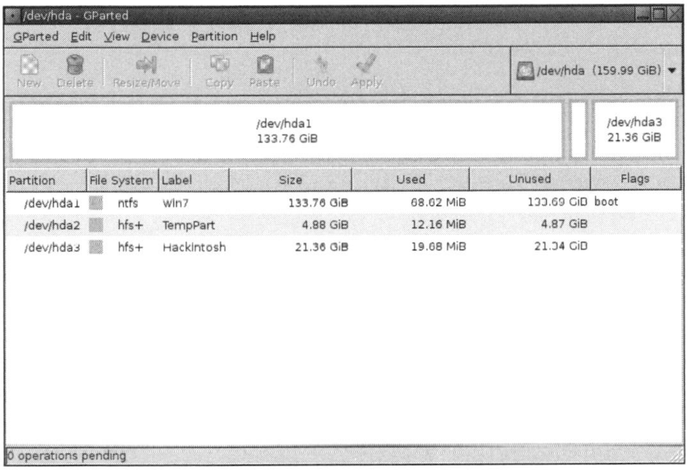

Figure showing GParted window with /dev/hda partitions

Partition	File System	Label	Size	Used	Unused	Flags
/dev/hda1	ntfs	win7	133.76 GiB	68.62 MiB	133.69 GiB	boot
/dev/hda2	hfs+	TempPart	4.88 GiB	12.16 MiB	4.87 GiB	
/dev/hda3	hfs+	Hackintosh	21.36 GiB	19.68 MiB	21.34 GiB	

Booting the Leopard Installer

In this section, you boot the Leopard retail DVD, ready to modify its installation parameters so that you can install it on your Windows disk.

Finding a boot disk

Because it is not a Macintosh, your computer cannot boot from your Leopard retail DVD. To install Leopard, you need to have your computer boot the way a real Macintosh does.

TIP

Many people have created boot disks for this purpose. In essence, they contain software that bridges the gap between your hardware and what Leopard expects to find in a genuine Apple.

You can find a collection of boot disks for specific motherboards at www.insanelymac.com/ forum/lofiversion/index.php/t125438.html. Many thanks to MACinized for collecting them together in one place. If your exact motherboard is not listed, try one from the same manufacturer.

Failing that, try one that sounds close. Remember, this is not an exact science!

NOTE

These boot disks are always supplied as an image file (.iso), which you need to burn to a CD. An image file is an exact image of what is on a CD. Because it is a bootable image, when you burn it to CD, the CD is bootable.

Creating your boot disk

You can't simply copy the .iso to a CD because it ends up as a file sitting on a CD and you won't be able to boot your computer. Because the .iso file is an exact image of the CD, you need to copy that image exactly to the CD.

CAUTION

Whatever CD/DVD-burning software you are using, be sure you use the option to burn an image. A very good, free program to burn CDs and DVDs is ImgBurn, available from `www.imgburn.com/`.

If you are using ImgBurn, follow these steps to burn your .iso file to your CD:

1. **Start ImgBurn running.**

2. **Insert a blank CD in your drive.**

3. **Click the "Write image file to disk" option.**

4. **Click the file finder icon (with the magnifying glass) and navigate to where your .iso file is located.**

5. **Check the Verify box to verify that the CD contains exactly the same data as the image file.**

6. **Click the large button to start the burn process.**

7. **Label your disk Leopard Boot.**

Specifying the hard disk identifier

This section explains how to boot the Leopard retail DVD using your boot CD as an intermediary.

Booting from the Leopard retail DVD is a two-step process, unless you are using a Macintosh. First, start the computer using the boot disk, and start the Leopard disk.

When your computer first starts, you see a screen that looks something like that shown in Figure 5.12.

Follow these steps to boot your computer:

1. **Insert your boot disk in the CD/DVD drive.**

2. **Restart your computer.**

3. **Press the key required to change your boot device.**

   Usually F12 works, but not always.

4. **Select CD/DVD, and press Enter.**

Figure 5.12

Boot menu

Boot Menu
Floppy disk
Hard disk
CD-ROM
Network
Use Arrow Keys to select
then press Enter

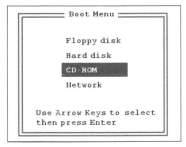

5. **Wait for the boot disk to start up and finish at a prompt.**

   You then see the screen shown in Figure 5.13, which is where you start the next stage of the boot process.

Figure 5.13

Darwin boot screen

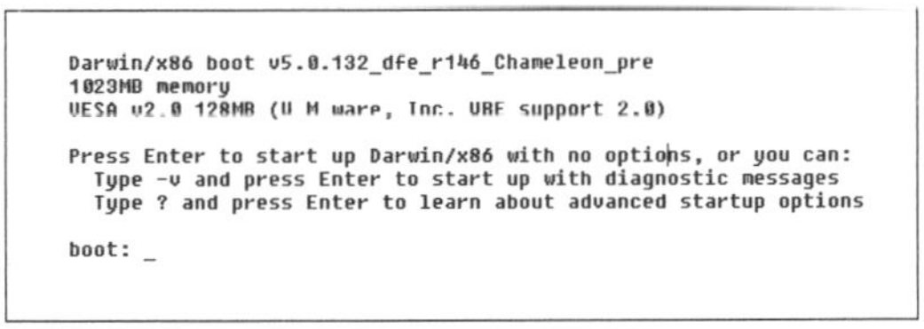
Darwin/x86 boot v5.0.132_dfe_r146_Chameleon_pre
1023MB memory
VESA v2.0 128MB (V M ware, Inc. VBE support 2.0)
Press Enter to start up Darwin/x86 with no options, or you can:
Type -v and press Enter to start up with diagnostic messages
Type ? and press Enter to learn about advanced startup options
boot: _

   At this point, the boot disk is waiting for you to boot Darwin, the Unix operating system on which Leopard is based. Of course, Darwin itself is not on that disk; it is on your Leopard retail DVD, so you need to tell it which disk that is and then swap disks.

6. **Press Esc.**

Now the boot prompt changes to look like the screen shown in Figure 5.14.

Figure 5.14

Darwin boot selector

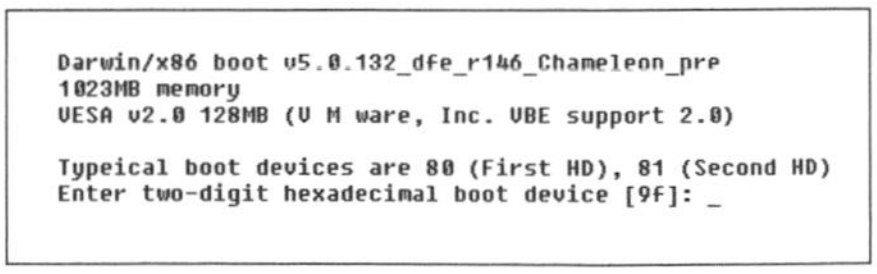
Darwin/x86 boot v5.0.132_dfe_r146_Chameleon_pre
1023MB memory
VESA v2.0 128MB (V M ware, Inc. VBE support 2.0)
Typeical boot devices are 80 (First HD), 81 (Second HD)
Enter two-digit hexadecimal boot device [9f]: _

In this case, the boot disk has identified the boot device as 9f, the decimal number 159 in hexadecimal.

NOTE

If you want to convert hexadecimal to decimal and vice versa, use the calculator at **http://easy calculation.com/hex-converter.php**.

Follow these steps to continue the boot process:

1. **Remove the boot disk from the CD drive.**

2. **Insert the Leopard retail DVD in the CD drive.**

3. **Wait a few seconds for the drive activity to stop, and press Enter.**

You see a second Darwin prompt, with the correct disk specified in the brackets.

Specifying boot options

This section explains how to specify boot options for the Leopard retail DVD and the effect of each.

At the boot prompt, you can type options that control the boot process. Table 5.3 lists the options you can type at the Darwin boot prompt.

Table 5.3 Darwin Boot Options

Option	Meaning
-v	Verbose: all output is sent to the screen
-f	Rebuild the kext cache
-x	Safe mode: similar to Windows safe mode
-s	Single-user mode

CROSS-REF

Appendix B contains explanations of various terms such as kext, kext cache, and so on.

At this point, don't worry about specifying any options other than -v because the kext cache can't be rebuilt; it's stored on the DVD, which can't be overwritten. Safe mode and single-user mode do not affect whether the disk boots.

1. **Type** -v**, and press Enter.**

A few lines of text appear on the screen, and then it clears and switches to graphics mode. The text continues down the screen.

At this point, the text looks like gibberish, but you should see one important line as highlighted in Figure 5.15.

Figure 5.15

Verbose boot screen

You should look for a line starting `BSD root: disk1s3`. The numbers you see may be different, but when you see it, you know that Leopard is at least going to boot on your computer.

NOTE

BSD root is the disk from which Darwin boots the main operating system. If Darwin can't identify it, then it can't boot.

After you see that line, you should see more messages scroll up the screen. The boot process takes quite a few minutes when you boot from the DVD. Be patient!

Finally, the screen goes blue and then black with the spinning beach ball in the top-left corner, and you see the Leopard Aurora desktop. Hooray!

Figure 5.16 shows the Leopard Aurora desktop.

Figure 5.16

Leopard Aurora desktop

Select the language you want to use to install Leopard and then pause at the next screen.

If you get stuck at a blank desktop, a blue desktop, or the spinning beach ball, turn to the troubleshooting section in Chapter 6.

Formatting your disks

Your computer is now running a bare-bones version of Leopard, running from the install DVD. Note that it has the Apple menu bar at the top of the screen. You now need to format the disk to which you want to install Leopard, as well as the temporary partition. To do that, you use Disk Utility, as shown in Figure 5.17.

Follow these steps to format your disks in preparation for installing Leopard:

1. **Click Utilities on the Apple menu bar.**

2. **Click Disk Utility.**

Figure 5.17

Start Disk Utility

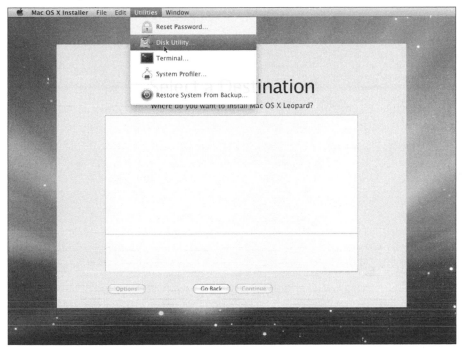

After some whirring from the DVD, Disk Utility starts up, showing you the disks connected to your computer. In this example, the only disk shown is a VMware virtual disk, because I captured the screens using VMware. Your disk should show three partitions, though the numbers on them may be different.

Select each partition in turn to be certain which is the new Hackintosh partition, which is the temporary partition, and which is your existing Vista partition. Follow these steps to format your disks:

CAUTION

Be very sure to select the correct partition: If you select the wrong one, you will erase your Vista or Windows 7 partition.

3. **Select Erase at the top of the Disk Utility window.**

4. **Select the small TempPart partition.**

5. **Select** Mac OS Extended (Journaled) **as the Volume Format.**

6. **Type the name for the partition.**

Figure 5.18 shows the small temporary partition ready to be erased and formatted.

Figure 5.18

Ready to format TempPart using Disk Utility

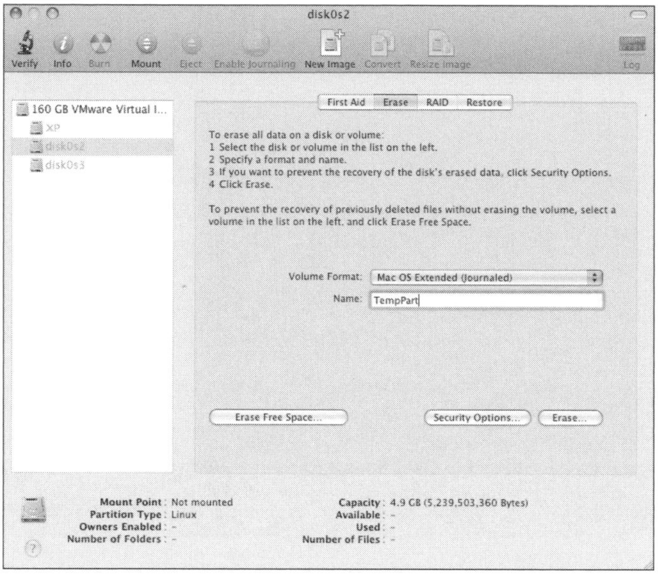

7. **Click Erase.**

Disk Utility then formats your disk ready for installation.

8. **Select the main Hackintosh partition.**

9. **Select** Mac OS Extended (Journaled) **as the Volume Format.**

10. **Type the name for the partition.**

Why not call it Hackintosh?

At this point, Disk Utility should look something like that shown in Figure 5.19.

11. **Click Erase.**

12. **When the erase has finished, click the red close icon in the Disk Utility window.**

You now return to the disk install select screen, as shown in Figure 5.20.

This time, your newly formatted partitions show up.

Figure 5.19

Disk Utility ready to format Hackintosh partition

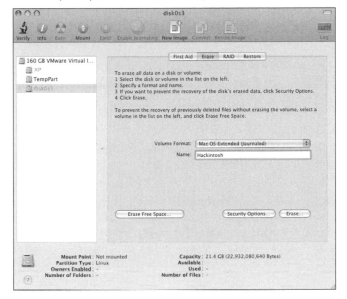

Figure 5.20

Select install disk

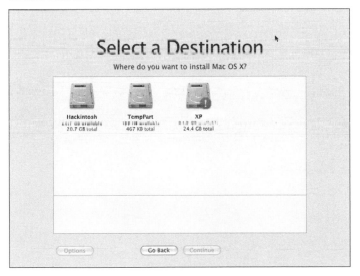

Modifying Your Leopard Installer

To install to an MBR disk, you need to remove the code in the installer that checks that the disk is formatted as GPT. As you would expect, while it sounds simple, you need to carry out a number of Unix commands and you need to get each one exactly right or it will not work.

For this method I am greatly indebted to Fredde87, llauqsd, and STLVNUB. The original article is on the Insanely Mac Web site at www.insanelymac.com/forum/lofiversion/index.php/t181287.html

CAUTION

Before you press Enter after entering each line of code, be sure to check your typing. If the command cannot be carried out, you receive an error message. If the command works, all that happens is that you get the prompt again. It works on the principle that no news is good news: If it didn't fail, then it must have worked!

Follow these steps to modify your installer:

1. **From the Apple menu bar, select Utilities, and then Terminal.**

This opens a terminal window as shown in Figure 5.21.

Figure 5.21

Terminal window in installer

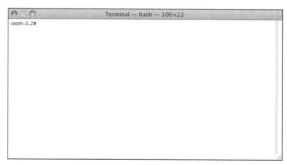

2. **Type the following code:**

```
cp -R /System/Installation/Packages/* /Volumes/TempPart
```

CAUTION

Be careful of spacing: there should be a space after cp, after –R and after *. Also be careful with capitalization as –r is not the same as –R. Be patient; it takes a while to copy the files.

This command copies everything in the System/Installation/Packages folder to your temporary partition.

3. **Type**

   ```
   cd /Volumes/TempPart
   ```

   This changes your working directory to the TempPart disk.

4. **Type**

   ```
   mkdir temp
   ```

   This creates a new folder called temp on your TempPart disk.

5. **Type**

   ```
   mv OSInstall.mpkg temp/
   ```

   This copies the installer to your new temp folder.

6. **Type**

   ```
   cd temp
   ```

   This changes your working directory to the temp folder.

7. **Type**

   ```
   xar -x -f OSInstall.mpkg
   ```

   xar is an archiving program. In this case you are using it to extract the files from the installer so that they can be modified.

8. **Type**

   ```
   cat Distribution | sed "s/eraseOptionAvailable='true'//g"¬
      > Distribution2
   ```

N O T E

The ¬ character is a line continuation character. You don't type it in; it is just there to show you that everything in that command should be on one line. Also, be careful of the single (') and double (") quotes.

This is a classic Unix command and explains why so many people love using Unix. First, cat reads everything in the file Distribution and writes it out to a new file Distribution2. If the command was simply cat Distribution > Distribution2 the two files would be identical.

But sed is a stream editor: it takes everything that is input to it, changes it, and writes it back out. The s/.../.../g means substitute everything between the first /.../ with whatever is in between the second /.../. The /g means globally.

So this compact command reads through everything in the file Distribution, replaces every occurrence of eraseOptionAvailable='true' with a blank then writes it out to a new file Distribution2.

9. **Type**

   ```
   mv Distribution2 Distribution
   ```

This command copies the new Distribution2 to overwrite the Distribution file.

10. **Type**

```
rm -Rf OSInstall.mpkg
```

This removes everything in the OSInstall.mpkg file.

11. **Type**

```
xar -c -f OSInstall.mpkg *
```

This repacks everything into the OSInstall.mpkg file.

12. **Type**

```
mv OSInstall.mpkg ../
```

This moves OSInstall.mpkg back into the top directory on the temporary disk.

13. **Type**

```
cd ..
```

This moves your working directory back up to the top directory.

14. **Type**

```
rm -Rf temp
```

This removes everything in the temp directory.

At this point your Terminal screen should look like the screen shown in Figure 5.22.

Figure 5.22

Terminal screen

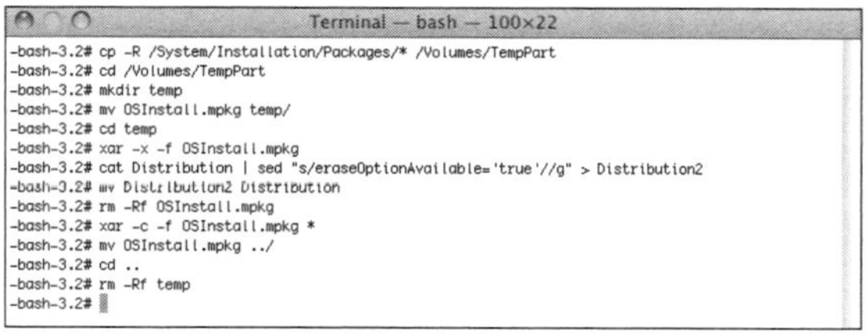

Don't close Terminal, as you require it again in the next part.

All the commands up to this point have been to create a modified Leopard installer. The remaining part of the exercise is to have the installer use your modified installer, rather than the one that is on the DVD.

If you have access to a Macintosh, you can create a new installation DVD with the modification, but this way is much easier if you don't have easy access to a Mac. If you want to create a modified DVD using a Mac, follow llauqsd's tutorial at `www.insanelymac.com/forum/lofiversion/index.php/t116505.html`.

Forcing the installer to use your modifications

Having created the new installer, you now need to be able to use it.

Follow these steps to set up your installer:

1. **Still using Terminal, type**

`mount`

This command shows all the disks that are mounted on your Leopard computer as shown in Figure 5.23.

Figure 5.23

Result of mount command

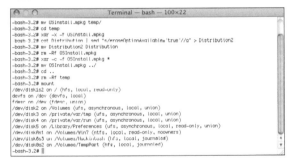

As you can see at the bottom of the window, the list of disks on my computer is:

- dev/disk0s1: /Volumes/XP
- dev/disk0s2: /Volumes/TempPart
- dev/disk0s3: /Volumes/Hackintosh

2. **In the list of disks shown by the mount command, look for one that is shown as** `/Volumes/TempPart`

In my case it is `/dev/disk0s2`

3. **Move up one level in the folder hierarchy by typing**

`cd /`

In other words, move to the root of the disk.

4. **Now unmount the disk by typing**

`umount /Volumes/TempPart`

C A U T I O N

Although the command is used to unmount the disk, it is written as umount: without the first "n". Also, be careful of spacing in the command.

5. **Type**

```
mount -t hfs /dev/disk0s2 /System/Installation/Packages
```

T I P

Remember to change the disk0s2 to whatever your TempPart disk is shown as.

This command remounts the disk, calling it `/System/Installation/Packages` so that when the installer looks for the packages, it finds the one on your disk, rather than the one on the install DVD.

6. **Close Terminal.**

This returns you to the part of the installation where you choose the disk to install to.

7. **Click the Back arrow to return to the Choose your Language screen.**

8. **Click the arrow to go through the copyright and licensing screens and then choose your Hackintosh disk for the installation.**

Note that your TempPart disk shows as a folder because you mounted the disk as / System/Installation/Packages which is a folder. This is shown in Figure 5.24.

Figure 5.24

Installation options showing disks and folder

CAUTION

Be very careful that you choose your Hackintosh disk, not your Vista or Windows 7 disk!

Specifying installation options

This section explains the Leopard installation options and how to select or deselect them. The Leopard retail version doesn't have many installation options. You have these options:

- Printer drivers
- Additional fonts
- Language translations
- X11, a Unix windowing system

Unless your specific printer is in the list, you need not install any printers because you can add these later.

If you plan to always use English as your language, you can leave out the language translations.

You should include the additional fonts, unless you are very short on hard disk space.

Figure 5.25 shows the customize options screen.

Figure 5.25

Customize options

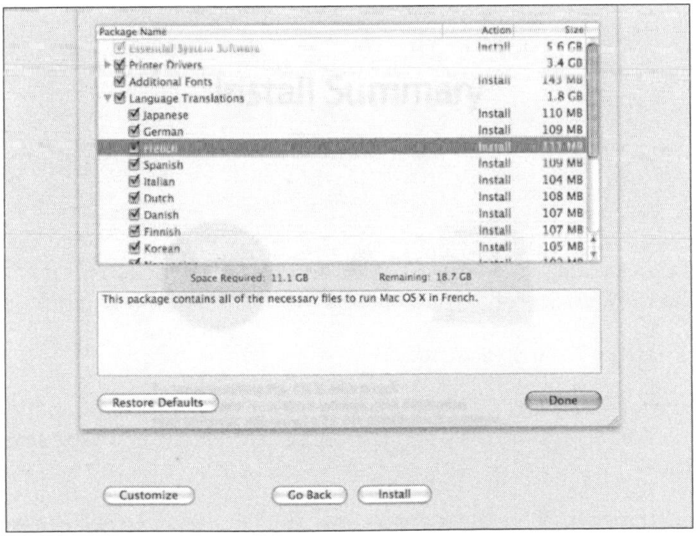

Follow these steps to select customize options:

Each small triangle beside a heading expands or contracts the list. If the individual box is blue, it means that option is selected. If the heading box is blue, it means that all options under that heading are selected.

1. **Place a check mark in each option that you want to select.**

2. **Click Done to proceed to the actual installation.**

Finally, you are ready to install Leopard. Figure 5.26 shows the Install Summary screen.

Figure 5.26

The Install Summary screen

3. **Click Install.**

Leopard first wants to check your DVD. Because you've got this far with it and it's the first time you've used it, checking the DVD is probably pointless, so you can click the Skip button.

Figure 5.27 shows this stage of the installation.

Leopard is now being installed. Normally, it takes between 20 and 60 minutes, depending on how fast your computer and disk drives are. The progress bar at the bottom of the screen gradually moves as the installation progresses, as shown in Figure 5.28.

Occasionally, this display stops moving, but it shows how much more time the installation will take, as shown in Figure 5.28. If this happens, wait until all CD and hard disk activity has stopped for two or three minutes, and then restart your computer.

Figure 5.27

Checking the installation

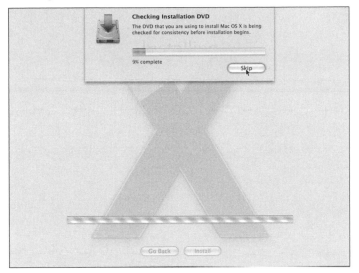

Figure 5.28

Installing Leopard

Otherwise, you eventually see the screen saying Leopard has been installed, as shown in Figure 5.29.

Figure 5.29

Installation succeeded

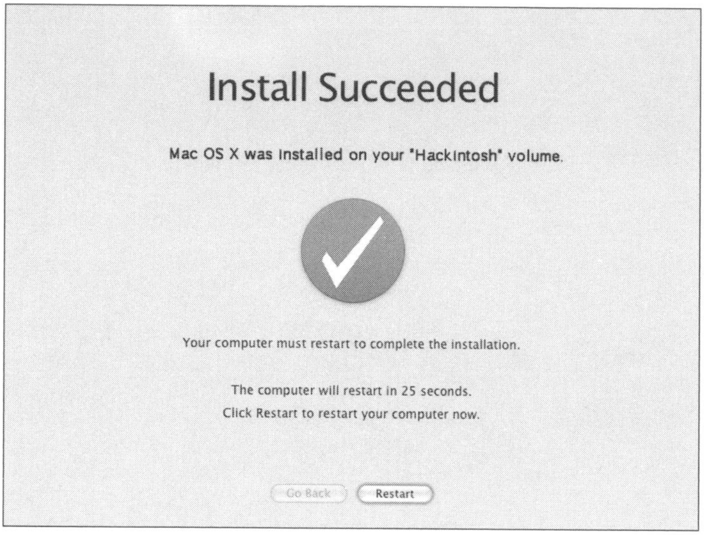

Install Succeeded

Mac OS X was installed on your "Hackintosh" volume.

Your computer must restart to complete the installation.

The computer will restart in 25 seconds.
Click Restart to restart your computer now.

Go Back   Restart

Restarting your computer

Now is the moment of truth! Will your computer restart?

Because Leopard was installed after your Windows installation, Darwin automatically becomes the default boot loader. So when you restart, you should see the Darwin boot prompt, this time with two choices, as shown in Figure 5.30.

Figure 5.30

Restart computer

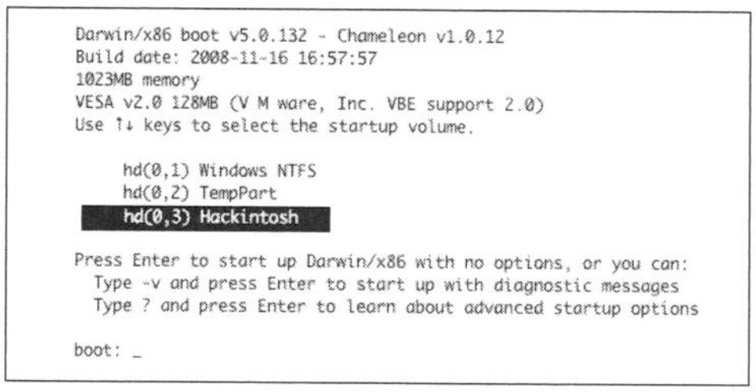

```
Darwin/x86 boot v5.0.132 - Chameleon v1.0.12
Build date: 2008-11-16 16:57:57
1023MB memory
VESA v2.0 128MB (V M ware, Inc. VBE support 2.0)
Use ↑↓ keys to select the startup volume.

    hd(0,1) Windows NTFS
    hd(0,2) TempPart
    hd(0,3) Hackintosh

Press Enter to start up Darwin/x86 with no options, or you can:
  Type -v and press Enter to start up with diagnostic messages
  Type ? and press Enter to learn about advanced startup options

boot: _
```

NOTE
If your XP disk is formatted with FAT file system rather than NTFS, your first line will read FAT instead of Windows NTFS.

Let's not try the OS X partition for a moment; let's try to start XP by selecting Windows NTFS at the Darwin boot screen.

Windows XP should load normally. If it doesn't, check Chapter 6.

Choosing Your Boot Loader

This section covers the three ways of dual booting either Windows XP or Leopard. These are your choices:

- Using the standard Darwin boot loader
- Using the Windows XP boot loader
- Using Chameleon, a graphical front end for the Darwin boot loader

Using the standard Darwin boot loader

If you are happy using the Darwin boot loader, you don't need to change anything. However, you must remember to press F8 each time you boot; otherwise, you cannot boot to XP. By default, Darwin simply loads Leopard.

Using the Windows XP boot loader

Because Leopard was installed last, it has set itself as the boot partition, so it is the first to boot. You need to change this, so the XP partition is restored as the boot partition. To do this, you need to do two things: Reset the boot partition, and install chain0.

Resetting XP as the boot partition

In order to return XP to being the boot partition, you need to restart your partition editor. In this case, we use GPartEd.

1. **Boot from the GPartEd CD.**

   Note that installing Leopard has set your Leopard partition to the boot partition. You need to set the boot partition to your XP partition.

2. **Right-click the first (XP) partition.**

3. **Select Manage Flags.**

4. **Select Boot.**

5. **Click Close.**

Installing chain0

Now that you have set XP as the boot partition, you need to tell it how to find the Leopard partition. This requires editing your `boot.ini` file. Follow these steps to install chain0:

1. **Use Notepad to open the file** boot.ini**.**

   It is located in the root folder (`C:\`) on your XP partition. You may need to open Windows Explorer change directory to the `C:\` folder. You may need to set folder options to show hidden files:

2. **Select Tools ⇨ Folder Options ⇨ View, and check Show Hidden Files and Folders.**

   This is shown in Figure 5.31.

   Figure 5.31

   Show hidden files and folders

   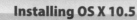

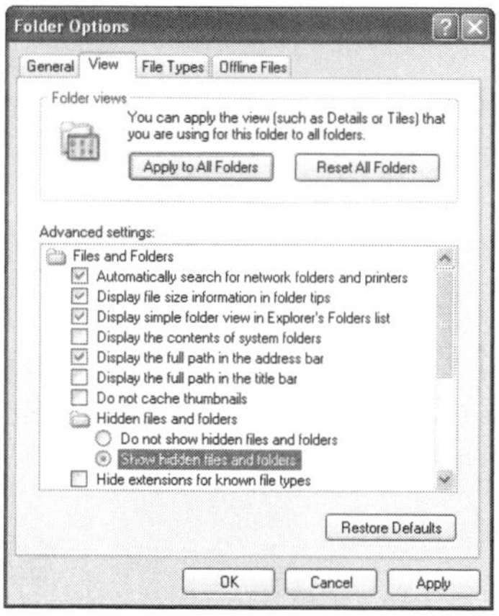

3. **Select the** C: **drive in Explorer.**

   Windows XP tries to prevent you from messing with any of its system files, so by default it doesn't allow you to list the files on the system drive, as shown in Figure 5.32.

4. **Click Show the contents of this folder.**

5. **Copy the file chain0 to** C:**.**

Figure 5.32

These files are hidden

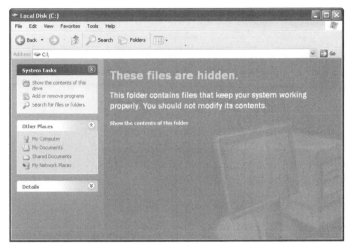

Editing boot.ini

In the `C:\` folder, you also find the file `boot.ini`, as shown in Figure 5.33.

Figure 5.33

Explorer showing `boot.ini`

1. **Open** boot.ini **using Notepad.**

   Figure 5.34 shows the normal content of `boot.ini`.

   Figure 5.34

   Content of `boot.ini`

   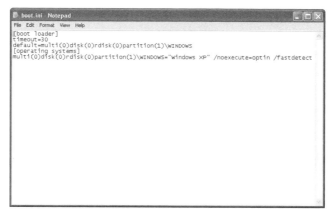

2. **At the end of the file, add the line:**

   ```
   C:\chain0 "Leopard"
   ```

3. **Save** boot.ini**.**

4. **Shut down XP.**

5. **Restart your computer.**

This time you should boot to a screen that gives you two choices to boot: One is for Leopard, the other for Windows XP. If the timeout is too long for you (the default is 30 seconds), you can change it by editing this line in boot.ini:

```
timeout=30
```

Using the Chameleon boot loader

A third boot loader you might want to use is the Chameleon v2 graphical boot loader. This is available from `http://chameleon.osx86.hu/static/some-words-about-donation?ref=file_download/22/Chameleon-2.0-r431.pkg.zip`.

To save you typing that long URL, I created a TinyURL to make it easier. This is `http://tinyurl.com/o97up5`.

1. **Boot into Leopard.**

2. **Download the file, saving it to your Leopard Downloads folder.**

3. **Double-click the download to extract the package from the zip file**

4. **Double-click the package file to install the boot loader.**

5. **Shut down Leopard.**

6. **Reboot your computer.**

This time, instead of the regular Darwin boot loader, you see a new graphic screen, as shown in Figure 5.35.

Figure 5.35

Chameleon 2 graphical boot loader

Your XP and Leopard disks are both shown: Your XP disk is titled Windows NTFS or FAT, and your Leopard disk has whatever name you gave it when you installed.

Use the arrow keys to change the selection from one to the other. If you want to enter startup options, simply type the options. The options you enter, such as -v, are shown on the screen. Press Enter in the usual way to start the boot process.

If you do not enter any boot options, you see the usual graphics screen, slightly modified with a shiny Apple logo and the usual clock timer, as shown in Figure 5.36.

Figure 5.36

Leopard boot screen

Summary

In this chapter, you backed up your XP disk and created space on it to fit a Leopard installation. After you installed Leopard, you installed a boot loader to allow you to select either operating system at boot time.

6

Troubleshooting Your Installation

Remember, Leopard was never designed to run on your computer, unless you have a genuine Apple Macintosh, so it rarely installs without a hiccough. Most computers will run Leopard to some extent; the most common issues are with video, sound, and wireless networking.

In this chapter, you find some hints on getting your Leopard installation to work, including things to try in order to get the install DVD to start and to get your Leopard installation to start.

If you decide it's too hard, you can find out how to restore your computer to the state it was in before you started.

Finally, I provide a method to change the Leopard boot parameters so you don't have to see the Darwin boot prompt each time you start Leopard.

Booting from the Install DVD

If you can't get the Leopard install DVD to start up, you are not going to get much further! In this section, you find some hints on how to at least get to the first Leopard installation screen where you select your installation language.

Starting the retail Leopard DVD

When you install the retail version of Leopard, you first boot from a special boot CD, generally the Kabyl-Bumby. The function of the boot CD is to get the Leopard install DVD to install the way it does on a real Macintosh. When this goes wrong, the result is a kernel panic.

Recovering from a kernel panic

In Macintosh OS X parlance, a kernel panic is the name given to an error that is completely unrecoverable, much like the infamous Blue Screen of Death (BSOD) of Windows.

Almost invariably the cause of a kernel panic is an inconsistency between your hardware and what the system is trying to do. For example, if you try to install retail Leopard on an AMD computer, it always panics.

6 | **In This Chapter**

Booting from the
install DVD

Booting Leopard

Restoring your computer
from your backup

Reinstalling with
different parameters

Restoring your XP
boot loader

Modifying the Apple
Property Lists to specify
future boot parameters

Kernel panics have many different causes, but the end result is the same: Your computer just stops.

One thing you can try is rebooting. It sounds strange, but sometimes a panic occurs the first time, but not subsequently.

If you consistently get a kernel panic, you should use a different boot disk. Many are available, each for a different combination of motherboard and other hardware.

One place to look is `www.insanelymac.com/forum/index.php?showtopic=114834 &start=0&p=934112&#entry934112`, which has boot disks for many different motherboards, thanks to a user called sonotone who collected them together.

I created a TinyURL (at `http://tinyurl.com`), `http://tinyurl.com/r49hnx`, to make finding them easier.

Start reading from under the dotted line (- - - -). If you find your own motherboard or computer listed there, download the file (which is most likely a .zip file), unzip it, burn it to a CD, and use it to start your computer.

If you can't find your exact computer or motherboard, try using one that is close.

Recovering from the "Still waiting for boot disk" error

"Still waiting for boot disk" means, obviously, that the Darwin boot loader can't find the disk it should boot from, even though it's sitting in the CD/DVD drive!

If you have a single hard disk, it is identified as disk0 as far as Darwin is concerned and your CD/DVD drive is disk1. If you have two hard disks, the second hard disk will be disk1 (disks are always counted starting from zero) and your CD/DVD drive is disk2.

At the Darwin prompt, as well as typing -v, you should also type the number of the CD/DVD drive, along with the partition number. (Partitions are always numbered starting with 1. Why? Who knows! They just are!)

So if you have a single hard disk, at the Darwin prompt, type `-v rd=disk1s1` and press Enter.

With luck, your CD/DVD then boots.

If your disk is formatted as GPT and not MBR, try `disk1s2`. This is because GPT creates a hidden 200MB partition as the first partition (disk1s1); Leopard is installed to the second partition, disk1s2.

Modifying your computer hardware

CAUTION

Modifying your computer hardware requires that you open your computer's system box, which may void your warranty. Unless you feel confident in doing this, don't!

Sometimes, the "Still waiting for boot device" error means the CD/DVD drive is not configured correctly.

CD/DVD drives (and hard disks) can be configured as Master or Slave. If you have a single CD/DVD drive, it should be configured as a master. If you have two, one should be a master, the other a slave. The reason for this is that the boot order for disks is master first, then slave. If you have no master (in other words, your drive is configured as a slave), then the system becomes confused and waits forever for a boot disk.

Each drive has a small panel on the back, alongside the power and data cable connections, that allows you to select either master or slave for that drive.

Figure 6.1 shows the rear view of a CD/DVD drive with the jumper block, power connector, and data connector.

Figure 6.1

Master-slave configuration

Rear view of CD drive showing jumpers

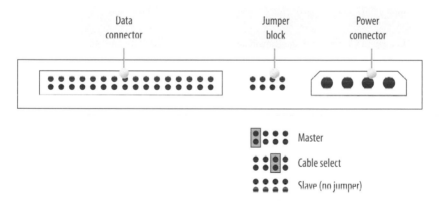

Master

Cable select

Slave (no jumper)

Position jumper over pins as shown

On the top surface of the drive, you find a diagram showing which pins are which. In this case, the drive is configured as a slave because there is no jumper. To configure it as a master, you need to place the jumper over the left-most pair of pins. You should use a pair of tweezers to do this.

CAUTION
Remember that opening your computer and making changes may void your warranty.

Enabling AHCI

One possibility that night prevent your retail install DVD from finding the correct disk drive to boot from is not having AHCI enabled, particularly if you are installing to a system using Windows XP.

AHCI stands for Advanced Host Controller Interface. You can find more information about this topic in Appendix B. If your computer uses Serial ATA (SATA) disk drives, it likely implements AHCI in the BIOS.

System Information for Windows will tell you whether you are using SATA disk drives. Figure 6.2 shows the SIW display for my computer.

Figure 6.2

SIW showing SATA drives

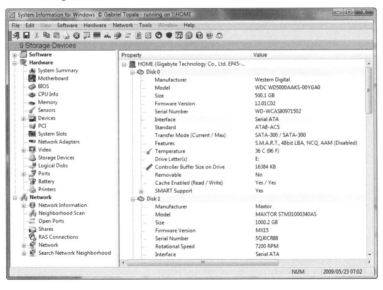

If you are running Windows XP, you probably don't use AHCI because XP requires special disk driver software that most computer manufacturers don't supply. If you are running Windows 7 or Vista, you may or may not have AHCI enabled. Both Vista and Windows 7 install either with or without AHCI. However, if it was installed with AHCI disabled, it can't be used after AHCI is enabled; it will crash with a blue screen error.

Leopard usually installs on an AHCI system if SATA drives are present.

To turn AHCI on, you need to go into your BIOS. In my BIOS, AHCI is under a top-level heading called Integrated Peripherals. I have these choices: Disabled, AHCI, and RAID.

Use whatever key you need to press to enter your BIOS. Search under various headings until you find one with a choice of AHCI. Enable AHCI and reboot.

You cannot run Windows XP with this setting; if Vista or Windows 7 was installed on a non-AHCI system, you cannot run them either. But Leopard is likely to install.

To switch between the two operating systems, you need to either enable or disable AHCI in the BIOS before trying to boot. Enable for Leopard; disable for Windows.

This is summarized in Table 6.1.

Table 6.1	Effect of AHCI on Dual Boot		
Computer Configuration	Installed Operating System	AHCI Status	Outcome
Parallel ATA drives only	Windows XP, Vista, or 7 installed	Ensure jumper is set to Master	Should boot to Leopard or a Windows operating system
Serial ATA drives	Windows XP installed	Need to enable AHCI in BIOS to install Leopard	Leopard boots with AHCI enabled; XP boots with AHCI disabled
Serial ATA drives	Windows Vista or 7 installed	Need to enable AHCI in BIOS to install Leopard	If AHCI was enabled when Vista or 7 was installed, can boot to Leopard or Windows; otherwise need to enable to boot Leopard

Trying another boot disk

Sometimes the DVD boots fine until it gets to the graphics screens, where it hangs with a screen that is blue all over, gray all over, or black. In most cases, you can move the cursor, but nothing more happens. In some cases, you also have the "Spinning Beach Ball of Death" or SBOD.

In almost every case, this occurs because the kexts that were installed from your boot disk are not correct.

In this case, the only thing to do is to try another boot disk. One good place to start looking is the list compiled by sonotone at http://tinyurl.com/r49hnx.

CAUTION

As always, be careful that you don't go over any download limits set by your ISP.

Starting a modified installation DVD

The above information applies to starting a modified installation DVD. These are the most likely errors:

- A kernel panic
- Can't find the boot device
- Hangs at some point with no progress at all

Recovering from a kernel panic

Restart your computer, and see whether the kernel panic occurs again. If it happens consistently, try specifying your boot disk CD/DVD drive using the `rd=diskXsY` boot option. If you have only one hard disk, your CD/DVD drive most likely is disk1; try `rd=disk1s1` and then try `rd=disk1s2`.

If you have two hard disks, your CD/DVD drive most likely is disk2. So try `rd=disk2s1` and then `rd=disk2s2`.

Recovering from the "Still waiting for boot disk" error

"Still waiting for boot disk" means, obviously, that the Darwin boot loader can't find the disk it should boot from, even though it's sitting in the CD/DVD drive!

One of the solutions in the kernel panic section should help here.

Modifying your computer hardware

CAUTION

This requires that you open your computer's system box, which may void your warranty. Unless you feel confident in doing this, don't!

Sometimes, the "Still waiting for boot device" error means that the CD/DVD drive is not configured correctly. See the section "Starting the retail Leopard DVD" earlier in this chapter for help on changing the configuration of your CD/DVD drive.

Enabling AHCI

One possibility that might prevent your install DVD from finding the correct disk drive to boot from is not having AHCI enabled, particularly if you are installing to a system using Windows XP.

Follow the instructions in the preceding section on enabling AHCI in your BIOS.

CAUTION

Remember that these are large files and may take you over any download limits imposed by your ISP.

Booting Leopard

So you've installed Leopard to your computer, but you can't get it running from the disk you installed to. Here are a few ideas to help you get it going.

Dealing with a kernel panic

If you have a kernel panic when starting up your installed Leopard, it is almost certainly because, when installing, you selected an option that is not compatible with your system.

As always, try rebooting: Sometimes a problem happens only on the first boot.

If it happens again, the only way out is to reinstall, making a note of the options you choose.

Identifying exactly what caused the kernel panic is difficult because, during the boot process, the boot loader starts several processes in rapid succession and several seconds could pass before the error appears on the screen, mixed in with result output from successful processes.

TIP

As always, less is more: Choose the minimum number of install options.

Dealing with the "Still waiting for boot disk" error

Normally this does not occur. If it does, you need to supply the appropriate `"rd=diskXsY"` parameter on the boot loader startup.

If you have installed to your first hard disk (for example, if you are intending to dual boot with Windows XP or Vista), you need to supply `rd-disk0s2`, assuming your primary partition on disk 0 is your Windows partition and Leopard is on the second partition.

If you have installed Leopard to its own disk, then it is disk1 or disk2, depending on how many other disks you have.

If you have installed to a USB drive, that is normally seen as disk0 because you have used the BIOS to set it as the boot disk.

It's a bit of a pain to have to tell Leopard where to boot from each time you do it, so later in this chapter you find a way to make the change permanent.

Dealing with the "Spinning Beach Ball of Death"

It is hugely frustrating to have Leopard get to the point where it's almost running, but not quite. Almost certainly this happens because you don't have the correct video kexts loaded.

If you can't find kexts for your exact graphics setup on the installation DVD, do not select any kexts at all. This usually allows you to get to the basic 1024 by 768 graphics screen.

Dealing with no welcome video

If you fail to see the Leopard welcome video, but you have normal graphics on screen, it means that your graphics setup is not capable of supporting Quartz Extreme/Core Image (QE/CI), which is similar to DirectX on a computer running Windows.

This means Leopard cannot use the hardware acceleration built into your video setup. This comes about for one of two reasons:

- You don't have the correct kext for your video setup.
- Your video setup uses part of your main memory, rather than having its own memory built in.

If your issue is the former, then you may be able to find the right kext by searching through the various forums. A list of forums is given in Appendix B.

As an example, if your video card is an nVidia 7600GT, search Google for `osx86 nvidia 7600gt kext`. You should be able to find an appropriate kext for your card.

Booting using safe mode

Just like Windows, Leopard provides a safe mode for booting. Safe mode does a disk check and then loads essential kexts, removes all font caches, disables all startup and login items, and removes the shared cache.

Booting into safe mode takes longer than usual because of the disk check. After you are running in safe mode, you may not have a network connection and your screen most likely runs in 1024 by 768 mode. This should get you through to a Leopard screen when all else has failed!

To start in safe mode, press F8 at the Darwin boot loader screen and type `-x`. I prefer to see what is happening during the boot, so I always use `-v -x` to set verbose mode as well.

After you have a Leopard screen, you can locate and install kexts to allow you to take full advantage of Leopard graphics.

Installing a kext using kexthelper

If your installation disk did not have an option to install your exact video system, then you may be able to find a kext online and install that.

To install a kext, the easiest way is to use an application called kexthelper b7. You can download this from `http://cheetha.net/`. You can download it to your Leopard disk or your Windows disk, provided that is available in your Leopard installation.

CAUTION

If you download any zip or dmg files to your Windows disk, don't try to open them in Windows because they contain components that are not visible to Windows.

After you have downloaded kexthelper, double-click the .zip file and place it in your Applications folder. Then, having downloaded your kexts, place them on your desktop.

Double-click kexthelper and drag the kexts you want to install into the main window of kexthelper; then enter your password into the Password box shown in Figure 6.3.

Figure 6.3

Kexts in Kexthelper window

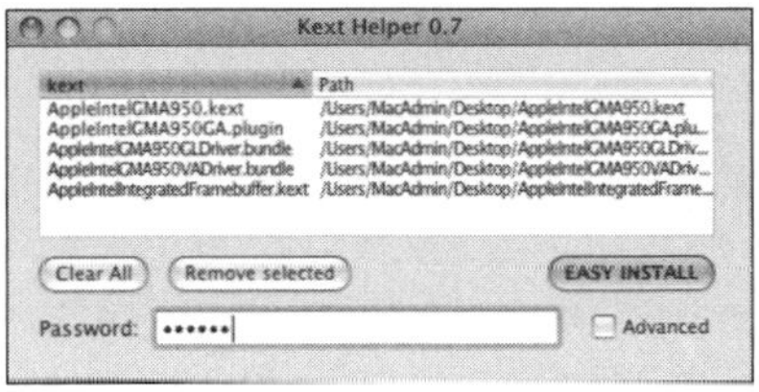

When you click Easy Install, kexthelper installs the kexts. Normally, after using kexthelper, you reboot, but if you've installed a graphics kext, it is essential that you reboot.

Installing injector strings using UInstaller

One final possibility to try is UInstaller, created by a Hackintosh genius called pcwiz. You can download it from his site at `http://pcwizcomputer.com/`.

1. **Click Downloads.**

2. **Click [Mac OSx86] Universal OSx86 Installer.**

   Then just after the bullet points, you see a link to Download Universal OSx86 Installer here (2.0MB).

3. **Click "here."**

   You can download it to either your Windows or Leopard disk.

4. **Place the .zip file on your Leopard desktop, and double-click it.**

5. **After the file is unzipped, open the folder and double-click UInstaller.**

   On the main screen of UInstaller, you find an option to select your video card, as shown in Figure 6.4a.

   UInstaller has several other options, but in this case all you're looking for is the video card you have.

6. **Click the drop-down box beside Apply EFI String for video card, and select your video card, if it is listed.**

   Figure 6.4b shows a selection of the video cards available.

CAUTION

If your exact video card is not listed, don't select anything. Remember that this video card selection goes into the EFI (see Appendix B) and must exactly match your actual video card.

Figure 6.4

UInstaller main screen (a); UInstaller video cards (b)

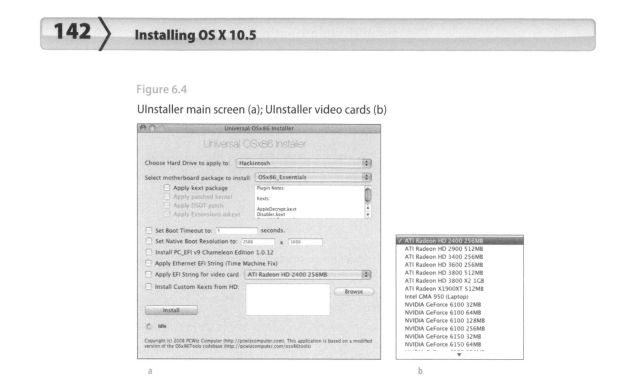

a   b

7. **If you do find your video card, click the check box and then click Install.**

8. **Reboot your computer.**

This should give you the correct video card kext and your video should work correctly.

Finding correct video kexts

Another possibility is to search for kexts for your video chip. Use a Google search string like "osx86 ati radeon 1150" if your video card is an ATI Radeon 1150.

At the very least you find other users with the same video chip looking for the same thing you are. You may find the correct kexts, or a work-around.

Changing your video card

While this is possibly a little extreme, if you really want to use Leopard and you are not afraid to open your computer, you can buy a new video card for which you know there are kexts available.

Appendix B has a table that lists the graphics chips used in most Macintosh computers. If you choose a chip type that has been used in a Mac, you can then search for a card that uses that chip, or one very similar.

Restoring Your Computer from Your Backup

In this section, you learn how to restore your hard disk using the disk image backup you made if you tried installing Leopard on your Windows 7, XP, or Vista disk.

Using the Vista Backup and Restore utility

If you used the Windows 7 or Vista Backup and Restore utility to back up your hard disk, you need to boot from your Vista (or Windows 7) install disk or the Vista (or Windows 7) recovery disk.

1. **Insert the install disk or recovery disk in your CD/DVD drive.**

2. **Restart your computer, and select to boot from the CD/DVD.**

3. **Click Repair Your Computer.**

   This is shown in Figure 6.5a.

   After searching for backups on your computer, the recovery disk comes to a selection screen as shown in Figure 6.5b.

   Figure 6.5

   The Repair your computer option (a); the System Recovery Options dialog box (b)

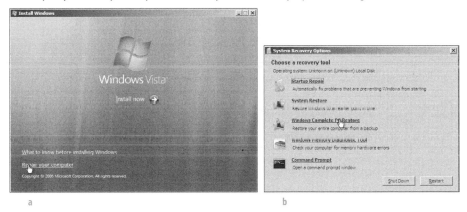

a   b

4. **Select Windows Complete PC Restore.**

Wait while Windows restores your computer to the point it was when you started installing Leopard.

Using other backup and restore programs

You need the restore disk for the program you used to back up your system.

Insert the restore CD or DVD in your drive, and boot from it. Then follow the instructions to restore your computer.

Reinstalling with Different Parameters

Assuming that none of the other troubleshooting hints fixed your installation, the only thing to do is to reinstall using different parameters.

If installing with different parameters does not work, you can try another distribution.

CAUTION

As always, remember that the files are large and may push you over your monthly download quota.

Restoring Your XP Boot Loader

So the worst has happened: You can't boot Windows XP after installing Leopard.

Windows XP contains a Recovery Console to allow for just such a contingency. You need your XP install CD to be able to use it.

1. **Insert your Windows XP installation CD.**

2. **Boot your computer from the CD.**

After loading required files, the boot process stops with a screen asking if you want to exit, continue to install XP, or enter the Recovery Console. Figure 6.6 shows the selection screen.

3. **Type R to enter the Recovery Console.**

Figure 6.7 shows the main Recovery Console screen.

Figure 6.6

Enter Recovery Console screen

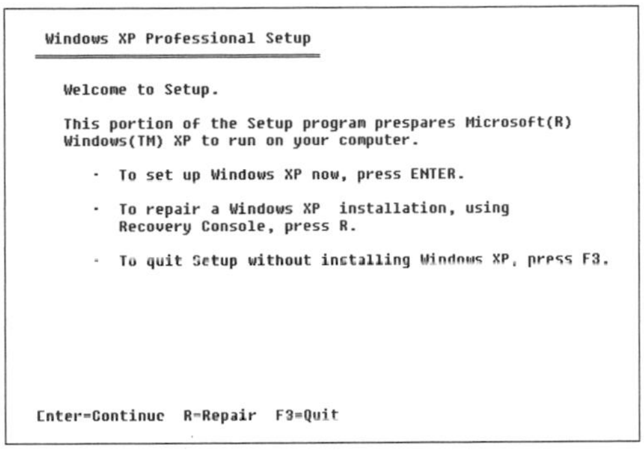

```
Windows XP Professional Setup

  Welcome to Setup.

  This portion of the Setup program prespares Microsoft(R)
  Windows(TM) XP to run on your computer.

     ·  To set up Windows XP now, press ENTER.

     ·  To repair a Windows XP  installation, using
        Recovery Console, press R.

     ·  To quit Setup without installing Windows XP, press F3.




  Enter=Continue  R=Repair  F3=Quit
```

Figure 6.7

Recovery Console

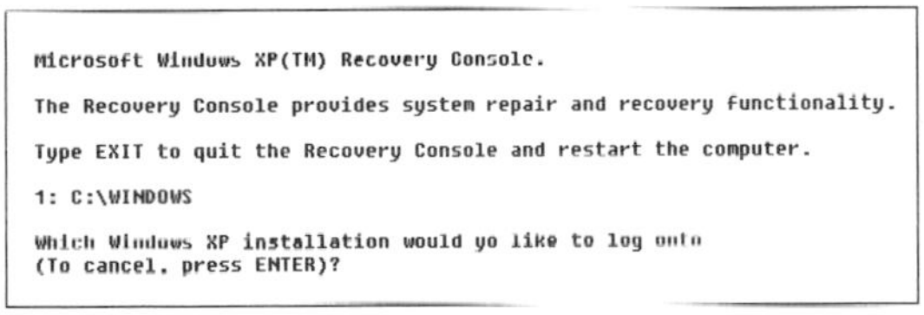

```
Microsoft Windows XP(TM) Recovery Console.

The Recovery Console provides system repair and recovery functionality.

Type EXIT to quit the Recovery Console and restart the computer.

1: C:\WINDOWS

Which Windows XP installation would yo like to log onto
(To cancel, press ENTER)?
```

You should see only one Windows installation listed, with the number 1.

4. At the prompt, type 1 and press Enter.

You need to supply an administrator password if you set one up when you originally installed XP.

5. Enter the password if prompted.

Recovery Console is not a graphical utility: It has a command line and requires you to type various commands. In this case, you need to use only a couple of the commands, but if you want to view all the commands, you can type Help at any time.

First you need to repair the Master Boot Record of your Windows disk.

6. Change the current directory to C:\ by typing cd \.

7. Type fixmbr, **and press Enter.**

8. **Confirm that you want to fix the Master Boot Record, and wait while Recovery Console rewrites the MBR.**

   You should also restore the XP boot loader files using Recovery Console. In these steps, I assume that your CD drive is the D: drive. If it is not, substitute your drive letter for `d` in the following commands.

9. **Type** `copy d:\i386\ntldr`**, and press Enter.**

10. **Respond with** `y` **at the prompt.**

11. **Type** `copy d:\i386\ntldr`**, and press Enter.**

12. **Respond with** `y` **at the prompt.**

Your XP boot sector and files should now be repaired and able to boot.

Modifying the Apple Property Lists to Specify Future Boot Parameters

In this section, you learn how to make Leopard boot with the same parameters each time, so you no longer need to type parameters into the boot loader.

Specifying boot parameters to the Darwin boot loader

In many cases, particularly when your video card is an exact match for the kexts you installed, Leopard boots and correctly identifies the maximum resolution of your screen. In some cases, however, that is not the case. In those cases, you can boot Leopard and tell it what resolution to use.

At the Darwin boot prompt, you type "`Graphics Mode`"="`1920x1080x32`".

You must include the quotes. This tells Leopard to start up with a screen resolution of 1920 x 1080 with 32-bit color.

Making the changes permanent

Needless to say, typing this each time you start Leopard is a little inconvenient. The way to avoid this is to edit the file that controls the boot parameters.

Locating the boot parameters file

This file is called `com.apple.Boot.plist`, and it resides in the `/Library/Preferences/SystemConfiguration` folder, as shown in Figure 6.8.

A .plist file is a property list file and is a text file of XML commands. Apple has its own document type definition (dtd), which defines what content a property list has.

Figure 6.8

Boot.plist folder

1. **Using Finder, navigate to** /Library/Preferences/SystemConfiguration.

Opening the boot parameters file

1. **Double-click the file** com.apple.Boot.plist **to open it in TextEdit, as shown in Figure 6.9.**

Figure 6.9

Boot.plist file open in TextEdit

2. **In the File menu for TextEdit, select Save.**

Saving the boot parameters file

First you need to save the file to your desktop because you don't have permission to save the file to the SystemConfiguration folder. Figure 6.10a shows the dialog box to save the file to your desktop. Follow these steps:

1. **In the Where: drop-down menu, select Desktop.**

2. **Add the extension .plist to the file; otherwise, it is saved as a .txt file.**

3. **Uncheck the box labeled If no extension is provided, use ".txt".**

4. **Click Save.**

TIP

Unlike Windows, capitalization is important in Leopard because it is based on a Unix platform. The files `com.apple.Boot.plist` and `com.apple.boot.plist` are different files. Never change the capitalization of system files.

If you accidentally try to save the file to the SystemConfiguration folder, you get an error message, as shown in Figure 6.10b.

Figure 6.10

Save Boot.plist file to desktop (a); insufficient privileges to save file (b)

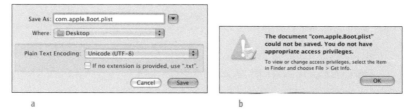

a   b

Editing the boot parameters file

Follow these steps to edit the boot parameters file:

1. **Using TextEdit, move down to the start of the line** `</dict>`.

2. **Press enter to insert a new line and move back up to the blank line.**

3. **Insert a Tab character, and** `<key>Graphics Mode</key>`.

4. **On the next line, insert another Tab, and** `<string>1920x1080x32</string>`.

Be sure to get the spelling and punctuation exactly as shown in Figure 6.11.

Figure 6.11

Inserting text using TextEdit

```
com.apple.Boot.plist
<?xml version="1.0" encoding="UTF-8"?>
<!DOCTYPE plist PUBLIC "-//Apple Computer//DTD PLIST 1.0//EN" "http://
www.apple.com/DTDs/PropertyList-1.0.dtd">
<plist version="1.0">
<dict>
        <key>Kernel</key>
        <string>mach_kernel</string>
        <key>Kernel Flags</key>
        <string></string>
        <key>Timeout</key>
        <string>5</string>
        <key>device-properties</key>
        <string></string>
        <key>Graphics Mode</key>
        <string>1920x1080x32</string>
</dict>
</plist>
```

5. **Save the file (File ➪ Save).**

6. **Quit TextEdit (TextEdit menu ➪ Quit).**

Replacing the old boot parameters file

Follow these steps to replace the old boot parameters file:

1. **Reopen the SystemConfiguration folder.**

2. **Drag the file** com.apple.Boot.plist **from your desktop to place it in the folder.**

Leopard gives you an error message, basically informing you that you don't have enough privileges to add the file to the folder, as shown in Figure 6.12a.

3. **Click Authenticate.**

You receive another message asking if you want to replace the old file with the new one, as shown in Figure 6.12b.

Figure 6.12

Insufficient privileges message (a); replace old file (b)

a   b

Of course you want to replace the old file!

4. **Click Replace.**

Now Leopard wants to be sure you can supply enough credentials to give you the privilege to replace the file, so it asks for your username and password, as shown in Figure 6.13.

Figure 6.13

Username and password prompt

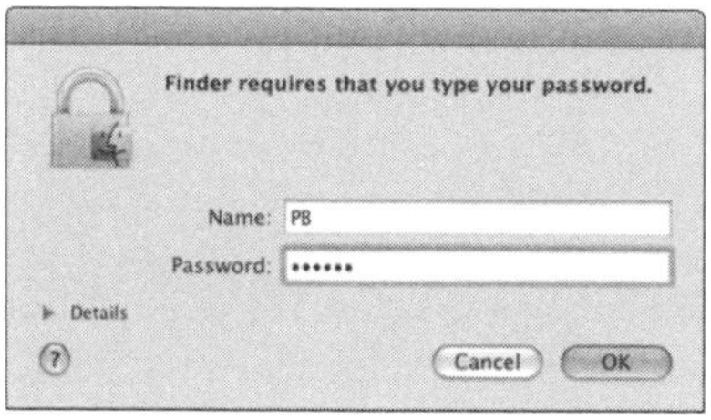

Finder requires that you type your password.

Name: PB

Password: ••••••

▶ Details

Cancel   OK

Finally Leopard replaces the file. This may all seem a little inconvenient, but it's actually a good thing. Files such as this are critical to the way Leopard works, so making a mistake can all too easily render your installation completely unusable.

Fixing file permissions

Leopard is very fussy about file permissions. The permissions attached to a file define who has permission (or privilege) to do what with the file. You can find a more extensive discussion of file permissions in Appendix B.

Finding file permissions

Leopard provides a simple way to find file permissions, as shown in Figure 6.14a.

This shows the permissions for the file: peterbaldwin has read and write permission; admin group has read-only permission, and the everyone group also has read-only permission.

Compare these permissions with those of another file in the same folder. Figure 6.14b shows the file permissions for `com.apple.network.identification.plist`, which is System read and write; wheel read-only; everyone read-only.

Leopard is very fussy about file permissions for system files; unless they are set exactly correctly, Leopard assumes that they have been tampered with and doesn't use them.

Figure 6.14

File permissions for Boot.plist (a); file permissions for
`network.identification.plist` file (b)

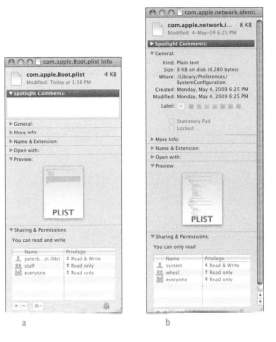

a   b

Using the file permissions database

Fortunately, Leopard contains a database of every system file and the correct permissions. It
also provides a repair utility called Disk Utility that is capable of setting them all back to their
correct values.

You can start an application in Leopard in several ways. In this case, we use Spotlight to search
for the file. Figure 6.15 shows a Spotlight search window for Disk Utility.

Figure 6.15

Spotlight search window for
Disk Utility

You can type only part of the application name, and Spotlight provides a list of possible matches. In this case, the file we want is the Top Hit.

1. **Click the Spotlight search magnifying glass on the top right of the screen.**

2. **Begin typing "disk utility" into the search box until you find Disk Utility listed.**

3. **Press Enter.**

This starts Disk Utility, as shown in Figure 6.16.

Figure 6.16

Disk Utility

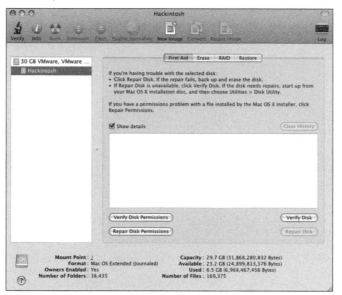

4. **Click Repair Disk Permissions.**

Disk Utility starts reading the permissions database, as shown in Figure 6.17.

As the screen says, it can take some time—up to five minutes in some cases. Finally it completes, and Disk Utility shows the files for which it has changed permissions, as shown in Figure 6.18.

Figure 6.17

Disk Utility reading disk permissions database

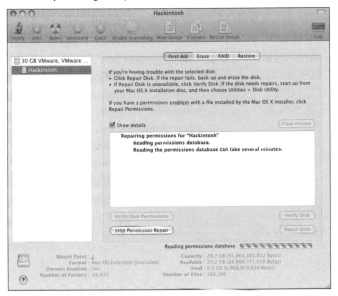

Figure 6.18

Disk Utility file permissions changes

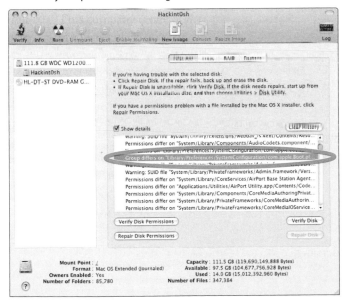

In this case, the changes made to `Boot.plist` are shown highlighted.

5. **Close Disk Utility.**

6. **Use Get Info for** `com.apple.Boot.plist` **to see the permissions as they are now set, as shown in Figure 6.19.**

Figure 6.19

File permissions for
`com.apple.Boot.`
`plist`

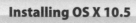

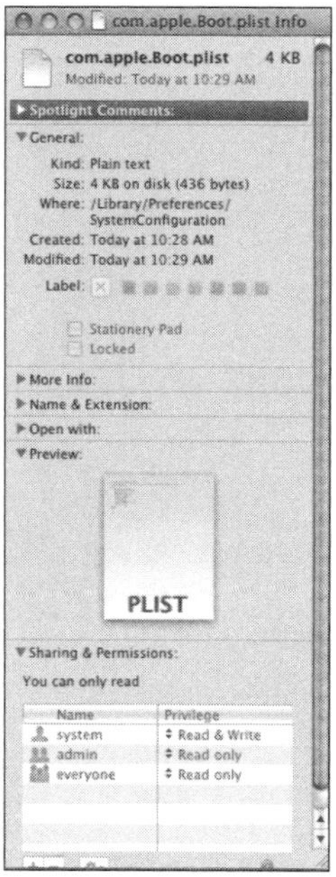

Testing the changes

Now comes the acid test! Does the changed `Boot.plist` file affect the graphics resolution?

1. **Restart your computer.**

2. **Boot from the correct disk by either using the boot manager or selecting the disk in the BIOS.**

If all has gone to plan, Leopard should start up in whatever resolution you have specified in the `Boot.plist`.

You may think that Leopard has ignored the graphics mode instructions in the file and has started in the basic 1024 x 768 mode. In this case, Leopard has not ignored the instruction, assuming you typed it correctly. It means, simply, that your graphics card is not capable of any other resolution at boot time.

Even though you can get different resolutions in Windows, you may not automatically get those same resolutions in Leopard. So much depends on your hardware and having the correct kexts.

Changing other parameters

You can change some other parameters in `Boot.plist`.

Changing the boot timeout

One of the parameters in `Boot.plist` is the boot timeout. This is the length of time Darwin waits at the boot prompt for a key press, before going on with the boot. Most distributions set this to five seconds, but you can make it any length you like, including zero.

1. **Open** `com.apple.Boot.plist` **with TextEdit as you did before.**
2. **Save the file to the desktop.**
3. **Look for the line** `<key>Timeout</key>`.

   On the next line is the number of seconds to pause, in this case:

   `</string>5</string>`
4. **Change the number to whatever you choose, and save the file.**
5. **Drag the file from the desktop into the SystemConfiguration folder.**
6. **Authenticate yourself.**
7. **Rerun Disk Utility to reset the file permissions.**
8. **Restart and verify that the timeout has changed.**

Getting Darwin to boot from a particular hard disk

This is useful if you need to specify the boot disk in the form of `rd=disk0s2` each time you boot.

Add two new lines to `Boot.plist`:

```
<key>Kernel Flags</key>
<string>rd=disk0s2</string>
```

Of course, replace the 0 and the 2 in the above to whatever you need.

Removing the Darwin boot prompt

If you don't want to see the Darwin boot prompt at all, add the following lines:

```
<key>Quiet Boot</key>
<string>Yes</string>
```

If, at some time in the future, you need to return to a Darwin prompt, press F8 quickly at boot time.

Seeing only a graphic boot screen

If you want your Hackintosh to look like a genuine Macintosh when it boots, add the following two lines:

```
<key>Boot Graphics</key>
<string>Yes</string>
```

Each time you make a change to `Boot.plist`, be sure to rerun Disk Utility to reset the file permissions.

Summary

In this chapter, you found several troubleshooting methods to help get Leopard working on your computer. In addition, you customized your Leopard boot process. In the event that the installation fails, you can return your computer to the state it was in before you started trying to install Leopard.

Again, Leopard was never built to run on your computer, and only with the help of many different experts and Apple developers can you possibly to do it. Without these experts sharing their knowledge, there would be no Hackintoshes.

Setting Up and Customizing Leopard

II

By this stage, you are feeling a great sense of achievement: You have successfully installed Leopard to your non-Apple computer and got it running.

Now it's time to explore the differences between Leopard and other operating systems, particularly Windows. Basically, all operating systems do pretty much the same things, but how they do things is what's important. In Chapter 7, you explore the many differences between the way you do things in Windows and how you do them in Leopard.

Like Windows, Leopard gathers all your preference settings together in one place. In Windows, it's the Control Panel. In Leopard, it's in System Preferences.

In all, Leopard has 54 panels for setting preferences, and they are divided into four major groups. Chapters 8 to 11 lead you through each of the major choices, explaining what each setting means and guiding you toward making the best choices for your personal preferences.

In This Part

7

Comparing Leopard and Windows

B y now you have seen one of the major differences between Windows and Leopard: installation. Windows can be installed quite easily on many different hardware platforms, with many different components, while Leopard is designed for a single manufacturer's platform, so it requires lots of effort to install on any other computer.

It's not just the ease of installation: Although Leopard and Windows do basically the same things, they look and feel quite different. In most cases, it's simply a matter of personal preference. Each platform has its fanboys, people who are simply fanatical about one platform or the other (or Linux!). Their favored platform has no faults or drawbacks, while any other platform is simply the work of the devil.

For most people, it's a matter of what works best for them. Macintosh gained a strong following in the graphics and publishing industries and is still dominant today. Windows gained a strong following in the business world and is still strong there.

In this chapter, we look at the differences in the user experience between the two platforms, assuming that you have reasonable expertise in using Windows.

Using the Keyboard

Apart from graphics, Web design, and other intensely graphical programs, almost everything in a Windows program can be controlled from the keyboard. If you like using keystrokes (as I do), rather than mouse movements, you may find the lack of keyboard equivalents in Leopard quite frustrating, but it's something you eventually get used to.

Most of the keystrokes used in Leopard are the same or very similar to those in Windows. Windows uses three modifier keys—Shift, Ctrl, and Alt—to modify the function of the key pressed, but Leopard has four modifier keys—Command (or Apple key), Control, Option, and Shift.

Figure 7.1 shows the symbols Apple uses to represent the modifier keys.

Figure 7.1

Apple keyboard modifier keys

Control (^) Key:

Option (⌥) Key:

Command (⌘) Key:

Different distributions of Leopard have slightly different key combinations. Most use the keys shown in Table 7.1.

Table 7.1 Key Mappings from Windows Keyboards to Macintosh Keyboards

Macintosh Key	Windows Key
Control	Ctrl
Command	Windows
Option	Alt

One keyboard feature that Leopard has in common is using the Command+Tab key combination to switch between running programs. In Windows, this is Alt+Tab. Figure 7.2 shows the result of the Command+Tab combination in Leopard.

Figure 7.2

Command+Tab

As in Windows, you can release the keys when the application you want to switch to is highlighted, or you can simply use the mouse to click the icon for the application.

Using the Single Menu Bar

One of the most striking differences between Windows and Leopard is the use of the single menu bar, which is permanently parked at the top of the screen. You can make it translucent if your graphics card allows it, but you can never remove it.

Figure 7.3 shows two different Windows applications both open with overlapping windows, each with its own menu bar.

Figure 7.3

Two menu bars in Windows

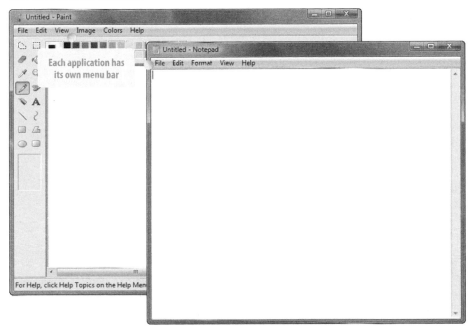

With Leopard, only one menu bar stays on the screen. It changes function depending on which application has the focus at present.

Finder is the Leopard equivalent of Windows Explorer, and it's always open, unlike Windows where you can close Explorer.

Figure 7.4 shows the menu bar when Finder is the focused application.

The menu bar has two main areas: The left side shows the menu bar for the current application; the right side shows several menulets. Officially, they are called Menu Extras by Apple, but everyone else knows them as menulets. On a standard installation of Leopard, the menulets shown in Figure 7.4 are usually installed, but you can install others as well. Figure 7.5 shows the menu bars for four common applications in Leopard.

Note that a constant on the left side of the menu bar is the Apple menu. This is always available, no matter what application is running.

Figure 7.4

Leopard menu bar for Finder

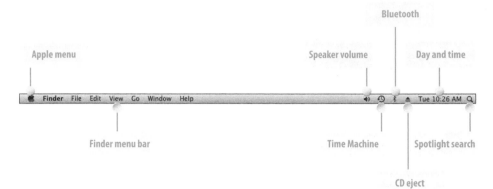

Figure 7.5

Menu bars for Finder, Safari, iCal, and Mail

Figure 7.6 shows the content of the Apple menu.

Figure 7.6

Apple menu

About This Mac

If you click About This Mac, it shows (naturally!) information about your computer, which it assumes is a Macintosh. Because you are not running a genuine Apple Mac, your display may not be quite correct, but Appendix B contains a method for putting the correct information into your display.

Figure 7.7 shows the About This Mac display from my Dell Mini 9 running retail Leopard updated to version 10.5.7.

Figure 7.7

About This Mac

Software Update

Software Update is similar to Microsoft Update on Windows computers, except that the default frequency of checking for updates is weekly, rather than daily. It not only checks your operating system for updates but also your Apple-supplied application software.

Figure 7.8 shows a display for software update from my Dell Mini Hackintosh.

Mac OS X Software

When you click Mac OS X Software, it opens the Safari Web browser and takes you to the software downloads pages on Apple's Web site. It naturally features Apple software, but it also includes software from third-party vendors.

Figure 7.8

Software Update

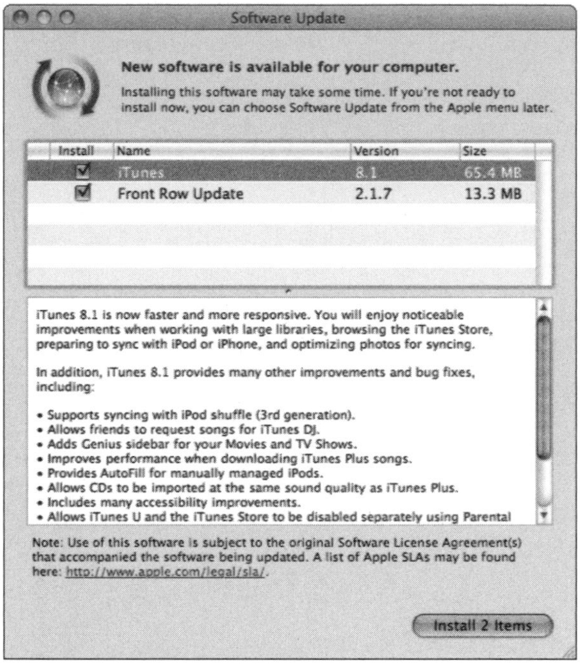

System Preferences

System Preferences is the Leopard equivalent of the Windows Control Panel and is explored in depth in Chapters 7 through 11.

The Dock

This is covered in depth in the next section.

Recent Items

This is exactly what you would expect and corresponds with Recent Items in Windows.

Force Quit

Sometimes an application hangs. Yes, even Macintoshes behave that way; it's not restricted to Windows! When this happens, you can invoke Force Quit to close the errant application.

This is exactly analogous to using Task Manager on a Windows computer, after pressing Ctrl+Alt+Del.

"Sleep," "Restart," "Shut Down," and "Log Out" do exactly what you would expect.

Using the Dock

At the bottom of the Leopard screen is the Dock. In essence, it works like a combination of the taskbar and the quick launch bar in Windows.

Figure 7.9 shows the dock with magnification turned on.

Figure 7.9

Dock

Each icon in the dock represents a software application you can start by clicking it. When an application is already running, it has a shiny dot underneath it

You can see in Figure 7.8 that Finder, Safari, and Preview are all running. Clicking the icon for a program that is already running brings its window to the front.

Adding an application to the Dock

You can add any application to the Dock simply by dragging its icon from the Applications folder to the Dock. Each time you run an application, its icon appears in the Dock. If you want to leave it there permanently, you can right-click it and click Keep in Dock, as shown in Figure 7.10.

Figure 7.10

Keep an application
in the Dock

Displaying folders in the Dock

In a gap in the Dock's shiny surface is a dotted line. Applications go to the left of this line; folders and minimized applications go to the right.

Not only can you add applications to the dock, but also folders. In fact, by default when you first install Leopard it creates two folders: Documents and Downloads. These two folders form the basis for stacks: Items in the folder appear on a spike, as shown in Figure 7.11a.

Other display possibilities exist for stacks. They were introduced with much fanfare, but in fact they are not terribly useful because of the amount of screen real estate they occupy. A more sensible display is as a grid.

If you right-click the Dock icon for the Downloads folder, you get the menu shown in Figure 7.11b.

Figure 7.11

Downloads stack in the Dock (a); Dock display menu (b)

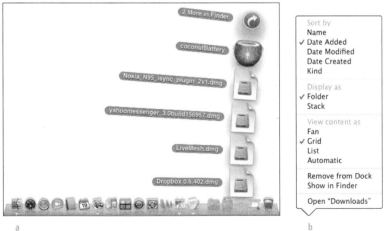

a   b

"Display as" refers to how the Downloads icon is displayed in the Dock—either as a folder or a stack. "View content as" refers to how the items in the folder are displayed when you click it. "Fan" is the normal style, but either "Grid" or "List" is generally more useful.

Figure 7.12 shows the Downloads folder displayed as a grid.

Figure 7.12

Downloads folder displayed as a grid

Adding a folder to the Dock

You can add your own applications and folders to the Dock. One very useful folder to add is your Applications folder. Here's how:

1. **Open a Finder window, and click your Applications folder.**

2. **From the title bar, drag the small icon (called a proxy icon) to the Dock and release it.**

   Your new icon appears in the Dock.

3. **Right click your Applications folder, and select View contents as a List.**

   Now your applications are all easily available from the Dock, as shown in Figure 7.13.

In Chapter 8, you look in more detail at how to set up the Dock to your liking.

Figure 7.13

Applications viewed as a list

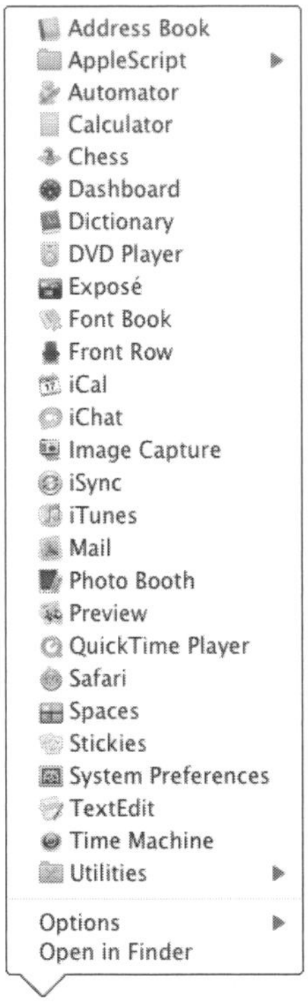

Using Application Software

Ever since the very first Macintosh, Apple has encouraged developers to use their user interface guidelines. As a consequence, almost all Macintosh software behaves in the same fashion.

In this section, we look at just one application: Finder, the Macintosh equivalent of Windows Explorer. The same principles apply to most applications.

As you become more familiar with Mac software, you will like some of the differences and you will find some of them irritating!

Finder is the Leopard equivalent of Windows Explorer. It performs all the same functions but has a different layout and different options. One thing to notice is that Finder is always running: You cannot easily shut it down, unlike Windows Explorer, which you can close when you no longer need it.

Using window control buttons

An application in Windows always has three buttons in the top-right corner: Minimize Window, Maximize Window, and Close Window.

Figure 7.14 shows the buttons in a Notepad window.

Figure 7.14

Minimize, Maximize, and Close

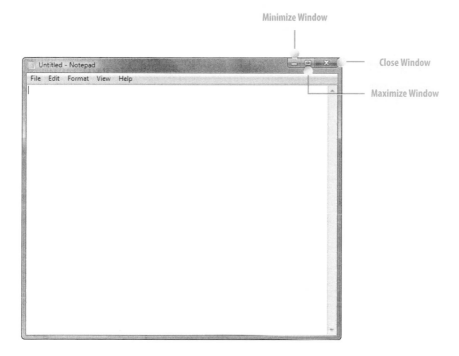

In a Leopard window, the three buttons in the top-left corner superficially look like the same buttons as in Windows, but they are different. Figure 7.15 shows the buttons in a Finder window.

Using the Close button

On the left side is the Close button, which works in exactly the same way as in Windows, with one difference: In Windows, closing the window closes the application if there is only one instance of the application running. In Leopard, closing the window closes the window but leaves the application running.

If you have a plenty of memory, it doesn't matter that much if several applications are running at once. One place where it does make a difference, though, is when you use Command+Tab to switch applications: All the inactive applications still show in the switcher, which causes some clutter.

Figure 7.15

Finder buttons

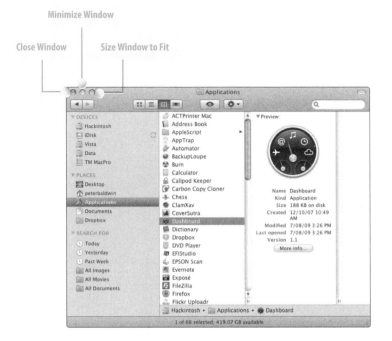

Using the minimize button

In the middle is the minimize button, which works in the same way as the minimize button in Windows. The window is minimized to the Dock to the right of the divider. Snow Leopard allows windows to be minimized to the application icon. Leopard has a couple of visual effects you can use on the minimizing process. The default is the genie effect, where the window appears to shrink back into the bottle like a genie! Figure 7.16 shows the genie effect as a window is minimized.

Using the zoom button

In Windows, the maximize button enlarges the window to the maximum size that the display can handle. Leopard doesn't have an equivalent button; instead it has the zoom button. Clicking this expands the window to either just large enough to show everything contained in the folder, or if Leopard can't show everything, the window expands to fill the available space on the desktop.

These same window control buttons appear in every Leopard application.

Finder is very customizable but quite different from Windows Explorer.

Figure 7.16

Genie effect

Resizing a window

One source of irritation for switchers from Windows to Macintosh is resizing a window. In Windows, you can click and drag any of the four sides of a window to resize it. Leopard has a single resizing handle in the bottom-right corner of the window. Figure 7.17 shows the resize handle in a Finder window.

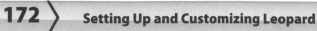
Figure 7.17

Resize handle

Resize handle

Controlling Finder

Because Finder is the one application that you use every single time you use Leopard, you should become familiar with it. It does the same job that Windows Explorer does, but you control it in different ways.

Figure 7.18 shows a Finder window, with its parts labeled.

Using the view buttons

Each Finder window can display in one of four different views, in just the same way as Windows Explorer. Each view has its advantages, just like in Windows Explorer. The views are Icon view, which is the default; List view, where each folder has an expansion triangle to show folders lower in the hierarchy; and Column view, which is good for rapidly traversing from one folder to another when they are both low in the hierarchy. The final view is Cover Flow view, unique to Leopard, which looks inside a file to show its contents, where possible. This view is copied directly from iTunes.

Figure 7.18

Finder window

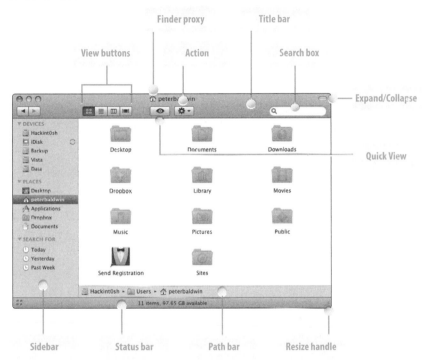

Figure 7.19 shows each of the four views, going from Icon view at the back, then List view, then Column view, and finally Cover Flow view on top.

Figure 7.19

Four views in Finder

Using Quick Look

Quick Look can look "inside" files and show their content. It can see into a large range of files, provided a file viewer is built into Leopard or you have software that can open the file. Figure 7.20 shows the quick view of this chapter in an early draft of this book as a Word document.

Double-clicking the title bar

This works exactly the opposite of Windows! In Windows, double-clicking the title bar maximizes the window; in Leopard, by default, it minimizes the window to the Dock. In Snow Leopard this has changed: it is no longer the default and has to be turned on in System Preferences (Appearance).

This works with every application, not just Finder, but it can be changed in System Preferences, as discussed in Chapter 8.

Figure 7.20

Quick Look

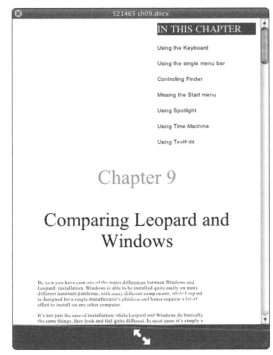

Arranging icons

In Icon view, you can rearrange the icons by right-clicking in the blank window area. On the pop-up menu, select Arrange By and then select how you want them arranged. The icons then snap to the grid, in the order you want. Figure 7.21a shows the pop-up windows to allow you to arrange icons in the window.

One trick that even many Mac users are unaware of is how to keep folders organized. "Arrange By" is just a one-off command. When you drag a new file into the folder, it is parked wherever you leave it, on top of other files.

If you hold down the Option key (usually the Alt key on a Windows keyboard) while you right-click in the Finder window, instead of "Arrange By" you see "Keep Arranged By." If you do that, any new files you drag into the folder will snap to their position on the grid, in whatever order you have specified. Figure 7.21b shows the pop-up windows.

Figure 7.21

Arrange By (a); Keep Arranged By (b)

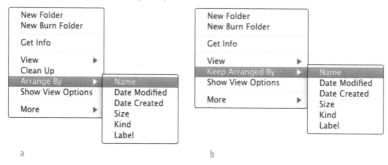

a   b

This is the default behavior in Windows Explorer folders. If you want to set all your Leopard folders to your Keep Arranged By order, right-click in a blank area of the Finder window and select Show View Options, as shown in Figure 7.22a.

In the window that pops up, click "Use as defaults," as shown in Figure 7.22b.

Figure 7.22

Show View Options (a); Set view as default (b)

a   b

Customizing Finder's toolbar

You can add extra functions to Finder's toolbar; here's how:

1. **Right-click anywhere in the Finder toolbar except over an icon**

2. **On the menu, click Customize Toolbar, as shown in Figure 7.23a.**

Each of the icons in the panel can be dragged into the Finder toolbar. Figure 7.23b shows the customize panel.

Figure 7.23

Customize Finder toolbar (a); Icons for customizing (b)

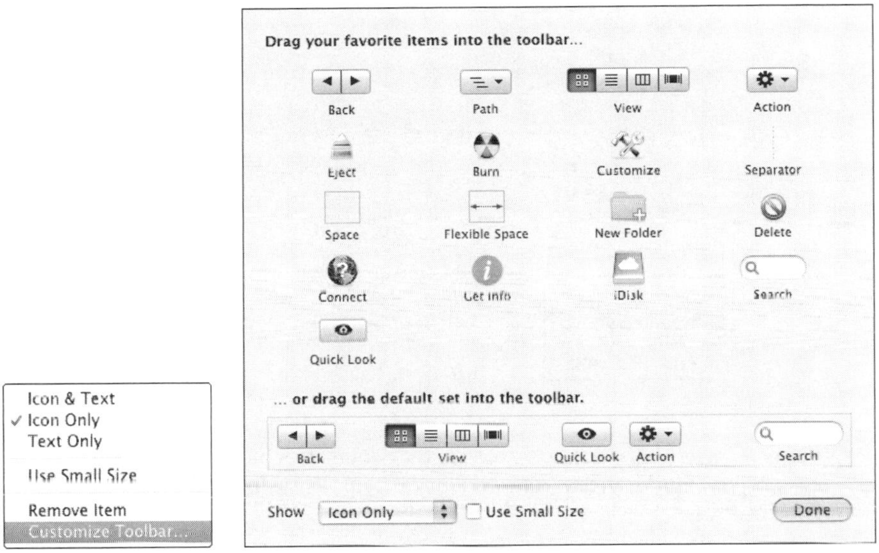

3. **Drag the Path icon into the toolbar, and click Done.**

Figure 7.24 shows the Finder window after adding the Path icon.

When you click the Path icon, it shows a drop-down list of all the folders above the current one in the folder hierarchy, as shown in Figure 7.25.

Figure 7.24

Finder with Path icon

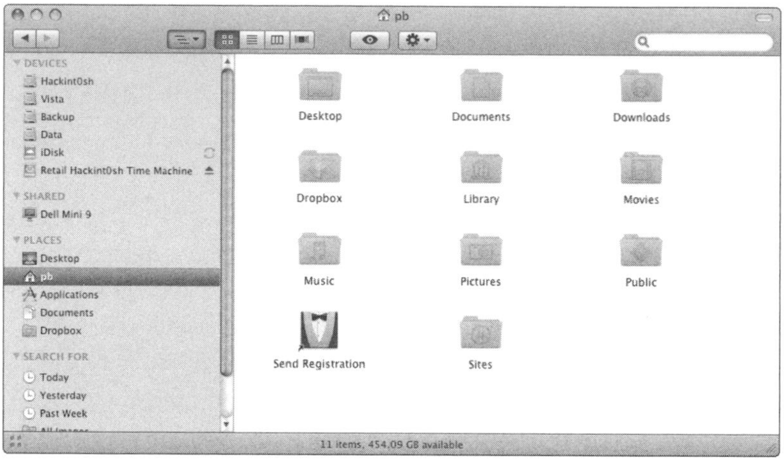

Figure 7.25

Path list

Many regular Mac users don't realize that you can achieve the same path information by right-clicking the Finder proxy (refer to Figure 7.18). The information is exactly the same as using the Path button.

Using a breadcrumbs bar

One feature of Windows Explorer in Vista and Windows 7 (but not XP) that I like and use often is the "breadcrumbs bar" at the top of an explorer window. Figure 7.26 shows the breadcrumbs bar.

In Finder, the equivalent is called a Path bar.

1. **Open a Finder window.**
2. **On the View menu, select Show Path Bar.**

At the bottom of the window, Finder adds a list of all the folders traversed to get to where you are. This is shown in Figure 7.27.

Figure 7.26

Windows Explorer breadcrumbs bar

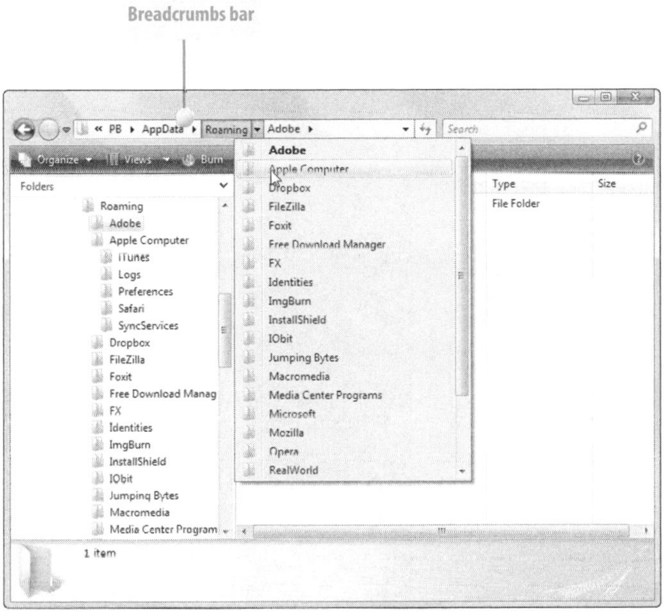

Figure 7.27

Finder with Path bar enabled

In Windows, each folder has a drop-down box to select the folder you want to go to. In Finder, it works a little differently: You double-click the folder icon.

Missing the Start Menu

Microsoft introduced the Start Menu with Windows XP and has enhanced and carried it on through Vista and Windows 7. The parts of the Start Menu are shown in Figure 7.28.

Figure 7.28

Components of the Vista Start menu

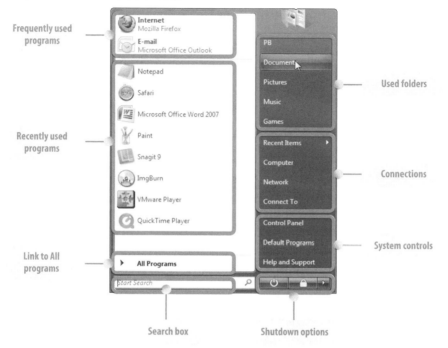

Leopard has no direct counterpart, having similar functions spread among different parts of the interface.

Saving frequently used applications in the Dock

Leopard's Dock corresponds with the frequently used programs part of the Vista Start menu. In Vista, you add a program to that section by "pinning" it to the Start menu. In Leopard, you start the application running, which places its icon in the Dock. Then you keep it in the Dock. Here's how:

1. **Open a Finder window, and move to Applications.**

2. **Double-click the Dictionary to start it running.**

3. Right-click the Dictionary icon in the Dock, and select "Keep in Dock," as shown in Figure 7.29.

Figure 7.29

Keep application icon in the Dock

4. Close the Dictionary, but note that its icon stays in the Dock.

Viewing all programs

In Windows, the link to All Programs shows you every application that is installed on the computer. In any Finder window, you can get the same view by selecting Applications in the sidebar.

Viewing user files and folders

When you installed Leopard, you were given a home folder, identified by a short version of your login name. This is identified by the little house icon in the Finder sidebar.

Using system controls

Most of the system controls for Leopard are contained in the System Preferences application, which is given extensive coverage in Chapters 8 through 11.

Using Spotlight

Spotlight was the headline new feature for OS X 10.4 (Tiger) when it was introduced in 2006.

In essence, it works similarly to the Search box in Vista and Windows 7. Spotlight indexes filenames and their content on your disks and allows you to quickly search for a file with a particular word in either its filename or its content.

For comparison with Spotlight, Figure 7.30 shows the result of a search for "10.5.7" using Vista, with the date of the file 9 June 2009 and the size less than 100KB.

Figure 7.30

Vista search result

To use Spotlight, click the magnifying glass icon on the top left of the menu bar.

You also can start Spotlight using the Command+spacebar keystroke.

Figure 7.31 shows the Spotlight search box.

Figure 7.31

Spotlight search box

As you type a word into the box, Spotlight goes to work straight away looking for instances of the word. As you type, the word becomes less ambiguous, so the selection narrows. Here's how it works:

1. **Open a Spotlight window, and type the word dictionary.**

    Figure 7.32 shows the result of a search for the word "dictionary" on my computer.

    Although that view of the search is useful, the real power of Spotlight comes when you click Show All.

2. **Click Show All.**

    Spotlight then opens a Finder window showing all the files found, as shown in Figure 7.33.

Figure 7.32

Spotlight search for Dictionary

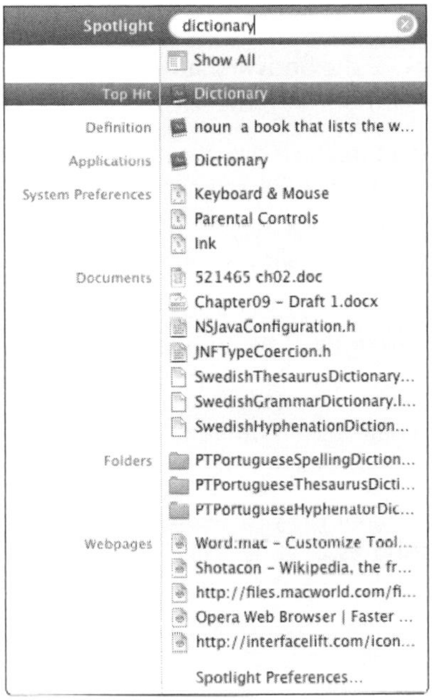

Spotlight	dictionary	⊗
	🔲 Show All	
Top Hit	📖 Dictionary	
Definition	📕 noun a book that lists the w...	
Applications	📖 Dictionary	
System Preferences	📄 Keyboard & Mouse	
	📄 Parental Controls	
	📄 Ink	
Documents	📄 521465 ch02.doc	
	📄 Chapter09 – Draft 1.docx	
	📄 NSJavaConfiguration.h	
	📄 JNFTypeCoercion.h	
	📄 SwedishThesaurusDictionary...	
	📄 SwedishGrammarDictionary.l...	
	📄 SwedishHyphenationDiction...	
Folders	📁 PTPortugueseSpellingDiction...	
	📁 PTPortugueseThesaurusDicti...	
	📁 PTPortugueseHyphenatorDic...	
Webpages	🌐 Word:mac – Customize Tool...	
	🌐 Shotacon – Wikipedia, the fr...	
	🌐 http://files.macworld.com/fi...	
	🌐 Opera Web Browser	Faster ...	
	🌐 http://interfacelift.com/icon...	
	Spotlight Preferences...	

Figure 7.33

Finder window showing Spotlight results

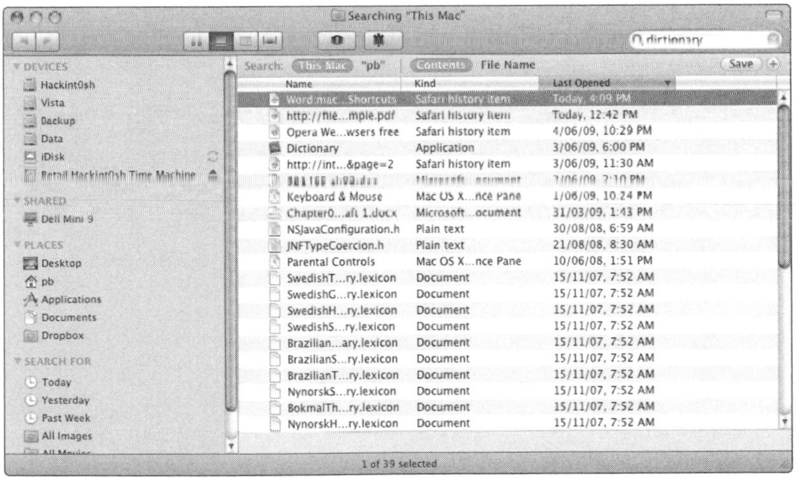

Name	Kind	Last Opened	
Word:mac...Shortcuts	Safari history item	Today, 4:09 PM	
http://file...mple.pdf	Safari history item	Today, 12:42 PM	
Opera We...wsers free	Safari history item	4/06/09, 10:29 PM	
Dictionary	Application	3/06/09, 6:00 PM	
http://int...&page=2	Safari history item	3/06/09, 11:30 AM	
521465 ch02.doc	Microsoft...document	7/06/09, 2:10 PM	
Keyboard & Mouse	Mac OS X...nce Pane	1/06/09, 10:24 PM	
Chapter0...aft 1.docx	Microsoft...ocument	31/03/09, 1:43 PM	
NSJavaConfiguration.h	Plain text	30/08/08, 6:59 AM	
JNFTypeCoercion.h	Plain text	21/08/08, 8:30 AM	
Parental Controls	Mac OS X...nce Pane	10/06/08, 1:51 PM	
SwedishT...ry.lexicon	Document	15/11/07, 7:52 AM	
SwedishG...ry.lexicon	Document	15/11/07, 7:52 AM	
SwedishH...ry.lexicon	Document	15/11/07, 7:52 AM	
SwedishS...ry.lexicon	Document	15/11/07, 7:52 AM	
Brazilian...ary.lexicon	Document	15/11/07, 7:52 AM	
BrazilianS...ry.lexicon	Document	15/11/07, 7:52 AM	
BrazilianT...ry.lexicon	Document	15/11/07, 7:52 AM	
NynorskS...ry.lexicon	Document	15/11/07, 7:52 AM	
BokmalTh...ry.lexicon	Document	15/11/07, 7:52 AM	
NynorskH...ry.lexicon	Document	15/11/07, 7:52 AM	

1 of 39 selected

From this window, you can narrow the search.

If you click your username (in this case, my username is shown as "pb"), the search is narrowed to show only files in your home folder.

3. **In the Finder window, click your username.**

By default, Spotlight shows results for the both filenames and the content of files. You can change it so Spotlight shows only filenames or content.

4. **Click File Name to show files with the word dictionary in their filename.**

In my case, there are none.

To narrow the search still further, Spotlight allows you to search by many other attributes.

5. **Click the small + (plus) sign on the right of the window.**

You can now select other attributes for your search. In the first drop-down box, you can select from Kind, Last opened date, Last modified date, Created, Name, and Contents.

If those selections are not enough to narrow your search, select Other and you can choose from a whole range of attributes, as shown in Figure 7.34.

Figure 7.34

Spotlight search attributes

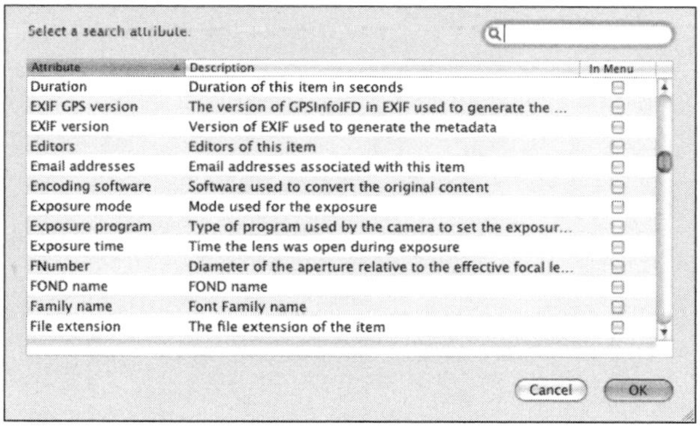

You can narrow your search even further by adding another selection line, as shown in Figure 7.35.

Figure 7.35

Figure 7.35

Two-line selection criteria

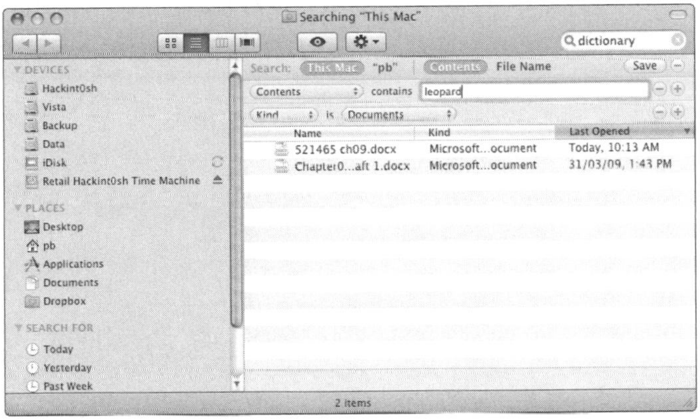

Finally, you can save your search and add it to the Finder sidebar, as shown in Figure 7.36.

Figure 7.36

Saving search selection

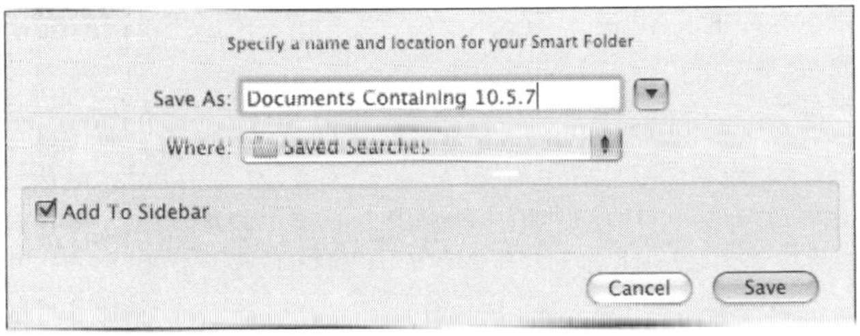

Anytime you want to perform the same search again, simply click the sidebar entry, as shown in Figure 7.37.

Figure 7.37

Search in sidebar

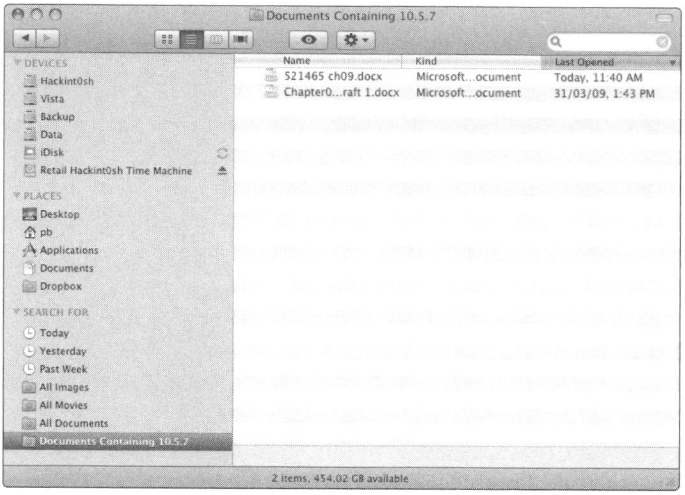

Using Time Machine

If Spotlight was the headline OS X application when Tiger (10.4) was introduced, Time Machine was the headline application with the introduction of Leopard.

It has no counterpart in Windows—not in the system software that comes with Windows—nor as yet do any third-party applications work like Time Machine.

Time Machine is brilliant in conception and very clever in execution. It saves you having to think about backing up your files because, after you connect an external drive, it automatically backs up your files every hour. After a day's backup, it consolidates those into a single daily backup. After 30 days, it consolidates your daily backups into a monthly backup. And it does all this automatically.

So you have no excuses for not backing up your files!

CAUTION

If your Leopard installation cannot utilize Quartz Extreme/Core Image graphics, you do not get the full experience of Time Machine because viewing the past backups requires QE/CI.

Figure 7.38 shows the System Preferences panel for Time Machine.

Figure 7.38

System Preferences for Time Machine

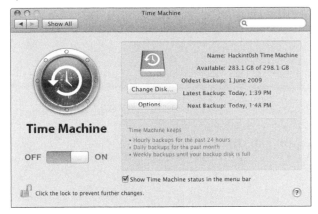

Setting up Time Machine

If you have other disk drives attached to the computer when you boot into Leopard for the first time, Leopard asks if you want to use one for Time Machine backup. Unless you want to reformat your disk and lose any information on it, you should say "No." If you plug an external drive (say a USB drive) into the computer, Leopard again asks if you want to use it for Time Machine. This time you can answer "Yes."

That's all there is to setting it up. If you check the box "Show Time Machine status in the menu bar," the menu bar gets a new icon (refer to Figure 7.4).

Clicking the Time Machine icon brings up a small menu, as shown in Figure 7.39.

Figure 7.39

The Time Machine menu

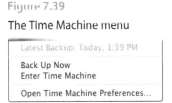

Excluding files from Time Machine

If you are using Microsoft Entourage for your e-mail, you find that it stores all your e-mails in one large file that grows as you use it. In this case, backing up your large file every hour will soon fill up your external hard disk.

This also occurs with, say, Parallels Desktop or VMware, because each virtual machine is stored in a large file. If Time Machine were to back up this file each time you quit the application, the backup would grow very large.

TIP
Don't forget to back up your e-mails in some other way.

Time Machine makes it possible to exclude such files from your backup. Here's how:

1. **Click System Preferences in the Dock.**

2. **Click Time Machine.**

3. **Click Options.**

   This brings up a sheet, as shown in Figure 7.40.

   Figure 7.40

   File exclusion pane for Time Machine

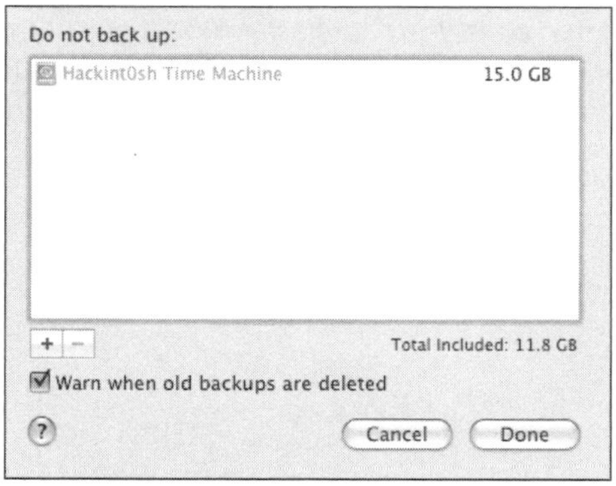

Do not back up:	
Hackintosh Time Machine	15.0 GB

   Total Included: 11.8 GB

   ☑ Warn when old backups are deleted

   (?)   (Cancel) (Done)

4. **Click the + (plus) sign and navigate to the files or folders you want to exclude.**

5. **Click Done.**

Retrieving files from Time Machine

Time Machine's cutest feature is the way you use it to recover files. Apple has consistently used the metaphor of a time machine, traveling back in time, even to the extent of having the Time Machine clock in the menu bar travel backward while it is backing up. You did notice that, didn't you?

So it's no surprise that when you select Enter Time Machine, you go on a journey back in time. The normal screen slides down your monitor to be replaced by a view of space seen through the window of your own time machine.

1. **On the menu bar, click the Time Machine icon and select Enter Time Machine.**

   Your Leopard screen slowly slides down, to be replaced with the view shown in Figure 7.41.

   Figure 7.41

   Leopard screen making way for Time Machine

2. **Use your mouse to click one of the time bars on the right of the display to go back to that date, as shown in Figure 7.42.**

TIP

Of course, if you've only just started Time Machine running, you can't go back very far! Come back to this exercise after Time Machine has saved a few backups.

Figure 7.42

Time bars in Time Machine

3. **Use the time bars to travel back to the date you want, and then use the Finder window to find the file you want.**

4. **Click Restore in Time Machine, and the file is placed in the folder from which it was deleted.**

Simple!

Troubleshooting Time Machine

One issue that occurs sometimes with Hackintoshes is that Time Machine will not back up. It has to do with the Ethernet setup on a Hackintosh. The fix is relatively simple and is given in Appendix B.

Using TextEdit

At first glance, TextEdit seems like Windows Notepad, but in fact it's more like a combination of Notepad and WordPad. Like Notepad, it can create and edit plain text files, but it also can create and edit more complex files. Figure 7.43a shows the file types it can handle.

In combination with Leopard's text-to-speech synthesizer, it can even read to you, though the voice gets a little monotonous after a while!

Although TextEdit can read and write Microsoft Word files, it cannot import the document styles from Word, so its usefulness is limited. But it is capable of some quite complex operations on text in its own right, such as kerning and creating ligatures, as shown in Figures 7.43b and 7.43c.

Figure 7.43

File types in TextEdit (a); TextEdit font menu (b); TextEdit text menu (c)

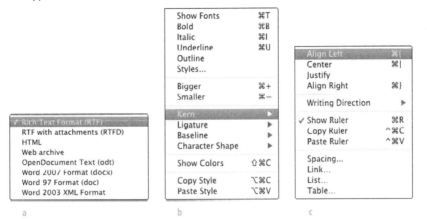

Using the Services Menu

This section explains the Services menu that is present in every Leopard application. It's one that is often overlooked, even by experienced Mac users, and has no real counterpart in Windows.

It provides some very useful features and is extendable. When you install a third-party application, quite often it adds its own services to the menu. Here's how to get at it:

1. **Start TextEdit running.**

2. **On the menu bar, click TextEdit and move your mouse down to Services.**

   This reveals the Services menu for TextEdit, as shown in Figure 7.44.

Figure 7.44

Services menu

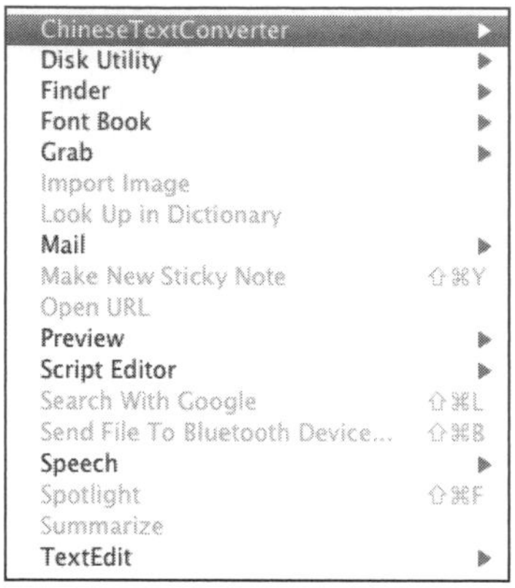

At this point, most of the options and suboptions are grayed out.

3. Using TextEdit, enter the following text:

```
In combination with Leopard's text-to-speech synthesizer
it can even read to you, though the voice gets a little
monotonous after a while!
Although TextEdit can read and write Microsoft Word
files, it cannot import the document styles from Word, so
its usefulness is limited. But it is capable of some quite
complex operations on text in its own right, such as
kerning and creating ligatures.
```

4. Highlight all the text in both paragraphs.

5. Now view the Services menu, as shown in Figure 7.45.

Note that all options are now black; hence, they are available.

6. On the Services menu, scroll down to Mail and select Send Selection.

This opens a new Mail document with the text already pasted into the body of the e-mail, as shown in Figure 7.46.

All you need to do is fill in the To field.

Play around with some of the other options in the Services menu. Few people find a use for the Chinese text converter, though!

After you install a few applications, you find that your Services menu grows as each application adds its own Services that you might want.

Figure 7.45

Services menu with text selected

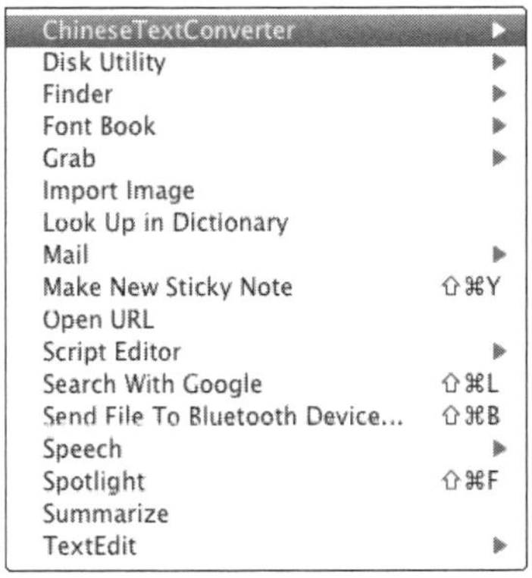

ChineseTextConverter	▶
Disk Utility	▶
Finder	▶
Font Book	▶
Grab	▶
Import Image	
Look Up in Dictionary	
Mail	▶
Make New Sticky Note	⇧⌘Y
Open URL	
Script Editor	▶
Search With Google	⇧⌘L
Send File To Bluetooth Device...	⇧⌘B
Speech	▶
Spotlight	⇧⌘F
Summarize	
TextEdit	▶

Figure 7.46

New mail message with copied text

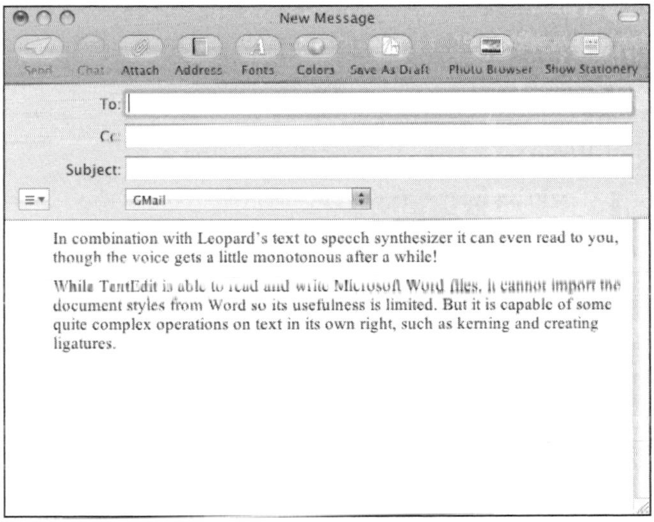

In combination with Leopard's text to speech synthesizer it can even read to you, though the voice gets a little monotonous after a while!

While TextEdit is able to read and write Microsoft Word files, it cannot import the document styles from Word so its usefulness is limited. But it is capable of some quite complex operations on text in its own right, such as kerning and creating ligatures.

If you find the menu grows beyond what you consider reasonable, bearing in mind that you might actually want some of these services, you can trim it using an application called ServiceScrubber. You can download this from `http://manytricks.com/service scrubber/`, but it can only remove services added by applications; it can't remove built-in Leopard services.

Using the Context Menu on Text

In this section, you use the Context menu obtained by right-clicking a word. Follow these steps:

1. **In the same TextEdit document, right-click the word "ligatures" at the end of the second paragraph.**

This brings up the Context menu shown in Figure 7.47.

Figure 7.47

Context menu in TextEdit

2. **Click Look Up in Dictionary.**

This brings up the Dictionary application with the word entered in the search box, as shown in Figure 7.48.

Figure 7.48

Dictionary results for Lookup

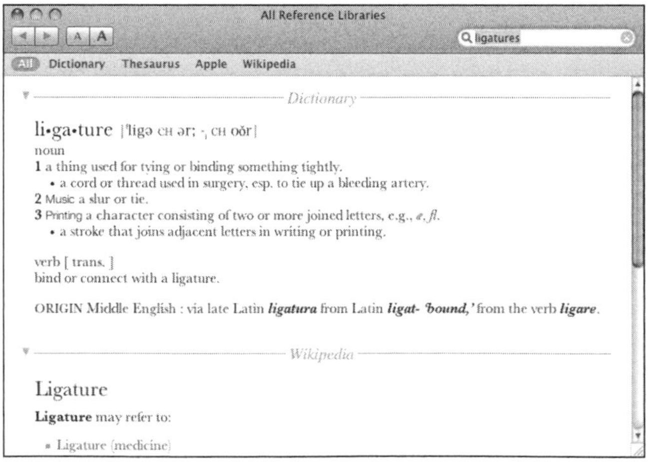

If looking up the word in the Leopard Dictionary and Wikipedia is not enough for you, you can also send it to a Google query. If you search in Spotlight, you get a Finder window that has all the files containing the word.

Summary

In this chapter, you examined some of the principal differences in behavior between Windows and Leopard.

Differences range from keyboard key assignments and how to change them to finding information about your Hackintosh. You have learned how to use the Dock to launch applications and fix them permanently for ready access.

You explored Finder's window layouts and ways it differs from Windows in its use of buttons, You had an extensive tour through Finder and learned to use it effectively, and you explored the differences between the Start menu in Windows and the Mac equivalents. You also learned how to search for files and save your searches for reuse.

You used Time Machine to back up and recover files, and you learned the basics of TextEdit, a combination of Windows Notepad and WordPad. In TextEdit, you were introduced to the Services menu, and you used the Context menu to look up a word definition.

Now you are ready to start setting up your Hackintosh in the way you want it.

8

Setting Up Personal System Preferences

N ow that you have some idea of the differences between Windows and Leopard, it's time to start setting up Leopard to your own satisfaction. Like Windows, no two people like exactly the same configuration for their computer.

As you saw in the preceding chapter, System Preferences is the Leopard equivalent of the Windows control panel. It is laid out differently from the control panel, but it performs pretty much the same functions.

In this chapter, you explore each of the options to set up your personal preferences for the way you want Leopard to behave. In later chapters, you set up other preferences.

System Preferences is accessed through the Dock by clicking the icon. Figure 8.1 shows the main screen.

Figure 8.1

Main screen for System Preferences

Setting Up Appearance

In this section, you see the effect of the various choices for setting up the appearance of your system. You can access the Appearance settings by clicking Appearance in the top-left corner of the screen.

Figure 8.2 shows Appearance options.

Figure 8.2

Appearance options

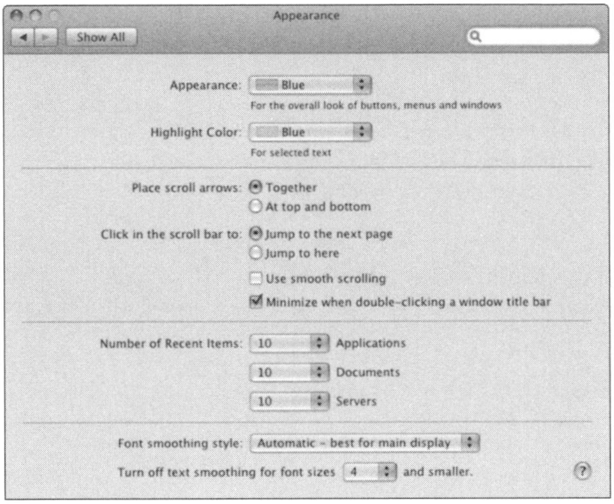

Setting general appearance options

Notice that Leopard has fewer customizing options than Windows does. Some may see this as a bad thing; my view is that it looks much more professional than the multicolored Windows setup.

You have only two options for Appearance, which governs the overall look of buttons and scroll bars: either blue or graphite. Blue is the default. You cannot change the colors of title bars, status bars, and so on, unlike Windows. Each version of OS X has had a slightly different look: Tiger used a brushed metal finish for the title bars of windows; Leopard has a plastic look to it.

Set the color to graphite, and see if you prefer that color.

Highlight color governs the color of text when you highlight it to cut or copy. Try different colors, and see which you prefer.

Setting scrolling options

As a Windows user, you probably won't feel comfortable with the default behavior for scrolling. By default, Leopard puts both up and down scroll arrows at the bottom of the window. To change the setting so it behaves like Windows, check the "At top and bottom" button for scroll bars.

Figure 8.3 shows the position of the scroll bars if set to Together.

Figure 8.3

Scroll bars
together

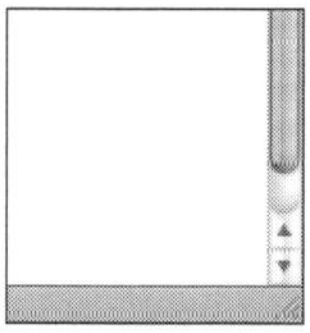

Scroll bar clicking defaults to the same as Windows: Clicking in that the scroll bar moves the scroll bar down one page at a time. If you select Jump to here, the screen jumps to that point in the document. For example, if you click three-quarters of the way down the scroll bar, the screen displayed is three-quarters of the way through the document.

Setting number of recent items

Number of recent items is a system-wide default that all applications implement, unlike Windows, where the number of recent items is shown on an application-by-application basis. "Recent servers" refers to other computers on your network: when you connect to another computer, it is considered to be a server by Leopard.

Setting font smoothing

Font smoothing works pretty much the same as Clear Type in Windows. Leopard turns it on by default, and you have very little reason to turn it off.

If your graphics setup does not automatically detect your display, you may need to select the particular font smoothing style for your monitor. Otherwise, leave it as Leopard sets it.

Setting Up Desktop and Screen Saver

In this section, you set up your desktop and screen saver to your preferences. Figure 8.4 shows the setting screen for Desktop and Screen Saver.

Figure 8.4

Desktop and Screen Saver settings

Setting up your desktop

When you first install Leopard, it defaults to using the Aurora picture from the set of desktops called Nature. By default, desktop pictures live in a folder called /Library/Desktop Pictures.

At the bottom is your Pictures folder. Notice that you can use any pictures you placed in that folder. Clicking the + (plus) sign at the bottom allows you to select any folder you choose, including your My Pictures folder on your Windows data disk, if you choose.

You can change the picture from every five seconds up to daily. You also can randomize the pictures.

If your graphics display is capable of Quartz Extreme/Core Image (QE/CI), you can make the menu bar translucent. I'm not exactly sure why this option is there, but I use it as a sign of whether the display is capable of QE/CI. If you don't want the translucency, uncheck the box.

Setting up your screen saver

In the same way you can set up your screen saver in Windows, you can do so in Leopard. To make changes or just to see what options are available, click the Screen Saver button at the top of the settings pane. Figure 8.5 shows the screen saver display.

As with the desktop, you can select a wide range of screen savers, both built in and external. You can select a folder to get pictures from, and they are displayed in various ways, but oddly, the amount of time that each slide is displayed can't be changed.

Figure 8.5

Screen saver

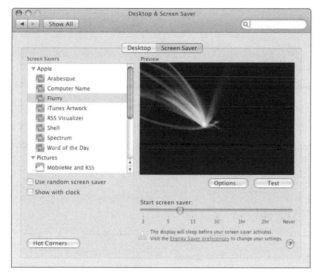

I don't use a screen saver: My display blanks before a screen saver kicks in. If I'm not using the screen, I shut it down. We look at changing energy saver preferences in Chapter 9.

Setting up hot corners

One very useful feature of Leopard that Windows doesn't emulate is *hot corners*. Hot corners allow you to mouse into a corner of the display and carry out various functions.

You can download an application that does something very similar for Vista. Download it from `http://programsforpeers.googlepages.com/hotcorners`.

I find it extremely useful in Leopard; Figure 8.6 shows how I have my hot corners set up.

Figure 8.6

Hot corners setup

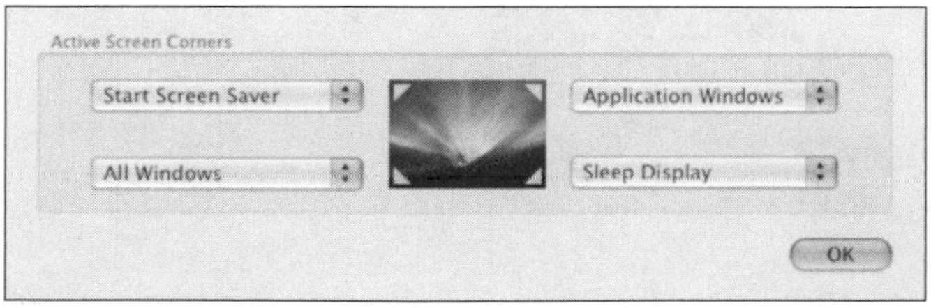

Table 8.1 lists the options available for each corner and explains the meaning of each.

Table 8.1 Hot Corners and Their Descriptions

Option	Description
Start screen saver	Starts the screen saver when you move the mouse into that screen corner.
Disable screen saver	Prevents the screen saver from operating when you move the mouse into that corner.
All windows	Shows all windows presently open, regardless of the application. The F9 key also does this.
Application windows	Shows all windows open within the application that is in the foreground. The F10 key also does this.
Dashboard	Brings the Dashboard to the foreground. The F12 key also does this. Find more information about the Dashboard later in this chapter.
Spaces	Splits the screen into the number of spaces you have set up, allowing you to choose which space you want to work in. The F8 key also does this. Spaces is covered later in this chapter.
Sleep display	Puts the display to sleep.

Figure 8.7 shows the screen with all application windows showing.

Figure 8.7

All applications hot corner

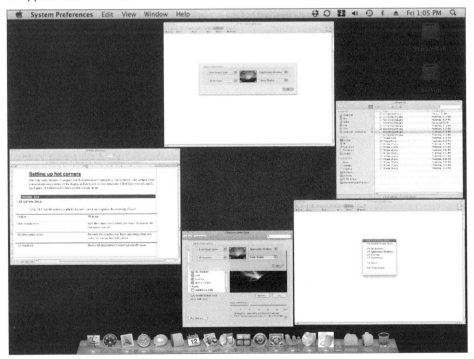

Figure 8.8 shows the screen with four spaces set up and different applications running in each space.

Figure 8.8

Spaces view of applications

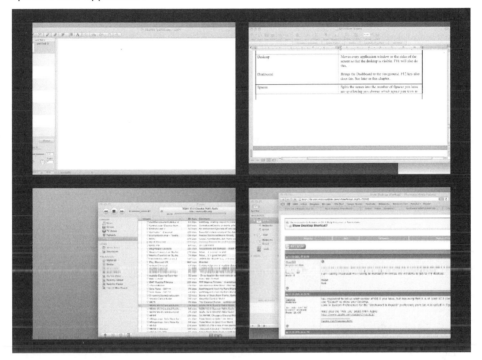

While working in Leopard, I use spaces extensively, and I find being able to view every open window very useful, so I have my computer set up that way.

Setting Up the Dock

As you have seen earlier, the Dock is an extremely useful part of the Leopard operating system.

From the main System Preferences screen, click Dock to bring up the settings panel shown in Figure 8.9.

Obviously, you can have the Dock as large or small as you like by moving the slider. At its largest, the Dock fills your screen. I prefer to have it occupy no more than about two-thirds of my screen.

Figure 8.9

Dock settings

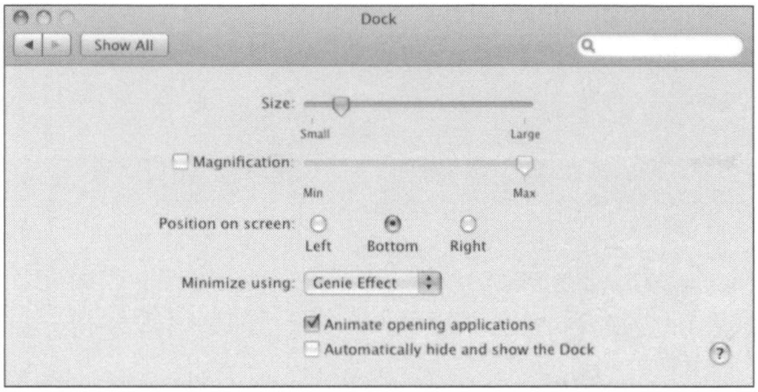

Magnification refers to the amount that an icon is magnified as you mouse over it. Figure 8.10 shows the maximum magnification on the Dock.

Figure 8.10

Dock magnification at maximum

My preference is to have magnification turned off, because when it's on I tend to feel almost seasick when I mouse over it.

Although displaying the Dock at the bottom of the screen is the default behavior, you can move it to the left or right of the screen. When it is displayed on either side of the screen, it no longer has the shiny table look as shown in Figure 8.11.

You have already seen the genie effect when minimizing an application to the dock. Rather than have the application funnel back into its icon, you can set it to simply shrink by selecting scale effect.

You may have noticed that when you click a Dock icon to open an application, it bounces a couple of times before it opens. Some people don't like that, feeling that it delays the opening of the application. I have never noticed a delay, and the bouncing doesn't worry me, so I leave it turned on.

Figure 8.11

Dock on the side
of the screen

As with the Windows task bar, you can hide the Dock until you actually need it. When you move your mouse down to the bottom of the screen, the Dock pops up. On my desktop, where I have plenty of vertical space, I leave it showing, but on my Dell Mini 9 I hide it because the screen is only 600 pixels tall. Your choice.

Setting Up Exposé and Spaces

Exposé complements the hot corners you can set up using Screen Saver. Exposé gathers the keyboard and mouse shortcuts to put them on the same screen. You also can set one or two of your mouse buttons to work one or two of the Exposé functions.

The Spaces feature allows you to set up a number of virtual screens. Each screen occupies the full area of your physical screen; in the case of my desktop, 1920 x 1080.

Figure 8.12 shows the pane used to set up Spaces.

Figure 8.12

Setup for Spaces

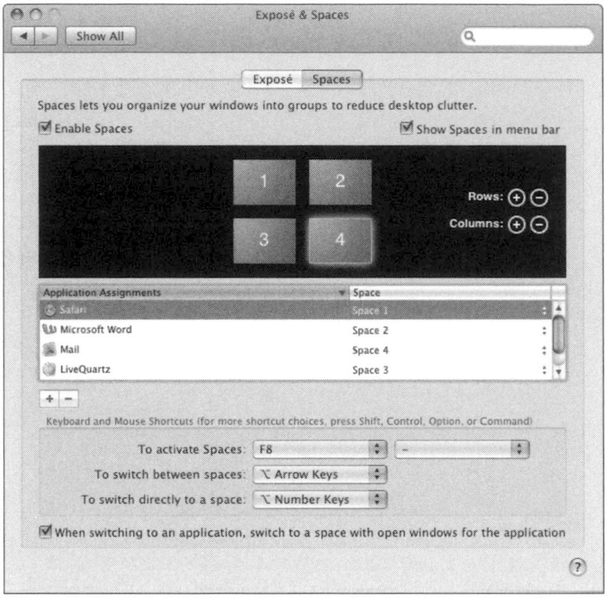

One really nice feature of Spaces is that it allows you to start an application in any space you wish. I keep my applications separated into separate spaces. For example, Safari always starts in Space 1, Microsoft Word in Space 2, as you can see in the middle of Figure 8.12.

You can switch between spaces using various key combinations. In my case, I've set it so the Option key (Alt key on a Windows keyboard) works with the arrow keys and the number keys. Leopard's default is to use the Command key with the arrow keys and number keys. Number keys are not just the numeric keypad keys: This also works with the number keys on the main keyboard.

TIP

You can move a window from one space to another by clicking and dragging the menu bar into the new space. For example, with a window open in space 1, click and drag it offscreen to the right and it moves into space 2. Move it down for space 3.

If you have Spaces shown in the menu bar, you can also use the mouse to switch spaces.

Setting Up International

Leopard is highly multicultural. In this section, you learn how to customize Leopard for your own location.

Setting languages

When installed, Leopard contains many different languages, as shown in Figure 8.13.

Figure 8.13

Languages available in Leopard

If, like me, you use only English, you can remove the other languages, although you get no particular benefit in doing so.

To remove a language, click Edit List and uncheck the languages you don't want to appear on your list. The list is shown in Figure 8.14.

Setting formats

Leopard allows you to completely customize how dates and times are displayed. In my case, I'm located in Australia, and Leopard has set up most of the preferences automatically.

Figure 8.15 shows the time and date display options.

Figure 8.14

Languages available

Figure 8.15

Time and date options

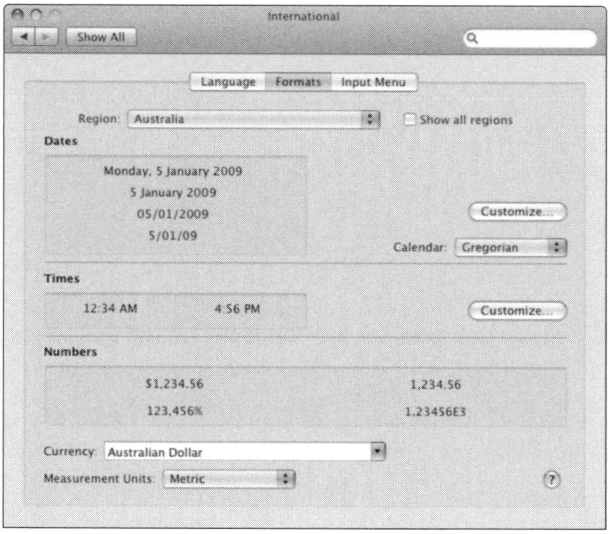

In my case, Apple got all the information correct so I didn't need to change anything. I assume this is true for other countries as well.

Using the input menu

Leopard's input menu is possibly a subject for a lifetime study! Just kidding. But it's absolutely crammed with features and very easy to use. The setting is shown in Figure 8.16.

Figure 8.16

Input menu

Figure 8.17

Character palette selection

At the top of the window are check boxes for the palettes available. When you check Character Palette, the flag for your country is placed on the menu bar. When you click the flag, you get a new menu, allowing you to select a character palette, as shown in Figure 8.17.

Figure 8.17

Character palette selection

If you click Show Character Palette, the character palette appears, as shown in Figure 8.18.

Figure 8.18

Character palette for Roman character sets

Leopard contains many different character sets. If you select All Characters from the drop-down box at the top left of the screen, you can see the number available, as shown in Figure 8.19.

Pressing the Insert button in the bottom right inserts the character into your document, provided the document can receive it.

If you put a check beside Keyboard Viewer in the languages preferences, you can have a keyboard onscreen for the chosen language. Figure 8.20 shows the keyboard for the Devanagari character set.

As you type, the onscreen keyboard shows each key as you press it. If the software you are using can display the characters (for example, TextEdit), you see the characters of the other language.

Figure 8.19

Character sets

Figure 8.20

Devanagari keyboard

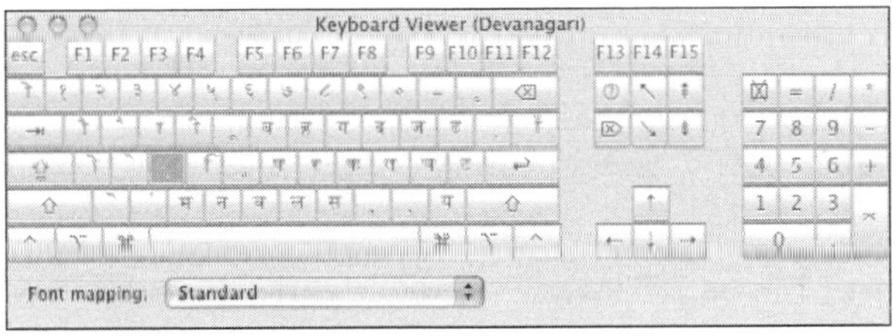

Setting Up Security

In this section, you learn about the various options governing security in Leopard and set up your computer in the way that best suits your circumstances.

General security options

Over the years, Microsoft has made significant security changes to Windows. For example, with Vista and Windows 7, you must set up an account even for the administrator. You can give either administrator or normal user privileges to each account.

By default, Leopard does not insist on the user logging in before using the computer. After your computer starts, you go straight through to the desktop without requiring any password. Although this is very convenient for you, it means that anyone who gets physical access to your computer also has access to all your files. This is particularly bad for a laptop used for business.

On the General tab of the System Preferences security panel, you can change some of the settings to make your computer and data more secure. Figure 8.21 shows the settings available.

Figure 8.21

General security settings

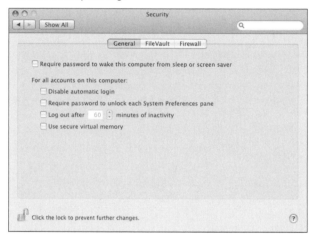

Require password to wake computer from sleep or screen saver

If your computer is in an area where other people are around and you don't want them to access your files, my recommendation is that you turn on the screen saver and then check the box to require the password.

When you check this box, Leopard also suggests that you disable automatic login. I recommend you do that.

Disable automatic login

Always check the box for Disable automatic login. That way, when you start your computer, it requires a password before getting to the point where your files are available.

If other people use your computer, be sure to set them up with their own accounts. Don't just allow everyone to use the same account. Chapter 11 gives you detailed information about setting up user accounts.

Require password to unlock each System Preferences pane

After you have your computer set up the way you want it, you should password-protect the System Preferences. After all, you don't want other people messing about with the system you have so carefully set up.

After you have set this up, the System Preferences pane has the lock in the bottom-left corner closed. If you click the lock, it requests your password just to be sure you actually have been given permission to change the settings.

Logout after inactivity

This is a setting that depends on the environment in which you use the computer. My own preference is to leave it unchecked.

Use secure virtual memory

If you use lots of software that has high memory requirements, such as Photoshop, when physical memory runs low on your computer, Leopard starts to write parts of memory out to the disk so that the memory is freed up for another operation. This is called virtual memory—memory that your computer can use but is not installed as physical memory.

Sometimes sensitive information (such as passwords for Web sites and so forth) is written to virtual memory. If your computer is stolen, someone with the right tools can comb through the virtual memory and retrieve the information.

If you check the Use secure virtual memory option, all the virtual memory on your disk is encrypted so the information is almost impossible to retrieve. When you check this box, Leopard requires you to restart before it is effective.

Figure 8.22 shows the security settings that I recommend.

Figure 8.22

Recommended security settings

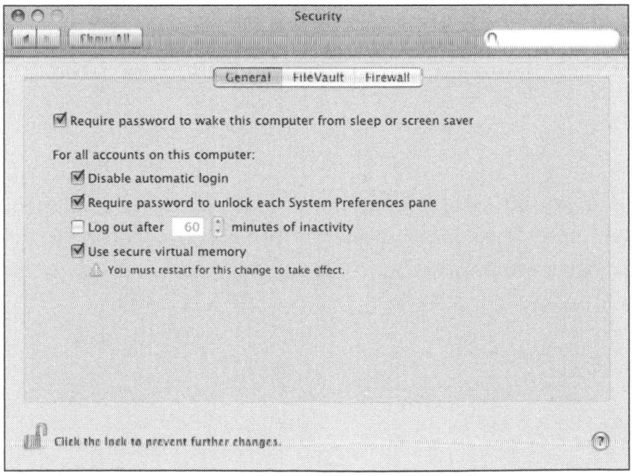

FileVault

FileVault is Leopard's file encryption service. Each file on your hard disk is encrypted so it can't be read by anyone who does not know the password.

Leopard has two passwords: One is your normal password, which is used in encrypting the files; the other is a master password, which can be used if you forget your own password.

Figure 8.23 shows the pane for FileVault security.

Figure 8.23

FileVault security pane

If you turn FileVault on, Leopard spends a while encrypting all the files in your home folders. Depending on how many files you have, this could take quite a while. From then on, all new files are encrypted.

CAUTION

Files are encrypted only when they are stored on your hard disk; they are not encrypted when you copy them to an external disk.

When the FileVault is turned on, files are not written on a file-by-file basis to your hard disk; they are written in a sparse image format. This means that you cannot recover single files; you must recover the whole user folder structure to another hard disk using your Leopard install disk. Figure 8.24 shows the warning message you get when you turn on FileVault.

Figure 8.24

FileVault warning

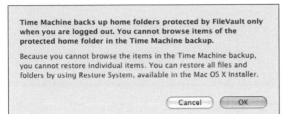

Time Machine backs up home folders protected by FileVault only when you are logged out. You cannot browse items of the protected home folder in the Time Machine backup.
Because you cannot browse the items in the Time Machine backup, you cannot restore individual items. You can restore all files and folders by using Restore System, available in the Mac OS X Installer.
Cancel
OK

Firewall

By default, Leopard is installed without a firewall. In my view, you should never use a computer without a firewall. Even though OS X computers are hacked very rarely, that's no reason for complacency.

TIP

I recommend that you turn on your firewall to the setting that allows only essential services.

The screen where you set this up is shown in Figure 8.25.

Figure 8.25

Firewall with essential services switched on

Show All
General
FileVault
Firewall
Allow all incoming connections
Allow only essential services
Set access for specific services and applications
option if you want to allow or block incoming connections for specific programs.
File Sharing (AFP)
Printer Sharing
Remote Login (SSH)
Screen Sharing
Advanced...
Click the lock to prevent further changes.

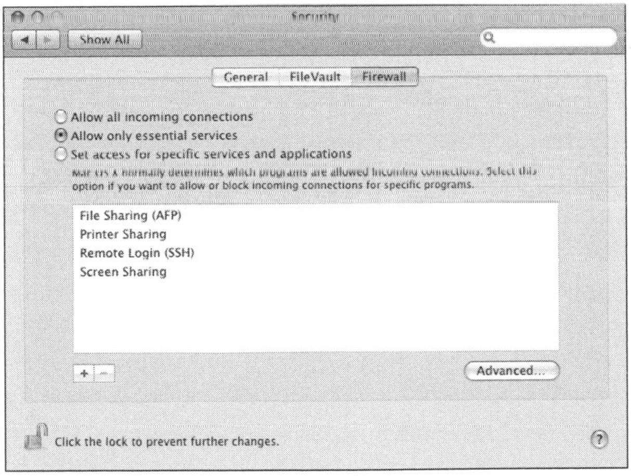

File Sharing, Printer Sharing, Remote Login (SSH), and Screen Sharing are listed in the services because I have them turned on in the Sharing pane that you see in Chapter 10.

If you click the Advanced button, you get an extra pane that allows you to log all firewall activity and, importantly, allows you to turn on stealth mode. This is shown in Figure 8.26.

Figure 8.26

Advanced firewall options

Logging firewall activity may be unnecessary, but I recommend you switch on stealth mode. What that means is that if a foreign computer attempts to contact your computer in a non-standard way, your computer does not respond at all. If you have stealth mode turned off, your computer sends a message back to the other computer saying, in effect, "I can't do anything." The problem is the foreign computer knows that your computer is connected and can try some other strategies to infiltrate your computer.

Setting Up Spotlight

With the Spotlight pane in System Preferences, you can set up where you want Spotlight to search and the results you want it to show. By default, Spotlight searches through all the categories listed, shown in Figure 8.27.

If you don't want Spotlight to look for fonts that match your search criteria, uncheck the box. My own preference is to let Spotlight search everything: Preventing this doesn't shorten a search significantly, because it's very quick anyway. And by letting it search everything, you'll be sure you haven't missed anything.

You also can exclude certain folders on your disk by specifically excluding them from a Spotlight search. Figure 8.28 shows two folders excluded from the Spotlight search.

TIP

My preference is to not exclude any folders from Spotlight search, but the choice is yours.

Figure 8.27

Spotlight search places

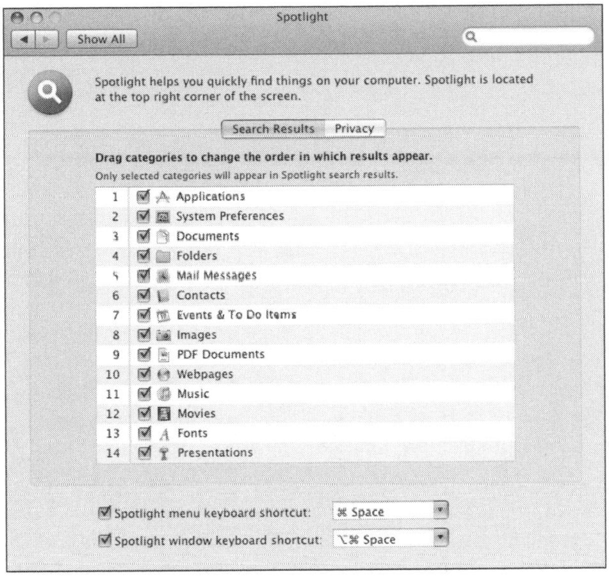

Figure 8.28

Folders excluded from Spotlight search

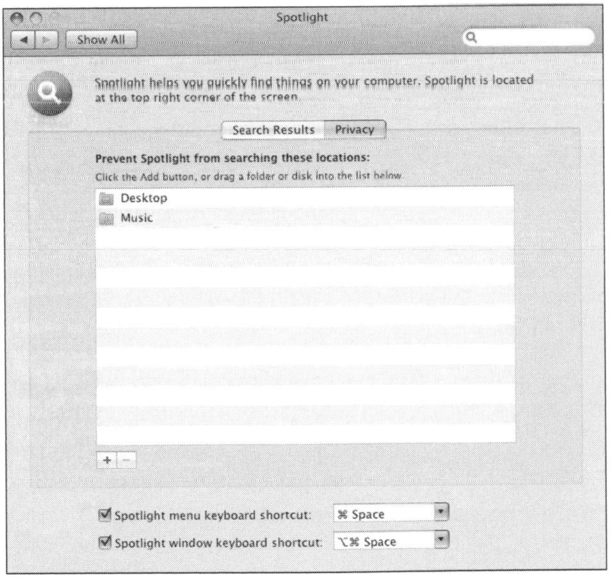

Using Dashboard

In a way, the Leopard Dashboard is very similar to the Vista sidebar. By default, it contains four widgets: clock, calendar, calculator, and weather forecast. Figure 8.29 shows the default Dashboard.

Figure 8.29

Leopard default Dashboard

By clicking the + (plus) sign in the lower left of the screen, you can show all the Dashboard widgets available. You also can download other widgets and add them to your set. And you can write your own widgets, as you do in Chapter 19.

By default, the F12 key is used to summon the Dashboard and to put it away. You also can set a screen corner to summon the desktop, in the Exposé and Spaces preferences pane.

Configuring widgets

When a widget is showing in the Dashboard, when you mouse over it a small "i" appears in the bottom right, as shown in Figure 8.30a.

When you click the "i," the widget rotates through 180 degrees so you can see the reverse, as shown in Figure 8.30b

Figure 8.30

Widget information button (a); reverse side of clock widget (b)

a   b

You can now specify the world region you want the clock to display and then the city within that region. Obviously if your city is not listed, you should select a city in the same time zone as you are.

Adding a widget

Adding another widget is easy. Just follow these steps:

1. **Click the + (plus) sign at the bottom of the Dashboard display.**

2. **Scroll to the second page, and drag the clock icon into your Dashboard.**

If your system is capable of Quartz Extreme/Core Image, you see a ripple effect as the widget settles into place.

3. **Use the "i" symbol to configure the time you want your new clock to show.**

Practice by adding a dictionary to your Dashboard, as shown in Figure 8.31.

Figure 8.31

Dictionary widget

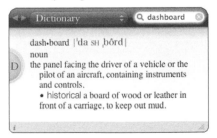

Some people love using widgets; others loathe them. I'm somewhere in the middle: I sometimes use them!

Summary

In this chapter, you learned about the personal preferences that are available through the System Preferences panels.

You set Appearance options to your liking and set up your desktop and screen saver using the options available. You configured the Dock to your liking and learned how to set up Exposé and Spaces to make your work easier and your Leopard experience more enjoyable.

You learned how to use Leopard as a multilanguage tool to write using many different character sets. Most importantly, you set up your computer with a firewall and other important security settings. You looked at how you can encrypt files so that, should your computer fall into the wrong hands, no one can glean your private information from it.

Finally, you saw how to configure the Spotlight search utility to give the results you need and learned how to use widgets on the Dashboard.

9 Setting Up Hardware System Preferences

So, you're feeling pretty good now: You got Leopard up and running on your computer, you set up your personal preferences using System Preferences, you feel satisfied, and you actually enjoy using Leopard.

Now is the time things start getting hard! Unless you have a genuine Macintosh, setting up your hardware is not easy. Some of it has been done for you because of the EFI and the kexts that other people have built.

If you're lucky, as I am with my Dell Mini 9, other people have done almost everything that needs to be done and it works out of the box. All I needed to do with the Dell was install my printer driver, though I don't often use it.

In this chapter, you learn how to set up much of your hardware on Leopard. Some of it is quite easy, but some is difficult.

Setting Up Bluetooth

In this section, you learn how to set up Bluetooth and how to pair it with another device, such as a mobile phone.

If you don't have a Bluetooth adapter, you can skip this section. However, you may want to buy one, because they're relatively cheap and can pretty much be guaranteed to work even on a Hackintosh.

Setting up your device

Obviously, before you can do anything, you need to set up the connection to your Bluetooth device. In this case, I go through the steps of connecting to my mobile phone. No, it's not an iPhone; it's a Nokia N95.

If you have an iPhone, its Bluetooth implementation is incomplete and you can't access the internal storage of your phone. If your iPhone carrier allows tethering, you can use your iPhone as a modem for your computer, but sadly you can't do much else with it.

Setting up your mobile phone

After I click Bluetooth in the System Preferences pane, the settings pane appears, as shown in Figure 9.1.

Figure 9.1

Setup pane for Bluetooth connection

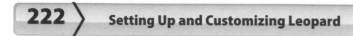

1. **Click Set Up New Device.**

   Leopard's Bluetooth Connection Assistant pops up. In Apple-speak, assistants are the equivalent of wizards in Windows. Figure 9.2a shows the assistant pane.

2. **Click Continue.**

3. **Click the radio button for the type of device you want to set up.**

   Figure 9.2b shows the button I clicked for setting up my mobile phone.

Figure 9.2

Bluetooth Setup Assistant pane (a); Setup Assistant for mobile phone (b)

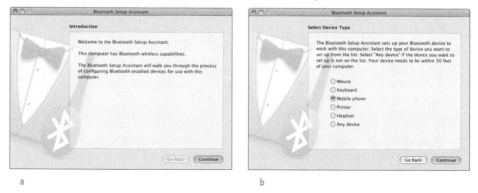

a   b

Setup Assistant then searches for any mobile phones it can find in the area. Figure 9.3a shows the result after finding my mobile phone.

This assumes that you have given your phone a name. If you haven't given it a name, it will have a MAC address like 00:29:61:88:00:00:1f:d0

4. **Click Continue.**

To pair successfully with the device, Leopard generates a number that you key into the other device. Figure 9.3b shows the phone number generated for my mobile phone, although I've obscured the actual digits.

Figure 9.3

Bluetooth phone discovered (a); passkey to pair with mobile phone (b)

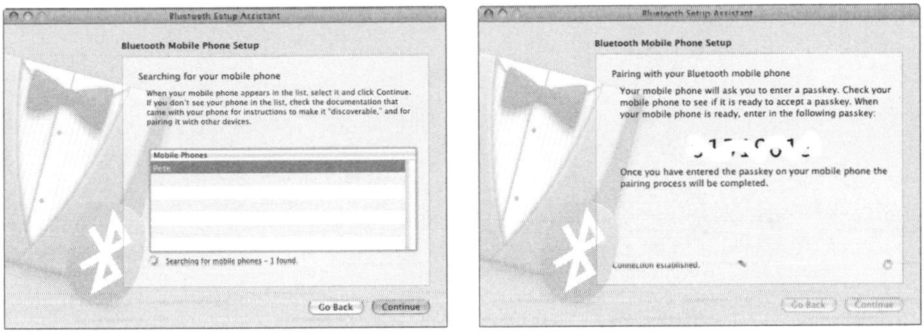

a   b

At this point, your phone should have received a message asking if you want to pair with your computer.

5. **Enter the passkey into your mobile phone.**

6. **Click Continue in Leopard.**

Finally, Leopard asks if you'd like to use your mobile phone as a modem to access the Internet. At the time of this writing, mobile phone companies are a little paranoid about doing this. It's known as *tethering,* and they are worried that it will overload their capacity. Figure 9.4a shows the screen.

7. **Leave the box checked if you're brave enough to try it!**

This depends on whether or not your carrier allows tethering. In my case, data is so much cheaper over my ADSL connection that I don't use the phone as a modem, even though my carrier allows tethering. When I'm away from home, I can usually get a wireless connection.

If you place a check in the box beside Show Bluetooth status in the menu bar, you can click the icon and have a menu, as shown in Figure 9.4b.

Figure 9.4

Use phone for Internet connection (a); Bluetooth menu (b)

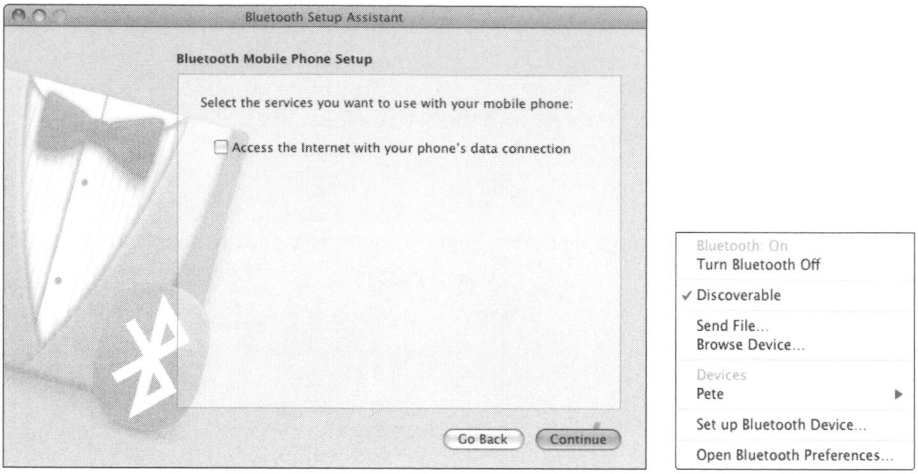

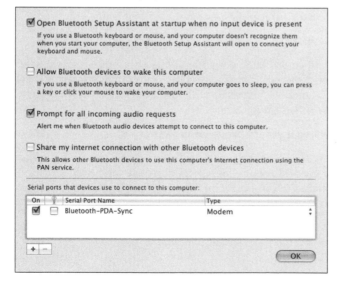

a

b

Setting advanced setup options

Bluetooth has some advanced settings, as shown in Figure 9.5

Figure 9.5

Advanced Bluetooth setup options

Each option is fairly self-explanatory. You may have encountered the first setting when you first started your computer if you are using a Bluetooth mouse or keyboard or if for some reason your computer doesn't recognize your keyboard when it boots.

Sharing your Internet connection with your phone is the opposite of tethering: It uses your computer's Internet connection to connect your phone to the Internet.

Browsing your mobile phone

Selecting Browse Device shows the logical disk drives on my phone, as in Figure 9.6a.

From there, it's a simple matter of opening a drive, opening folders, and finding the file you want.

Remember, you can't do this if you are using an iPhone.

Moving files from the computer to the phone and back is simple, as shown in Figure 9.6b.

Figure 9.6

Browse phone folders (a); file transfer menu for Bluetooth phone (b)

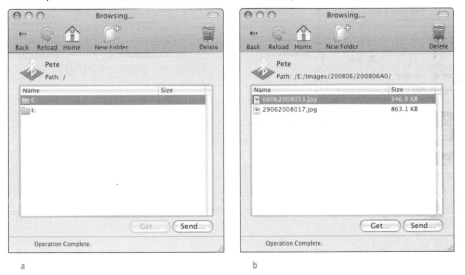

a   b

Setting Up CDs and DVDs

As you can see from Figure 9.7a, you have only a few options to configure with CDs and DVDs.

Options available for each type of medium inserted are shown in Figure 9.7b.

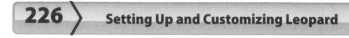

Figure 9.7

Options for CDs and DVDs (a); selections for disk media (b)

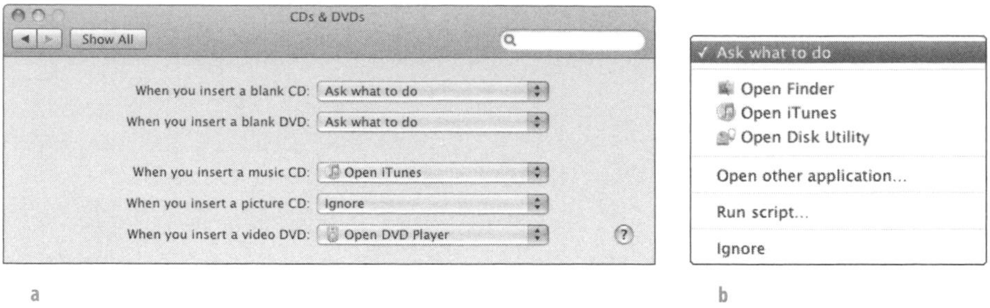

a   b

I have never touched the default actions because they work for me.

Setting Up Your Display

In this section, you set your display to the best settings for your graphics card and monitor, as well as for your own comfort.

Setting up a display is one of the most problematic areas of building a Hackintosh. The resolution choices for your display depend on your graphics card as well as your monitor. Thanks to the hard work of lots of people, you can use many different graphics displays.

TIP

If you are thinking of buying a new computer to run Leopard, particularly a laptop or netbook, check very carefully that the graphics adaptor is supported in Leopard. The hardware compatibility lists are in Chapter 1.

If you are buying a netbook, you can find a good table listing compatibility at `http://gadgets.boingboing.net/2008/12/17/osx-netbook-compatib.html` or `http://tinyurl.com/4z3d9g`.

Setting your screen resolution

As shown in Figure 9.8, Leopard can detect the name of my display and all the different resolutions it is capable of.

To change resolution, click the desired resolution and your screen resets to the new resolution. Leopard doesn't always quite get it right, and Leopard says a couple of resolutions are available, but in fact they are not. A couple of times I've been left with a display setting that my monitor can't display, and I had a black screen! I had to restart by specifying the resolution at the boot time using the parameter `"Graphics Mode"="1920x1080x32"` as shown in earlier chapters.

Figure 9.8

Display settings

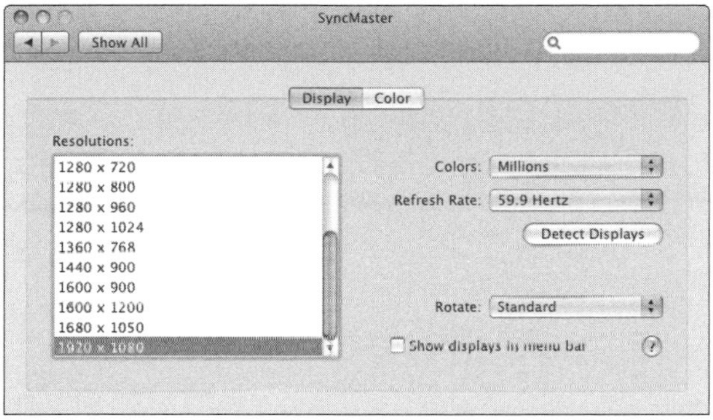

Substitute your monitor's resolution for the 1920 and 1080; remember to include the quotes.

Appendix B contains a table of the different graphics cards used by different Macintoshes. With the exception of nVidia displays, unless your exact graphics chip has been used in a Mac, you are unlikely to be able to extract the most performance from your adapter.

For the most part, an unsupported graphics card displays only in 1024 x 768 pixel mode and without any hardware acceleration. Lack of hardware acceleration means that you can't browse your Time Machine backups, nor can you access any of the features of Quartz Extreme/Core Image. Chapters 20 and 21 cover topics in using QE/CI.

OSX86 Tools by pcwiz has many different kexts available for different graphics cards. I hope yours is among them.

You can download OSX86 Tools from the Web site at `http://code.google.com/p/osx86tools/downloads/list`.

Setting up a color profile

You also can set up a specific color profile for your computer. To do so, click the Color tab on the display pane, as shown in Figure 9.9.

Unless you are working in the graphic arts industries, I recommend that you don't touch the color profiles! I never do.

Click Open Profile to look at your color profile.

Leopard also lets you calibrate your display, providing an assistant for you. The first screen is shown in Figure 9.10.

Figure 9.9

Color pane of display settings

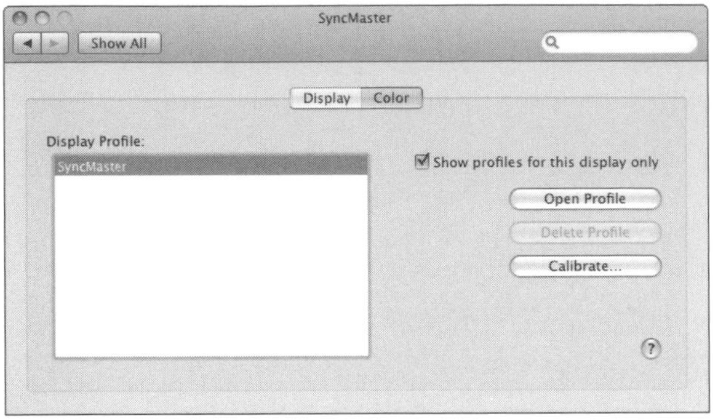

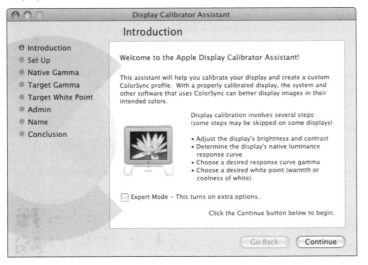

Figure 9.10

Display Calibrator Assistant

Again, because I don't do any work that requires exact color matching, I haven't bothered to calibrate the display other than to go through and look at some of the other profiles. Unless your display is obviously showing wrong colors or you do lots of work where you need to match colors, you can probably ignore it too.

Setting Up Energy Saver

In this section, you find out the best settings for your computer to both save energy and enhance your Leopard experience.

Setting sleep options

As explained in Chapter 8, I don't bother with a screen saver, either with Windows or with Leopard. I set up my display to blank after ten minutes and put the computer to sleep after an hour, although I change that if I'm downloading large files during my off-peak download allowance. This is shown in Figure 9.11.

Figure 9.11

Sleep options settings

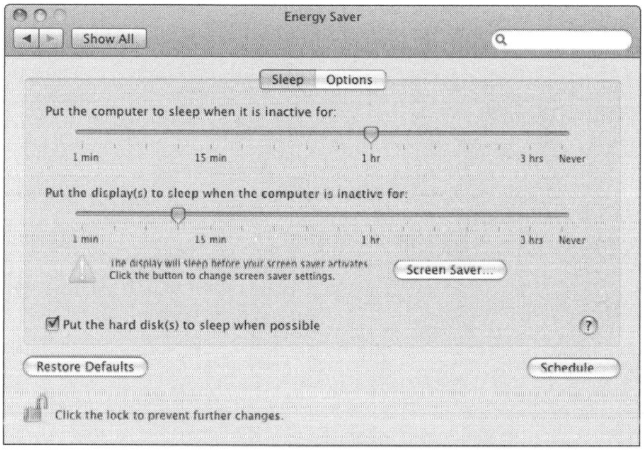

Your needs and preferences will obviously differ from mine, so choose whatever suits you best. You also can access the screen saver setup screen by clicking the Screen Saver button.

Be warned, though, that some Hackintoshes go to sleep without problems, but they do not wake up from sleep. A bit like me, really!

You can schedule when you want the computer to start up or wake plus sleep, shutdown, or restart by clicking the Schedule button. This is shown in Figure 9.12.

I also let my disks sleep whenever possible, by checking the "Put the disks to sleep" check box. The only downside to this is that if I want to access a file on one of my Windows disks, it takes around five seconds for the disk to spin up and become available.

Figure 9.12

Schedule options

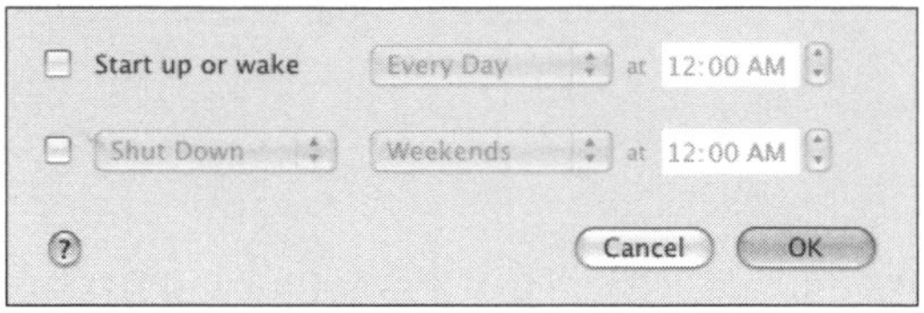

☐ Start up or wake	Every Day ⬍	at	12:00 AM ⬍
☐ Shut Down ⬍	Weekends ⬍	at	12:00 AM ⬍
⑦		Cancel	OK

Setting wake and power down options

Clicking the Options button displays the wake and other options pane, as shown in Figure 9.13.

Figure 9.13

Wake and power down options

Energy Saver

Show All

Sleep | Options

Wake Options:
☑ Wake for Ethernet network administrator access

Other Options:
☑ Allow power button to sleep the computer

⑦

Restore Defaults   Schedule...

🔓 Click the lock to prevent further changes.

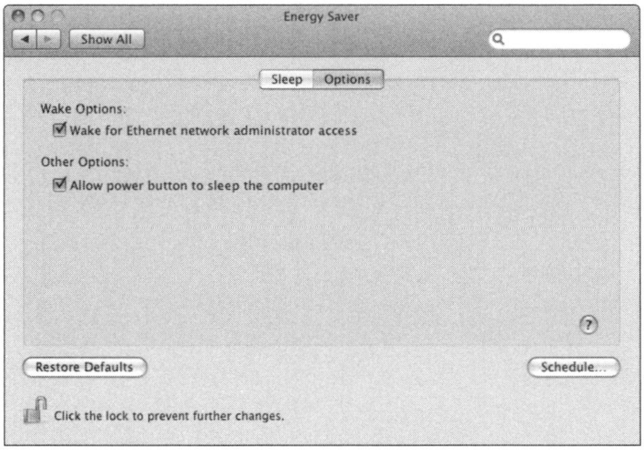

This pane has only two settings: Wake for Ethernet administrator access means that you can wake your computer by sending a special Ethernet packet to the Ethernet port. It does not work with Airport or other wireless setups.

The option called Allow power button to sleep the computer has no effect with my computer. The power button on my keyboard brings up the dialog box shown in Figure 9.14.

Figure 9.14

Power button dialog box

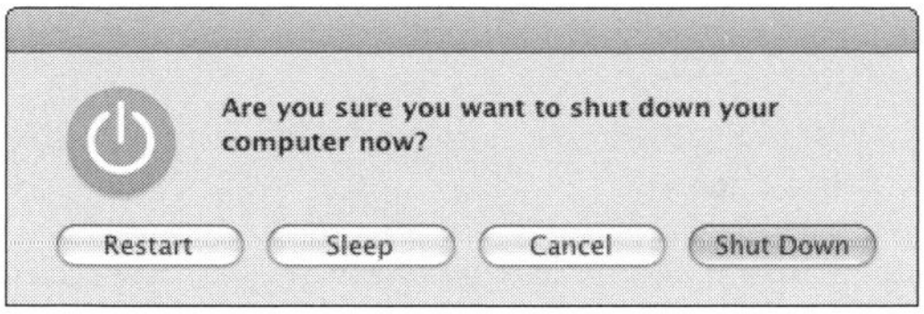

Setting Up Keyboard and Mouse

In this section, you explore the options for setting up your keyboard and mouse to suit your preferences. As shown in Figure 9.15, the preferences panel has four panes.

Figure 9.15

Keyboard and mouse settings panel

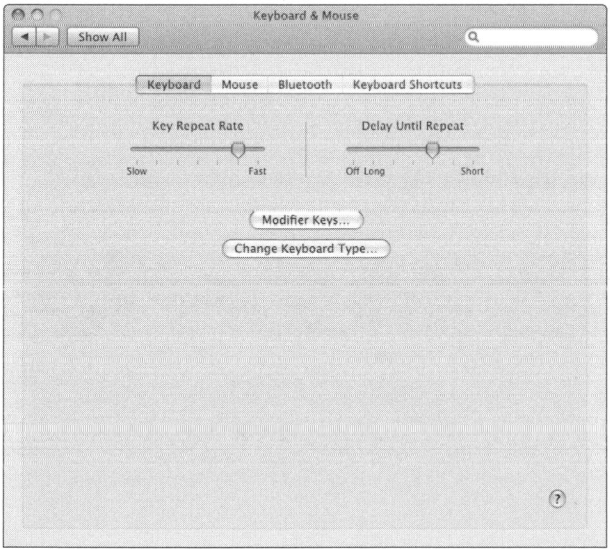

Setting up your keyboard

Use the sliders to set your desired keyboard repeat rate and the delay until repeat. The repeat rate is the rate at which extra characters are typed: Make the rate very slow for people who have difficulty with fast motor actions.

Delay until repeat is the length of time it takes before the key starts repeating. If needed, you can switch off key repeat.

Changing modifier keys

Click the Modifier Keys button to change the assignment of your Option, Control, Command, and Caps Lock keys. Figure 9.16 illustrates the choices.

Figure 9.16

Set modifier keys

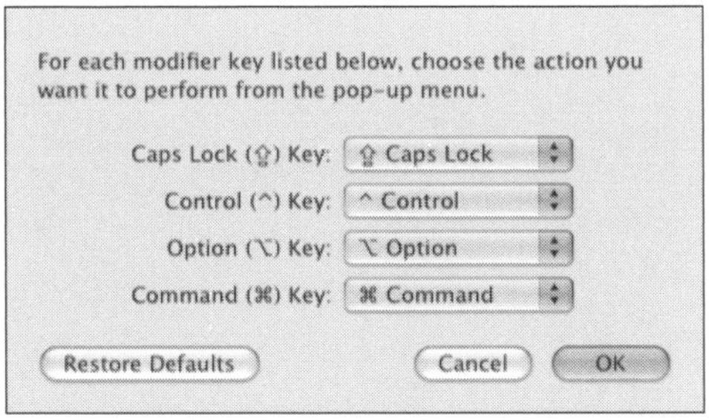

For each modifier key listed below, choose the action you want it to perform from the pop-up menu.

Caps Lock (⇧) Key: ⇧ Caps Lock

Control (^) Key: ^ Control

Option (⌥) Key: ⌥ Option

Command (⌘) Key: ⌘ Command

Restore Defaults   Cancel   OK

If you prefer them the same as they were when originally installed, click the Restore Defaults button.

For most Hackintosh installations, the default key settings are shown in Table 9.1.

Table 9.1 Keyboard Equivalencies for Windows Keyboard to Leopard	
Windows Keyboard Key	*Leopard Keyboard Key*
Ctrl	Control
Windows key	Command
Alt	Option

Changing your keyboard type

Click the Change Keyboard Type, and Leopard starts an assistant to set up your keyboard. This is the same one that ran when you started Leopard for the first time after installation.

Used in conjunction with the International settings you explored in Chapter 8, it allows you to connect keyboards for foreign languages and use them to enter text in that language.

You may also want to check whether any multimedia keys above your function keys work with Leopard. The mute, volume up/down, play/pause, prev/next track, and stop keys work on mine.

Setting up your mouse

Figure 9.17 shows the settings pane for your mouse.

Figure 9.17

Mouse settings pane

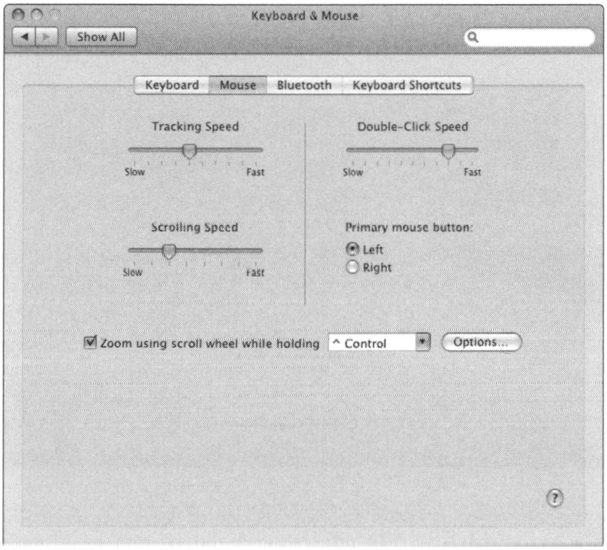

These settings are very similar to the settings in Windows. Tracking speed is the amount the mouse pointer on the screen moves in relation to the amount you move the mouse.

If the box for Zoom using scroll wheel while holding is checked, you can hold down the Ctrl key and zoom the whole screen display to focus on a small area.

To see how it works, press and hold the Ctrl key while you move the scroll wheel on your mouse toward the screen. Figure 9.18 shows my screen magnified to about double normal size.

If you have a mouse with a scroll wheel, try this for yourself. When you do it, note how the screen moves as you move the mouse pointer. If this makes you seasick, set the option to Only when the pointer reaches an edge, as shown in Figure 9.19.

Figure 9.18

Leopard screen magnified (image blurred because of magnification)

Sat 10:23 AM Peter Baldwin
Apple
http://www.apple.com/
Google
Apple Yahoo! Google Maps YouTube Wikipedia News (299) Popular
Apple
Store
Mac
iPod + iTunes
iPhone
Hackintosh
Vista
Data
MacPro Time Machine
FRAY
Th
Now

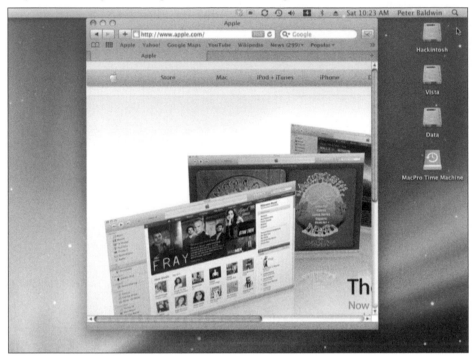

Figure 9.19

Scroll options for magnified screen

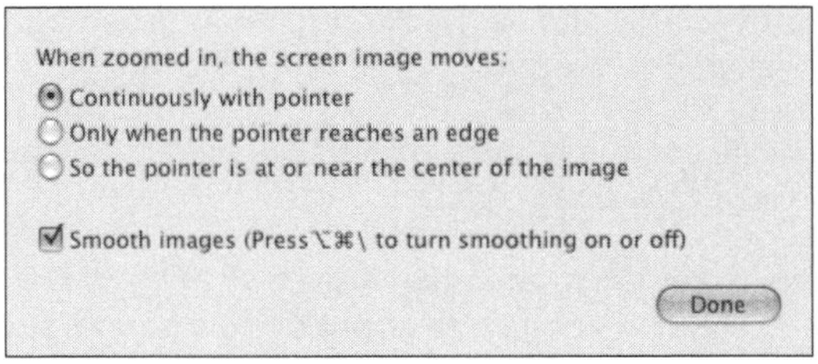
When zoomed in, the screen image moves:
Continuously with pointer
Only when the pointer reaches an edge
So the pointer is at or near the center of the image
Smooth images (Press ⌥⌘\ to turn smoothing on or off)
Done

Using a Bluetooth mouse and keyboard

Bluetooth allows you to name your mouse and keyboard and to monitor the battery charge, as shown in Figure 9.20.

Figure 9.20

Bluetooth mouse and keyboard dialog box

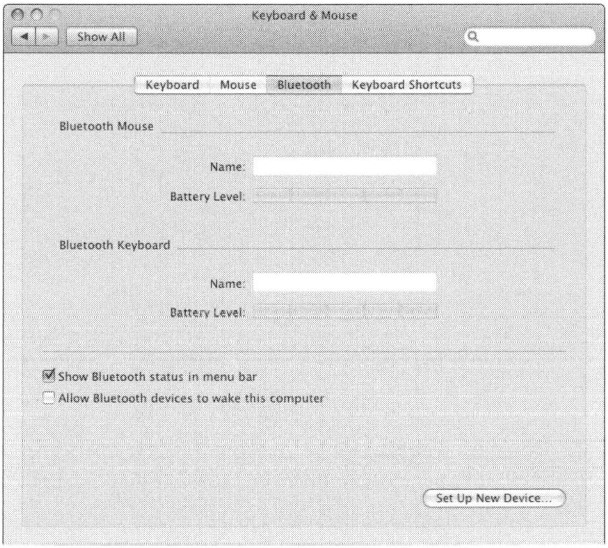

Because I don't use a Bluetooth mouse or keyboard, the illustration can't show you what these look like!

Setting keyboard shortcuts

Leopard allows you to change many of the standard key assignments to something of your choice and to add your own keyboard shortcuts, as shown in Figure 9.21.

Figure 9.21

Keyboard shortcuts

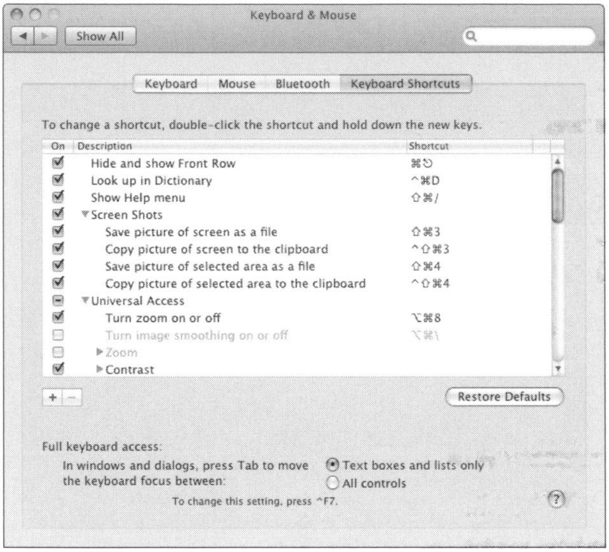

Personally, I don't find much use for adding shortcut keys: Leopard already has all the ones I need. But let's create a keyboard shortcut to allow you to import text into a new sticky note.

If you haven't used sticky notes yet, open Spotlight and type **Stickies**. Follow these steps:

1. **Open Spotlight by pressing Cmd+spacebar.**

   On your Windows keyboard, it's probably the Windows key and the spacebar.

2. **Type** Stickies **and press Enter.**

   If this is the first time you've used Stickies, it displays two sticky notes explaining what you can do with them.

3. **Close both notes, saving them if you wish.**

4. **Open System Preferences, click Mouse and Keyboard, and then click Keyboard Shortcuts.**

5. **Scroll to the bottom of the window, and click the + (plus) sign at the bottom.**

   This pops up a new window, as shown in Figure 9.22.

Figure 9.22

Adding a keyboard shortcut for a new application

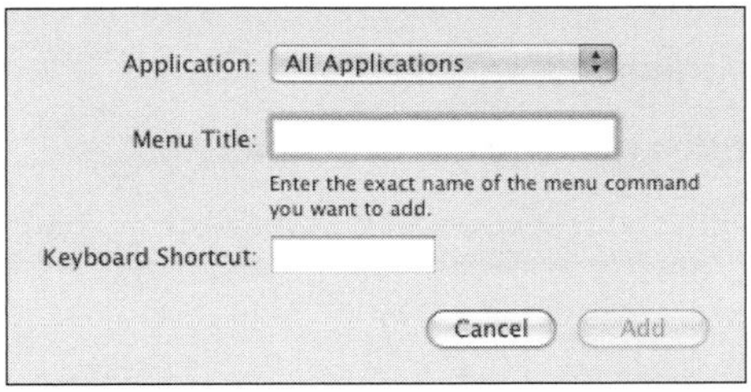

6. **Click Application, scroll down until you come to Stickies, and select it.**

7. **Click in the Menu Title box, and type** Import Text.

   In the Stickies menu, Import Text has an ellipsis (…) following it. It may look like three full periods, but it's actually a character in its own right. To enter an ellipsis, use the Option+; keystroke. In other words, hold down the Option (Alt) key while you type a semicolon.

8. **Enter the ellipsis, and tab to the next field.**

   This is where you enter your keystroke shortcut.

9. **Hold down the Control, Command, and Option keys (Ctrl+Windows+Alt), and press T.**

   This enters the keystroke into the Keyboard Shortcut box. Figure 9.23a shows the result.

10. **Click Add to add your new shortcut to the keystrokes for Stickies.**

11. **Click the File menu for Stickies, and check that your new keystroke is there.**

    Figure 9.23b shows the File menu with the new keystroke.

    Now you need to test your new shortcut.

Figure 9.23

Set Stickies shortcut keystroke (a); Stickies File menu (b)

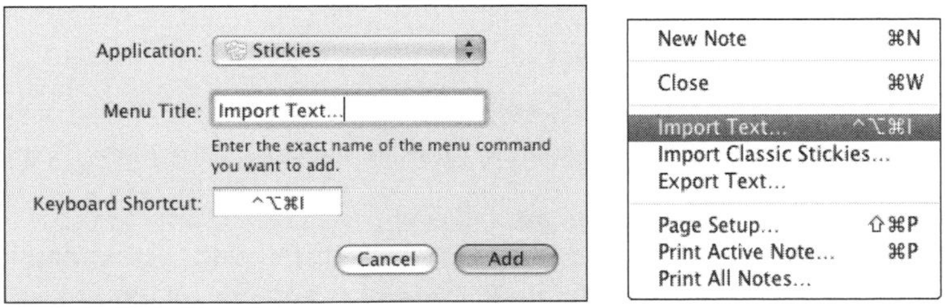

a   b

12. **Launch TextEdit, and create a new file with a couple of lines of text.**

13. **Save the file to your desktop.**

14. **Bring Stickies to the foreground using Cmd+Tab.**

15. **Press your Ctrl+Cmd+Option+T keystroke combination.**

This creates a new sticky with the text you saved in the note as shown in Figure 9.24.

Figure 9.24

Text in TextEdit and Stickies

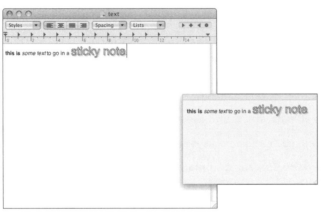

Obviously you wouldn't go to the bother of creating a text file just to put into a sticky note, but it's useful to be able to add text files. Note that Stickies also show any formatting you have in the note.

Setting Up Print and Fax

In this section, you learn how to set up your printer and fax, if you have a modem.

Setting up your printer

Before you can set up Print & Fax in System Preferences, you need to have a printer installed. Most recent printers have drivers available for download from the manufacturer's site.

If your printer does not have a driver available, you may still be able to use it because a CUPS driver may be available. CUPS stands for Common Unix Printing System, and it has drivers for many printers. Because of its Unix heritage, OS X and Leopard can use CUPS drivers. In fact, the driver for my printer, downloaded from the manufacturer's site, is a CUPS driver, as shown in Figure 9.25.

Figure 9.25

Print & Fax setup

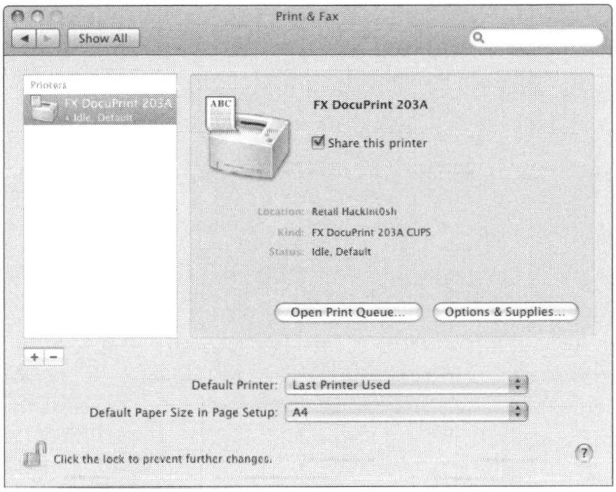

Printer drivers are normally supplied as disk image (.dmg) files, so you simply double-click the file to start the Installer. Most printer drivers require that you reboot after installation.

Sharing the printer is simply a matter of checking the Share this printer box.

As you can see, very little can be changed here; the same is true on the Driver and Supply Levels panes. With a genuine Macintosh, using an Apple printer, more information is shown, including a blatant plug for buying more supplies!

Setting up faxing

If you don't have fax modem, you won't see any reference to it in System Preferences. But you can still use something similar to faxing if you want to send sensitive information over the Internet. The problem with simple e-mail is that unless you have arranged with the recipient to encrypt the file, it is sent as plain text and can be intercepted.

To get around this, you can create a document the mimics the fax you want to send and print it to a PDF file. This is available on the Print menu for all Leopard applications, as shown in Figure 9.26.

Then simply e-mail the PDF file to the recipient. The main advantage is that you are not sending plain text over the Internet, so hijacking the information is much harder, though not impossible.

Figure 9.26

Printing to a PDF file

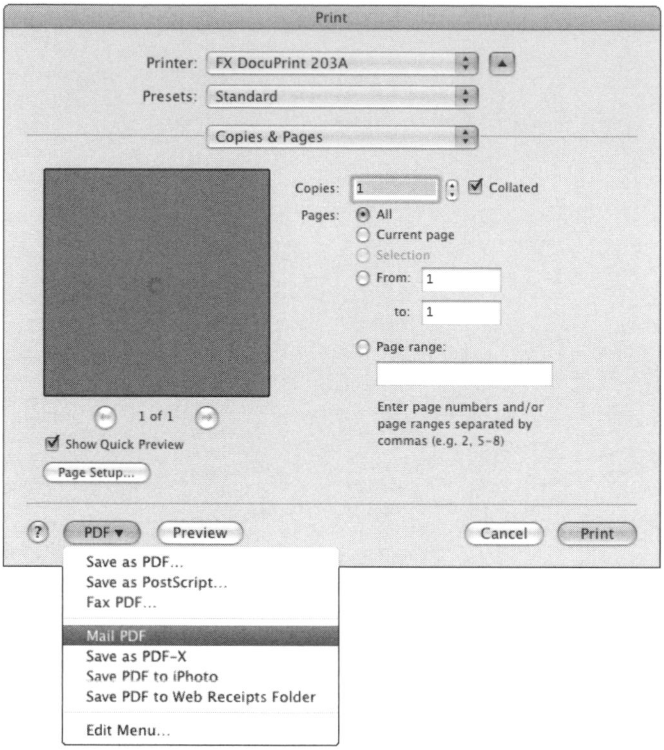

You can password protect the PDF file, though of course you have to let the recipient know the password. You can do this through a simple phone call.

Setting Up Sound

Apart from wireless networking, sound is generally the most difficult part of Leopard to set up correctly. It's definitely not something you can do on your own. In this section, you learn how to install the correct drivers (kexts) for your computer system and how to configure System Preferences for sound.

Finding the correct audio drivers

If you are lucky, you have installed the correct drivers when you installed Leopard. If you installed the retail Leopard, having the correct drivers is impossible, so you need to search for them.

CROSS-REF
In Chapter 1, you created a table showing all the hardware in your computer. Now is the time to go back and find the Vendor ID and Device ID for your sound system.

First, obviously, you want to search the Internet. A good place to start is `www.insanelymac.com/forum/index.php?showtopic=97811`, which I converted to a TinyURL for you: `http://tinyurl.com/mxojbe`

If you are using a well-known brand and model of computer, search for sound drivers for that computer. Otherwise, search for your motherboard or your sound chip.

If you can't find what you need, try some of the forums, such as `insanelymac.com`, `osx86 project.org`, `pcwizcomputer.com`, and `osx86scene.com`. Correct etiquette is that you must do your own searches before you ask someone for help. Don't expect to log in to the forum and ask that someone send you the correct kexts. You are likely to get some abuse!

After you have your kexts installed, you can then use System Preferences to set up your sound.

CROSS-REF
After you find the correct drivers, install them using kexthelper, as described in Chapter 6.

If, after all this, you can't find kexts that work with your computer, you can try using a USB sound device. These are available online, particularly through eBay. Many are less than $10 and may or may not work. For a bit more money, you can buy something that comes with OS X drivers on CD.

Simply plug it into a spare USB slot and plug your amplifier into its sound outputs.

Setting up sound in System Preferences

As with many System Preferences, sound has three panes: Sound Effects, Output, and Input.

Setting sound output

After installing your kexts and rebooting, I suggest you start with the second pane—Output—because you could spend time worrying that your sound isn't working, when all that's happening is that you are trying to set it for the wrong output. This pane is shown in Figure 9.27.

On my computer, all the outputs work, except possibly Digital Out because I don't have anything to test it with.

In my case, the correct output is Built-in Speaker, even though I don't have built-in speakers! Still, who cares? It works!

Figure 9.27

Sound output pane

Setting sound effects

This allows you to choose the sound effects you hear when Leopard wants to get your attention, as shown in Figure 9.28.

Figure 9.28

Sound effects

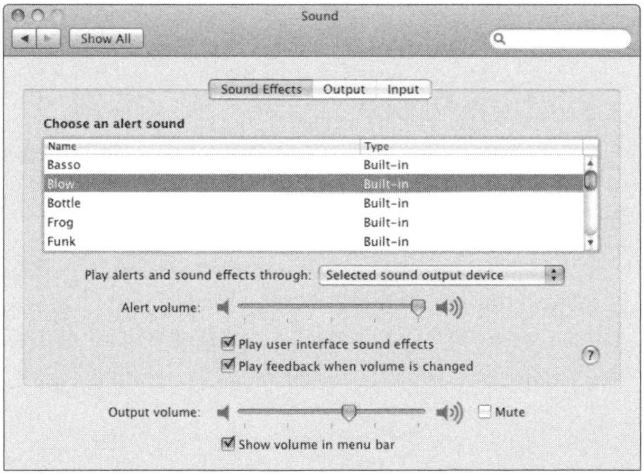

All the alerts use the same sound, unlike Windows, which has dozens of sounds, including the highly irritating (to me!) Start Navigation sound that clicks every time you search for a new Web site or folder on your computer.

Setting sound input

Figure 9.29 shows the sound input settings. On my system, the internal microphone and webcam both work. I've never tested the line in. I'm not sure how the line out can show as a line in port!

Figure 9.29

Sound inputs

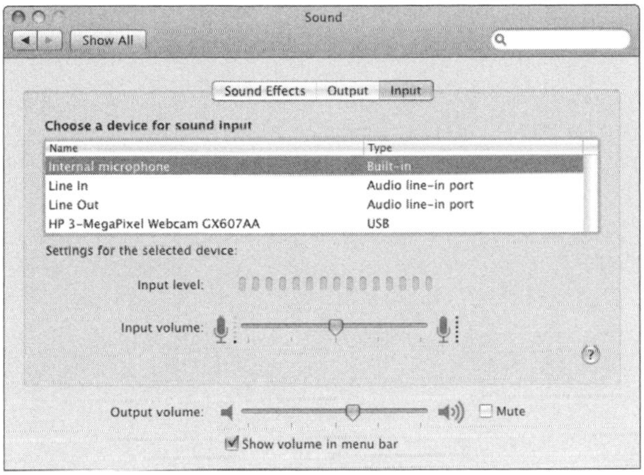

Interestingly, Leopard detected my webcam as soon as I booted for the first time and offered to take my photo for my user account.

Summary

In this chapter, you set your system preferences for most of your hardware. This included simple devices such as Bluetooth devices, CDs and DVDs, Energy Saver, and keyboard and mouse, as well as more complicated devices such as your display, printer, and sound.

By now, you should be getting to know your way around Leopard and feeling comfortable with using it.

In the next chapter, you set up more of your system preferences, including networking.

Setting Up Internet and Network Preferences

Once upon a time, computers weren't connected to the Internet! Once upon a time, they weren't even connected to each other, but those days are long gone.

It's almost impossible to imagine using a stand-alone computer that doesn't connect to any other computer, whether on a local area network or the Internet.

In this chapter, you go through the process of setting up your Hackintosh to connect with the Internet and with other computers for sharing files and hardware resources. You also set up QuickTime on your computer.

Setting Up Your Network

In this section, you learn how to configure your networking connections. For most desktop computers, this is relatively simple, and Leopard generally finds your wired network connections automatically. For laptops that use wireless networking, the story is not so straightforward.

Using a wired connection

Leopard has detected and pretty much automatically set up networking on every desktop computer I've installed it on. This is because only a few networking chips are used in both generic computers and Apples.

My motherboard has two Ethernet connectors, identified as Ethernet Adaptor (en0) and Ethernet Adaptor (en1). By default, each of them connects to the router/modem using DHCP.

DHCP stands for Dynamic Host Configuration Protocol. When you connect a computer to the router, the router acts as a DHCP server and assigns the computer an IP address. This happens automatically after the computer connects to the router. Addresses are in a private range of addresses, allocated by international agreement. Private means they are located inside a single network and cannot be directly accessed from outside. Each computer inside the network uses Network Address Translation (NAT) to direct information packets that come through a single IP address to the appropriate computer.

T I P

You can find out more about DHCP and private IP addresses by consulting Wikipedia.

Different router manufacturers use different ranges of private IP addresses, but most are in the 192.168.x.y range of addresses. The manual for your router will tell you the range of address used.

Figure 10.1 shows the configuration of my desktop computer before connecting an Ethernet cable.

Figure 10.1

Network adaptors before connection

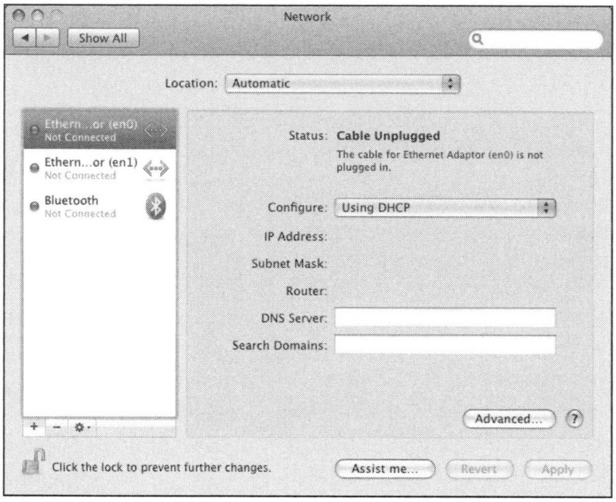

A few seconds after the cable was plugged in, the computer was given its own IP address by the router, as shown in Figure 10.2

Each network adaptor has an identifier known as its Media Access Control (MAC) address. Every adaptor manufactured by every manufacturer has its own unique MAC address. If you're interested (although I have no idea why you would be!), you can find your adaptor's MAC address by clicking Advanced on the network pane and then clicking Ethernet. Every computer on the planet has a different address.

Many routers keep an internal table of network adaptor identifiers and assign the same IP address to it each time it connects.

Figure 10.2

Network adaptors after connection

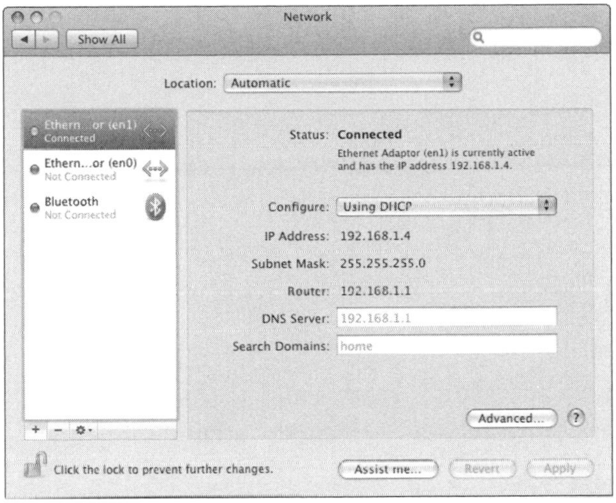

Giving the adaptors sensible names

I always rename my adaptors. In my case, my fixed Ethernet adaptors are stacked one on top of the other, so I named one of them Top Port and the other … yes, Bottom Port.

At the bottom of the panel showing the adaptors is a button with a cogwheel and a down arrow on it. Click that to give your connections new names.

Figure 10.3a shows the menu for renaming the adaptors. Figure 10.3b shows the drop-down box for entering the new name.

Figure 10.3

Menu for configuring services (a); renaming adaptor (en0) (b)

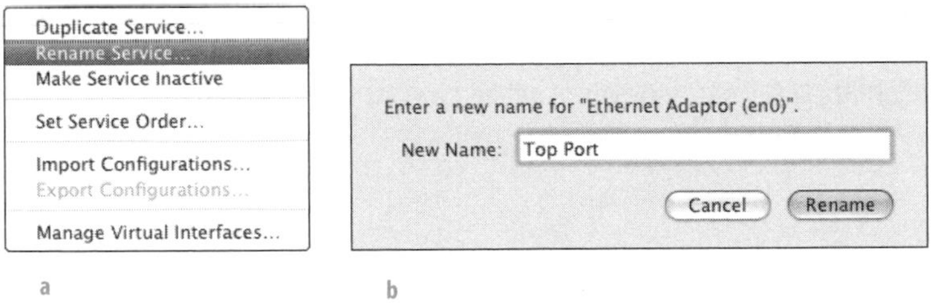

a   b

Setting your own IP address

It may happen that your router doesn't automatically set your IP address, so Leopard provides a method of setting it yourself. To do it, you need to know a little bit about your network and router. Figure 10.4 shows the menu to set your own address.

Figure 10.4

Setting IP address manually

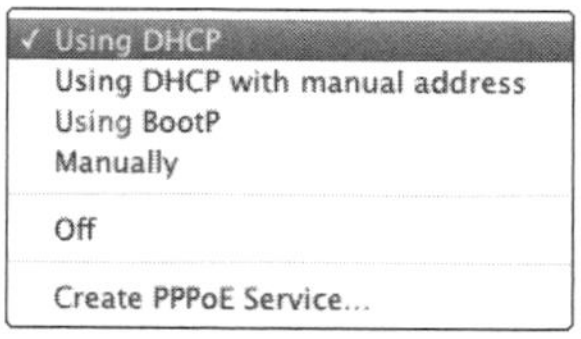

✓ Using DHCP
Using DHCP with manual address
Using BootP
Manually
Off
Create PPPoE Service…

Before you can complete the dialog box, you need to know the following:

- The address of your router
- The address range your router will accept

Follow these steps to set your IP address:

1. **Click Using DHCP to open the drop-down box.**

2. **Select Using DHCP with manual address.**

3. **Enter the IP address you want to use, ensuring that it is in the range for your router.**

4. **In DNS Server, enter the private IP address for your router.**

Figure 10.5 shows this information for my computer and router.

Using the network assistant and diagnostics

If you click the Assist me… button on the Network pane, you can start either the network assistant or network diagnostics. In my experience, neither of them is at all helpful; maybe with a real Macintosh they help, but they've never provided me with much help. Use them if you have problems, but you most likely will have to look elsewhere.

Figure 10.5

Manual DHCP configuration

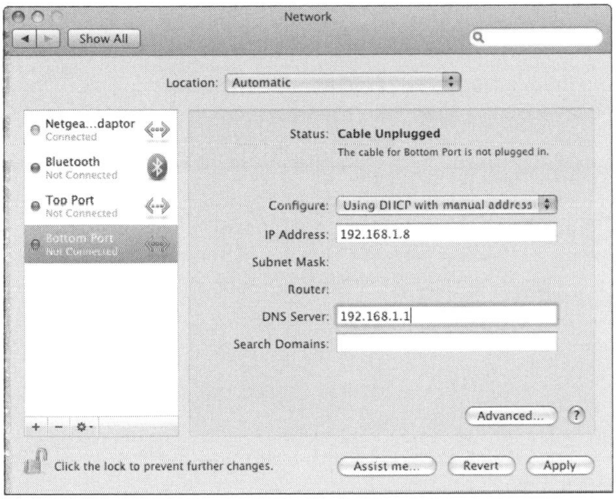

Using a wireless connection

As mentioned in the earlier chapters, setting up wireless networking is one of the most difficult parts of getting a Hackintosh up and running. The reason is simply that Apple only uses a small number of wireless adaptor chips, and if yours is not one of them, you will have difficulties.

Some Dell computers use the same wireless adaptor as Apple uses, so they work out of the box. Or to misquote Apple: "They just work."

Finding network adaptors that work

After trying several different internal wireless cards for my computer and failing to get any of them to work, I settled on a USB wireless adaptor.

I have tried several different USB adaptors, and these are the only ones that have worked for me.

- Netgear WG111v2
- RokAir
- Asus WL-167g

I bought each of them from eBay. RokAir supplied a CD containing the Mac drivers, the Netgear drivers came from their site, and I found the Asus drivers through `insanelymac.com`. Good luck!

Installing driver software for the wireless network

After you have inserted the USB adaptor, you need to install drivers. These can be downloaded from the Internet normally as disk image (.dmg) files. These are installed using the standard Leopard installer.

This sequence of steps shows the installation of the Netgear wireless adaptor. Your wireless adaptor may be different, but the steps are essentially the same:

1. Unzip the file you downloaded, if required.

This mounts the disk image or opens the folder containing the installer package, as shown in Figure 10.6.

Figure 10.6

Netgear installer package

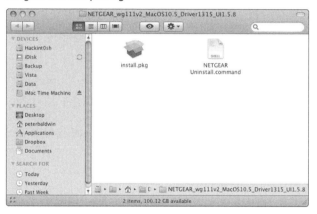

2. Double-click the package to start the installer, as shown in Figure 10.7a.

When the installation completes, you are required to restart your computer, as shown in Figure 10.7b.

3. Restart your computer.

When your computer has restarted, the Netgear control application asks you to enable the WLAN card, as shown in Figure 10.8a.

4. Open System Preferences, and go to the Networking panel.

You may see nothing different, or you may have a new Ethernet Adaptor listed. In this case, nothing is listed.

Figure 10.7

Installer for Netgear wireless adaptor (a); installation completion (b)

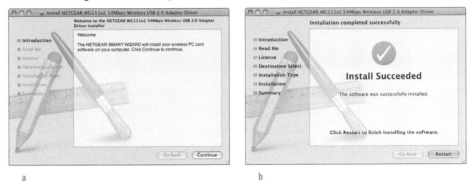

a   b

5. **Click the + (plus) sign at the bottom of the adaptors pane.**

This opens a dialog box to allow you to add the new adaptor, as shown in Figure 10.8b.

Figure 10.8

Enable WLAN Message (a); add new network adaptor dialog box (b)

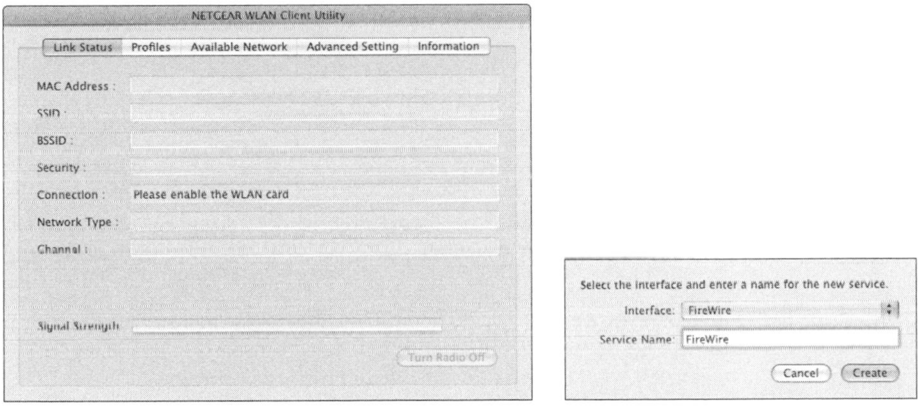

6. **Click the drop-down box for FireWire interface. This shows the existing adaptors as well as the new adaptor you just installed, as shown in Figure 10.9a.**

7. **Select the new adaptor (en4 in this case).**

8. **Give it a meaningful name in the Service Name box.**

In this case, I used the name Netgear WG111, as shown in Figure 10.9b.

Figure 10.9

Add new Ethernet adaptor (a); naming the adaptor (b)

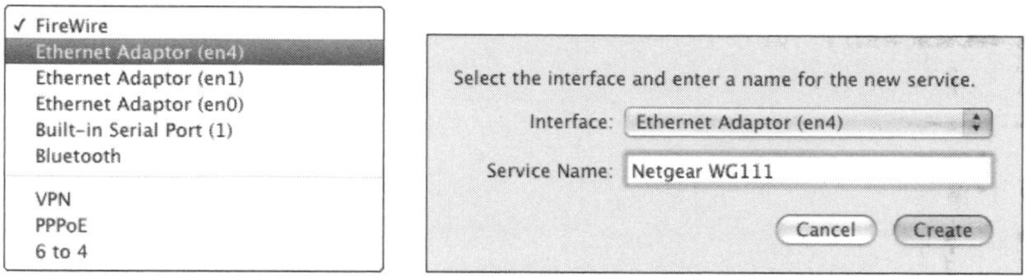

a   b

9. **Click Create.**

After a few seconds delay, the new adaptor appears in your Adaptors pane on the left, and it should use DHCP to get an IP address. If it doesn't get one automatically, assign one manually, as in the section above.

10. **Click Using DHCP to open the drop-down box.**

11. **Select Using DHCP with manual address.**

12. **Enter the IP address you want to use, ensuring that it is in the range for your router.**

13. **In DNS Server, enter the private IP address for your router.**

14. **Return to the Netgear application, and click Available Network.**

Figure 10.10 shows the networks visible in the area around my home router.

If you haven't already set up secure networking on your router, you should drop everything and do it now! These days, WEP encryption is pretty easy to crack, so you should use WPA2_PSK encryption because it's more secure.

15. **Click Connect.**

Your adaptor detects the type of encryption you are using, so you now have to provide your encryption key. Figure 10.11 shows this screen.

Figure 10.10

Available networks

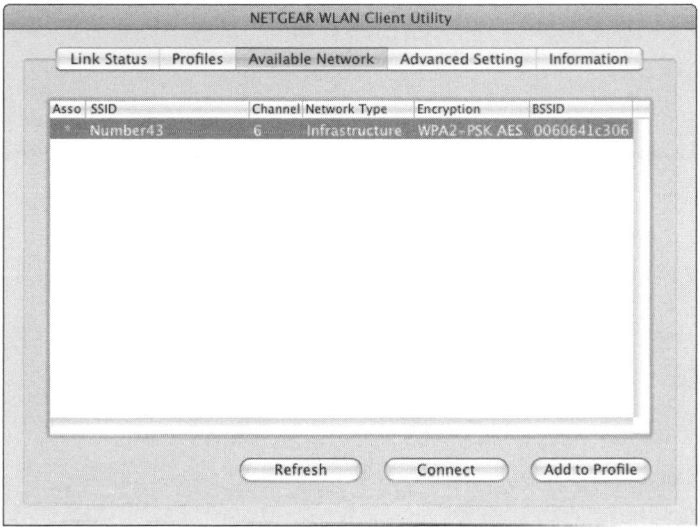

Figure 10.11

Network security properties

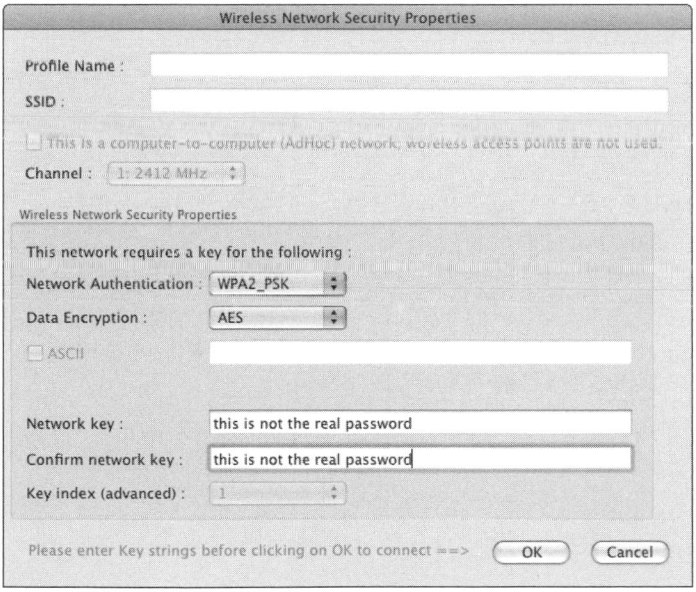

16. **Enter the key into the Network key field and again into the Confirm network key field.**

No, it won't let you copy and paste!

17. **Click OK.**

Hooray! At last you're connected wirelessly. Figure 10.12 shows the Netgear connected screen.

Figure 10.12

Netgear connected wirelessly

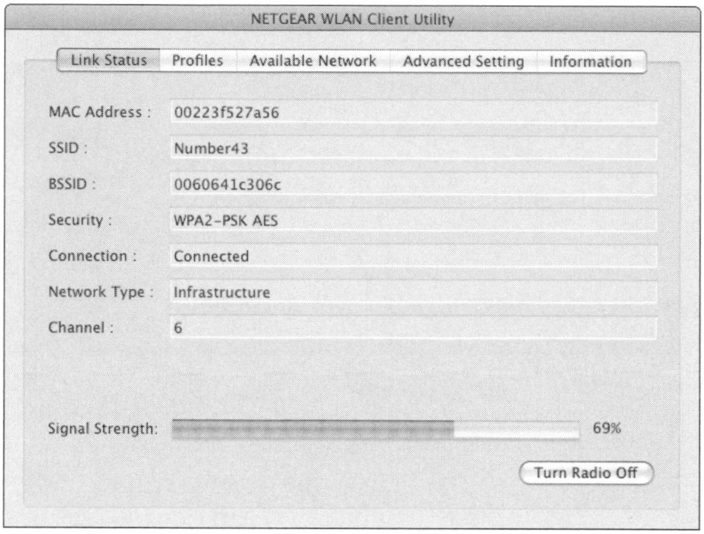

```
                    NETGEAR WLAN Client Utility

  [ Link Status ]  Profiles   Available Network   Advanced Setting   Information

  MAC Address :   00223f527a56

  SSID :          Number43

  BSSID :         0060641c306c

  Security :      WPA2-PSK AES

  Connection :    Connected

  Network Type :  Infrastructure

  Channel :       6




  Signal Strength: [████████████████████        ]      69%

                                              ( Turn Radio Off )
```

From now on, each time you start Leopard, this screen pops up for a second or two, and then, if you are connected, it hides itself, though you see its icon in the Dock.

Of course, the procedure for connecting your own wireless network adaptor will be different. The Netgear and RokAir use the same Realtek chip, so the setup is very similar. The Asus adaptor uses a Ralink chip, and the installation is not quite as smooth.

In my experience, and that of others, the Asus adaptor is a bit hit or miss. Sometimes you have to unplug the adaptor and then plug it in again before it will work. Sigh.

Managing without networking

Can you manage without networking? Possibly, depending on what you do with your computer. For me, it would be almost impossible.

Setting Up Sharing

In this section, you learn how to set up your Hackintosh to share files and printers with other computers, running both Macintosh and Windows.

You can set up your Hackintosh to share CDs and DVDs, and Web sites stored on your computer, but most often you will want to share just files and printers, and occasionally control your computer remotely. You also can set up screen sharing, but, apart from the novelty value, it's probably not much use to you.

Setting up file sharing

Setting up file sharing is a relatively simple process. It allows you to share files with Macintosh and Windows computers, as well as via File Transfer Protocol (FTP). Follow these steps:

1. **Open System Preferences, and select Sharing.**

   Figure 10.13 shows the opening screen in the sharing panel.

   Figure 10.13

   Sharing panel

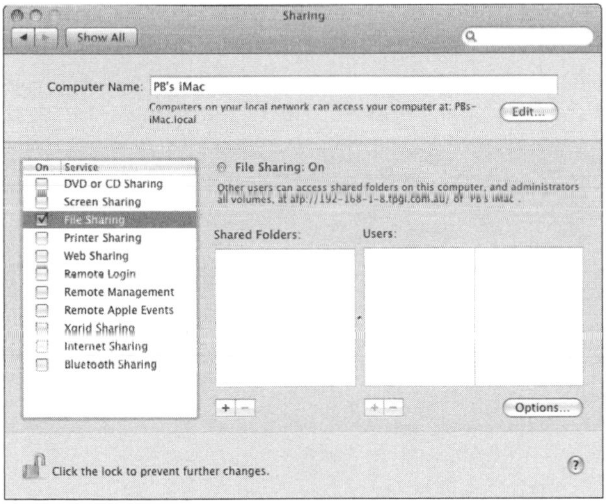

2. **Check the box beside File Sharing.**

   This switches on file sharing, but at present you're not sharing anything.

3. **Click the + (plus) sign under Shared Folders.**

4. **In the drop-down sheet, navigate to the folder you want to share.**

Figure 10.14 shows the sheet with the Public folder selected.

Figure 10.14

Folder selection sheet

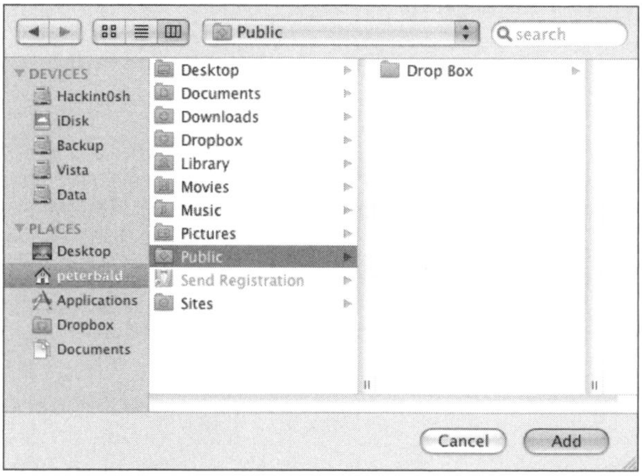

5. **Click Add.**

Figure 10.15 shows the panel after adding the Public folder for file sharing.

Figure 10.15

File sharing users

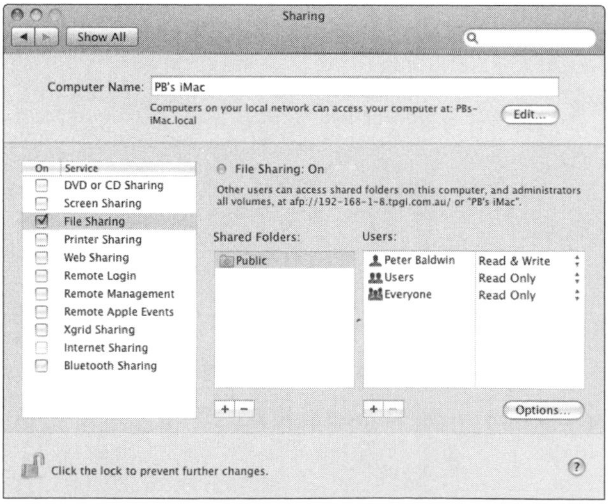

Note the default permissions applied.

CROSS-REF

Appendix B gives more information on file permissions.

Because this folder is in your home folder, as shown in Figure 10.16, you are the owner of it.

Figure 10.16

Path to shared folder

Users refers other users with accounts on the computer; Everyone means anyone who is not a user of the computer.

You can change the permission for each group of users; you can take anyone off the list, or you can add anyone who is in your Address Book.

Permissions that are available for each group are shown in Figure 10.17a.

Write only is an interesting option. It allows you to set up the folder so you have complete control. Others can't see what's in the folder, but they can add their own files. In Leopard it's known as a Drop Box and is quite a useful option in some circumstances.

6. Change the permissions for any group of users.

Be sure not to change your own permissions; otherwise, you may not be able to read or write from a different computer.

7. **Click the Options button.**

Figure 10.17b shows the options available for the types of sharing.

Figure 10.17

Permissions for groups allowed to access the folder (a); type of sharing options (b)

AFP stands for Apple Filing Protocol and is the protocol used for sharing data between Apple computers.

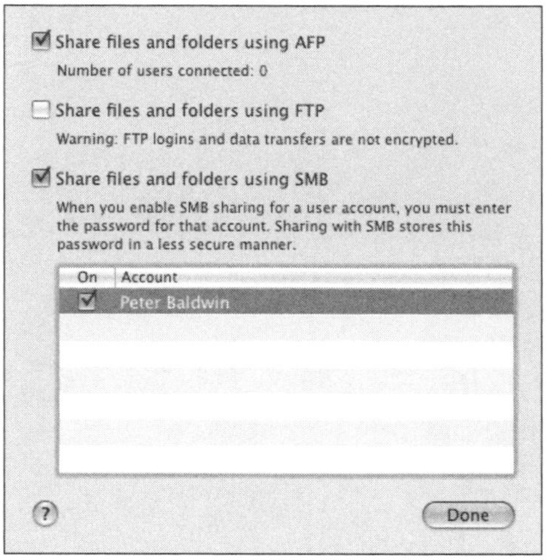

FTP stands for File Transfer Protocol and is a standard protocol for sharing files between very different types of computer systems. Every networked computer operating system can implement some form of FTP.

SMB stands for Server Message Block and is used mainly by Windows computers. No, it's not that Apple couldn't bear the thought of writing Windows instead of SMB; it's just that it fits the same form as the other two protocols.

8. **If you are going to access your files from a Windows computer, check the SMB box, and then click Done.**

Setting up printer sharing

If you have a printer set up, it should show when you click Printer Sharing, as shown in Figure 10.18.

To share your printer, check the box beside Printer Sharing.

Figure 10.18

Printer sharing

To connect to the printer from another Mac, open its System Preferences to the Printers pane. Click the + (plus) sign and add the printer from the dialog box that pops up, as shown in Figure 10.19.

It really is that simple!

Figure 10.19

Add Printer dialog box

Setting Up MobileMe

In this section, you learn about MobileMe, Apple's file-sharing and synchronizing service. It allows you to synchronize your calendar, contacts, and e-mails across several different computers, as well as an iPhone or iPod Touch. You can get a free trial, use it for 60 days, and then decide whether you want to pay for it or not.

If your network is not yet set up and operating, skip ahead to the next section. Otherwise, you can set up your account from your Windows computer. Follow these steps:

1. **Use your Web browser to go to** `http://me.com` **and sign up for a free trial.**

Figure 10.20 shows the signup screen.

Figure 10.20

MobileMe signup screen

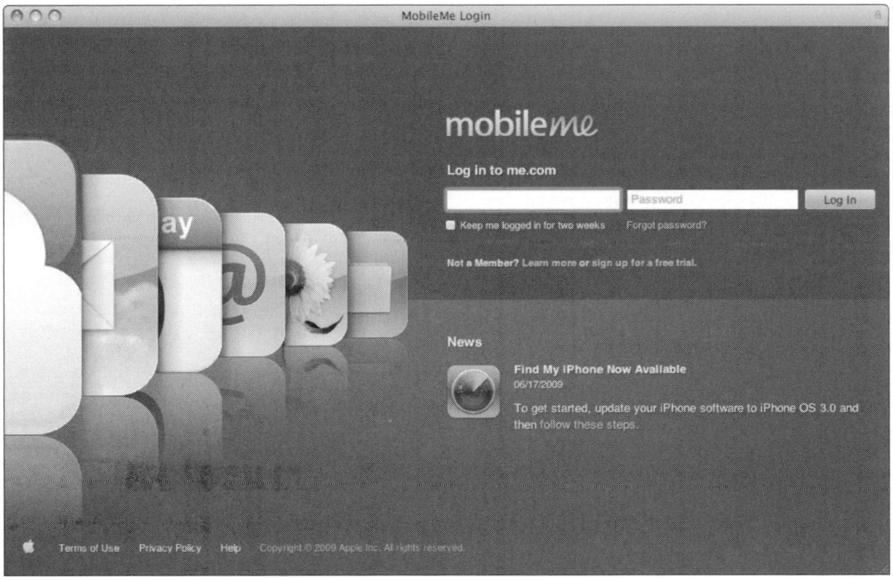

2. **After you are signed up, open System Preferences and click MobileMe.**

Figure 10.21 shows the pane for connecting to MobileMe on your computer.

3. **Log into your account by providing your username and password.**

Your MobileMe status appears in the pane, as shown in Figure 10.22.

Figure 10.21

MobileMe installer pane

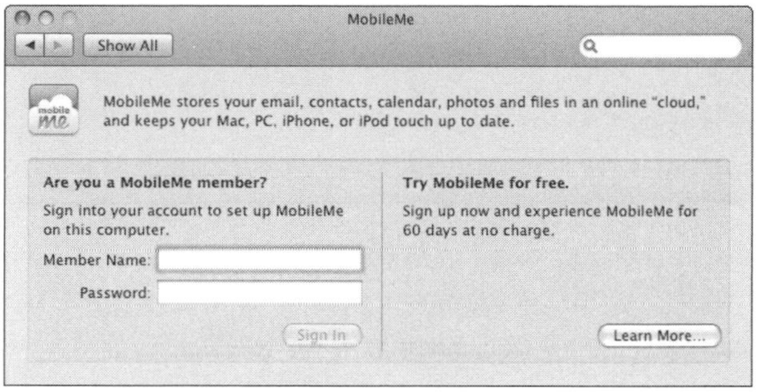

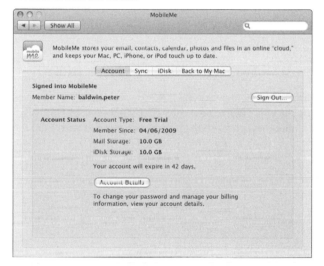

Figure 10.22

MobileMe account details

Synchronizing with MobileMe

On the next pane is the MobileMe synchronization page, shown in Figure 10.23.

You can choose to sync automatically or manually, and you can choose exactly what you want to synchronize. Place a check in each box for the items you want to sync and how often, choosing from hourly, daily, weekly, or manually.

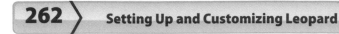

Figure 10.23

MobileMe synchronization frequency

Using your iDisk

Part of your subscription to MobileMe covers a 10GB backup disk. This is stored centrally on Apple's computers, but you can download a copy of it to all your computers. You can then access your files from your computer, and they are synchronized with MobileMe. In this way, you can keep the same files on all your computers in sync. This pane is shown in Figure 10.24.

Figure 10.24

iDisk properties pane

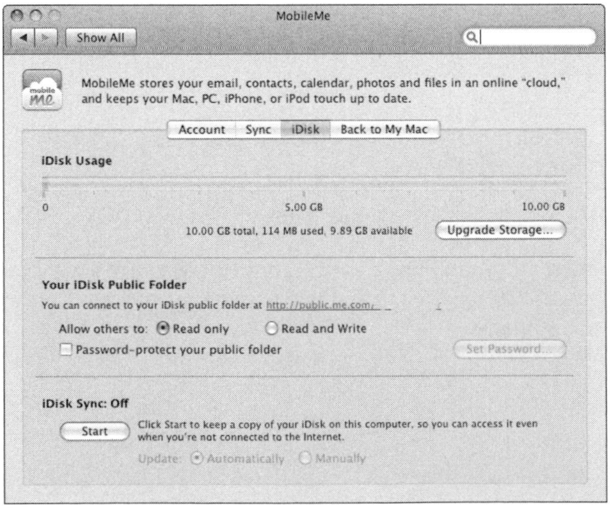

When you connect to your iDisk, a new disk icon appears on your desktop, as shown in Figure 10.25.

Figure 10.25

iDisk desktop
icon

You edit files in your iDisk and then synchronize them with your MobileMe account. You can then access them from another computer (or iPhone or iPod Touch) when you synchronize that computer.

Using the Back to My Mac feature

Back to My Mac is a very neat feature that allows you to easily connect from another Mac (or Hackintosh!) anywhere in the world to your Mac at home, provided it is switched on, of course!

Connecting Back to My Mac from another Mac

If you have an Apple modem, which is unlikely, given that you're reading this book, setting it up is apparently pretty simple. If you don't have an Apple modem, you may have to do a bit more work, and your modem must be capable of being set up that way.

My modem-router is a Netcomm NB6Plus4W, and it worked fine straight away. On the Back to My Mac pane of MobileMe in System Preferences, click Start. If your modem is working well, you should see the display in Figure 10.26.

On the other Mac (or Hackintosh), you should see an entry in the sidebar allowing you to connect to your remote. In my case, I named my desktop computer PB's iMac and then connected to it from my Dell Mini 9. Figure 10.27 shows the folders on my desktop, with the screen shot taken from the Dell Mini 9.

Of course, from the desktop I also can connect to the netbook. And, with a little bit of work, I can connect to either from my Windows computer, although my desktop computer does double duty: sometimes it runs Vista, sometimes Leopard.

Figure 10.26

Back to My Mac is turned on.

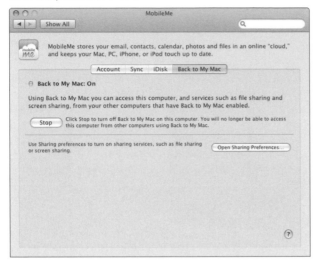

Figure 10.27

Connecting to my desktop Hackintosh from the netbook Hackintosh

Just for fun, I also turned on screen sharing and took a screen shot from my Dell Mini 9, showing the desktop of my desktop computer. This is shown in Figure 10.28.

Figure 10.28

Screen sharing from netbook to desktop computer

Connecting Back to My Mac from Windows

If you want to set up Back to My Mac on your Windows computer, read this online article:
http://lifehacker.com/366940/back-to-my-mac-from-a-pc.

If your modem doesn't work straight away, you need to set up Port Forwarding on it. Consult the manual for your router for Port Forwarding.

On my router, the setup for Port Forwarding is under Advanced. Figure 10.29 shows the screen on my router after I set up Port Forwarding.

First, you need to know the IP address of your computer. This is shown on the System Preferences Network pane.

You need to set up TCP forwarding on port 443 and UDP forwarding on port 4500.

Figure 10.29

Port Forwarding setup

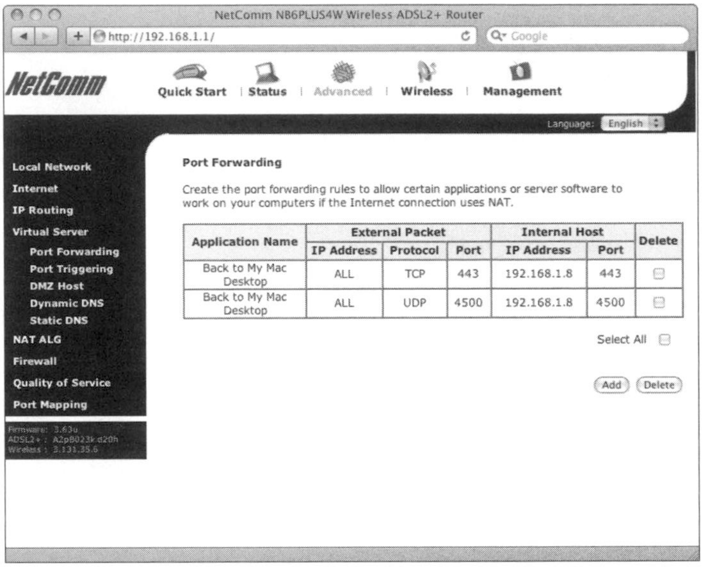

Setting Up QuickTime

By comparison with setting up networking, setting up QuickTime is a dream! In this section, you learn about some of the options available and how to set them. Figure 10.30 shows the first pane in QuickTime System Preferences.

When you first open the QuickTime settings panel, you are invited to buy QuickTime Pro. The Pro version adds some features that are not in the standard, free version. These features include the ability to convert formats and to capture video from webcams and other things with both audio and video.

Go ahead and buy it if you choose, but I suggest you look around for other applications first.

On other panes, you can configure how you want your browser to handle QuickTime movies and updating with other CODECs. CODEC means COmpress-DECompress. It is how information in audio and video is compressed for delivery and then decompressed by the player. Figure 10.31 shows the pane that takes you to Apple's Web site to update your CODECs.

QuickTime as a standard cannot play many different formats, such as DivX, XVid, and .wmv files. If it tries to play a file it can't decompress, it asks you to install the new CODEC. Unfortunately, it doesn't offer much guidance as to which CODEC is required.

Figure 10.30

QuickTime settings

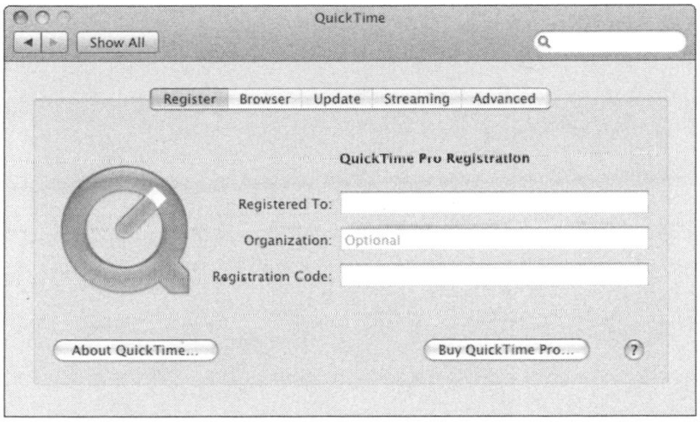

My advice is to install Perian (http://perian.org/). Its creators describe it as the Swiss Army knife for QuickTime. After you install it, QuickTime plays just about everything you try to load. I haven't found anything yet that it can't decode.

On the Streaming tab, you can control how long QuickTime waits until it starts playing streamed media. Normally, you buffer media coming from the Internet so that if a packet of the media is delayed, the file can keep playing from the buffer and the buffer fills up again when packets start flowing in again.

You can control the size of the buffer with the slider, as shown in Figure 10.32.

Figure 10.31

Install new CODECs

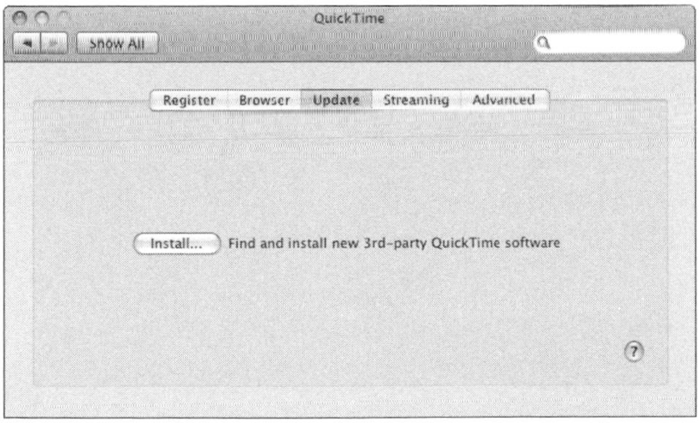

On the Advanced pane are some options for handling different media types, all of which I leave alone!

Figure 10.32

Buffer size control

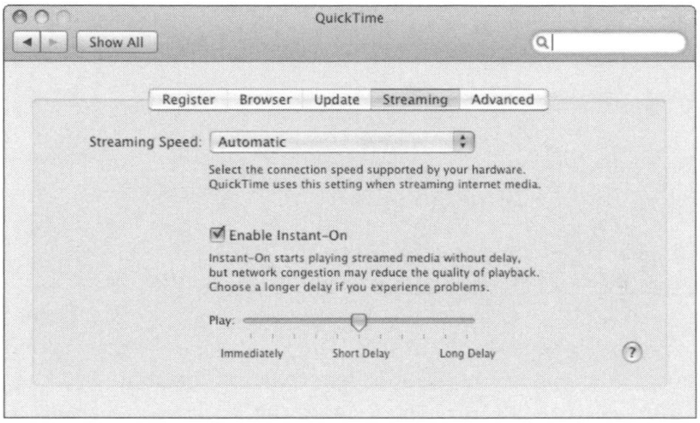

Summary

If you went through everything in this chapter, you configured all the really hard stuff, and you have a Hackintosh that is almost completely set up. Hopefully, your choice of hardware was such that it was possible to get everything working.

You set up your networking and sharing options so that you can connect to the Internet and share files with other computers. You should also now be able to share your printer with other computers.

If you signed up for a MobileMe account, you learned how to synchronize bookmarks, contacts, and other items between your computers and an iPhone or iPod Touch, if you have one. You learned how to connect to another computer using Back to My Mac.

11

Setting Up System Preferences

You're on the home straight toward getting your Hackintosh set up completely, the way you want it. If you've been working through the book chapter by chapter, you have set up the most difficult preferences. From now on, it's mostly about housekeeping.

In this chapter, you find how to set up accounts for other users, set the date and time, and explore differences in the way time is handled between Windows and Leopard and the headaches it can cause.

This chapter helps you set up a new account and apply parental controls so you can control what your children do with the computer. You also set up Time Machine and the assistive technology built in to Leopard.

Setting Up User Accounts

One big difference between Leopard and Windows 7 and Vista is how user accounts are handled. Vista and Windows 7 force you to create a user account with password and force you to log in to an account when the system boots. As you've already seen, Leopard forces you to create an account but then allows you to boot directly into that account.

I don't recommend doing that for two reasons. One is that anyone who steals your computer can go straight to your files without knowing your login or password. The other is that the default account is an administrator account and has complete control over everything on your computer.

In this section, you create a new account with normal user permissions and then set Leopard not to log in automatically.

Setting login options for your account

Follow these steps to set your login options:

1. **Open System Preferences, and select Accounts.**

   Figure 11.1 shows the greeting screen for Accounts.

Figure 11.1

Accounts main screen

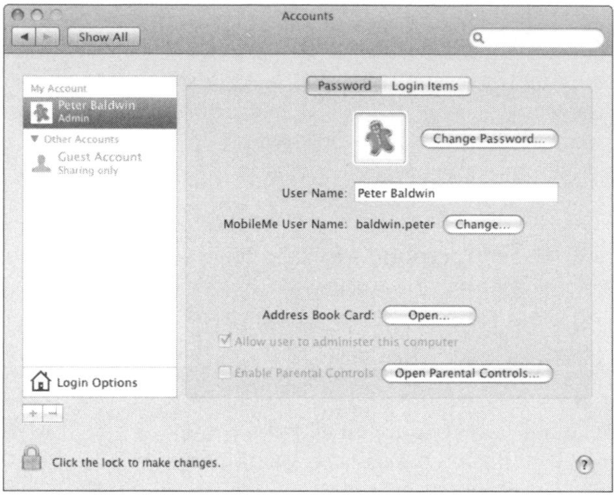

2. **Click the lock icon, and enter your account password in the pop-up window.**

3. **Click the Login Options button at the bottom of the left panel.**

   This opens a new dialog box, as shown in Figure 11.2.

Figure 11.2

Login options dialog box

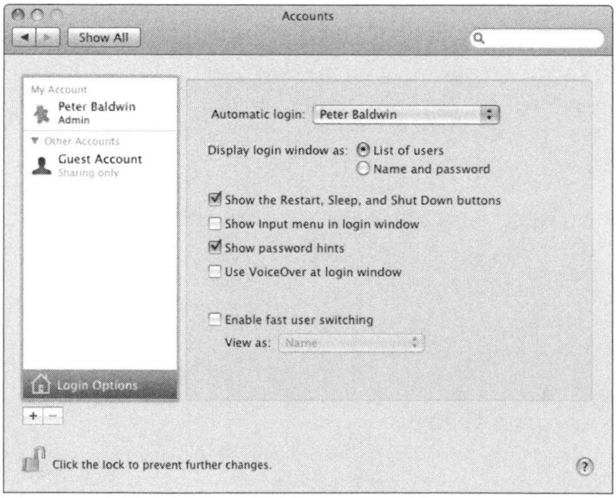

Table 11.1 explains what each option on the screen does.

Table 11.1 Login Options

Option	Meaning
Automatic login	Each time you start the computer, it asks for a username and password before letting you do anything.
Display login window as list of users	This lists the name of each user. Click one to allow password entry.
Display login windows as name and password	This does not display any usernames. It requires you to know a username and password.
Show Restart, Sleep and Shut Down buttons	This one's pretty obvious!
Show Input menu in login window	This allows you to choose a different language setting at the time of logging in.
Show password hints	Again, this one's pretty obvious.
Use VoiceOver at login window	This speaks prompts at the user login. VoiceOver is explained later in this chapter.
Enable fast user switching	This allows you to switch users without having to log in; your login name appears on the right side of the menu bar.

Whether to use the other language input window and whether to use VoiceOver are personal choices depending on the needs of other users of your computer.

Disabling the Restart and other buttons seems a little pointless, because the unauthorized user can still turn the power off.

On my desktop computer, VoiceOver does not work at the login window, although it works on all other occasions. It does work on my Dell Mini 9.

TIP
For greatest security, disable automatic login, display the login windows as name and password, and don't show password hints.

Creating a new account

In this section, you create a new account with standard user permissions and with parental controls implemented. Follow these steps:

1. **Open System Preferences and the Users panel.**

2. **Click the lock, and enter your password in the box.**

3. **Click the + (plus) sign below the Login Options button.**

4. **Select Managed with Parental Controls as the type of account.**

5. **Enter a name, password, and password hint for the account.**

    Obviously, you would not type the same password hint as I have, as shown in Figure 11.3.

Figure 11.3

Creating a managed account

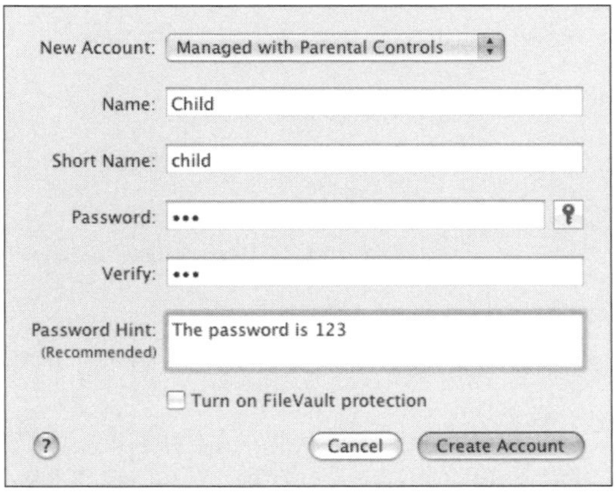

6. **Click Create.**

If automatic login is still turned on, Leopard asks whether you want to leave automatic login switched on. Needless to say, you don't want to leave it on if you have gone to the trouble of creating a new user account.

Setting Finder options

Figure 11.4 shows the options available to manage the new account.

The Use Simple Finder option is suitable only for inexperienced users (not necessarily young!). By clicking the Only allow selected applications option, you can control exactly what applications the managed user can use.

Controlling content

On the second panel, you control the type of content the managed user can access, as shown in Figure 11.5.

Figure 11.4

Managed account options

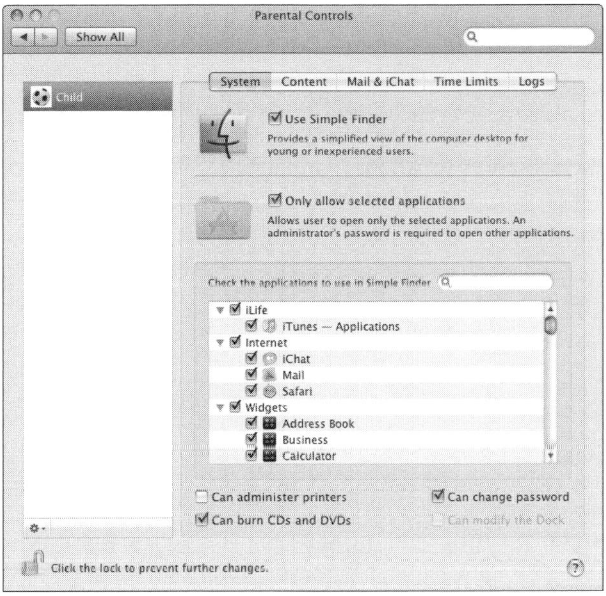

Figure 11.5

Content management

Controlling mail and chat

On the Mail and iChat pane, you can list the addresses the user can contact either through mail or chatting.

Adding time limits

One very useful feature is being able to set time limits on when the user can use the computer,

Of course, you need to keep track of school vacations manually.

Gathering logs of user activity

As a concerned parent, you can see exactly what your child has been doing by viewing the logs on the Logs panel. If you find the user has visited sites you think are inappropriate, you can add restrictions that prevent it from happening again.

Using fast user switching

Fast user switching means that you don't have to log out of your account to log into another account. Your open applications keep running in the background. Here's how to switch users:

1. **Check the box for Enable fast user switching.**

   Note that your name now appears on the menu bar.

2. **Click your name.**

   A new menu appears, as shown in Figure 11.6.

   Figure 11.6

   Fast user switching menu

3. **Click Login Window…**

   Your screen turns into a box that rotates and brings you the login window. To return to where you were, type your username and password. Or enter another username and password.

Setting login items

Each time you log in, Leopard can automatically start applications for you that may run in the background. By default, Leopard starts a couple of applications, but you can add any others you like. For example, you may want to open Mail and Safari each time you log in. You can add them to the list of login items.

1. **Open System Preferences, and click Accounts.**

2. **Click Login Items to see the applications that start up each time you log in.**

   Figure 11.7 shows the applications that start automatically when I log in.

   Figure 11.7

   Login items

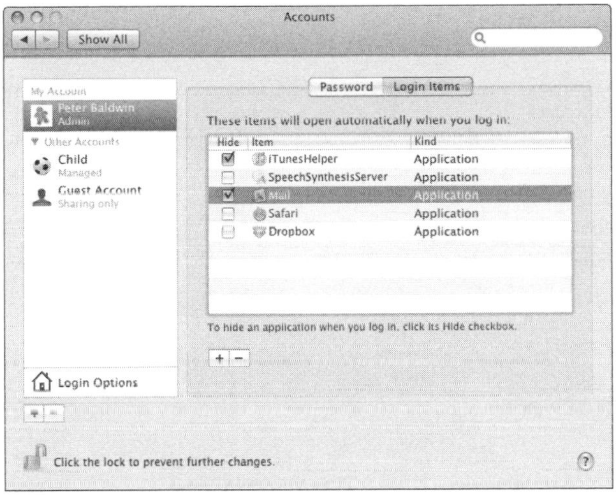

3. **Click the + (plus) sign, and navigate to your applications folder.**

4. **Select Mail, and click Add.**

5. **Click + (plus) again, select Safari, and then select Add.**

If you decide you no longer want an application to start automatically, simply highlight it in the list and click the – (minus) button.

Use the check box beside each login item to hide it when you login. My own preference is to open Mail but leave it hidden when I log in. Because I'm always using the Web for research, I always open Safari.

Setting Up Date and Time

If you are dual booting Leopard and Windows, keeping the time and date synchronized between the two operating systems can be a big issue. Be sure to work through the second part of this section.

Setting Date and Time is simply a matter of opening System Preferences and going to the Date and Time panel. When you installed Leopard, you set the time and date. After you connected to the Internet, Leopard located your nearest time server (in my case, Apple Asia) and set the date and time automatically.

If you need to change the date or time for any reason, uncheck the box for Set date & time automatically. You then can change the date or time. This is shown in Figure 11.8.

Figure 11.8

Setting the date and time

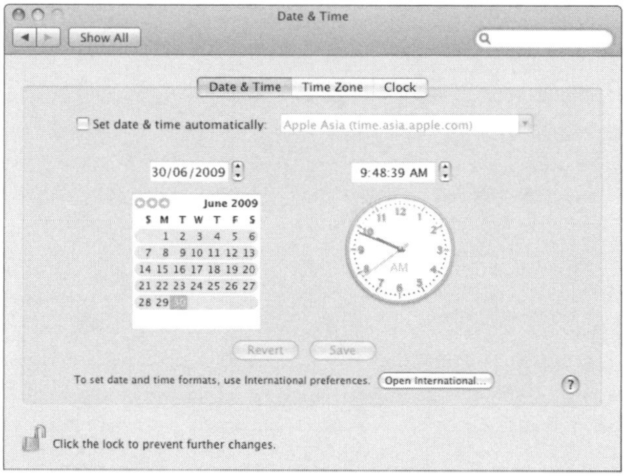

Setting your time zone

When you installed Leopard, you set your time zone, and you have no need to change it for a desktop. If your Hackintosh is a laptop or netbook, you need to change the time zone as you travel.

To change it, simply click the world map somewhere near where you are located and choose the Closest City from the drop-down box. This is shown in Figure 11.9.

In my case, the nearest city to me is Sydney, which is where I live. Snow Leopard can use geo-data about your location to set your time zone automatically.

Figure 11.9

Closest city drop-down box

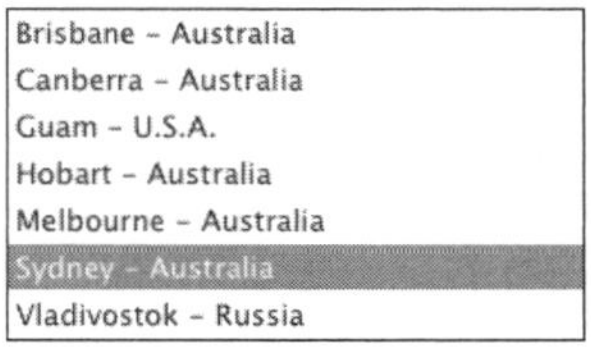

Brisbane – Australia
Canberra – Australia
Guam – U.S.A.
Hobart – Australia
Melbourne – Australia
Sydney – Australia
Vladivostok – Russia

Setting clock options

Leopard lets you set a number of options for how you use the clock. These are shown in Figure 11.10a.

Not everyone likes it, but I like Leopard to announce the time to me every half hour. I find Alex's synthesized voice soothing. Maybe I'm just weird! You can set how fast "he" speaks and the volume so he doesn't startle you. These options are shown in Figure 11.10b.

Figure 11.10

Clock options (a); customizing Leopard's time announcements (b)

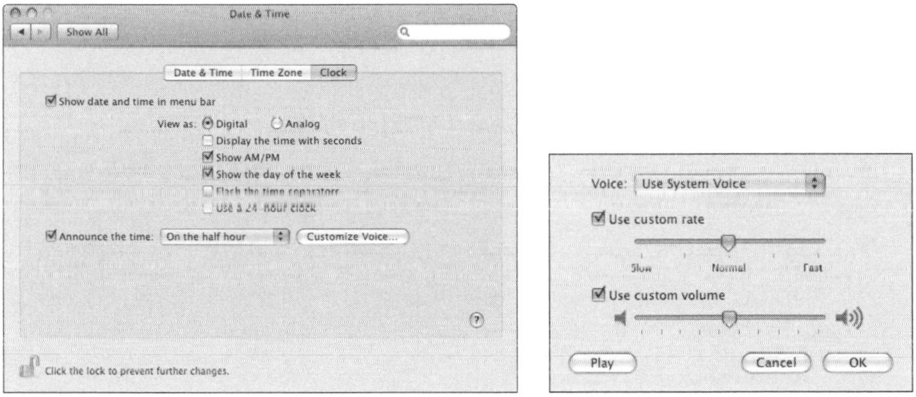

a   b

Synchronizing time with Windows

Windows uses your local time as the base for its timekeeping; Leopard (and, incidentally, every other operating system) uses Greenwich Mean Time (GMT) as the base for its timekeeping. What this means is that, after running Leopard and returning to your Windows system, the time is out of sync by the difference between your local time and Greenwich Mean Time.

Sydney, Australia, is 10 hours ahead of GMT, except during summer, when we are 11 hours ahead.

When I shut Leopard down and restart in Windows Vista or 7, the time is 10 hours (or 11 hours in summer) behind local time in Sydney. It's a pain to have to remember to change the time immediately on starting Windows.

You might think that it really doesn't matter if you set your time zone to somewhere that removes the difference between the two systems, but if you then go to a different time zone, you once again have the incorrect time. More importantly, in an international setting, time zone differences are important when people are located in two different time zones.

If you search the Internet, you will find several purported fixes for this, mostly involving changing the Windows Registry. Although they may work in Windows XP and they appear to work for a time in Windows 7 and Vista, in fact they are not permanent fixes.

I have found that the only reliable fix is that created by Zephyroth, which is available at `www.hackint0sh.org/forum/f184/68045.htm`. I created a TinyURL at `http://tinyurl.com/ktvylg`.

Follow these steps to fix this time discrepancy:

1. **Download the package.**

   Unfortunately the standard unarchive utility in Leopard can't open it, so you need to download another application: The Unarchiver, available for download on the Apple site at `www.apple.com/downloads/macosx/system_disk_utilities/theunarchiver.html`.

2. **Download The Unarchiver from the Apple site.**

3. **Open your Downloads folder in Finder, and drag The Unarchiver to your Applications folder.**

4. **Right-click the Zephyroth package, and select The Unarchiver to open it.**

   Because the file is so small, it unarchives almost instantly and creates a new package called Localtime-Toggle.pkg.

5. **Double-click the package.**

   This opens Leopard's Installer to install the package.

That's all there is to it. Now, when you shut down Leopard, your time is set back to your Windows time. No more setting the time when you start Windows.

Running Software Update

Software Update is a service similar to Windows Update: It updates the software on your computer as new software modifications become available. In this section, you use Software Update to update your Leopard installation.

In my experience, Software Update poses no problems if you installed the retail version of Leopard. My desktop and netbook both have retail installs, and Software Update has never caused me a problem. Follow these steps to get it set up:

1. **Open System Preferences, and select Software Update.**

   As you can see in Figure 11.11, I leave Check for updates set to Weekly, and I check the option to Download important updates automatically.

Figure 11.11

Software Update scheduled check

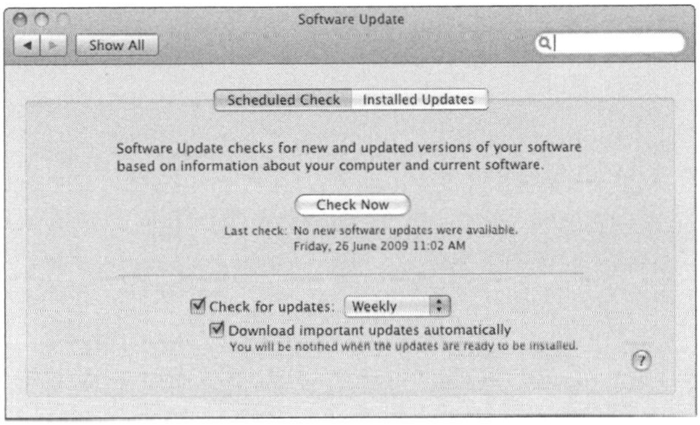

2. **Set your frequency of checking to what you require.**

To see the updates that have been added to your system, click the Installed Updates tab. Figure 11.12 shows the updates that have been installed to my Dell Mini 9.

Figure 11.12

Installed updates

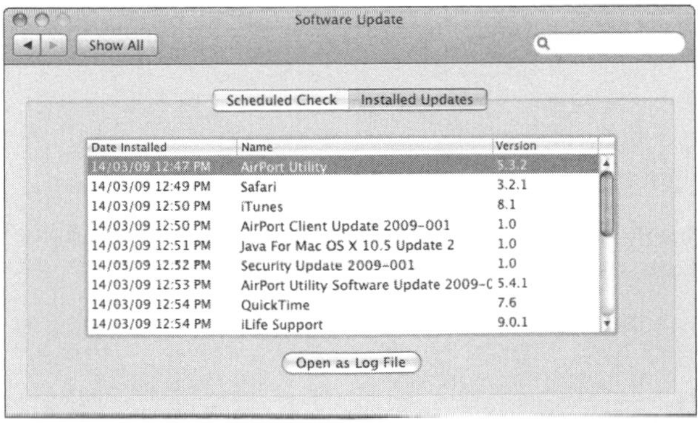

Setting Up Speech

Apple has done a huge amount of work on assistive technology in Leopard, from voice synthesis, voice recognition, magnified text, and keyboard assistance. You explore the other facets of the technology in the last section of this chapter. In this section, you look at speech recognition and speech synthesis.

Setting up Speech Recognition

To set up speech recognition, you obviously need a microphone. Many webcams have built-in microphones, and Leopard can use them. Follow these steps to work with speech recognition:

1. **Open System Preferences, and select Speech Recognition, as shown in Figure 11.13.**

Figure 11.13

Speech Recognition setup screen

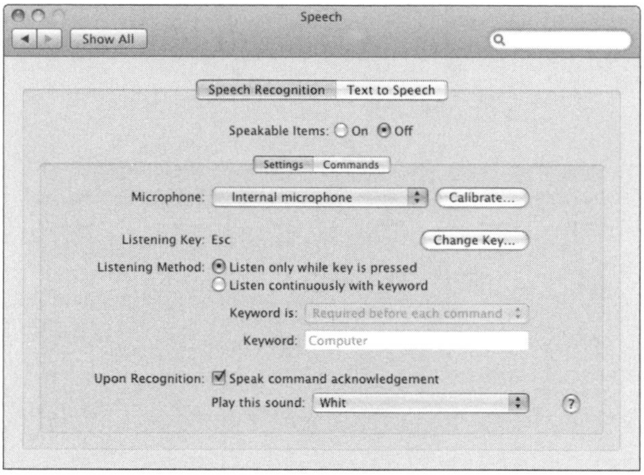

2. **Select your microphone—most likely Internal microphone—from the drop-down box.**

3. **Click Calibrate....**

   This brings up the screen shown in Figure 11.14a.

4. **Speak into the microphone, and move the slider until the level is mostly in the green section and going to the red at times.**

5. **Say each of the phrases on the left.**

   When each phrase is recognized, the words flash.

6. **Keep adjusting the volume slider until each phrase is recognized.**

7. **Click Speakable Items On.**

A new icon appears on your desktop—the speech recognition symbol, as shown in Figure 11.14b.

Figure 11.14

The microphone calibration screen (a); Speech Recognition On symbol (b)

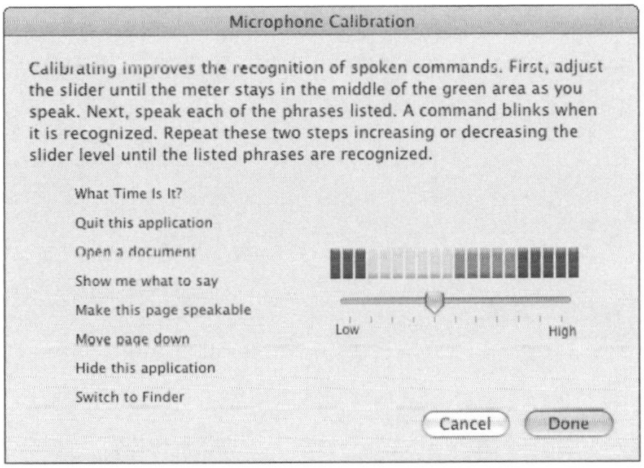

a

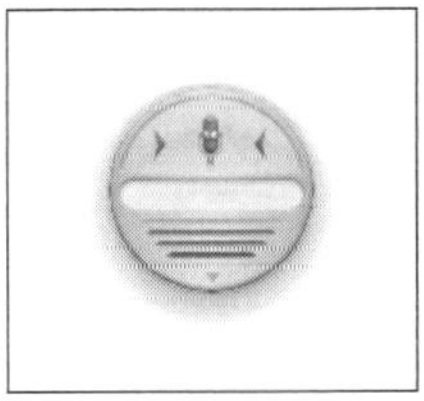

b

8. **Put a check in the Speak command acknowledgment check box.**

9. **Click Commands to find the commands that Leopard recognizes.**

10. **Click Open Speakable Items Folder.**

This lists all the commands that Leopard understands, as shown in Figure 11.15.

Try out some of the commands by speaking them and seeing how accurate Leopard is. Remember to press the ESC key to make Leopard start listening.

My experience is that, after I have trained the speech recognition engine, it understands my commands about 90 percent of the time.

Remember that speech recognition is designed to be an assistive technology to aid people with limited motor skills. I can't imagine what it would be like in an office with 30 people speaking commands into their computers.

Figure 11.15

Speakable commands

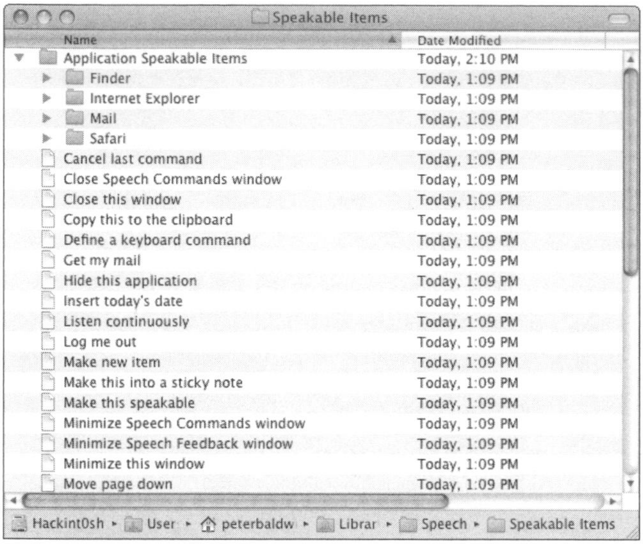

Exploring Text to Speech

Most people either love or hate Leopard's text-to-speech capabilities. I'm somewhere in the middle. I have it set tell me the time every 30 minutes and when alerts are displayed, which I find useful when I'm not sitting at the computer.

1. Open System Preferences, and then open Text to Speech.

This opens the panel as shown in Figure 11.16.

2. Click Set Alert Options....

This opens the sheet shown in Figure 11.17a.

By default, Leopard uses the name of the application as the alert, but you can change that.

3. Click the drop-down box for Application name.

You then set Leopard to use a phrase from the standard list either using the next one or one chosen at random. If you don't like any of the standard phrases, you can enter your own.

4. Select Edit Phrase List....

A new window pops up, as shown in Figure 11.17b.

Figure 11.16

Text to Speech preferences

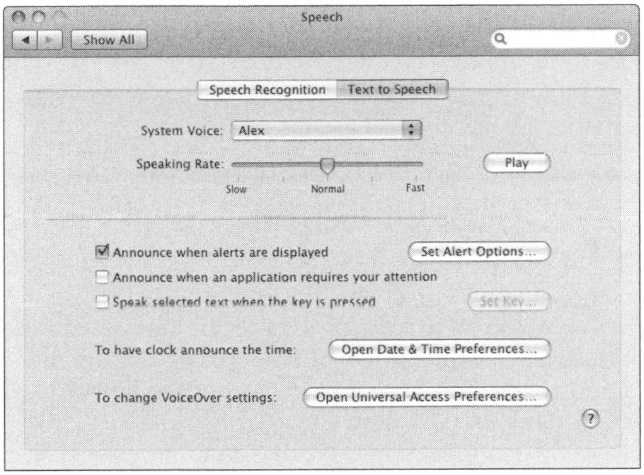

Figure 11.17

Alert options sheet (a); Alerts phrase list (b)

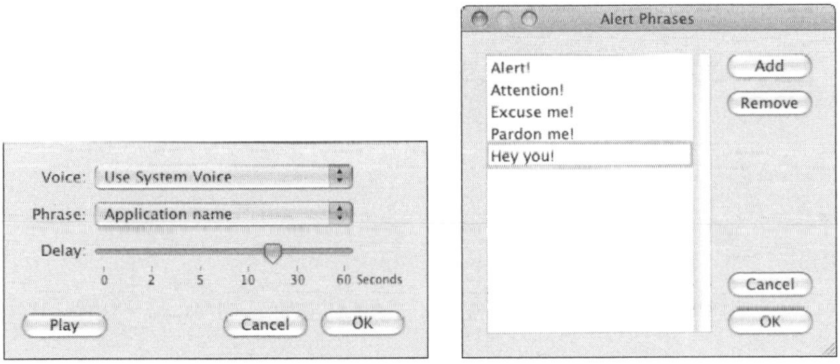

a   b

5. **Click Add, and enter your new phrase in the box.**

You may prefer a phrase a little less imperative than what I've added; but it's your choice!

6. **Set the delay before Leopard alerts you.**

Exploring Leopard's voices

Leopard comes with a range of voices: male, female, and "novelty," according to Apple's description. Most of them are understandable, barely, but Alex sounds very much like a real person. Unfortunately, many installations leave Alex out because he takes up around 750MB on the install disk.

If you have the retail version, you have Alex installed.

Setting Up Startup Disk

For your Hackintosh, you are not likely to have any choice but the disk you started. When using a real Macintosh connected to a network, you may have options to start your computer from a networked Mac. Even if you are connected to a network, your Hackintosh can be guaranteed not to start from a disk that starts a regular Mac.

Figure 11.18 shows the setup screen for Startup Disk.

Figure 11.18

Startup Disk setup

One option you may want to explore is using your computer as a target disk for another computer. You need a FireWire port on each computer. After they're connected in this way, your computer's hard disk becomes available for the other computer.

Setting Up Time Machine

As explained in Chapter 8, Time Machine is a brilliant backup system. Basically, after it's set up, you can forget about it, secure in the knowledge that all your files are being backed up. If you accidentally erase a file, you can get it back using Time Machine.

In this section, you set up Time Machine and use it to recover a deleted file.

Setting up a separate hard disk

As soon as you plug a hard disk into a fresh installation of Leopard, it asks if you want to use it as a Time Machine backup. This is shown in Figure 11.19.

Figure 11.19

Time Machine backup disk

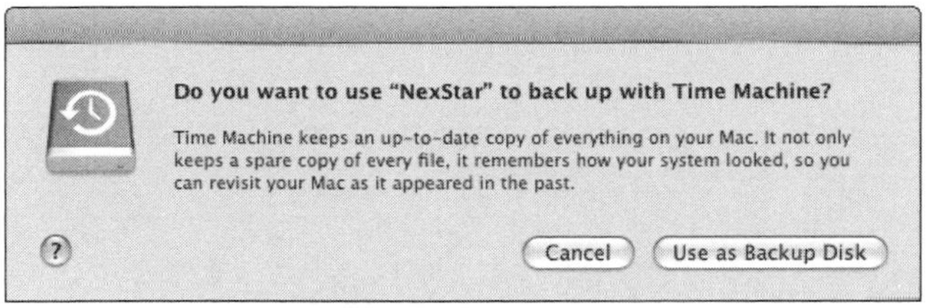

Do you want to use "NexStar" to back up with Time Machine?

Time Machine keeps an up-to-date copy of everything on your Mac. It not only keeps a spare copy of every file, it remembers how your system looked, so you can revisit your Mac as it appeared in the past.

(Cancel) (Use as Backup Disk)

The disk does not have to be empty, but it does have to be formatted for HFS+. If it is not formatted for HFS+, Leopard offers to format it for you. After it is set up, you need to do very little.

You can prevent Leopard from backing up some files and folders. You might use this if you have large files that change frequently. One example is virtual machines.

If you are using Parallels or VMWare, each time you exit the application, a new file is written to the disk. Because these files are often 1 to 2GB in size, backing up a different one each hour could be a waste of space, particularly because both allow you to save a snapshot of the state of the system.

To exclude files or folders, click Options on the Time Machine panel. A sheet appears that allows you to add files or folder to be excluded from backup. This is shown in Figure 11.20.

Figure 11.20

Files or folders to exclude from Time Machine

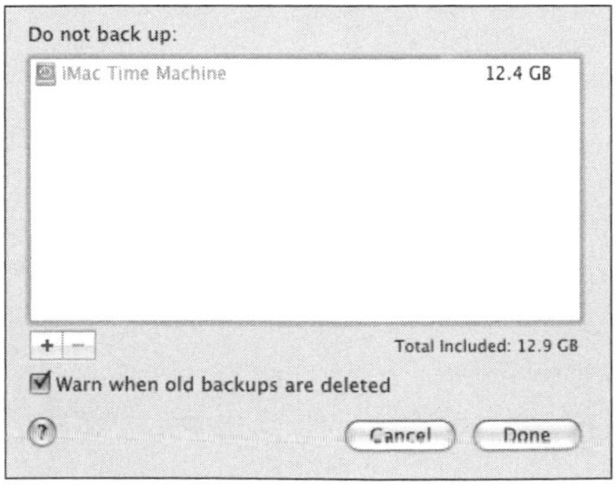

Do not back up:

iMac Time Machine   12.4 GB

+ −   Total Included: 12.9 GB

☑ Warn when old backups are deleted

(Cancel) (Done)

Click the + (plus) sign and use the Finder window to search for the files or folders.

Recovering a file using Time Machine

C A U T I O N

If your Leopard installation does not have Quartz Extreme/Core Image working, you can't recover files this way. If you have a translucent menu bar, QE/CI is working.

Time Machine has one of the coolest interfaces in Macland. When you click the Time Machine Dock icon, the whole screen slides down, and you see into the vast reaches of space! Well, not quite. Figure 11.21 shows the screen as it's sliding down.

Figure 11.21

Entering Time Machine

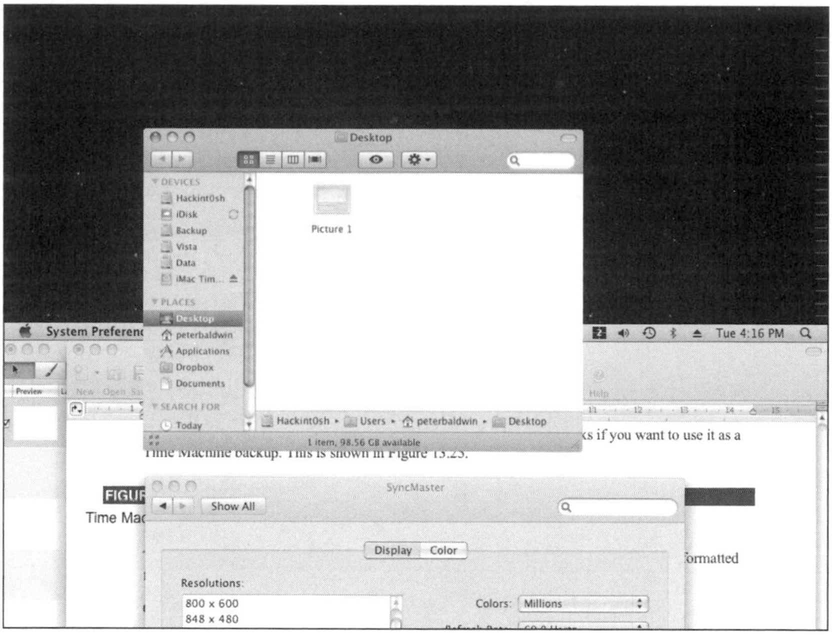

To see how to recover files using Time Machine, we do something completely artificial here, but the principles apply regardless. Follow these steps:

1. **Open TextEdit, and create a new file.**

2. **Enter the text This is a test of Time Machine.**

3. **Save the file to your desktop as Lazarus.**

4. **Force Time Machine to do a backup by clicking the icon in the menu bar and selecting Back Up Now.**

   Time Machine should only take a few seconds to do the backup.

5. **When the backup is complete, delete the file from your desktop and empty the Trash.**

6. **Select Enter Time Machine from the menu bar icon.**

7. **When you are in Time Machine, click the Finder window behind the one on top.**

   You should see the file you just deleted.

8. **Highlight the file, and click Restore on the bottom right of the Time Machine display.**

9. **Exit Time Machine.**

   Lo and behold, your file is restored to the desktop.

Fixing the networking kernel extension setup

With a Hackintosh, sometimes Time Machine doesn't like the disk you use. Typically, it accepts the disk, but when you do your first backup, it complains with an error. I haven't had it happen with the retail version, but I have had trouble with other versions.

Fixing it is relatively easy, although it requires a bit of confidence and the ability to follow instructions! But if you've reached this point in the book, you should be fine.

CROSS-REF
See Appendix B for instructions on fixing the problem.

Setting Up Universal Access

Apple has spent lots of time setting up access for people with eyesight, hearing, and motor skill difficulties. In this section, you explore the various assistance options and suit them to your needs. Figure 11.22 shows the main panel for Universal Access.

Setting up for seeing difficulties

VoiceOver is the utility to give voice prompts for users who have sight difficulties. To open the utility, click Open VoiceOver Utility....

The options are too many to go through here. Figure 11.23 shows the main screen.

Figure 11.22

Universal Access main panel

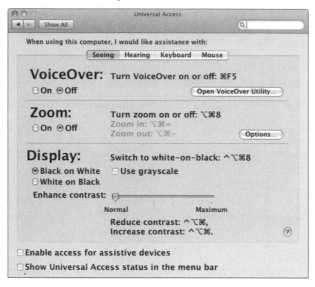

Figure 11.23

VoiceOver setup utility

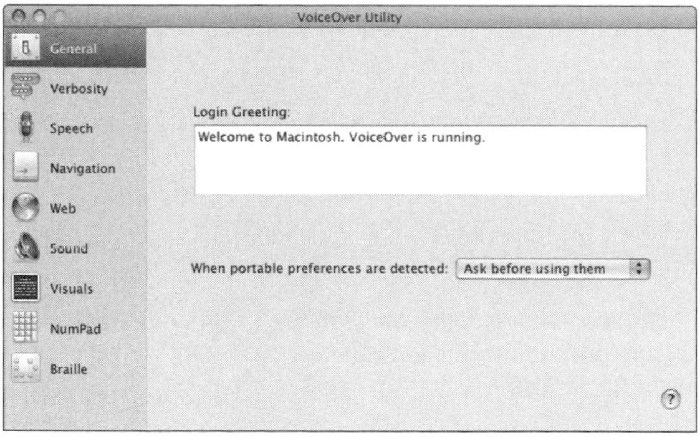

If you need to set up VoiceOver for another user, you and the user should explore the options together.

For milder sight difficulties, you may simply turn zoom on or invert the colors on the screen.

Zoom can be turned on from the keyboard using the Command-Option-8 keystroke. That is Windows key-Alt-8 on most Hackintoshes. To zoom in on the screen, use Command-Option-= (equal sign); to zoom out, use Command -Option- - (minus sign).

Setting the display to invert colors may help, as well as setting the screen to use only grayscale. You also can increase or decrease screen contrast.

One cute trick you can play the next time you go into an Apple store is to press the Control-Command-Option-8 key combination. That's Ctrl-Windows key-Alt-8 on most Hackintoshes. Try it for yourself.

Setting up for hearing difficulties

Coping with hearing difficulties is easier than coping with eyesight difficulties, so you don't need to make many adjustments for hearing impairment. The only real option is to flash the screen when an alert sound occurs. Some people prefer to turn the sounds off anyway and just use the screen flash. Try it and see if you like it.

Setting keyboard options for assistance

Sticky Keys is the major way of coping with physical disabilities related to keyboard use. The options are shown in Figure 11.24.

Figure 11.24

Assistive keyboard options

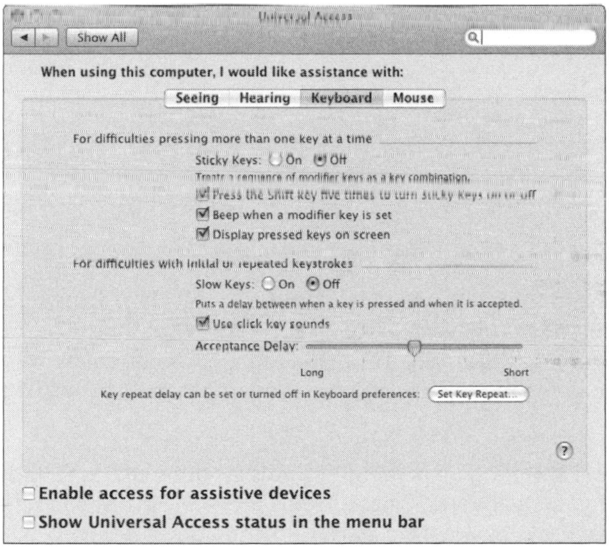

When Sticky Keys is turned on, rather than pressing a modifier key (Shift, Command, and so on) at the same time as the alphanumeric key, you can press the modifier key first, release it, and then press the alphanumeric key.

Setting mouse options for assistance

If you have a vision difficulty, you can increase the size of the mouse pointer. In addition, you can use the numeric keypad in place of the mouse. Figure 11.25 shows the options available for changing mouse behavior.

Figure 11.25

Assistive mouse options

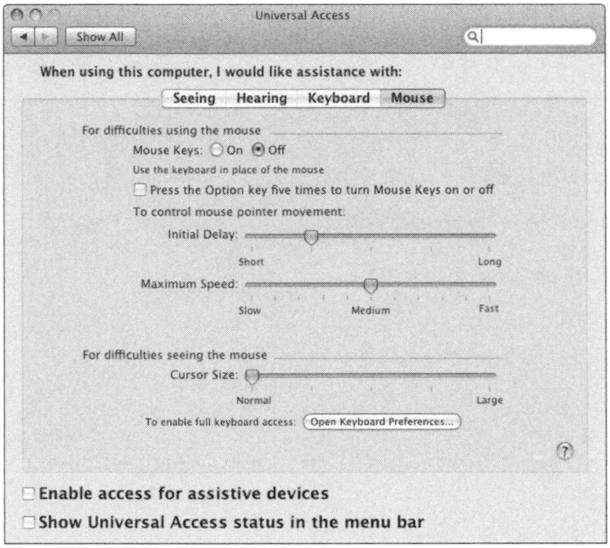

Summary

In this chapter, you completed setting up your Hackintosh the way you want it, taking into account any physical limitations you may have. You set up accounts for other users. You set up your desired date and time preferences, and added a small program to change the way time is handled in the Macintosh so no time difference exists when you return to Windows after using Leopard.

You saw how versatile Leopard is at setting up parental controls for other users. You set Leopard speech options to suit your needs and updated your software. Finally, you set up Time Machine to perform incremental backups and used assistive technology if required.

Now you are ready to start exploring the software applications that come with Leopard.

Using Your Macintosh

III

Now that you have your HackIntosh set up the way you want it, and you're up to speed on the differences between Windows and Leopard, it's time to do some real work!

With guidance, you work your way through using the six main applications that are installed with Leopard:

- Safari for browsing the Web
- Mail for managing e-mail
- Address Book for managing contacts
- iCal for managing calendars
- Preview for viewing many different types of graphics content
- iTunes for managing music collections

After learning about how to make your Windows NTFS disks writable, you then explore methods of running Windows within OS X. You install and use Parallels and VMware enabling you to use Windows, either as a fresh installation or using your existing installation.

To continue the virtualization theme, you finally install Leopard on a virtual machine in Windows.

12

Using the Main Macintosh Software

Leopard comes with a good range of basic software to handle many of the common tasks you use a computer to do, such as Web browsing, e-mailing, keeping lists of your contacts, managing your schedule, and playing music.

Of all the applications used on a computer, the Web browser is probably the most frequently used. Leopard comes with Safari, a pretty capable browser. Mail for Leopard is a basic e-mail package that allows you to send and receive messages.

Leopard's Address Book application can store all your contact details, while iCal is a quite sophisticated calendar application. Preview can view many different types of files, not just graphics files, and iTunes has become almost the default music manager, not just on Leopard, but on Windows as well, in the same way that the iPod has virtually become the only music player.

In this chapter, you explore how to set up each application to your liking and how to synchronize between other software and your faux Mac.

Using Safari

At the time of this writing, Safari is at version 4.03. If you do not have this version, you should update to the latest version using Software Update. As vulnerabilities are discovered in every application that deals with the outside world, they are updated and patched. So for your own peace of mind, be sure you are always using the latest version.

In this section, you explore the Safari Web browser and learn how to set it up to your liking.

Starting Safari for the first time

When you first start Safari, its home page is set to `http://apple.com`, as shown in Figure 12.1.

Of course, you can change your home page to any site you like.

Safari also has a default set of bookmarks when you first start. Apple has made an attempt to include the most popular sites in the bookmarks, but you can change these too.

Figure 12.1

Safari top sites screen

Safari opens with the Top Sites display. This starts out with sites chosen by Apple, but as you browse the Web, sites that you view frequently replace the defaults that Safari uses to start.

Working with bookmarks

Although Safari has a default set of bookmarks, it's highly unlikely that they will meet all your needs, so you should change them as you wish.

Adding new bookmarks

Follow these steps to add a new bookmark to the bookmarks bar:

1. **Type the URL you want to bookmark into the address bar.**

2. **Wait for Safari to navigate to the page.**

3. **Drag the URL displayed in the address bar down to the bookmarks bar.**

4. **Edit the name of the bookmark.**

   Remember that the shorter the name, the more you can fit on the bookmarks bar.

5. **Click OK.**

Deleting bookmarks

Deleting bookmarks is simply a matter of dragging the bookmark from the bar to anywhere else on the desktop. The bookmark disappears with a puff of smoke.

Editing bookmarks

You can edit bookmarks in a couple of ways. You can edit each one singly or several at once, as shown in Figure 12.2.

Edit several bookmarks at once by following these steps:

1. **Click the open book icon at the left of the bookmarks bar.**

   This shows all your bookmarks in two columns.

2. **Click the name of the bookmark to edit it, or click the address to edit that.**

3. **When you have finished, click the open book icon to return to the site you were viewing in that tab.**

Figure 12.2

Editing bookmarks

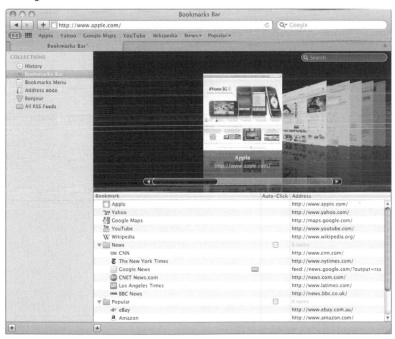

Setting Safari preferences

Like all applications, Safari has its own preferences settings. Not all of what I would call preferences are available on that menu, however; some are set using the View menu.

Setting preferences on the View menu

Settings in the View menu are not classified as preferences, but to me they are, because they change the way Safari looks on your screen. Figure 12.3a shows the preferences that can be set through the View menu.

My personal preference is to always have the bookmarks bar, toolbar, and status bar visible, except on my Dell Mini 9 because the screen is only 600 pixels tall.

Setting other preferences

Safari has many different preferences located, in the usual Leopard fashion, on a series of panes with tabs, as shown in Figure 12.3b.

Figure 12.3

View menu (a); Preferences pane for Safari (b)

a

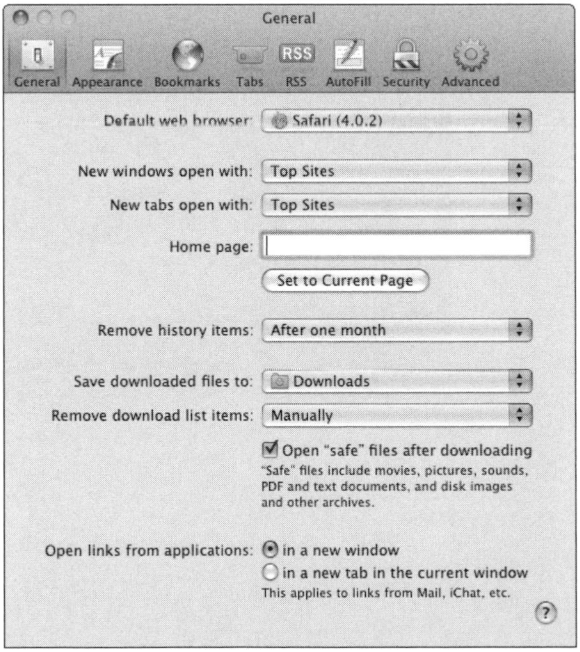

b

General preferences

On the General Preferences pane, you get to choose the page that Safari loads when it opens. By default, the Top Sites pane is loaded, but you can choose what it starts with. Figure 12.4a shows the menu to choose the default page when opening a new window or a new tab.

If you select Tabs for Bookmarks Bar, the new window opens with all your bookmarks as tabs. My own preference is to open new tabs and windows with a blank page. You choose what you want to see.

You can choose how long Safari keeps your links to visited sites and whether to automatically remove links to downloaded files. Note that this doesn't delete the actual files you've downloaded; just the links. The files stay in your download folder.

Appearance preferences

On the Appearance tab, you can choose the default fonts that Safari uses. This is almost useless nowadays because most pages you visit specify the fonts to use. This is shown in Figure 12.4b.

Figure 12.4

Preference menu for new page or tab (a); Appearance preferences (b)

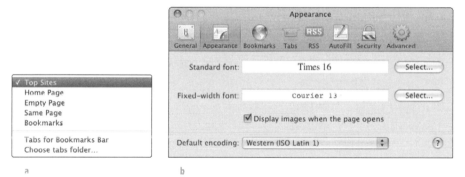

a

b

One useful switch is Display images when the page opens. If you uncheck this, Safari loads the text on the page without loading the images. If you're on a slow connection, this speeds up page loading quite dramatically. Note that after you uncheck the preference, you may need to quit Safari and restart.

Bookmarks preferences

On the Bookmarks preferences pane, you can select the bookmarks you want displayed. This is shown in Figure 12.5a.

Top Sites is the button with the 3x3 grid of square dots in the top-left corner of the title bar. Personally, I never use it, so I don't have it displayed. If you check Address Book, Safari searches through your address book and displays any links to pages it finds in there. By default, Leopard has a page in your address book for the Apple Web site. This is displayed if you check the box.

Bonjour is Apple's implementation of the zero configuration network protocol. If you install iTunes in Windows, it automatically loads Bonjour. It allows your computer to easily search the network and show any other computers on the network. My home network doesn't have any Web sites available, so I don't bother with having Bonjour on the bookmarks bar.

Tabs preferences

Figure 12.5b shows the preferences on the Tabs pane.

Figure 12.5

Bookmarks preferences (a); Tabs preferences (b)

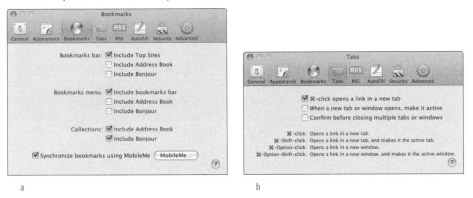

a   b

You cannot set much here. Command-click is checked to open a link in a new tab. My own preference is to use a right-click and choose Open Link in a New Tab rather than Command-click.

When you click a link, you can have it bring that link to the foreground by checking the preference for When a new tab or window opens, make it active. My preference is to have links open in background tabs (the default behavior) because it better suits my way of working. You may want to change this.

RSS preferences

RSS stands for Really Simple Syndication. Most Web sites these days have an RSS feed to bring new articles to you without you having to go to sites. This preference pane allows you to set Safari as your default RSS reader, as shown in Figure 12.6.

Figure 12.6

RSS preferences

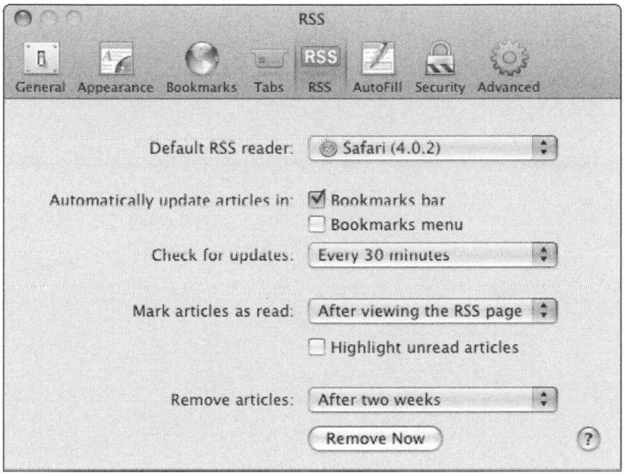

By default, the other choice you get is Mail, but I prefer to use Google Reader with Safari. If you choose to use Safari, when you visit a Web site with the RSS link in the toolbar, click it. Safari displays the newsfeed for the site.

If you want to aggregate all your newsfeeds into one tab, follow these steps:

1. **Create a new bookmark called RSS Feeds.**

2. **Visit a site whose RSS feed you want to add to your aggregated feeds.**

3. **When the site has loaded, click the RSS button at the right end of the address bar.**

4. **When the URL says "feed:// …", click and drag the URL into your new bookmark folder.**

   Note that the bookmark folder shows the number of unread items beside the label.

5. **Click the bookmark, and select the feeds you want to see.**

   This is shown in Figure 12.7.

Figure 12.7

Menu showing newsfeeds

Autofill preferences

Safari can copy data from your card in Address Book to fill in forms you find on Web sites. This is shown in Figure 12.8.

Figure 12.8

Autofill preferences pane

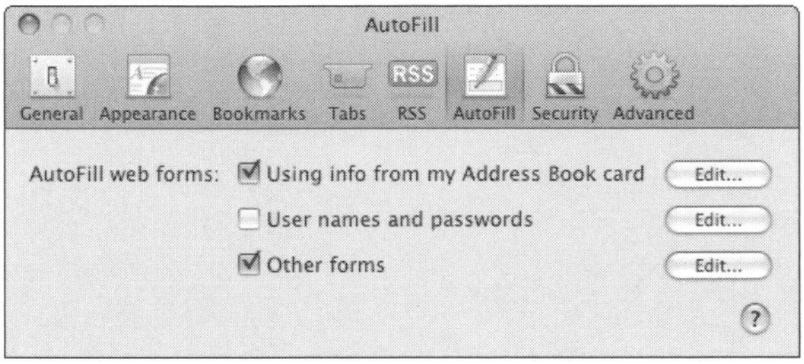

Maybe I'm a little paranoid, but I prefer to fill in that data myself, so I don't use Autofill. Choose whether or not you want to use it.

Security preferences

Security preferences allow you to make your Web surfing a little more secure. You can enable or disable plug-ins, Java, and JavaScript, and block pop-up windows. The preferences are shown in Figure 12.9.

My own view of secure browsing on the Web is that I restrict permissions as much as possible. If I need to enable something to view a particular Web site, then I enable it. For example, I disable plug-ins and Java, although I leave JavaScript on by default. Most Web sites these days require JavaScript.

I also block cookies from third-party sites. Although cookies can be very useful for Web sites that you visit, cookies from sites that serve advertisements for example can find out which sites you've visited and when you visited.

You also can disable the ability of some Web sites to create databases on your computer. I have never used a site that wants to create a database.

Finally, you can set Safari so that if you attempt to send a nonsecure form to a secure Web site, it alerts you. By the way, you can tell whether a site is secure by the lock icon in the toolbar.

Advanced preferences

Surprisingly, Safari has very few advanced preferences. This is shown in Figure 12.10.

Figure 12.9

Security preferences pane

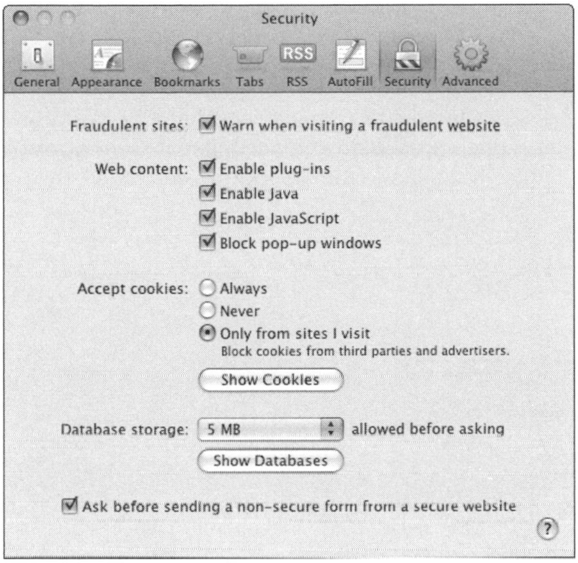

Figure 12.10

Advanced preferences pane

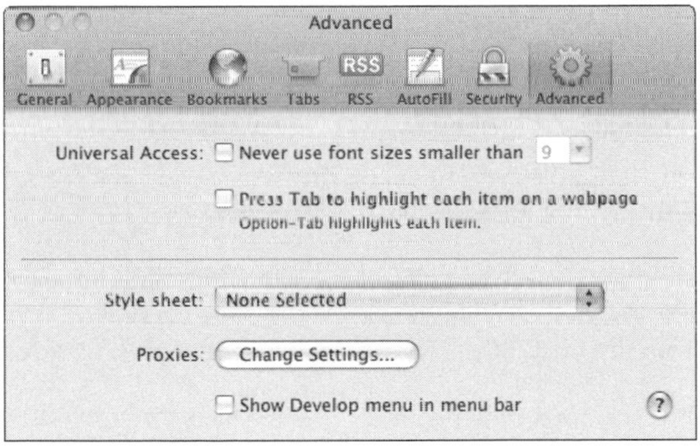

Not using font sizes smaller than a certain size and using Tab to highlight items on a Web page are intended for accessibility. For people with eyesight difficulties, small text is hard to read; for people who have difficulty moving the mouse, pressing the Tab key allows you to move from link to link on the page.

Again for visual impairment, you can set your own style sheet that might have very large fonts. This overrides the style sheet used on the Web site so it doesn't look like it was designed to look.

Surfing privately

One final option for Safari is the ability to surf privately. This means that it does not save your history of Web sites you visit, it deletes references to downloaded files, it saves no information (including passwords), and so on. Figure 12.11 shows the greeting screen for when you enable private surfing in Safari.

Figure 12.11

Private surfing in Safari

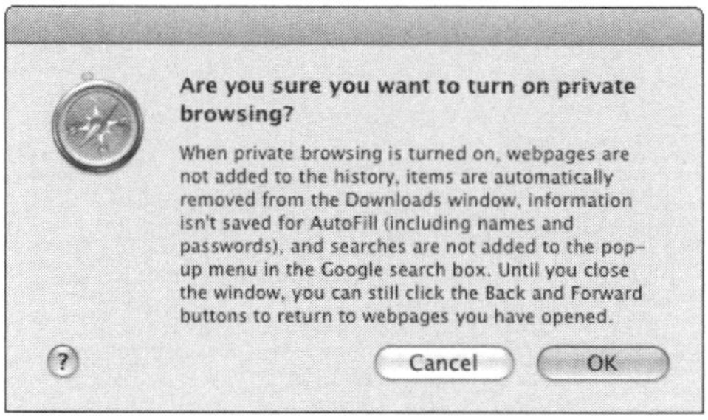

Using Mail

In this section, you learn how to set up and use Leopard Mail.

Leopard Mail is a useful e-mail client. It enables you to set up and use several different accounts. It can use either POP (Post Office Protocol) or IMAP (Internet Message Access Protocol).

POP is the oldest protocol and uses offline mail storage. Every so often, the mail client connects to the post office server and downloads any new mail. All processing is done on the local computer, and generally the mail is deleted from the post office server after it has been downloaded.

IMAP, on the other hand, is used in a pseudo online fashion where mail is downloaded from the server to the client but is not deleted on the server, so it can be accessed from a different computer. This means that if you access your mail from your computer at home and then access it from your computer at work, you see the same mailbox. Mail stays there until you explicitly delete it.

Most ISPs offer POP mailboxes for free. Many also offer IMAP, but for an extra fee. Unless you really must access your mail from several different computers, you probably don't need to pay extra for it.

Linking to your e-mail provider

Before you can start doing anything with Mail, you must have an account set up. If you have a POP e-mail account with your ISP, you probably should set up a new mail account with a Web-based server. If you use your POP account in both Windows and Leopard, you need to be sure that you don't delete the mail from the server when you retrieve it into each mail client.

In this example, I choose Google mail because you can easily set up an IMAP account.

To set up your account with Mail, carry out the following steps:

1. **Use Safari to go to gmail.com.**

2. **Click Create an account, and follow the prompts to create a new account.**

   Figure 12.12 shows the new e-mail account set up in Gmail.

   Figure 12.12

   New account in Gmail

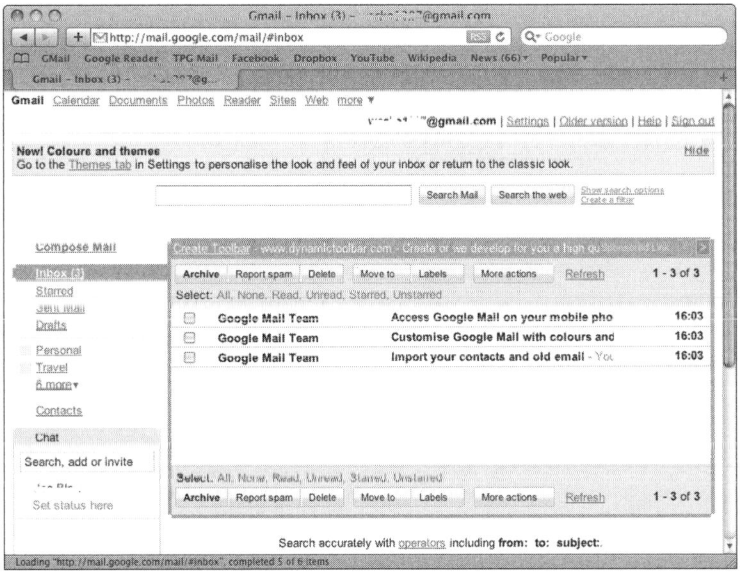

3. **After you have created the account, start Leopard Mail.**

4. **Select Preferences from the Mail menu.**

5. **Click the Accounts button.**

   Figure 12.13a shows the accounts panel with no account set up.

6. **Click the + (plus) sign at the bottom of the accounts pane.**

7. **Fill in the detail on the first screen of the Mail Setup Assistant.**

   Figure 12.13b shows the first screen.

Figure 12.13

Accounts panel before setting up an account (a); first screen of mail setup assistant (b)

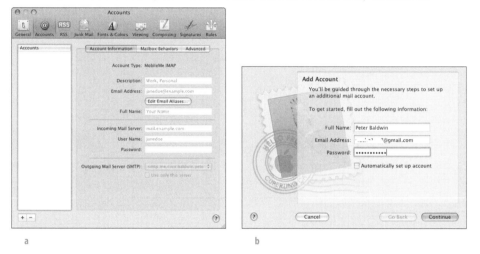

a   b

8. **Uncheck the box for Automatically set up account, and press Continue.**

9. **Select IMAP as the Account Type, and fill in the User Name and Password.**

   Figure 12.14a shows this screen.

10. **Click Continue.**

11. **Enter a description for the outgoing mail server, and reenter the User Name and Password, as shown in Figure 12.14b.**

12. **Check the account details in the Summary screen.**

    Figure 12.15 shows this summary screen.

Figure 12.14

Incoming mail server setup (a) outgoing mail server setup (b)

a   b

Figure 12.15

Mail setup assistant summary screen

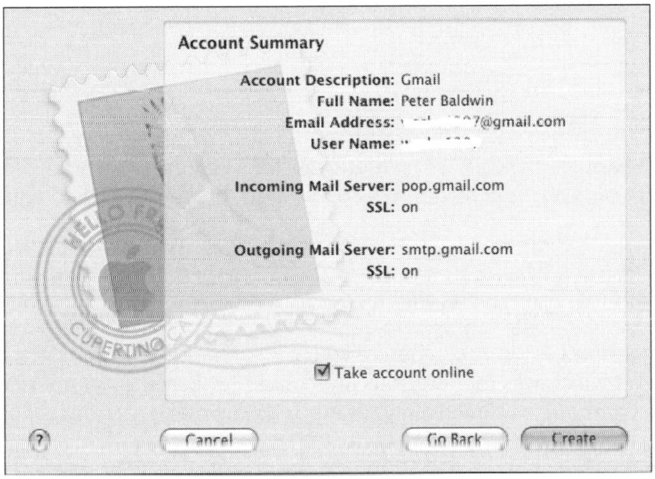

Account Summary

Account Description: Gmail
Full Name: Peter Baldwin
Email Address: ' ' '7@gmail.com
User Name: " ' ' ' '

Incoming Mail Server: pop.gmail.com
SSL: on

Outgoing Mail Server: smtp.gmail.com
SSL: on

☑ Take account online

13. **Finally, select Get all new mail from the Mailbox menu.**

Mail now shows your Inbox with the same e-mails you saw using Safari when you created the account. This is shown in Figure 12.16.

Adding any other accounts is simply a matter of following Steps 4 through 13.

Figure 12.16

Inbox view of new mail

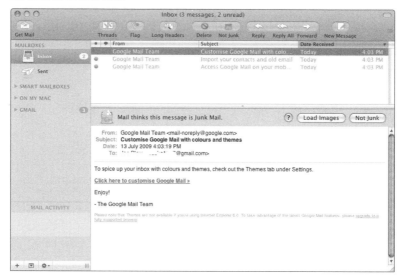

Setting Mail preferences

As with every Mac application, you set preferences for Mail under the Mail menu. It has nine sheets. In this section, you work through each of the sheets to set it up to your liking.

Setting General preferences

Figure 12.17 shows the General preferences panel.

Under General preferences, you can change your e-mail handler, which defaults to Mail. You can set how often Mail checks for new mail. If you use MobileMe as your e-mail address, it uses *push mail* so your mail arrives directly in your inbox as soon as it arrives at MobileMe.

One useful action for Mail is to have it show you the count of unread messages on its Dock icon, as shown in Figure 12.18.

If you get a meeting request via e-mail, you can choose to add it to your iCal calendar.

Figure 12.17

General preferences

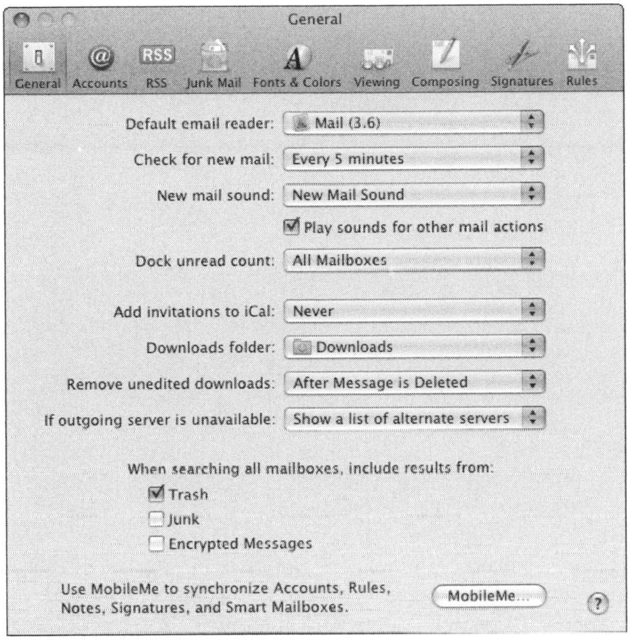

![General preferences window showing Mail settings]

Figure 12.18

Unread mail count

Setting Accounts preferences

As you can see from Figure 12.19a, you can use Mail to check several different e-mail addresses.

By clicking the Mailbox Behaviors tab, you control how Mail handles messages. Figure 12.19b shows the Mailbox Behaviors pane.

Figure 12.19

Accounts preferences (a); Mailbox Behaviors pane (b)

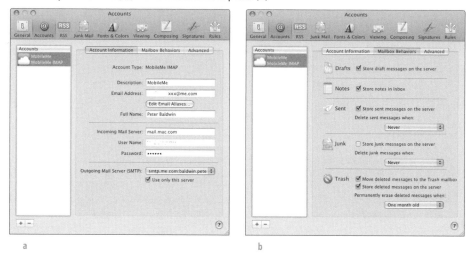

a   b

By default, your incoming e-mail is stored on the server if you are using IMAP; my recommendation is to always use the server to store your sent messages. In the event you have to reinstall Leopard and you don't have a recent Time Machine (or other) backup, you don't lose all your sent mail if you use this option. And you never know when it might be useful legally!

On the final pane for Accounts preferences, you can set some advanced preferences. These are shown in Figure 12.20.

My recommendation is to leave these alone. Obviously, you almost always want the account enabled, and by keeping copies for offline viewing, you can download your mail quickly, log out, and check your messages after you disconnect. You can write your replies and send them the next time you connect to the Internet. Obviously, this is very useful when traveling.

Setting RSS preferences

If you choose to use Mail as your default RSS reader, you can change it here, as shown in Figure 12.21.

This is similar to the RSS preferences tab in Safari.

Setting Junk Mail preferences

Mail has good junk-mail filtering. I have never bothered to change any of these preferences, because I find it works perfectly for me; very rarely does any junk mail get through.

Figure 12.20

Accounts Advanced preferences

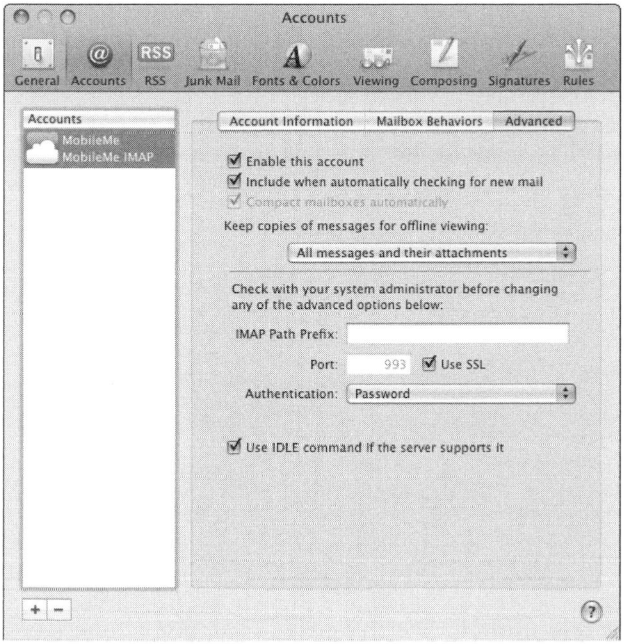

Figure 12.21

RSS preferences

Setting Fonts & Colors

I'm pretty happy with all the default choices of fonts for displaying my mail. These are shown in Figure 12.22a.

One font I'm not keen on is that chosen for notes. It's not too bad on the note itself, but it looks garish in the inbox. This is shown in Figure 12.22b.

Figure 12.22

Fonts & Colors preferences (a); default font for Notes (b)

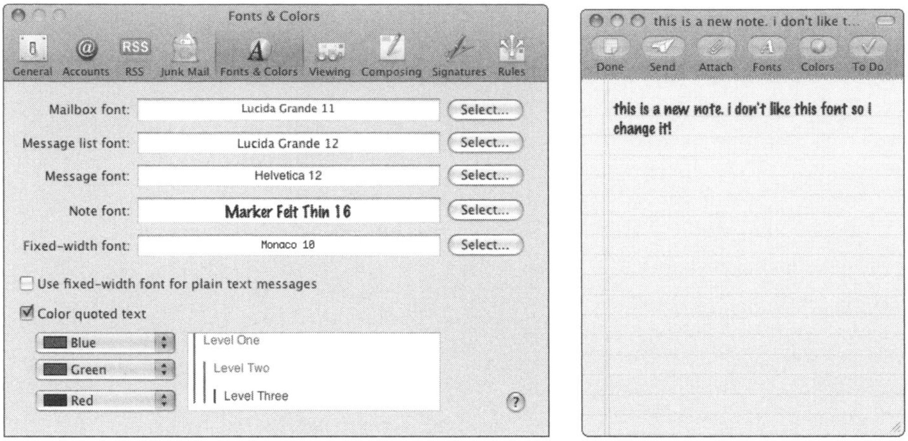

a   b

I changed it to Georgia 14 Italic. Nice.

Setting Viewing preferences

Viewing preferences affect the way messages are displayed in your mailboxes. Figure 12.23 shows the preferences pane.

A couple of comments are in order here. Although Mail puts a blue dot beside unread messages, most e-mail systems use a bold font to indicate unread messages. I prefer to turn that on.

The option Display remote images in HTML messages means that when you receive an HTML message with embedded images, these are stored on a server external to your e-mail server, so Mail has to download the images from another server. This could compromise your security because you are letting the external images site know that your computer is there.

Personally, I leave it unchecked, but I'm very careful about how I treat e-mail, particularly mail from someone I don't know. Like most things, it's a compromise between security and convenience. Make your own choice!

One option that can help you here, although it is complicated, is to view the full headers of a suspect e-mail, but that's beyond the scope of this book!

Setting Composing preferences

I prefer to leave the Composing preferences at their default settings.

Figure 12.23

Viewing preferences

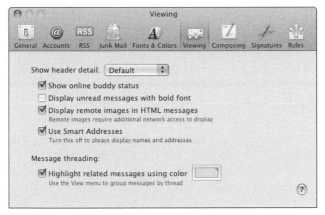

Setting up signatures

A signature is the text at the end of a message identifying the sender and the organization, often having a legal disclaimer. If you need to add these, you set them in the Signatures pane.

Using other mailboxes

Leopard Mail allows you to create new mailboxes in which to store messages. These are not the same as new accounts; think of a new mailbox as being like a new folder in an existing e-mail account. They are useful to keep messages sorted in ways that make sense to you. For example, you could put all the messages from a group you belong to in the same mailbox, making them easier to find.

First you need to create a new mailbox and then tell Mail how to select messages to go in the mailbox.

Creating a new mailbox

To create a new mailbox, follow these steps:

1. **On the Mail menu, click Mailbox and then click New Mailbox.**

Figure 12.24a shows the menu.

2. **Select where you want to create the new mailbox and what you want to call it, as shown in Figure 12.24b.**

You may or may not be able to create a new mailbox on your server. If you are using MobileMe you can; with other e-mail providers, probably not.

Figure 12.24

Creating a new mailbox (a); naming your new mailbox (b)

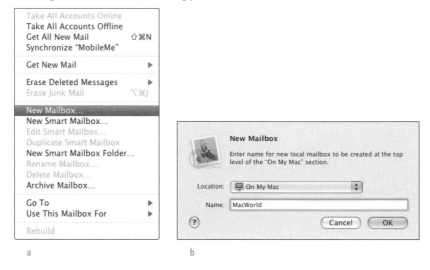

a   b

3. Create the mailbox on your "Mac."

For this example, I used the name "MacWorld" to store messages from MacWorld. Figure 12.25 shows the result of creating the new mailbox.

Figure 12.25

New mailbox showing in sidebar

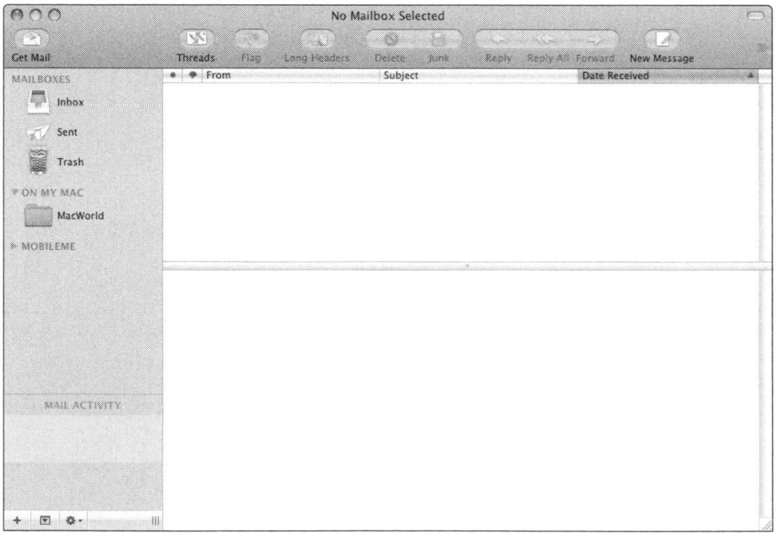

Setting up rules

After you have the new mailbox set up, you need to tell Mail how to put messages into it. To do this you create a new rule, from the Rules preferences pane, as shown in Figure 12.26.

Figure 12.26

Rules preferences pane

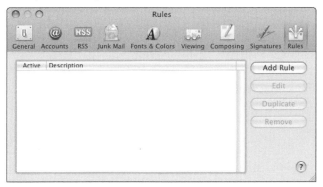

Before you start on the following instructions, be sure your Inbox is selected in Mail.

To set up a new rule, follow these steps:

1. **Click Add Rule.**

   Figure 12.27a shows the dialog box to create a new rule.

   In this example, I called the rule MacWorld and told it that if the From: field of the message contains the word "macworld," then move the message to the MacWorld folder.

   Note that case is ignored in the Contains field.

   You can add many more conditions, but for this example, we just use one condition.

2. **Click OK after entering your conditions.**

3. **On the sheet that drops down, as shown in Figure 12.27b, click Apply.**

   Since you selected your Inbox, Mail applies the rule to messages already in the Inbox. Mail automatically applies the rules to any new messages you receive.

Figure 12.27

Create a new rule (a); apply rules to selected mailbox (b)

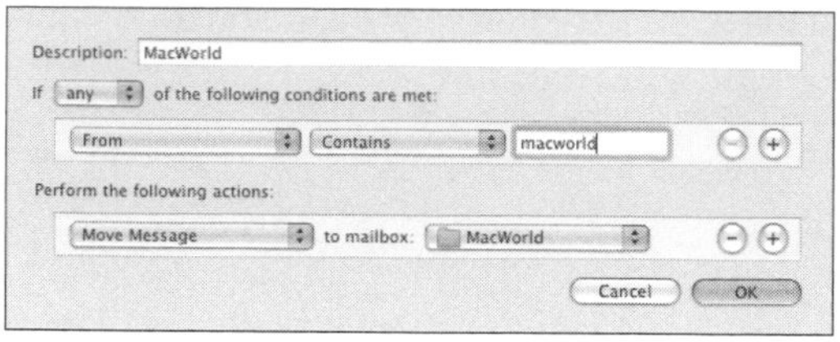

a

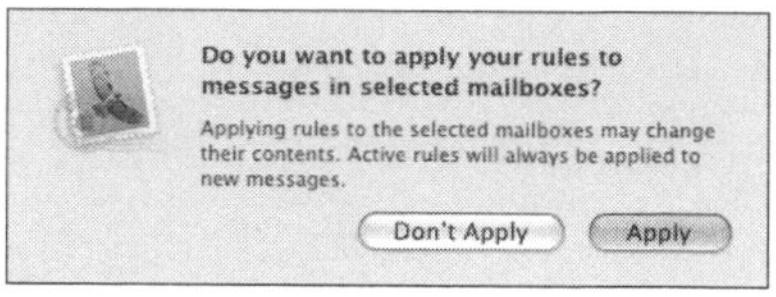

b

4. **Select the new mailbox (MacWorld in this case) to see the messages that have been moved from your Inbox.**

This is shown in Figure 12.28.

Figure 12.28

Messages moved to new mailbox

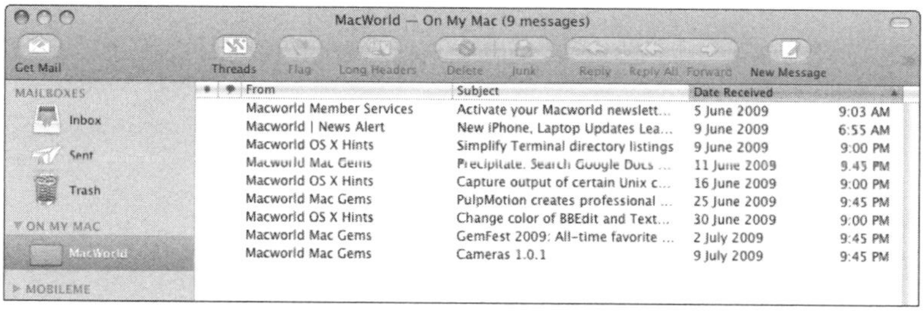

Using smart mailboxes

Creating a new mailbox and applying rules to messages moves your messages around. Mail has Smart Mailboxes that present a different view of your e-mails without moving them. Smart mailboxes gather messages that meet your conditions.

For example, you might create a smart folder that shows messages from your family. Go through the following steps to create a new smart folder:

1. **From the Mailbox menu, select New Smart Mailbox.**

Figure 12.29 shows the drop-down sheet.

Figure 12.29

Sheet for defining a smart mailbox

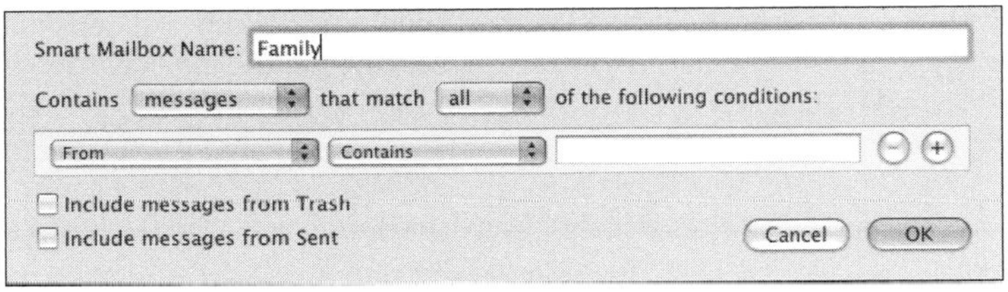

In this case, you want to include everyone with the same surname as you (Baldwin in my case) but exclude yourself, so leave the condition as all.

2. **Enter your surname in the first line, and then click + (plus).**

3. **In the second line, select From and Does not contain, and then select your first name.**

Figure 12.30 shows the definition sheet for my family.

Figure 12.30

Definition sheet for smart mailbox

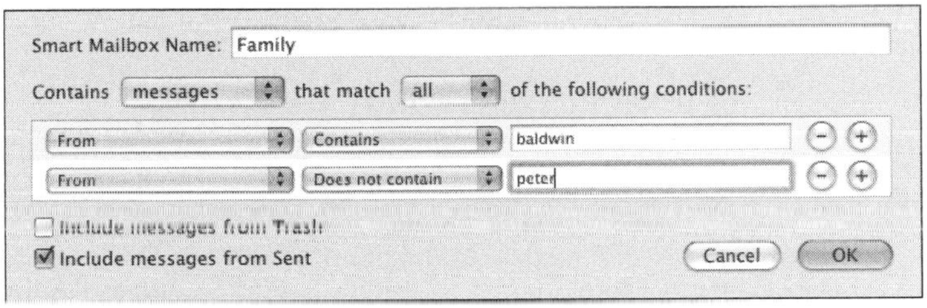

You finish up with a new folder with a star icon in the middle.

When you view the content of the folder, it shows the messages that meet your criteria, but they are not moved to the smart folder; they remain in their mailbox.

Smart Mailboxes can be very useful for gathering messages together that are stored in different mailboxes but relate to a common theme.

Using Address Book

Address Book is a simple application that aims to do one job and succeeds quite well. It uses the metaphor of cards with an index. As you select each name, the index card is displayed on the right, as shown in Figure 12.31.

Figure 12.31

Address Book

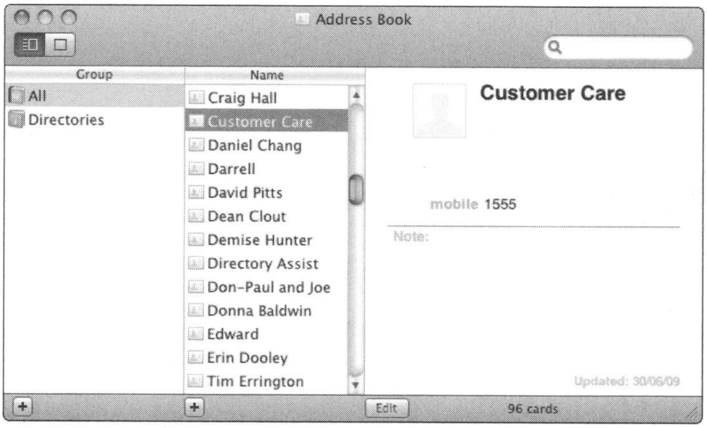

If you want to edit a card, simply select the card and click Edit.

Setting preferences

In keeping with the simplicity of the application, the preferences also are quite simple. If the default fields are not sufficient for your needs, you can add more fields. Figure 12.32a shows the default fields listed in the preference pane.

Each of the double triangles leads to a pop-up menu that allows you to select a different item name. Figure 12.32b shows the choices available for a phone number.

If you choose to, you can share your address book with other MobileMe users. Use the Sharing pane in preferences.

Figure 12.32

Default fields for Address Book (a); telephone number choices (b)

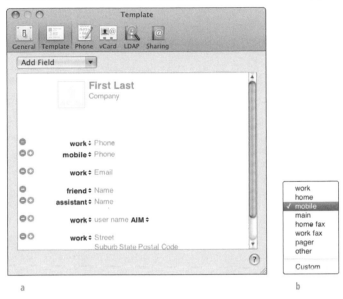

a   b

Synchronizing with a mobile phone

Although Address Book can't directly synchronize with a phone, Leopard has an application that allows you to do so if you have Bluetooth enabled on both devices. It's called iSync and can synchronize between Address Book and iCal and your mobile phone. Unfortunately you can't sync an iPhone this way: You need to use iTunes and the USB cable. Figure 12.33a shows the simple iSync screen.

To use iSync, you must first set up Bluetooth. Follow the instructions at the start of Chapter 9.

Your phone may require an additional driver to enable it to synchronize with your computer. Consult your phone manufacturer's Web site.

My phone is a Nokia N95, and I downloaded a driver to enable it to sync with iSync.

If you attempt to sync your phone before downloading the correct driver, you probably will receive an error message saying that iSync cannot connect to the phone. After you have installed the driver, you should receive a message saying that your device was found, as shown in Figure 12.33b.

Figure 12.33

iSync screen (a); Device found screen (b)

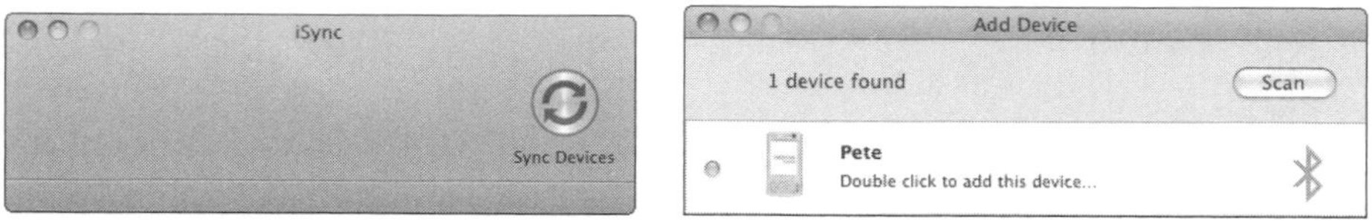

a

b

Double-click the phone's name to add it to iSync. After you have done that, you see a drop-down sheet asking what it is you want to synchronize, as shown in Figure 12.34.

Figure 12.34

Data to synchronize

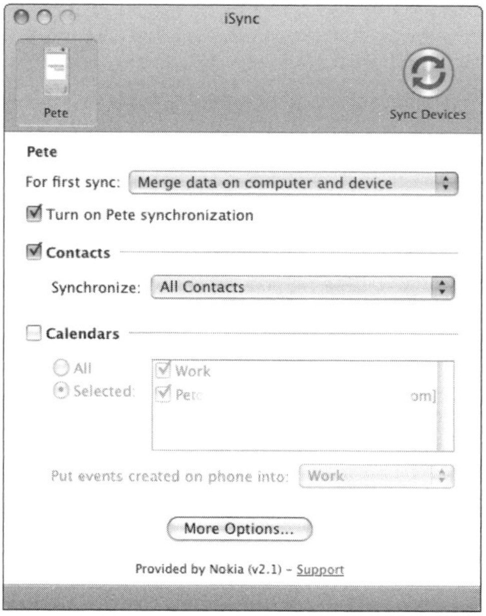

Now click Synchronize, and wait while the devices are synchronized.

Synchronizing with Yahoo

Synchronizing your Address Book with your Yahoo contacts is easy and built into Address Book. Follow these steps to synchronize with Yahoo contacts:

1. **Open Address Book.**

2. **Click Preferences on the Address Book menu.**

3. **On the Preferences pane, check the box Synchronize with Yahoo.**

4. **Click the Yahoo button, and click Accept to accept the terms of service.**

5. **Enter your Yahoo ID and password.**

6. **Start iSync.**

7. **Check the boxes for Enable syncing on this computer and Show status in menu bar.**

   You now find a new icon consisting of two half circles with arrows on them. This is the Synchronize button.

8. **Click the Synchronize button, and wait while Address Book is synchronized with your Yahoo contacts.**

   You should receive an alert warning you that you are about to synchronize contacts with Yahoo, as shown in Figure 12.35.

   Figure 12.35

   Yahoo synchronization alert

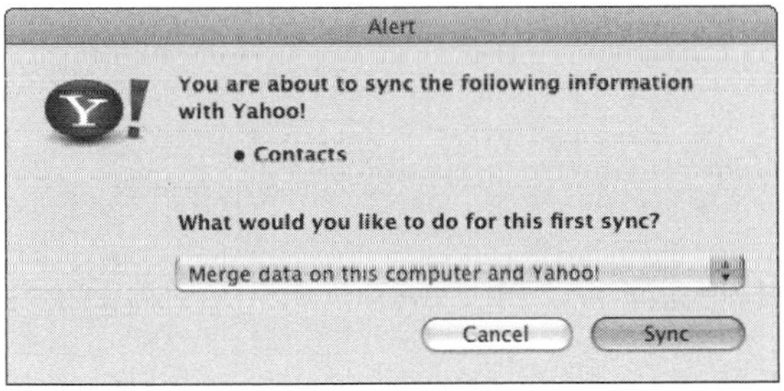

9. **Check your Address Book and your Yahoo contacts to ensure that the synchronization worked.**

Synchronizing with Google contacts

Although the help file for Address Book says it's a simple matter of checking the Synchronize with Google check box on the General tab in preferences, it works only for iPhone and iPod Touch.

However there is a workaround at `http://lifehacker.com/393855/enable-google-contact-sync-without-an-iphone-or-ipod-touch` or `http://tinyurl.com/3o5pdu`. It's not for the faint-hearted. Be sure to read the comments.

Using iCal

Leopard has a calendar application called iCal. Although it is not hugely sophisticated, it is certainly worth using as a basic calendar. It is capable of synchronizing with other devices and of viewing calendars located on other systems.

Figure 12.36 shows the default calendar view.

Figure 12.36

Default iCal view

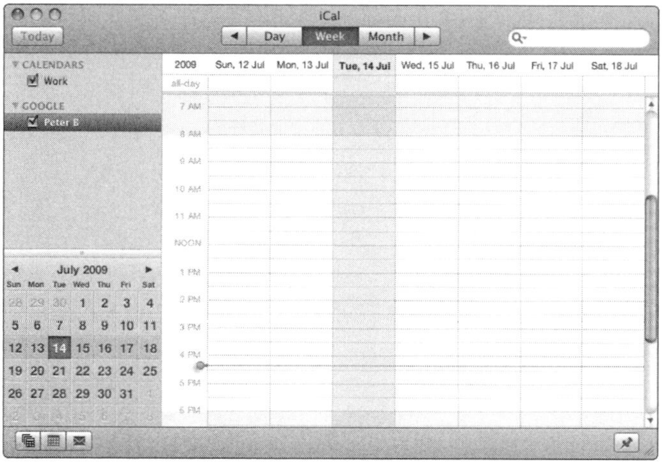

Synchronizing with a mobile phone

Follow the instructions above on synchronizing Address Book with your phone, using iSync.

Synchronizing with Google calendar

Unlike Address Book, iCal is very easy to synchronize with Google calendar. In fact, I use Google calendar as my master calendar and synchronize Outlook calendar in Window, iCal, and my mobile phone.

Follow these steps to synchronize iCal with Google calendar:

1. **Open iCal, go to the Preferences pane, and click the Accounts tab.**

2. **Click the + (plus) button to add an account.**

3. **Type Google for the description.**

4. **Type your Google username and password.**

5. **Click the triangle to open a new prompt for Server Options.**

6. **Type** https://www.google.com/calendar/dav/YOUREMAIL@gmail.com/user, **replacing YOUREMAIL by your Gmail username.**

Figure 12.37 show your screen at this point.

Figure 12.37

iCal new account settings

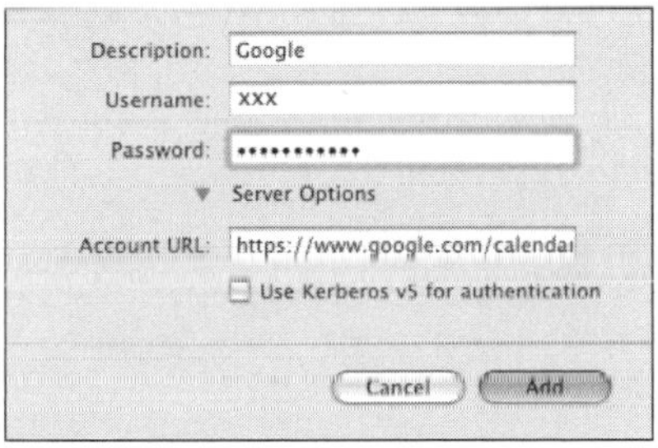

Description:	Google
Username:	XXX
Password:	••••••••••
	▼ Server Options
Account URL:	https://www.google.com/calendar
	☐ Use Kerberos v5 for authentication

Cancel   Add

7. **Close iCal preferences.**

You now see a new entry in your calendar sidebar showing your Google account. While the calendars are synchronizing, you see the usual Leopard rotating wheel.

Synchronizing with Yahoo calendar

At the time of this writing (July 2009), you must use the new beta of Yahoo calendar. If you are using the old calendar, log in and go to http://switch.calendar.yahoo.com to accept the terms of service.

Follow the instructions above for Google calendar, but use your Yahoo username. For the server, type **https://caldav.calendar.yahoo.com**.

Using Preview

Preview is a neat application: Not only does it preview graphics files, like Windows Picture and Fax viewer, but it also previews many other types of files as well, especially Adobe Reader documents. And if that's not enough, it allows you to do simple edits, including resizing, of your photos. Snow Leopard extends its capability even further by adding annotation tools.

For a complete list of the file types that Preview can open, go to `http://en.wikipedia.org/wiki/Preview_(software)`.

Setting Preview preferences

Preview has very few preferences to set. Figure 12.38 shows the main preferences pane for Preview.

Figure 12.38

Preview preferences pane

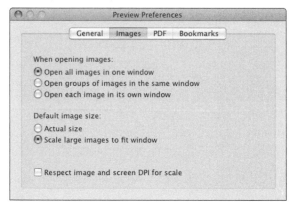

Preview's default behavior is to open each image in a separate window, but I prefer to set it to always use the same window and have images displayed actual size.

With those settings, as you open each new image, it gets added to the sidebar so that you can move from one image to the next. For me, coming from Windows, there is one minor irritation: Windows Picture and Fax Viewer moves from one image to the next just by using the arrow keys. Preview doesn't do that. You have to remember to select all the images you want to preview at once or be prepared to add each one individually.

Editing with Preview

With Preview, you can make minor edits to graphics files. The Edit menu has the usual Cut, Copy, and Paste entries. Using the selection and moving tools on the toolbar, you can extract a section of the image and cut it or copy and paste to a new location. You also can paste the selection into a different image. Figure 12.39a shows the selection menu.

On the Tools menu, you find many options to change the image. This menu is shown in Figure 12.39b.

The Adjust Color menu allows you to make many adjustments to the image, more so than Windows Photo and Fax Viewer, although it lacks an automatic correction mode that most photo processing packages have. Figure 12.39c shows the color adjustments possible with Preview.

Figure 12.39

Preview selection menu (a); Preview tools menu (b); Preview color adjustments (c)

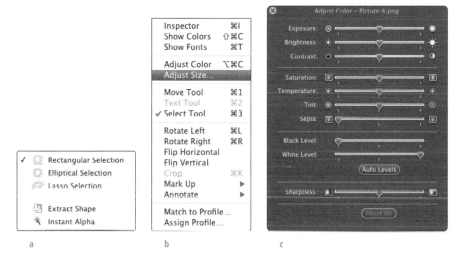

a   b   c

Using Preview with PDF files

One very useful feature of Preview when used with PDF files is the ability to store notes inside the PDF file. Figure 12.40 shows a note stored within a PDF file.

Figure 12.40

Note stored within a PDF

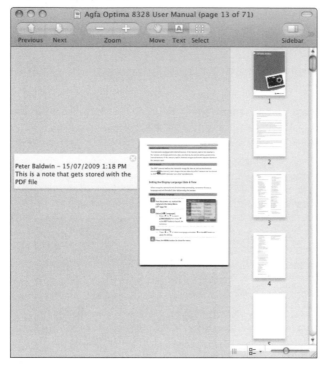

Using iTunes

In the same way that the iPod and iPhone have become almost ubiquitous, so iTunes has become more or less ubiquitous for managing them. In this section, you look at using your Windows-formatted iPod on your "Mac."

Synchronizing with your iPod

If, like me, you set up your iPod using a Windows computer, it is formatted as a FAT volume. Because Leopard can read from and write to FAT volumes, you can easily copy music to it from your Leopard computer. Remember, though, that you can't take the music from your iPod and store it in Leopard, but you can connect it and play music from it.

Figure 12.41a shows the message I got on first connecting my Windows-formatted iPod to Leopard.

After it is connected, it becomes available in just the same way as it does in Windows. The display shows that it was formatted in Windows, as shown in Figure 12.41b.

Figure 12.41

Synchronization message from iTunes (a); iPod formatted under Windows (b)

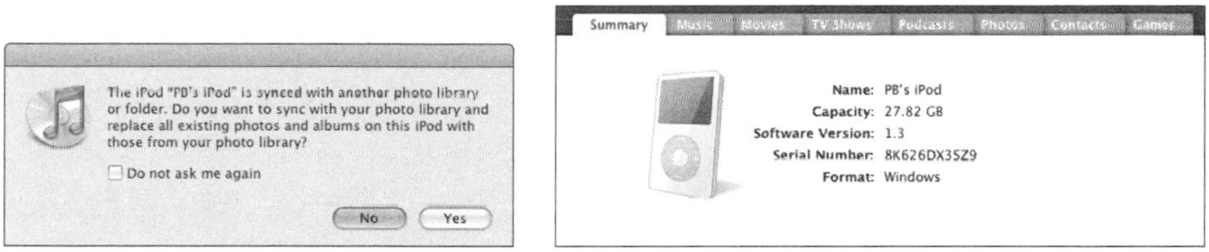

a   b

You can use iTunes in Leopard to play your iPod files created on your Windows computer.

Playing files on your Windows disks

iTunes in Leopard plays any music file that's stored on your Windows disks. Its default behavior is to copy the files to your music library in Leopard, which is probably not what you want. To prevent this from happening, follow these steps:

1. **Open iTunes preferences.**

2. **Go to the Advanced tab.**

3. **Uncheck the box for Copy files to iTunes Music folder when adding to library.**

   Figure 12.42 shows the Advanced pane.

4. **To add a folder on a Windows disk, select Add to library... on the File menu, navigate to the folder you want to add, and click Open.**

   iTunes leaves the original files on your Windows disk, but they become part of your iTunes music in Leopard. After all, your iTunes library is simply a file that points to where the actual music files are stored.

5. **On the File menu, select Library, Consolidate library....**

   Figure 12.43 shows the warning you receive.

Now you see the selected folders on your Windows disk added to your iTunes library. You can play any of them, provided that your Windows disk is available to Leopard.

Figure 12.42

iTunes Advanced pane

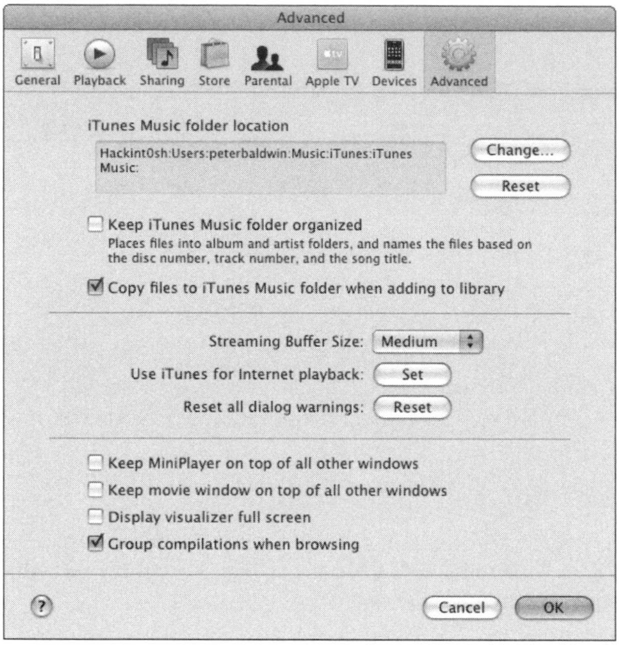

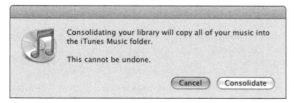

Figure 12.43

iTunes consolidate library warning

Summary

In this chapter, you explored the standard software applications that are included with Leopard.

These covered the basics of using a computer, including a very good Web browser, as well as a good e-mail client, address book, and calendar application, all of which can be linked together to manage your personal and business life.

In addition, you explored the Preview application that allows you to make simple manipulations to graphics images in many different formats and you can view and add notations to PDF files.

Reading and Writing to Windows Disks

U p to now, you have been concentrating on what's happening with your Leopard disk. But you need to be able to access other disks as well. If you're like most Windows users, you have at least one physical hard disk and two or more partitions.

If these disks and partitions are formatted in the very old Windows format, using a File Allocation Table (FAT), Leopard can both read and write to them. But If you're using disks and partitions formatted with NTFS (New Technology File System), and you should, then it's not quite so easy because, by default, Leopard can read from but not write to them.

In this chapter, you find out how to read and write both formats and about some of the pitfalls.

Reading and Writing to FAT Partitions

In this section, you see how to read and write to FAT partitions and how to view hidden files in Leopard. You also learn about the functions of hidden files and why Leopard uses them.

Initially, In MS-DOS, the file allocation table consisted of 12 bits, which limited the total capacity of a disk to 32MB. Yes, 32 MEGAbytes! Because the majority of personal computers used only floppy disks, this wasn't a big issue; even hard disks at the time were no more than 20MB. My first hard disk was 10MB and cost an arm and a leg.

Pretty soon, however, 32MB became way too small, so Microsoft introduced first a 16-bit FAT, then a 32-bit FAT. Most USB keys and camera cards use the 16-bit FAT; the 32-bit FAT is used with other disks.

The FAT system has several limitations:

- Disks and partitions are limited to 2GB maximum for 16-bit FAT.
- Files are limited to 4GB maximum, even with 32-bit FAT.
- Time and date of a file are specified in increments of two seconds.

- You can't restrict file permissions for individual users.
- They're not very fault tolerant; disk-writing errors are difficult to recover from.

All in all, FAT disks are not a very good choice for hard disks. If your Windows disks are format-ted as FAT volumes, I recommend you convert them to NTFS using the `convert.exe` utility from Microsoft.

Viewing hidden files

One thing you find as you begin using your Hackintosh is that each time you access a disk, Leopard creates some hidden files. This happens regardless of whether the disk is formatted with HFS, FAT, or NTFS.

Normally, you don't see these files because Finder hides them from you. But you can make them visible by carrying out the following steps:

1. **Start Terminal running.**

2. **Type the following command:**

`defaults write com.apple.Finder AppleShowAllFiles YES`

Figure 13.1 shows the Terminal window.

Figure 13.1

Terminal window with command

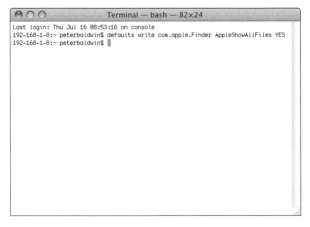

```
Last login: Thu Jul 16 08:53:16 on console
192-168-1-8:~ peterbaldwin$ defaults write com.apple.Finder AppleShowAllFiles YES
192-168-1-8:~ peterbaldwin$ 
```

3. **Type the following command:**

`killall Finder` and press Enter.

This stops Finder running and then it restarts, showing the hidden files on your desk-top. Be careful to spell Finder with a capital F.

Using TinkerTool

TinkerTool is a freeware application that allows you to easily make changes to the way Leopard behaves. It is very safe to use because by pushing a single button, you can restore your system to the way it was before you started the TinkerTool session, or you can reset everything to the standard Leopard defaults.

You can download TinkerTool from `www.bresink.com/osx/TinkerTool.html`.

We can't explore the whole of TinkerTool here; you can do that on your own. We just use it to show hidden files in Leopard.

After downloading and installing it, start it running. The first option on the first screen is the one you want to show hidden files. Check the box, and click the Relaunch Finder button.

The figure shows the TinkerTool home screen.

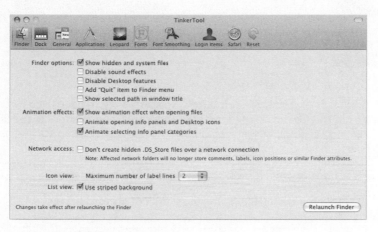

When you want to return to hiding the hidden files, carry out Steps 1 to 3, but type this:

```
defaults write com.apple.Finder AppleShowAllFiles NO
```

TIP

If you don't feel comfortable using Terminal to type commands, refer to the sidebar.

On your desktop, you now see two new icons: One is `.DS_Store`; the other is `.localized`, as shown in Figure 13.2.

Not only does Leopard put hidden files on your desktop, it also puts hidden files in every folder, including any disks formatted with other file systems to which you connect.

One file that is always present is `.DS_Store`. This stores attributes of a folder such as the position of the icon, the background image, and so forth. Another common file is called `.localized`. It is always 0 bytes and simply indicates that the folder name can be stored in the local language.

Figure 13.2

Hidden files on Leopard desktop

Another file you find on your FAT formatted disks after they've been used by Leopard is `.fseventsd`. This file can be used by applications to detect changes to the file system, such as creating a new folder. For example, if you are using iPhoto, it can detect when you create a new folder and put files in the folder.

Appendix B contains more information about these hidden files.

Figure 13.3 shows the hidden files in the root folder of my Hackintosh.

The red "No Entry" signs on the `.fseventsd` and `.Spotlight-V100` folders mean that these are system folders, and normal users have no access to them at all.

Windows also hides files by default so they don't show up. To view hidden files in Windows, follow these steps:

1. **Start Windows Explorer.**
2. **Press the Tab key to show the menu.**
3. **Select Folder Options.**
4. **Click File Types.**
5. **Scroll down to the radio buttons to show hidden attributes.**
6. **Select Show hidden files, and click OK.**
7. **Navigate to the root folder of your disk.**

Figure 13.3

Hidden files on Hackintosh hard disk

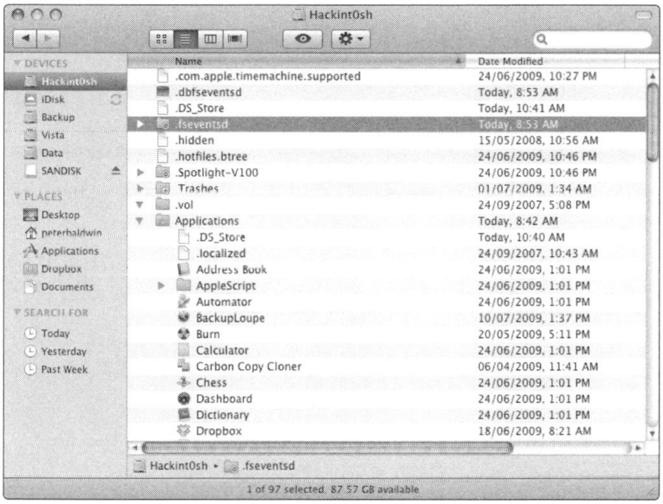

Provided you have written files to the disk, you see a number of hidden files. Figure 13.4 shows the hidden files in the root folder of my Windows Vista system disk, viewed using Leopard Finder.

Figure 13.4

Finder view of Windows hard disk hidden files

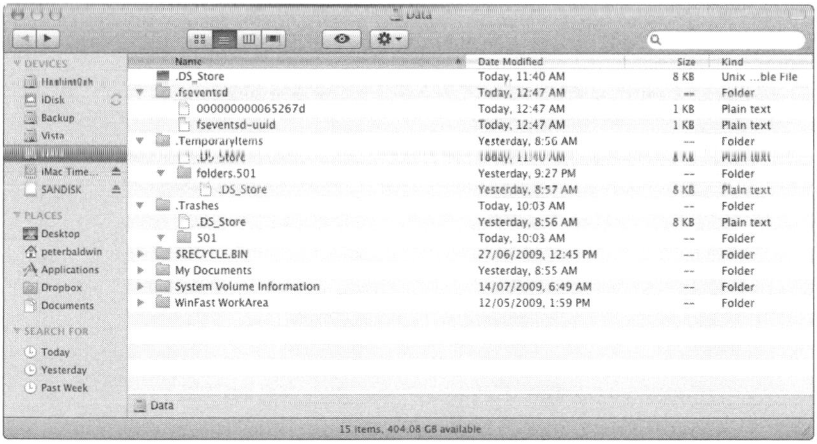

Figure 13.5 shows the Windows Explorer view of the same disk with hidden files visible.

Figure 13.5

Explorer view of hard disk

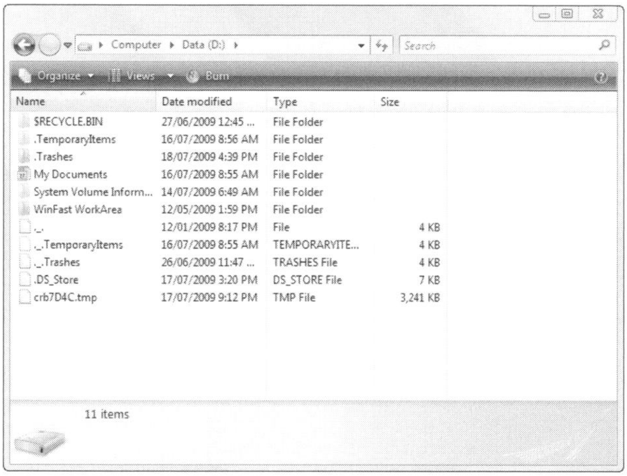

Deleting hidden files

Hidden files are kept hidden by Finder for a good reason: Unless you know exactly what you're doing, you can render Leopard unworkable by willy-nilly deleting hidden files on your Leopard disks. Generally, it's quite safe to delete them from your Windows disks if they annoy you; otherwise, leave them alone.

Reading and Writing to NTFS Partitions

As you know, by default Leopard can read from but not write to NTFS partitions. I know two ways around this limitation, both involving additional software. One uses two freeware applications; the other uses purchased software.

Installing MacFUSE

MacFUSE is an enabler application that installs as part of Leopard and allows you then to connect to many different file systems. On its own, all it does is provide a platform to be able to install drivers to connect to file systems of any other operating system (such as Linux) or even define your own file system.

In this case, we're only interested in using it to read and write NTFS disks.

Carry out the following steps to install MacFUSE:

1. **Navigate to** `http://code.google.com/p/macfuse/`**, and click the Download tab.**

   As usual, it downloads as a disk image (.dmg) file.

2. **When Safari opens the Finder window, double-click the MacFUSE.pkg file.**

3. **Follow the Leopard Installer prompts, and then restart your computer.**

4. **Open System Preferences, and note the new icon in the Other section.**

   Figure 13.6 shows the System Preferences pane with MacFUSE added.

   Figure 13.6

   System Preferences with MacFUSE icon added

5. **Click the MacFUSE icon in System Preferences.**

Figure 13.7 shows the very sparse MacFUSE pane.

Figure 13.7

MacFUSE pane in System Preferences

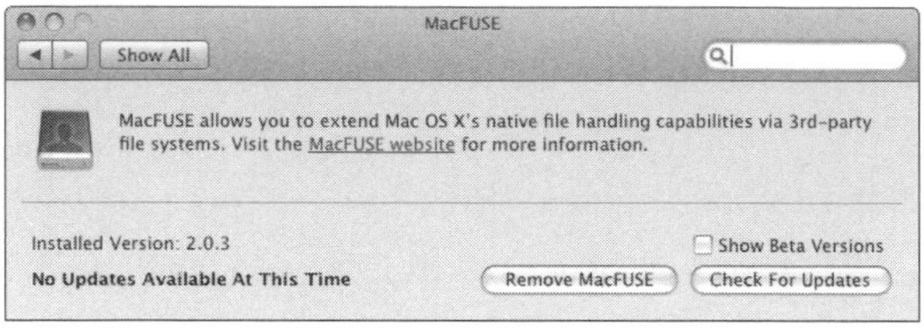

Installing NTFS-3G

NTFS-3G is the other part of the solution to being able to write to NTFS disks. To install it, carry out the following steps:

1. **Navigate to** www.ntfs-3g.org/.

2. **Click NTFS-3G for Mac OS X.**

3. **Scroll down to the Download: prompt, and select the latest build.**

   Again, it is supplied as a .dmg file.

4. **When Safari opens the disk image, double-click Install NTFS-3G and wait while it installs.**

Figure 13.8 shows System Preferences with NTFS-3G installed.

Now you can read and write to your Windows disks to your heart's content.

Installing ntfs-mac

Another option for writing to NTFS disks is Paragon Software's ntfs-mac. This comes with a package that can read Macintosh HFS+ disks from Windows Vista, though I have tried only the free trial, which doesn't include the Windows application.

If you decide to install ntfs-mac, it's probably a very good idea to uninstall NTFS-3G so you don't risk corrupting your Windows disks by using two applications to write.

Figure 13.8

System Preferences with NTFS-3G

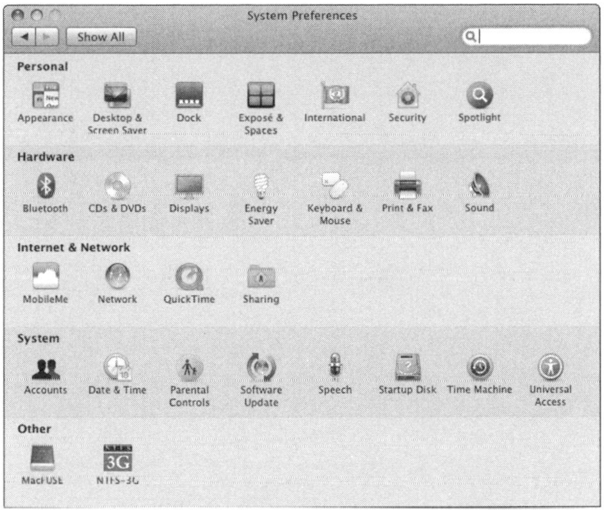

Follow these steps to install ntfs-mac:

1. **Use Safari to navigate to** www.paragon-software.com/home/ntfs-mac/.

2. **Click the Try Now button.**

3. **After the disk image file has downloaded, double-click the Installer package.**

4. **Restart your computer.**

You should now be able to write files to your Windows disk.

Summary

In this chapter, you learned about the limitations of Leopard in using Windows disks. You learned how to view hidden files on both your Hackintosh and Windows disks. Finally, you learned how to install software to be able to read and write to any Windows disk.

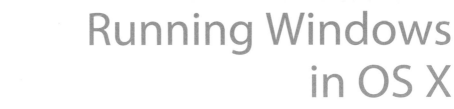
U p to now, you have been running both Leopard and Windows, choosing which disk you want to boot from. After you are using one operating system, getting to the other one is difficult: It requires a reboot.

Virtualizing software provides a solution. You can run Windows without leaving Leopard. It doesn't run as fast as native Windows runs, but you can have the best of both worlds with a single boot.

At present, two competing solutions are available on the Leopard platform: Parallels and VMware. Both are available in trial versions that can be downloaded, and both cost the same: around $80 at the time of this writing. Both applications install and run on a Hackintosh.

In this chapter, you install trial versions of both applications and install virtual machines to use from your computer.

CAUTION

Virtual machine files are very large, and each time you make changes, the state of the virtual machine changes. If you use Time Machine to back up, the files will rapidly fill your disk.

Using Parallels Desktop

Parallels began in 1999 and has produced a large range of virtualization solutions. In this section, you learn how to install and use Parallels Desktop for Macintosh.

Installing Parallels Desktop

Follow these steps to download and install a trial version of Parallels Desktop:

1. **Navigate to the Parallels Web site at** www. parallels.com/.

2. **Click Download.**

   You need to register and provide a valid e-mail address so they can send you an installation key.

3. **After the download is complete, double-click the .dmg file to install it.**

Before you can use Parallels, you need to install an operating system.

Creating a virtual machine

In this section, you create a new virtual machine from an installation disk for a Windows version. You can use your existing Windows install disk. If your computer did not come with the complete installation disk, you can use your existing Windows installation.

CAUTION

If you use your existing installation (called your Boot Camp partition in Macintosh terminology), be aware that any changes you make to the virtual machine also happen to your real Windows partition.

Follow these steps to create a new virtual machine:

1. **Start Parallels running.**

2. **From the menu bar, click File, New Virtual Machine.**

This starts the New Virtual Machine Assistant, as shown in Figure 14.1a.

3. **Click Continue.**

4. **If you have your operating system on a CD or DVD, select Real CD/DVD. If your operating system exists as an .iso file on your hard disk, select CD/DVD image and navigate to the image file.**

In this example, the image file was the release candidate for Windows 7, located on my Windows data disk, as shown in Figure 14.1b.

Figure 14.1

New Virtual Machine Assistant (a); Operating System Detection (b)

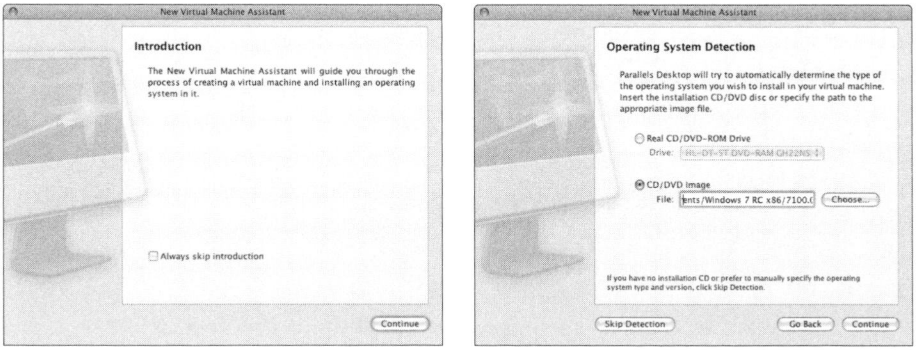

![New Virtual Machine Assistant screenshots showing Introduction panel (a) and Operating System Detection panel (b)]

a   b

5. **Click Continue.**

Parallels detected the operating system and displayed it on the next screen, as shown in Figure 14.2a.

If you want your Hackintosh home folder to be shared with Windows, leave the box checked. If you want Windows to be able to share user folders and desktop objects, leave the box checked.

6. **Click Create.**

Parallels creates a desktop icon to refer to the new virtual machine and then takes you to the point where you install the operating system, as shown in Figure 14.2b.

Figure 14.2

Detected System (a); Prepare to Install Operating System (b)

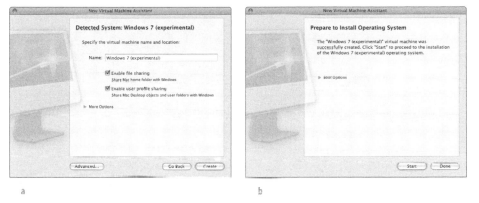

a   b

7. **Click Done.**

Parallels displays a window showing your newly created virtual machine, as shown in Figure 14.3.

Before you can use your new virtual machine, you must install an operating system. Figure 14.4 shows partway through the installation of Windows 7 Release Candidate.

After the installation has finished, you should install the Parallels Tools, which allow better performance from peripherals attached to your computer, as well as better video performance.

Figure 14.3

Virtual machine created

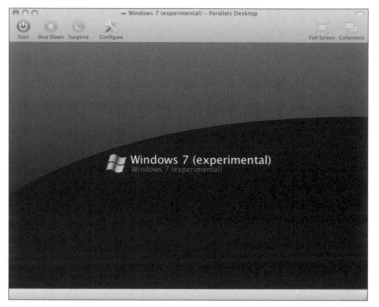

Figure 14.4

Installing Windows 7

8. **From the Virtual Machines menu, select Install Parallels Tools.**

   Wait while the tools are installed, and then restart your virtual machine.

   Figure 14.5 shows Parallels being installed.

   Figure 14.5

   Installing Parallels Tools

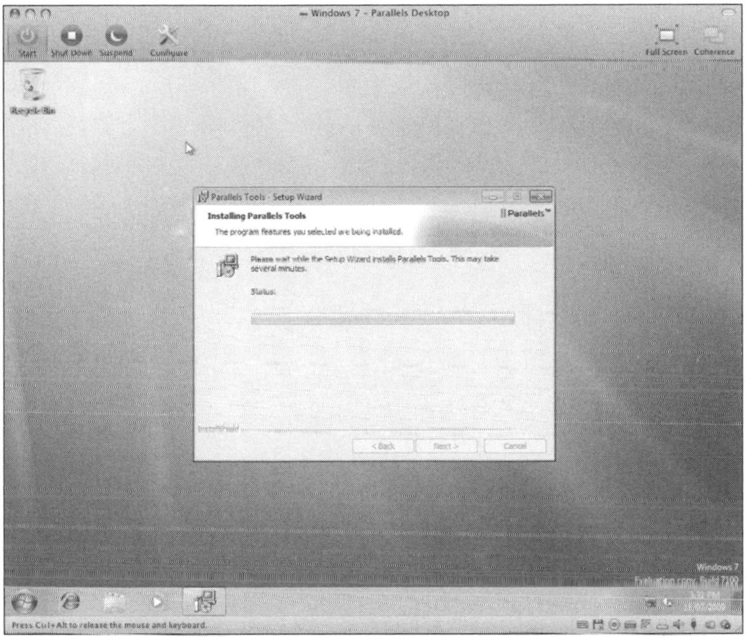

Parallels modes

A Parallels Virtual Machine can operate in one of three modes:

- Windowed mode
- Full-screen mode
- Coherence mode

Using windowed mode

In windowed mode, your virtual machine runs in a window on your desktop, just like all your other applications. Figure 14.6 shows Windows 7 running in a window, along with Safari.

Figure 14.6

Windows 7 and Safari running

Using full-screen mode

Full-screen mode means exactly what it says: Your virtual machine takes over your whole screen. When it is running in full-screen mode, you cannot distinguish it from the real thing. You need to remember the keystroke combination to get back to windowed mode: Alt-Command-Return.

Using coherence mode

Coherence mode is when each Windows application runs in its own window on your desktop. You can have several Windows and Macintosh applications running at the same time, each in its own separate window, as shown in Figure 14.7.

Figure 14.7

Parallels running in coherence mode

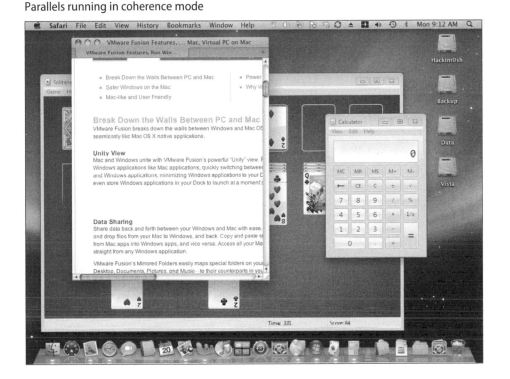

Note that each running Windows application has its own icon in the Dock, as shown in Figure 14.8.

Figure 14.8

Coherence mode icons in the Dock

Using snapshots

One useful feature of virtual machines is that you can take a snapshot of the machine at a given point and save it to disk. You can then return to this snapshot later, to capture the state. It's a bit like Windows System Restore on a grand scale.

To take a snapshot, select Take Snapshot from the Virtual Machine menu in Parallels, as shown in Figure 14.9.

To revert to a previous snapshot, select Revert to Snapshot.

Figure 14.9

Snapshot menu

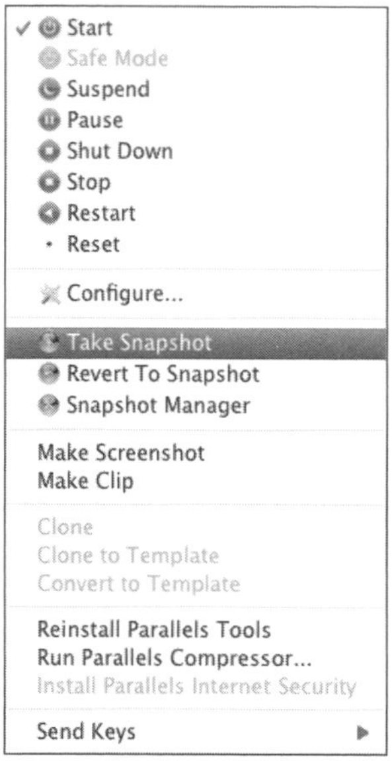

Using VMware

In this section, you download, install, and use VMware. The VMware for Windows platform has been around a little longer than Parallels; the Mac version, not quite as long.

Installing and creating a virtual machine

1. **Navigate to the WMware Web site at** www.vmware.com/products/fusion/.

2. **Click Get Free Trial.**

   You need to register and provide a valid e-mail address so they can send you an installation key.

3. **After the download is complete, double-click the .dmg file to install it.**

When you first install VMware, it wants to create a virtual machine from your Windows disk as a Boot Camp partition, so I installed my existing Vista installation as a Boot Camp virtual machine.

Follow these steps to create your Windows disk as a virtual machine:

1. **Click the right arrow in the Virtual Machine Library screen, as shown in Figure 14.10.**

Figure 14.10

Virtual Machine Library

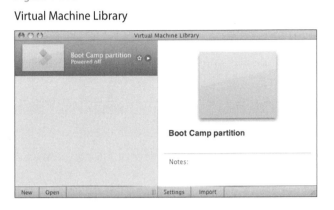

2. **Wait while VMware creates your virtual machine.**

CAUTION

As with Parallels, any changes you make to your virtual machine are reflected in your Windows partition.

To create a new virtual machine, follow these steps:

1. **On the File menu, select New....**

   This starts the New Virtual Machine Assistant, as shown in Figure 14.11a.

2. **If you have the CD/DVD with the operating system, insert it in the drive; otherwise, click Continue without disk.**

3. **If you are using an .iso image file, select it in the Choose operating system image file box, shown in Figure 14.11b.**

4. **Fill in your details in the Easy Install dialog box shown in Figure 14.12a.**

   Easy install fills in those details for you while the installation proceeds.

5. **Click Continue.**

   If you don't enter a product key, Easy Install prompts you for one.

Figure 14.11

New Virtual Machine Assistant (a); Choose Operating System (b)

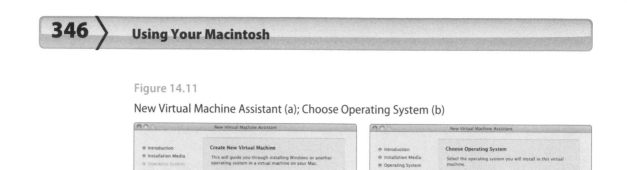

a   b

6. In the Sharing dialog box, choose the files and folders you want to share with the virtual machine, as shown in Figure 14.12b.

Figure 14.12

Easy Install dialog box (a); Sharing dialog box (b)

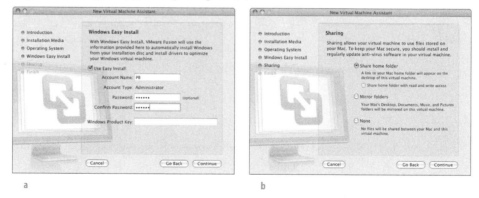

a   b

7. Click Continue.

Now you are ready to start the installation, as shown in the summary in Figure 14.13a.

8. Choose where you want to store your new virtual machine, and click Save, as shown in Figure 14.13b.

Figure 14.13

Finish dialog box (a); Save dialog box (b)

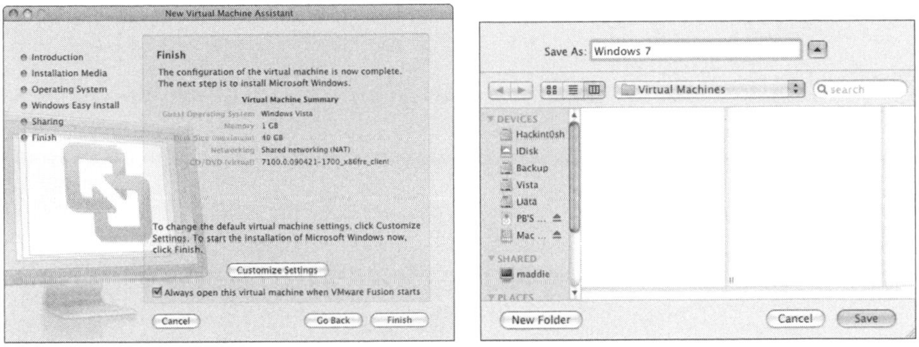

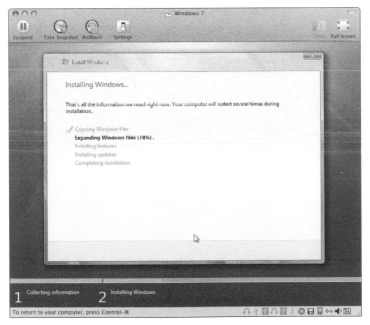

a   b

VMware then gets very busy creating your new machine. It boots from the image file and then installs. Figure 14.14 shows a screenshot during the installation process.

Finally, when the installation is complete, you can log in and start using your virtual machine.

Figure 14.14

Windows 7 installation

VMware modes

Just as Parallels can run in three modes, so can VMware.

Using windowed mode

Figure 14.15 shows VMware running Windows 7 in windowed mode.

Figure 14.15

Windowed mode

Using full-screen mode

When VMware is running in full-screen mode, it fills the screen and is indistinguishable from the real application. To leave full-screen mode, use the keys Ctrl+Cmd+s (that's Ctrl+Windows key+s on your PC keyboard.

Using unity mode

VMware has unity mode, corresponding with coherence mode in Parallels. As with Parallels, applications running in the guest operating system have icons in the Dock, as shown in Figure 14.16.

Figure 14.16

WMware applications running in the Dock

Measuring performance

While processor speed, memory speed, and disk access speeds are affected slightly by virtualizing the operating system, it is in graphics speed that the most performance loss occurs.

Figures 14.17 and 14.18 show the results of measuring the Windows Experience Index on my real computer and comparing it with the same computer using VMware. Notice the large drop in performance on both graphics measures.

Importing other virtual machines

With both Parallels and VMware, you can import virtual machines created elsewhere. Figure 14.19 shows a virtual machine created in VMware on Windows (for Chapter 15) running on my Hackintosh after being imported into VMware Fusion for Macintosh, running in windowed mode.

Unfortunately, VMware won't let you run a virtual machine inside another virtual machine!

Figure 14.17

Performance information for my virtual computer

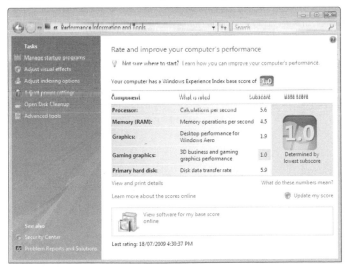

Figure 14.18

Performance information for my real computer

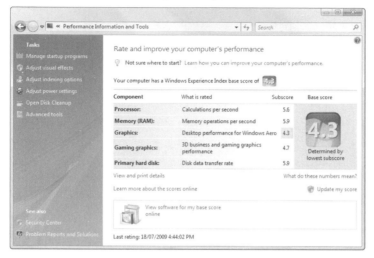

Figure 14.19

Leopard virtual machine running in Leopard

Summary

In this chapter, you have downloaded and installed two virtualization products that run on Leopard that allow you to run a guest operating system such as Windows Vista or Windows 7 on your Hackintosh. You compared both products to see the strengths and weaknesses of each.

In particular, you saw the effect of virtualization on the speed of graphics. You need to determine for yourself whether the loss of performance in graphics is worth the convenience of being able to run both operating systems, as well as others, without needing to reboot your computer.

In the next chapter, you look at carrying out the exact opposite: Instead of running Windows in a virtual machine in Leopard, you experiment with running Leopard as a guest operating system in Windows.

Running OS X on Windows Using VMware

U p to now, you have installed and used OS X running natively on your computer, with Leopard having direct connection with your hardware.

In the previous chapter, you downloaded and used two virtualization applications, using them to install and run Windows operating systems. You also may have used them to install a completely different operating system such as Linux, but that is beyond the scope of this book. You saw some of the advantages and disadvantages of running an operating system this way.

The Macintosh platform has two virtualization hosts; Windows has four major ones:

- VMware workstation
- Parallels workstation
- Virtualbox
- Virtual PC

In this chapter, you download and install the VMware client for Windows and install Snow Leopard as the guest operating system.

Creating a Virtual Snow Leopard Installation

Installing OS X natively on your computer is not an easy task, and neither is installing it in a virtual machine. Remember: OS X is not meant to run on anything other than Apple-labeled hardware.

On the Mac, both VMware and Parallels provide tools that increase the speed of the virtualization, but those tools are not available if you run Snow Leopard on a Windows computer, so you have a pretty slow Snow Leopard, but no worse than some older Macintosh hardware.

In this chapter you install Snow Leopard to VMware, running in Windows. I used Vista, but it will also work with Windows 7.

I am extremely grateful to plastikman for developing this method and to prasys for putting it on his blog at `http://prasys.co.cc/2009/11/snow-leopard-boot-132-for-vmware-workstation-7-and-vmware-player-3/`. I've created a TinyURL for you: `http://tinyurl.com/yjpljjc`.

Creating an install disk image

Before you start, you need to purchase a retail copy of Snow Leopard because you will use that to install your virtual machine.

Although VMware is able to read a real CD or DVD, it works much better if you use a virtual disk. In Windows a very simple way of creating an image (or iso) is to use ImgBurn. Other products are capable of creating one, but ImgBurn is free and works nicely.

Follow these steps to create an iso of your retail Snow Leopard install disk:

1. **Download ImgBurn from their Web site at** `www.imgburn.com/`.

2. **Install it and then start running it.**

3. **Insert your Snow Leopard install disk in your DVD drive and wait for it to be recognized by ImgBurn.**

   Figure 15.1 shows the ImgBurn screen with my retail Snow Leopard install disk in the drive.

   Figure 15.1

   ImgBurn screen

   Note that ImgBurn sees the disk as a WindowsSupport disk, but it will nevertheless copy all the Macintosh files as well as the Windows files.

4. **If you want to change where ImgBurn saves the iso, click the folder icon to select the folder.**

5. **Click the Disk to Folder icon and then wait while ImgBurn creates your iso.**

Sourcing the other files you need

Plastikman, who created this method, has made your job easy for you by providing all the files you need, except for your Snow Leopard install DVD.

Follow the links on prasys's blog to download these files. They are archived together into a tbz2 archive file. Windows cannot unpack tbz2 files, but 7-Zip can. 7-Zip is available from the Web site at `www.7-zip.org/`. This is another example of the fantastic free software available.

Be sure to make a donation at all the sites where you get free software. By donating, you ensure that developers continue to develop free software.

Follow these steps to install 7-Zip:

1. **Download and install 7-Zip from the 7-Zip site.**

2. **Start the program running and navigate to the folder where you stored the Snowy_Vmware_files.tbz2 archive.**

3. **Double-click to open and unpack it.**

   Figure 15.2 shows this.

   Figure 15.2

   Unpacking archive file with 7-Zip

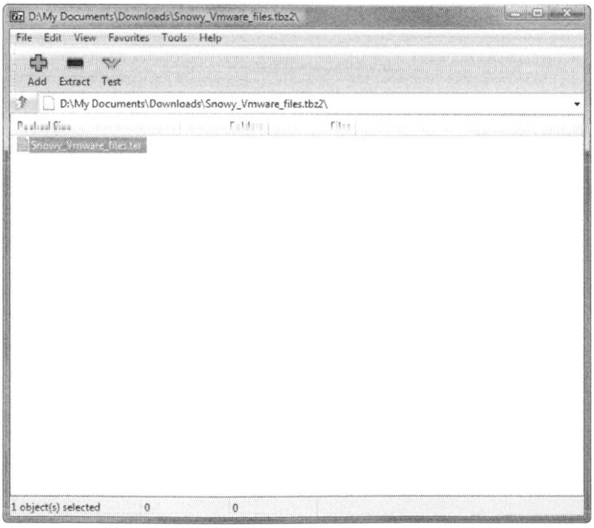

Creating a VMware Virtual Machine

In this section you learn how to set up VMware ready to install Snow Leopard, boot from your Snow Leopard install disk, and install Snow Leopard.

Obtaining your VMware software

As with VMware in Leopard, you need to download the VMware Workstation host software. This is available from the VMware site: `www.vmware.com/products/ws/`.

You need a product key before you can use it. The product key is for a 15-day trial, so if you decide you like it, you can then buy the full product. Obtain the product key by registering at the VMware site. After you have logged in you receive an e-mail with the trial product key.

Another option is to create the virtual machine using VMware Workstation and then use VMware Player to use it.

Booting your Snow Leopard install disk

To create a virtual machine, follow these steps:

1. **Start VMware Workstation running.**

2. **On the greeting screen, select Open Existing VM or Team.**

   Figure 15.3 shows this screen.

   You open the existing VM that plastikman created for you. This has all the correct parameters set so that you can install Snow Leopard to your virtual machine.

3. **Navigate to the folder where you unpacked the archive and select the correct vmx file.**

CAUTION

Don't try to install the file with a . in front of its name; that is a file that Macintoshes use, but Windows does not know how to treat it.

4. **Click OK to go to the Virtual Machine Settings panel, shown in Figure 15.4.**

   Next you need to tell VMware to boot from the boot iso that plastikman has also created.

5. **Click Edit virtual machine settings.**

   This brings up a panel where you can change parameters. The only one you need to change is where to find the boot disk.

Figure 15.3

Greeting screen for VMware

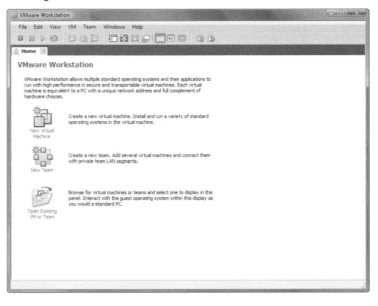

Figure 15.4

Virtual Machine Settings panel

6. **Double-click CD/DVD and use the Browse button to find the darwin_snow.iso file that was included in the Snowy_vmware archive.**

Figure 15.5 shows the selection screen.

Figure 15.5

Boot CD selection screen

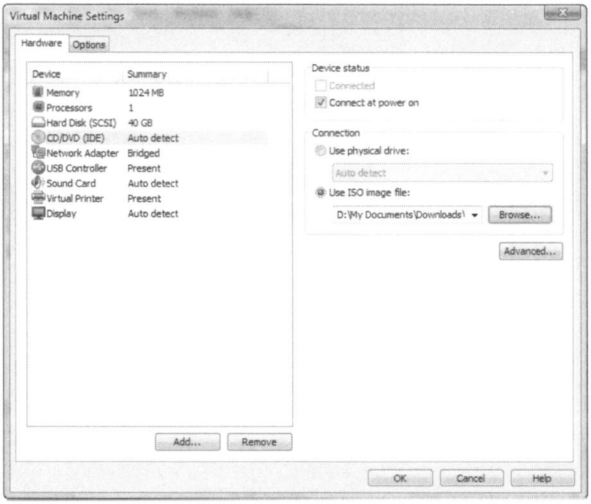

7. **When you return to the Virtual Machine Settings panel, click Power on this virtual machine.**

Within a few seconds, the virtual device starts and boots from the boot iso.

8. **Click your mouse anywhere in the virtual machine screen and press the F8 key.**

This brings up the bootloader, as shown in Figure 15.6.

At this point you need to swap the bootloader for your Snow Leopard install disk. If you were using your hardware CD/DVD drive, you would open the door and replace the disk.

In this case you are using virtual disks, so you need to change it virtually.

9. **Press Ctrl+Alt together to release your mouse pointer from the virtual machine.**

Figure 15.6

Snowy bootloader

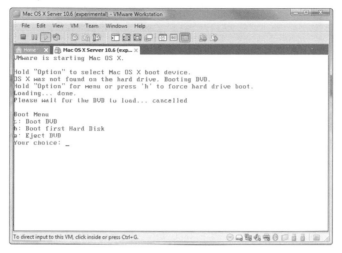

10. **In the status bar at the bottom of your virtual machine, click the small DVD symbol.**

    A small menu pops up with two choices: Connect and Settings.

11. **Click Settings and browse to find the Snow Leopard iso you created earlier.**

12. **Click OK, then click on the DVD symbol again.**

13. **Click Connect, then click back in the main window.**

    You have now connected your Snow Leopard disk to the virtual machine.

14. **In the main window, press C to select Boot DVD.**

15. **When the Darwin prompt appears, press F8 so that you get the boot prompt.**

16. **Type** −v **(for verbose boot) and press Enter.**

You should see a screen looking like Figure 15.7 at some point during the process.

Then sit back and relax until you get to the first install screen, looking like Figure 15.8.

In my experience, the installation always gets to this point.

Figure 15.7

Boot progress screen

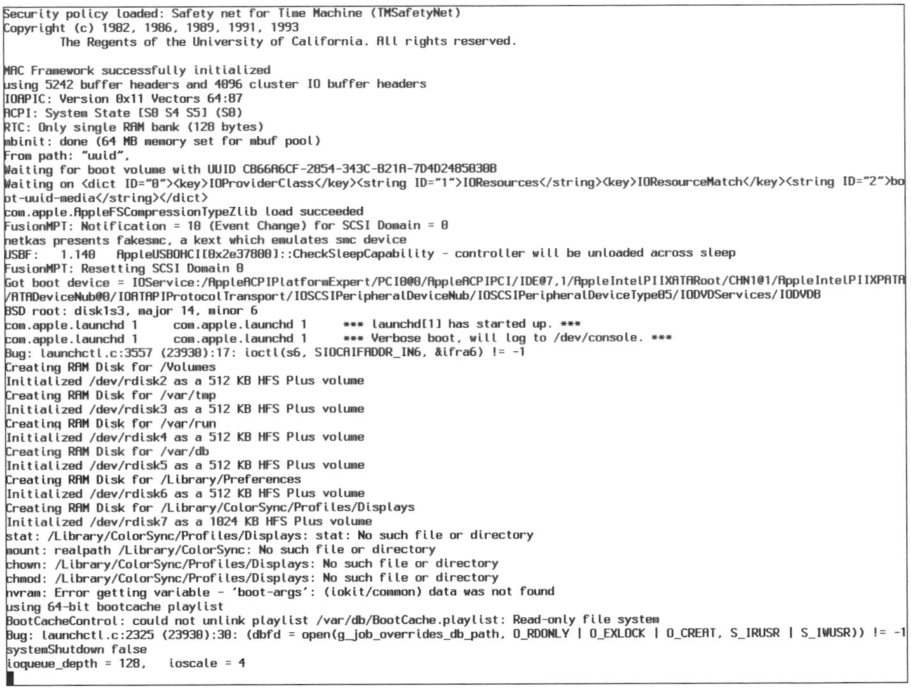

```
Security policy loaded: Safety net for Time Machine (TMSafetyNet)
Copyright (c) 1982, 1986, 1989, 1991, 1993
        The Regents of the University of California. All rights reserved.

MAC Framework successfully initialized
using 5242 buffer headers and 4096 cluster IO buffer headers
IOAPIC: Version 0x11 Vectors 64:87
ACPI: System State [S0 S4 S5] (S0)
RTC: Only single RAM bank (128 bytes)
mbinit: done (64 MB memory set for mbuf pool)
From path: "uuid",
Waiting for boot volume with UUID CB66A6CF-2854-343C-B21A-7D4D2485030B
Waiting on <dict ID="0"><key>IOProviderClass</key><string ID="1">IOResources</string><key>IOResourceMatch</key><string ID="2">bo
ot-uuid-media</string></dict>
com.apple.AppleFSCompressionTypeZlib load succeeded
FusionMPT: Notification = 10 (Event Change) for SCSI Domain = 0
netkas presents fakesmc, a kext which emulates smc device
USBF:    1.148   AppleUSBOHCI[0x2e37800]::CheckSleepCapability - controller will be unloaded across sleep
FusionMPT: Resetting SCSI Domain 0
Got boot device = IOService:/AppleACPIPlatformExpert/PCI000/AppleACPIPCI/IDE07,1/AppleIntelPIIXATARoot/CHN1@1/AppleIntelPIIXPATA
/ATADeviceNub@0/IOATAPIProtocolTransport/IOSCSIPeripheralDeviceNub/IOSCSIPeripheralDeviceType05/IODVDServices/IODVDB
BSD root: disk1s3, major 14, minor 6
com.apple.launchd 1     com.apple.launchd 1     *** launchd[1] has started up. ***
com.apple.launchd 1     com.apple.launchd 1     *** Verbose boot, will log to /dev/console. ***
Bug: launchctl.c:3557 (23930):17: ioctl(s6, SIOCAIFADDR_IN6, &ifra6) != -1
Creating RAM Disk for /Volumes
Initialized /dev/rdisk2 as a 512 KB HFS Plus volume
Creating RAM Disk for /var/tmp
Initialized /dev/rdisk3 as a 512 KB HFS Plus volume
Creating RAM Disk for /var/run
Initialized /dev/rdisk4 as a 512 KB HFS Plus volume
Creating RAM Disk for /var/db
Initialized /dev/rdisk5 as a 512 KB HFS Plus volume
Creating RAM Disk for /Library/Preferences
Initialized /dev/rdisk6 as a 512 KB HFS Plus volume
Creating RAM Disk for /Library/ColorSync/Profiles/Displays
Initialized /dev/rdisk7 as a 1024 KB HFS Plus volume
stat: /Library/ColorSync/Profiles/Displays: stat: No such file or directory
mount: realpath /Library/ColorSync: No such file or directory
chown: /Library/ColorSync/Profiles/Displays: No such file or directory
chmod: /Library/ColorSync/Profiles/Displays: No such file or directory
nvram: Error getting variable - 'boot-args': (iokit/common) data was not found
using 64-bit bootcache playlist
BootCacheControl: could not unlink playlist /var/db/BootCache.playlist: Read-only file system
Bug: launchctl.c:2325 (23930):30: (dbfd = open(g_job_overrides_db_path, O_RDONLY | O_EXLOCK | O_CREAT, S_IRUSR | S_IWUSR)) != -1
systemShutdown false
ioqueue_depth = 128,    ioscale = 4
```

Figure 15.8

Snow Leopard language selection screen

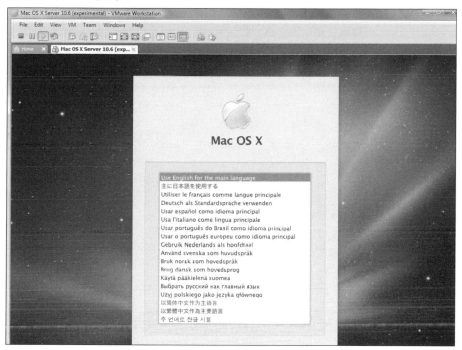

Installing Snow Leopard

Not only has plastikman created all the files for you, he's also set up a 40GB hard disk, which should be large enough for you. So it's now simply a matter of installing Snow Leopard to that hard disk.

Follow these steps to install Snow Leopard:

1. **Click the arrow to proceed to the next step.**

2. **Click Accept for the license details.**

    You arrive at the screen asking where you want to install Snow Leopard, as shown in Figure 15.9.

Figure 15.9

Disk selection screen

3. **Click the image of the disk and click Install.**

You could go through and select Customizing options, but in my opinion it's simpler to install the whole lot. It doesn't take up much space.

Now it's a matter of waiting while Snow Leopard installs. The first time I did it, the installation crashed with a kernel panic after about 30 minutes, but in fact the installation had gone to completion.

In subsequent installations, it has gone right through to the success screen, as shown in Figure 15.10.

Figure 15.10

Installation successful screen

At this point you can either stop your virtual machine by clicking the red button at the top or you can wait for it to shut itself down.

Setting Up Snow Leopard

Now that you've installed Snow Leopard, it should be plain sailing from here. You need to go through the normal setting up process of creating your user account and so on.

Booting for the first time

First you need to boot your new installation. As suggested by plastikman, it may be necessary to boot several times before you get through to the first screen. In my experience it has never taken more than four boots to get there, but plastikman suggests that it may take up to ten boot attempts.

Follow these steps to boot your virtual Snow Leopard:

1. **Select your Snow Leopard virtual machine in WMware and click Edit virtual machine settings.**

2. **Double-click CD/DVD settings and browse to find the darwin_snow.iso file you originally booted from.**

   This is needed because your virtual disk does not have a boot loader. If this was a real machine rather than virtual this would be a nuisance, but in this case it's not a problem.

3. **Click OK and then click Start this virtual machine.**

4. **After the BIOS has signed on you get a message saying Operating system not found.**

   This is because the CD/DVD drive is not active. If you look in the status bar, you will see it's grayed out.

5. **Click the red stop button, then click the CD/DVD symbol in the status bar and select Connect.**

6. **If you receive an error message saying the Mac OS is using the CDROM device, click OK then shut down the virtual machine.**

7. **Again, select Start this virtual machine.**

   This time, after the BIOS has signed on, you see a message asking you to press F8 NOW. You only have a very short time to respond so I suggest you put your finger ready to press the F8 key!

8. **Press F8 and then enter –v –x to launch Snow Leopard in verbose, safe boot mode.**

   I have found using both together reduces the number of reboots. If you don't react in time to press the F8 key, Snow Leopard goes ahead and boots in normal mode. If this happens, your screen display looks like that shown in Figure 15.11.

   You then see the gray screen with the Apple logo and the rotating clock symbol.

   On the first boot, Snow Leopard normally takes quite a while to start. On my computer, the usual time can be up to five minutes, so be patient. Watch the little hard disk icon in the status bar. When it gets to the point where it is only blinking briefly every ten seconds or so, it probably indicates that the boot is not going to succeed.

9. **Repeat Steps 7 and 8 until you succeed in getting to the welcome screen.**

   In my experience it has never taken more than four boot attempts. Be patient. Eventually you will be able to complete the installation.

   Because your virtual machine is not capable of Quartz Extreme/Core Image graphics, you do not see the greeting video and instead go straight to the welcome screen, as shown in Figure 15.12.

Figure 15.11

Normal boot screen

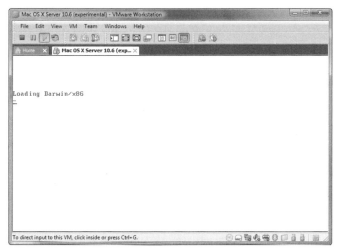

Figure 15.12

Snow Leopard welcome screen

10. Select your country on the Welcome screen and click Continue.

11. Go through the remaining screens, entering your details where needed.

If you have a MobileMe membership you can enter details. Your Snow Leopard installation should be connected to the Internet at this point.

12. Set up your account name and password, and finally you arrive at the Snow Leopard main screen.

13. Check that everything has installed by looking at the Dock.

14. Open Safari and check that you can connect to the Internet.

Saving a snapshot

One really nice feature of virtual machines is that you can save snapshots. These capture the exact state of the virtual machine and save it to disk. If you reload a snapshot you recreate your virtual machine in exactly the same state as it was when you saved it. Trust me; it can be a real lifesaver.

At this point, save a snapshot of your virtual machine by following these steps:

1. Use Ctrl+Alt if you need to, to free the mouse pointer from the Snow Leopard virtual machine.

2. Click VM on the VMware window.

3. Select Snapshot, then Take snapshot.

4. Call the snapshot First boot and save it.

Now, whenever you want to return to that point, simply select Snapshot, Load snapshot and select the one you want.

Using Your Virtual Machine

From this point on, your virtual Snow Leopard behaves exactly the same as the real Snow Leopard, except that it can't use Quartz Extreme/Core Image. It can connect to the hard disks on your host computer.

If you click About this Mac from the menu bar, you see that it is running version 10.6 of OS X. Figure 15.13 shows the display on my virtual Snow Leopard.

Figure 15.13

About this virtual Mac

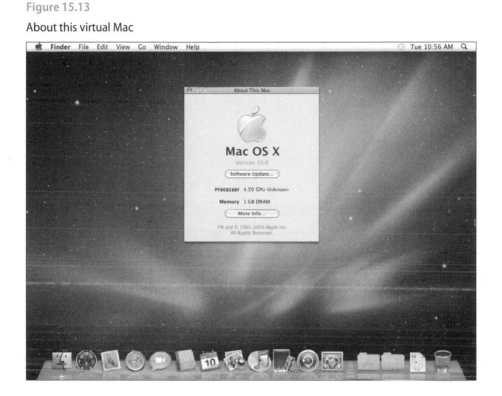

Note that it is wrong about my processor speed. If only it really was that fast!

If you click on the More Info button on the About this Mac display, you see details about the installation. Figure 15.14 shows the first panel of information about my computer.

Figure 15.14

More info about my Snow Leopard

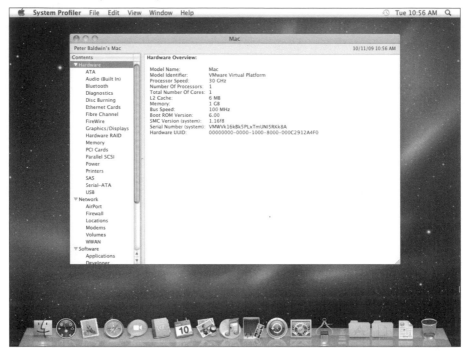

If you open a Finder window, you should see your Windows host computer listed.

Figure 15.15 shows the Finder window for my installation, with the Windows host computer (HOME) and my real Mac Mini.

Figure 15.15

The Finder window for my installation

Sharing your Windows files

Before you can connect with your virtual machine, you must share the files and folders on your Windows computer. To do this, follow these steps on your Windows host computer:

1. **Use Windows Explorer to navigate to the folder you want to share.**

   In this case, I will share My Documents.

2. **Right-click the folder, and select the Sharing tab, as shown in Figure 15.16.**

3. **Click Advanced Sharing, and place a check mark in Share this folder, as shown in Figure 15.17.**

Figure 15.16

Sharing tab

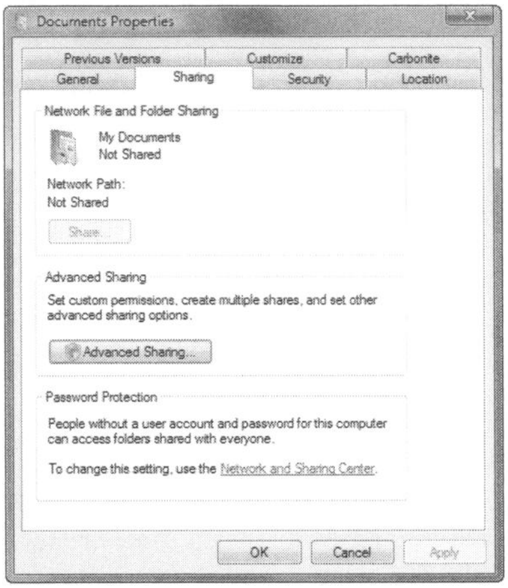

Figure 15.17

Advanced sharing

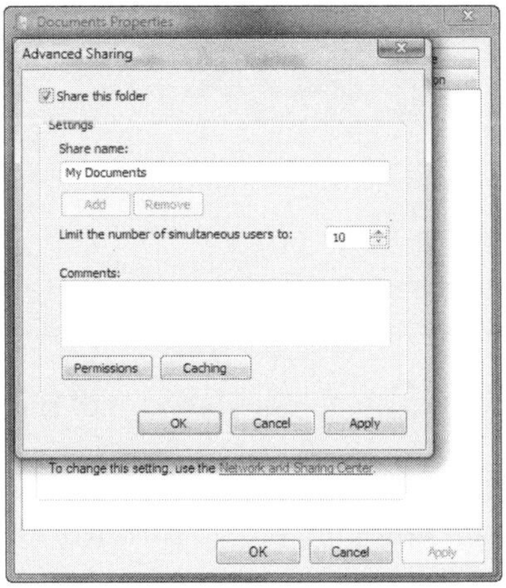

4. Click OK, followed by OK after you have checked that the folder is now shared, as shown in Figure 15.18.

My Vista computer is named HOME so the share name becomes \\HOME\My Documents, and this becomes the server name in Leopard.

Figure 15.18

My Documents shared

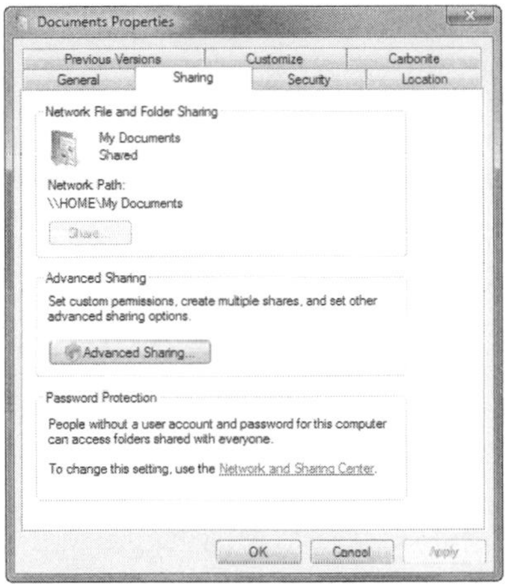

5. **In your virtual machine, make sure Finder is the front application and select Go, Connect to Server..., as shown in Figure 15.19.**

Figure 15.19

Connect to server

6. **In the server box, type** smb:// **followed by the name of your server from the shared folder above.**

In this case, the server name is smb://home, as shown in Figure 15.20. Remember that while Windows uses the double backslash (\\), Leopard uses the double forward slash (//).

Figure 15.20

Connect to server dialog box

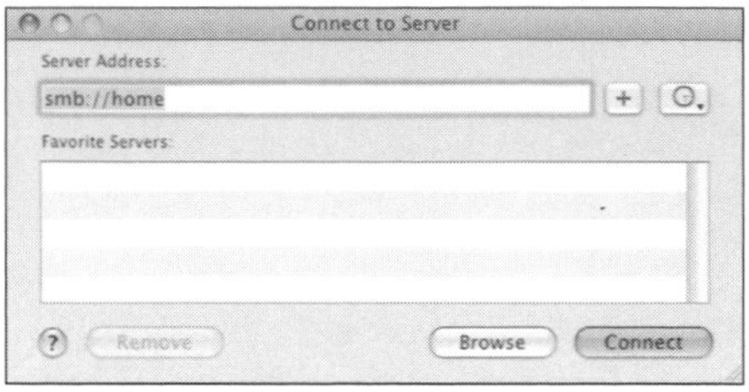

The folks at Apple can't bring themselves to use the word "Windows," so they refer to the server as SMB (standing for Server Message Block)!

If your virtual Leopard can't find your computer by its server name, try using its IP address. In my case the server then becomes smb://192.168.1.2.

7. **In the name and password box, enter a username and password for the account on the Windows computer and allow Leopard to save the name and password in your keychain of passwords, as shown in Figure 15.21.**

Figure 15.21

Connect to a username

8. **Click Connect.**

9. **Select the name of the volume to mount.**

In this case, as shown in Figure 15.22, the only shared folder is My Documents, but if you had shared other folders, they would be shown as well.

10. **Leopard mounts the volume and opens it in your default view, as shown in Figure 15.23.**

Figure 15.22

Volume to mount

Figure 15.23

My Documents shared

Finally, so that the volume is available each time you use the virtual machine, you can save it to your desktop as a shortcut. Follow these steps to do that:

1. **In the My Documents window, right-click the folder alias icon in the toolbar.**

   Remember that the folder alias icon is the little icon at the top of the toolbar, to the left of the name of the folder.

2. **Select the highest folder in the hierarchy (Peter Baldwin's Mac Pro, in this example), as shown in Figure 15.24.**

3. **Press and hold the Command and Option keys (Windows key and Alt) while you drag the icon to the desktop.**

   This places an alias to the My Documents folder on your desktop. Now whenever you want to view files on your Windows computer, simply double-click on the desktop alias to open the folder.

Figure 15.24

Top of folder hierarchy

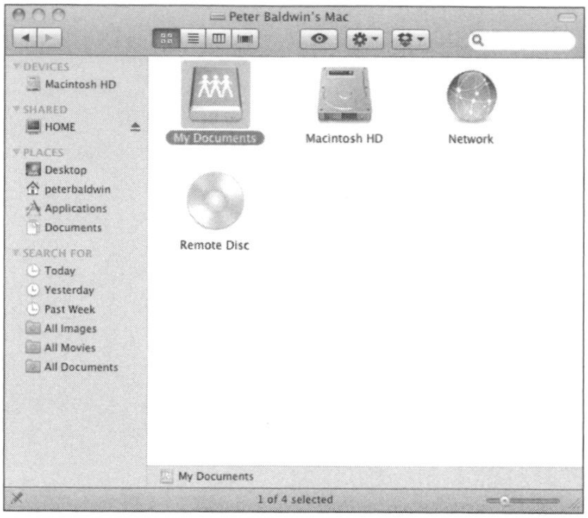

4. **Save a snapshot of your system so that you don't have to reconnect and save the alias every time you start Leopard.**

TIP

When you finish your session with Snow Leopard, you should suspend the virtual machine rather than simply shut it down. That way, any changes you made are saved until your next session.

Summary

In this chapter, you installed a standard retail copy of Snow Leopard to create a virtual machine using VMware. You then set it up to connect with your Windows computer and saved a snapshot of it for ease of using it at a later date.

Virtual machines are becoming more frequently used in computing, particularly in relation to servers. Four products are available for virtualizing other operating systems on the Windows platform, but at this time only one of them can install and run OS X. For other operating systems running as guests, the providers of virtualizing software provide systems that can optimize the virtual machines. Because Apple permits OS X to be installed only on Apple-labeled computers, the manufacturers of virtualizing software for Windows do not provide optimizations, so the virtual machines suffer from low graphics performance.

IV
Enhancing Your Macintosh

N ow you're on the home stretch. By the time you work through all of this part, you will have done more than probably 95 percent of Mac users. As with Parts II and III, the exercises in this part can be done on a Macintosh computer.

While each chapter in this part focuses on programming your Hackintosh to do new things, for the most part, the programming is not particularly difficult, nor is it difficult to understand.

Before you start the exercises in these chapters, you need to become an Apple Developer. You can do this for free and avail yourself of many free applications and utilities, as well as access to a whole library of information.

First you use Automator, which is designed so you can automate tasks that you do regularly and that have a number of steps in them. Having mastered Automator, you create some scripts in AppleScript to link applications together.

If you find Leopard's Dashboard useful, you will enjoy creating your own widgets to install into Dashboard. Next you use Quartz Composer, a very powerful graphics processing application that allows you to manipulate graphic images in many different ways. Finally, you develop a complete, albeit simple, stand-alone application and learn the rudiments of the Objective-C programming language.

Automating Your Work

N ow that you've built your Hackintosh and got it working to your satisfaction, what are you going to do with it? Pretty much all the software you might have used on your Windows computer has an equivalent on the Macintosh. In some areas, particularly in publishing, graphic arts, and video, the Mac has always enjoyed a reputation for being the best in the field. In some areas, the Windows platform has caught up and even surpassed the Macintosh, but for many fields, using a Mac is still almost de rigueur.

One feature of every Mac that does not have an exact analog in the Windows world is Automator. This is built-in software that, as the name suggests, can automate many tasks you undertake using the computer. For example, if you often have to prepare a set of photographs to a specific size for publication, you can create an Automator script to do it automatically.

In this chapter, you look at Automator, run some sample scripts, and create your own script to back up your files.

Getting Around in Automator

Automator is the Leopard application that allows you to create scripts to carry out repetitive tasks without requiring user intervention. It takes small building blocks called Actions and links them together to automate a task.

In this section, you launch Automator, orient yourself to the screen layout, and experiment with the actions library.

Preparing to launch Automator

Before you can launch Automator, you must switch on access for assistive devices. Follow these steps to turn it on:

1. **Open System Preferences.**

2. **Choose the Universal Access pane.**

3. **Check the box for Enable access for assistive devices, as shown in Figure 16.1.**

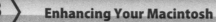

Figure 16.1

System Preferences pane for Universal Access

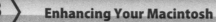

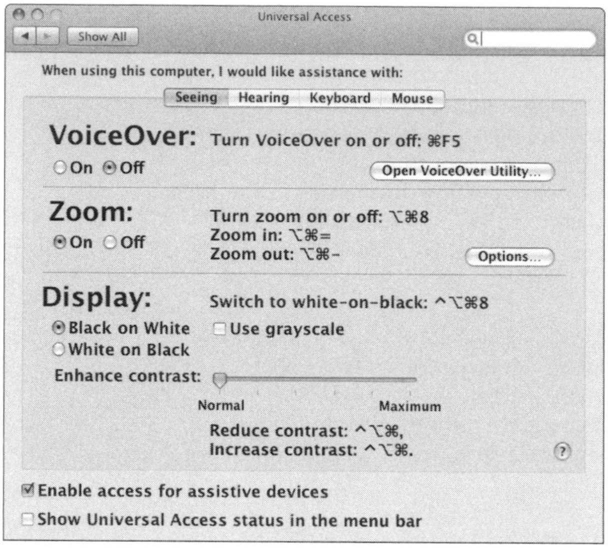

Orienting yourself to Automator

When you launch Automator, the first screen you see is the main window of the application, with a sheet overlaying it. The overlay sheet is the starting point sheet, as shown in Figure 16.2.

Figure 16.2

Automator starting point sheet

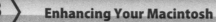

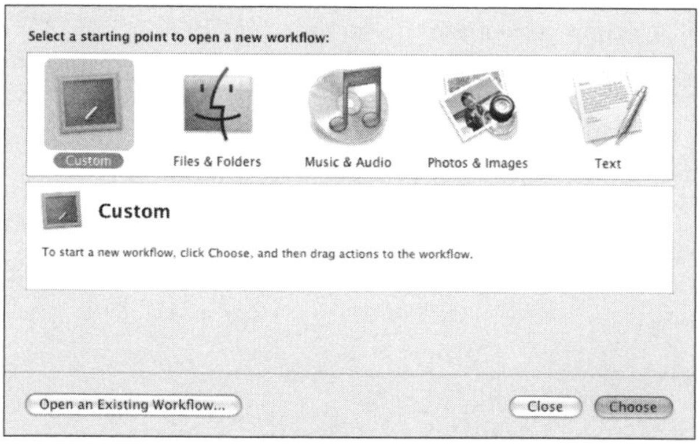

If you choose to create a new workflow, you arrive at the main workflow menu, as shown in Figure 16.3.

Figure 16.3

Automator workflow items

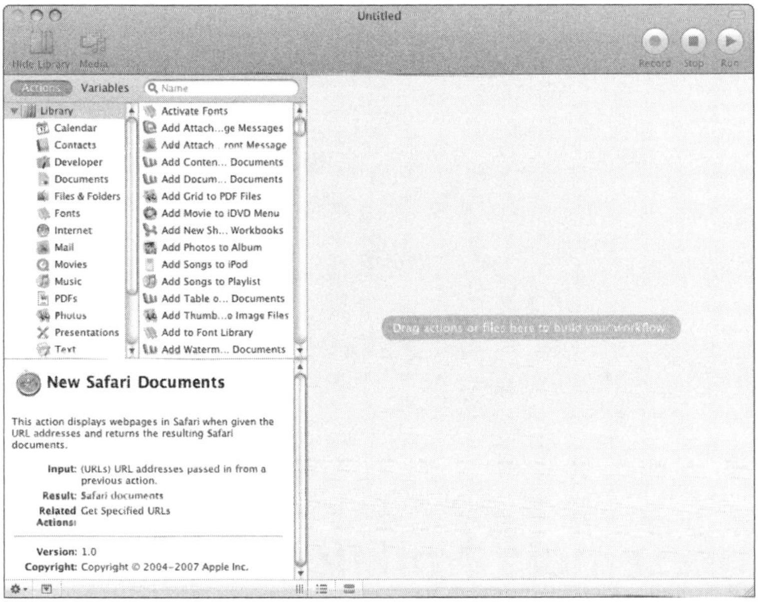

The example shown here is from my computer with Microsoft Office installed. Many applications add their own actions to the library: In this case, Office added two extra library categories—Documents and Presentations. These aren't in your library unless you have installed Microsoft Office.

At the top of the main screen is a selector to switch from Actions to Variables. The Variables view is shown in Figure 16.4.

Figure 16.4

Variables view

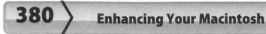

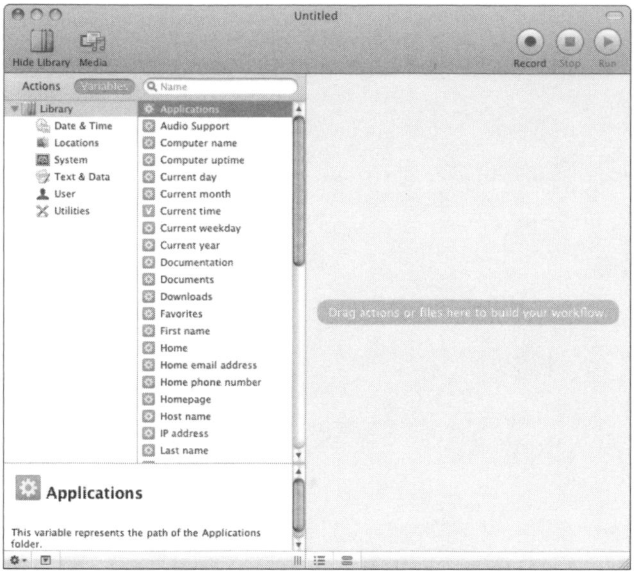

Running a Sample Workflow

In this section, you download and run a sample workflow provided by Apple. This workflow takes some selected files and creates a new disk image containing the files.

Preparing to run workflows

Before you start on this section, copy some picture files from your Windows disk to the Pictures folder in your home folder. Four or five pictures are plenty.

Downloading and running the workflow

To run the workflow, follow these steps:

1. **Create a new folder called Workflows in your Documents folder.**

2. **Navigate to** www.macosxautomation.com/automator/examples/ex06/ pkg/workflow.zip **(or** http://tinyurl.com/la58or**), and save the down-loaded file.**

3. **Unzip the file, and drag it to your Workflows folder.**

4. **Double-click the file, and wait while Automator opens it.**

Figure 16.5 shows the workflow open in Automator.

Figure 16.5

Create disk image workflow

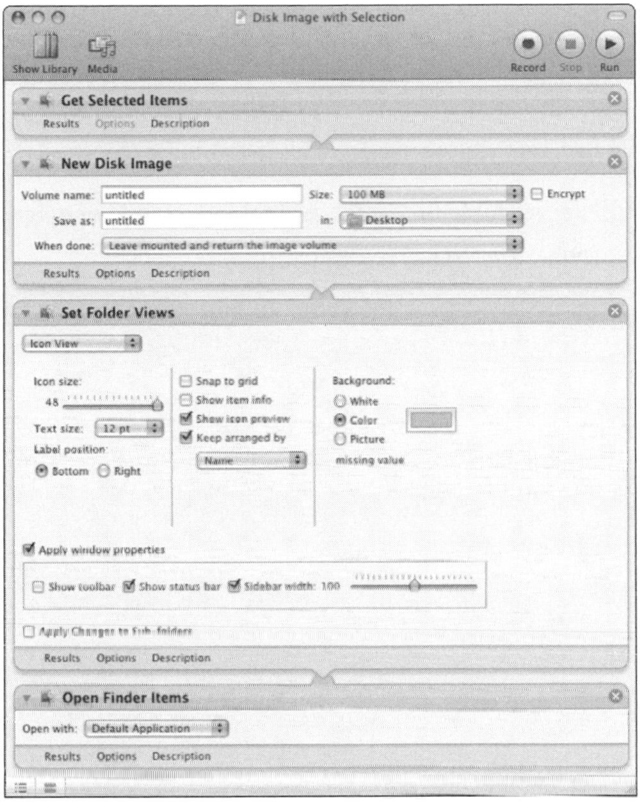

There are four steps in the workflow:

Step 1: Open the selected files.

Step 2: Ask for the names of the disk image and the filename.

Step 3: Set the Finder view parameters.

Step 4: Open the image in a Finder window.

Each step in a workflow takes its input from the step before it and passes its output to the step that follows it.

In Step 1, Finder opens the selected files and passes them to Step 2. Step 2 gets a filename and volume name as input from the user and creates a new disk image file. Step 3 sets the appropriate parameters for Finder. Finally, in Step 4, the disk image is mounted and the contents displayed in Finder.

Before you start, you need to open a folder and select two or more files. After the workflow runs, it asks you to enter two names, one as the volume name for the disk image and the other as the filename for the image; the two can be different. It then sets a view in Finder, creates the disk image and the file, and finally opens the disk image.

To run the workflow and create the new disk image, follow these steps:

1. **Open your Pictures folder in Finder, and select a couple of items.**

2. **Run the workflow by clicking the Run button.**

3. **At the prompt, enter** Test Volume **as the Volume name and** Test Image **for Save as, as shown in Figure 16.6.**

Figure 16.6

Volume and image name

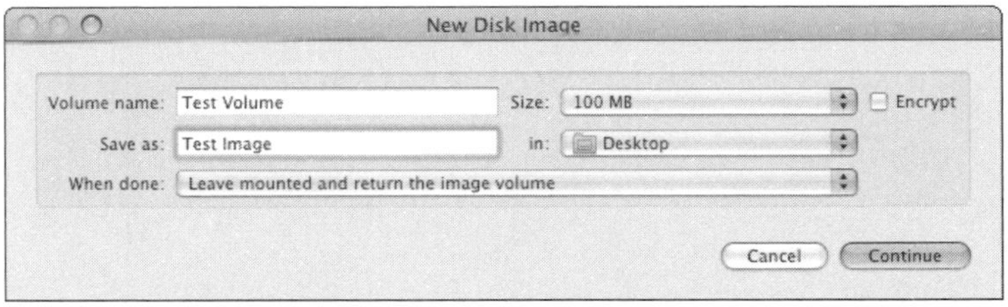

After a few seconds, a new disk image appears on your desktop. Shortly after, Image Mounter mounts the image, as shown in Figure 16.7a.

4. **Finally, Finder opens the disk image and shows the files, as shown in Figure 16.7b.**

Figure 16.7

New disk image and volume (a); Finder view of disk image (b)

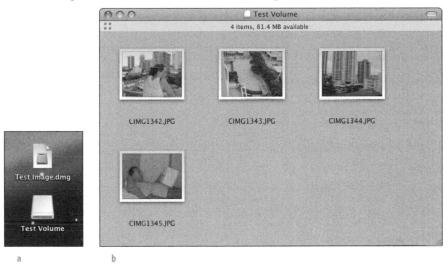

a   b

Viewing the results and the log

If you click the Results button on a step, Automator shows the results of the step. Figure 16.8 shows the result of the first step.

Figure 16.8

Step result from Automator

While it is running, Automator also keeps a log of what happens in each step and how long each step took. To view the log, click the icon in the bottom left of the Automator window. Figure 16.9 shows the log for the run.

Figure 16.9

Log for the run of disk image with selection

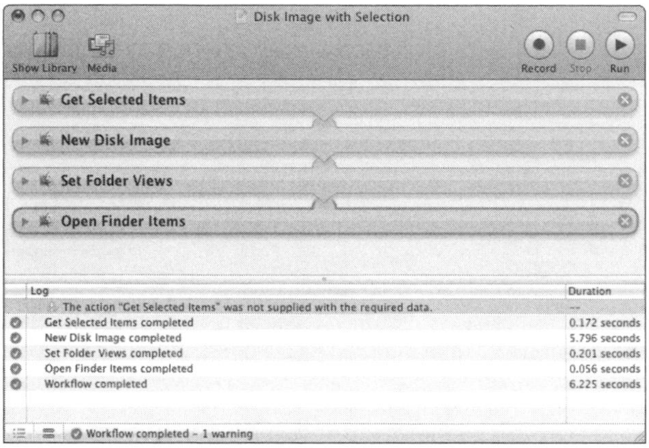

Note the error message in the first line. You can ignore it. The whole process took just over six seconds.

Modifying the Sample Workflow

A limitation of the workflow is that you must remember to select files in a folder before you start the workflow; otherwise, you finish up with an empty volume. In this section, you modify the workflow so it asks you which files you want to include in the workflow.

Follow these steps to modify and run the workflow:

1. **Close the original workflow without saving any changes, and reopen it in Automator.**

2. **Click the close button (located on the right of the action) on the Get Selected Items action to remove it from the list of actions.**

3. **Click the Show Library button.**

4. **Select Files and Folders, select Ask for Finder Items, and drag it to the first position on the workflow, as shown in Figure 16.10.**

Figure 16.10

New workflow

5. **Select Allow Multiple Selection, and set Start at: to Pictures.**

6. **Run the workflow, selecting multiple documents in the Pictures folder when prompted.**

7. **Save the workflow to your Workflows folder as** Disk Image Prompted Selection.

Looping

What if the files you want to add to the disk image are from different folders? The Ask for Finder Items action allows you to select from only one folder. To add extra files, you need to be able to rerun the Ask for Finder Items action and add the new files to the existing list.

Automator has a loop action that allows you to accomplish exactly this.

To create a looping workflow, follow these steps:

1. **Reload the Disk Image Prompted Selection workflow.**

2. **From the Library, select Utilities, Loop and drag it as the second item in the work-flow, as shown in Figure 16.11.**

Figure 16.11

Adding the loop action

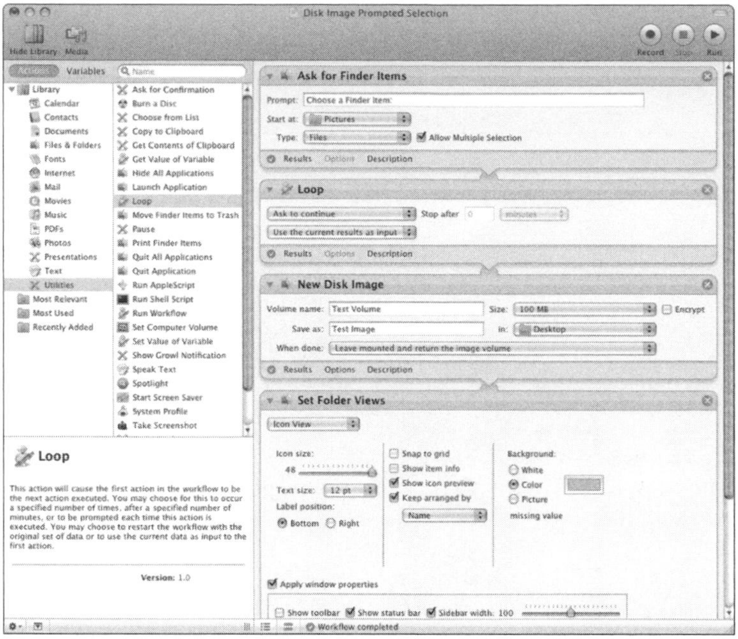

3. **Set looping to Ask to continue, and select Use the current results as input.**

   By using current results as input, you add the new items the second time through the loop to those from the first time through.

4. **Save the workflow as** Looping Disk Image with Prompted Selection.

5. **Run the workflow and select one or two files from the Pictures folder.**

6. **Click Choose.**

7. **On the loop sheet that drops down, select Continue, as shown in Figure 16.12.**

8. **Navigate to a different folder, and select one or two files from that folder.**

9. **Click Choose, and then on the drop-down sheet, select Don't Continue.**

10. **Enter the names of the disk volume and disk image you want to create.**

11. **Wait until the workflow completes, and then examine the files included in your disk image.**

Figure 16.12

Continue Looping

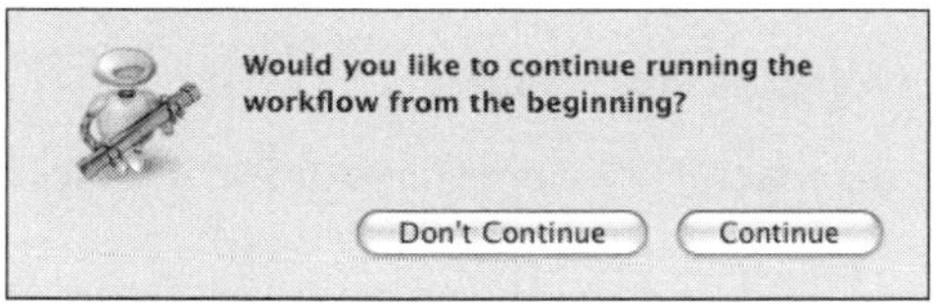

Using variables

If you want to include all the files in a particular folder, rather than ask the user to input the files individually, you can define a variable and then use that as the input into a workflow.

Follow these steps to use variables to specify the files to include in the image:

1. **Delete the Ask for Finder Items and Loop actions.**

2. **In the Library, select Variables, Locations and drag Pictures to be the first action, ahead of New Disk Image, as shown in Figure 16.13.**

Figure 16.13

Using a variable for input

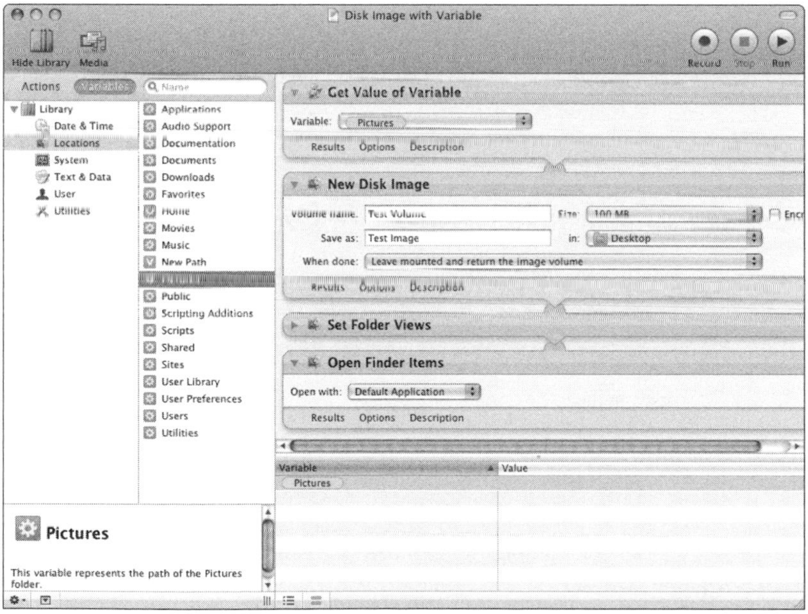

Remember that the output for each action is the input for the next, so by using the variable Pictures, you find the path to that folder and use it as input to the New Disk Image action.

3. **Save the workflow as** Disk Image with Variable**.**

4. **Run the workflow, and see that all the items in your Pictures folder are added to the disk image.**

Creating a New Workflow

In this section, you create a new workflow from the start rather than modifying an existing workflow.

Using the actions library

Let's create a very simple Automator workflow to take a number of files and create an archive (zip file) from them. Follow these steps:

1. **Start Automator running.**

2. **On the starting point sheet, select Files and Folders and then select Get content from My Mac and Search for files and folders when my workflow runs, as shown in Figure 16.14.**

Figure 16.14

New Files & Folders workflow

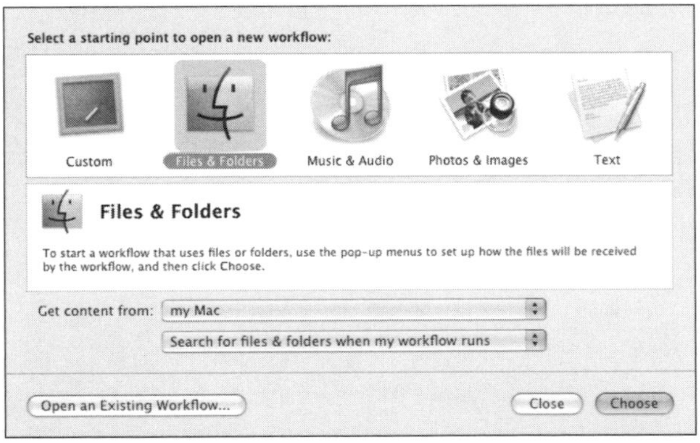

3. **Click Choose.**

Figure 16.15 shows your Automator window at this point.

Figure 16.15

Automator Window with Search for Finder Items

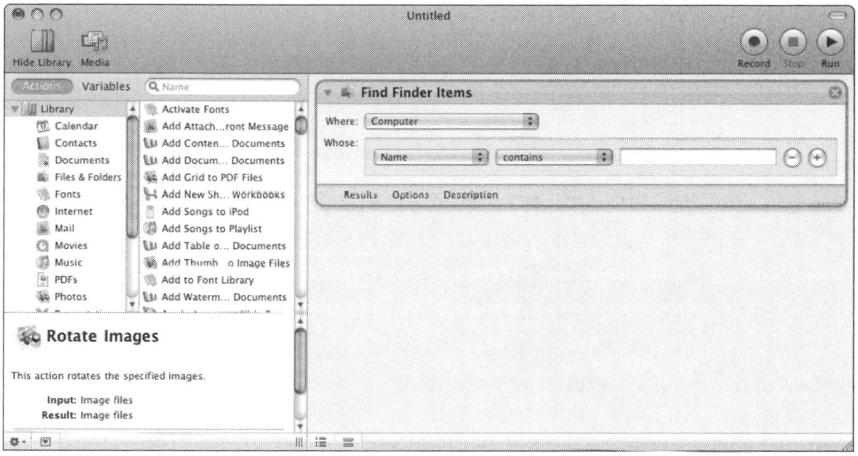

4. **In the Where drop-down box, choose your username (peterbaldwin in my case).**

5. **In the Whose drop-down box, choose Kind, is, and Image.**

6. **Save the workflow in your Workflows folder as** Archive Images.

   That completes the first part of the workflow.

7. **Run the workflow, and click Results to see the files that were found.**

   My results are shown in Figure 16.16.

   Where did all those files come from? In my case, most of the files are images created for this book, but some are files cached by Safari and sundry other files.

   Now I add the action that creates the zip file.

8. **In the Library pane of Automator, select Files & Folders, then select Create Archive, and drag it to the Actions pane, as shown in Figure 16.17.**

9. **In the Where drop-down box, select Desktop.**

10. **Save the workflow.**

    Now it's time to run it.

11. **Click the Run button in the toolbar of Automator.**

    When the workflow completes, you see two green check icons beside Results in the Actions pane.

12. **Open the Archive.zip file on your desktop.**

Figure 16.16

Image files on my computer

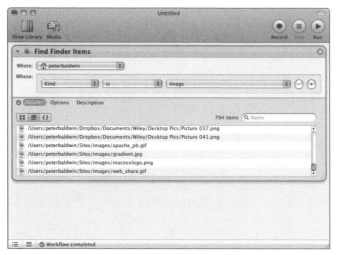

Figure 16.17

Create archive in Actions pane

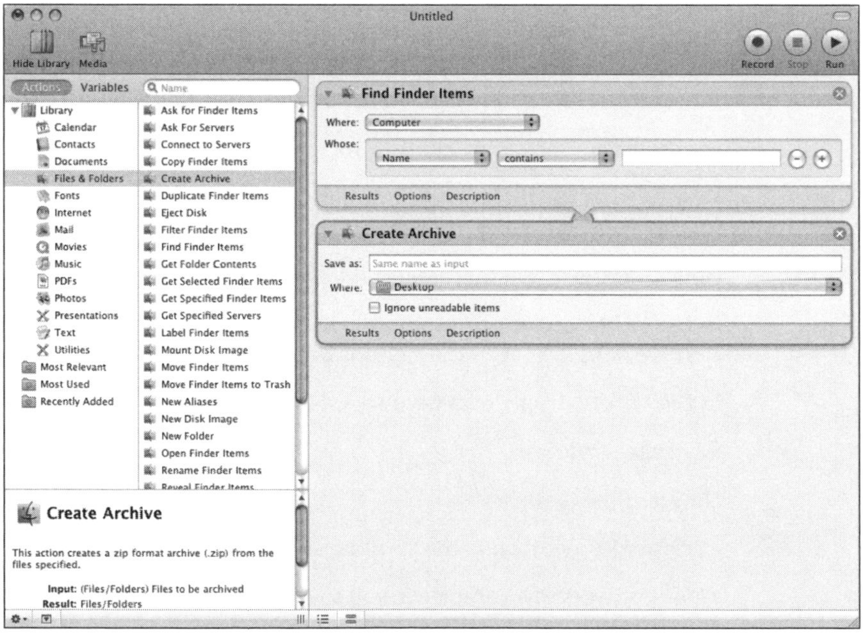

Saving a Workflow as a Plug-in

Automator's real power lies in the fact that any of the workflows you create can be turned into plug-ins for Finder or folders. Finder plug-ins are available in any folder; folder plug-ins are specific to the folder to which they are attached.

In this section, you create a Finder plug-in from the workflow you created earlier and use it in any folder. You also create a new folder plug-in.

Creating Finder plug-ins

Previously you created a workflow to find files meeting certain criteria and create an archive file containing those files. Now you extend this to make a Finder plug-in that can be used from any folder.

Follow these steps to create a Finder plug-in to archive files:

1. **Start Automator, and create a new workflow, selecting Custom as the start point.**

2. **Add the Get Selected Finder Items and Create Archive actions.**

3. **Open your Pictures folder, and select a couple of pictures.**

4. **Run your workflow, and check that it creates a new file called Archive.zip in the same folder.**

5. **Save the workflow as a Finder plug-in by selecting File, Save as Plugin. . . .**

6. **Name the plug-in** Make Archive, **and click Save, as shown in Figure 16.18.**

   Figure 16.18

   Save workflow as Finder plug-in

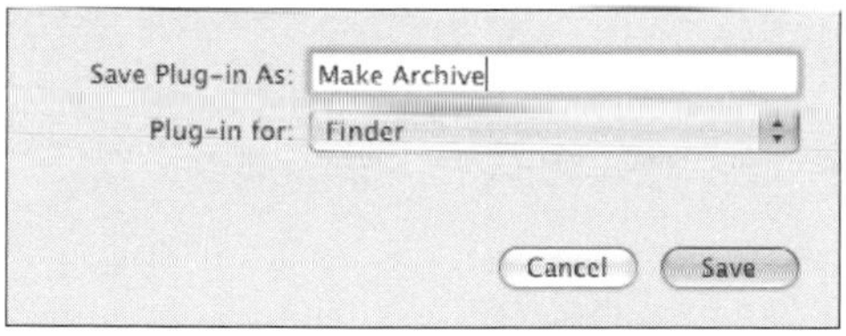

7. **Remain in your Pictures folder, and move Archive.zip to Trash.**

8. **Select some files, right-click anywhere in the folder blank space, and select More on the context menu.**

9. **Select Automator, and then select Make Archive, as shown in Figure 16.19.**

   Your Pictures folder dims for a second or two, then returns with a new file called Archive.zip.

Figure 16.19

Context menu choice to run Finder action

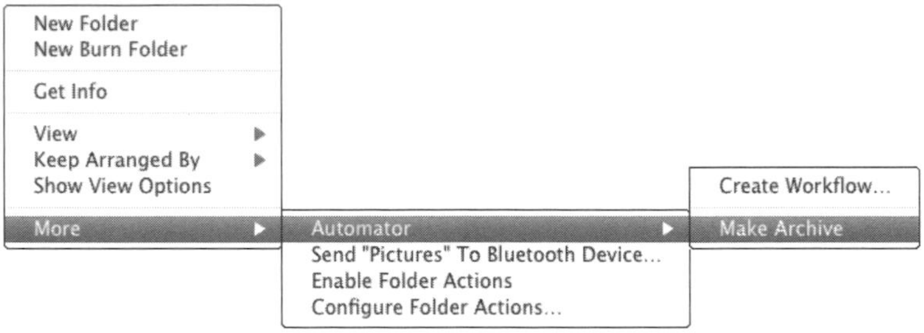

Because this is now a Finder action, it can be run from any folder and creates a new zip file containing all the files you specify.

All your workflow plug-ins are saved in your Library folder. This is located at `~/Library/Workflows/Applications/Finder`. The ~ tells you to start at your home folder; that's the one that has your login name. In my case, my home folder is called peterbaldwin.

As you can see from the Automator library, there are many, many possibilities for creating workflows, limited only by your imagination and need.

And if you don't want to reinvent the wheel, search the Internet for "automator sample workflows." Places to start include `http://automator.us/downloads.html`, `http://automatorworld.com/`, and `http://automatoractions.com/`.

Using Folder Actions

Folder actions are scripts (or small programs) that can be attached to a folder. Chapter 19 takes you into more detail with scripts, even creating your own. For now, we just use scripts created by other people.

In this section, you add folder actions to folders on your computer.

Detecting files added to a folder

Each installation of Leopard has a folder called Drop Box inside your Public folder. If you use Get Info to examine the details about the Drop Box folder, you find it has permissions that give everyone the ability to save files to your Drop Box, but they can't view any files in there, as shown in Figure 16.20.

This can be useful in large organizations where you collect files from other people for processing. But how do you know when someone leaves a file in your Drop Box? You attach a folder action to notify you.

Figure 16.20

Drop Box permissions

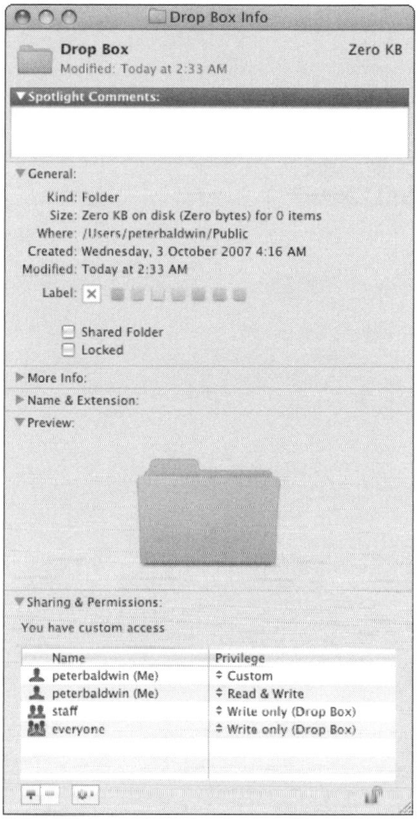

In this section, you can't use the Drop Box because it's unlikely you're connected to other users. You can, however, see how it would work.

Follow these steps to add a folder action to your Pictures folder:

1. **Open your Pictures folder, using Finder.**

2. **Right-click in the window, and select More, Enable Folder Actions, as shown in Figure 16.21.**

3. **Right-click again, and select More, Attach a Folder Action, as shown in Figure 16.22.**

4. **If needed, navigate to the folder** /Library/Scripts/Folder Action Scripts**, select** add - new item alert.scpt**, and click Choose, as shown in Figure 16.23.**

Figure 16.21

Enable folder actions

Figure 16.22

Configure folder actions

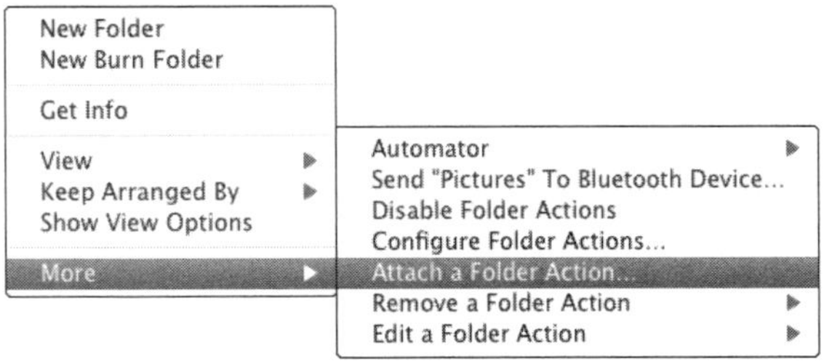

Figure 16.23

Choosing a folder action script

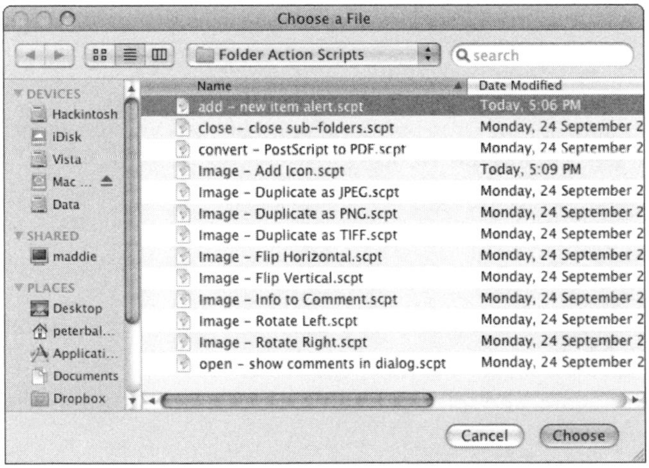

Test the script by dragging a new picture into the folder. You should get a pop-up window telling you a new item has been added to the folder, as shown in Figure 16.24.

Figure 16.24

New item alert

Converting graphics files to other formats

You can use folder action scripts for many other things. One use is to convert graphics files to another format as you add them to a folder.

Follow these steps to add a new folder action to convert graphics files:

1. **Open the Pictures folder, right-click in the window, and select Configure Folder Actions.**

   This opens a new window, as shown in Figure 16.25a.

   The left part of the window shows the folders that have actions attached. The right half shows the actions attached to each folder.

2. **Disable the** add - new item alert **action by unchecking the box.**

3. **Click the + (plus) sign below the right half of the window, and select** Image - Duplicate as .PNG **script, as shown in Figure 16.25b.**

4. **Click Attach, and then close the window by clicking the Close button.**

5. **Drag a new image file from your Windows My Pictures folder.**

   Two new folders appear: Original Images, which contains the file you dragged into the folder, and PNG images, which contains the converted graphics file. This is shown in Figure 16.26.

Needless to say, you can attach many other folder actions to any folder. And if you can't find enough built into Leopard, you can even create your own, as you see in Chapter 19.

Figure 16.25

Folder actions setup window (a); actions set up with Duplicate as PNG selected (b)

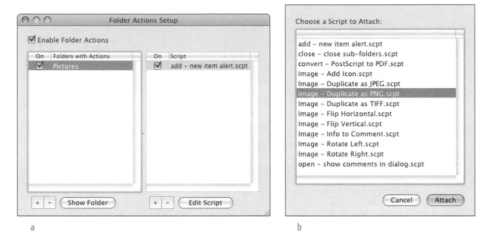

a   b

Figure 16.26

New images folders

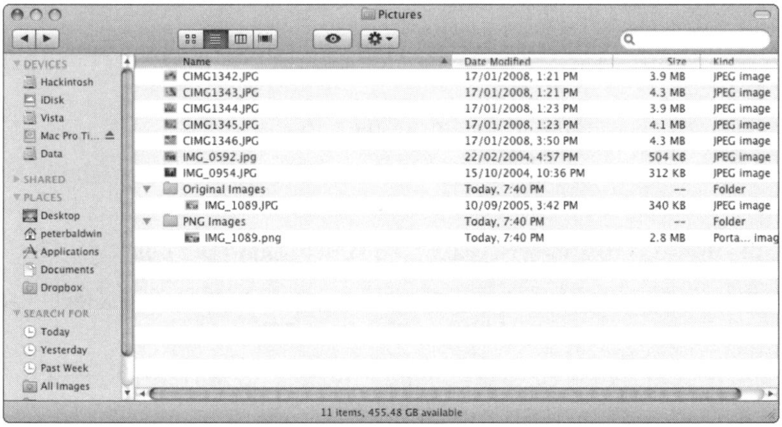

Summary

In this chapter, you saw some of the automation power of Leopard. You downloaded and modified some Automator workflows and created an Automator workflow of your own. You also looked at the power of folder actions and how they can be used to automate workflows.

Leopard is unique because you can easily customize the system using relatively simple tools. Doing the same things in Windows or Linux is quite a bit more complicated.

Creating and Editing AppleScript Macros

I n the preceding chapter, you saw how easy it is to extend the functionality of Leopard by using Automator to create new commands to control the way Leopard behaves, and using folder actions.

AppleScript provides the power behind Automator and folder actions. This programming language is quite easy to read, and more importantly, you can easily create new programs with it. Its genealogy can be traced back to HyperTalk, the programming language for HyperCard, which appeared on the Macintosh in 1987.

In this chapter you examine some prepared scripts that come with Leopard to understand how they work. Then you modify them and finally create your own scripts. And if we don't call it programming, you might not be scared off!

Starting with AppleScript

In this section, you orient yourself to the AppleScript environment and use ScriptEditor to run a simple script.

Starting ScriptEditor

To start working with scripts, you need to run ScriptEditor. The following steps start it running and allow you to set up your scripting environment:

1. **Use Spotlight to start ScriptEditor by typing** script **and clicking ScriptEditor.**

   Because this is the first time you've run ScriptEditor, it starts the AppleScript Utility that displays a dialog box, as shown in Figure 17.1.

2. **Check Enable GUI Scripting and Show Script Menu in menu bar.**

   Note that a new icon appears in the menu bar. If you click it, you get quick access to any of the scripts that are preinstalled in Leopard.

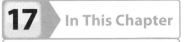

Figure 17.1

AppleScript utility setup

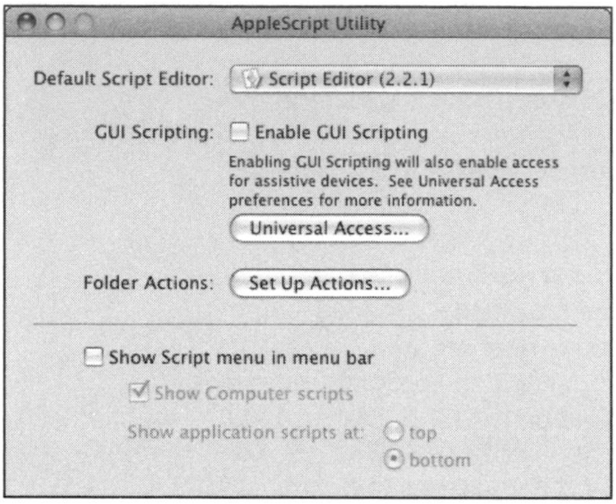

3. **Close the dialog box to leave you at the ScriptEditor start screen, shown in Figure 17.2.**

Figure 17.2

ScriptEditor start screen

Orienting to the ScriptEditor screen

At the top of the ScriptEditor window is the title bar, which has four main buttons:

- **Record:** This records menu and keystrokes.
- **Stop:** This stops recording.
- **Run:** This runs a script.
- **Compile:** This checks a script before running it and gets it into a form where it will run.
- **Bundle contents:** You won't see this active very often, but it allows you to look inside bundles. A bundle is a directory that contains executable code and the resources it needs.

Using a Prepared AppleScript

In this section, you open a very simple AppleScript, run it, examine the code inside the script, and make a modification to it.

Finding prepared scripts

Leopard comes with a large number of prepared scripts that you can use and modify. To locate them, click the scripts icon on the menu bar. Figure 17.3 shows the drop-down list of scripts.

Figure 17.3

Available prepared scripts

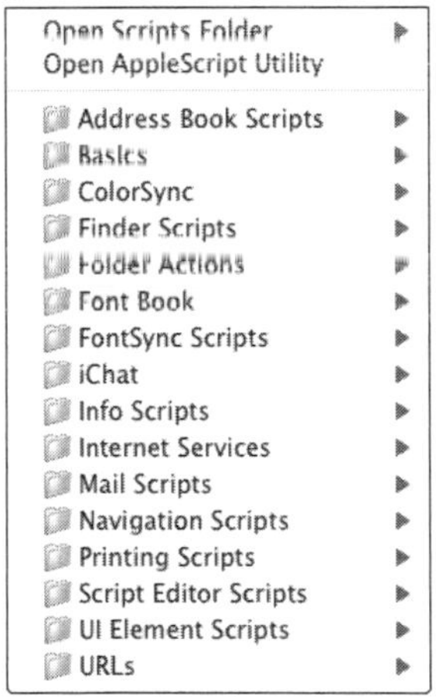

```
Open Scripts Folder          ▶
Open AppleScript Utility

  Address Book Scripts        ▶
  Basics                      ▶
  ColorSync                   ▶
  Finder Scripts              ▶
  Folder Actions              ▶
  Font Book                   ▶
  FontSync Scripts            ▶
  iChat                       ▶
  Info Scripts                ▶
  Internet Services           ▶
  Mail Scripts                ▶
  Navigation Scripts          ▶
  Printing Scripts            ▶
  Script Editor Scripts       ▶
  UI Element Scripts          ▶
  URLs                        ▶
```

Running the script

In this example, we use about the simplest script possible: one that hides all the open Finder windows.

Follow these steps to open the script:

1. **Start ScriptEditor running.**

2. **Click File, Open, and navigate to /Library/Scripts/Finder Scripts.**

3. **Select Finder Windows - Hide All.**

Figure 17.4 shows the ScriptEditor window with the script loaded.

Figure 17.4

ScriptEditor window

4. **Click the Compile button.**

When the script runs, it hides any open Finder windows, minimizing them to the Dock.

Reading the AppleScript code

Each AppleScript is made up of several parts. This section explains those parts.

Reading comments

Because AppleScripts are really programs, or applications, they can contain comments. Comments are information for the human reader and are ignored by the computer when the program runs.

In AppleScript, comments are enclosed between (* and *) characters. These are the standard keyboard symbols for *, (, and).

In this simple example, the comment is by far the major part of the script.

Reading commands

A command is an instruction to the computer to do something. In this example, the command is tell. The command has to work on something, so the rest of the line says what the command has to work with: application "Finder".

At the end of the command, end tell says that the command has completed.

Using if statements

In the middle of the command are three lines:

```
if the (count of windows) is not 0 then
    set collapsed of every window to true
end if
```

The first line makes sure the script only executes if at least one Finder window is open. This is called a *conditional statement*: It determines whether a particular condition is true.

If no Finder windows are open, then the conditional statement is false, so the next line is skipped.

If at least one Finder window is open, then the condition becomes true, so the next line is executed. Each window has several properties, and collapsed is one of them. The collapsed property has only two possibilities; it can be true or false. In other words, a window is either collapsed to the Dock, or it isn't. So the line set collapsed of every window to true sets the collapsed property to true for every window. The result is that every window minimizes to the Dock.

See how it works by following these steps:

1. **Open two or three Finder windows.**

2. **Click the Run button to start the script running.**

3. **Watch while the windows collapse, one at a time, to the Dock.**

    If you want to see it happen slowly, hold down the Shift key when you click Run.

Did you happen to notice the order that the windows collapsed to the Dock? It was in the order that they appear on the screen: The topmost window collapsed first and then the other windows in order down to the bottom-most.

Changing the script

It is always easier to modify a script from somewhere else rather than create your own scripts from scratch. As Isaac Newton said, this is "standing on the shoulders of giants."

Reversing the action

Obviously, one very easy change you can make is to reverse the action if the condition is met: Instead of collapsing the windows, resurrect them from the Dock. If the windows shrink to the Dock when the collapsed property is set to true, then they should return if the property is set to false.

Edit your script so it now reads:

```
tell application "Finder"
  if the (count of windows) is not 0 then
    set collapsed of every window to false
  end if
end tell
```

Run your script, and check that the windows rise from the Dock and resume their place on your desktop.

Coping with errors

What if no Finder windows are open? Your AppleScript appears to do nothing, if that is the case. So let's test for whether any Finder windows are open.

```
tell application "Finder"
  if the (count of windows) is 0 then
    display dialog "There are no Finder windows open!"
  end if
end tell
```

Figure 17.5 shows the dialog box you see when you run the script with no open Finder windows.

Figure 17.5

Error dialog box

Now let's combine the two scripts so that something happens.

```
tell application "Finder"
  if the (count of windows) is 0 then
    display dialog "There are no Finder windows open!"
  else
    set collapsed of every window to true
  end if
end tell
```

Now, if no Finder windows are open, we get the error message; if windows are open, then all the windows are collapsed to the Dock.

If you have sound working, close all your Finder windows and try this version:

```
tell application "Finder"
  if the (count of windows) is 0 then
    say "Oops!"
    display dialog "No Finder windows are open!"
  else
    set collapsed of every window to true
  end if
end tell
```

Creating Your Own Scripts

So far we haven't even remotely scratched the surface of what you can do with scripts. In this section, we look in some more detail at Finder scripts, opening windows, setting views, and much more.

Creating Finder scripts

Finder is one of the most used applications in Leopard; it's hard to imagine getting through a day without using It.

Opening a new Finder window

Let's start by opening a new Finder window. Follow these steps:

1. **Start ScriptEditor, and enter the following code:**

   ```
   tell application "Finder"
     activate
     make new Finder window to startup disk
   end tell
   ```

2. **Compile the script, and run it using the toolbar buttons.**

   Figure 17.6 shows the outcome on my disk.

Figure 17.6

Output of script to create new Finder window

3. **Save the script as "Open Finder Window.scpt" to your Library/Scripts folder; use the default options for now.**

   You will look at the other options later.

Setting the window's target

Generally, you are not going to want to open a Finder window at the top level of your startup disk; you want to open the window in a given folder. Let's open the Finder window in your Music folder. If you have more than one Finder window open, you need to specify which Finder window you want to control. You do this by specifying the number of the window.

How do you know what number your new window is? Well, in this case it's quite simple: Windows are numbered from front to back on the screen. Because your new window has just opened, it is at the front, so it's window 1.

Follow these steps:

1. **Add an extra line so your script now looks like this:**

```
tell application "Finder"
  activate
  make new Finder window to startup disk
  set target of Finder window 1 to folder "Music"
end tell
```

2. **Save the script as "Open Music Folder.scpt" in your Library/Scripts folder.**

3. **Run the script.**

Note that exactly the same window opened up as before: Finder has ignored your instruction to set the target to your Music folder. Why is this? Finder is dumb, and it needs to be explicitly told how to find your Music folder, so ScriptEditor displays the error message shown in Figure 17.7a.

Not a very helpful message, is it? What you need to do is to tell Finder exactly how to find the Music folder, starting from your startup disk. The easiest way to do this is to use that Finder window and follow these steps.

4. **On the View menu of the Finder menu bar, select Show Path Bar.**

This is shown in Figure 17.7b.

Figure 17.7

AppleScript error message (a); Show Path Bar (b)

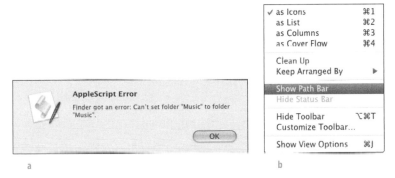

a

b

This makes the path to the folder visible at the bottom of the window. In my case, the Music folder is located at /Hackintosh/Users/peterbaldwin/Music.

To tell Finder how to get there, you start at the highest level, working down to the startup disk.

5. **Change the set target line of your script to read as follows:**

```
set target of Finder window 1 to folder "Music" of folder¬
    "peterbaldwin" of folder "Users" of startup disk
```

Note the ¬ symbol in the line of code above. This is the line continuation character and is used to spread a long line over two or more lines, because of the limitations of the size of the page in this book. You don't need to type it into ScriptEditor; it automatically recognizes the line as being a long line.

Figure 17.8 shows the result of this new command.

Figure 17.8

Folder opened with correct path

Obviously, your username is not peterbaldwin, so substitute your own name.

An easier way is to use the alias `home` to replace "`peterbaldwin`" `of folder` "`Users`" and so on. So that line becomes this:

```
set target of Finder window 1 to folder "Music" of home
```

6. **Save your script.**

Setting view options

Now that you can write a script to open a particular folder in Finder, you need to tell it how to display it onscreen. Suppose you want the new window to display with a path bar, no toolbar, always the same size, and always in a certain place on the screen.

Follow these steps to set some view options:

1. **If you don't have your Open Music Folder script open, open it in ScriptEditor.**

2. **Add the following line just before the end tell:**

```
set current view of Finder window 1 to icon view
```

3. **Run the script.**

Check that the window opens up in icon view. Obviously, if you want it to open in any other view (List, Column, or Cover flow), you use that name as the view. Cover flow is shortened to just `flow`.

4. **Add the following line after the current view line:**

```
set bounds of Finder window 1 to {1000, 200, 1800, 700}
```

A window's bounds are the screen coordinates of its corners; the first two numbers are the x,y coordinates of the top-left corner; the second two are the x,y coordinates of the bottom-right corner.

Simplifying the script

Right now, your script looks like

```
tell application "Finder"
  activate
  make new Finder window to startup disk
  set target of Finder window 1 to folder "Music" of home
  set current view of Finder window 1 to list view
  set bounds of Finder window 1 to {1000, 200, 1750, 700}
end tell
```

We can simplify the script in a couple of ways. First, I can show you a simpler way to open a new Finder window. Simply use the command `open folder "Music" of home` to replace the third line.

All the `set` commands refer to the same window, so we can put them inside a new `tell` command.

Follow these steps to simplify your script:

1. **Replace line 3 in your script with this line:**

```
open folder "Music" of home
```

2. **Enter a new line 4:**

```
tell Finder window 1
```

3. **Remove the** of Finder window 1 **from each of the other lines.**

4. **Add the line:**

```
end tell
```

Now your script should look like

```
tell application "Finder"
  activate
  open folder "Music" of home
  tell Finder window 1
    set current view to list view
    set bounds to {1000, 200, 1750, 700}
  end tell
end tell
```

Saving and running scripts

So far, you have just saved your scripts using the default options and run them by clicking Run in ScriptEditor.

When you save a script, you have a choice of how you save it. These choices are shown in Figure 17.9.

Figure 17.9

Formats for saving scripts

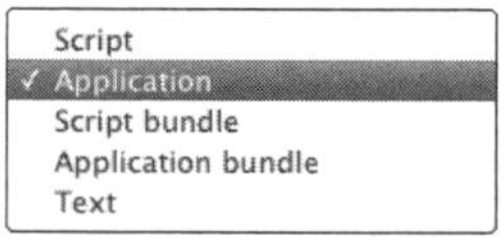

Table 17.1 shows the properties of each of the formats.

Table 17.1 Properties of Each File Format for Scripts

Type	Extension	Editable?	Properties
Script	.scpt	Yes *	Needs ScriptEditor to run
Application	.app	No	Runs as stand-alone application
Script bundle	.scptd	Yes *	Packaged so other applications can use it
Application bundle	.app	No	Packaged so other applications can use it
Text	.applescript	Yes	Plain text; can be edited with TextEdit

* Can be made noneditable by checking the Run only box.

Of these file formats, the only ones you need to use until you become an experienced developer are the Script and Application types.

When you save the script as an Application, it becomes a standard Leopard application and can be run simply by double-clicking it. It can even be placed in the Dock so it is always available. I do that so I can quickly get to a particular folder without having to open a new Finder window and navigate to where I want.

Other options in the Save dialog box are:

- **Startup Screen:** The script displays a warning message before it starts running, as shown in Figure 17.10.
- **Stay Open:** After the script has run, it stays running. This is useful if you want to loop the script and do other things.

Figure 17.10

Startup screen for script

Getting user input

Rather than having a script that is just a one-trick pony, being able to gather user input and make use of it can be very helpful. For example, we can make the Open Music Folder more general by asking the user to enter a folder name and then open that.

To do this, we need to allow the user to enter the folder name. AppleScript has a very simple way of doing this using the `display dialog` command. If you use `display dialog` on its own, it puts a box on the screen with two buttons: OK and Cancel.

If you add the command `default answer`, the dialog box has room for the user to enter something. So to capture the user's desired destination folder, you would use something like this:

```
display dialog "Enter the folder name:" default answer myFolder
```

Notice that we have to specify a container (called a *variable*) `myFolder` to store the user's input.

Before we can use a variable, we have to tell AppleScript to expect it, so it needs to be defined before it is used. This is done using the `set` command that you encountered earlier.

Unlike many other programming languages, AppleScript isn't that fussy about what types of variables you use. If the application requires a sequence of characters (known as a *string*) and you enter a number, AppleScript happily converts it (if possible) in a process known as *coercion*. This happens behind the scenes, and you will be unaware of it, as long as the coercion makes sense.

For example, if the script requires a number and you enter "123e," that doesn't make sense as a number, so the script stops with an error.

In this example, let's set the value of `myFolder` to be *Music*. We do this using the command:

```
set myFolder to "Music"
```

Follow these steps to modify your Open Music Folder script:

1. **Open your Open Music Folder script using ScriptEditor.**

2. **Enter a new first line:** set `myFolder` to "Music".

3. **Click the Compile button.**

Note that ScriptEditor puts the variable `myFolder` in green. This is the default color ScriptEditor uses to display variables.

4. **On the next line, enter this:**

```
display dialog "Enter the folder name:" default answer¬
    myFolder
```

5. **Save the file, and then click Run.**

Now your dialog box is displayed, as shown in Figure 17.11.

Figure 17.11

Dialog box to get user input

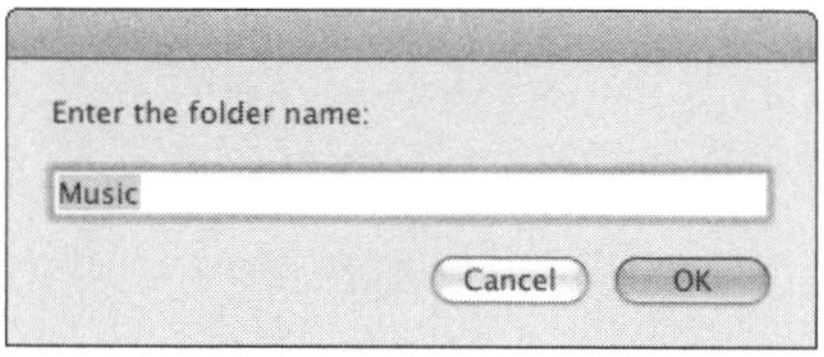

Note that the value of `myFolder` that you set in the first line shows as the default answer.

6. **Click Cancel, because you haven't finished yet.**

Now you need to change the value of `myFolder` to whatever the user typed. To do this, you use another `set` command. When the user clicks OK, whatever is in the dialog box is returned as the `result`.

7. **Add the line:**

```
set myFolder to text returned of the result
```

Now you need to start Finder and have it carry out the main part of the script. But rather than use Music as the folder to open, we want to open the folder corresponding to what the user typed. To do this, we substitute the variable `myFolder` for Music in the `open folder` command.

8. **Edit the** open folder **line to read:**

```
open folder myFolder of home
```

Now your script should look like:

NOTE

Don't type the line continuation character ¬ in the second line; just enter the text all as a single line.

```
set myFolder to "Music"
display dialog "Enter the folder name:" default answer¬
    myFolder
set myFolder to text returned of the result
tell application "Finder"
  activate
  open folder myFolder of home
  tell Finder window 1
    set current view to list view
    set bounds to {1000, 200, 1750, 700}
  end tell
end tell
```

9. **Save and then run your script.**

10. **In the dialog box, type** Documents **and click OK.**

You should see the Finder window as shown in Figure 17.12.

Figure 17.12

Documents folder in Finder

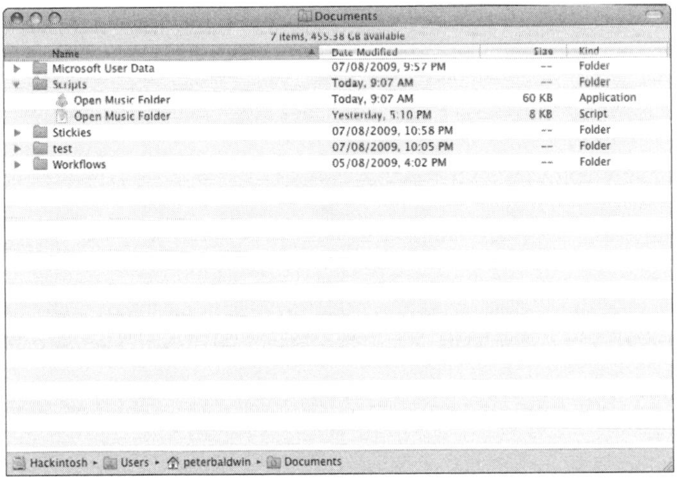

Of course, the content of your Documents folder will be different from mine.

Note that the script doesn't care about capitalization because Finder doesn't care. *dOcUmEnTs* is treated just the same as *Documents*.

You can open folders that are below the level of the top folder by using a : to separate the names. For example, to open the iTunes folder that is a subfolder of the Music folder, you would enter **Music:iTunes.**

One small modification you can make to the script to make it look a little more professional is to add an icon to the dialog box.

11. Modify the display dialog command to read:

```
display dialog "Enter the folder name:" default answer¬
    myFolder icon note
```

NOTE
Don't type the line continuation character ¬ ; just enter the text all as a single line.

This time your dialog box displays with an AppleScript icon, as shown in Figure 17.13.

Figure 17.13

AppleScript icon in dialog box

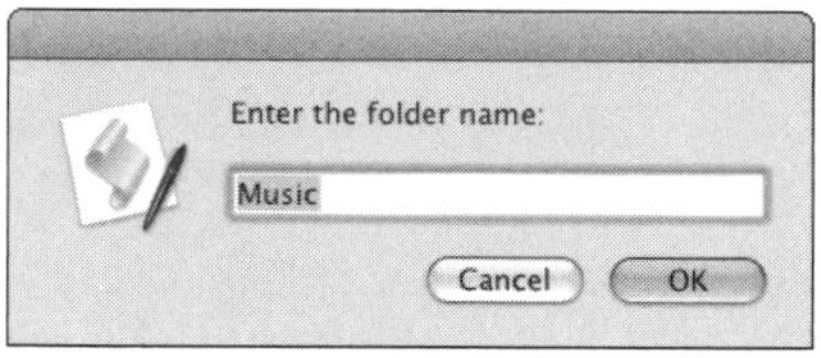

Handling errors

What happens if you type a folder name that doesn't exist at the top level of your home folder? Find out!

Run your script but enter a folder name that you know doesn't exist.

Note how the Dock icon for ScriptEditor bounces up and down. Check with AppleScript, and you find that ScriptEditor is displaying an error message, as shown in Figure 17.14.

Figure 17.14

ScriptEditor error message

AppleScript Error
Finder got an error: Can't get folder "junk" of folder "peterbaldwin" of folder "Users" of startup disk.

OK

Obviously, you can't depend on the user always entering valid data—even when you are the user! So rather than have the application eventually end with a ScriptEditor error, your application should handle it and display the error message to the user.

AppleScript uses the `try` and `on error` commands to handle errors. You can think of these as the script trying to do something. If it succeeds, there's no problem. If it doesn't succeed—in other words, on error—do something else.

What we need to do is to get the user input, activate Finder as before, and then try to open the folder the user specified. If it succeeds, go ahead and do the rest of the script. If it doesn't succeed, show an error message and quit.

Follow these steps to add error handling to your script:

1. **Open your Open Music Folder script with ScriptEditor.**

2. **Immediately after the** activate **command, insert this line:**

   ```
   try
   ```

3. **Immediately after the first** end tell**, add these lines:**

   ```
   on error
      display dialog "Oops! There is no folder with that¬
      name" with icon stop buttons "Sorry!"
   end try
   ```

NOTE

Don't type the line continuation character; just enter the text all as a single line.

In this case, we've jollied it up a little by putting a stop icon in the dialog box, and then naming the button "Sorry!"

Your script should now look like:

```
set myFolder to "Music"
display dialog "Enter the folder name:" default answer¬
   myFolder with icon note
set myFolder to text returned of the result
tell application "Finder"
   activate
   try
      open folder myFolder of home
      tell Finder window 1
         set current view to list view
         set bounds to {1000, 200, 1750, 700}
      end tell
   on error
      display dialog "Oops! There is no folder with that¬
         name" with icon stop buttons "Sorry!"
   end try
end tell
```

4. **Test that your application still works by leaving the default as Music.**

5. **Check that your error handling works by entering nonsense text in the dialog box.**

You should get an error message like that shown in Figure 17.15.

Figure 17.15

Error message for nonexistent folder

To polish your script just a little more, you should tell the user why the error message appeared. To do that, show what the user typed in the dialog box. You do this by changing the text slightly and adding the variable (*myFolder*) that the user typed.

You do this by showing a fixed part of the error message (*Oops! There is no folder called*) and then add what the user typed to the end of it. This is called *concatenation* and is like addition but for strings of characters. The symbol for concatenation is the ampersand character (&).

6. **Change your** on error **dialog box line to the following:**

```
display dialog "Oops! There is no folder called " &¬
    myFolder with icon stop buttons "Sorry!"
```

Now your error message should look like that shown in Figure 17.16.

Figure 17.16

Error message showing incorrect input

Making your application user proof

How can you prevent users typing the wrong thing? You can't! But you can eliminate the need for the user to type anything. If you could present a list of possible choices, the user can simply choose one of the options. Then there's no possibility of making an error.

This section is going to introduce several new concepts. First, AppleScript has a type of data called a *list*. You can create a list of numbers or strings. The list is enclosed in curly brackets { }.

This is a list of numbers: {1, 2, 3}. Each item in the list is separated from the others by a comma. This is a list of folder names: {"Documents", "Music", "Desktop"}. Note that strings are still enclosed in quotes.

Here's a way to eliminate user error: Show a list on the screen, and have the user select just one correct item. You know it's correct because you drew up the list!

AppleScript has a command to display a list and then have the user choose an item. It is the `choose from list` command.

Follow these steps to create new script:

1. **Start ScriptEditor, and create a new file.**

2. **Enter the following line:**

   ```
   choose from list {"Documents", "Music", "Downloads"}
   ```

3. **Save the script as a script with the name** Open User Folder.

4. **Run the script.**

   You should see a selection box, as shown in Figure 17.17a.

   Note that the OK button is grayed out until you select one of the options. Then you can click OK.

   Look in the bottom frame of ScriptEditor after you have selected a folder. You should see something like Figure 17.17b.

   ScriptEditor displays the selection made. Note that it displays as a list with only one element: {"Music"}.

Figure 17.17

Folder selection box (a); result of folder selection (b)

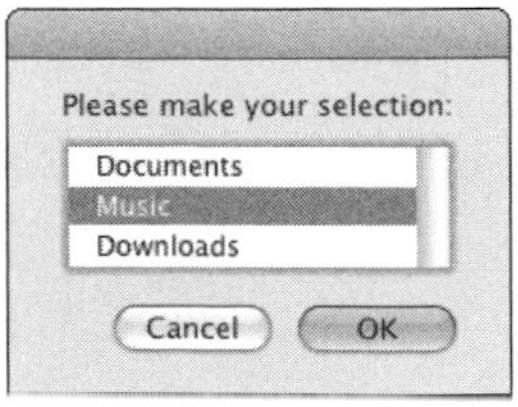

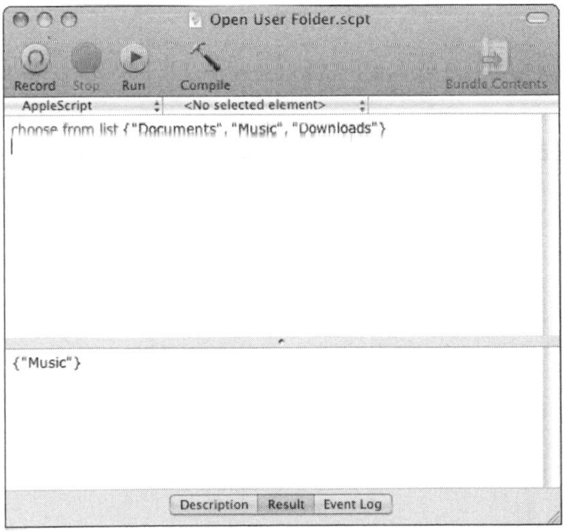

a   b

So far so good: We created a list so the user just makes a selection. Of course, the drawback is that we have to enter the folder names manually. Aren't computers supposed to save us that drudgery? Of course. So let's get the computer to tell us the names of the folders.

Follow these steps to create a script that creates and displays a list of all the folders in the top level of the user's home folder:

1. **Delete the only line in your script because you're starting from scratch.**

2. **Create a new empty list called listOfFolders**

```
set listOfFolders to {}
```

Now you want to get Finder to trawl through the user's home folder and get the names of all the folders.

3. **Add these lines:**

```
tell application "Finder"
  set folderlist to every folder of home
```

4. **Run the script.**

You should receive a lengthy error message from ScriptEditor that looks like Figure 17.18.

Figure 17.18

Error message

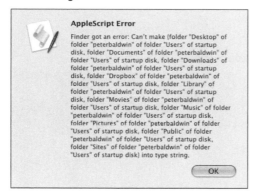

Unfortunately, the variable folderlist is not a string, so it can't be coerced into a list. We have to do that in our program.

To do this, we need to step through every item in folderlist, convert it to a string, and add it to the end of the list of folders. This requires a repeat loop, which tells ScriptEditor to keep repeating an operation until it can't repeat any longer.

5. **Add the following line to the script:**

```
repeat with currentFolder in folderlist
  set currentFolderName to (the name of currentFolder)
  copy currentFolderName to the end of listOfFolders
end repeat
```

Note that the loop is enclosed in a *repeat … end repeat* pair of commands.

The loop sets a variable currentFolderName to the name of the currentFolder in the folderlist and then adds the currentFolderName to the end of the list of folders, called listOfFolders.

6. **Now let's see if it has worked by adding a choose from list command:**

```
choose from list listOfFolders
```

7. **Save the file, and then click Run to see what happens.**

You should see a choose box like that shown in Figure 17.19.

Figure 17.19

Choose box showing folders

Hooray! We've achieved the first part of our aim of fool-proofing our script.

First, let's tidy up the choose box by replacing the generic prompt with one of our choosing.

8. **Change the choose command to read as follows:**

```
choose from list listOfFolders with prompt "Which folder¬
    do you want to open?"
```

9. **Give the choose box a title:**

```
choose from list listOfFolders with title "Open a folder"¬
    with prompt "Which folder do you want to open?"
```

10. **Make the default selection the first folder in the list read as follows:**

```
choose from list listOfFolders with title "Open a folder"¬
    with prompt "Which folder do you want to open?" default¬
    items item 1 of listOfFolders
```

11. **Change the default buttons on the choose box by adding text to the last line:**

```
choose from list listOfFolders with title "Open a folder"¬
    with prompt "Which folder do you want to open?" default¬
    items item 1 of listOfFolders OK button name {"Open¬
    Folder"}
```

N O T E

Although that line is spread over several lines in the book, it is all one line. Don't type the ¬ characters.

This results in a choose box that looks like Figure 17.20.

Figure 17.20

Final choose box

Now you can do something with whatever the user chose from the list. If you run the script, the user's choice is shown in the bottom Result pane, as shown in Figure 17.21.

In this case, I chose Downloads from the list.

What remains now is to get that choice as the input to the remainder of the script. As you can see, the value that the choose function returns is a list because it's inside the curly brackets: {"Downloads"}.

So we need to capture that list returned and then convert it to a string. To get the list returned from the choose command, we just set a new variable as the result as in:

```
set returnValue to choose …
```

Figure 17.21

User's choice shown in Result pane

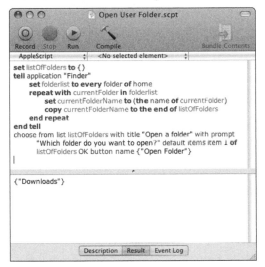

Then we need to coerce the returned list to a string value. This is very simple in AppleScript because sometimes the conversion is automatic. In this case, though, it isn't, so we simply tell AppleScript to do it using as text.

Follow these steps to do this:

1. **Open the Open User Folder script if it is not already open.**

2. **At the start of the** choose... **statement, insert the following:**

   ```
   set returnValue to choose from list listOfFolders...
   ```

3. **After the choose statement, add this line:**

   ```
   set myFolder to returnValue as text
   ```

   Yes, it's that simple! Now you simply open the folder.

4. **Just before the** end tell **line, insert the following line:**

   ```
   open folder myFolder of home
   ```

Now your complete script should look like this:

```
set listOfFolders to {}
tell application "Finder"
  set folderlist to every folder of home
  repeat with currentFolder in folderlist
    set currentFolderName to (the name of currentFolder)
    copy currentFolderName to the end of listOfFolders
```

```
    end repeat
    set returnValue to choose from list listOfFolders with title¬
     "Open a folder" with prompt "Which folder do you want to¬
     open?" default items item 1 of listOfFolders OK button name¬
     {"Open Folder"}
    set myFolder to returnValue as text
    open folder myFolder of home
end tell
```

NOTE

As always, remember not to type the continuation character; just put everything on one line. AppleScript formats it when you compile the script.

Now you have a fool-proof script that opens a folder starting at the user's home folder. Of course, now the user cannot specify a folder at the next level down (such as Music/iTunes), but that's the price you pay for error-proofing the script.

Creating an Application

Up to now you've been saving your scripts as .scpt files. These are editable, but they require ScriptEditor to run. One of the options for saving scripts is as an application, as you saw earlier. Follow these steps to use your script as an application:

1. **If it's not already open, open your Open User Folder script.**

2. **Select Save As, choose Application, and uncheck the Startup Screen box.**

3. **Open a Finder window if one is not already open, and navigate to your Library/ Scripts folder off your home folder.**

    Figure 17.22 shows the content of my Scripts folder; yours may be different.

    Note that you see two versions of the Open User Folder script: One has the script symbol inside a document icon while the other just has the script icon. The document is the editable script; the script icon alone indicates that it is an application.

TIP

Always save an editable script copy as well as the application so that if you need to modify the script later, it's possible to do it. You can't edit an application.

4. **Double-click the application icon.**

    Your application runs, asking you which folder you want to open, then opens the folder. Success!

Figure 17.22

Scripts folder

Making the script available to other users

So far the script has been for your exclusive use because you saved it to your own Library/ Scripts folder. You can make it available to other users by putting it in the systemwide scripts folder. That's where the scripts that appear on the script menulet on your menu bar come from.

Follow these steps to make the script available to all users:

1. **If it's not open already, open your Library/Scripts folder and copy the Open User Folder script.**

2. **Navigate to the folder startup disk (Hackintosh, in my case) /Library/Scripts/ Finder Scripts, and paste the script there.**

   This is shown in Figure 17.23.

3. **Click the Script menulet on your menu bar, select Finder Scripts, and check that Open User Folder is listed.**

   This is shown in Figure 17.24.

4. **Create a new user account.**

   Can you remember how to do it? Hint: Open System Preferences, select Accounts, click the Lock icon, enter your password, and click the + (plus) sign under the Accounts pane.

5. **Log out of your account and log in to the new account.**

Figure 17.23

Global Finder scripts

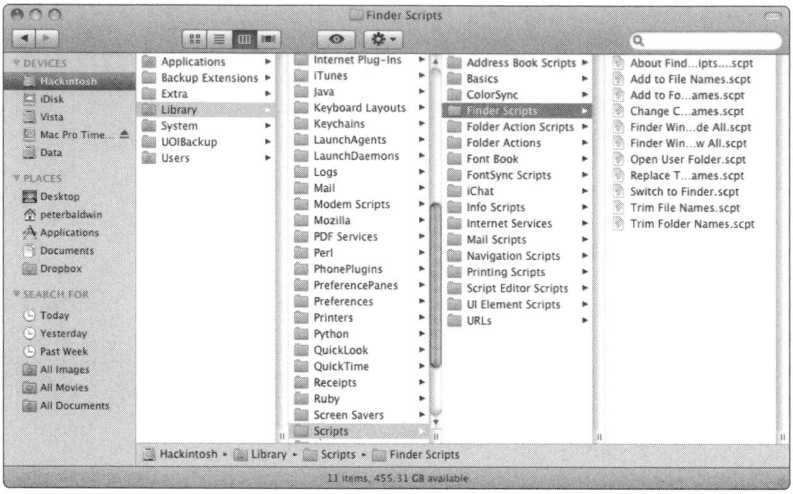

Figure 17.24

Open user folder in Finder scripts menu

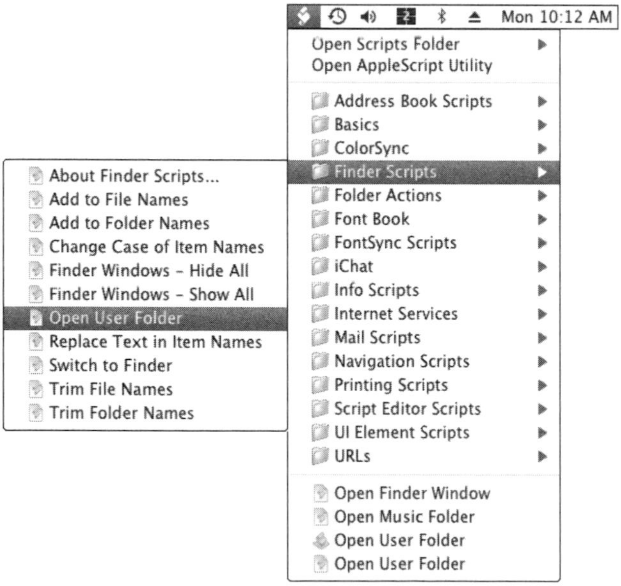

6. **Turn on the Scripts menulet in the menu bar.**

   Remember how? Hint: Run the AppleScript utility, and check the box for Show Script menu in menu bar.

7. **Open the script menu to Finder Scripts, and run the Open User Folder script.**

Does the script run? It should! Which folder does it select? It should select a folder in the other user account, not yours. Is the script editable? That depends!

When you save the script, whether it's in your own Scripts folder or the global Scripts folder, it has permissions; because you are the owner, you have read and write permission, but everyone else has read-only permission. You can see this by selecting Get Info on the script file. Figure 17.25 shows the permissions for the script in my global library (Hackintosh/Library/Scripts/Finder Scripts).

Figure 17.25

Permissions for script file

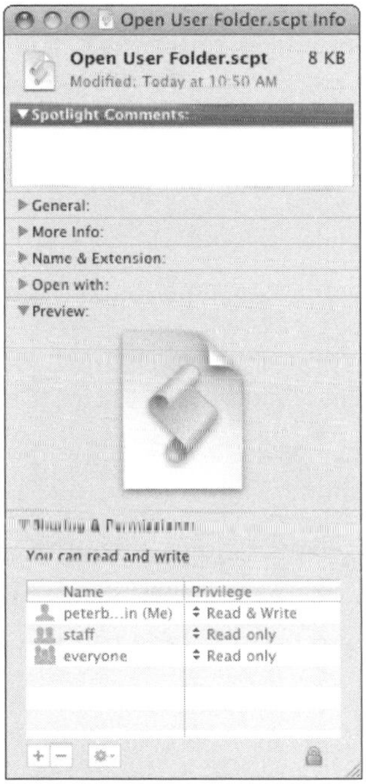

You can change permissions by clicking the lock icon and setting whatever you want for "staff" and "everyone."

When you created the new account, if you gave the new user Admin permissions, then he can't write the file. But he can change permissions on the file, even to the point of locking you out! In other words, the new user can give you read-only permission! That's a good reason to be careful about how you set up accounts for other users!

Using scripts in other applications

We've spent a lot of time with Finder scripts, so you pick up the basic concepts of scripting with AppleScript. As you can see from the scripts menu, lots of scripts are available to you. Most applications designed for Leopard install their own scripts when you install them.

Some of the default scripts have limited usability or duplicate what you can already do with Preferences for each application.

In this section, you create a script that takes e-mail addresses from your Address Book and creates a message to send to all members, letting them know that you'll be on vacation for a certain period.

Creating an e-mail list

Before you start, you should make sure that you have a few contacts with e-mail addresses in your Address Book. They don't need to be genuine, nor do the e-mail addresses need to be actual addresses: You won't be sending the message—unless you really want to!

Follow these steps to create an e-mail list from your Address Book contacts:

1. **Open ScriptEditor, and create a new file.**

2. **Save it as Get Email Addresses.**

   Next we need a variable to store the e-mail addresses. This will be a string of zero characters. Remember that a string is always enclosed in " " characters; to create an empty string, we use "".

3. **Type** `set emailAddresses to " "` **as the first line.**

   Next, you're going to work with Address Book, so tell the script the name of the application.

4. **Type** `tell application "Address Book"`**, and press Enter a couple of times to insert some blank rows.**

5. **Type** `end tell`**.**

Address Book stores information such as birth date, company, name, and so on as *properties* of a person, but e-mail addresses are not stored as properties. The reason for this is easy to understand: A person has only one birth date (except at parties!), only one title, but may have more than one e-mail address, phone number, and so on.

Because of this, we can't just use a line like: set emailList to email of every person as you might expect. Instead, you need to explicitly retrieve the *value* of the e-mail address using a statement like: set emailList to the value of email of every person.

In this example, we ignore the fact that some people have only one e-mail address, while others may have several. We retrieve only the first e-mail address for each person.

Follow these steps to create your script to read the e-mail addresses from Address Book:

1. **After the** tell **statement, enter the following:**

```
set emailList to the value of email 1 of every person
```

That loads the value of all the e-mail addresses into emailList.

2. **Check the output of the script by setting the return value for the script to show the value of emailList; add the following line just before the** end tell:

```
emailList
```

The output is shown in Figure 17.26, which I ran on a fake Address Book.

Figure 17.26

Results of running e-mail script

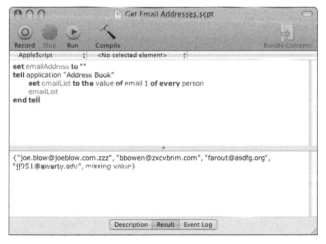

The result is not a list but a string of four e-mail addresses plus a missing value. This occurs because one name in the Address Book has no e-mail address.

Next we need to be able to extract a single e-mail address so we can pass it to Mail to create the e-mail.

3. **Add a new line after the** end tell**:**

```
set emailAddress to (text item 1 of emailList) as text
```

4. **To check that we have the first e-mail address, add this line at the end, just before the** end tell**:**

```
emailAddress
```

This last line in effect prints the value of emailAddress to the Result window.

When I ran this on my e-mail list, I got the output shown in Figure 17.27.

Figure 17.27

Output showing first e-mail address

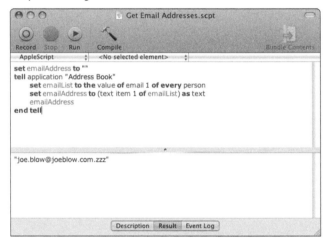

Creating a new e-mail using Mail

Now that we've got an e-mail address, the next step is to pass it to Mail and create an e-mail. First, let's create a script that creates a new e-mail. Follow these steps:

1. **Create a new script called Create New Email.scpt, and save it.**

   We'll be working with Mail, so we need tell and end tell commands.

2. **Type** tell application "Mail".

3. **Enter two or three blank lines, and then add** end tell**.**

Creating a new mail message could hardly be simpler. The command is `make new outgoing message`. A message has several properties, such as "subject," "content," "sender," and so on. Note that recipient is not a property of an e-mail message because it can have several values; properties such as subject, content, sender, and so on can have only one value.

Follow these steps to create your first outgoing message:

1. **Add the following line after** tell application "Mail".

```
set newMessage to make new outgoing message with ¬
   properties {subject:"Test email", content:"Testing¬
   1-2-3" & return & return & "Thanks", sender:"me@my.com"}
```

NOTE

Remember to enter as one line; the continuation characters are only for clarity in the book.

So you can see the new message when it's created, you need to tell Mail to make the new message visible. How will you do this? With a `tell` statement, of course—this time, directed at the new message.

2. **Add the following lines to the script:**

```
tell newMessage
  set visible to true
end tell
```

Now you can run the script and check that it creates a new mail message. Figure 17.28 shows what happened when I ran it.

Note that the message contains the subject line specified, the text in the body of the e-mail, but no recipient in the To: line. What you can't see is that the sender is identified as me@my.com.

Now we need to add a recipient. Because it's possible to have multiple recipients, the way to do it is to add another recipient at the end of the existing list of recipients. Of course, at present there are no recipients, so that creates a single recipient.

3. **Still inside the tell newMessage block, add this line:**

```
make new to recipient with properties¬
   address:"joe@joe.com"}
```

Figure 17.28

Running the create new mail message script

4. **Save and run the script.**

You should get a new mail message created as before, but this time with joe@joe.com in the To: line, as shown in Figure 17.29.

Note how Mail has looked inside your Address Book, found Joe's e-mail address, and put his name as the recipient, rather than just the bare e-mail address. Neat, huh?

Figure 17.29

New e-mail with recipient

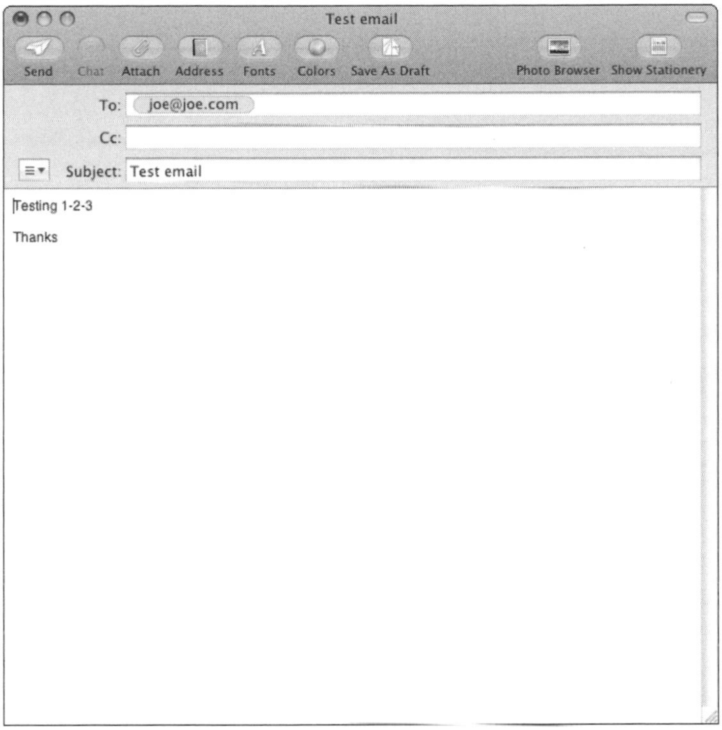

Combining the two scripts

Now we have two scripts: one to get e-mail addresses from your Address Book; the other to create a new e-mail message using Mail. We need to put them together so the output from the Address Book script feeds the e-mail addresses into the Mail script.

Your Mail script needs to sit inside the Address Book script. Follow these steps to combine the two scripts:

1. **Open both scripts, and copy and paste from the Mail script into the Address Book script.**

2. **Remove the joe@joe.com address, and replace it with emailAddress, the address that your Address Book returns.**

After doing this, your script should look like:

```
set emailAddress to ""
tell application "Address Book"
  set emailList to the value of email 1 of every person
  set emailAddress to (text item 1 of emailList) as text
  tell application "Mail"
    set newMessage to make new outgoing message with¬
      properties {subject:"Test email", content:"Testing¬
      1-2-3" & return & return & "Thanks",¬
      sender:"me@my.com"}
    tell newMessage
      set visible to true
      make new to recipient with properties¬
        {address:emailAddress}
    end tell
  end tell
end tell
```

This now creates an e-mail with the recipient being the first address in your list.

Creating more than one recipient

Even though you have retrieved a list of e-mail addresses from your Address Book, at the moment you send the e-mail only to the first person in your list. You now have to cycle through the list of addresses and add each of them as a recipient.

Up to now we've used the first address in the list (joe.blow@joeblow.com.zzz). The way we selected it is `text item 1 of emailList`. Instead of only getting the first value, we want to get all the values. To do this, we have to set up a loop so that as each address is retrieved, we add it as a recipient and then get the next address.

In this case, we set up a `repeat while` loop.

In English, we can write this as:

- Set the count to 1, and get address 1.
- Add 1 to the count, and get address 2.
- Keep doing this until no more addresses are left to get; in other words, while the count is less than the number of addresses.

In AppleScript, we write this as follows:

```
set emailNumber to 1
repeat while emailNumber is less than or equal to totalEmails
... add the recipient ...
set emailNumber to emailNumber + 1
end repeat
```

It sounds more complicated than it actually is! Follow these steps to add the looping statements:

1. **As the second line of the script, insert the following:**

```
set emailNumber to 1
```

2. **After the line** set visible to true **insert these lines:**

```
repeat while emailNumber is less than or equal to totalEmails
  set emailAddress to (text item emailNumber of emailList)¬
    as text
  make new to recipient at end of to recipients with¬
    properties {address:emailAddress}
  set emailNumber to emailNumber + 1
end repeat
```

Note that the third line adds a new recipient to the end of the existing list of recipients.

Let's go through how it works. At the start, emailNumber is set to 1. The value for totalEmails is defined earlier so the repeat line tests to see if the emailNumber is less than or equal to totalEmails. If it is less, as it is at the start, then it retrieves the text of the emailAddress corresponding to emailNumber. In other words, if emailNumber is 2, then it retrieves the second emailAddress.

Then it creates a new recipient using the e-mail address it just retrieved and adds it to the end of the list of recipients. Then it adds 1 to the emailNumber.

In the case here, there are five e-mail addresses so the repeat goes through five times, adding to the e-mail recipients.

After the repeat loop has done its work, the e-mail is created and we can close the tell newMessage loop.

At this point, your script looks like:

```
set emailAddress to ""
set emailNumber to 1
tell application "Address Book"
  set emailList to the value of email 1 of every person
  set totalEmails to count of emailList
  tell application "Mail"
    set newMessage to make new outgoing message with properties¬
      {subject:"Test email", content:"Testing 1-2-3" & return &¬
      return & "Thanks", sender:"me@my.com"}
    tell newMessage
      set visible to true
      repeat while emailNumber is less than or equal to ¬
        totalEmails
        set emailAddress to (text item emailNumber of emailList)¬
          as text
        make new to recipient at end of to recipients with¬
```

```
            properties {address:emailAddress}
        set emailNumber to emailNumber + 1
      end repeat
    end tell
  end tell
end tell
```

Figure 17.30 shows what happened when I ran it on my Address Book.

Figure 17.30

E-mail with all recipients

This is looking good, except for that "missing value." Remember, one person in my Address Book doesn't have an e-mail address. So we need to detect that and remove it.

Removing the missing values

We need to remove the missing values by testing to see whether emailAddress is a "missing value." If it is, we don't create a new recipient.

Follow these steps to remove the missing value:

1. **Immediately before the** make new recipient… **line, insert the following:**

   ```
   if emailAddress is not equal to "missing value" then
   ```

2. **Immediately after the** make new recipient… **line, insert the following:**

   ```
   end if
   ```

3. **Run the script.**

   Figure 17.31 is my output when I ran the script.

   Figure 17.31

   Final output with no missing value

Entering a Subject line

Now you have a script that scans through your Address Book for all your e-mail addresses, creates a message, and inserts all the e-mail addresses as recipients.

One problem with this script is that, if you want to run it with a different subject line and different body, you have to edit the script. That's not a good policy: You should always make scripts (and in fact any type of computer program) as generic as possible.

Why not add a line to query the user for the subject of the e-mail? Follow these steps:

1. **Immediately after the line** set emailNumber to 1**, enter the following line:**

   ```
   set emailSubject to ""
   ```

2. **Immediately before the line** tell application "Address Book"**, insert the following lines:**

   ```
   display dialog "What is the Subject of the email?"¬
      default answer ""
   set emailSubject to text returned of the result
   ```

   Figure 17.32 shows the dialog box.

   Figure 17.32
   Dialog box to get subject of the e-mail

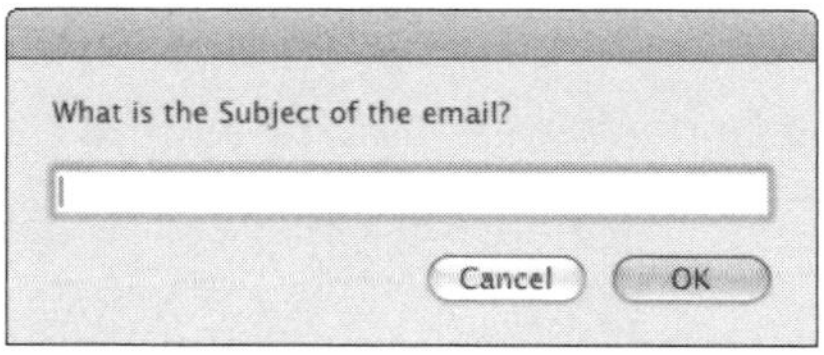

Getting the content text from a file

Using a display dialog command to get the subject line for the e-mail is fine, but it's not suitable for getting the body of the message, because of its complete lack of any editing functions. A much better solution is to use TextEdit, which is designed for entering and formatting text.

So how can we get text from a file into TextEdit and then into the e-mail? Follow these steps to do that:

1. **Open TextEdit, and create a new file.**

2. **Enter some text, such as "Hi everyone, here is my new e-mail address: me@ my.com. Regards."**

3. **Save it to your Scripts folder as** email content.txt.

4. **Close TextEdit.**

5. **Open your combined file in ScriptEditor, if it's not already open.**

6. **Immediately before the** tell application "Address Book" **line, insert the following new lines:**

```
tell application "TextEdit"
   activate
   set theFilename to choose file
   set theDocument to open theFilename
   set theContent to text of theDocument
   close theDocument
   quit
end tell
```

Let's walk through this script segment step by step.

The first two lines start TextEdit running. The line `set theFilename to choose file` opens a standard File Open dialog box. The `choose file` part returns with a variable called `theFilename`, which is the name of the file you selected.

In the next line, the `open` command opens your file and sets a variable called `theDocument` to the content of the file you just opened.

In the fourth line, the text of the file is copied to a variable called `theContent`.

The last two lines close the document and quit TextEdit, leaving the contents of the document in the variable `theContent`.

Figure 17.33 shows the text to go in my e-mail.

Figure 17.33

E-mail message

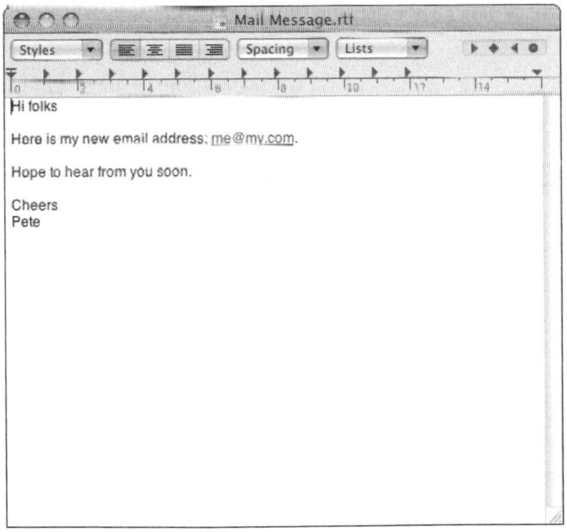

Note that I've included my e-mail address as a hyperlink. To insert an e-mail address as a hyperlink in TextEdit, you select the text and use Format, Text, Link… from the TextEdit menu. A hyperlink to mail is `mailto:me@my.com`.

All that remains now is to use the variable `theContent` in the e-mail.

7. **Inside the** tell application "Mail" **block, change the** set newMessage **line to read as follows:**

```
set newMessage to make new outgoing message with¬
    properties {subject:emailSubject, content:theContent,¬
    sender:"me@my.com"}
```

8. **Test the script by running it; enter a subject line, then open your file in TextEdit, and send the text to the e-mail.**

Figure 17.34 shows the e-mail created when I run the script.

Figure 17.34

Final e-mail

Note that the mail hyperlink doesn't show up; but it does show in the message when the other person receives it.

Adding a little more refinement

Running your script requires you to create the file containing the body of the e-mail in advance. In a year's time, you'll have forgotten that you need to do that, and unless you specifically tell them, nobody else would have any idea that they need to do that. So why not add a prompt asking if you've created the text file for the body of the e-mail?

Follow these steps to add a prompt:

1. **Immediately after the** set email subject to text returned ..., **insert the line:**

```
display dialog "Have you created your text file for the¬
    content?" buttons {"No", "Yes"} default button 2 with¬
    icon caution with title "You need to create a text¬
    file."
```

If the user clicks the "Yes" button, you want to go on with the rest of the script.

2. **Enter the following as the next line:**

```
if result is {button returned:"Yes"} then
```

This does the remainder of the script. If the user clicks the "No" button, the script terminates.

3. **As the very last line in the script, enter this line:**

```
end if
```

Your completed script now should read:

```
set emailAddress to ""
set emailNumber to 1
set emailSubject to ""
display dialog "What is the Subject of the email?" default answer "" with icon
    note
set emailSubject to text returned of the result
display dialog "Have you created your text file for the content?" buttons
    {"No",¬
    "Yes"} default button 2 with icon caution with title "You need to create a
    text¬
    file."
if result is {button returned:"Yes"} then
  tell application "TextEdit"
    activate
    set theFilename to choose file
    set theDocument to open theFilename
    set theContent to text of theDocument
    close theDocument
    quit
  end tell
tell application "Address Book"
    set emailList to the value of email 1 of every person
    set totalEmails to count of emailList
```

```
tell application "Mail"
   set newMessage to make new outgoing message with properties¬
      {subject:emailSubject, content:theContent, sender:"me@my.com"}
   tell newMessage
      set visible to true
      repeat while emailNumber is less than or equal to totalEmails
         set emailAddress to (text item emailNumber of emailList) as text
         if emailAddress is not equal to "missing value" then make new to¬
            recipient at end of to recipients with properties¬
            {address:emailAddress}
         end if
         set emailNumber to emailNumber + 1
      end repeat
   end tell
end tell
end tell
end if
```

Refining even further

What if you want to send the e-mail only to certain people in your address book? Say you only want to send it to anyone with a ".com" e-mail address.

One way to do this is to show the users a list of top-level domain names such as.com, .org, .edu, .gov, or country suffixes such as .au, .uk, .ca, and so on, and ask the user to choose which ones to include.

The following code allows the user to select one or more top-level domain names (TLDs):

```
set listOfTLD to {".com", ".org", ".gov", ".edu"}

choose from list listOfTLD with title "Which domains?" with¬
   prompt "Select all the TLDs:" default items item 1 of¬
   listOfTLD with multiple selections allowed
```

Use ScriptEditor to try it out. Figure 17.35 shows the result, with two TLDs selected.

Figure 17.35

Select top-level domains

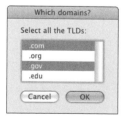

I'll leave it as an exercise for you to modify your code to pull all the matching e-mail addresses from your Address Book before sending them to Mail.

You might also want to include an error-checking script to make sure that Address Book, Mail, and TextEdit are available on the computer. It would be an unusual Macintosh that didn't have them, but you never can be certain.

Summary

In this chapter, you explored the basic concepts and techniques of using AppleScript to create small utility programs that carry out a specific task. If you are an experienced programmer, you probably picked up the concepts and techniques pretty quickly. If not, I hope you didn't find it too challenging and are motivated enough to try writing your own scripts.

With both sample scripts, I tried to take you from the most basic concepts through more advanced ones and create scripts that are useful into the future. I haven't used the e-mail script myself, but I use a version of the Open Folder script every day to open the folder where I store these files.

Modifying the Dashboard

I n Chapter 10, you looked at Leopard's Dashboard, which in many ways is Apple's equivalent to the sidebar in Windows Vista. In the same way as with the sidebar, Dashboard has widgets that you can download and add to your Dashboard.

You have already seen how to add new widgets to your own Dashboard and use them. In this chapter, you develop some of your own and add them to your Dashboard.

Creating new widgets from scratch is not easy, because it requires some fairly sophisticated HTML and JavaScript programming skills. Delving in that deeply is beyond the scope of this book, but if you want to do it, many resources are available to help you.

Before you can start doing anything about developing for the Dashboard, you need to first install the Apple Developer Tools. You will use this comprehensive set of applications in this and the next few chapters.

In this chapter, you use the developer tools to create your own widgets to place in your Dashboard.

Installing the Apple Developer Tools

Apple makes a set of developer tools available for Leopard that contains many different applications enabling you to develop your own applications, not just for Leopard but for iPhone as well. Some of the developer tools included are listed in Table 18.1.

Many different utilities are available that allow you to see what is happening inside your applications.

In This Chapter

Installing the Apple Developer Tools

Getting around with Dashcode

Creating a basic computer gauge

Creating a map widget

Creating a countdown timer

Table 18.1 Apple Developer Tools

Tool	Use
AU Lab	Mixes digital audio
Dashcode	Develop new Dashboard widgets
Core Image Fun House	Apply many different graphics effects to images
Pixie	Magnify screen
Quartz Composer	Create many transformations of images
Interface Builder	Create an interface for an application
XCode	Build many different applications from templates

Downloading the developer tools

Apple supplies the developer tools as a downloadable disk image. Be warned: It is a big image file, around 1GB. When it is installed on your computer, it takes up almost 4GB, so be sure you have enough disk space.

At the time of this writing, the current version of the developer tools was 3.1.3, which is what I used in these chapters.

Before you can download the tools, you need to become a member of the Apple Developer Connection (ADC). Several levels of membership are available, but the free level gives you access to the developer tools and all the documentation you could ever want! The top level memberships cost $3,500, but the online membership is free, and until you get serious about developing applications, it's all you'll need.

Follow these steps to register and download the developer tools:

1. **Go to the Apple Developer site at** `http://developer.apple.com/.`
2. **Click Mac Developer Program.**
3. **Click Register, and complete the enrolment form.**
4. **After you have registered, log in and download XCode.**

CAUTION
XCode is a big file, so be aware of any download limits on your Internet account.

Installing the developer tools

After the disk image has downloaded, you need to install the tools. Follow these steps to install them:

1. **After the disk image has been mounted, double-click XcodeTools.mpkg and go through the installer process.**

All the developer tools are installed to a "Developer" folder on the startup disk. In my case, it's at Hackintosh/Developer.

2. **Open the folder in Finder, and drag the folder alias (remember that?) to your Dock.**

3. **Right-click the Dock icon, and set your preferences.**

I set mine to Display as a Stack and View content as List, as shown in Figure 18.1.

Figure 18.1

Developer tools display in the Dock

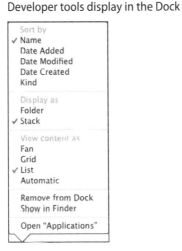

Getting Around with Dashcode

Dashcode is the first developer tool you'll use. As the name implies, it allows you to create code (or programs) to take their place in the Dashboard.

Reviewing the Dashboard

Figure 18.2 is to remind you of what the Dashboard looks like. Your display will be slightly different, but the essentials are the same.

You bring the Dashboard into view by pressing the F12 key, clicking on the Dashboard icon in the Dock, or moving the mouse to a corner of the screen if you have set up Exposé that way.

Figure 18.2

Dashboard display

Each of the objects on the screen is a widget. In this view, you can see the weather forecast, clock, calculator, and calendar widgets, but more are available by clicking the + (plus) in the bottom-left corner. This brings up a selection bar where you can choose another widget and simply drag it onto the display, as shown in Figure 18.3.

Starting with Dashcode

Launch Dashcode; remember that it isn't in your Applications folder, but in your Developer folder. If you don't have it in the Dock, just use Spotlight to launch it.

Your first view of Dashcode is a screen allowing you to choose the type of template you want to use, as shown in Figure 18.4.

In version 3.1, the highlighted template type is Web Application, which is used to develop iPhone and iPod touch applications. But that's for another book. For now, select Dashboard Widget. This brings up a new template selection menu, this time for developing Dashboard widgets.

Figure 18.3

New widgets

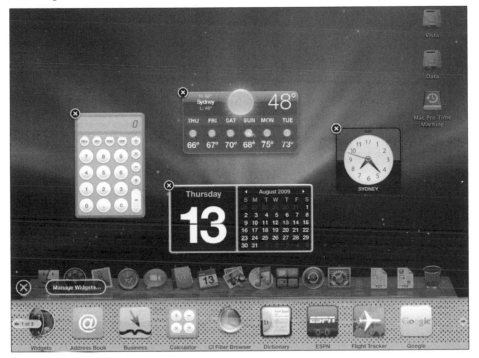

Figure 18.4

Dashcode template view

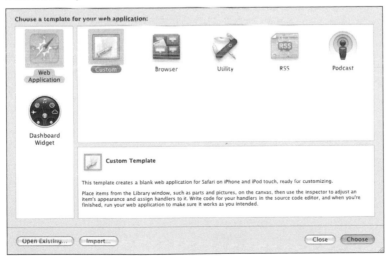

Creating a Basic Computer Gauge

In this section, you develop a basic computer gauge to monitor various activities on the computer. Select from the project screen shown in Figure 18.5.

Figure 18.5

Template selection for computer gauge

Follow these steps to create your computer gauge:

1. **Click Computer Gauge, and then click Choose.**

Figure 18.6 shows the gauge project window.

Figure 18.6

Gauge project window

Table 18.2 shows the various parts of the project window and explains what each part is used for.

Table 18.2 Project Window Explanation

Part	Location	Use
Toolbar	Top of the window	Runs your widget; shows buttons for the inspector and the components library
Parts outline	Top part of left side	Switches among the tools available to create the project
Workflow steps	Bottom part of left side	Shows milestones for development of a widget
Canvas	Right side	Designs the widget's interface

To create a project, follow the workflow steps, marking each stage completed as you finish it. From the screen display, you can see the stages in the workflow:

- Provide data
- Set attributes
- Preview default image
- Design widget icon
- Test and share

Some of these steps are very complex and require high levels of programming knowledge and ability. Fortunately, you are not required to do any of that for this chapter! You work just with the look and feel of the widgets, leaving the inner workings alone.

Testing the gauge

In this example, all the work of designing the inner workings has been done, so let's just see how the gauge works. Follow these steps to test the gauge:

1. **On the toolbar, click Run.**

Did you note the water ripple effect when the gauge starts? Provided you have QE/CI running, this is the normal behavior when you add a widget to your Dashboard.

2. **Watch the gauges for a few seconds.**

Note that the processor dial increases and decreases in speed as your computer works, doing things in the background.

3. **Open TextEdit to create a file, and quickly click in the Dashcode window.**

You should see the processor needle increase, and some disk activity shows on the disk activity gauge.

4. **Enter some text in TextEdit, and save the file.**

5. **Quickly click in the Dashcode window again to see the gauges change.**

6. **Open Safari, and quickly click in the Dashcode window.**

Hopefully, the CPU, disk, and network gauges all show activity.

From this limited testing, you can see that the gauge does actually work, getting input about the processor load, disk activity, and network activity. Later, you see how to drag the gauge to your desktop so you can watch it in operation.

Modifying the gauge

Now that you've seen that the gauge actually works, you can change its look to something you prefer. The changes are restricted to just the look because doing anything more requires programming knowledge.

Changing gauge sizes and text

Follow these steps to make changes to the gauges and the text in the widget:

1. **In the toolbar of the Dashcode window, click Inspector.**

The Inspector window opens to the right of the canvas.

2. **Click the gauge.**

A bounding rectangle with a blue border now surrounds the gauge. The Inspector window shows the properties of the gauge, as show in Figure 18.7.

Figure 18.7

Inspector window for processor gauge

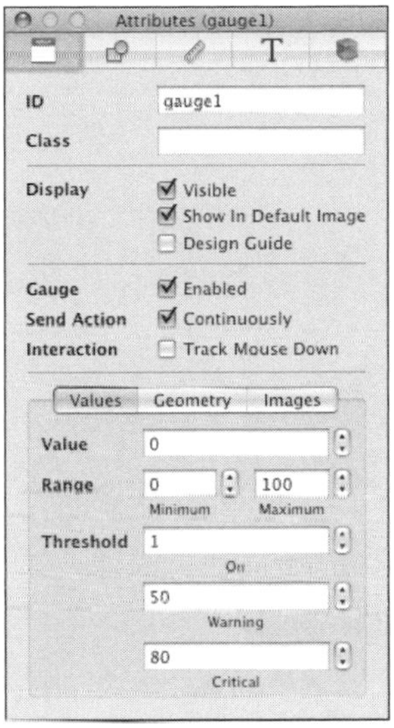

3. **Click the various buttons on the Inspector, while leaving the gauge selected.**

Figure 18.8 shows the other settings panes for the gauge properties.

On the Style and Effects pane, the only options you can change are the opacity. On the Metrics pane, you can change the size of the gauge and where it sits in the whole panel. Because there is no text on the actual gauge, you cannot change any settings on the text panel.

4. **Click the Metrics pane.**

5. **Change the size of the gauge to 90 pixels wide by 90 pixels high.**

6. **Change the top position to 20 pixels and the left position to −100 pixels.**

This puts it in the top-left corner of the front panel.

7. **Select the text** PROCESSOR**.**

8. **Drag the right edge of the blue bounding rectangle until the blue line marking the center of the box aligns with the center of the needle of the gauge.**

Figure 18.8

Properties setting panes for gauge

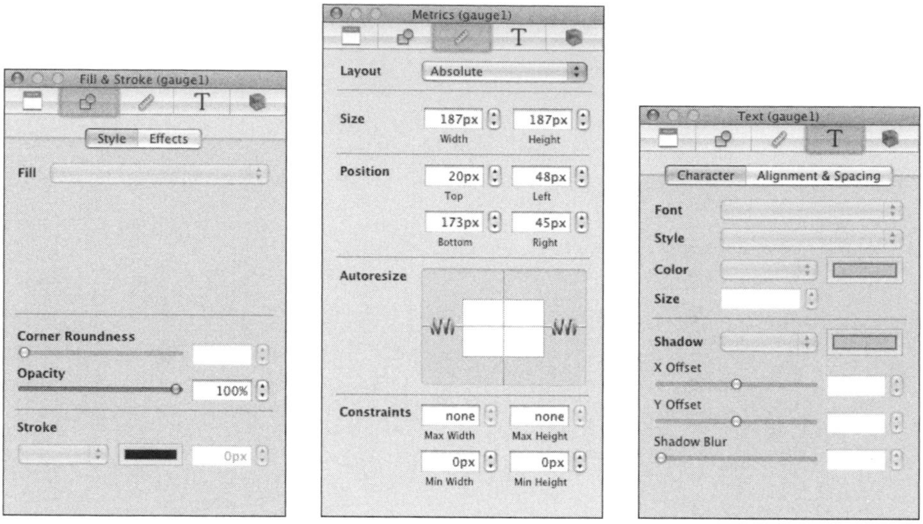

a   b   c

9. **Drag the text up until it sits just below the gauge.**

In my example, the settings are width: 100 pixels; height: 18 pixels; top: 110 pixels; left: 17 pixels.

10. **Change the text to** Processor **instead of** PROCESSOR**.**

11. **Set the font to Lucida Grande Bold, 11 pixels, and 25 percent gray.**

Use the Leopard color selector, as shown in Figure 18.9, to set the color.

12. **Set the shadow to white with a 1-pixel offset in each direction.**

This gives the text an engraved look in the final panel.

13. **Shrink the Disk Activity bar to 100 pixels by 20 pixels, and drag it up so it sits just below the word** Processor**.**

14. **Move the DISK ACTIVITY label so it sits just below the bar.**

15. **Set the font and color properties the same as for the processor label, and change the text to mixed case.**

Figure 18.9

Leopard color selector

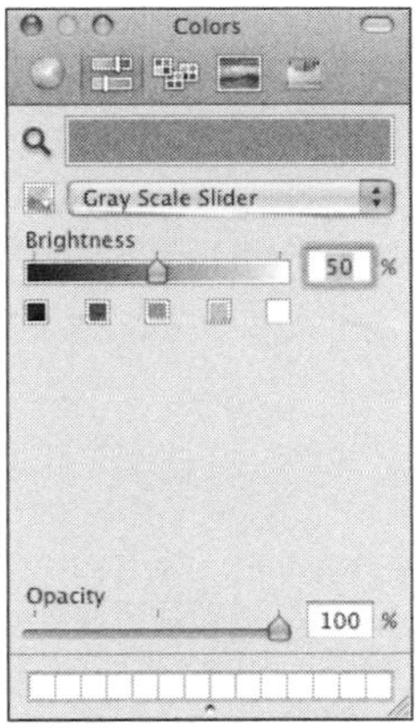

16. **Select the three labels and the two buttons for disk activity as a group.**

    Selecting by drawing a bounding box won't work; you need to select each one while holding down the Shift key.

17. **With the three labels and two buttons selected, move them under the disk activity gauge and set the text to the same as the other labels.**

18. **Select the front image (the whole background) by clicking the resize handle in the bottom-right corner of the bounding box.**

19. **Drag the resize handle until the dimensions are around 140 pixels by 240 pixels.**

    Oops. The processor gauge is now partly outside the gauge background.

20. **Drag the processor gauge back inside the background.**

    Figure 18.10 shows my gauge at this point.

21. **Click the Run button to see your gauge working.**

Figure 18.10

Gauges in final positions

Changing colors and patterns

I prefer the gauge to look less shiny and something like brushed aluminum. Follow these steps to change the look of your gauges:

1. **Select the Fill and Stroke panel for the background to the gauges.**

2. **On the effects pane, deselect Glass and select Recess.**

3. **Set the recess depth to 5 pixels, shadow to 20 percent, and highlight to 50 percent.**

4. **On the Style panel, select a gradient fill of 50 percent gray at the top, 75 percent at the bottom, and opacity of 75 percent.**

5. **Set the stroke to solid, 75 percent, and 2 pixels.**

    Your gauge should now look like Figure 18.11

6. **Run your gauge again.**

Figure 18.11

Finished gauge

Using the gauge

Dashcode uses the term *deploy* to mean adding your widget to your Dashboard.

Deploying your gauge

Now that you are happy with its design, follow these steps to add it to your Dashboard:

1. **Save your widget.**

2. **Select File, Deploy Widget.**

3. **Move some of your other widgets around to clear space for where you want the gauge to sit.**

   Figure 18.12 shows the arrangement of my Dashboard before I added the gauge.

4. **Click Keep to keep the widget as part of your Dashboard.**

Figure 18.12

Dashboard showing widget being deployed

Using your gauge on your desktop

You may want to place your gauge on your desktop. Few Leopard users know this trick, but you can drag any widget off your Dashboard and place it on your desktop. To place your gauge on your desktop, follow these steps:

1. **Start Terminal running.**

2. **Enter the following command:**

```
defaults write com.apple.dashboard devmode YES
```

This puts Dashboard into developer mode.

3. **Enter the command:**

```
killall Dock
```

This stops the Dock, which controls Dashboard, and restarts it. Your Dock disappears for a second or two, and then reappears.

4. **Press F12 to show the Dashboard.**

Don't hold the F12 key down, or it opens your CD/DVD drive.

5. **On your Dashboard, click the widget you want to place on your desktop and drag it to where you want to place it.**

6. **Before you release the mouse button, press the F12 key again.**

Your Dashboard disappears, but you can still drag your widget to wherever you want to place it on your desk.

Be careful where you place it, because it will always be on top of anything that is at the same location.

7. **Reverse developer mode by typing the following into Terminal:**

```
defaults write com.apple.dashboard devmode NO
killall Dock
```

Of course, you can do this with any widget, not just your gauge. To bring the widget from your desktop back into your Dashboard, set developer mode to on (YES) and click the widget before you press F12. After your Dashboard has appeared, drag the widget back into the Dashboard.

Don't forget to turn developer mode off (NO).

Deploying your widget for anyone to use

Your own widgets are all stored in your <home>/Library/Widgets folder. Systemwide widgets that are available for anyone to use are stored in <startup disk>/Library/Widgets.

To make your widget available to all users, simply copy it from your widgets folder to the systemwide folder.

Creating a Map Widget

In this section, you create a map widget using Google maps. Before you start, you need to have a Web site publicly available on the Web. You don't actually need to have anything on your Web site; you simply need a URL. Normally your ISP provides facilities to host your own Web site: Check the ISP's documentation.

Google made its API (Application Programming Interface) publicly available so the owner of a Web site can create a map to show potential customers where they are located, points of interest, and so forth. You can harness that very simply using the maps widget. After you have created your widget, you can distribute it to other people.

For this example, I created a very rudimentary map with points of interest for Sydney Harbor.

Creating your widget

Follow these steps to create your widget:

1. **Start Dashcode running, and select New Project, Maps.**

Figure 18.13 shows the starting screen.

Figure 18.13

Map widget start screen

2. **Save your project as My Map 1.**

3. **Change the text** *Map title shows here* **to** *My First Map Widget.*

4. **Change the colors and size of the map if you wish.**

I left everything at the defaults.

Creating your Google map

Before you can create your widget, you need to create a map using Google maps.

Follow these steps to create your map:

1. **Use your browser to go to** `http://maps.google.com`.

2. **Sign into your Google account.**

   If you don't already have a Google account, follow the instructions on the site to create one.

3. **In the location bar, type a search term for the place you want your map to show.**

4. **When the map is on the screen the way you want it, click My Maps at the top left of the screen.**

5. **Click Create New Map.**

6. **Give your map a title and description, and check the Unlisted button, unless you want to share your map publicly.**

7. **Click Edit.**

8. **Click the Placemark button, the one that looks like an upside-down blue teardrop.**

9. **Drag the placemark on to your map, and enter a name and some descriptive text.**

10. **When you are happy with your map, click Done.**

    That's it. You've created your own Google map. Figure 18.14 shows my Google map.

Figure 18.14

Google map of Sydney

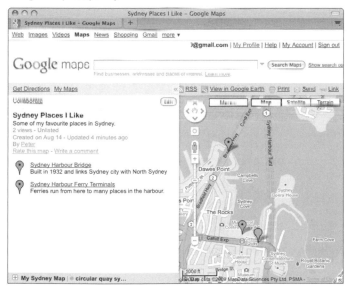

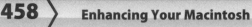

11. **To get the URL for your map, click Link on the far right of the Google map.**

12. **Copy the URL to the clipboard.**

    You may want to save it in a TextEdit document so you can refer to it later.

Getting your mashup code

Return to Dashcode to continue creating your widget. Follow these steps to set your map to display in your widget:

1. **In the Workflow Steps pane, click the arrow icon to the left of the heading Maps properties.**

   Figure 18.15 shows the screen at this point.

   Figure 18.15

   Project properties screen

   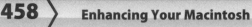

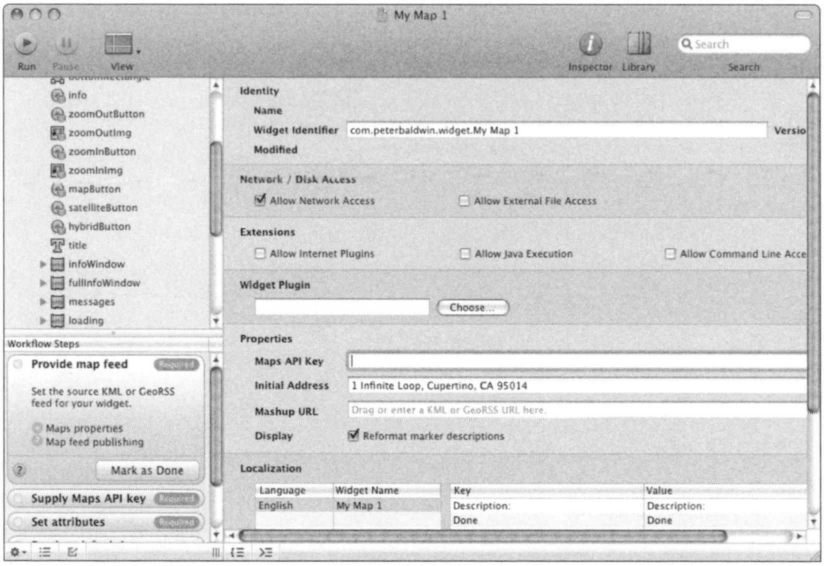

2. **In the Mashup URL box, paste the URL you copied to the clipboard.**

3. **Click Mark as Done.**

4. **Collapse the workflow step by clicking the title line Provide Map Feed.**

5. **Click Supply Maps API key.**

6. **Click Maps API Signup.**

   This takes you to the Google maps signup page.

7. **Read the terms and conditions of using the Google maps API.**

8. **Enter your Web site's URL in the box, and click the Generate key.**

   On the next page, your API key is in green in the top box.

Putting it together

Now you have all the details to set up your maps widget. Follow these steps to complete it:

1. **Copy the API key, and paste it into the Maps API key box in Dashcode.**

2. **In the Initial Address line, delete the address 1 Infinite Loop, Cupertino, CA 95014.**

3. **Click Mark as Done in the Supply Maps API key workflow step.**

4. **Click the Set Attributes box in the workflow steps.**

5. **Dashcode has created an identifier for you, and if you're happy with that, save your project.**

6. **Click Run.**

Now watch as your widget starts up, bounces with ripples on the screen, and takes you to the map you just created in Google.

Figure 18.16 shows my map widget.

Figure 18.16

Map widget showing map of Sydney

If you want to look at the map I created, its URL is `http://tinyurl.com/ma6opc`. To retrieve the actual URL, follow these steps:

1. **Go to** `http://tinyurl.com`.

2. **Click Preview Feature in the left menu bar.**

   Check that the message says you have preview turned on.

3. **In your browser address bar, type** `http://tinyurl.com/ma6opc`.

4. **Click Proceed to this site.**

Creating a Countdown Timer

A countdown timer is provided as one of the standard Dashcode projects. It displays a countdown in days, hours, minutes, and seconds to a particular event. It can take an event from your iCal calendar and use that as the end of the countdown. In this section, you create a countdown timer that counts down the time until the next event in your calendar.

You can use iCal if you choose or any other calendar application that can create .ics files. I use Google calendar as my main calendar, but you may choose another.

Setting the event

Create your countdown timer by following these steps:

1. **Start Dashcode, and choose the countdown template.**

2. **Save your timer as Time Until Next Appointment.**

Using iCal calendar application

If you are using iCal as your calendar application, follow these steps to connect to your countdown timer:

1. **Open iCal, and select the calendar you want to use.**

2. **On the File menu, select Export... and save the calendar to your Documents folder.**

Using Google calendar

If you are using Google calendar, follow these steps:

1. **Open your calendar.**

   On the left side of the screen is the My Calendars box.

2. **Click the down arrow, and select calendar settings.**

3. **Scroll down to Calendar Address.**

4. **Click the iCal button.**

5. **Copy the URL to the clipboard.**

Using MobileMe calendar

Follow these steps to publish your iCal calendar and then use it in the countdown timer:

1. **Open iCal.**

2. **Highlight your calendar, and select Publish from the Calendar menu.**

3. **In the dialog box, select the options you want, as shown in Figure 18.17.**

Figure 18.17

Publish to MobileMe dialog box

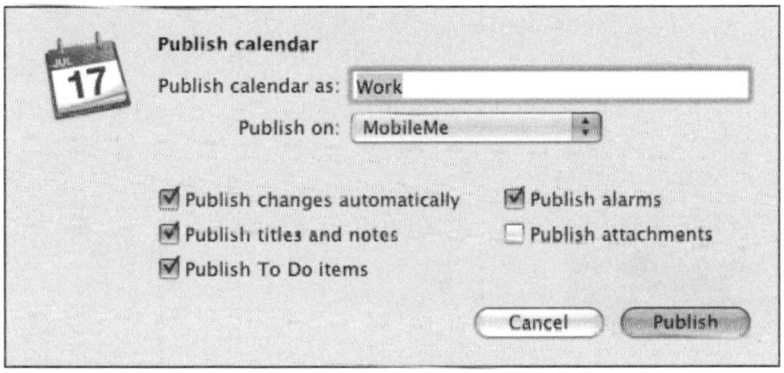

4. **Click Publish.**

5. **On the dialog box that returns after publishing, copy both the webcal:// and the http:// links.**

Linking the countdown timer to the calendar

Now that you have a published calendar, either on your local computer or on the Web, you can link it to your timer by following these steps:

1. **In Dashcode, select Widget Attributes.**

   Part of that screen is shown in Figure 18.18.

2. **In the Network / Disk Access section, be sure that Allow Network Access and Allow External File Access are both checked.**

Figure 18.18

Countdown timer properties

3. **In the Target Kind drop-down box, select Shared Calendar and paste the address of the .ics file.**

4. **Save your widget.**

5. **Run your widget.**

    Figure 18.19 shows my widget counting down until the next appointment in my calendar.

Figure 18.19

First run of countdown widget

Changing the look of the timer

I don't manage my day down to the last second, so the seconds display on the timer is of no importance to me. Also, I don't particularly like the look of the timer.

Removing the seconds display

To remove the seconds display on the time, follow these steps:

1. **In the Parts Outline panel, expand the display of the front of the timer until you can see the label timer colons, as shown in Figure 18.20.**

2. **Right-click colon3, and select Delete.**

3. **Right-click remaining-seconds, and select Delete**

4. **Expand countdown-label, and delete label-seconds.**

    It is important that you delete them this way, rather than simply deleting them from the display. If you simply delete the items that appear onscreen, the widget still expects to find them there when it runs, so it gives you an error.

Figure 18.20

Front image properties

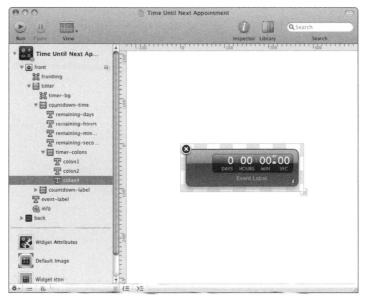

5. **Using Command+Shift, highlight remaining-days, remaining-hours, remaining-minutes, colon1, colon2, label-days, label-hours, and label-minutes.**

   Your screen should look like that shown in Figure 18.21.

6. **Move all these to the right side of the display.**

   By doing it this way, you retain the relative positions of all the elements.

7. **Highlight timer-bg, and shrink it by dragging the left side to the right.**

8. **With timer-bg still highlighted, open the property inspector if it's not already open.**

9. **On the Fill and stroke pane, select Effects and then uncheck the Glass box.**

10. **Check the Recess box, and set the depth to 10 pixels, shadow to 100 percent, and highlight to 100 percent.**

    These changes have the effect of making the black panel appear to be recessed in the main widget panel. The shadow appears at the top and the highlight at the bottom, giving the effect of light coming from overhead.

11. **Select frontimg, and uncheck the Glass box.**

    For this timer, we give it the look of a standard Leopard toolbar with the subtle gradient from bright at the top of the box to slightly darker at the bottom.

Figure 18.21

Labels, colons, and times highlighted

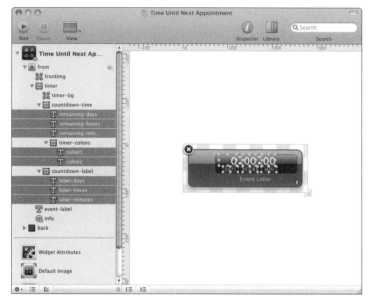

12. **With the frontimg still highlighted, select Style in the property inspector.**

13. **In the Fill drop-down box, select Gradient.**

14. **Click the top color panel.**

The standard Leopard color selection box appears, as shown in Figure 18.22.

Figure 18.22

Leopard color selection box

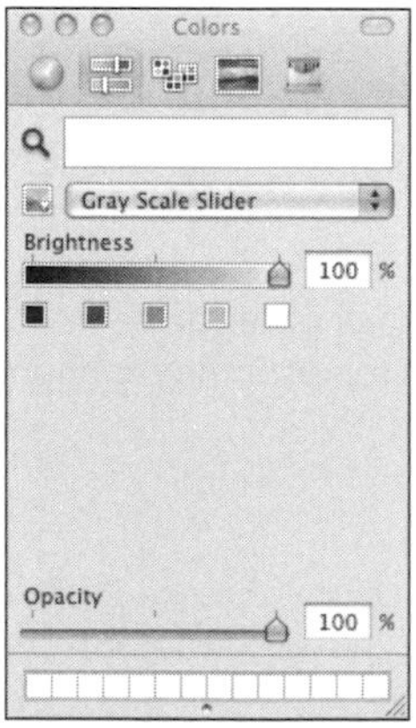

15. Click the magnifying glass icon, place it over the very top of the toolbar in Dashcode, and then click.

This gives a gray color of 77 percent.

16. Click the lower color panel on the inspector, and then click the magnifying glass icon.

17. Click the magnifying glass over the bottom edge of the toolbar.

This gives a gray color of 60 percent. Now your timer has the color gradient of a Leopard toolbar, but with a blue outline.

18. In the inspector, select None for Stroke to remove the blue outline.

Now the event label telling you what the countdown refers to is no longer visible.

19. Highlight event-label in the elements pane.

20. In the property inspector, select Text and Character.

21. Set the Style to Bold and the color to Black.

22. Move the event-label box so it sits just to the left of the info button.

23. Highlight frontimg, and drag the handle at the bottom right so the box is symmetrical around the timer panel.

24. You may need to adjust the position of the event-label for balance.

Finally, because you know it's a countdown timer, you don't need to have the text *Countdown to* in the label.

25. Select Widget Attributes, as shown in Figure 18.23.

26. In the area shown highlighted, delete the words *Countdown to,* leaving just the %s.

27. Save your widget, and then run it.

Figure 18.24 shows my widget running. The first appointment in my calendar is Dinner with Michael, in 5 days' time.

Figure 18.23

Widget attributes

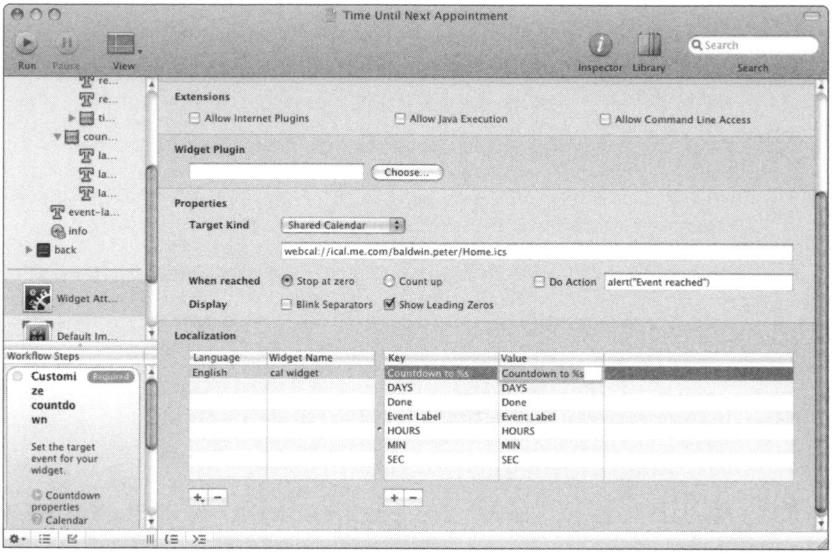

Figure 18.24

Countdown timer running

Adding another element

One minor difficulty with the timer as it now stands is that, while the countdown time is in a panel recessed into the widget, the event just appears as flat text on the top surface of the widget.

Follow these steps to make a recessed background panel for the text appear like the count-down time:

1. **Highlight front in the parts outline panel.**

2. **In the right panel, drag the size handle so the image of the front is quite large.**

   This is just to give you some canvas to work on.

3. **In the Toolbar, click the Library button.**

   This opens the Library panel, as shown in Figure 18.25.

Figure 18.25

Dashcode library panel

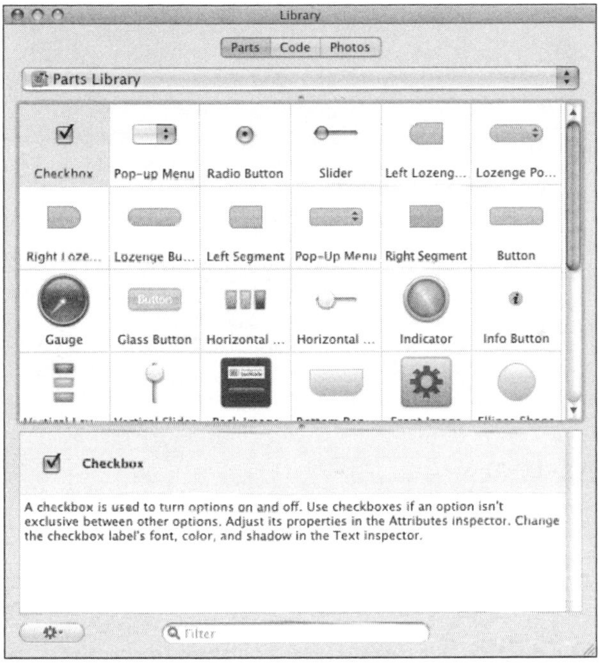

4. **Select the rounded box and drag it into your timer box.**

   Note that a new element is added to the parts outline panel, as shown in Figure 18.26a.

5. **Click twice on the title "box" (but not too quickly, or it will register as a double-click), change the title from *box* to *event,* and expand the box.**

6. **In the Library, select Rounded Rectangle Shape and drag it onto your image.**

   This adds another part to the parts outline.

7. **Change its name from *roundedRectangleShape* to *event-bg.***

8. **Expand the event-bg to slightly smaller than the event box.**

9. **In the properties inspector, select Fill and Stroke for event-bg.**

10. **Set the Fill to solid, and in the color selection box, choose black.**

11. **In the Effects panel, set the Recess to 10 pixels, 100 percent shadow, and 100 percent highlight.**

12. **In the parts outline box, select event-label and drag it down so it sits under event-bg, as shown in Figure 18.26b.**

Figure 18.26

Parts outline (a); parts outline showing event-label moved (b)

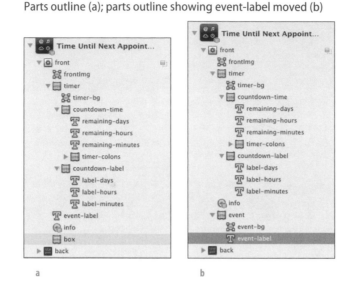

a   b

13. Highlight event-label, and use the inspector to change the text color to white.

14. Drag it into the event background box, and then resize and move them all so they sit under the countdown box.

15. Drag the resize handle for the front image so everything looks nicely symmetrical.

One small, final touch is to make all the text the same color.

16. In the parts outline, select all the elements that contain text (remaining days, hours, and minutes; labels days, hours, and minutes; event label) and set the text color to 80 percent white.

Figure 18.27 shows my final countdown timer.

Figure 18.27

Final countdown timer

Adding some programming

Programming in Dashcode looks extremely complex! The files window shows a large number of JavaScript files. In the standard projects, these are all supplied for you and you don't need to modify any of them. If you are creating your own widgets from scratch, you can reuse some of the standard code, but it requires a higher level of ability and is beyond the scope of this book.

You can, however, do a small amount of programming easily in Dashcode. In this section, you add a button to your widget that takes you to your calendar.

Adding a button to the widget

Follow these steps to add a button to your widget:

1. **Open your Time Until Next Appointment widget.**

2. **Enlarge the canvas using the resize handle.**

   Don't worry about the size; you can adjust it later.

3. **Open the Library panel, and select a button, as shown in Figure 18.28.**

Figure 18.28

Library panel showing button selected

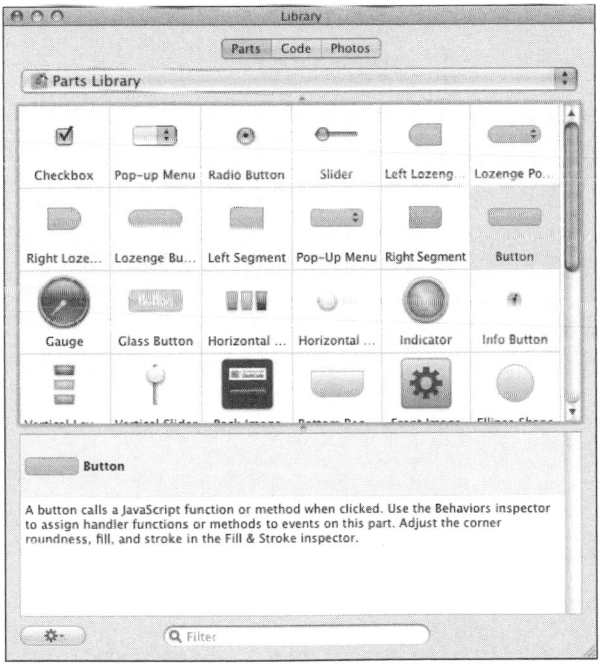

4. **Drag the button to your canvas, inside the boundary of the widget.**

5. **Open the properties inspector with the button selected.**

6. **Select Attributes for the button.**

7. **In the ID field, enter** calendarButton, **and in the Key field, enter** View Calendar, **as shown in Figure 18.29a.**

8. **Resize the widget so the button and the panels are centered, as shown in Figure 18.29b.**

Figure 18.29

Button Attributes (a); Final Widget View (b)

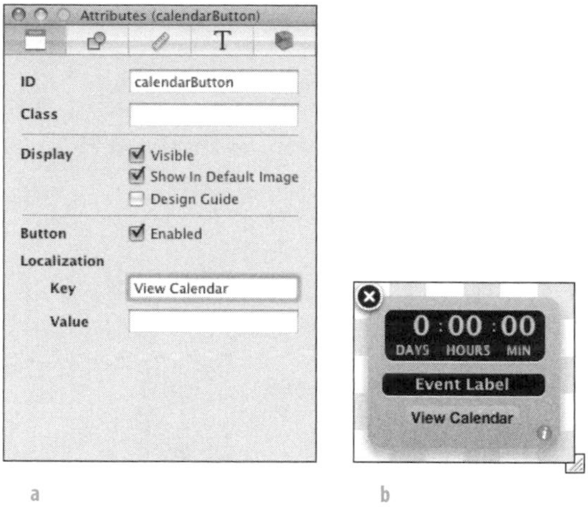

a   b

9. **Save the widget, and check that it still works by clicking Run.**

Adding some code to the widget

At the moment, you have a button on the widget that doesn't do anything: click it to check. In this section you add some simple code to get the button to open your calendar.

Follow these steps to add the code:

1. **Open the property inspector if it is not already open.**

2. **Click the icon for the Behaviors panel (the rightmost button).**

   Figure 18.30a shows the property inspector panel for Behaviors.

   In this case, you want to add a behavior that is triggered when the button is clicked. This is the onclick event.

3. **In the Handlers column for onclick, double-click, enter the text** showCalendar, **and press Enter.**

The property inspector adds the text (event) after the handler, as shown in Figure 18.30b.

Figure 18.30

Behaviors panel (a); Behaviors window (b)

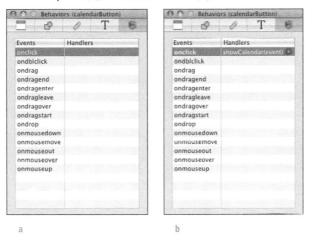

a   b

It then opens the code window at the end of the main.js program, as shown in Figure 18.31.

Figure 18.31

Code window

```
410
411  // Initialize the Dashboard event handlers
412  if (window.widget) {
413      widget.onremove = remove;
414      widget.onhide = hide;
415      widget.onshow = show;
416      widget.onsync = sync;
417  }
418
419
420  function showCalendar(event)
421  {
422      // Insert Code Here
423  }
424
```

Now you need to add code to open the calendar. You can choose either of the code samples to open your calendar.

Adding code to open the iCal application

Follow these steps to add code to open iCal:

1. **Open the Library panel if it is not already open, and select the Code panel.**

   Figure 18.32 shows the library in code view.

   Figure 18.32

   Library panel in code view

2. **To make it a little easier to find the item you want, click the gear wheel icon in the bottom-left corner and change the view to View Icons and Descriptions.**

3. **Scroll down until you find Show Application.**

4. **In the code window at the bottom, highlight the code, as shown in Figure 18.33.**

5. **Copy the code (Command+C), and paste it into the code window where it says //** *Insert Code Here.*

   Note: // indicates a comment. After the paste, your code window should look like Figure 18.34.

Figure 18.33

Open application code highlighted

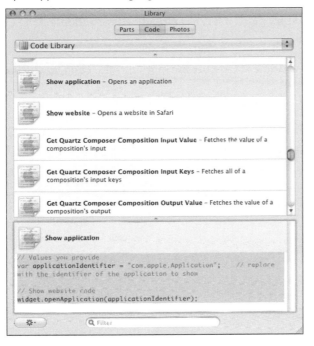

Figure 18.34

Code window after pasting code

6. **Replace the word** *Application* **in the purple text** *com.apple.Application* **with** *iCal* **so the line should now read** *com.apple.iCal.*

7. **Save your widget, and then run it.**

8. **Click the View Calendar button.**

   Your iCal application should open.

Adding code to open the calendar in a web browser

Follow these steps to add code to the button to open your calendar in a Web browser:

1. **Open the Library panel if it is not already open, and select the Code panel.**

2. **Scroll down until you find *Show Website*.**

3. **In the code window at the bottom, highlight the code, as shown in Figure 18.35.**

Figure 18.35

Open Web site code highlighted

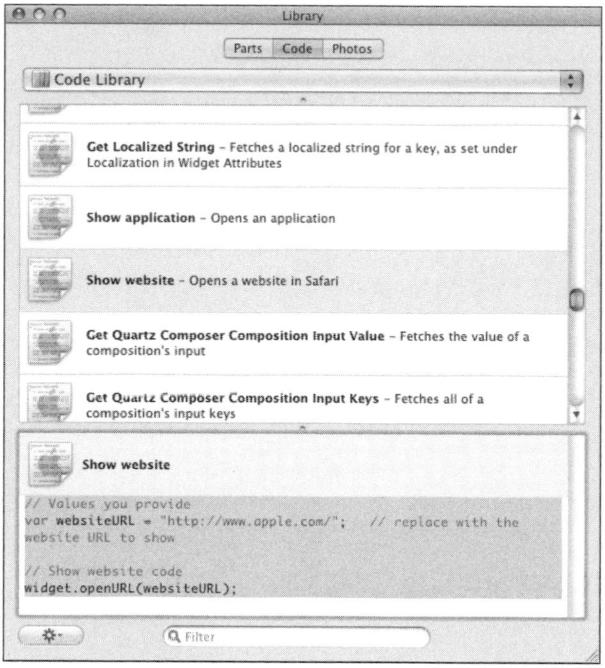

4. **Copy the code (Command+C), and paste it into the code window where it says //** *Insert Code Here.*

   Note: // indicates a comment.

5. **Replace the word *website* for Apple with the Web address of your calendar, replacing the purple text.**

   If you used Google calendar, you should use the HTML address of your calendar, not the .ics version you used for the Target of your application.

6. **Save your widget, and then run it.**

7. **Click the View Calendar button.**

   Your calendar should open in your Web browser.

8. **If you're happy with your widget, deploy it.**

Summary

In this chapter, you created three widgets from the templates supplied with Dashcode:

- Computer gauge
- Map
- Countdown timer

You used the Dashcode editor to modify the look and feel of each widget and then linked them to information on the Internet.

Although this is just a basic introduction to widget creation, it should allow you to experiment further in creating your own widgets that don't rely on a template.

19

Using Quartz Composer

Quartz Composer is a very powerful tool for creating three-dimensional moving images. Several screen savers for the Macintosh are Quartz Composer files with a filename extension of .qtz.

Some of Apple's existing online documentation refers to an earlier version of Quartz Composer, and the screen illustrations will look a little different from the version you are using, assuming you downloaded it fairly recently.

In this chapter, you create some simple Quartz Composer compositions and learn your way around the application.

Introducing Quartz Composer

Quartz Composer is one of the Apple developer tools. Before you can use it, you need to install the Apple Developer Tools. If you haven't already done this, follow the instructions in Chapter 18. In addition, you must have Quartz Extreme/Core Image enabled on your computer; otherwise, you will not be able to manipulate the graphics.

In effect, Quartz Composer is a programming language but with a very different interface. It is very complex and powerful, but it's much easier to understand and use than a traditional programming language carrying out the same tasks.

Understanding the main windows

When you start Quartz Composer running, it displays two windows:

- The editor window
- The viewer window

In the editor window is the canvas that you use to create your composition. Each item on the canvas is known as a patch, in an analogy with a patch panel dating from the old manual telephone switchboard days. These days, patch panels are found behind the scenes in any organization where there are large numbers of computers connected to a central system. Patch panels allow technicians to connect a particular wall outlet to a particular port on the router.

Understanding patches

In Quartz Composer, a patch is like a cable that connects one part of the system to another. In programming terms, a patch is like a subroutine. It takes a certain input and produces an output. What the inputs and outputs are depends on the patch itself.

There are several types of patches:

- Composites that combine two or more images to produce a composite image
- Controllers that take input from hardware devices such as the mouse and Apple remote
- Filters that apply various visual effects to an image
- Generators that generate constant colors, text, and star shine effects to add to an image
- Modifiers that crop, resize, and rotate images
- Numeric patches that do various numeric calculations and apply them to images
- Renderers that take image inputs and output them to the screen
- Many and varied tools, such as stopwatch, time, and iterators
- Transitions, such as ripple, dissolve, page curl, and so on

Figure 19.1 shows the editor window with several patches applied, taken from the template Graphic Transition.

Figure 19.1

Quartz Composer editor window

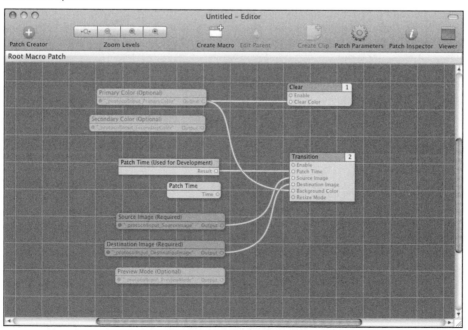

Figure 19.2a shows the viewer window for the patches shown in Figure 19.1.

Note that in the viewer window, the Run button is dimmed. This is because Quartz Composer is really based around animation. Although it's not apparent, that window has two images. The first image loads and then transitions into the other. At the time this image was captured, it was running at 60 frames per second, drawing the second image 60 times every second.

Fundamental to Quartz Composer is the Patch Creator. This is a selection panel that allows you to select a pre-prepared patch to use in your composition. Figure 19.2b shows the Patch Creator.

Figure 19.2

Viewer window (a); Patch Creator window (b)

a   b

Each patch has a number of input ports and output ports. The exact number depends on the patch. An image importer, for example, has no input ports and only a single output port: the image.

Because the entire operation of Quartz Composer is graphical, each patch is represented by a graphical element. Figure 19.3 shows a Pixellate patch. The input ports are on the left: Image, Center (X), Center (Y), and Scale.

Figure 19.3

Patch showing input and output ports

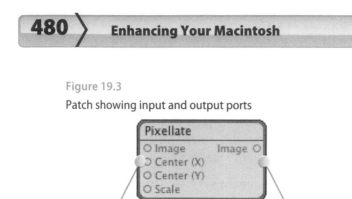

Input ports   Output ports

Understanding the coordinate system

At first, Quartz Composer can be very confusing because different patches require different coordinates. Some require dimensions in pixels; others require dimensions in Quartz Composer's own coordinate system.

Before you can start using Quartz Composer, you need to understand the three-dimensional coordinate system, because that's the system that QC works in. Our senses perceive three dimensions in space around us: left-right, forward-backward, and up-down. By convention, we call the left-right direction the X axis, the forward-backward direction the Z axis, and the up-down direction the Y axis.

Figure 19.4 shows this graphically.

Our computer screens are all two-dimensional; nevertheless, we can simulate movement in three dimensions. Movement along the X axis occurs when the image moves left or right. Movement along the Y axis occurs when the image moves up or down. Movement along the Z axis is when the object gets closer to or farther away from our viewpoint. Obviously, this can't happen on a flat screen; instead, we simulate movement along the Z axis by making the object smaller or larger. Making it smaller makes it appear to be farther away; making it larger makes it appear closer.

Quartz Composer normalizes coordinates from −1 to +1 for the X axis so the full width of a composition is two units in the X dimension—or from −1 to +1.

In the Y dimension, the full extent of the boundaries depends on the aspect ratio of your screen or display area. In the case of a 1024 x 768 screen, the aspect ratio is 4:3, so your maximum Y value is +1 divided by the aspect ratio, shown as 1/(AR) in Figure 19.4. This is 1 / (4/3), which is 0.75. So the Y values range from −0.75 to +0.75. My monitor is 1920 x 1080, an aspect ratio of 16:9. So the Y values range from −0.56 to +0.56. Z axis values range from −1 to +1.

For these exercises, though, we'll ignore the aspect ratio of the screen and use both X and Y coordinates from −1 to +1.

Figure 19.4

Three-dimensional axes

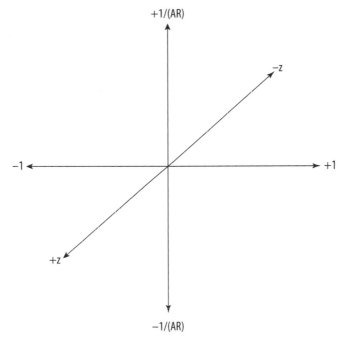

Creating a Rotatable Picture

In this section, you prepare a very simple composition consisting of a two-dimensional image that you can rotate in two dimensions using your mouse.

Preparing your picture

Before you start, you need to have a picture that you can rotate. The simplest way to do this is to use a picture from your Windows disk. The picture should be around 600 pixels square, though the exact dimensions are not critical.

If you don't have a picture of suitable size, follow these steps to create one from an image on your Windows disk:

1. **Open an image on your Windows disk, using Preview.**

2. **Click the Select button, and select a rectangular portion of the image.**

3. **Copy the rectangular section (Edit, Copy).**

4. **Select File, New from Clipboard.**

5. **Save the file as Image01.png.**

6. **On the Tools menu, select Adjust size.**

7. **Enter 600 pixels for the width.**

   Be sure that Scale proportionally and Resample image are both checked, as shown in Figure 19.5.

Figure 19.5

Image resizing

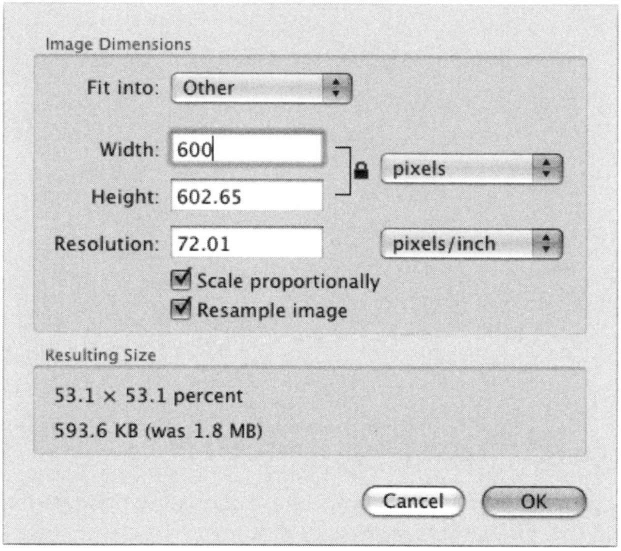

8. **Click OK.**

9. **Save as Image01.png.**

Using sprite rendering

There are two major renderers in Quartz Composer: sprites and billboards. Sprites operate in all three dimensions; billboards operate in only two dimensions. Because we want to simulate movement in three dimensions, we use sprite rendering in this exercise.

Follow these steps to create your first Quartz composition:

1. **Start Quartz Composer.**

2. **On the greeting screen, shown in Figure 19.6, select Blank Composition.**

Figure 19.6

Quartz Composer template screen

As you would expect, this brings up two blank windows: the editor and the viewer. The editor window is where you place and link your patches; the viewer window is where you view the output.

Importing an input image

Earlier you created an image to use for your first composition. Follow these steps to use this image as input to the editor:

1. **In the Quartz Composer editor window, click Patch Creator.**

2. **In the search box of the Patch Creator, search for *import*.**

3. **Drag the result (Category: Source, Name: Image Importer) into the editor window.**

    Figure 19.7 shows your editor screen at this point.

Figure 19.7

Editor with Image Importer patch

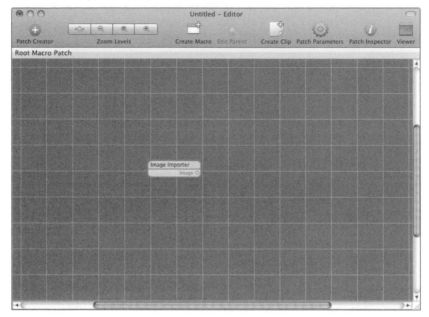

4. **Save your composition as Image Rotator.**

Now that you have an Image Importer patch, you have to tell it which image to import.

5. **Highlight the Image Importer patch, and click Patch Inspector.**

This brings up another window, shown in Figure 19.8a.

6. **In the drop-down menu box, select Settings.**

Figure 19.8b shows the Settings pane.

7. **Click Import From File…, and select Image01.png, the image you prepared earlier.**

Note that nothing appears in the viewer window. That's because you imported the image, but you haven't done anything with it yet.

Figure 19.8

Image Importer patch properties window (a); Image importer patch settings pane (b)

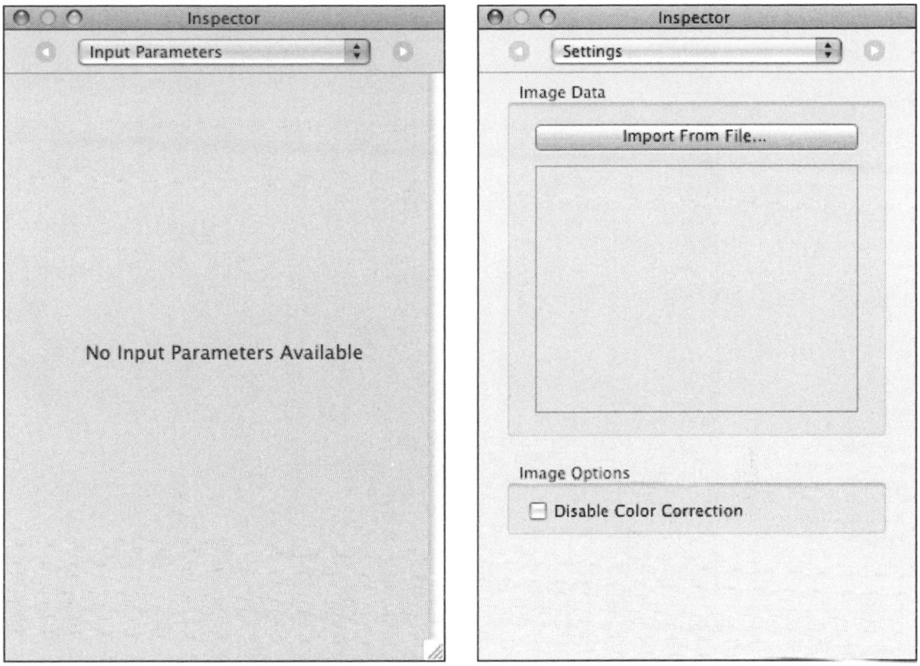

a   b

Making the Image visible

Now that you have an image available, you need to do something with it. In this example, you use the Sprite renderer, which works in three dimensions. Follow these steps to make the image visible:

1. **In the Patch Creator window, search for *sprite*.**

2. **Drag the Sprite renderer to your editor canvas.**

   Your editor canvas should now look like Figure 19.9.

3. **Look at the property inspector window for the Sprite renderer.**

   Figure 19.10a shows the properties of the Sprite renderer.

Figure 19.9

Editor canvas

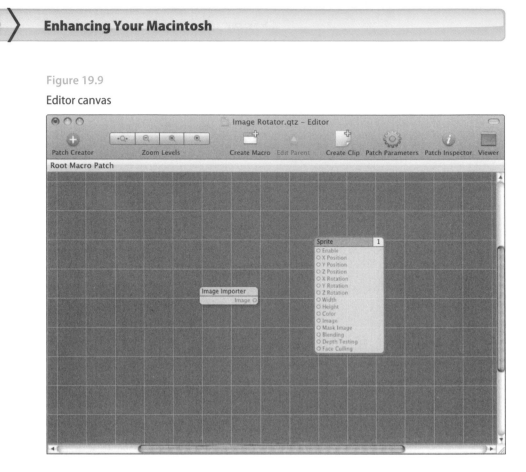

4. **Save your work.**

   Now you have to give the Sprite renderer an image to work with.

5. **Click in the small circle on the right side of the Image Importer patch.**

   This is the output image port.

6. **While holding down the mouse button, drag to the small circle labeled Image in the Sprite renderer.**

   This creates a line linking the two image circles. Your editor canvas should now look like Figure 19.10b.

   This is how programming is done in Quartz Composer: linking input ports and output ports. Each patch does something to the image.

7. **If you can't see the viewer window, click the Viewer button on the editor window.**

   Figure 19.11 shows my viewer window at this point.

Figure 19.10

Sprite renderer properties (a); Image Importer linked to Sprite renderer (b)

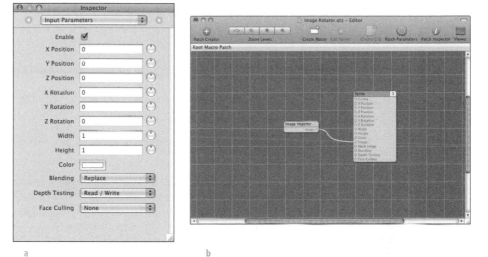

a   b

Figure 19.11

Viewer window

Reading mouse movements

So far, all we have is a static image in the viewer window. Now let's get it to respond to mouse movements. To do this, you need another patch: mouse controller.

Follow these steps to add a mouse controller to your canvas:

1. **If it is not already open, click Patch Creator to open the Patch Creator window.**

2. **In the search box, type** mouse.

3. **Drag the mouse controller onto your canvas.**

   Now you need to take the output from the mouse controller, and send it as input to the Sprite renderer.

   You might expect that you would take the mouse's X position (its position on the left-right axis) and feed it to the X position input to the sprite. But that's not what you want. To make the mouse movement seem natural, you connect its X axis output to the Y axis of the sprite. Figure 19.12 should make this clearer.

Figure 19.12

Mouse movement to shape rotation

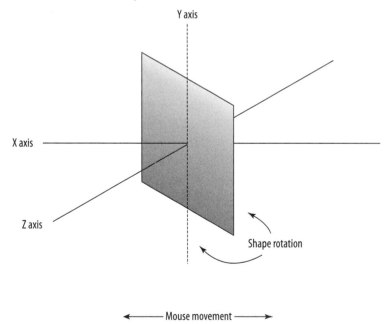

4. **Join the X Position port on the mouse controller to the Y Rotation port on the Sprite renderer.**

Your canvas should now look like Figure 19.13.

Figure 19.13

Canvas with mouse controller connected

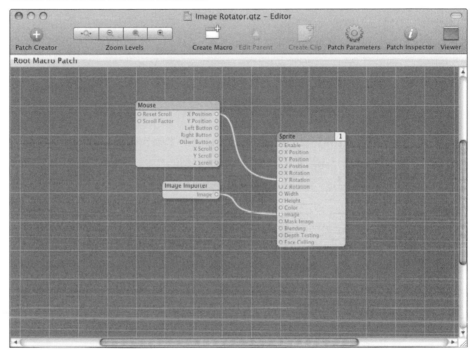

5. **Click in the viewer window, and move the mouse from right to left.**

If you look closely and move the mouse through large distances, you should see the left and right borders of the image move slightly as it rotates.

Applying mathematical transforms

Even with large mouse movements, the image rotates only by a very small amount, so you need to amplify the mouse movements. You do this by using a Math patch.

Adding a Math patch for left-right motion

A Math patch can carry out any mathematical operation on its input and send it to its output.

Follow these steps to add a Math patch to magnify your mouse movements:

1. **In the Patch Creator, search for *math*.**

2. **Drag the Math patch onto your canvas, and place it near your Mouse Controller patch.**

3. **Disconnect the output port for X position of the mouse controller from the Sprite renderer, and connect it to the Initial Value port of the Math patch.**

4. **Connect the Resulting Value port of the Math patch to the Y Rotation input port of the Sprite renderer.**

   Figure 19.14a shows your canvas at this point.

   Now you need to tell the Math patch what to do to the input value before sending it as the output value. You want to multiply the mouse movement so it has a greater effect on the image.

5. **Click the Math patch, and open the Patch Inspector if it is not already open.**

6. **In the drop-down box for operation #1, select Multiply.**

7. **In the Operand #1 box, enter 50.**

   Your Patch Inspector window should now look like Figure 19.14b.

Figure 19.14

Math patch added to the canvas (a); Math patch inspector (b)

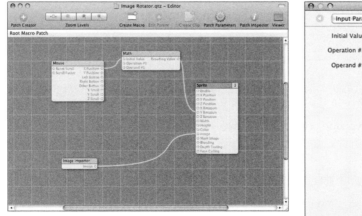

a   b

8. **Click in the viewer window, and move your mouse from left to right.**

   Now your image rotates much more. You should be able to rotate it so it reverses.

Adding a Math patch for back-forth motion

Your Mouse patch can output its Y position as well as its X position. This time, you need to connect the Y motion to rotation about the X axis.

Again, its output is not great enough to move the image very much, so you need another Math patch. Set it up as for the X position: Set the operation #1 to **Multiply** and operand #1 to **50**.

This time, you should be able to rotate the image around two axes. Figure 19.15a shows your editor canvas after this step.

Figure 19.15b shows my image rotated in both directions.

Figure 19.15

Editor canvas with mouse movement linked (a); image rotated in two directions (b)

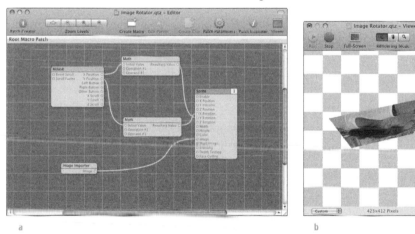

a   b

Filtering the image

Between the image importer and the renderer, we can introduce a patch that does some filtering of the image. Quartz Composer comes with almost 80 filter patches. Most of them have other inputs besides the image to be filtered. In this example, we use a simple filter: sepia tone. This changes the image to something that looks like an old photograph.

Adding a sepia tone filter

Follow these steps to insert a sepia tone filter in the image:

1. **In the Patch Creator, search for** *sepia* **and drag the filter to the canvas.**

2. **Connect the output image port on the image importer to the input image port on the left of the sepia tone patch.**

3. **Connect the right image port on the patch to the input image port on the Sprite renderer.**

4. **Make the viewer window visible to view the image in sepia tone.**

Adding another filter

You can choose from many other filters. See what happens when you take the Color Invert patch and link the image output port from the sepia tone filter to the input port of the color inverter, and then link the output of the color inverter to the input of the renderer.

Creating a Rotating Cube

Quartz Composer has a patch for creating a rotating cube from an image. It places an input image on all six sides of the cube. Rather than being a simple patch like the Math patch, it is actually a macro: It contains several patches that are encapsulated into a single unit.

Follow these steps to create a rotating cube of your image:

1. **Create a new Quartz composition using the blank template.**

2. **Save it as Rotating Cube.**

3. **Open the Patch Creator if it is not already open.**

4. **Type** importer **in the search bar.**

5. **Double-click Image Importer in the Patch Creator to add it to your canvas.**

6. **Type** cube **into the Patch Creator search bar.**

7. **Double-click Clip: Rotating Cube to add it to your canvas.**

   At this point your view window shows a gray, rotating cube.

8. **Connect the output image port of the importer to the input image port of the Rotating Cube patch.**

   Your canvas should look like Figure 19.16a.

   Your view window now shows your image on all six faces of a cube, rotating.

9. **Click inside the Rotating Cube patch.**

10. **Open the Patch Inspector if it's not already open.**

11. **From the drop-down box, select Input Parameters.**

   Your Patch Inspector should look like Figure 19.16b.

Figure 19.16

Rotating cube canvas (a); inspector view of Rotating Cube patch (b)

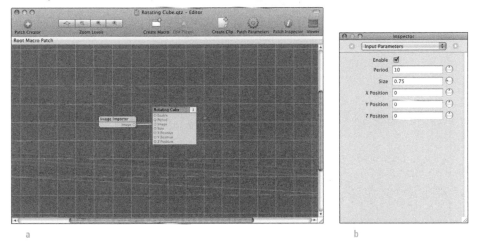

a   b

Default parameters for the Rotating Cube patch are shown in Table 19.1:

Table 19.1 Default Rotating Cube Parameters

Parameter	Meaning	Default Value
Enable	Whether the patch is visible	Checked
Period	Time in seconds for the display to repeat itself	10
Size	Magnification factor used to display the image	0.75
X Position	X axis position for the center of the image	0
Y Position	Y axis position for the center of the image	0
Z Position	Z axis position for the center of the image	0

Experiment with changing the parameters. Watch the effect of each change in the viewer window.

Adding interpolations

In the preceding composition, you used the mouse to control the animation. In this composition, you use a patch called Interpolation. Interpolation means inserting a value between two fixed points. The Interpolator patch generates values between maximum and minimum values that you specify. If you connect the output to one of the inputs for the rotating cube, you can vary the value.

Table 19.2 describes the meaning of each of the input parameters for the Interpolator patch.

Table 19.2 Input Parameters for the Interpolator Patch

Parameter	Meaning	Default Value
Start value	First value that the interpolator creates	0
End value	Last value that the interpolator creates	1
Duration	Time of the interpolation in seconds	1
Tension	Amount of curvature to the interpolation line (ranges from −1 to +1)	0
Repeat mode	Whether and how the interpolator repeats: None, Loop, Mirrored Loop, Mirrored Loop Once	Loop
Interpolation	The shape of the line joining the start and end values; thirteen possible values	Linear

Interpolating the size of the cube

By adding an Interpolation patch and connecting its output to the Size input parameter of the Rotating Cube patch, you can change the size of the cube while it is rotating.

Follow these instructions to add an Interpolation patch to your canvas and connect it to the rotating cube:

1. **In the patch creator window, type** interp.

2. **Press Enter to place the patch on your canvas.**

3. **Highlight the Interpolation patch, and set the following values in the Patch Inspector:**
   - Start value: 0.5
   - End value: 1
   - Duration: 10
   - Repeat mode: mirrored loop

4. **Connect the result of the interpolation port patch to the size port of the rotating cube.**

   Your rotating cube now changes in size from half (start value = 0.5) its input image size to actual image size. Remember, the default for the Rotating Cube patch is 0.75.

Interpolating other cube parameters

In the same way as you control the size of the cube using an Interpolation patch, you can control the other settings.

Follow these steps to add more interpolations to your cube:

1. **Add three more interpolation patches to your canvas.**

Your canvas should look like that shown in Figure 19.17.

Figure 19.17

Canvas with four interpolation patches

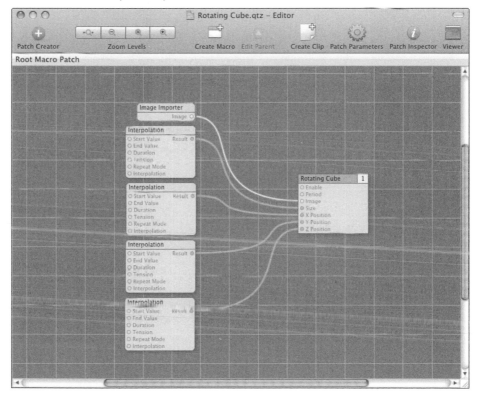

2. **For each patch, set the start value to −0.5 and the end value to +0.5.**

3. **Set the repeat mode to Mirrored Loop for all three patches.**

4. **Set a different duration for each patch.**

If you specify a prime number for the duration of each patch, the repeat cycle for the animation becomes very long.

5. **Connect the Result port of each patch to one of the X Position, Y Position, and Z Position ports for the Cube renderer.**

6. **Save your composition.**

Creating a screen saver

Using your composition as a screen saver is very simple. All you need to do is to copy it to your Library/Screen Savers folder if you want it only for you to use or to /Library/Screen Savers if you want to make it available to every user.

Placing the composition in your screen saver folder

Follow these steps to make your composition available as a screen saver:

1. **Save your composition to your Library/Screen Savers folder, as shown in Figure 19.18.**

Figure 19.18

Saving composition to Screen Savers folder

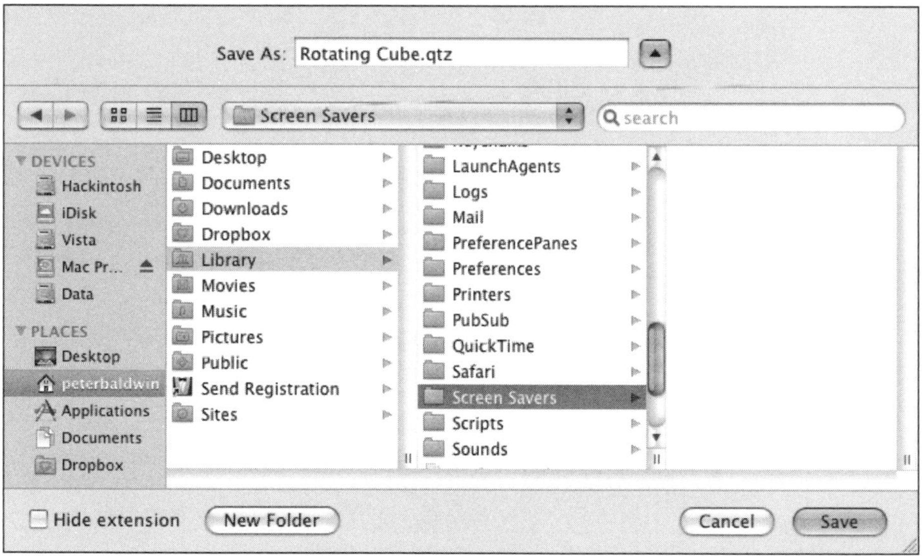

2. **Open System Preferences, and select Desktop and Screen Saver.**

3. **In the Screen Savers panel, scroll down to Other and click the expansion triangle, as shown in Figure 19.19a.**

4. **Select Rotating Cube.qtz.**

   You immediately notice that the screen saver is behaving oddly, as shown in Figure 19.19b.

   Figure 19.19

   Screen Saver system preferences (a); screen saver behaving oddly (b)

   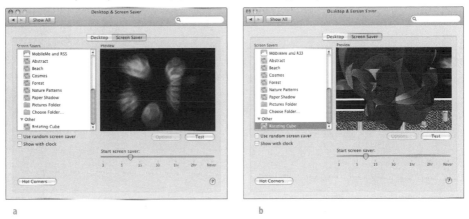

   a   b

Your cube is being redrawn, but the background image is not being cleared. As the screen saver runs, it draws more and more copies of the cube, but doesn't clear the background. Before each frame in the composition, the screen should be cleared so each image Is drawn on a fresh background.

Fixing the screen saver

To make the screen saver redraw the background after each time It draws the cube, you need to add a Clear patch to your composition.

Follow these steps to add a Clear patch:

1. **In Quartz Composer, show the Patch Creator if it is not already visible.**

2. **Type** clear **in the search box, and double-click Renderer Clear to add it to your canvas.**

   Figure 19.20a shows the Clear patch added to your canvas.

3. **If your view window is not showing, click the Viewer button and click Start.**

   Figure 19.20b shows the view when you click the Start button.

Figure 19.20

Canvas with Clear patch added (a); blank viewer window (b)

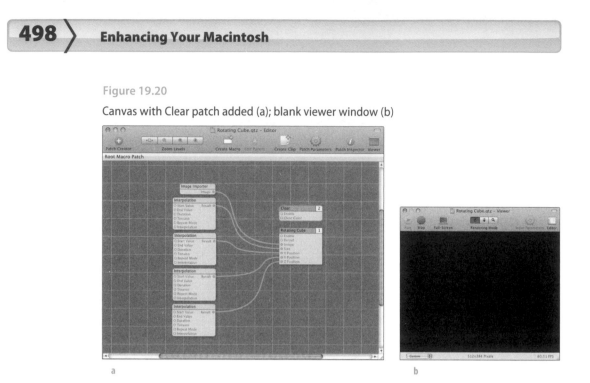

a   b

Your view is black because the clear filter you added clears the display to black immediately after your rendered image is drawn. The result is that you don't see your cube.

Up to now, you probably either have not noticed the yellow numbers in the top-right corner of the renderer patches or have not understood their significance. Figure 19.21 shows the two renderers, showing their numbers.

Figure 19.21

Renderer patches showing layer IDs

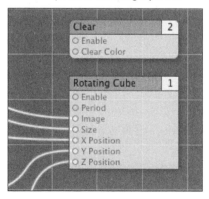

These numbers show the layer numbers of the renderers. In Quartz Composer, layers are numbered from front to back, and renderers operate in the order of their layer number. So in your composition, the clear renderer is on layer 2, while the Cube renderer is on layer 1. To fix your composition, you need to move the clear renderer so it executes after the Cube renderer.

Follow these steps to reverse the order of the renderers:

1. **Click the number 2 in the top right of the clear renderer.**

2. **On the pop-up menu, select Layer 1.**

   Now your composition displays correctly, against a black background.

3. **Save your composition as a screen saver again, and test it.**

   It should work correctly now as a screen saver.

Using Image Effect Filters

Quartz Composer comes with a large range of image effects filters. In this section, you use some of the filters to create special effects.

Using a single filter

Follow these steps to see some of the filter effects available in Quartz Composer:

1. **Create a new composition, and save it as Filters.qtz.**

2. **Search for the Billboard Renderer patch, and add it to your canvas.**

3. **Add an Image Importer patch, and select the image you used in the preceding exercise.**

4. **Connect the output image port of the importer to the Input image port of the renderer.**

5. **Use the Patch Inspector to set the width of the image to 2.**

6. **Search for *pixel,* and add the Pixellate filter to your composition.**

7. **Connect the output image port of the image importer to the input image port of the Pixellate Filter patch.**

   Note that the connection from the importer to the renderer stays intact. You can take the output from a patch and send it to as many inputs as you wish, but each patch has only one input.

8. **Connect the output image port of the Pixellate patch to the input image port of the renderer.**

9. **Use the viewer window to see the effect on your image.**

   Figure 19.22 shows the effect of the Pixellate patch on my image.

   Figure 19.22

   Pixellate patch applied to image

10. **Click the Pixellate patch in the canvas, and then open the Patch Inspector.**

11. **See what happens as you use the slider to increase and decrease the scale.**

12. **Try several of the other filter patches to see their effects.**

13. **When you have examined several of the patches, return to the Pixellate patch.**

Using more than one filter

Because each filter has both an input and an output, you can connect the output of one filter to the input of another, and then the output of the second filter to a third filter or to the renderer.

Follow these steps to see the result of linking two filters together:

1. **Open your canvas with the Pixellate patch.**

2. **Find a Bloom patch, and add it to your canvas.**

3. **Connect the output port of the Pixellate patch to the input Image port of the Bloom patch.**

4. **Connect the output Image port of the Bloom patch to the input Image port of the renderer.**

   Note what the output looks like in the viewer window.

5. **Add an Addition patch, and connect the Image Importer output Image port to the input Image port of both the Pixellate and Bloom filters.**

6. **Connect the output Image port of the Pixellate filter to the Background Image port of the Addition patch.**

7. **Connect the output Image port of the Bloom filter to the input Image port of the Addition patch.**

8. **Connect the output port of the Addition patch to the input Image port of the Renderer.**

   Figure 19.23 shows your canvas at this point.

Figure 19.23

Canvas with filters

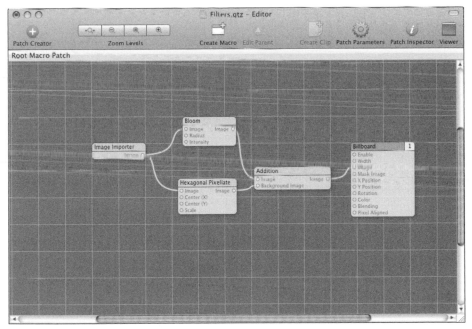

9. **Compare the output of this canvas with the output of the simple daisy chain you had before.**

   Figure 19.24 shows the output from my image.

   Figure 19.24

   Comparison of image with and without the Addition patch

   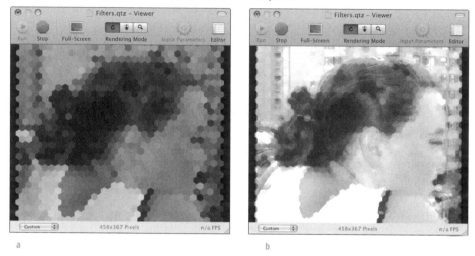

   a   b

Note how the output using the Addition patch is much brighter. This is because the output of the two filters is added together, resulting in a brighter image. This may or may not be the effect you want.

Using Image Masks

In this section, you create and use image masks to modify the way the image is displayed on the screen.

Image masks are images that are added to another image, but in a special way. Rather than being a simple addition of two images, dark areas in the mask image let the other image show through; white areas in the mask prevent the underlying image from showing.

Understanding alpha channels

Computer monitors use the RGB color model. This means the image is made up of three colors: red, green, and blue. Any pixel on the screen has a value between 0 and 255 for each color. That's eight bits each for three colors, giving a total of 24 bits to represent the value of each pixel on the screen.

Most operating systems these days allow a fourth channel called the alpha channel. It is sometimes referred to as a transparency layer or a mask and represents the transparency of each pixel. When two images are overlaid, the composite image depends on the colors of the pixels and their transparency.

An alpha of 0 means the pixel is completely opaque; in other words, zero transparency. An alpha of 255 means the pixel is completely transparent. Because alpha has values requiring eight bits, this means the total number of bits to represent each pixel is 32: eight bits each for red, green, and blue, and eight bits for alpha.

Some image formats allow saving transparency information. One reason that .png graphics have become so widespread is that the format allows transparency information to be saved in the file. JPEG images do not allow transparency.

Your Leopard menu bar uses an alpha channel to allow it to be shown as translucent, though you have no control over the actual alpha value.

Creating an image mask

Any image can be used as an image mask. Because the alpha channel uses only eight bits, it appears like a black and white (monochrome) image. In this section, you use an Addition patch to add two images together; in the next section, you create an alpha mask using the same images.

Creating an addition image

Follow these steps to create an addition image render:

1. **Open your /Library/Desktop Pictures/Abstract, and copy the file Abstract 4.jpg to your composition work folder.**

2. **Create a new blank composition, and add two Image Importer patches.**

3. **Use the first patch to import your Image01.png image.**

4. **Add a Billboard patch to your canvas.**

5. **Use the second Image Importer patch to open the Abstract 4.jpg file.**

6. **Add an Addition patch to your canvas.**

   Because the two images are of different sizes, you need to resize the abstract image.

7. Add an Image Resize patch to the canvas.

8. Connect the output Image port of the Image Importer to the input Image port of the Image Resize patch.

9. Set the resize mode to Stretch, the resize condition to Always, and the width and height to the same as your Image01.jpg.

   If you've been following the exercises, your image should be 600 x 600 pixels.

10. Click the Resize patch, and hover over the output Resized Image circle.

    A yellow box pops up with a preview of the image and details of the size of the image, as shown in Figure 19.25a.

11. Connect the output Image port of the first Image Importer to the input Image port of the Addition patch.

12. Connect the output Resized Image port of the Image Resize patch to the Background Image port of the Addition patch.

13. Connect the output Image port of the Addition patch to the input Image port of the Billboard renderer.

14. Save your composition as Image Masking.qtz.

    Your canvas should look like that shown in Figure 19.25b.

15. If it is not open, open the View window.

Figure 19.25

Image resize preview (a); Composer addition canvas (b)

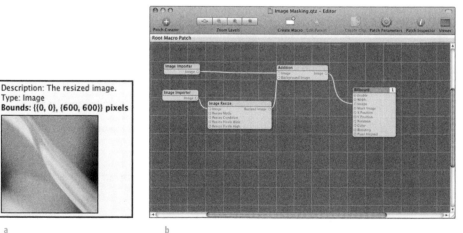

a   b

Creating a masked image

Follow these steps to create a masked render, using the same images as in the previous section:

1. **Delete the Addition patch by clicking it and pressing the Delete key.**

2. **Connect the output Image port of the Image Importer to the input Image port of the Billboard renderer.**

3. **Add a Mask To Alpha patch.**

4. **Connect the output Image port of the Image Resize patch to the input Image port of the Mask To Alpha patch.**

5. **Hover over the input Image to the Mask patch, and compare it with the output Image.**

Figure 19.26 shows the two images side by side.

Figure 19.26

Input and output of the Mask To Alpha patch

 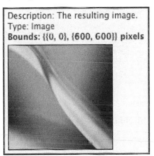

Input image   Output image

Note that the masked image output is monochrome only because it only uses eight bits.

6. **Connect the output port of the Mask To Alpha patch to the Mask Image Input port of the renderer, as shown in Figure 19.27.**

Compare the output of the masked image to the addition image you created earlier. Where the mask image is white, it is the most opaque and lets the least amount of color of the main image show. Where the mask is black, it is most transparent.

Figure 19.28 shows a comparison of the output from the Addition patch compared with the mask.

Figure 19.27

Canvas for Mask input to renderer

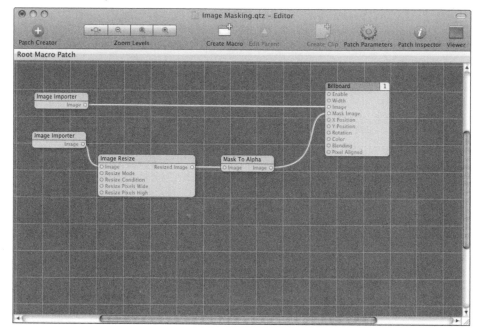

Figure 19.28

Comparison of addition versus masking

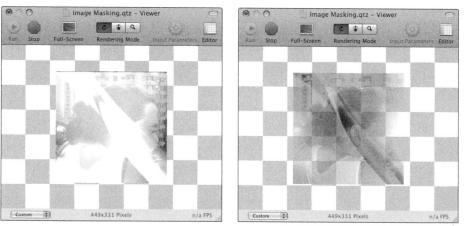

Addition   Mask

Major uses of alpha channel masking are for making image cutouts.

Using Render in Image Macros

One of the most powerful features of Quartz Composer is the ability to take an image with several different patches and encapsulate them into a single macro. You can then take this macro and add other patches. In effect, it works like a subroutine in programming. By rendering part of the final image, you can use it in the same way as you would any other image.

Render in Image is the name of this macro. You start with your rotating cube composition, which itself is a macro, and modify it to add another effect.

Creating the Render in Image macro

Follow these steps to create a new Render in Image macro:

1. **Open your Rotating Cube composition.**

   In this exercise, we use a simple rotating cube without the Interpolation patches you applied previously.

2. **Delete the four Interpolation patches.**

3. **Set the Rotating Cube input parameters to the following:**

   a. Period: 10

   b. Size: 1

   c. X Position, Y Position, and Z Position to 0

4. **From the Patch Creator, add a Render in Image patch.**

5. **Save your canvas as Rotating Cube Render in Image.qtz.**

6. **Select all the patches except the Render in Image patch.**

7. **Cut the patches (Command+X).**

   Do not use Delete because you want to save these patches to the clipboard.

8. **Double-click the Render in Image patch.**

   This opens what appears to be a blank canvas, but in fact it is the next level down in the patches. The line below the toolbar now shows Root Macro Patch > Render in Image.

9. **Paste (Command+V) the patches.**

   Your canvas should now look like that shown in Figure 19.29.

Figure 19.29

Render in Image macro

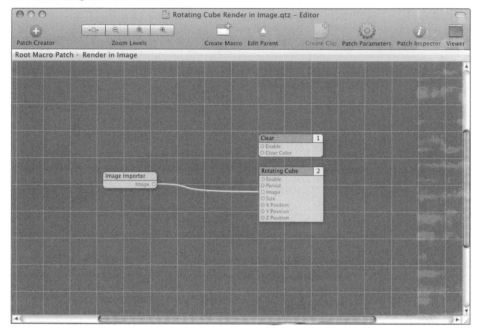

10. **On the toolbar, click Edit Parent to go to the root level.**

   All you see now is the Render in Image macro. You can tell the difference between a standard patch and a macro patch because a standard patch has rounded corners while a macro patch has square corners.

11. **Add a Billboard renderer.**

12. **Connect the image output port of the Render in Image macro to the image Input port of the renderer, as shown in Figure 19.30.**

13. **Open the Viewer window.**

   Your rotating cube now appears. Although it filled the view window before, it now only fills half the window. This is because the default width parameter for the Billboard patch is 1.

14. **Change the Width parameter in the renderer to 2.**

   Remember that the X coordinates for Quartz Composer go from −1 to +1: That's a width of 2.

15. **Save your composition.**

Figure 19.30

Render to Billboard renderer

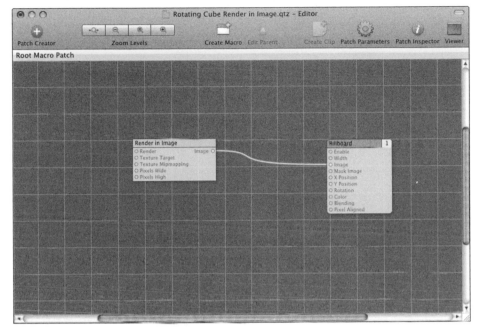

So far, this seems like lots of work to finish up where we started! But in fact we have created a new patch that behaves exactly like an image you load from your disk, except that in this case it is animated.

Using the Render in Image macro

Now that you have the rendered image available as a patch, you can add some other effects to it. To add a pixellate effect to the rotating cube, follow these steps:

1. **Add a Pixellate Filter patch to your canvas.**

2. **Connect the output image port from the Render in Image macro to the input image port of the Pixellate filter.**

3. **Connect the output image port of the Pixellate filter to the input image port of the Billboard renderer.**

   Figure 19.31 shows the results. You can then add any other patches to create special effects.

Figure 19.31

Render in Image macro with Pixellate filter

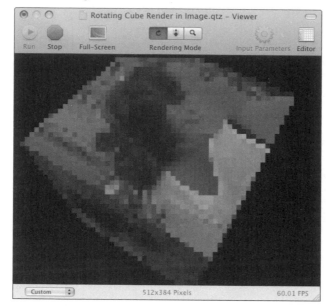

Publishing a port to the macro

In your original image that is now inside the Render in Image patch, you used Clear patch to set the background color. In this case, the color was black. But it may happen that you want to be able to change the color when you use the macro. To do this, you need to publish the port in the Clear patch. This then makes the port available at the top level of the macro.

Follow these steps to publish the color port of the Clear patch:

1. **Open your Rotating Cube Render in Image.qtz composition if it is not already open.**

2. **Double-click the Render in Image macro.**

3. **Right-click the Clear Color port of the Clear patch.**

4. **On the menu, select Published Inputs, Clear Color.**

   A small pop-up appears that allows you to change the name of the published port if you wish. For now, just leave it as it is.

5. **Press Enter to accept the name Clear Color.**

   Now when you look at the Clear Color patch, the Clear Color label has quotes around it and the port itself is filled in rather than the circle it was before.

6. **Click Edit Parent to return to the top level of your composition.**

Figure 19.32 shows the top-level view of your composition now.

Figure 19.32

Top-level view of Render in Image composition

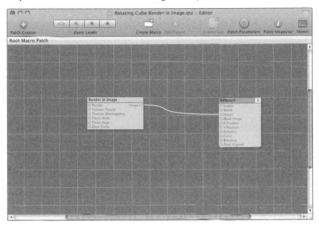

Look closely at your Render in Image macro and note that it now has a Clear Color input port that it did not have before. Compare Figure 19.32 with Figure 19.30. This allows you to use a different clear color for your new patch.

Changing the clear color

Rather than setting a single clear color for the macro, we add a clear color that varies over time using a Color Mixer patch and an Interpolation patch. The Color Mixer patch allows the color to vary between two different colors, while the Interpolation patch controls the time scale and the variation.

Follow these steps to add a varying clear color to your composition:

1. **Add a Color Mixer patch to your composition, and connect its output port to the Clear Color input port on your macro.**

2. **Click the First color panel to set the first color.**

You can choose any color you want; I set mine to yellow.

3. **Click the Second color panel to set the second color.**

I set mine to blue; you choose yours. Figure 19.33 shows the color settings for my patch.

Figure 19.33

Color settings for Clear Color patch

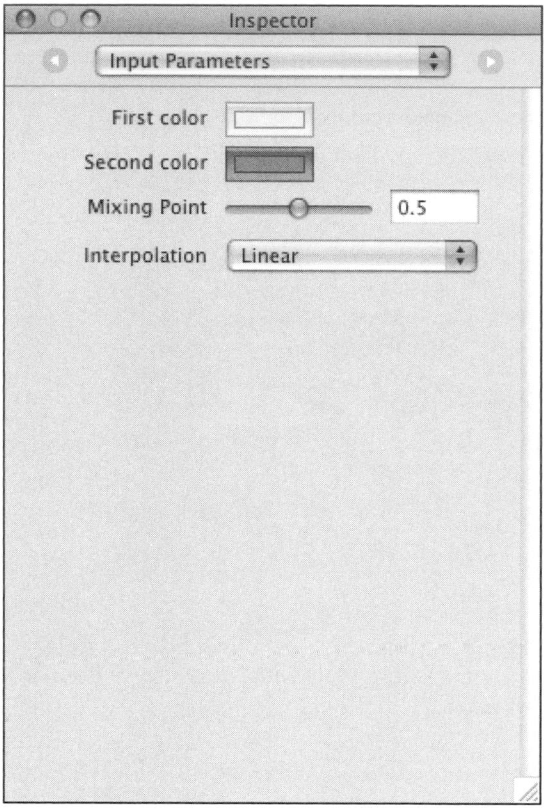

4. **If it is not already open, open the Patch Inspector.**

5. **Move the Mixing Point slider, and see what happens at various points.**

6. **Add an Interpolation patch, and set the Start Value to 0, End Value to 1, and Duration to 10 (seconds).**

7. **Set Repeat Mode to Mirrored Loop, and leave Interpolation at Linear.**

8. **Connect the Result port of the interpolator to the Mixing Point input of the Color Mixer patch.**

   Now watch as the background color slowly cycles from yellow to blue, through gray, in my case.

9. **Save your composition as Rotating Cube Render in Image 2.qtz.**

Creating a Audio Spectrum Display

For this innovative use of Quartz Composer, I am grateful to Alex Clarke, who posted a tutorial at Machine Codex at `http://machinecodex.com/codexmachina/?q=node/8`. It displays the spectrum of an audio signal as a series of bars. Each bar displays the volume of a different frequency range.

Unfortunately, it's not a trivial exercise to take the output from, say, iTunes, and use it as input to your computer. If Apple made it easy to do that, nothing would stop you from playing some copy-protected music and re-recording it without copy protection.

For this exercise, you need either a microphone you can plug into your audio input or some other form of audio (maybe a DVD player) that goes to the line input on your audio device. In this example, I use the microphone of my webcam.

Obtaining audio input

In order to get input into the composition, you need to change System Preferences to set your audio input to either your microphone or to your line input. Figure 19.34 shows my preferences set to my USB webcam.

Figure 19.34

System Preference for sound

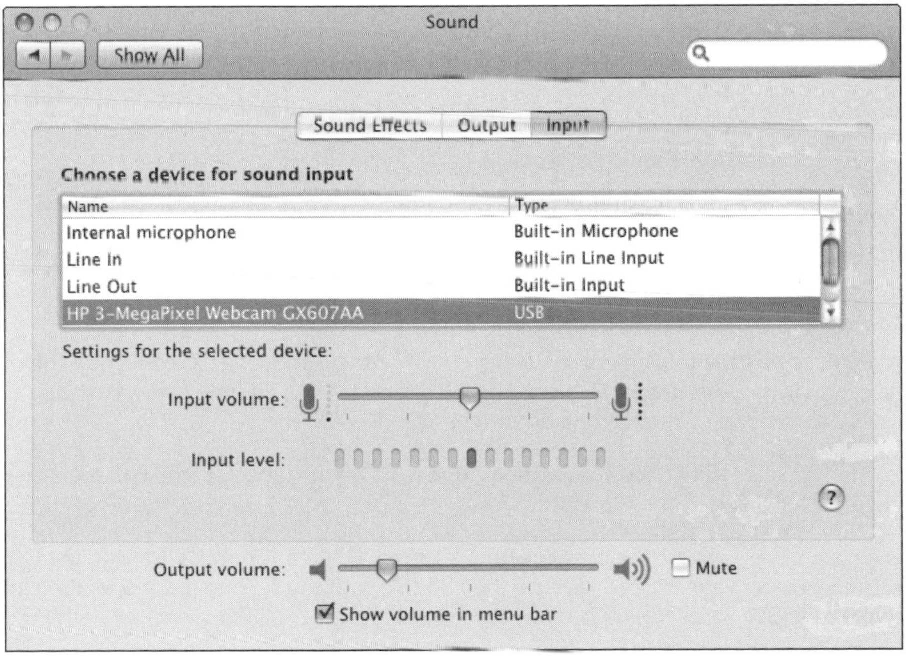

To start creating your meter, follow these steps:

1. **Open System Preferences, and set the input to a suitable input.**

    Be sure that either a microphone or some other sound source is connected. If there is input, you should see the level on the System Preferences bar move.

2. **Open Quartz Composer, and create a blank composition.**

3. **Place a Clear renderer and a Cube Renderer patch on your canvas.**

4. **Set the Clear renderer to layer 1.**

5. **Place an Audio Input patch on your canvas, and connect the Volume Peak port to the Height port on the Cube renderer.**

    You should see a small bar in the Viewer window that fluctuates slightly in height as the sound level varies. Because the variation in height may be small, you may need a Math patch to amplify it.

6. **Add a Math patch to your composition, and connect its Initial Value port to the Volume Peak port on the Audio Input patch.**

7. **Use the Patch Inspector to set Operation #1 to multiply.**

    You need to experiment a little with the operand value so the bar fills the viewer window when it has full volume input. In my case, the multiplier is 1, but yours will be different.

8. **Set the width of the cube to 0.02, so it appears slim in the viewer, and set its depth to 0.**

9. **Save your composition as Level Meter 1.qtz**

    Your canvas should now look like that shown in Figure 19.35a.

    In your viewer, you should see something like Figure 19.35b at a moderately high level of input.

Making a unidirectional bar

At the moment, the movement of the bar is symmetrical about the X axis: it goes below the axis the same distance as it goes above the axis. Conventionally, volume bars move only above the X axis, so we need to subtract the bottom part.

To do this, we need two math operations: one to halve the length of the bar, the other to position it on the Y axis.

As an example, suppose the bar goes from +150 to −150 on the Y axis. Halving the length of the bar makes it go from +75 to −75. If we then add 75 with the second math operation, it goes from 0 to +150.

Figure 19.35

Canvas for Level Meter 1 (a); Level Meter 1 in operation (b)

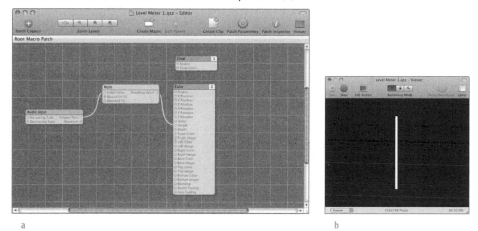

a   b

Follow these steps to create the new bar:

1. **Double-click inside the title bar of the Math patch, and enter the name** Amplifier.

   Eventually there will be three Math patches on your canvas, so it's a good idea to give each one of them a name.

2. **Add two more Math patches, naming one of them** Divider **and the other** Adder.

3. **Connect the Resulting Value port of the Amplifier to the Initial Value port of the Divider.**

4. **Connect the Resulting Value port of the Divider to the Operand #1 port of the Adder.**

5. **Connect the Resulting Value port of the Adder to the Y Position port of the Cube renderer.**

   Your canvas should now look like that shown in Figure 19.36a. Your viewer should now look like Figure 19.36b when a high peak is reached.

Continuing development of the meter

From here the project increases in complexity. I recommend you work through the tutorial by Alex Clarke at `http://machinecodex.com/codexmachina/?q=node/8`.

Figure 19.36

Canvas for single-bar volume meter (a); single-bar volume meter (b)

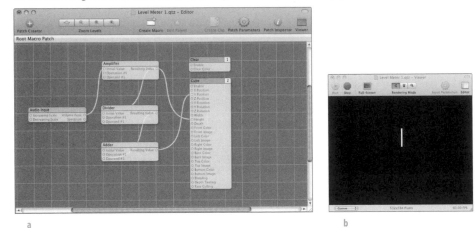

a   b

Summary

In this chapter, you discovered the utility and power of Apple's Quartz Composer. It allows developers to create very powerful graphics effects and incorporate them into other programs.

You created three projects:

- A two-dimensional picture that rotates in tune with mouse movements
- A spinning cube with an image on each face that bounces around the screen and acts as a screen saver
- A single bar that varies in height, depending on the volume of sound input

Other resources are available on the Web for creating Quartz compositions. Remember, as always, that Google is your friend.

I n this chapter, you look at three of the smaller and less-technical applications that come when you install the Developer Toolkit.

Each is a stand-alone program developed to demonstrate another facet of OS X. Many of the additional tools debuted with Tiger (OS X 10.4) and have been carried forward to Leopard.

Using Core Image Fun House

Before you can use Core Image Fun House you must download the Apple Developer Tools, as shown in Chapter 18. You also must have Quartz Extreme/Core Image enabled.

Core Image Fun House is an application that is designed to show the power of core image graphics. It allows you to open an image file and then apply what it terms image units. These are essentially small programs written in the CIKernel language. This is a derivative of the Open GL language.

Core Image exists as a go-between, sitting between the application software and the Open GL language. Figure 20.1 shows where CI sits in the generation of graphics.

If application software such as QuickTime acted directly on the graphics hardware, every different graphics card would require a different version of QuickTime—one built specifically for that card.

Instead, the Open GL language layer communicates directly with the graphics card. This means that every graphics card requires a different version of the Open GL layer. This is why, during installation, you had to install specific kexts for your graphics card. If the exact kext is not available, then your graphics card doesn't work at its best, or even at all in some cases.

Core Image adds another layer of abstraction to the programming process, meaning that the programmer doesn't need to know all about Open GL but instead can learn Core Image and use that. Core Image then translates instructions into what Open GL expects.

Figure 20.1

Graphics processing

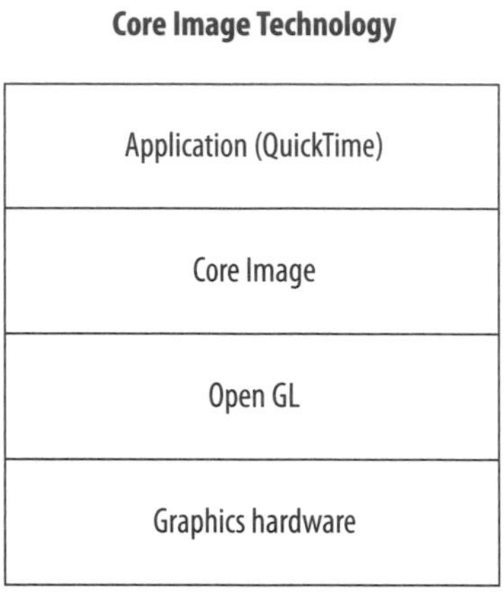
Core Image Technology
Application (QuickTime)
Core Image
Open GL
Graphics hardware

In this section, you use Core Image Fun House to load an image and experiment with different image units. An image unit is a small subprogram that manipulates pixels in the original image to produce a new image.

Starting Core Image Fun House

Core Image Fun House is located in the Graphics Tools folder in Developer Tools. Follow these steps to start Core Image Fun House and load an image:

1. **Start Core Image Fun House, and select an image to process.**

   By default, CIF starts in its own Example Images folder.

2. **Choose the Wolf.jpg image, and click Open.**

   CIF opens the graphic image in a window and displays the Effect Stack, shown in Figure 20.2.

   You can use an image of your own if you choose.

Figure 20.2

Effect Stack

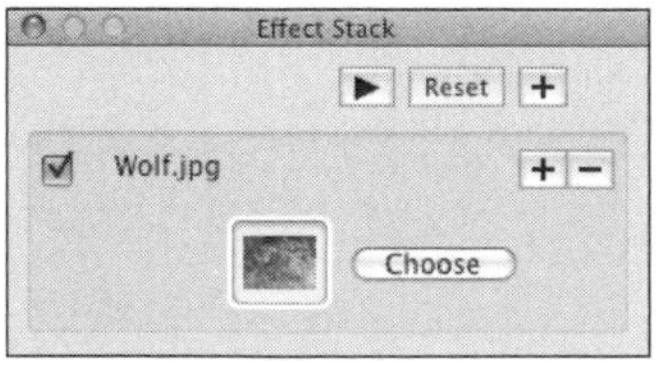
Effect Stack
Reset
Wolf.jpg
Choose

Using the Effect Stack

As the name implies, the Effect Stack is a stack of different effects you can add to the image. As each is applied, it works on the result of all the other effects. Effects in the stack are applied in order from top to bottom.

Effects are grouped into several categories such as distortion effects, color adjustment, stylizing effects, and so on.

Follow these steps to play with the image you opened:

1. **Click the + (plus) alongside Wolf.jpg.**

   We want to give the wolf a narrower, more peaked nose.

2. **In the Image Units window, select Distortion Effect and then Pinch Distortion.**

   In the bottom left is the center of the pinch distortion, as shown in Figure 20.3. You can drag this around the image and place it where you like.

Figure 20.3

Image after Pinch Distortion effect was applied

3. **Drag the pinch distortion center to the tip of the wolf's nose.**

4. **Adjust the pinch distortion radius to about 300 and the scale to about 0.8.**

This gives the wolf a very long peaked nose.

Just to show that the wolf has no evil intent, let's add a halo.

5. **Click the + (plus) alongside Pinch Distortion.**

Remember, the effects are added from top to bottom.

6. **Select Generator, Lenticular Halo.**

7. **Move the center of the halo so it frames the wolf's head.**

8. **Adjust the various parameters until you have an effect you are happy with.**

Unfortunately, you can't save your picture as a JPEG or PNG image, but you can save it as an image that can be reopened in Fun House.

Saving your work

It's diverting to play around with the Fun House, but it's a pity you can't save any of your images directly as graphics files, though you can do it using Leopard's built-in screen capture.

Follow these steps to save your image:

1. **After your image is onscreen, press and hold Shift+Command+4.**

2. **When the crosshairs appear, press the spacebar.**

3. **Move the camera icon around until the window you want to capture is highlighted in blue.**

4. **Click the left mouse button.**

Leopard takes your screen shot and, by default, places it on your desktop. If you press and hold the Control key as well (Control+Command+Shift+4), the capture is placed in the clipboard, ready to paste into another application.

If you want to change the defaults, the simplest way is to use TinkerTool. In the General tab, you can change the file type for saved screen shots, as shown in Figure 20.4.

Figure 20.4

Using TinkerTool to change screen capture defaults

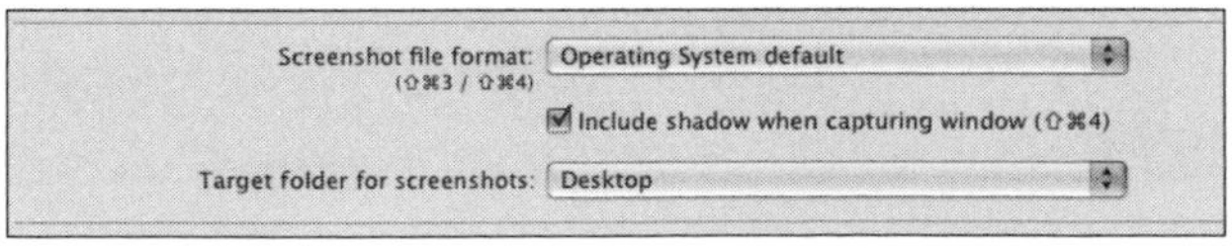

5. **Open Preview, and select File ⇨ New From Clipboard.**

6. **To remove the small bar at the top, use the Rectangle selection tool to copy the remainder of the image.**

7. **Select File ⇨ New From Clipboard again.**

8. **Save the new image.**

   Photoshop, it isn't! But it's much cheaper if you just want to change one or two pictures.

Using Repeat After Me

Repeat After Me is a utility application that comes as part of the Developer Toolkit. It is a tool for programmers who want to use a synthesized voice in their application. Although we cannot delve that deeply into speech synthesis here, Repeat After Me gives some insights into the process. And besides, it's a bit of fun to play with!

In this section, you use Repeat After Me to enter some text, have it converted into phonemes, record your own voice saying the same words, and then modify the output so the synthesized voice more closely resembles your own speech pattern.

A phoneme is a distinct unit of sound that distinguishes one word from another. Apple uses its own representations of phonemes. Unless your installation of Leopard is customized for a non-English language, the phonemes it uses are for a North American accent.

Starting with Repeat After Me

Follow these steps to start using Repeat After Me to play some speech:

1. **From the developer applications, select Utilities, Speech and Repeat After Me.**

   Figure 20.5 shows the start screen of Repeat After Me.

2. **In the Text field, type** I can't do that Dave.

3. **Click the "To Phonemes" button to show the phonemes representing the phrase.**

   You can find a list of the phonemes that Apple uses and how they sound when spoken at http://tinyurl.com/neyvwe.

4. **Click the "Build Graph" button to build the waveform of the speech.**

5. **Save your file as 2001.ramd.**

6. **Play the speech using Command+/.**

Figure 20.5

Repeat After Me start screen

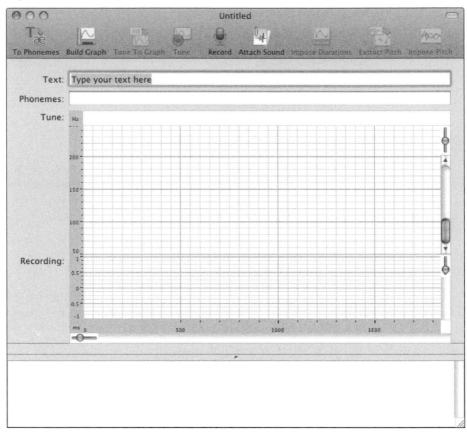

Exactly how it sounds depends on your system voice. Needless to say, it sounds best if you use the Alex voice, but any of the others will do.

Modifying the inflection of the voice

After you have the Leopard voice speaking the text, you can modify the phonemes used. For example, you can lengthen the "a" sound in "can't" so it becomes longer, sounding like "car-n't."

To change the phonemes, follow these steps:

1. **Open the Web site with the list of phonemes used by Apple.**

2. **Find the phoneme corresponding with the "a" in "can't.**

   It is "AE," which Apple says is pronounced like the "a" in "bat."

3. **Change the phoneme to "AA," which is pronounced like the "a" in "father."**

4. **Play the voice now, and listen for the difference.**

Change any of the other phonemes that you choose and listen to the differences. There are no phonemes in the Apple set that correspond with many other accents. For example, it's impossible to render some of the sounds in Australian or the many British accents.

Changing the voice to match your inflexion and pitch

To make the voice more realistic, you can say the words yourself and then modify the way the synthesizer speaks the text.

Follow these steps to modify the voice to be more like yours:

1. **On the Toolbar, click the Record button.**

   A mini-recorder appears on your screen, as shown in Figure 20.6.

   Figure 20.6
   Mini-recorder

2. **Click the Record button on the recorder, and say the text into your microphone.**

3. **Click the Stop button when you have finished.**

4. **Click Save.**

   Your recorded sound appears in the bottom part of the display, as shown in Figure 20.7.

5. **Click Impose Durations.**

   This moves the synthesized speech on the time line so it aligns with your speech.

6. **Play the sound again.**

   Unless you spoke very quickly or slowly, you probably won't hear any difference.

Figure 20.7

Synthesized speech with recorded voice

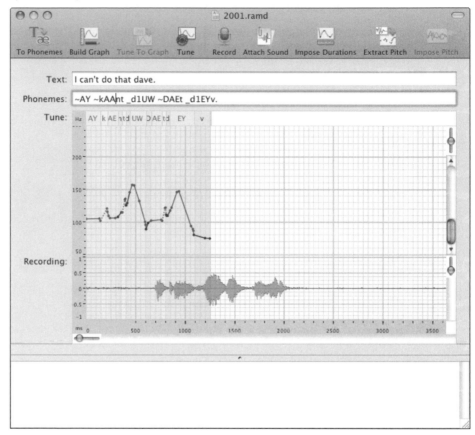

7. **Click Extract Pitch.**

This superimposes a graph on the chart that shows the pitch changes in your voice when you spoke the words, as shown in Figure 20.8.

Figure 20.8

Human voice pitch superimposed

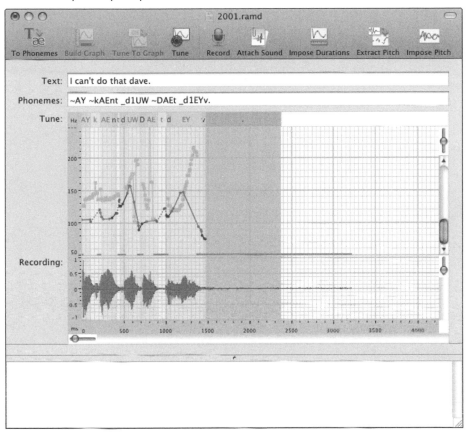

8. **Click Impose Pitch.**

   Figure 20.9 shows the result of imposing the pitch.

   Playing the speech now should give a sound that approximates the rhythm and pitch of your voice when you spoke the words.

Figure 20.9

Human voice pitch applied

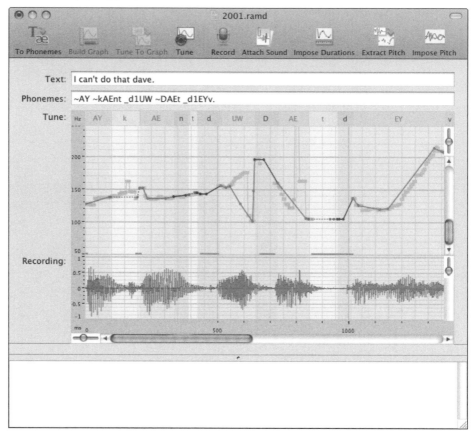

Making other changes

You can make these changes as well:

- Change the duration of the speech, thus slowing it down or speeding it up by moving the end of the duration in the Tune bar.

- If the voice doesn't follow your pitch accurately, add more points to the graph by holding down the Shift key while placing the mouse on the line.

- To move a single point while keeping the others fixed, use the Option key with the mouse.

Playing the output in another application

It is possible to play the output from Repeat After Me in another application, such as TextEdit. Follow these steps to play the speech in TextEdit:

1. **Click the Tune button on the toolbar.**

   Repeat After Me produces a text output that is a text representation of the speech, as shown in Figure 20.10.

   Figure 20.10

   Text representation of speech

   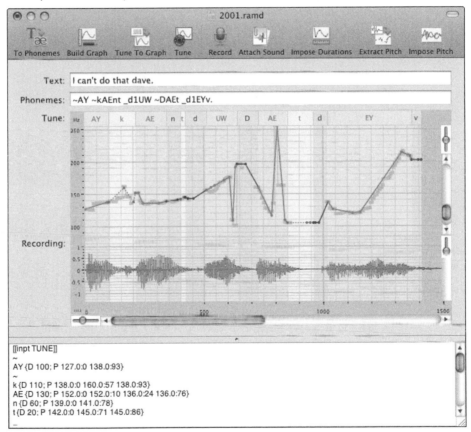

2. **Copy all the text that appears in the bottom pane.**

3. **Open a new TextEdit document, and paste the text.**

Figure 20.11 shows the text highlighted in TextEdit.

Figure 20.11

Speech text highlighted in TextEdit

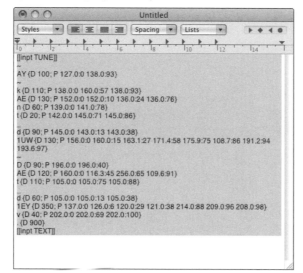

4. **Highlight the whole text, and then right-click and select Speech ⇨ Start Speaking.**

Summary

In this chapter, you used two of the small developer applications that are part of the Developer Tools. Core Image Fun House allows you to experiment with the various image filters and tools to change graphic images. Using the Fun House and Preview is like creating a poor person's Photoshop.

Repeat After Me allows you to experiment with Leopard's speech synthesizer and create new sounds to incorporate into applications.

21

Using XCode to Create New Programs

Before you start this chapter, you need to have installed the Apple Developer Tools. Chapter 18 gives instructions on how to do this.

Until now you have been using the higher level programming facilities of Leopard.

As you already know, OS X is built on a foundation of Darwin, which handles all the low-level interfaces to the hardware. You have used some higher level features such as Core Image, which provides a toolkit to allow graphics manipulation without requiring programming at the very lowest levels.

In this chapter, you use the programming language and tools that are used to build Leopard itself. You use the XCode development environment to create a Cocoa application, using the Objective-C programming language that sits behind Leopard. The application is really very simple: it has a single screen that allows you to enter a number of inches. When you press the Convert button, it converts that distance to centimeters.

Developing a Cocoa Application

Like any highly graphical operating system such as Windows or the graphical layers of Linux such as Gnome or KDE, OS X uses a layered model. At the very lowest level is the kernel that interacts directly with the hardware. At successively higher levels are the application program interfaces (APIs) such as Quartz and QuickTime, then the user interface level (Aqua in the case of OS X), then finally the application environment.

This is shown graphically in Figure 21.1. Bear in mind that this is a greatly simplified view.

Figure 21.1

Application architecture of OS X

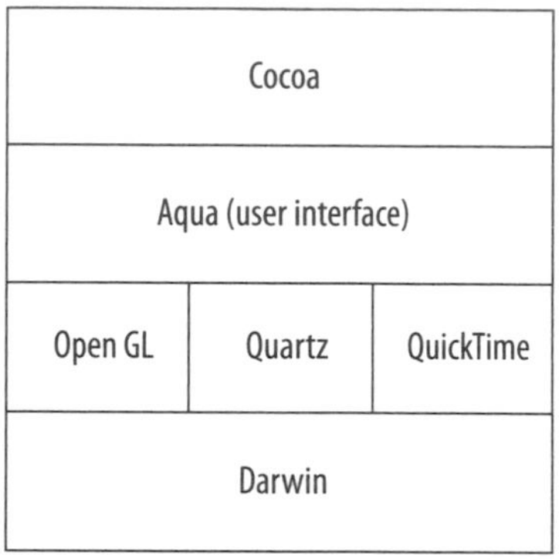

Cocoa
Aqua (user interface)
Open GL / Quartz / QuickTime
Darwin

Understanding Cocoa

Cocoa is a high-level object-oriented programming environment for OS X. It comprises a collection of frameworks and application program interfaces. Cocoa is programmed in Objective-C, which is a derivative of the standard C programming language, modified for object orientation, in a similar way to the language C++.

Object-oriented programming is suited to a highly graphical environment such as OS X. An object-oriented program defines objects. An object has methods associated with it. An object, for example, may be an input box that the user types into. A method defines what the input box does with the text after the user has typed it.

Understanding Aqua

Aqua is the user interface to OS X. It defines details of the appearance of the standard user interface components such as dialog boxes, windows, menus, and controls. By following the Aqua guidelines, an application can look like it was designed as part of the operating system.

Aqua defines the look of objects right down to details of how deep the shading around a text input box should be, the placement of elements on the window for the application, and the layout of the menu choices. It even defines details, such as that the default button should be colored blue and should pulse slowly while waiting for input; that the three buttons on the top left of the window should be red, amber, and green; and that they should show x, – and + symbols when the mouse is placed over them.

To make your application give the user the best experience possible, it's important that you design it so that it looks and acts like other applications they have used. Nothing turns users off faster than a design that behaves in unexpected ways.

Using XCode

Because of all the programming tools Apple makes available in the XCode package, developing an application for Leopard is relatively easy, though by no means trivial. In the remainder of this chapter you develop a very simple application using the interface designer and the bits of program that tie things together.

Your application is a simple, single-screen application that asks the user to input a distance in inches. It then computes the distance in centimeters and outputs the result. While very simple in intent, it allows you to learn the basics of developing for OS X.

Designing the User Interface

In the old days of computer programming, there was no such thing as a user interface. In fact, users were seen as a hindrance, getting in the way of the high priests ministering to the computer. Output was either on dense lines of printout or on a screen that scrolled so fast it was almost impossible to read.

Today, however, the user is paramount. These days, application program design starts out with the screens that users see when using the program. Software companies spend millions of dollars on getting the design to be the optimum for the users.

Starting a new project

In this project, you use the XCode development environment with its various components.

Follow these steps to create a new project:

1. **Start XCode.**

   XCode greets you with its welcome screen, as shown in Figure 21.2.

   You can stop the display of this screen each time you start XCode by unchecking the box in the lower left corner.

Figure 21.2

XCode welcome screen

2. **Click the text under the heading Create your first Cocoa application.**

This brings up the XCode documentation set, as shown in Figure 21.3.

3. **This is much too complicated for our purposes here, so simply close both windows.**

Figure 21.3

XCode documentation set

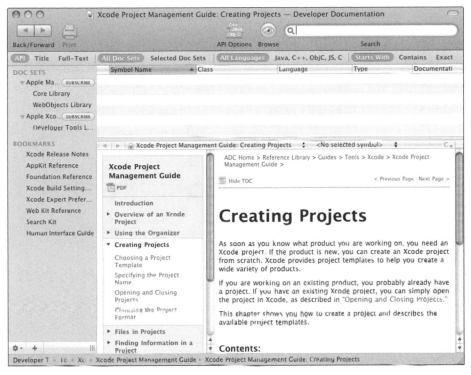

4. **Click File, New Project.**

   XCode then asks you to choose the type of project you want to create, as shown in Figure 21.4.

   Note the wide variety of project types you can create using XCode. If you have not installed MacFUSE for reading NTFS disks, yours will not show MacFUSE.

5. **Under Mac OS X, be sure Application is selected and then select Cocoa Application in the right panel.**

   Before you click the Choose button, just watch it for a few seconds. Note that it pulses subtly. That is a standard Aqua interface feature. Subtle, but when it's not there in an application, you miss it.

6. **Click Choose.**

Figure 21.4

Project type selection screen

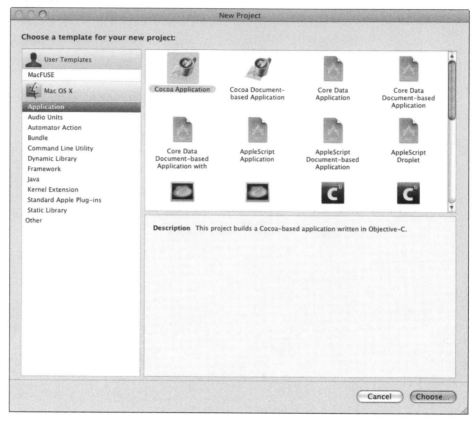

7. **Name your project Distance Converter, and save it in a new folder called Distance Converter.**

   After your project is saved, XCode displays the screen shown in Figure 21.5.

   For the moment, ignore the complexity of the display. Much of it becomes clearer during the development of your application.

Figure 21.5

XCode project window

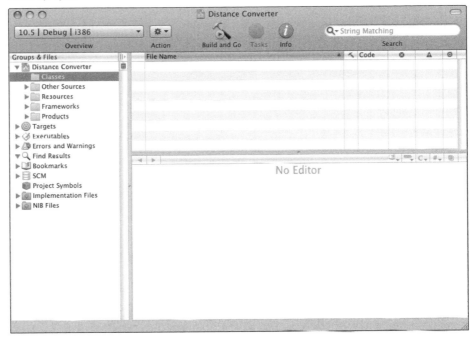

Using Interface Builder

When creating a new Cocoa application, the first step is to design the user interface. XCode provides a complete interface builder to do just that.

Creating the main window

Follow these steps to create the main window of your user interface:

1. **In the project window, locate the Resources folder and click it.**

2. **Highlight MainMenu.xib, as shown in Figure 21.6.**

Figure 21.6

Resources folder in project window

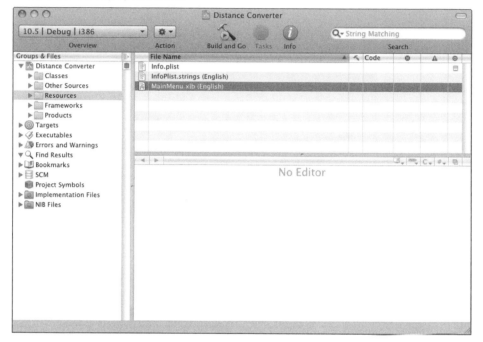

3. **Double-click MainMenu.xib to start Interface Builder.**

This opens several new windows, each showing a different aspect of building your interface.

The windows are:

- Application main window
- Document window
- Library window
- Inspector window

We examine each window as we need it in developing the application.

Figure 21.7a shows your application's main window. This is the view that the user sees when running the application.

Obviously, there is more work to be done!

Your document window is shown in Figure 21.7b.

Figure 21.7

Application main window (a); project document window (b)

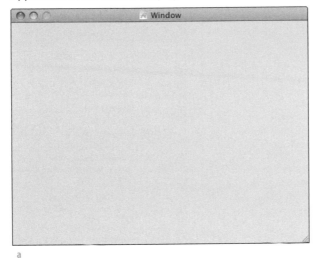 

a

b

4. **Click Window in the document window.**

   This switches the focus of your Inspector window to the main window. The Inspector should look like Figure 21.8a.

5. **Click inside the Title text field of the Inspector, type** Distance Converter, **and press Enter.**

   Note that the title of your application window now has changed to Distance Converter.

   The Controls section in the Inspector determines which buttons appear on the top-left corner of the window. These are Close, Minimize, and Resize.

6. **Because you won't need a resize button, uncheck the box.**

   See how the change is reflected in your document window.

7. **Save your project.**

Adding two input fields

So far you have a blank window, so you need to add a place in which the user can enter a distance and a place for the application to output the converted distance. To do this, you need to use the Library, which is shown in Figure 21.8b.

Figure 21.8

Inspector window for main window (a); Library window (b)

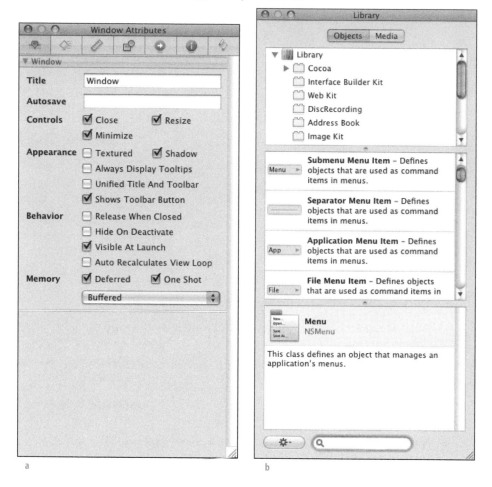

a   b

Follow these steps to add two input fields to your main window:

1. **Be sure that Objects is selected in the Library window.**

2. **Scroll down and expand the headings through Cocoa ⇨ Views & Cells ⇨ Inputs & Values, as shown in Figure 21.9a.**

3. **Select Text Field, and drag it to your application main window.**

4. **Place it in the top-right corner of your window, as shown in Figure 21.9b.**

Figure 21.9

Library window with Inputs & Values selected (a); Main window with text field added (b)

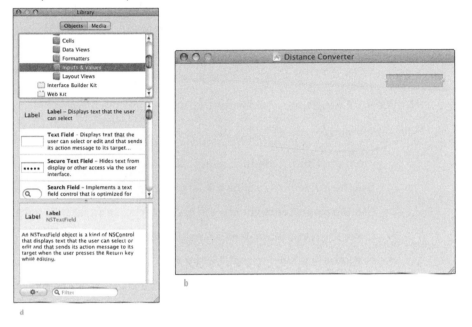

Note that blue dotted guidelines appear on your main window. These are guidelines generated by Interface Builder to ensure that you place your objects in accordance with the Aqua user interface standards. You are not obligated to do so, but it makes sense to have your application comply with all the Aqua interface standards.

5. **Ensure that the text field is highlighted, and in the Inspector window, enter 1 as the Title.**

    This is the number that will appear in the field when the application runs. Because the window will take only numeric values, it should be right aligned.

6. **Click the right align button in the Alignment section of the inspector.**

7. **Open the size pane by clicking the Ruler icon at the top of the Inspector window.**

8. **Set the width to 80.**

9. **Check that the field is still aligned with the Aqua guides by moving it so you see the blue guidelines.**

10. **Drag another text field from the Library to your window.**

    Note that once again Aqua guidelines appear so you can align your second text field with the first.

11. **Use the Inspector to set the width to the same as the input field (80).**

12. **On the Text Field Attributes pane, uncheck the Editable box in the Behavior line.**

    You do this so the field is used only to display the output of the conversion.

13. **Save your project.**

Adding text labels

Now you need to tell the user what the text fields are for. This requires the use of labels.

Follow these steps to add labels to your project:

1. **From the Library window, select Label and drag it to your window.**

2. **Use the guidelines to align the label with the top text field.**

3. **Use the Inspector to change the text to Inches: and set it to right aligned.**

4. **Move the label beside the text field it refers to.**

5. **Drag another label onto the window.**

6. **Change its text to read Centimeters:, right justify it, and move it so the colon lines up under the Inches: label using the guidelines.**

Adding a button

So far you have a window with an input field for the user to enter a distance to be converted and a field to display the converted value. Now you need some way to start the process. In other words, you need a button.

Follow these steps to add a button to your project:

1. **In the Library window, select Cocoa ⇨ Views & Cells ⇨ Buttons and drag a Push Button to your window.**

2. **In the Inspector window, set the Title to Convert.**

3. **Select the Key Equiv. field, and press the Enter key on the main keyboard (not on the numeric keypad).**

    This puts a return symbol in the field and makes the Convert button the default, even though it is the only button. This means that the user can simply press Enter to start the conversion.

4. **Set the width of the button to 80 characters, the same as the two text fields.**

5. **Align the button with the centers of the text fields using the guides.**

6. **Save the project.**

Tidying up the window

At present you have all the controls crowded into the top-right corner of the window. Let's move them and resize the window.

Follow these steps to finish designing the application window:

1. **Ensure that the size of the two labels is just bigger than the text they contain.**

Do this by selecting each label in turn and moving the left edge of the containing box so it is up against the left edge of the label.

2. **Select all the controls by lassoing them.**

3. **Drag them to the top left of the window, using the guides.**

4. **Use the resize handle on the window to shrink the window so it is just large enough to contain the fields.**

Again, use the guides.

5. **Save your project.**

Your application window should now look like that shown in Figure 21.10.

Figure 21.10

Final design on application window

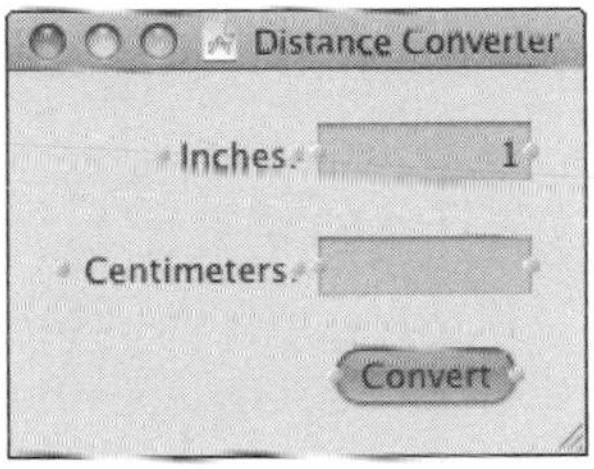

Trying out your design

Interface Builder contains a simulator so you can check your designs as you progress.

Follow these steps to check your design using the simulator:

1. **On the Interface Builder menu, select File, Simulate Interface, or press Command+R.**

2. **Type some text into your Inches text field.**

You should be able to, as shown in Figure 21.11.

3. **Try to type some text into your Centimeters field.**

   You should not be able to. If you are able to enter text into your Centimeters field, it's because you forgot to uncheck the Editable box for the field.

4. **Check that the Convert button is highlighted in blue and is pulsating slowly.**

   If it is not highlighted, it's because you didn't set the Enter key as the Key Equiv.

5. **Click the Convert button.**

   It should darken slightly when you click it and return to the normal state after you release the mouse.

6. **Exit the simulator by typing Command+Q or using Quit Cocoa Simulator on the menu bar.**

Figure 21.11

Using the simulator to check your design

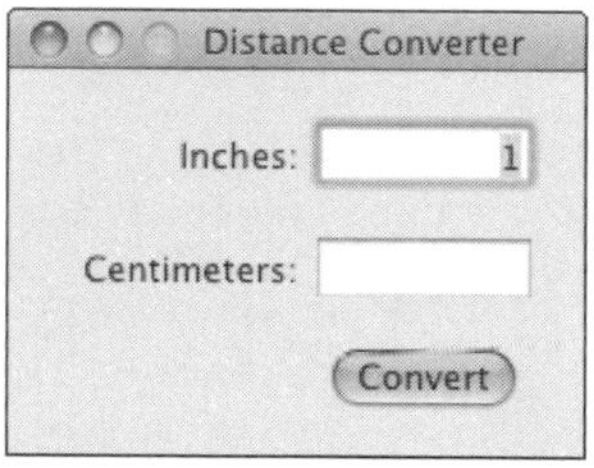

Adding the Programming

So far we've got a nice window for the application, one that meets all the Apple guidelines for developing in Cocoa. But it doesn't do anything yet! In this section, you add the programming code that makes it work.

Understanding object-oriented programming

Until the early 1990s, most computer programming was done in procedural languages. A procedural language is one that focuses on procedures—things that have to be done. The procedures act on various types of data structures.

Object-oriented programming (often abbreviated *OOP*) takes a different view. It defines *objects* that have certain *attributes* (data structures) and *methods* that describe the things an object can do.

An object, however, is an instance (or example) of a more general category called a *class*.

This is shown diagrammatically in Figure 21.12.

Figure 21.12

Concepts of object-oriented programming

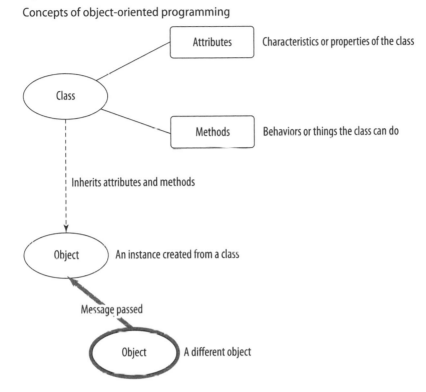

Using a concrete analogy

A lion is a class of animal. It has various characteristics or attributes, and various things it can do or methods. Some of these are summarized in Table 21.1.

Table 21.1 Attributes and Methods of Class Lion

Class	Attributes	Methods
Lion	Four legs	Can growl
	Large teeth	Can run
	Long tail	Can use forelegs to hold prey

Inheritance is the process whereby an object inherits the attributes and methods of the parent class.

Leo the Circus Lion is an instance of the class lion or an object of the class lion.

Leo inherits all the attributes and methods of the lion class, but may also have additional attributes and methods of his own. For example, Leo can jump through hoops, so an additional method is can jump through hoops.

Message passing is a very important concept in object-oriented programming. Another object, such as the lion tamer, can pass a message to Leo saying "jump through the hoop now."

The lion tamer is an instance (or object) of the class person, so it inherits the attributes and methods of person, but adds an extra method: can get lions to jump through hoops.

Putting it into a programming context

So far you have created your application's main window. The window is an object (or instance) of a class called window. You have an input text box that is an instance of a more general text box. It inherits the characteristics of a text box, but yours is different from the general text box class because it has the numeral 1 in it at the start.

You can see the attributes of the application window using the Inspector, as shown in Figure 21.13.

Figure 21.13

Application window attributes

Although this is very similar to the Inspector window when you started (refer to Figure 21.9), you can see that it has one attribute of its own: Title.

Using Objective-C

Now that you have an interface with controls that have various attributes, you need to define some methods that act on them. These are implemented using a programming language: Objective-C, in this case.

First you need a method to convert inches to centimeters. That's a pretty trivial conversion: simply multiply by 2.54. A method such as this is derived from a Model class.

Because of a restriction on the Implementation in OS X, your *converter* method cannot interact directly with the user interface but instead has to work through another method called a *controller* method.

Linking the parts together

Now that you have your user interface designed with its text fields and buttons, you need to create two new methods: one to do the computation, the other to act as the interface between your user interface and the computation method. The Convert button starts the whole process.

Figure 21.14 shows the linkages diagrammatically.

Figure 21.14

Linkages between user interface and methods

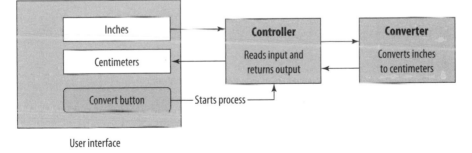

User interface

Creating the Converter method

In the next few sections, you are exposed to some Objective-C code. On the way, I explain what each line does so you can follow along. You won't learn how to become an expert Objective-C programmer by the end of this, but hopefully you will understand the basic concepts and terminology. If you already have some background in programming, making the switch to Objective-C should not be that difficult.

First, let's look at the converter method. It exists in two separate files: Converter.h and Converter.m. Converter.h is the class definition file, while Converter.m is the definition of a specific instance of a class (an object). Remember that a class is the general structure (a lion), while an object is a specific instance (Leo the lion).

Understanding the Converter header file

Here is the code for the file Converter.h:

```
#import <Cocoa/Cocoa.h>
@interface Converter : NSObject {
    float inches;
}
@property(readwrite) float inches;
- (float) convertToCentimeters;
@end
```

NOTE

A semi-colon (;) is used to end each statement, though not necessarily each line.

Here is a line-by-line commentary on the code:

Line 1:

```
#import <Cocoa/Cocoa.h>
```

This is a directive that tells the compiler to include a file called Cocoa.h. This contains definitions of the major classes in Objective-C from which our converter class is derived.

NOTE

A compiler is a program that takes the programming language file and converts it into the program code that the computer uses when it runs the program.

Line 2:

```
@interface Converter : NSObject { float inches; }
```

Although this is written over three lines in the code, it is really a single line because the braces (curly brackets) enclose what follows. The convention is to write the opening brace at the end of the first line, put anything inside the braces on the next line(s), and then write the closing brace on its own on the last line.

@interface Converter means that it is the definition of our class called Converter. The : (colon) indicates that it is derived from a super-class or NSObject. This particular NSObject is a floating-point (decimal) number called "inches."

NOTE

The NS part of the super-class name comes from NextStep, which was an operating system developed for the NeXT computer that first went on sale in 1986. Apple bought NeXT in 1996, and parts of the operating system live on.

Line 3:

```
@property(readwrite) float inches;
```

This line defines a property of our class. It can be read and written to (in other words, changed). It is a floating-point number called "inches."

Line 4:

```
- (float) convertToCentimeters;
```

The - (minus) sign indicates that this is a method of our instance of a converter. It sends a floating-point number to another method called convertToCentimeters. That method is in the method (.m) file.

Line 5:

```
@
```

Just as the @ was used at the start of the definition of the class Converter, so it is needed to end the definition.

Creating the Converter header file

Follow these steps to create the Converter.h header file:

1. If it is not already open, open your Distance Converter project file.

2. In the Groups & Files pane, select Classes, as shown in Figure 21.15.

Figure 21.15

Project window with classes selected

3. **From the menu bar, select File ⇨ New File or press Command+N.**

This opens the new file template selection window, as shown in Figure 21.16.

Figure 21.16

File template selection window

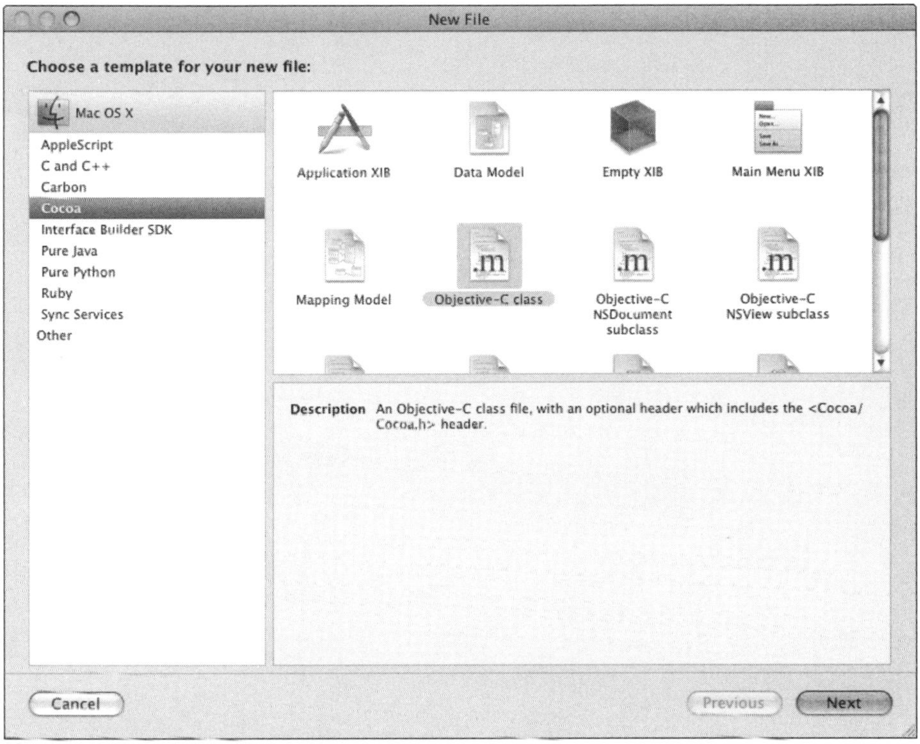

4. Select Objective-C class, and click Next.

5. Name the file Converter.m, and ensure that the Also create Converter.h box is checked, as shown in Figure 21.17.

Figure 21.17

Creating Converter.m and Converter.h

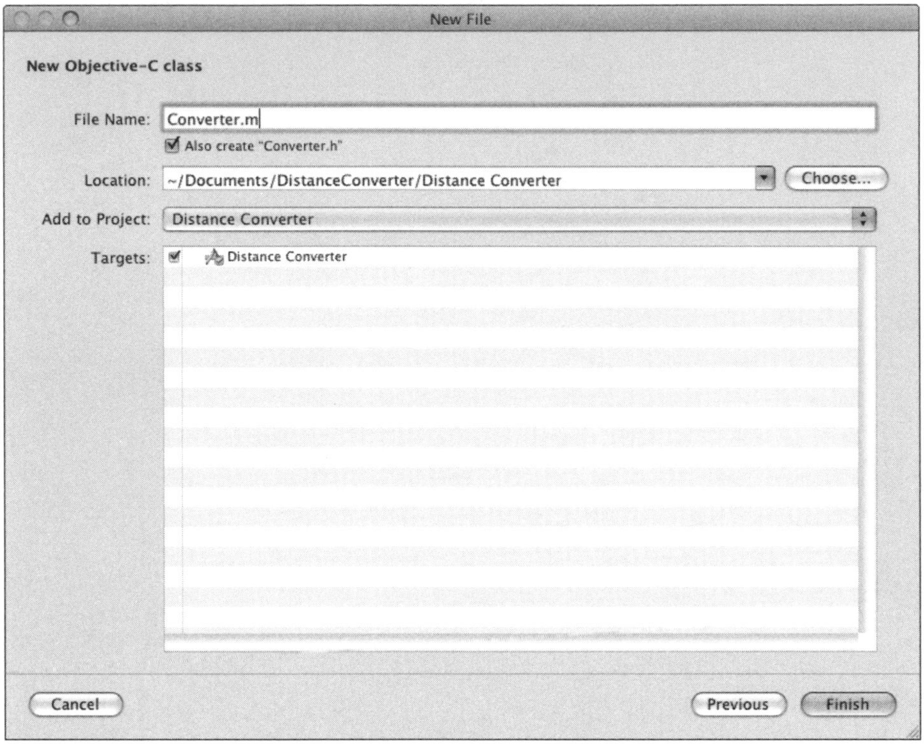

6. **Click Finish.**

   Your project screen should now look like that shown in Figure 21.18.

7. **Double-click Converter.h, and enter the following code:**

```
#import <Cocoa/Cocoa.h>
@interface Converter : NSObject {
    float inches;
}
@property(readwrite) float inches;
- (float) convertToCentimeters;
@end
```

   Be sure there is only one #import and one @end line.

8. **Save the file.**

Figure 21.18

Project window with new files created

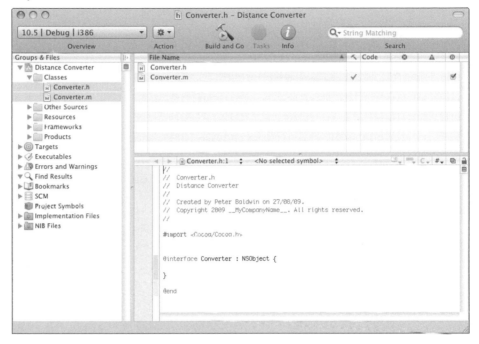

Understanding the Converter method file

Here is the code for the method file, Converter.m:

```
#import "Converter.h"
@implementation Converter
@synthesize inches;
- (float) convertToCentimeters {
    return (self.inches *2.54);
}
@end
```

Again, here is a line-by-line commentary on the code:

Line 1:

```
#import "Converter.h"
```

This line simply imports the class definitions you have defined in Converter.h.

Line 2:

```
@implementation Converter
```

This line starts the definition of how the converter is implemented.

Line 3:

```
@synthesize inches;
```

This creates a variable called inches.

Line 4:

```
- (float) convertToCentimeters { return (self.inches *2.54); }
```

Although this line is written over three lines in the code, it actually behaves as a single line.

Remember the – (minus) sign from the header file? It is used to define a method. In this case, the method is convertToCentimeters and is a floating point. The return means that it sends back a value to whatever sent it a value. The self.inches * 2.54 is the heart of the method. It tells the program to take the value of inches and multiply it by 2.54.

Line 5:

```
@end
```

As before, this ends the definition of the implementation of the converter.

Creating the Converter method file

Follow these steps to edit the method file:

1. **Double-click the Converter.m file in the project window.**

2. **Enter the following code:**

```
#import "Converter.h"
@implementation Converter
@synthesize inches;
- (float) convertToCentimeters {
    return (self.inches *2.54);
}
@end
```

3. **Save the file.**

Creating the Controller method

Again in this section, you get immersed in Objective-C code. The code for the Controller is more difficult than the code for the Converter because the controller needs to interact both with the visible parts of the application that you created with Interface Builder and with the converter that does the actual number work.

Understanding the Controller header file

Here is the code for the header file Controller.h:

```
#import <Cocoa/Cocoa.h>
@interface Controller : NSObject {
    IBOutlet NSTextField *inchesField;
    IBOutlet NSTextField *centimetersField;
}
- (IBAction)convert:(id)sender;
@end
```

Here is a line-by-line commentary on the code:

Line 1:

```
#import <Cocoa/Cocoa.h>
```

Again, the code begins with a directive that tells the compiler to include a file called Cocoa.h containing definitions of the major classes in Objective-C, from which our controller class is derived.

Line 2:

```
@interface Controller : NSObject {
    IBOutlet NSTextField *inchesField;
    IBOutlet NSTextField *centimetersField;
}
```

Although this is written over four lines, because of the braces it is treated as just a single line.

It is a declaration of the class Controller that is made up of objects derived from the class NSObject. The attributes of the class are derived from another object class known as IBOutlet.

IBOutlet is a class of objects defined in Interface Builder (which is what the IB means). There are two IBOutlet classes, each corresponding to one of the text fields you created with Interface Builder. The class of each outlet is from a higher class called NSTextField.

Finally the name of each field is written with a * in front. The *inchesField means "the data contained in the field called inchesField." The same is true for centimetersField.

Translating that into English, it means: this IBOutlet is an NSTextField that contains the value of the inchesField in the interface. Obviously, the other IBOutlet is the field that contains the value of the centimetersField.

You will see how these names are used when you come to make the connections between the interface and the code.

Line 3:

```
- (IBAction)convert:(id)sender;
```

Finally we have an instance method. IBAction is a method from Interface Builder, and it is attached to the Convert button. This method is defined in the Controller.m file.

Creating the Controller header file

Follow these steps to create the header file:

1. **If it is not already open, open your Distance Converter project file.**

2. **In the Groups & Files pane, select Classes.**

3. **From the menu bar, select File ⇨ New File or press Command+N.**

4. **Select Objective-C class, and click Next.**

5. **Name the file Controller.m, and ensure that the Also create Controller.h box is checked.**

6. **Click Finish.**

7. **Double-click the Controller.h file.**

8. **Enter the following code:**

```
#import <Cocoa/Cocoa.h>
@interface Controller : NSObject {
    IBOutlet NSTextField *inchesField;
    IBOutlet NSTextField *centimetersField;
}
- (IBAction)convert:(id)sender;
@end
```

9. **Save the file.**

Understanding the Controller method file

The final part of the jigsaw is the method file for the Controller. Here is the Controller.m code:

```
#import "Controller.h"
#import "Converter.h"
@implementation Controller
- (IBAction) convert:(id)sender
{
  Converter *converter = [[Converter alloc] init];
  [converter setInches:[inchesField floatValue]];
  float centimeters = [converter convertToCentimeters];
  [centimetersField setStringValue:[NSString stringWithFormat:@"%.2f",¬
    centimeters]];
  [inchesField selectText:self];
  [converter release];
}
```

```
- (BOOL) applicationShouldTerminateAfterLastWindowClosed:(NSApplication¬
    *) theApplication
{
  return YES;
}
@end
```

Here is a line-by-line commentary on the code:

Line 1:

```
#import "Controller.h"
```

As before, we need to import the header file.

Line 2:

```
#import "Converter.h"
```

This time we also need to import definitions from the other header file, Converter.h.

Line 3:

```
@implementation Controller
```

This line begins the implementation of the Controller class. It ends with the last line, @end.

Line 4:

```
- (IBAction) convert:(id)sender
```

This line sets an instance method for the Interface Builder convert action sent by the Convert button.

Lines 5–12:

```
{
  Converter *converter = [[Converter alloc] init];
  [converter setInches:[inchesField floatValue]];
  float centimeters = [converter convertToCentimeters];
  [centimetersField setStringValue:[NSString stringWithFormat:@"%.2f",¬
   centimeters]];
  [inchesField selectText:self];
  [converter release];
}
```

Without going into too much detail, these lines allocate the memory required for the convert method. This is done by the keyword `alloc`.

`InchesField` is set to a floating-point (decimal) value so the math can be carried out.

CentimetersField is also set to a floating-point value with two digits after the decimal point and then converted to a string to display in the text box on the window.

Finally the memory allocated earlier is released. This is very important: If a program doesn't release the memory it allocated for itself, gradually memory fills up with memory that is no longer in use.

Lines 13–17:

```
- (BOOL) applicationShouldTerminateAfterLastWindowClosed:(NSApplication¬ *)
    theApplication
{
  return YES;
}
```

Finally the last part of the application is pretty self-explanatory. The NSApplication class defines a method called applicationShouldTerminateAfterLastWindowClosed. This is set to a Boolean value (BOOL), which can have two values: Yes or No (or True or False). It is explicitly set to return a value of YES so the application terminates when the last window is closed.

If that line is set to return NO, it means that the application keeps running, even after the last window has closed, hence using more and more memory each time you run the application. For an application this size it won't make much difference, but for bigger applications with extensive data structures the difference can be large.

Creating the Controller method file

Follow these steps to create the method file:

1. **Double-click the Controller.m file.**

2. **Enter the following code:**

```
#import "Controller.h"
#import "Converter.h"
@implementation Controller
- (IBAction) convert:(id)sender
{
  Converter *converter = [[Converter alloc] init];
  [converter setInches:[inchesField floatValue]];
  float centimeters = [converter convertToCentimeters];
  [centimetersField setStringValue:[NSString¬
    stringWithFormat:@"%.2f", centimeters]];
```

```
    [inchesField selectText:self];
    [converter release];
}
- (BOOL) applicationShouldTerminateAfterLastWindowClosed:¬
    (NSApplication *)theApplication
{
    return YES;
}
@end
```

3. **Save the file.**

NOTE

Note the line continuation characters (¬). In Objective-C, it is not essential that the line doesn't break at the end, but it is more convenient to enter it as one line.

Connecting the pieces

Now that you have the header and method files for your application, you need to connect them to the interface you built for the application.

Follow these steps to complete your project:

1. **Open the project if it is not already open.**

2. **Open mainmenu.xib.**

   This opens the Interface Builder that you used to create the converter.

3. **Open the Library window (Command+Shift+L) if it is not already open.**

4. **In the Library window, select Cocoa ⇨ Objects & Controllers, as shown in Figure 21.19a.**

5. **Drag an Object into mainmenu.xib window, as shown in Figure 21.19b.**

6. **Open the Inspector if it is not already open, and go to the Information panel (Command+6).**

Figure 21.19

Library window with object selected (a); object added to Mainmenu.xib window (b)

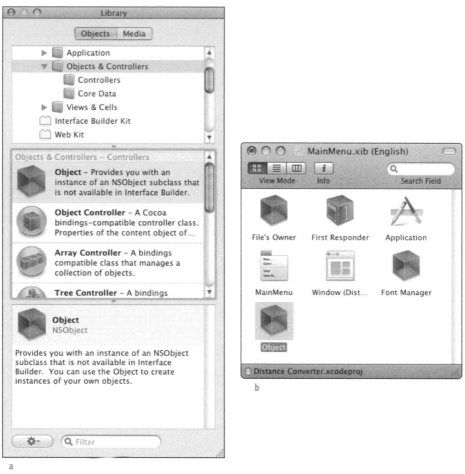

7. **In the Class field, type** Controller**, as shown in Figure 21.20a.**

Note that the inspector automatically adds the information from your Controller.h file, and the name of the object in the mainmenu.xib window is changed to Controller.

8. **In the mainmenu.xib window, right-click the Controller icon.**

This opens a HUD window that allows you to create the connections

N O T E

A HUD is a Heads Up Display and is the name Apple gives to this type of window that appears with a black background.

The HUD window is shown in Figure 21.20b.

Figure 21.20

Adding controller class to Mainmenu (a); Heads Up Display of controller connections (b)

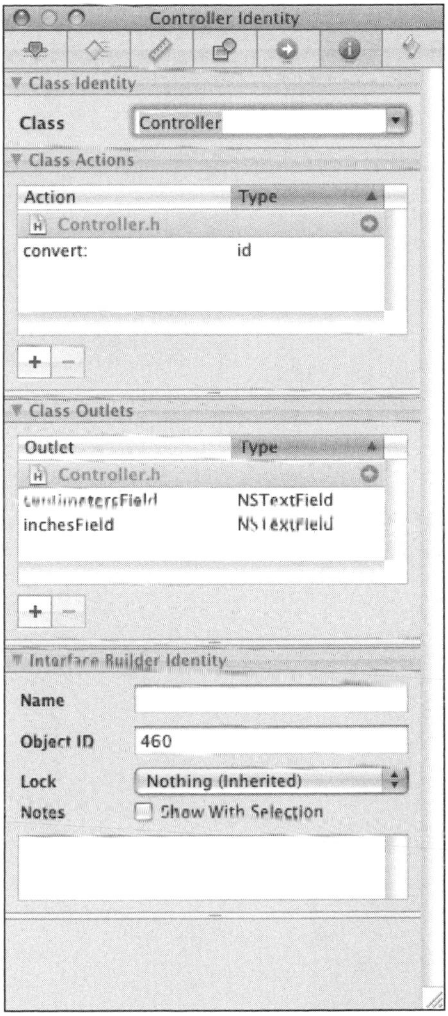

a

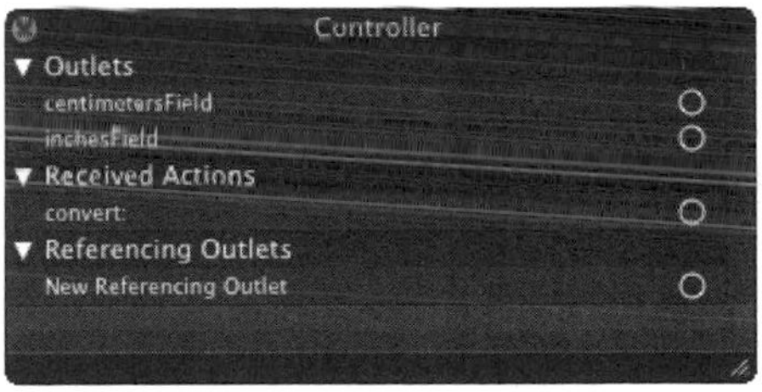

b

9. **Drag the circle to the right of the outlet centimetersField to the centimeters field on your application window, as shown in Figure 21.21.**

Figure 21.21

Dragging the outlet to the application window

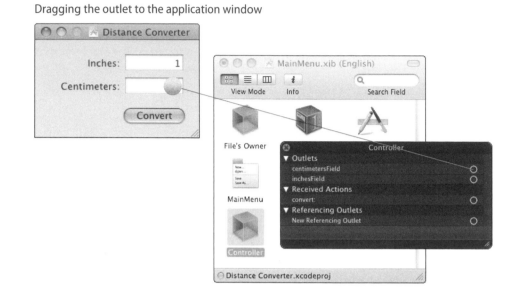

10. **Repeat Step 9 for the inchesField outlet, dragging it to the Inches field on your application window.**

11. **Connect the Convert circle in the Received Actions line to the Convert button on your window.**

By now your Controller HUD should look like Figure 21.22.

Figure 21.22

Controller HUD

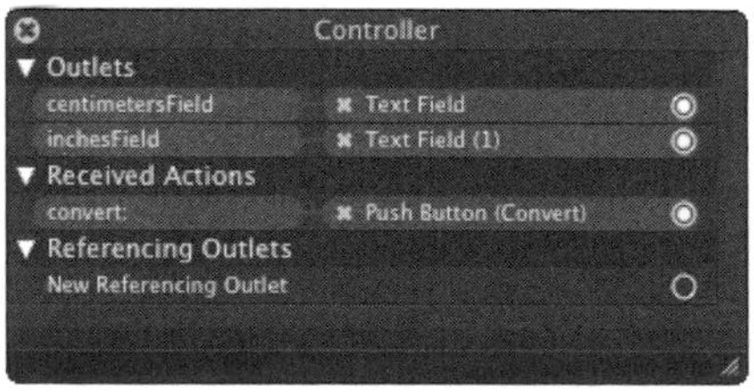

12. **Click the circle beside New Referencing Outlet in your HUD, and drag it to the File's Owner in mainmenu.xib, as shown in Figure 21.23.**

13. **When the label delegate appears above File's Owner, click it to set it as the referencing outlet.**

Now your Controller HUD should look like Figure 21.24a.

Figure 21.23

Setting new referencing outlet

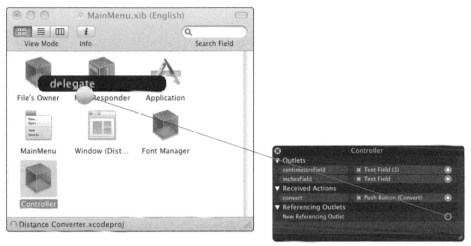

14. **Save your mainmenu.xib.**

15. **Open the Inspector window if it is not already open, and select Controller Connections (Command+5).**

    Your connections should look like those shown in Figure 21.24b.

Figure 21.24

Completed controller HUD (a); Controller connections (b)

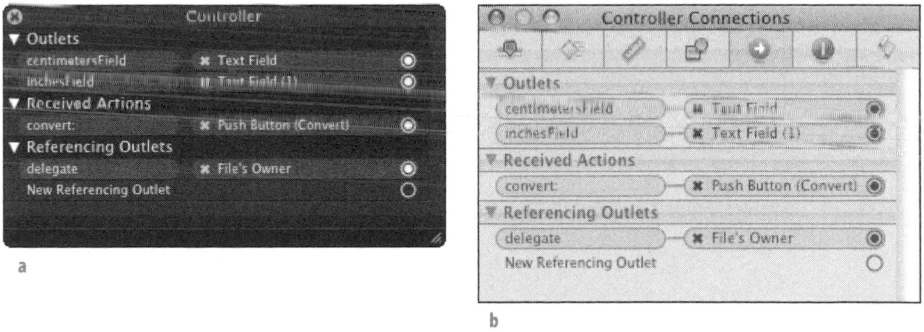

16. **If your connections do not look exactly like those shown, go through these steps carefully.**

17. **Save mainmenu.xib, and quit Interface Builder.**

Building the Application

Building your application means converting it into an application that can run on your computer and could hardly be easier. The XCode window has a Build & Go button. Click that button, and the compiler starts. Assuming you made no errors, as soon as the program is compiled, it runs as an application.

When building an application, two major types of errors can occur: compile-time errors and run-time errors. As you'd expect, compile-time errors happen when the application is being compiled into code that the processor can understand.

Fixing compile-time errors

Compile-time errors are the only ones that are likely in a simple application like Distance Converter.

If you make a typo when entering the code, XCode picks it up when you compile. You cannot miss the errors because the compiler highlights them and explains what the error is.

Figure 21.25 shows a compile-time error caused by me misspelling convertToCentimeters. I spelled it convertToCentimetres.

Figure 21.25

Compile-time warning error

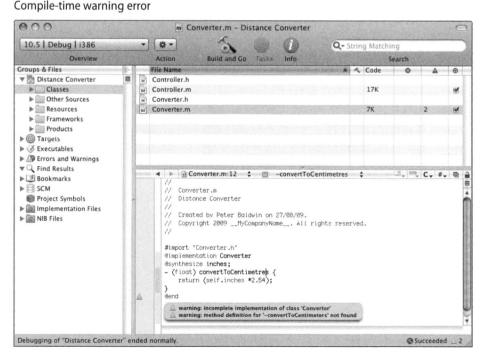

In this case, the error is a warning error: The compiler couldn't find a method for convertToCentimeters. It doesn't prevent the application from compiling, but when it runs, because it can't find a method to convert the inches, nothing happens when you press the Convert button.

Try it for yourself. Figure 21.26 shows a fatal compile-time error.

To create this error, I removed the closing } (brace) from the second-to-last line of Controller.m. In case you can't read the print, the error says `error: syntax error before 'AT_NAME' token`. That's not terribly helpful!

The error message says something is missing just before the @end statement (or token).

Note that a warning error indicates that an @end is missing. The @end is actually there, but the earlier error throws the compiler out.

Figure 21.26

Compile-time fatal error

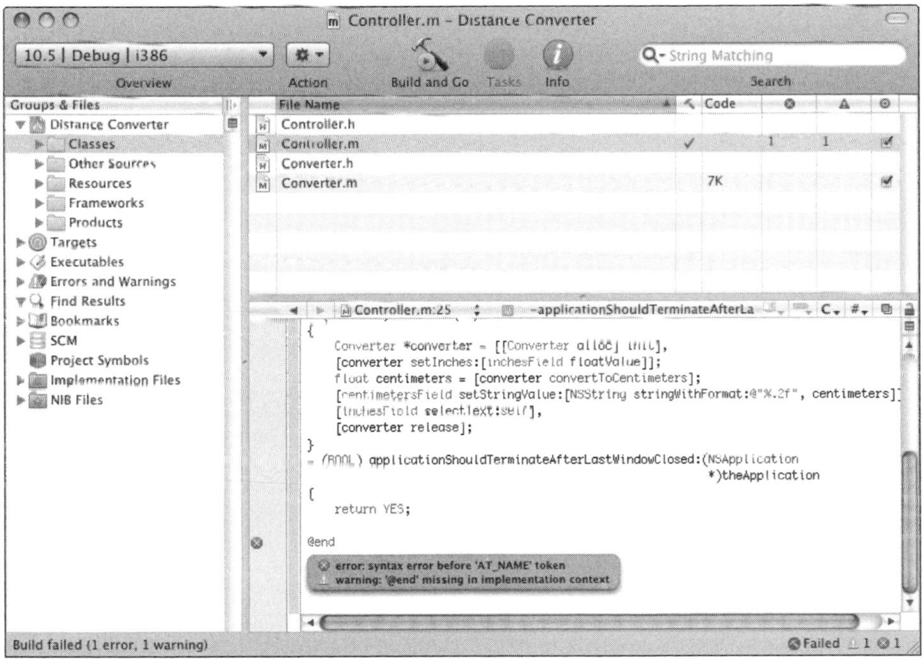

Fixing run-time errors

In an application this small, you are unlikely to find any run-time errors. Run-time errors occur when all the code for the application compiles without error, but the application crashes when it runs. Now that's something very familiar to Windows users and less familiar to Mac users!

Running the Application

Assuming that your application compiles and builds, it will also run and you see the window you designed onscreen, waiting for input.

In the Inches box, enter a number and click the Convert button. Check that the answer shown in the Centimeters box is 2.54 times the number you entered.

Figure 21.27 shows the output for my Distance Converter.

Figure 21.27

Distance Converter working

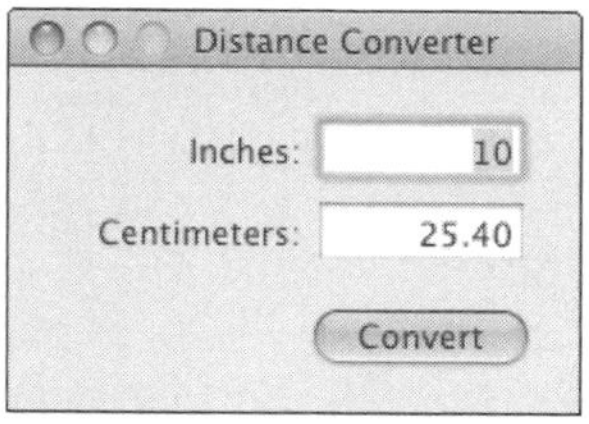

Success!

Refining the Application

At present, your application compiles, runs, and even gives the correct answer! What more could you want?

Well, if you look carefully, you'll notice that when you click Distance Converter on the menu bar, it shows About NewApplication, Hide NewApplication, and Quit NewApplication on the submenu. This is shown in Figure 21.28.

Changing the submenus

Changing the default submenu items could hardly be simpler. Follow these steps to change the submenu:

1. **If it is not already open, open Distance Converter in XCode.**
2. **Open MainMenu.xib in Interface Builder.**
3. **Navigate to the menu builder.**
4. **Click the NewApplication menu.**
5. **On the drop-down menu, double-click About NewApplication.**

6. **Change the text to** About Distance Converter, **and press Enter.**

7. **Repeat Steps 5 and 6 for Hide NewApplication and Quit NewApplication.**

8. **Click Help on the menu.**

9. **Change NewApplication Help to** Distance Converter Help.

10. **Quit Interface Builder, and click Build & Go in XCode.**

11. **Check that your menus are correct.**

Figure 21.28

Distance Converter menu bar

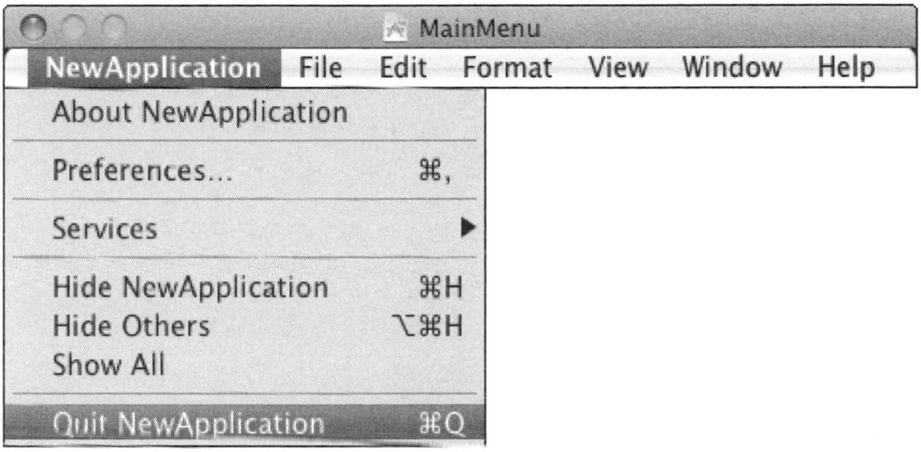

```
  ○ ○ ○                    MainMenu
  NewApplication    File   Edit   Format   View   Window   Help
    About NewApplication
    Preferences...                     ⌘,
    Services                             ▶
    Hide NewApplication                 ⌘H
    Hide Others                        ⌥⌘H
    Show All
    Quit NewApplication                 ⌘Q
```

Changing the application icon

Did you notice that when you run the Distance Converter, its icon in the Dock is a generic application icon? Figure 21.29 shows the generic icon in the Dock, beside the XCode icon.

Figure 21.29

Generic application Dock icon

Follow these steps to change your application's icon:

1. Find some suitable clipart.

I found a public domain image of a calculator by searching the Web using Google.

2. Copy the image from the Web site, and open Preview.

3. Select File, New from Clipboard.

Figure 21.30a shows the resulting image.

4. Select Tools, Adjust Size to set the image to either 512 wide or 512 tall, depending on your image.

Figure 21.30b shows the drop-down sheet in Preview.

Be sure that the Scale proportionally and Resample image boxes are both checked.

5. Save the image as Distance Converter.png into your XCode Distance Converter folder.

Figure 21.30

Clipart image pasted into Preview (a); Preview resize image sheet (b)

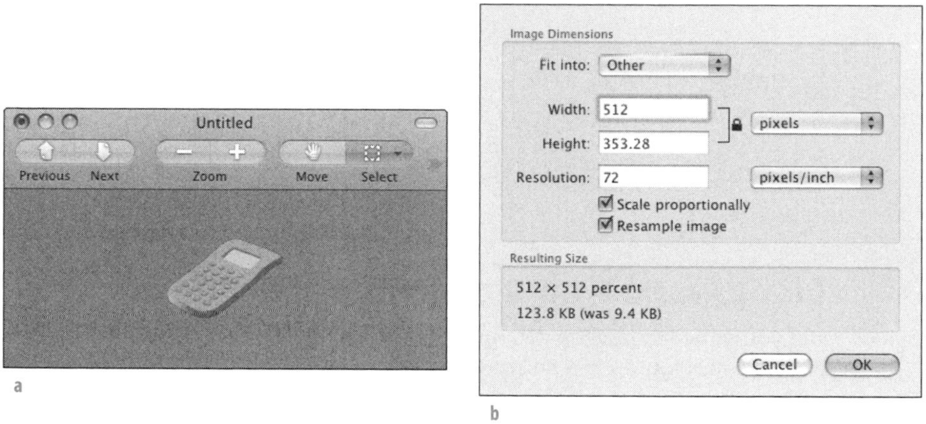

6. In Developer Tools Utilities, open Icon Composer.

The greeting screen of Icon Composer is shown in Figure 21.31.

Icon Composer is designed to allow you to convert ordinary images to Apple's icon image format files, .icns.

7. Open a Finder window in your Distance Converter folder, and drag the Distance Converter.png image into the large (512) window of Icon Composer.

8. **Select Copy to all smaller sizes, and press Import, as shown in Figure 21.32a.**

   Icon Composer then creates the smaller icon sizes automatically.

9. **Save the file as Distance Converter.icns to your Distance Converter folder.**

10. **Close Icon Composer.**

11. **If XCode is not already open, launch it and open your Distance Converter project.**

12. **Drag the Distance Converter.icns file from your Finder window into the Resources section of XCode.**

    On the drop-down sheet, shown in Figure 21.32b, you don't need to check the Copy items into destination group's folder because the file is already there.

    Figure 21.33 shows your XCode project window.

    So your application icon is incorporated when you build your project, you need to add it to the Info.plist file.

Figure 21.31

Icon Composer screen

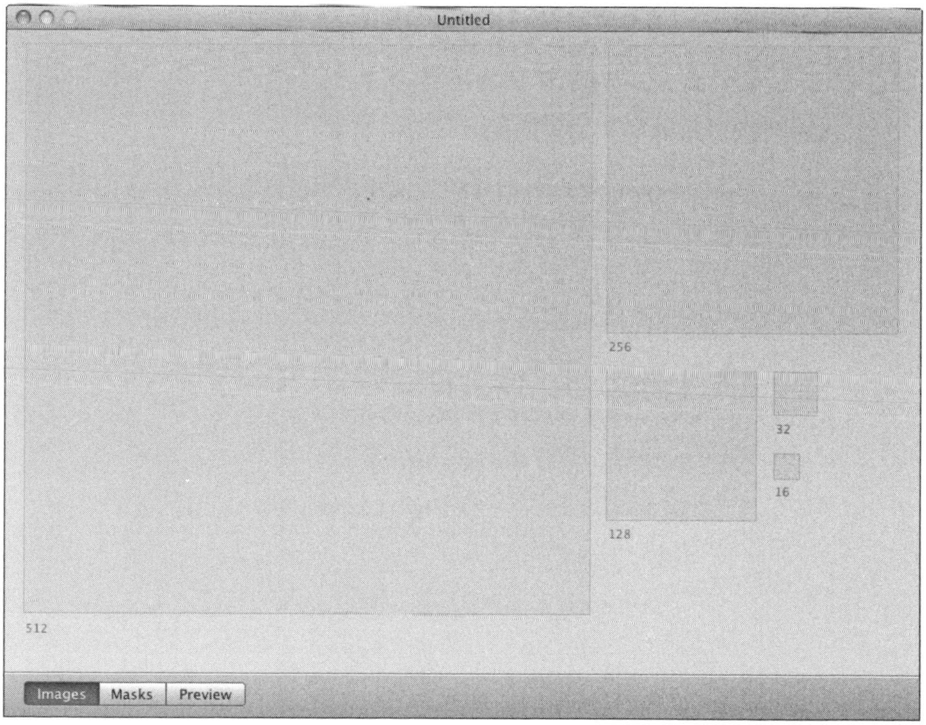

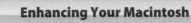
Figure 21.32

Icon Composer creating icons (a); XCode project drop-down sheet (b)

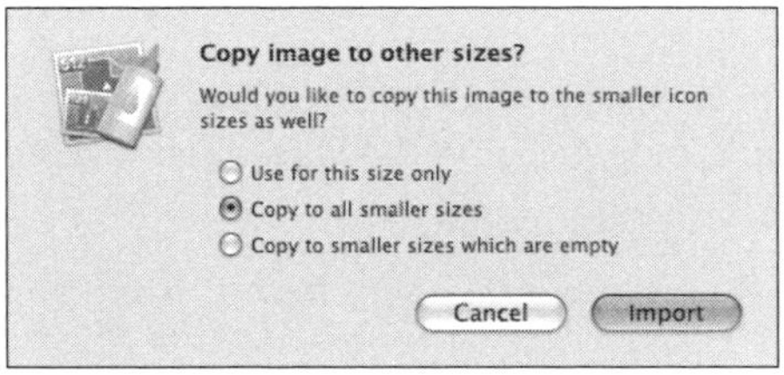

☑ Copy items into destination group's folder (if needed)

Reference Type: Default

Text Encoding: Unicode (UTF-8)

● Recursively create groups for any added folders
○ Create Folder References for any added folders

Add To Targets

☑ Distance Converter

Copy image to other sizes?

Would you like to copy this image to the smaller icon sizes as well?

○ Use for this size only
● Copy to all smaller sizes
○ Copy to smaller sizes which are empty

Cancel   Import

Cancel   Add

a

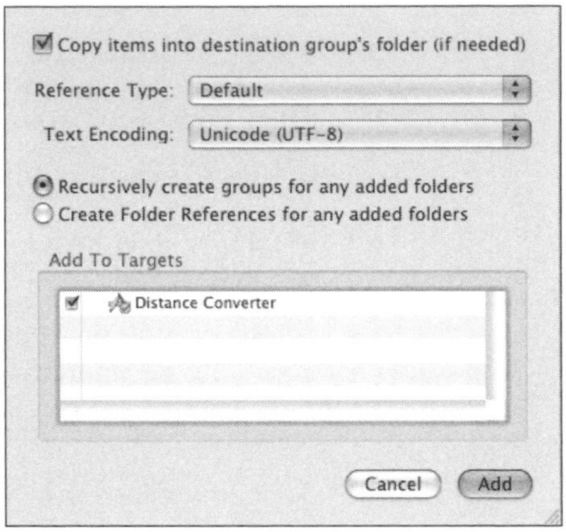

b

Figure 21.33

XCode project window

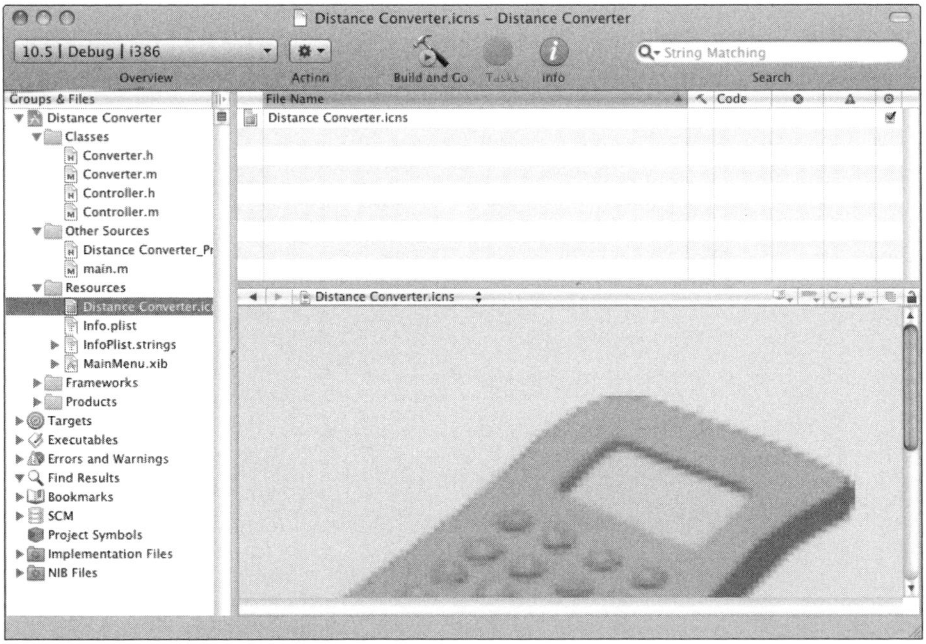

Distance Converter.icns – Distance Converter

10.5 | Debug | i386

Overview   Action   Build and Go   Tasks   Info   Search

String Matching

Groups & Files   File Name   Code

▼ Distance Converter   Distance Converter.icns
  ▼ Classes
      Converter.h
      Converter.m
      Controller.h
      Controller.m
  ▼ Other Sources
      Distance Converter_Pr
      main.m
  ▼ Resources
      Distance Converter.ic
      Info.plist
    ▶ InfoPlist.strings
    ▶ MainMenu.xib
  ▶ Frameworks
  ▶ Products
▶ Targets
▶ Executables
▶ Errors and Warnings
▼ Find Results
▶ Bookmarks
▶ SCM
    Project Symbols
▶ Implementation Files
▶ NIB Files

Distance Converter.icns

13. **Highlight Info.plist in the top window.**

14. **In the lower window, move the highlight to Icon file and enter Distance Converter, as shown in Figure 21.34.**

There is no need to add the .icns extension to the file because XCode automatically looks for a file with that extension.

15. **Save your project, and then click Build & Go.**

After your project is compiled, it runs. Your new Icon should appear in the Dock, as shown in Figure 21.35a.

16. **While your application Is running, select About Distance Converter.**

Your new icon appears here as well, as shown in Figure 21.35b.

17. **If you choose, save the Distance Converter.app file to your Applications folder.**

Figure 21.34

Icon file in XCode window

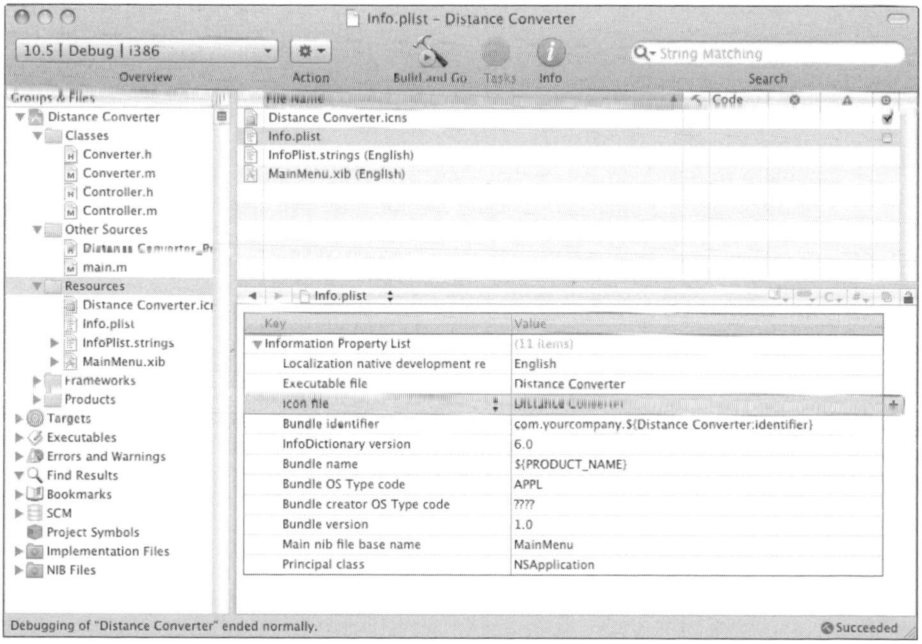

Figure 21.35

New Dock icon (a); About Distance Converter (b)

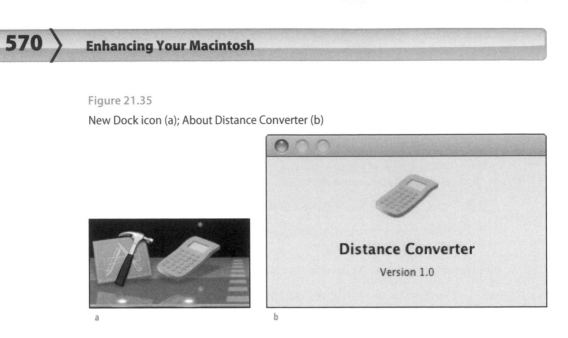

a   b

Summary

For many, this chapter has been pretty heavy going! If you have programming expertise, I hope it triggered some enthusiasm for programming in the OS X environment. If you are already familiar with object-oriented programming, such as C++, then the jump to Objective-C is not that high. The major differences are in the syntax.

If you do not have prior programming expertise, I hope this chapter has inspired you to try some programming. As you have seen, OS X makes it somewhat easier to build applications because of the many tools, such as XCode, Interface Builder, and Icon Composer to help the process.

Apple provides a wealth of documentation to help you along your path.

Some Successful Case Studies

22

By now you have installed and been using your Leopard installation on your non-Apple computer. In this chapter, I discuss some installations I have carried out on different computers, the difficulties encountered, and how I overcame them.

While writing this book, from Chapter 7 on, I have almost exclusively used Leopard with only an occasional trip back to Vista.

Installing to a Gigabyte Motherboard

My first installation was to my trusty old bitzer (bits o' this and bits o' that) computer that had been running Vista for six months or so. It's a computer that I've tinkered with, replacing the motherboard, graphics card, hard disks, and other components over a couple of years.

Purely by chance, I found I had a system that was a relatively easy fit with Leopard.

It has a gigabyte EP45-DS3P motherboard with an Intel CoreDuo E8400 processor. This combination turned out to be one of the easiest boards for getting Leopard running. From the start, I used a retail copy of Leopard using the Boot-132 boot disk.

Graphics was also a breeze. The computer has an nVidia 7600GS graphics card. Apple has used several different nVidia graphics cards over the years, so I found a wealth of knowledge about using them in Hackintoshes. The kexts used are nVkush, which is generic for nVidia on Hackintoshes. It can automatically detect the card at boot time and load the correct drivers. It supports Quartz Extreme/Core Image.

Overcoming difficulties

Major difficulties were with the Wi-Fi and sound. Sound was easily fixed by posting on a forum. Within a few hours, I had an answer and sound kexts tailor-made for my motherboard, thanks to Gary Malec.

Wi-Fi proved much more problematic. Wired Internet worked right from the start, but because the ADSL modem must be in a different room, I had to get Wi-Fi working. I tried five different wireless adaptors, including two PCI bus internal cards. The only ones to work were a Netgear WG111 USB adaptor and a Rokair USB adaptor. The Rokair was supplied with an install disk, and I downloaded the Netgear driver from the Web site.

The problem with most generic Wi-Fi adaptors is that their manufacturers don't bundle the drivers with them, simply because almost every Mac has wireless built in, so the market is very small.

Viewing a success

Every application I have loaded, bar one, has worked with no tweaking required. That applies to all Apple system applications as well as third-party apps. While writing this book, I used Microsoft Word for the bulk of the writing and PowerPoint for creating some of the diagrams. LiveQuartz, a free graphics program, did the bulk of the diagrams.

Figure 22.1 shows the About This Mac panel for the computer.

Figure 22.1

About This Mac for gigabyte/nVidia computer

Installing to a Dell Mini 9

My other computer is a Dell Mini 9 that I bought with the express purpose of running Leopard. I bought it about two months after getting Leopard running on the desktop computer. I checked with various Web sites and found that, at the time (March 2009), it was rated just about the easiest computer of all to run Leopard.

Gadgets.boingboing.net updated a chart roughly once a month that shows compatibility for lots of netbooks. Find the chart at `http://gadgets.boingboing.net/2008/12/17/osx-netbook-compatib.html` or `http://tinyurl.com/4z3d9g`. As you can see, the Mini 9 gets a green check mark for everything.

A Web site dedicated to the Mini 9 (and other Dell minis) has a forum dedicated to OS X installation and difficulties at `www.mydellmini.com/forum/mac-os-x/`.

Overcoming difficulties

This may sound odd, but in fact I had almost no difficulties to overcome! The Hackintosh has such a large fan base, especially on the My Dell Mini Web site, that all the issues have been overcome by folks more talented than I am.

I started with a retail copy of Leopard 10.5.2 and installed it from a USB key because the Mini doesn't have a DVD drive. Installation went smoothly, and on the second boot up, it worked fine. Wi-Fi worked from the start: All I had to do was enter my password for my wireless network.

One item that gets broken when Leopard is updated is sound. This is easily fixed by redoing the DellEFI custom install and is well documented on the My Dell Mini Web site.

I also updated the boot to use Chameleon v2.

Viewing a success

My install started out with the Type 11 install method. This is now a superseded method, but it was all that was available at the time. Since then, I have upgraded through 10.5.6, 10.5.7, and 10.5.8. In every case, the upgrade has worked perfectly with nothing broken. I also have upgraded all the software every time it becomes available on Apple's Software Update site.

Not only does the Mini 9 make a great netbook, it also is usable as a desktop machine. I have a wireless keyboard and mouse: I don't like the Mini 9 keyboard, and I don't like trackpads. I also have an old 17-inch LCD monitor that connects through the video out slot and gives me a dual screen. Because the menu bar is movable between the two screens, the external monitor can be used as the main monitor.

Figure 22.2 shows the About This Mac panel for the computer.

Figure 22.2

About This Mac for Dell Mini 9

Summary

I've shown you that after much experimenting and many failures, you can definitely run Leopard on a wide range of hardware. Some hardware gives excellent results, while other hardware gives mediocre or poor results.

For most users, unless the computer can connect to the Internet, either wired or wireless, and can make best use of the graphics and sound hardware, there is little point in installing Leopard.

If you have an existing computer you want to try Leopard on, use the Hardware Compatibility Lists to get an idea of how difficult it will be.

If you want to buy a computer specifically to run Leopard, refer to the compatibility lists at `http://wiki.osx86project.org`. The fact that someone has managed to get a particular computer to run doesn't mean it will be easy: It simply means that it's possible!

Is it worth it? In my case, definitely. When I started this project, I had almost no Macintosh expertise. Now I prefer to use Leopard than any Windows operating system and I've bought my own genuine Macintosh.

Leopard seems easier on the hardware as well. Under Vista, my hard disk light is on for maybe 10 percent of the time. In Leopard, it flicks on only when I save a file.

a

References

I n Table A.1, all the references from previous chapters are gathered together. In addition, you find general reading references on topics of interest to builders of Hackintoshes.

Table A.1 Web References from all Chapters

Topic	URL*
System Information for Windows	www.gtopala.com/
Find manufacturer of PCI device	www.pcidatabase.com
Hardware Compatibility Lists	http://wiki.osx86project.org/wiki/index.php/Main_Page
Update Leopard	www.apple.com/downloads/macosx/apple/macosx_updates/
pcwiz	http://pcwizcomputer.com
Downloads site	www.mediafire.com/
Downloads site	http://rapidshare.com/
Macrium Reflect (Free)	www.macrium.com/reflectfree.asp
DriveImage XML (Free)	www.runtime.org/driveimage-xml.htm
Drive Backup Free	www.paragon-software.com/home/db-express/features.html
Acronis True Image	www.acronis.com/
Norton Ghost	www.symantec.com/norton/ghost
Paragon Hard Disk Manager	www.paragon-software.com/home/hdm-personal/
O&O Disk Image 3	www.oo-software.com/home/en/products/oodiskimage/index.html
Terabyte Image for Windows	www.terabyteunlimited.com/image-for-windows.htm
Acronis Partition Manager	www.acronis.com/
Partition Magic	www.symantec.com/norton/partitionmagic
Paragon Partition Manager	www.paragon-software.com/home/pm-personal/
CD/DVD burner for Windows	www.imgburn.com/
Disk partitioning	http://gparted.sourceforge.net/
EasyBCD	http://neosmart.net/
Chain 0 to dual boot	http://rs279.rapidshare.com/files/118576025/Chain0_.rar

continued

Table A.1 Continued

Topic	URL*
Leads to forum on .iso for different motherboards	`http://tinyurl.com/r49hnx`
Kexthelper b7	`http://cheetha.net/`
UInstaller and other software	`http://pcwizcomputer.com/`
Remove services from Leopard	`http://manytricks.com/servicescrubber/`
Leads to table of netbook compatibility on Boing Boing Gadgets	`http://tinyurl.com/4z3d9g`
OSX86 Tools	`http://code.google.com/p/osx86tools/downloads/list`
Audio drivers	`http://tinyurl.com/lqbw67`
Back to my Mac from a PC	`http://lifehacker.com/366940/back-to-my-mac-from-a-pc`
Leads to change time Leopard to Windows	`http://tinyurl.com/ktvylg`
The Unarchiver	`www.apple.com/downloads/macosx/system_disk_utilities/theunarchiver.html`
Yahoo calendar in iCal	`http://switch.calendar.yahoo.com`
File types opened by Preview	`http://en.wikipedia.org/wiki/Preview_(software)`
TinkerTool	`www.bresink.com/osx/TinkerTool.html`
MacFuse	`http://code.google.com/p/macfuse/`
NTFS3G	`www.ntfs-3g.org/`
Ntfs-mac	`www.paragon-software.com/home/ntfs-mac/`
Parallels desktop	`www.parallels.com/`
VMware Fusion	`www.vmware.com/products/fusion/`
VMware workstation	`www.vmware.com/products/ws/`
WinRAR	`www.rarlab.com/download.htm`
7-Zip	`www.7-zip.org/`
XBench - benchmarks for OS X	`www.xbench.com/`
Workflow example	`www.macosxautomation.com/automator/examples/ex06/pkg/workflow.zip`
Apple Developer Site	`http://developer.apple.com/`
Audio spectrum display	`http://machinecodex.com/codexmachina/?q=node/8`
Phonemes for Apple speech	`http://tinyurl.com/neyvwe`
Dell Mini Forum	`www.mydellmini.com/forum/mac-os-x/`
Boot-132 Loaders for Retail Vanilla Leopard Install in a Disk Partition	`www.insanelymac.com/forum/lofiversion/index.php/t125438.html`

Topic	URL*
Retail Leopard Install with Boot-132-Chameleon w/ EFI-strings Loader	`www.insanelymac.com/forum/lofiversion/index.php/t128274.html`
Boot from EFI partition, zero modification installs on Intel SSE2 or better	`www.insanelymac.com/forum/lofiversion/index.php/t127330.html`

* All URLs were correct and working at 29 September, 2009.

NOTE

Where a URL is broken over two lines, there is no space in it; type it as a single line.

The Missing Theory

This appendix provides background material gathered in one place.

It covers some theoretical topics from the rudiments of how processors work, disk formats, what happens when you boot your Leopard and Windows computers, kernels and kexts, and a general history of OS X on the Macintosh.

In practical topics, it details some fixes for issues that arise during installation, as well as some general troubleshooting advice.

Processor Instructions

In general, you do not need to know very much about processor instructions to install Leopard. However, you should be aware of some terms that will help you understand the process of installing Leopard.

For compatibility with older software, modern processors still have to work with instructions from earlier processors. Intel developed the technique of using one instruction to operate on more than one set of data. This allows the code required to be much smaller because, rather than having one set of instructions for each bit of data, one instructions works with all of them, effectively carrying out operations in parallel.

This technique is called Single Instruction, Multiple Data, abbreviated to SIMD. It is especially useful in putting graphics on the screen because several pixels can be processed at once.

Table B.1 explains the meaning of each of the newer instruction types and what they do.

Table B.1 Processor Instruction Types

Instruction	Meaning	Explanation	Introduced
MMX	Multimedia Extension	Only worked on integers	1997
SSE	Streaming SIMD Extension	Added floating-point support	1999
SSE2	Second version	Adds double precision floating point	2001
SSE3	Third version		2004
SSSE3	Supplemental SSE3	Additional instructions for MMX registers	2005
SSE4	Fourth version	Instructions not specific to graphics	2006
EM64T	Intel 64	Supports 64-bit programs	2004

The instruction types supported by the processor are important because Leopard will not run on instruction sets earlier than SSE2, and preferably SSE3.

Table B.2 shows the instruction sets supported by each of the Intel chips since 2001.

Table B.2 Instruction Sets Supported by Intel Processors

Chip	Year	SSE2	SSE3
Pentium 4	2001	Yes	No
Itanium 2	2002	Yes	No
Celeron 4	2002	Yes	No
Pentium 4M	2002	Yes	No
Pentium 4	2004	Yes	Yes
Celeron D	2004	Yes	Yes
Centrino	2003	Yes	No
Core Duo	2006	Yes	Yes
Core 2	2006	Yes	Yes
Atom	2008	Yes	Yes
Core i7	2008	Yes	Yes

Because Leopard will not run on any processor that does not support at least SSE2, you can see that it will not run on any Intel chips earlier than the Pentium 4 of 2001.

Graphics Systems in Macintosh Computers

If Apple has used a particular graphics processor in a Macintosh, getting it working in a Hackintosh is relatively easy. If your graphics card has not been used in a Mac, you are likely to have difficulty getting it to work satisfactorily.

Quartz Extreme/Core Image is Apple technology that uses the power of modern graphics cards to take lots of the processor load away from the central processor. It requires your graphics system to have hardware acceleration. If your graphics system does not have hardware acceleration, it is unlikely to support Quartz Extreme/Core Image.

Table B.3 shows a summary of the graphics chips that have been used in Macintoshes. The list is by no means exhaustive, but it can be used to get an indication of how likely you are to have the best graphics performance.

Table B.3 Graphics Chips Used in Macintoshes

Mac Model	Graphics Chip
Mac Mini Core Solo	Intel GMA950
iMac Core Duo 17"	Intel GMA950
iMac Core Duo 20"	ATI Radeon X1600
MacBook Core Duo 13"	Intel GMA 950
MacBook Pro Core Duo 15"	ATI Radeon X1600
MacBook Pro Core Duo 17"	ATI Radeon X1600
Mac Mini Core Duo	Intel GMA950; NVIDIA GeForce 9400M
iMac Core 2 Duo 17"	Intel GMA950; ATI Radeon X1600
iMac Core 2 Duo 20"	ATI Radeon X1600; ATI Radeon HD 2400 XT; ATI Radeon HD 2600 PRO; NVIDIA GeForce 9400M
iMac Core 2 Duo 24"	NVIDIA GeForce 7300GT; NVIDIA GeForce 8800 GS; NVIDIA GeForce 9400M; NVIDIA GeForce GT 120; NVIDIA GeForce GT 130
MacBook Core 2 Duo 13"	Intel GMA950; Intel GMA X3100; NVIDIA GeForce 9400M
MacBook Air Core 2 Duo 13"	Intel GMA X3100; NVIDIA GeForce 9400M
MacBook Pro Core 2 Duo 15"	ATI Radeon X1600; NVIDIA GeForce 8600M; NVIDIA GeForce 9600M GT
MacBook Pro Core 2 Duo 17"	ATI Radeon X1600; NVIDIA GeForce 9600M GT

The computers are listed roughly in order of their release date.

MacTracker is a very useful little utility to find out what's inside any given Macintosh. It's available at `http://mactracker.dreamhosters.com/`.

A Primer on Disk Formats

Hard disks are divided into cylinders and sectors. Firmware built into the disk controller generally conceals the actual number of platters, cylinders, and sectors, though this is unimportant to the operating system. The disk controller translates what the operating system requests to the actual layout of the disk.

Master boot record

The first sector of a hard disk used in Windows computers is known as the master boot record. It consists of a table containing information about how the disk is divided up. The original specification developed by IBM said that a disk might contain up to four partitions, allowing up to four operating systems to be installed on the same disk.

Partition table

A hard disk can be split into *partitions*. In Windows, each partition becomes a separate disk drive (C:, D:, etc) and can hold operating system and application software, or only data, or a mixture. Each partition also can carry a separate operating system and software.

An MBR disk can contain only four primary partitions: This is a limitation forced by the definition of a partition table. Although the disk can contain only four primary partitions, it can replace up to three of those by *extended partitions*. An extended partition can contain up to 24 logical partitions, though this would be very unwieldy.

Figure B.1 shows a disk divided into four partitions.

Figure B.1

Disk partitioned into four partitions

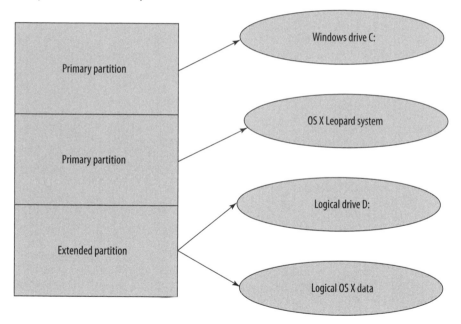

As you can see, the disk has two primary partitions: one to run Windows and one to run OS X. It also has an extended partition that is divided into two logical partitions.

Most Windows computers these days are shipped from the manufacturer with a single hard disk with two partitions. One is the C: drive for the Windows installation; the other is the D: drive, which contains a backup image of Windows and the relevant drivers so you can reinstall it relatively easily, should it become corrupted.

If you want to run more than one operating system, you must have more than one partition.

Each partition on an MBR disk can have a maximum size of 2TB (2,000 gigabytes).

Active partition

One, and only one, partition must be marked as the active partition. This can be any one of the primary partitions. It is the active partition that contains the boot loader, which in turn loads the operating system.

If you are going to install OS X and Windows Vista on the same disk, either operating system can be on the active partition. But you need a boot loader to allow you to choose which operating system to start.

GUID Partition Table

As you would expect, Apple takes a different approach from Microsoft. Rather than having a disk with a master boot record, Apple uses a different partitioning scheme. This is the GUID Partition Table (GPT). Unlike MBR, there is no limit of four primary partitions.

GUID is an acronym itself, meaning Globally Unique Identifier. A GUID is a randomly generated number of 32 hexadecimal bytes, or 128 bits. Although it is theoretically possible to randomly generate the same code twice, in practice it is almost impossible. Using 128 bits, there are 2128 possible identifiers, or over 3 x 1038. That's 3 followed by 38 zeros.

A typical GUID might be {3F2504E0-4F89-11D3-9A0C-0305E82C3301}. Conventionally, GUIDs are written in blocks: 8 digits – 4 digits – 4 digits – 4 digits – 12 digits and enclosed in braces { }. If you have ever delved into the Windows registry you will have encountered GUIDs. Each software manufacturer creates their own GUID. Although there is no central registry of GUIDs, it is almost impossible that two manufacturers will create the same GUID.

Each disk has its own GUID.

EFI partition

When Leopard partitions a GPT disk it creates an extra, hidden, partition of 200MB. This is the EFI partition, and it is always the first partition and always hidden. That is why when you boot from your Leopard disk it always uses, say, disk0s2. Disk numbers start from zero; partition numbers start from 1.

Up to now, Apple has never used the EFI partition, leaving it blank.

Protective MBR

At the start of a GPT disk is what's known as a Protective MBR. This is a part of the disk that looks to the computer like an MBR, but it has an unknown type so applications like disk partitioning and formatting software for other operating systems do not accidentally change it and make it unusable.

Table B.4 shows the ability of each Windows operating system to use a GPT disk.

Table B.4 Windows Operating Systems and GPT Disks

Operating System	Bits	Read	Write	Boot From
XP	32	No	No	No
XP	64	Yes	Yes	No
Vista	32	Yes	Yes	Yes, but only on EFI systems
Vista	64	Yes	Yes	Yes, but only on EFI systems
Windows 7	32	Yes	Yes	Yes, but only on EFI systems
Windows 7	64	Yes	Yes	Yes, but only on EFI systems

A retail copy of OS X can read and write MBR disks but cannot be installed to one. This creates an issue if both operating systems are to be installed on the same disk: OS X can only be installed on a GPT disk, but Vista cannot!

Reading and writing NTFS disks in Leopard

Leopard can both read and write to disks formatted with the File Allocation Table (FAT) method. This is the default format for all USB thumb-drives, camera storage cards, and so on.

By default, Leopard can read from but not write to the more common method of formatting Windows drives, the New Technology File System (NTFS). Why this is so is not immediately clear.

Nevertheless, a free solution to the problem is available. A combination of MacFuse and NTFS-3G allows you to read and write to NTFS disks. This is discussed in Chapter 13.

Hidden files used by Leopard

When Leopard writes to your Windows disks, it creates hidden files. In Leopard, these are hidden by the operating system, although you can view them.

Follow these steps to view hidden files on your Leopard disks:

1. **Run Terminal.**

2. **Type** defaults write com.apple.finder AppleShowAllFiles TRUE **and press Enter.**

3. **Type** killall Finder **and press Enter.**

   This is shown in Figure B.2.

At least two hidden files now appear on your desktop: .DS_Store and .localized.

To return Finder to not showing hidden files, follow the steps above, but replace TRUE with FALSE in Step 2.

Figure B.2

Terminal commands

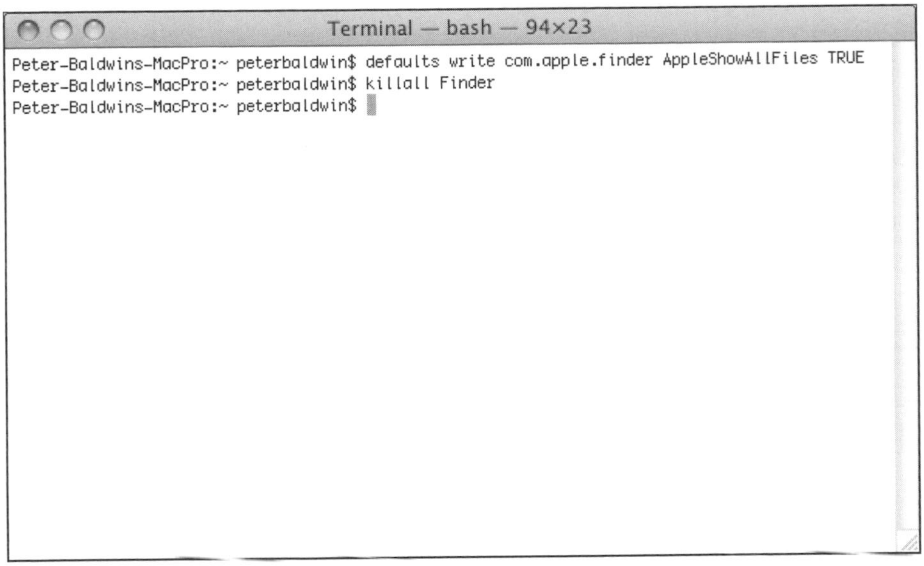

```
○ ○ ○              Terminal — bash — 94×23
Peter-Baldwins-MacPro:~ peterbaldwin$ defaults write com.apple.finder AppleShowAllFiles TRUE
Peter-Baldwins-MacPro:~ peterbaldwin$ killall Finder
Peter-Baldwins-MacPro:~ peterbaldwin$ ▌
```

The .DS_Store file

This is the Desktop Services Store and is a hidden file created by OS X to store custom attributes of a folder such as the position of icons or the choice of a background image. By default, the Mac OS X Finder creates a .DS_Store file in every folder that it accesses, even folders on remote systems (for example, folders shared over a Windows or Apple connection) and even if the user has customized the appearance of the folder only by moving its Finder window.

The .localized file

In Leopard, a folder's name is always the same, regardless of the localization. But Finder has the ability to show some names in a localized form. When a .localized file (always 0 bytes in size) is stored in a folder, it tells Finder that the folder is a "localizable" folder, meaning that it can be given a local name. For example, the Documents folder is localizable to Dokumenter in Norsk. Likewise, Library is Bibliotek and so on. If Finder sees .localized in any folder, it automatically uses the folder name appropriate to the language being used.

Any folders you create are not localizable so you won't find a .localized file.

On your Windows disks

In the root of your Windows disks, you probably will find .DS_Store, .TemporaryItems, and . Trashes hidden files. These also are visible in Windows Explorer if you set it to display hidden files.

Reading and writing HFS+ disks in Windows

Unfortunately, no open-source software is available for Windows to read and write Macintosh HFS+ disks.

HFS Explorer is free and open source, but it can only read but not write to HFS+ disks. Get it from `http://hem.bredband.net/catacombae/hfsx.html`.

Two commercial products can read and write HFS+ disks: Transmac (`www.acutesystems.com/`) and MacDrive (`www.mediafour.com/products/macdrive/`). Both work, and cost around the same. Try the trial version of each before deciding if you need it and to compare them.

Booting Your Computer

The term "boot" comes from back in the dim, dark days of computing when the computer basically had no instructions telling it how to start. The operator had to set some switches to put the first instructions into the computer. Only a few instructions were needed to give the computer enough information to start loading the next part of the instructions, which may have come from a paper tape or punched cards.

Because it appeared as though the computer was practically starting itself, it became known as "bootstrapping" as in "lifting yourself up by your own boot straps." The name became shortened and has stuck.

Booting a Windows computer

Here are the steps a Windows computer goes through when it starts from cold.

Power-on self-test

When you first switch on your computer, the BIOS (Basic Input Output System) takes over. It carries out what is known as the POST, or power-on self-test, that does things like checking the hardware, especially the memory and the keyboard. If it encounters a problem, it gives a series of beeps; you can find out what these beep codes mean by referring to the documentation for your BIOS or at `www.computerhope.com/beep.htm`.

Find boot device

Next, the BIOS carries out instructions, trying to find a device that can be used to carry out the next stage. Normally this is a hard disk, but most BIOSs allow you to set a boot priority: the order in which it checks devices to find out which to boot from.

Assuming that your boot device is a hard disk, the BIOS then reads the first sector of the first hard disk. This first hard disk sector is known as the Master Boot Record and is 512 bytes long, regardless of the size of the disk. It contains the Partition Table for the disk, as well as up to 446 bytes of instructions.

Boot loader

After the BIOS has found the active partition, it loads the boot loader. In Windows XP, this is a file called *NTLDR*; in Vista and Windows 7, it is called *bootmgr*. Figure B.3 shows the Windows boot process.

Figure B.3

Windows boot process

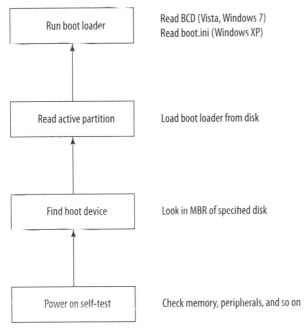

NTLDR uses a file called *boot.ini* to tell it where to find the next part of the boot process. This is normally in C:\windows. Boot.ini is a simple text file.

Bootmgr uses a boot configuration database, which is no longer a simple text file. As a consequence, you cannot edit the boot configuration with a simple editor, such as Notepad.

Finally, Windows itself gets control and loads the remainder of the operating system.

Macintosh computer

As you might expect, Apple does things a little differently from Microsoft. We will look at what happens in the boot process of Intel Macs; this is different from what happened with earlier generations of Apple hardware.

Apple uses the Extensible Firmware Interface (EFI) rather than a simple BIOS. This has much more functionality than the Windows BIOS.

Power-on self-test

First the EFI carries out a power-on self-test, just like the BIOS. It then performs an inventory of all the hardware devices connected and loads drivers for them. On a Windows computer, this phase doesn't happen until Windows itself is loading. You can see this for yourself by watching the light on your mouse: It may turn on when you first boot, because the BIOS recognizes it, but it switches off and comes on again only partway through the Windows startup.

OS X stores the address of the normal boot drive in nonvolatile RAM so that on booting it knows immediately which drive to boot from.

It then initializes the graphics hardware and puts a gray background screen on the display.

Find boot file

When booting from the hard disk, rather than looking simply at the code located in the MBR, OS X looks on the startup disk for a *blessed* file. This file is the main operating system file. *Bless* is an OS X command that writes the name of the file and the disk into the nonvolatile RAM in the EFI ready to be found at boot time. Figure B.4 shows this.

Figure B.4

Leopard boot process

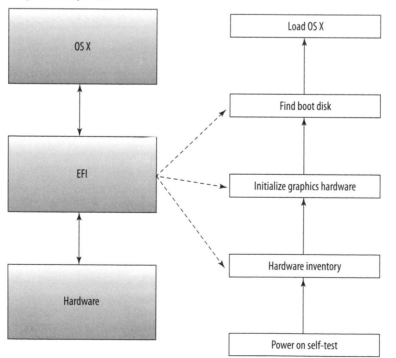

When OS X is running on non-Apple hardware, obviously there is no EFI, so another method of booting must be found.

The installation boot CD

When you first booted your computer to install OS X, you used a boot CD you downloaded from the Internet. This boot disk is based on *syslinux*. Syslinux is an open-source project, created specifically to allow operating systems to be booted from devices such as floppy disks, USB memory sticks, and CDs.

In this case, its main function is to provide an environment from which to launch the Darwin boot loader.

If you look at the disk's contents in Finder, you see something like that shown in Figure B.5a.

Exactly what appears on your disk may differ slightly, but the basics are there: a BOOT file, MBOOT.C32, an ISOLINUX folder, and a small ISOLINUX executable file.

Inside the INITRD.IMG file is where all the magic occurs. You can view the content of INITRD.IMG by opening it with Disk Mounter and navigating to the Extra/Extensions folder. It contains several kexts, as shown in Figure B.5b.

Figure B.5

Install CD files (a); INITRD.img kexts (b)

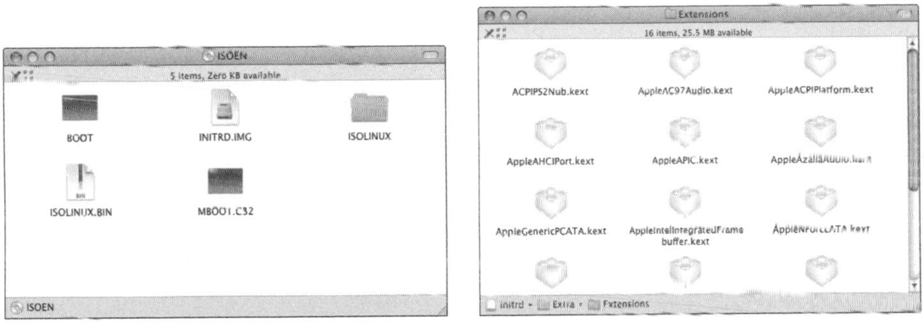

a

b

Each of these kexts is loaded when the disk boots (while the ..... are crawling across the screen). All these kexts together comprise a fake EFI, to have the Installer DVD install as if it's running on a real Macintosh. This is how it's possible to boot and install the retail Leopard DVD.

These files are copied to the hard disk drive so the Darwin boot loader can load them first. This then allows the rest of the retail installation to boot. Figure B.6 shows the kexts in the boot disk.

Table B.5 lists each of these kexts and what they are used for.

Table B.5 Kexts and Their Purpose

Kext	Purpose
ACPIPS2Nub	PC PS/2 keyboard and mouse driver
AppleAC97Audio	Realtek AC97 audio driver (but not specific to a chip)
AppleACPIPlatform	Power control, specifically computer sleep
AppleAHCIPort	Driver for SATA systems with AHCI enabled
AppleAPIC	Driver for Intel Advanced Programmable Interrupt Controller
AppleAzaliaAudio	High-definition audio driver
AppleGenericPCATA	Driver for generic ATA drives
AppleIntelIntegratedFrameBuffer	Driver for GMA900 graphics
AppleNForceATA	Driver for SATA drives on NForce motherboards
ApplePS2Controller	Controller for PS/2 keyboard and mouse
AppleSMBIOS	Fixes hardware information for system profiler
AppleVIAATA	Driver for hard disk and CD/DVD controller
Dsmos	Translates system information that may be encrypted
IntelCPUPMDisabler	Disables the Intel power management
NVkush	Autodetects nVidia graphics cards
SMBIOSEnabler	Enables the System Management BIOS

Some Hackintoshers are working on putting most of the kexts permanently into the EFI partition on the hard disk (see earlier) so booting is simply a matter of reading that.

Kernels and Kexts

For any operating system, the kernel is the very innermost core that interacts directly with BIOS or the EFI firmware and the hardware. A kext, in Apple terms, is a kernel extension.

Kernel

Any application software (browser, word processor, etc.) interacts with the kernel, rather than directly with the hardware.

In the retail OS X, the kernel used is called the *mach kernel*, which was developed at Carnegie Mellon University. The unmodified mach kernel is known as *vanilla kernel*. This is important because it means that if your computer can run the vanilla kernel, you can install all OS X updates without breaking the installation.

Kexts

Sitting between the kernel and the application software in the Windows world are small programs called *drivers*. They allow your computer to send correct output to a display monitor, a network card, or your sound card, formatted in a way that the hardware can understand.

In the Macintosh world, these drivers are called *kexts*—short for "kernel extensions." When you install OSX86 and specify drivers for your video hardware, network hardware, and so on, you are installing kexts.

Frequently, many kexts are bundled together into a new file called an *mkext*. This is done for faster loading and caching of the kexts; rather than load each individual kext, the boot loader loads them all in one file.

Writing kexts, or even understanding how they work, is not a trivial exercise! That's why so few people are capable of writing them!

Installing kexts sometimes requires use of the terminal to enter commands because you have to save the old kexts, install the new ones in the right location, and set the permissions on the new kexts.

File Permissions in OS X

Every OS X file has an owner. The owner is generally the account that created the file.

File permissions are **read**, meaning the user has permission to read the file; **write**, meaning the user has permission to change the file, and **execute**, meaning the user has permission to start the file running as a command. These are abbreviated to rwx.

NOTE
Having write permission implies read permission as well.

In addition, there are three types of users: the owner, the group the owner belongs to, and other users. Each file has three sets of permissions specified. In other words, each file has nine possible permissions.

These could be written as:

Owner: r w x
Group: r w -
Others: r - -

The – means "no permission."

More commonly, they are written on a single line as rwxrw-r--.

A file that is listed as -rwxr----- means the owner has read, write, and execute permission; other members of the group have only read permission, while everyone else has no permission.

In the example above, the - in front of the rwx means that the object is a file. If it is a folder (directory) the – is replaced by a d. For example, a user's Documents folder is shown as:

Documents: drwxrwxr--

For a folder, the meanings are slightly different: w gives write permission, which also gives permission to delete files, even if the user does not have write permission for the file! An x determines whether the user can see what is in the directory. In this case, the owner can do everything with the folder; other members of the group can read and write to the folder, but everyone else has read access to the folder but can't see what's in it! This means that if you know the exact name of the file, you can read it, but you can't browse the folder to find it.

Owners and groups

Ordinary users can be grouped together: for example, while working on a project so that each member of the group has access to the same files. They could all be made members of the ProjectX group.

Superuser

In addition to ordinary users, there is one major system user: superuser, known as *root*. Root has read, write, and execute permission for every file on the computer. Needless to say, you should not give someone root permission lightly!

Root is the only member of a group called *wheel*.

It is possible to change the permissions of a file (but only if you own it) by using the command *chmod*.

You also can change the owner of a file, again only if you own it, using the *chown* command.

In OS X, you can easily find the permissions on a file by right-clicking the filename and selecting Get Info. Figure B.6a shows the permissions for a data file owned by the user.

To change permissions, you must be the owner. In the Get Info window, click the padlock. This changes the display to that shown in Figure B.6b.

Operating system permissions

When you do anything to Leopard's kexts or kernel files, you must ensure that they have the correct permissions set. Otherwise, Leopard refuses to use them.

Fortunately you don't need to remember the permissions every file requires: Leopard keeps a database. Disk Utility can read that database, check all your system files' permissions, and then correct them.

Figure B.6

Get Info for data file (a); change permissions (b)

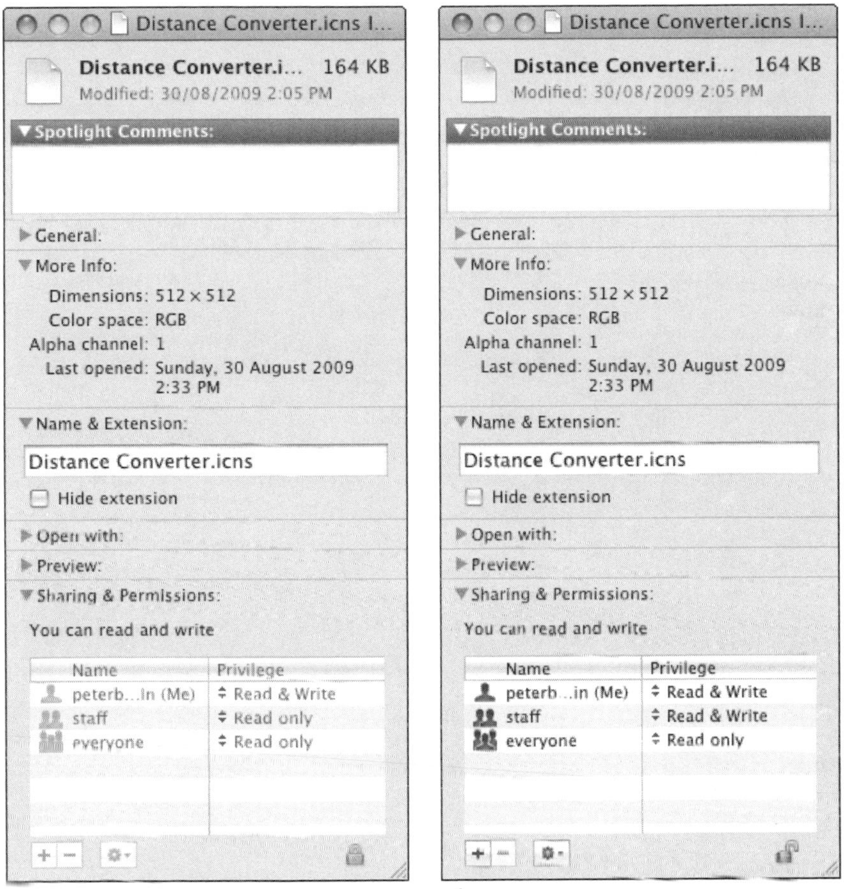

a   b

Follow these steps to fix the permissions:

1. **Start Disk Utility.**

2. **Select your system disk (Hackintosh, in my case).**

3. **On the First Aid tab, click Repair Disk Permissions.**

4. **Close Disk Utility when the repair is complete.**

Figure B.7 shows Disk Utility after it has repaired my permissions.

Figure B.7

Permissions repaired

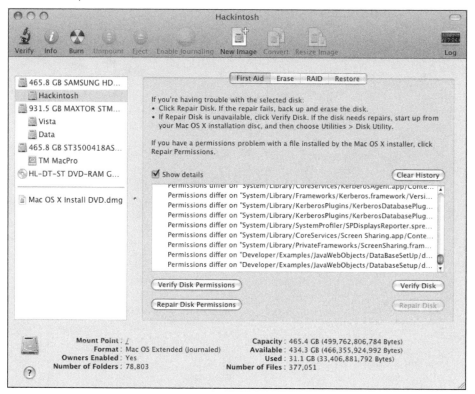

Some Apple History

Mac OS X is the tenth Macintosh operating system (X being the Roman numeral for 10). It was released in its first version, known as *Cheetah*, in March 2001, running on the Mac Power PC computer.

Version 10.1, known as *Puma*, was released later the same year. Other versions followed—10.2: *Jaguar* and 10.3: *Panther*—in late 2003 and late 2004, respectively.

In January 2006, Apple introduced its first computers based on the Intel platform. This represented the second major change of chip supplier for Macintosh. The first Macs, from 1984, were based on the Motorola 68000 series of chips and were phased out in 1994 in favor of the PowerPC chip, some made by Motorola, others made by IBM.

Since switching to the Intel platform, all PowerPC models have been discontinued but still are supported by operating systems up to Leopard. Snow Leopard does not run on PowerPC Macs.

OS X version 4, *Tiger*, released in early 2005 for the PowerPC, was the first version to run on the Intel platform. Since then, Version 5, *Leopard*, was introduced in October 2007. Version 6 (*Snow Leopard*) was introduced in late August 2009.

Each major version has gone through several minor versions. These are shown by an extra decimal point, so the eighth minor version of Tiger is known as 10.4.7. Numbering begins at zero. The final version of Leopard is 10.5.8.

Each major version of OS X introduces a major new feature. For Tiger, it was *Spotlight*, a powerful indexing and search utility, similar to the *Search* feature in the *Vista Start button* menu. For Leopard, the major new feature was *Time Machine*, a fantastic backup utility with no equivalent on the Windows platform that comes even close to being as useful and user-friendly.

Upgrading your version from one major revision to the next requires purchase of the new version, but upgrades to minor versions are free by download from the Apple Web site.

Be warned, though, that Apple updates do not work on many of the OSX86 distributions. Back up your files before you try it! I always create two partitions and install onto one. Then I use Carbon Copy Cloner (find it online) to create a bit-for-bit image on the other partition.

Troubleshooting Your Installation

This is not a comprehensive guide to what can go wrong. It covers the most likely occurrences and how to overcome them.

Still waiting for root device

If you get stuck at the *Still waiting for root device* line, here are a couple of things you can try.

Serial ATA

If your computer uses Serial ATA (SATA) hard disks, be sure that your DVD drive is also SATA; otherwise, OS X cannot utilize it. System Information for Windows (as in Chapter 1) can tell you what types of drives you have.

Master-Slave configuration

If your computer only has parallel ATA drives (not SATA), then you must be sure that your DVD drive is configured as the Master, not the Slave. How can you tell? Unfortunately, the only way to tell is to take the drive out of the computer and look at the jumpers, which are small pins on the back of the drive that allow you to select whether the drive is the Master or the Slave. If Slave is selected, swap the jumper to select Master.

Your drive has a small sticker on it, near where the cables connect. It tells you where to put the jumper to make the drive the master.

If you have a hard disk connected to the same cable as your CD/DVD drive you may have to set the hard disk to slave so you can boot the DVD, then change it back to master to boot from the hard disk.

AHCI

AHCI stands for Advanced Host Controller Interface. If your computer has SATA drives, it almost certainly has AHCI capability. This may or may not be enabled. If it is not enabled, it is highly unlikely you can boot your Leopard installation disk.

AHCI is enabled through the BIOS and is unique to each motherboard. On my Gigabyte motherboard, it is under the heading Integrated Peripherals. It is called SATA RAID/AHCI Mode and has three settings: Disabled, RAID, and AHCI.

Enter your BIOS setup, and ensure that AHCI is on.

HPET

An HPET is a High Precision Event Timer. If your motherboard allows you to enable or disable it, you should enable it.

On my motherboard, it is under Performance Management Settings. It has two headings: HPET support Enabled or Disabled and HPET mode 32 bit or 64 bit. I recommend you enable HPET and set it to 64 bit.

Post-Installation Fixes for Leopard

After you have installed Leopard, you usually need to apply one or two fixes.

Leopard time versus Windows time

One issue that can drive users to the brink is the difference between how Windows measures time and how Leopard measures it. The problem arises from the fact that Windows sets your local time to the time your hardware clock shows.

Here in Sydney, we are 10 hours ahead of Greenwich Mean Time (GMT). If my hardware clock shows 9 AM, Windows sets its time to 9 AM.

Leopard, however, assumes the hardware clock is showing GMT. Because I told it that I'm in Sydney, 10 hours ahead of GMT, Leopard sets its time to 7 PM. If I get the time from Apple's timeserver, it sets my clock to my actual local time.

When I return to Windows, however, my hardware clock has been set back 10 hours, so Windows thinks it's now 1 AM. This is shown diagrammatically in Figure B.8.

If you search the Web, you can find many solutions to the problem. From experience, no solution that tries to get Windows to show the correct time works. The only solution that works is to get Leopard to adjust its time.

Figure B.8

Leopard time versus Windows time

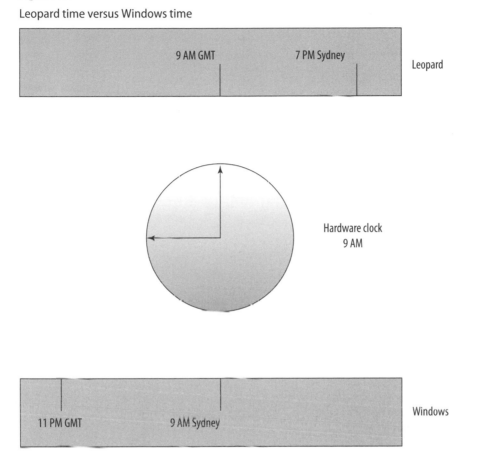

While it may seem that the way Windows uses the clock is the better way, in fact every other operating system uses the same method as Leopard: using GMT as the base time.

To fix it, download a file from `www.one4house.com/iamges/Zephyroth_Dual_Boot_Time_Fix.pkg.tgz` and install it to Leopard. I've created a TinyURL for you: `http://tinyurl.com/n9cu7a`.

Fixing the *About This Mac* display

Generally, when you install Leopard to any computer other than a genuine Apple, it doesn't auto-detect the details of your processor, usually displaying something like *2.83 GHz Unknown*. Although it won't affect anything you do with your Hackintosh, most people prefer it to show the correct display.

To fix this, Zephyroth has created an About This Mac Modifier. You can download it from `www.mediafire.com/?429xddziskv`. Just double-click the package file to install it.

An alternative is to use ~pcwiz's OSX86 Tools. This tool is able to make many other modifications to your installation. Figure B.9 shows the greeting screen of the tool.

Figure B.9

OSX86 Tools greeting screen

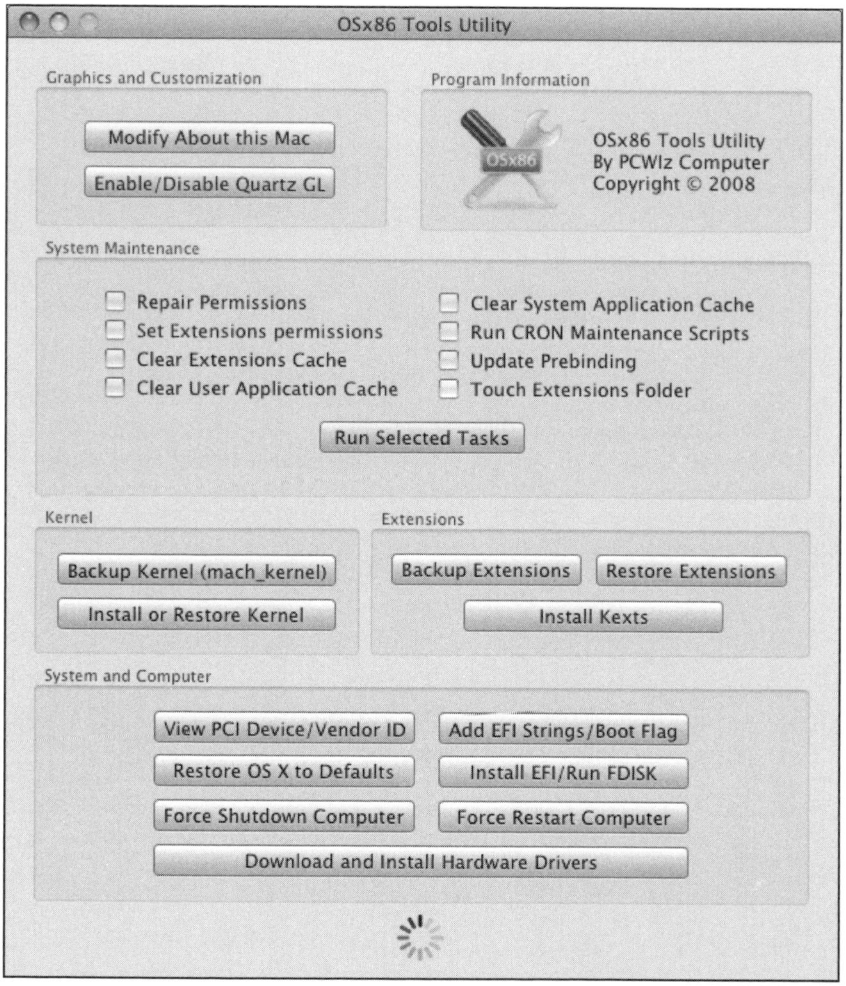

Fixing Time Machine issues

One other issue that often arises with non-Apple installations of Leopard is that Time Machine refuses to work because it can't identify the UUID of the system disk. The simplest fix for it is to again use OSX86 Tools.

Follow these steps to apply the fix:

1. Run OSX86 Tools.

2. Click Add EFI Strings/Boot Flag.

This opens the boot editor, as shown in Figure B.10.

Figure B.10

Boot editor of OSX86Tools

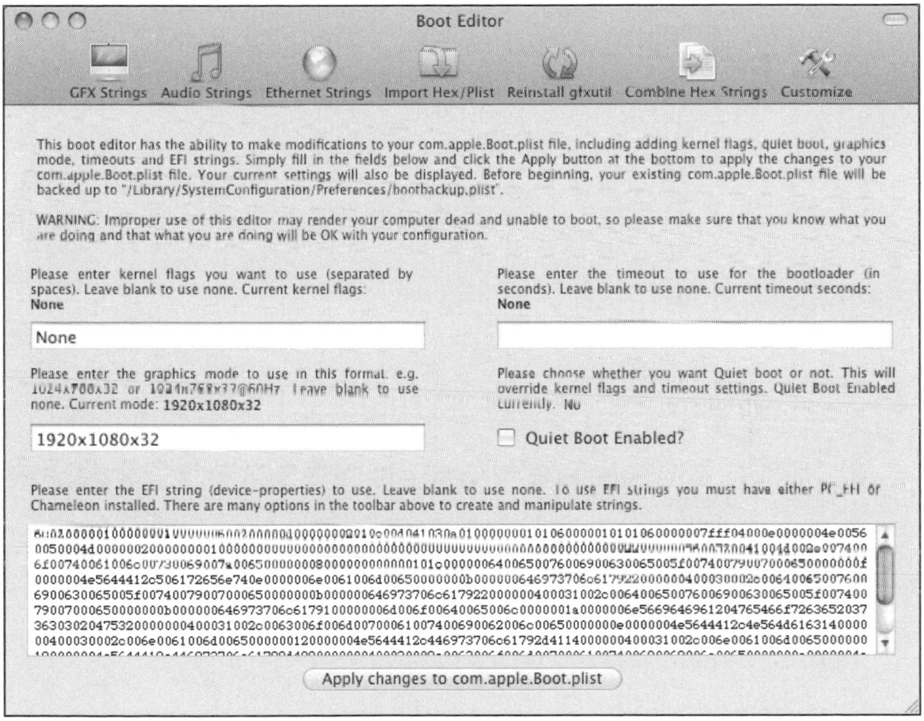

3. Click Ethernet Strings.

This opens the Ethernet Strings Creator, as shown in Figure B.11, and creates the string you need.

Figure B.11

Ethernet strings creator

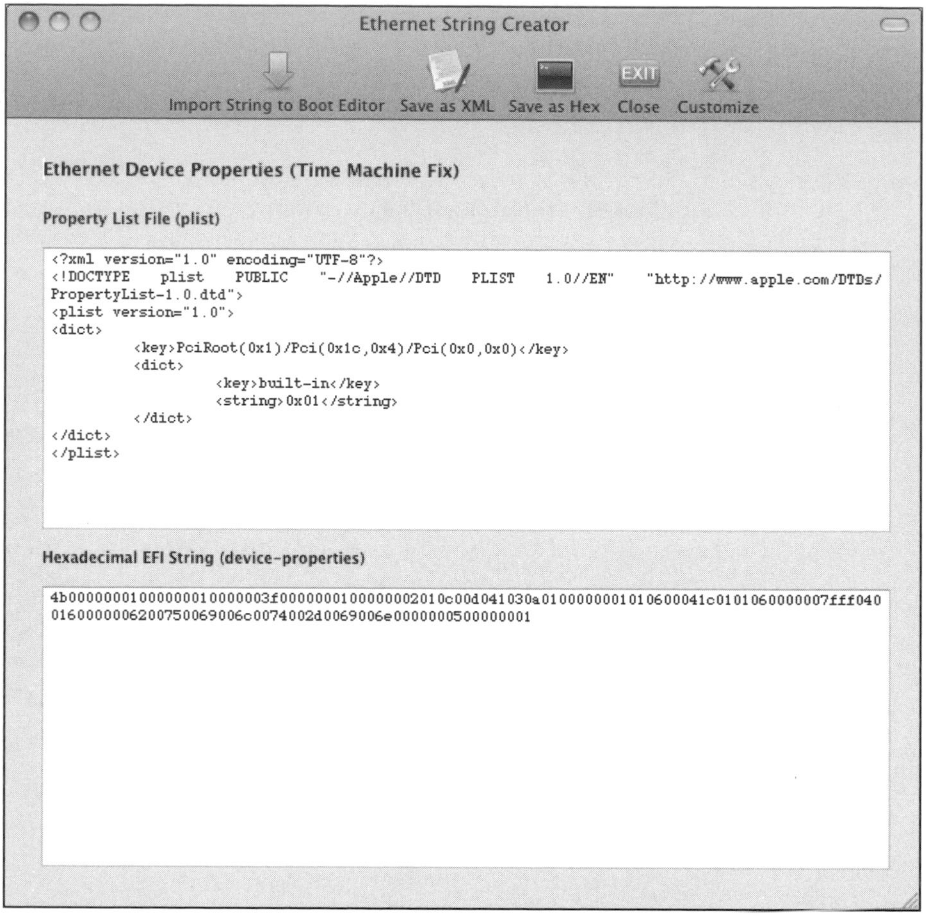

4. **Click Import String to Boot Editor.**

5. **At the bottom of the Boot Editor screen, click Apply changes to com.apple.Boot. plist.**

6. **Reboot.**

   Your Time Machine should now work.

Installing Snow Leopard

Apple released Leopard in October 2007, and a large body of expertise around installing it on non-Apple computers is available. Although Snow Leopard did not add any new "must have" features, it has changed many of the ways in which the operating system interacts with the hardware.

One very simple change is that Snow Leopard now reports hard disk capacity in base-10 giga-bytes, the same way disk manufacturers have measured them for several years. A more subtle change is that file sizes for many system files in Snow Leopard show as zero length in Finder. This is because Apple has changed the way many system files are stored.

Obviously changes such as these mean the developers of Hackintoshes have to make substan-tial revisions to the way things work, and it will be some time before installing Snow Leopard to non-Apple hardware is as easy and well-defined as installing Leopard.

If you're using a genuine Macintosh, you just insert the Snow Leopard Install Disk and upgrade. As you'd expect, it's not that simple if you're using a Hackintosh.

At this time, the only installations possible are on specific computers and motherboards. Most methods require starting with a working Leopard installation, but this can be a Hackintosh installation.

Several people have Snow Leopard running on a Gigabyte motherboard, very similar to mine. The Dell Mini scene has one of the more active user communities, and several people have it running on either a Dell Mini 9 or 10v.

This appendix is a brief introduction to the installation on a Gigabyte motherboard and a Dell Mini 9.

Installing to a Gigabyte Motherboard

A few different experts have put together guides showing how to install Snow Leopard on a Gigabyte motherboard. The boards chosen are very similar: Gigabyte EP45-UD3P, EP45-UD3R, and EP45-DS3L.

Three guides to installing to these motherboards are available and are shown in Table C.1.

I chose Blackosx's guide because that is closer to my motherboard (DS3P) than the UD3P. Because of time constraints, I didn't create my own DSDT.aml file as recommended by Blackosx. Everything works pretty much perfectly, except for Bonjour networking and Time Machine.

Bonjour is Apple's zero configuration networking protocol, and because it is not running, I can't connect to my Dell Mini 9. Time Machine crashes with a kernel panic about three or four min-utes into the first backup.

Table C1 Installation Guides for Gigabyte Motherboards

Motherboard	Author	URL
EP45-UD3P	Adam Pash	`http://lifehacker.com/5351485/how-to-build-a-hackintosh-with-snow-leopard-start-to-finish`
EP45-DS3L	Blackosx	`www.insanelymac.com/forum/index.php?showtopic=180954`
EP45-UD3R	d00m42	`www.insanelymac.com/forum/lofiversion/index.php/t181903-0.html`

Wireless networking is a continuing problem. None of my USB adapters work in 64-bit mode. The Netgear and the RokAir both appear to work in 32-bit mode, but they never give a network connection. Wired Ethernet worked right from the start.

Figure C.1 shows Snow Leopard running on my desktop computer. It has been updated to version 10.6.1 with Apple Software Update.

Figure C.1

Snow Leopard on my desktop computer

Installing to a Dell Mini 9

Thanks to a huge amount of work by meklort and great documentation by bmcclure937, installation to the Mini 9 is relatively pain-free and "just works," including Wi-Fi networking, sound, sleep, and Time Machine

To install Snow Leopard to the Dell Mini, you need a Leopard installation to create the required files. This need not be a genuine Mac: I used my desktop running retail Leopard 10.5.8.

Complete instructions are at `www.mydellmini.com/forum/os-x-snow-leopard/` `12338-official-snow-leopard-mini-netbookbootmaker-method-updated.` `html` or `http://tinyurl.com/mbrqb6`.

If you have a Mini 9 or 10v, follow those instructions: They work.

Figure C.2 shows the About This Mac screen from my Mini 9.

Figure C.2

Dell Mini 9 running Snow Leopard

Figure C.3 shows my Mini 9 having its desktop shared from the Leopard retail installation on my desktop computer.

Figure C.3

Dell Mini 9 desktop using Screen Sharing

Installing to Other Computers

At the time of writing, a few methods are available for installing to other computers, but so far they are highly specific to the computer or motherboard and use only the retail copy of Snow Leopard.

As always, Google is your friend. Simply search on Google for Snow Leopard and your computer or motherboard. You are very likely to find something.

Psystar's RebelEFI

In late October 2009, Psystar, the company producing Macintosh clones, released an EFI boot disk at `http://store.psystar.com/home/rebel-efi-preview.html` saying that it can be used to install Snow Leopard on a non-Apple computer. The trial download is free, and if you decide to use it, it costs $50.

I downloaded the free version of the file and burned to a CD using ImgBurn in Vista.

My computer booted fine from the boot disk, prompting me to swap to the Snow Leopard install disk. This started fine and allowed me to format my disk and then install Snow Leopard.

Installation stopped with the progress bar at about 75 percent and saying 15 minutes to go. Although the installation appeared to have failed, in fact it worked fine when booting from the RebelEFI disk.

When Snow Leopard started, it led me through the usual screens, creating a new user, selecting language, location, and so on. Finally, I arrived at the Snow Leopard home screen.

Unfortunately, the only resolution available was 1024 x 768, although QE/CI appeared to be working as the greeting video played at first boot.

As in the instructions, I opened the CD in Snow Leopard and double-clicked to install the RebelEFI package. This is to make the hard drive bootable without using the RebelEFI boot disk. This appeared to install, but on restarting did not boot, giving a boot0 error. On a second attempt it worked, and the computer booted from the hard disk.

Snow Leopard appeared to work fine, given the video limitation.

Table C.2 summarizes my experience with RebelEFI.

Table C.2 Summary of RebelEFI on EP45-DS3P / 7600GS

Item	Working?
Installation	Yes, though it appeared not to
Boot from hard disk	Yes, after second installation of RebelEFI
Video	Only 1024 x 768
QE/CI	Appears to work, but not properly tested
Wired networking	Worked fine
Audio drivers	Caused kernel panic on installation
Wi Fi drivers	Did not work

As you can see, my trial was only partly successful. Remember that this was a very early version of RebelEFI and was only the free version. It may be that on purchasing the full version, parts that do not work on the free version may work.

By all means, try it. It may provide a simple, easy way of installing Snow Leopard on your system.

.plist Apple Property list; written in XML; used to store system properties; *see* XML

ACPI Advanced Configuration and Power Interface; a standard for managing power

AFP Apple Filing Protocol; Apple's networking file service

Alpha channel Measures the transparency of a pixel; 0 is transparent, 1 is opaque

AMD Advanced Micro Devices; manufacturer of processor and graphics chips

API Application Programming Interface; defines the way application programs interface with the operating system

Apple menu Menu in the top-left corner of the Leopard menu bar

AppleScript High-level scripting language for Macintosh computers

Aqua Graphical user interface and primary visual theme for OS X

Assistant Automated setup program used to guide the user through an Installation process

ATA Interface standard for connection of storage devices; derived from AT (the original IBM-PC/AT) Attachment

ATI Major supplier of graphics processing units; now owned by AMD

Attributes (OOP) Properties of an object

Automator Apple programming system to create automated actions

Billboard renderer Part of Quartz Composer; creates a flat 2D image from inputs

BIOS Basic Input Output System; lowest level of programs that control the computer

Bluetooth Open wireless protocol for exchanging data over short distances

Boot Process of starting a computer from a cold start

Boot CD CD used to load components so that the remaining system can be loaded from another source

boot.ini File used by Windows XP to specify startup options

Boot loader Program that runs as part of the boot process and allows the user to select the desired operating system

chain0 Small program used to pass boot control to the Darwin operating system

Chameleon Boot loader program with graphical interface; developed specifically for Hackintoshes

Class (OOP) A blueprint for objects of a specific type

Cocoa Native object-oriented-programming (OOP) environment for Macintosh

CODEC COmpressor-DECompressor for video

Combo update Apple update for OS X for updating more than one dot (.) update (say, from 10.5.1 to 10.5.8)

Concatenation Operation to join strings together; "the"&"cat" results in "thecat"

Context Menu Menu obtained by right-clicking an object

Control Panel Application that allows users to customize how Windows looks and behaves; compare with System Preferences in Leopard

Core Image Applies filters, transforms, and other effects to images at the pixel level

Darwin Underlying operating system for OS X and iPhone OS; derived from NextStep OS

Dashboard OS X application used to host widgets

Dashcode Programming environment for creating widgets to place in Dashboard

Device Manager Control Panel applet in Windows that allows users to control the computer hardware

DHCP Dynamic Host Configuration Protocol; allows computer to automatically obtain an IP address from a router when connecting to a network

Disk Image (.dmg) Macintosh file containing an exact image of a disk

Disk partitioning Dividing a hard disk into separate data storage areas, each independent of the others

Disk Utility Macintosh utility for managing disks and disk images

diskpart.exe Windows utility for manipulating disk partitions

Display adapter Card to generate and output images to a display

Dock Macintosh bar of icons that allows quick access to application software

DSDT.aml Differentiated System Description Table; describes the system hardware in a way that is independent of the platform; written in ACPI Machine Language, hence the .aml

EasyBCD Windows program for managing the Vista (Windows 7) boot loader, using a graphical interface

EFI Extensible Firmware Interface; Apple's replacement for the BIOS, it's larger and more complex

Exposé Allows users to quickly find all open windows or open windows for a given application

FAT File Allocation Table; early Windows disk allocation system

File permissions Defines which users have ability to read, delete, and modify files

File Vault Apple's encrypting file system

Finder Application for finding files and devices; equivalent to Windows Explorer

FTP File Transfer Protocol; allows file transfer between computers with different operating systems

GPartEd Free partition editor

GPT (GUID Partition Table) Globally Unique IDentifier; GPT is a disk partitioning system based on a GUID; compare with MBR

Hardware acceleration Graphics adaptors that have extra hardware to take graphics processing load of the computer's central processor

HFS+ Hierarchical File System extended; file system developed by Apple for Mac OS (including OS X)

HPET High Precision Event Timer; a fixed-rate counter with up to 32 independent timers; normally built into the motherboard

HUD Heads Up Display; a type of display used in OS X with white text on a black background

HyperCard Very early hypertext system; available only for Mac and discontinued in 2004

iCal Macintosh calendar application

iDisk Part of MobileMe; allows files to be stored remotely and accessed from any computer

Image backup Backup of a whole disk; stores every byte without regard for file structures

Image file (.iso) Contains a bit-by-bit image of a disk

Integrated video Graphics adaptor is not a separate card but is built into the computer motherboard

Intel CPU manufacturer; chosen by Apple to build the computers to replace the PowerPC chip

Intel GMA950 Graphics processor chip used in several Apple computers

Interface Builder Part of XCode; allows design of user interface when developing application software for OS X

Interpolation Method of constructing new data points within a range of fixed data end-points

IP address Unique address of a computer used for networking; written as four numbers separated by dots; for example, 192.16.1.2

Kabyl-Bumby Boot disk for Leopard installation

Kernel Innermost part of an operating system that interacts directly with the hardware and the EFI or BIOS

Kernel panic Occurs when the kernel encounters an error; cannot be recovered from

Kext Kernel extension; used to integrate hardware into the kernel without modifying the kernel

Kexthelper OSx 86 utility to allow kexts to be easily incorporated into the operating system

Leopard OS X version 5 (10.5)

Linux Operating system based on Unix

MAC address Media Access Control; a unique identifier given to each network adapter

MacFUSE Allows extension of OS X's file handling to cover other file systems

Mail OS X application for e-mail

MBR Master Boot Record; the first 512-byte sector of a hard disk for use with Windows and other operating systems; compare with GUID Partition Table or GPT

Menubar The fixed menu at the top of the display of OS X

Method (OOP) The abilities of an object; the things it can do

mkext Bundle of kexts combined into a single file for faster loading and caching

MMX MultiMedia eXtensions; single instruction, multiple data instructions introduced by Intel in 1997

MobileMe Apple's Web-based mail, calendar, and data sharing application

Motherboard Major component in a computer; includes the processor; allows other devices to connect

NAT Network Address Translation; a technique used to hide internal IP addresses while presenting a single IP address to the outside world

NTFS New Technology File System; file system used by Windows

NTFS-3G Software that allows OS X to read NTFS file systems; requires MacFUSE plug-in

ntfs-mac Commercial software to allow OS X to read NTFS file systems

Object (OOP) An example of a class; contains data structures and methods used to manipulate the data structures

Object-Oriented Programming (OOP) A type of programming based on objects and methods that act on the objects

Objective-C An OOP language used by Apple in developing applications

OOP *see* Object-Oriented Programming

OSx86 A contraction of OS X and x86 referring to x86 processors; projects designed to run OS X on non-Apple hardware

Parallels Virtualization software that allows OS X to run Windows programs

PC_EFI A method of faking an EFI on non-Apple hardware

Peer-to-peer (P2P) Method of sharing files between computers without going through a central server

Peripheral A device connected to a computer that expands the host's capabilities, such as a printer

Pixie Screen magnifying application; part of XCode

QE/CI *see* Quartz Extreme and Core Image

Quartz Composer Visual programming language; part of XCode

Quartz Extreme Utilizes the graphics processor to draw images without using the CPU

Quick look OS X feature to allow viewing the content of a file using Finder

QuickTime Multimedia framework allowing creation and playback of digital media clips

Recovery console Part of Windows XP; allows repair of a computer that will not boot; replaced by tools on the System Recovery Options menu on the Vista boot disk

Retail DVD Installation DVD for Leopard purchased from Apple

RSS Feed Really Simple Syndication; allows viewing of only the frequently updated parts of a Web site

Safari Leopard's Web browser

SATA Serial ATA; interface standard based on serial (rather than parallel) connection; *see* ATA

Services menu Menu available in every OS X application

SIMD Single Instruction Multiple Data; allows one processor instruction to act on several data objects to give a degree of parallel processing

SMB Server Message Block; Applespeak for file access to Windows computers

Spaces OS X application that allows use of virtual screens to separate different applications

Spotlight OS X search facility that indexes the entire computer system

Sprite renderer Part of Quartz Composer; creates a pseudo 3D image that can be moved around the screen

SSE2 Streaming SIMD extension version 2; extends SSE; *see* SIMD

SSE3 Streaming SIMD extension version 3

String A group of alphabetic, numeric, and punctuation characters treated as a single unit

System disk Leopard disk that contains the operating system; *also* known as a boot disk

System Information for Windows Free software that can determine the hardware installed in a Windows system

System Preferences Application that allows users to customize how Leopard looks and behaves; compare with Control Panel in Windows

TextEdit Text editing application supplied with Leopard

Time Machine Easy-to-use backup system supplied with Leopard

tinyurl.com Web site that allows long URLs to be shortened

Universal OSx86 Installer Allows setting of many boot parameters and install kexts for Leopard; *also known as* UInstaller

Unix Multitasking operating system dating from the 1970s but still in use today

Virtual machine A software implementation of a computer that requires no additional hardware

VMware Virtualization software that allows OS X to run Windows programs

WEP encryption Wired Equivalent Privacy; outdated encryption system for securing wireless networks; *see* WPA2 encryption

Widget Small program that sits in the Leopard Dashboard

Wired Network Network where computers are connected by wires; usually Category 5 or Category 6 Ethernet cables

Wireless Network Network where computers are connected without using wires; *also* Wi-Fi

WPA2 encryption Wi-Fi Protected Access version 2; recommended encryption system for Wi-Fi networks, usually with a Pre-Shared Key (PSK) set on the router

X11 X Window System that provides a graphical user interface for networked computers

XCode Application programming system for Leopard and iPhone developers

XML eXtensible Markup Language; a set of rules for marking up documents

Index